THE
Illustrated
History *of*
Canada

THE
Illustrated
History *of*
Canada

EDITED BY CRAIG BROWN

KEY PORTER BOOKS

Canadian Cataloguing in Publication Data

The Illustrated history of Canada / general editor, Craig Brown. -- Rev. ed.

Includes index.

ISBN 978-1-55263-920-7

1. Canada--History. I. Brown, Robert Craig, 1935-

FC165.I44 2007   971   C2007-901829-7

The publisher gratefully acknowledges the support of the Canada Council for the Arts and the Ontario Arts Council for its publishing program. We acknowledge the support of the Government of Ontario through the Ontario Media Development Corporation's Ontario Book Initiative.

We acknowledge the financial support of the Government of Canada through the Book Publishing Industry Development Program (BPIDP) for our publishing activities.

Key Porter Books Limited
Six Adelaide Street East, 10th floor
Toronto, Ontario
Canada M5C 1H6

www.keyporter.com

Design: Peter Maher

Electronic formatting: Jean Lightfoot Peters

Printed and bound in Canada

07 08 09 10 11 5 4 3 2 1

Foreword

*T*HE *ILLUSTRATED HISTORY OF CANADA* is a book about Canadians. It is a story of how Canadians have lived and worked, how they have seen themselves, how they have thought about each other. It is a history of how Canadians realized their ambitions in their several communities, across generations of huge colonial empires and, more recently, as citizens of a nation in the international world. In this book six Canadian scholars—historians and historical geographers—have interpreted the words and illustrations of our past for all readers.

The book begins with Arthur Ray's vivid description of the first Canadians, the Amerindian and Inuit peoples, at the moment when their world was broken into by Europeans—fishermen, traders, and explorers who crossed the Atlantic seeking out the riches of North America. The encounter stretched over nearly three centuries, from the middle years of the sixteenth to the early decades of the nineteenth century, following the paths of the European adventurers from Newfoundland to the

Pacific and into the Arctic. Almost as soon as contact had been made, colonizers and settlers began to establish their first tentative footholds in North America. Christopher Moore traces these initial, precarious settlements at Port-Royal and Quebec, how they grew into a vast continental empire, and how the settlers of New France founded a way of life that became a permanent influence on our society and our identity as Canadians.

Great Britain ultimately prevailed over France in the long rivalry of North American empires. Graeme Wynn takes up the story; British peoples, between 1760 and 1840, braved 4,800 kilometres (3,000 miles) of rolling ocean to develop stable communities and to establish British institutions and law in the British North American colonies. The stage was set for consolidation, for political union, for expansion westward, aiming to control the Hudson's Bay territory before Americans got it. Confederation, the restless ambitions of its creators, and the sometimes desperate gambles they took to achieve continental nationhood, are the dramatic centrepiece of Peter Waite's chapter on the remaining years of the nineteenth century.

Canadians began the twentieth century with hearty optimism. A buoyant economy transformed our society. In his portrait of Canada between 1900 and 1945, Ramsay Cook sketches the transformation, the growth of cities, the diversification of industry, the emergence of a vibrant western Canada, the commitment of Canadian lives and treasure in two world wars, and the despair of the Great Depression. Unprecedented wealth, a legacy of a wartime economy, Desmond Morton relates, stimulated even greater changes in Canadian society in the last half of the twentieth century. Our society became more compassionate than in the past, prepared to use the instruments of government to protect and enhance the welfare of our citizens. It became a more tolerant society, more willing to welcome new immigrants, more conscious and respectful of the distinctive cultures and traditions of all Canadians. And we are a more confident nation, determined to make a significant contribution to international amity and well-being.

Each of these authors offers a distinctive view of his subject, and readers will discover new insights into our past. Familiar themes will be found, but freshly observed, newly minted.

Canadians regard our multicultural character as a mark of our national identity. Politicians and editorialists celebrate multiculturalism as a Canadian virtue and programs at every level of government promote recognition of our several traditions. The authors of this book remind us that Canadians have always been many peoples.

That was so long before Native Canadians encountered Europeans in the mid-1500s. At first Europeans, crudely, tended to lump all Amerindians together as "savages." But Champlain, La Vérendrye, Franklin, Hearne, Thompson, Pond, and a host of others who followed Cartier's quest of exploration, quickly discovered that there were, in fact, many nations of Native Canadians. Beothuk, Mi'kmaq, Algonquin, Iroquoian, Chipewyan, Cree, Assiniboine, Babine, Kwakwaka'wakw, and Inuit spoke different languages and dialects, organized their societies and governments differently, developed distinctive cultures and economies, and made their own ingenious accommodations to climate and landscape. Nor were Europeans of one piece either. Fishermen who put ashore in Newfoundland to cure cod, whalers who penetrated the Arctic, and explorers who charted the waterways of the continent came from several lands, Portugal, Spain, France, and Britain.

Less diverse were the founders of New France. They were mostly Catholic. Perhaps as many as half of the men, and nearly all of Louis XIV's *filles du roi*, were townspeople rather than land-bound peasants. They established an empire that extended from Ile Royale through the Great Lakes watershed and down the Mississippi to Louisiana. More important, they founded a unique society, rich in custom, tradition, and memory; their language has become a permanent component of what it means to be a Canadian.

The British victors of 1760 had already established a presence in Nova Scotia decades before Wolfe challenged Montcalm on the Plains of Abraham. After the Treaty of 1763 their numbers swelled and swelled again in the aftermath of the American Revolution. Like the French before them, many of the early settlers were soldiers who took up land after a term of imperial service in the New World. Others, from the south, created an enduring niche in Canadian mythology as Loyalists, though an expert witness, Governor Parr of Nova Scotia, skeptically observed that most were "not much burthened with Loyalty." Others still, a small minority of the settlers, were state-sponsored emigrants from Britain after the Napoleonic wars.

What attracted all these people, and the thousands of Scots, Irish, English, and Welsh who came out from Great Britain, was land. British North America was a place of opportunity, of promise. "The prospects for you here are ten to one above what they are in the old country," wrote one enthusiastic settler. Land, not free but cheap and abundant, meant the promise of a farm, of raising a family, of making a go of it in the new land. Most, albeit modestly, realized their expectations in the several British North American colonies. By mid-century the farming frontier had pushed up against the Canadian Shield. It was time to move on. Spokesmen for these rest-less, acquisitive farmers had already spotted another world to conquer, the great North-West, the seemingly empty lands of the Hudson's Bay Company. Here was an empire, said George Brown, waiting to be conquered, developed, controlled.

The filling up of the pre-Confederation colonies had been something of a hap-hazard process, sometimes assisted, sometimes hindered by the policies of the imperial government. Conquering the North-West was different. It was an enormous project of nation building by the new Dominion government. It required promises of free land and promotion of the North-West as the Land of Opportunity, the Last Best West. Most of all, it required many more newcomers than ever before. British settlers were wanted: Americans too—their experience with dry-land farming was an invaluable asset in the North-West. That was the key, and it prompted a dramatic new initiative in settlement policy. Long-harboured doubts about whether immi-grants from continental Europe could "fit in" were cast aside. If these Europeans were farmers, individually and in groups they were encouraged to come. Men, women, and children who could endure a prairie winter, who would break the tough prairie sod, were destined to fulfil the expansionist dreams of the nation builders. The new-comers came in unprecedented numbers, almost two million of them between 1891 and the Great War, and well over half of them went to the North-West.

The Great War, post-war immigration restrictions, the Depression, and yet another world war temporarily slowed the flow of immigrants to Canada. But after 1945 Canada again became a land of hope and opportunity for people seeking a new life in a new country. Two million arrived between 1946 and 1961, another one and a half million in the next decade. In earlier times the government's appeal to new-comers had always been preferential and restrictive. Blacks had been pointedly discouraged, and severe limitations had been applied to immigrants from Asia. Gradually, after the Second World War, restrictions based on race, colour, and coun-try of origin were eased, and newcomers formerly unwanted added new dimensions to the reality of Canada as a nation of many peoples.

Canadians have also had to learn how to live with each other. It has never been easy; throughout our history that accommodation has been marked by incompre-hension, suspicion, fear, and prejudice. Native Canadians thought the Europeans they encountered were intruders. In the early stages of contact between the two worlds, reciprocal interest in the exploitation of fur-bearing animals created an unstable but working partnership between them. All too quickly, however, it eroded into a dependence for the Native Canadians that weakened their societies and ultimately ruined their centuries-old way of life.

French imperial power in North America was destroyed in 1760. French-Canadian society was not. More out of necessity than liberality, the imperial government in London promised religious freedom and wrote guarantees for the French language and the civil code into the Quebec Act of 1774. Subsequent generations of British officials and British colonists worried about their relationships with the French Canadians. Some even regarded the work of the Conquest as unfinished. Lord Durham found "two nations warring in the bosom of a single state"; he recommended a legislative union of the Canadian colonies that he believed would swamp and assimilate the French Canadians and assure progress for the colony. A generation later, George Brown, surveying the Quebec Resolutions that would soon become the provisions of the British North America Act, crowed to his wife: "…a complete reform of all the abuses and injustice we have complained of!! Is it not wonderful? French Canadianism entirely extinguished!" Led by far-sighted and determined political leaders, the French Canadians stood the expectations of both Durham and Brown on their heads. But the matter did not end there. John A. Macdonald's opinion that trying to finish the work of the Conquest "would be impossible if it were tried, and it would be foolish and wicked if it were possible" did not represent the views of all of his English-Canadian backbenchers. Like Macdonald, every prime minister from Sir Wilfrid Laurier to Jean Chrétien has had to learn that the political, economic, social, and cultural adjustments required to accommodate both French and English Canadians are offered grudgingly.

That is also true of the acceptance of newcomers by the host society. Canadians, French and English alike, have continually fretted about the presence of too many Americans in their midst. Lady Aberdeen, the outspoken wife of the Governor General, summed up that concern in 1895. The "U.S.A. ideas" that American farmers brought to the North-West in their cultural baggage, she said, "must be dealt with ruthlessly." The brash, populist notions of the Yankees were unsettling. Still more disturbing were the "foreign navvies" who manned the railway construction gangs, the immigrant labourers in the factories and mines, and the European settlers on the prairies. Their multiplicity of languages, customs, and traditions threatened, most Canadians feared, to undo Canadian society altogether. These peoples were "strangers within the land." English Canadians wanted "to instill in their minds the principles and ideals of Anglo-Saxon civilization." As one Protestant minister in

Montreal put it, "one of the best ways of Canadianizing, nationalizing, and turning all into intelligent citizens, is by means of a good English education." The chosen vehicle on the prairies was the creation of single, state-controlled, secular, "National" public school systems. But that, in turn, upset existing understandings and rekindled fear and suspicion in the minds of French Canadians. In the post-war years, and especially in the last decades of the twentieth century, new fears and suspicions were kindled by the arrival of newcomers from Asia and Africa as well as Europe and by a renaissance of confidence and self-determination among Canada's First Nations. Still, in recent years we have begun to understand that living together, for all Canadians, is a demanding, subtle, and continuous process of accommodation.

Canadians have also had to learn how to live with their environment. The explorers hoped to find easy treasure and a quick route to the wealth of the East. Instead they discovered an immense continent, a tough, sometimes unforgiving terrain, and a severe climate. The journals of the adventurers echo that sentiment again and again. Survival itself was sometimes in question and the Europeans soon learned that the Native Canadians were masters at it. Captain John Franklin, astonished at the elegant design and utility of an igloo his Inuit guide had built, wrote that "one might survey it with feelings somewhat akin to those produced by the contemplation of a Grecian temple...both are triumphs of art, inimitable in their kinds."

The wealth of Canada is hard come by. Both finding it and extracting it require ingenuity and technological sophistication. Our history is replete with examples: the toggled harpoon head of the Inuit hunter, the canoe of the Indian and the *voyageur*, the York boat of the Hudson's Bay trader, the notched-log cabin of the pioneer farmer, the chilled steel plough that cut the prairie sod and the new wheat strains developed by our agricultural scientists, the bush pilot's Noorduyn Norseman, the satellite sensors of the modern geologists and foresters. Many of these machines, tools, and techniques are of Canadian inspiration and design; others have been imported and adapted to the Canadian environment.

No technological innovation had a more radical and long-lasting impact on Canadian society and the Canadian economy than the railway. For generations distance and winter kept Canadians apart in narrow parochial villages and loyalties. Distance hindered communication. Winter shut down commerce, froze mill-streams, closed factory doors, and imposed distinctly seasonal lifestyles on Canadians. Beginning in the 1850s, railways changed the ways Canadians went about their work, regarded their prospects, thought about each other. When the iron horse came to town a person's perceptions of space, time, and opportunity slowly, inexorably, expanded outward. Breaking the bonds of distance and winter, railways took goods to markets; brought customers from home; delivered newspapers, books, and magazines to readers; carried settlers to homesteads; penetrated the Shield to tap new resources. Railways inspired daring political ambitions; they built nations. The Intercolonial, from Montreal to Halifax, was a condition of Confederation; and only the Canadian Pacific would make a Dominion *a mari usque ad mare* a reality.

The idea that there could be a Dominion from sea to sea developed slowly. There was, and is, a strong sense of self-sufficiency about Canadians. A royal official noted it among the *habitants* of New France in the 1750s. They would, he complained, "follow only their own will and fancy." A British officer, Lieutenant-Colonel Gubbins, observed the same in his travels about New Brunswick in the early 1800s. Self-sufficiency, of course, was a necessary condition of survival for pioneering societies and it fostered a vigorous sense of local community and local identity. Lord Durham was particularly struck by it. "There are many petty local centres," he observed, "the sentiments and the interests...of which, are distinct and perhaps opposed."

The union of the Canadas that followed Durham's Report, colonial self-government (itself a reflection of self-sufficiency) achieved in the province and the other colonies in the 1840s and 1850s, and the prospects created by railways all set the stage for Confederation. Union, politicians and governors agreed, would raise British North Americans above the parish squabbles of local politics. Confederation would enable Canadians to reach outward, realize expansionist ambitions, acquire and control new lands. Thus could be built a continental nation.

There was little thought of independence, of emulating the American colonies of 1776. The goal of the Confederationists was, rather, to achieve self-sufficiency within the British Empire. That meant expanding self-government to a widening range of responsibilities, transforming the imperial relationship into what Macdonald called a "healthy and cordial alliance." There were dangers in this, as Macdonald and his successors, Laurier and Borden, all discovered. Each step was accompanied by sharp debate and often profound disagreement between French and English Canadians. There were also awful, unanticipated costs. Autonomy within the Empire–Commonwealth and recognition of Canada's national status were the rewards Borden demanded for Canadian participation in the Great War of 1914–18.

In the interwar years a few Canadians, like John Dafoe, editor of the *Winnipeg*

Free Press, argued that Canada's new status was a hollow shell unless Canadians were prepared to fulfil their responsibilities in the League of Nations. That kind of argument made politicians nervous. What with tidying up the constitutional niceties of our new status, dispatching a Canadian minister to Washington, and looking out for our own interests in relations with foreign states, was there not enough on our international agenda? Had not the question of Canada's obligations beyond her own shores always caused more discord among Canadians than any other issue? If there was another European war, and by 1938 all the signs pointed in that direction, Mackenzie King knew that there would be an irresistible demand from Canadians that Canada fight at Britain's side. King was determined to lead a united nation into the war and to avoid the disastrous policies, like conscription, that had very nearly torn Canada apart in the First World War. In large measure he succeeded in doing just that.

A difficult question remained to torment post-war diplomats and political leaders: had not Canadian isolationism, the shunning of responsibilities in the international community, only served to encourage Hitler's vicious tyranny? Many, like Lester Pearson, thought so. And if Hitler was gone, another problem, the Soviet Union, remained, locked in an aggressive imperial rivalry with the United States in Europe and throughout the world. Canada was caught between them—"the ham in the Soviet–American sandwich" was the way the Soviet ambassador described the new geopolitical reality in a Calgary address in the early 1960s. Self-sufficiency in international affairs was a luxury Canadians could no longer afford.

Involvement and collective security were the bywords of Canadian diplomacy in the post-war years: involvement at the United Nations, in the Commonwealth, in the so-called Third World; and collective security through NATO and NORAD. The confident diplomats of External Affairs boasted of many achievements by their "quiet diplomacy": recognition of a distinctive role for "middle powers," especially Canada; imaginative mediation and peace-keeping in international crises; constructive contributions to international aid. A heady optimism characterized Canadian diplomacy in the 1950s and 1960s, a sense of confidence that energetic involvement in international politics would both assert and enhance the Canadian identity for Canadians.

That confidence eroded as the twentieth century drew to a close. There was a growing concern among many Canadians about dependence upon the United States, the dominant super-power in the world following the collapse of its rival, the

Soviet Union. The concern is very different from the interwar attitude to foreign affairs when a minimalist perception of Canada's responsibilities to the international community preoccupied both diplomats and politicians. Rather, it was how best to maintain a significant and distinctive Canadian presence in international affairs. A major contribution was Canada's service in peace-keeping missions around the globe. At the beginning of the 1990s Canadian men and women were on fifteen different peace-keeping assignments. By the end of the decade others, including Kosovo and Indonesia, had been added to the list. Canadians remain convinced that they can make valuable contributions to reducing the dangers of war, to lessening gross economic disparity between nations and to adapting to change in an emerging global economy.

Over the centuries since Europeans first encountered Native Canadians on the Atlantic coast, Canadians have created a transcontinental nation of many peoples. Learning to live together remains a challenge to all of us. Luck and persistence, ingenuity and expertise, have enabled us to convert our resources into wealth. Slowly, but surely, we have developed an awareness of our national responsibilities to ourselves and to the international community. These are major themes in our history and of this book.

The idea of an illustrated history of Canada was suggested by Louise Dennys and Malcolm Lester of the publishing house Lester & Orpen Dennys. They wanted to produce a book that would capture in text and illustrations the excitement of our past, the variety, the richness and the subtlety of our history, and what it means to be a Canadian. That is what we have tried to do in this book.

Since the first edition was published in 1987, two French editions, *Histoire général du Canada*, have been published by Editions du Boréal (1988 and 1990), a Spanish edition, *La Historia Ilustrada de Canada*, by Fondo de Cultura Económica of Mexico (1994) and updated English editions by Lester Publishing Company (1991 and 1996) and Key Porter Books Limited (1997 and 2000). With the encouragement of Ms. Anna Porter of Key Porter Books, and especially Ms. Linda Pruessen, our editor, we have revised *The Illustrated History of Canada* for this new edition.

Craig Brown
Toronto
June, 2002

A Note on
the Illustrations

THE PICTURES IN THIS WORK are intended not just as a page-by-page representation of the text, but rather as a parallel commentary. We have tried to strike a balance between the familiar and the little known: the former because they are classic images of our heritage, with no comparable substitutes; the latter because they testify to the extraordinary wealth of our archives, both public and private. We have attempted not only to represent all sectors of our society and all regions of our geography, but also to do justice to one of Canada's most precious resources—her arts.

In the past, historical illustrators and picture editors have too often had to rely on secondary sources, and to reproduce from copies of copies. The systematic photographing of collections has at last made it possible for high-definition images to replace the smudgy woodcuts, engravings, and halftones of earlier days. Also, relatively inexpensive printing and reprographic techniques now allow us to go back to original works, and thus to minimize distortion and loss of quality.

"A tangible object," proclaimed the dean of Canadian historical artists, C. W. Jefferys, "cannot lie or equivocate so successfully as a word." But he warned that certain images are less trustworthy than others. "Official" art, whether portraits, monuments, murals, wartime propaganda, or political icons, tends to tell us more about the biases of its propagators than about its purported subjects. If *The Illustrated History of Canada* includes relatively few examples of such self-aggrandizing works, it reflects the modern interest in the lives of ordinary citizens, rather than military campaigns, heads of state, and individual feats. This shift from the mythic and heroic to the social and material can be seen in Jefferys' pioneering *Picture Gallery of Canadian History* (1942–50): early volumes specialized in "visual reconstructions" of "dramatic episodes," but later he asserted the primacy of "Old

buildings, early furniture, tools, vehicles, weapons and clothing, contemporary pictures of people, places and events" which "much be examined to fill out the story."

In the spirit of this declaration of faith, we have attempted to fill out our story
with images of people, places, and events as they appeared to their beholders, not as
"interpreted" in later years. The resulting picture gallery reveals that there are as
many visions of Canada as there are versions of what it means to be Canadian.

Robert Stacey
Picture Editor

Contents

When Two Worlds Met

ARTHUR RAY

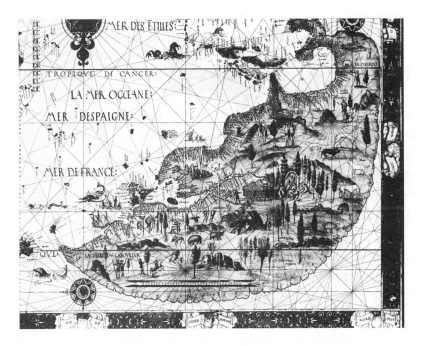

This is one of the first maps to portray the geographic information Cartier
obtained during his first two voyages to Canada. Hochelaga and Stadacona are
located, the mythical Kingdom of the Saguenay is included, and whalers appear
in the coastal waters. The orientation is north-south rather than south-north,
as later became usual. Extract from Pierre Descelliers's world map, 1546
(nineteenth-century copy).

The land should not be called New Land, being composed of stones and horrible rugged rocks.... I did not see one cartload of earth and yet I landed in many places... there is nothing but moss and short, stunted shrub. I am rather inclined to believe that this is the land God gave to Cain.

THESE WERE JACQUES CARTIER'S first images of Canada, and they were the impressions of a bitterly disappointed explorer. Jacques Cartier had been commissioned by François I to look for gold in the New World and a passage to Asia. With these goals in mind he had set out from the small port of St-Malo, France, on April 20, 1534, with two ships and sixty-one men. After navigating his ships around numerous menacing icebergs off the foggy coast of northern Newfoundland, Cartier had crossed the Strait of Belle Isle in early June, and probed the Labrador coast south-westward for a distance of some 200 kilometres (125 miles). Along this coast he met a few "wild and savage folk" who "clothed themselves in the furs of animals" and wore their hair "tied up on the top of their heads like a handful of twisted hay, with a nail or something of the sort passed through the middle...into which they weave a few bird's feathers." What a rude contrast these Aboriginal people were to the wealthy Asian merchants or the gold- and silver-rich Aztecs of Mexico Cartier hoped to find! Given his mission and expectations, his initial disappointment and harsh characterization of Canada and of the people he first encountered is understandable. The Native world of the early sixteenth century was far more complex and wealthy than Cartier could have known. And we can only guess at what the Indians thought of Cartier. What we do know is that they loved their homeland and had a deep spiritual attachment to it.

Archaeologists believe that the ancestors of Canada's Native peoples migrated across the Bering landbridge from Siberia more than 12,000 years ago, towards the end of the ice age. Hunters of prehistoric bison, caribou, elk, mammoth, mastodon, and other large mammals, they advanced rapidly—an average of about 80 kilometres (50 miles) a generation—until, some 10,500 years ago, they had settled all the habitable areas of North and South America below the waning ice-sheets. A few thousand years later the glaciers had retreated far enough that some of the Native peoples were able to occupy Central Canada, around Hudson Bay and James Bay.

Despite enduring legends of Carthaginians, Phoenicians, the Irish Saint Brendan the Navigator, and other wanderers dating from the Bronze Age to late medieval times, contact between Canada and Europe seems to begin with the Vikings nearly one thousand years ago. The Norse were an adventurous sea people and they spread rapidly across the northern Atlantic in the ninth century. Norse sagas describe several voyages to North America after they had settled in Greenland late in that century; the most famous of these heroic stories tells of Leif Ericsson's wintering at a place he called "Vinland" around the year 1000. The Greenlanders probably made occasional forays across Davis Strait to Baffin Island, Labrador, and Newfoundland, and the Norse settlement excavated at L'Anse aux Meadows in northern Newfoundland must be one of many places where they landed or wintered. The sagas, and evidence excavated from Native sites, suggest that the Norse explored the northern coast quite widely, and that there was sporadic contact between them and the Native peoples of northern North America over many years. There was, however, little basis for trade or friendly exchange between them, and the Native peoples appear to have defended their territory effectively against the intruders until the decline of the Norse colony in Greenland put an end to these encounters in the thirteenth century.

These contacts were made during a warm phase in the climate which lasted two centuries. It was apparently the deterioration in the climate that led the Norse to abandon the area. It was not until five hundred years after Leif Ericsson, in 1497, that John Cabot's voyage from Bristol in England reopened European contact with Canada. Again there are legends and possibilities of prior voyages, but even if Cabot's was not the first, it was certainly the one with consequence. His voyage was part of the explosive fifteenth-century maritime expansion that took the Europeans right around the world by 1520. Cabot (born Giovanni Caboto) understood, like his Italian contemporary Christopher Columbus, that a direct and possibly shorter route

L'Anse aux Meadows, Epaves Bay, on the north-east tip of Newfoundland: the first Norse settlement found so far in North America. Here eight Viking house-sites and four boatsheds dating from *c.* 1000 AD were excavated, between 1961 and 1968, by seven archaeological expeditions.

Cartier rencontre les Indiens de Stadacona. This romanticized image of Cartier's first encounter with the Stadacona shows the explorer making a bold approach to shy, retiring Indians; in fact, Cartier's own accounts indicate that the roles were reversed. Most often the newcomers were welcomed. This 1907 oil painting is by Marc-Aurèle De Foy Suzor-Côté.

to the spice trades of the Far East might be found by sailing west. Finding backers in England for a reconnaissance on a more northerly latitude than Columbus's, he probably landed in northern Newfoundland, spent a month sailing this new coast, and returned to Bristol to acclaim and a royal pension.

Cabot's reconnaissance, and ones that followed by João Fernandes (1500), the Corte-Real brothers (1500), João Alvares Fagundes (1520–25), and Giovanni da Verrazano (1524–28), showed that no easy westward route to the Indies existed. Cabot, however, had on his return announced a different kind of wealth: cod. Already there was a strong market in Europe for these fish—Europeans had been catching cod in the North Sea and off Iceland for generations. Soon after Cabot's voyage, fishermen from Portugal, France, and Britain began to fish for cod on the banks of Newfoundland and Nova Scotia. By the 1550s the Newfoundland cod trade employed hundreds of ships and thousands of men travelling annually between European ports and the new fishing grounds.

Along with the fishermen came whalers, particularly Basques from northern Spain and south-western France. They focused on the Strait of Belle Isle where the narrow waters facilitated their hunt. In the 1560s and 1570s more than a thousand whaling men were summering—and sometimes wintering—there every year. The fishermen and whalers were more interested in Canadian waters than Canadian land, but they gradually developed a third trade through contact with the Native peoples. There was a luxury market for furs and pelts in Europe, which the fishermen could tap once they entered into amicable exchanges with the Natives. By the latter half of the sixteenth century, voyages were being organized specifically for this trade.

In 1534, when Jacques Cartier explored the Gulf of St. Lawrence, he not only encountered fishing boats and visited harbours already named by Basque whalers, but also traded furs at Chaleur Bay with the Mi'kmaq (Micmac). Cartier, however, had a different agenda. By then it was clear that Columbus's westward search had discovered not the Indies but a new continent, which was already being called America. A route through this continent was still hoped for, but the Spanish experience in Mexico and Peru had established a new motive for exploration. By Cartier's time, the *conquistadores* had conquered Aztec Mexico and Inca Peru and seized treasure troves as valuable as the riches of the Far East. Accordingly, the King of France's commission to Cartier authorized him to discover "certain isles and countries where it is said there must be great quantities of gold and other riches."

Although Cartier's initial disappointment with Canada proved unfounded, his assessment was accurate in one fundamental respect. By comparison to most of western Europe, Canada is a harsh land. Except for the prairies and the Pacific coast, the Canadian climate north of the 49th parallel is like that of Europe north of the 60th parallel: Norway, central Sweden, and Finland. In other words, Canada is primarily a northern country. South of the 49th parallel, in southern Ontario, the St. Lawrence valley, and on the prairies, the climate is like that of eastern central Europe and the western Soviet Union. Only coastal British Columbia and the Maritimes, with the exception of Newfoundland, are comparable to France and the British Isles. Only southern British Columbia, the prairies, southern Ontario, the St. Lawrence valley, and the southern Maritimes have growing seasons in excess of 160 days, enough to make large-scale agriculture possible. As a result, most of what is now Canada was better suited to the lifestyles of Native hunters and fishermen than it was to the

Captain Cook's Ships Moored in Resolution Cove, Nootka Sound. Vancouver Island. March 1778. The trade between the British and the Nootka was, in James Cook's words, "carried on with the strictest honesty on both sides." After completing his trading and repairing his ships, the great explorer sailed on to the Sandwich Islands (Hawaii), where he was killed in a dispute with the Natives. Watercolour by M.B. Messer after John Webber.

European peasant farmers who followed in the footsteps of the early explorers.

This fundamental fact of Canadian geography greatly influenced the course of the relationship between the Native peoples and the European intruders. In contrast to the land that was to become the United States, few areas of this northern world were suitable for farming. This meant that the conflict between them over possession of land was substantially less in the early days than it was in the United States, where the climate and geography made an agricultural way of life possible, and had led the Aboriginal people to clear and settle some of the best land; there, conflict was inevitable when the newcomers took it over for their own use. In Canada, until the nineteenth century, Europeans mostly prized the rich fishing they found along the Atlantic coast and the wealth that the Native people harvested from the forests.

The scramble for the wealth of the forests began slightly more than half a century after Cartier cast disapproving eyes on the Montagnais of the Labrador coast. In 1588 two of his nephews sought and obtained from Henry III of France a short-lived monopoly on trade with the Montagnais and other Natives. This signalled the beginning of a fight for control of the fur trade that was to last until the middle of this

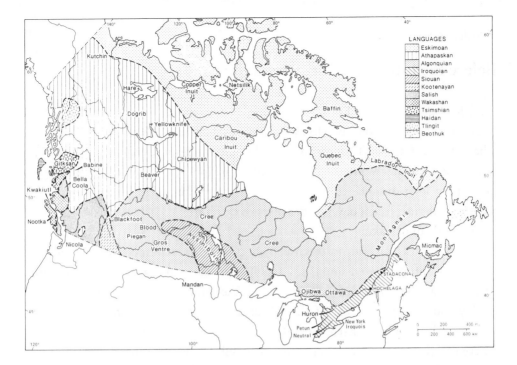

Native Canada at the time of early European contact. This map illustrates the distribution of Native groups in relationship to language areas. The incomplete records of the period and the high mobility of the Native peoples make the establishment of precise historical boundaries difficult to determine; many are disputed to this day.

century—a contest which quickly became enmeshed in the imperial struggle between France and England for control of the northern half of the continent. It was one of the driving forces behind the European invasion, and its outcome influenced the shape of the modern political map of North America. The fur trade itself would disrupt the Native world by fostering conflicts between groups who jockeyed to control the supply of furs to the Europeans and the trading routes to the interior, by spreading epidemic diseases, by stimulating the migration of whole populations, and by introducing iron-age technologies into stone-age economies, and drawing Native people into an international commodity marketing system in the process. These developments did not have the same impact on all of Canada's Native peoples. Native Canada, on the eve of contact by the Europeans, was too rich and complex a world for that—both geographically and culturally. Nevertheless, the coming of the Europeans would change it forever.

Before the Intruders: The Face of the Land

Canada is nearly as big as Europe; it is some thirteen times larger than the combined territories of the country's two founding nations, France and England. Indeed, size is a basic fact of Canada. Those who wanted to tap the resources of this vast territory and those who later wanted to weld it into a nation had to meet the challenge of developing long-distance transportation and communications systems. From the beginning to the present day, this has been an extraordinary achievement—as well as a very costly undertaking.

Canada's vast size and northern climate provide an extremely varied landscape. The mossy, shrub-covered land that Cartier observed on the Labrador coast is typical of a large part of Canada north of the treeline: the wind-swept Arctic tundra of northern Labrador, Ungava, most of the Northwest Territories, and the Arctic islands. Although the land had a barren look to it, game was not scarce. The northern forest, where it meets the tundra, was home—as it still is today—to the muskox and once abundant barren-ground caribou, a small, tough, deerlike animal. The herds summer north of the treeline and, unlike the thick-coated muskox, they retreat south to the woods in winter. Here, the arctic hare, arctic fox, wolf, and wolverine are the most important fur-bearing animals. Lake trout, whitefish, pike, and arctic char abound in the coastal rivers. The northern coastal waters are the home of the ringed and bearded seal, walrus (except in the western Arctic), narwhal, beluga whale, and polar bear.

South of the treeline, most of Canada east of Lake Winnipeg and the Mackenzie valley is part of the Canadian Shield, where thousands of years ago large rocky areas were scraped bare of soil by massive continental ice sheets. Between these barren regions the land is covered with an evergreen forest of pine, spruce, and tamarack, known as the "boreal" or northern forest. In the twentieth century Canada's Group of Seven attempted to capture the essence of this landscape on canvas. Theirs are romantic images. European explorers and early fur traders saw it much differently—they had to come to grips with its harsh reality in order to survive. The great nineteenth-century explorer, geographer, and fur trader David Thompson put it succinctly:

I have called [it] the Stoney Region....It is little else than rocks with innumerable Lakes and Rivers....The summer is from five to six months, or more properly the open season, with frequent frosts, and heats, but always tormented with Musketoes and other flies...even the timid Moose Deer on some days is so distressed with the flies, as to be careless of life, and the hunters have shot them in this state, and the cloud of flies about them so great, and dense, that they did not dare to go to the animal for several minutes.

In the eighteenth century, the Hudson's Bay Company men regarded this wooded Shield country as a "food desert"; they believed game was too scarce there to support a string of trading establishments.

In the heart of the Shield country, Hudson Bay and James Bay provide one of the great water entries into the North American continent. From the Nelson River on the west to the Rupert River on the south-east a vast swampland borders these bays and extends inland for distances up to several hundred miles. In the nineteenth century, this insect-infested swamp was dubbed the "land of fog and bog" by Hudson's Bay trader James Hargrave. Aptly named, it would be the Hudson's Bay Company's Canadian base for its first two centuries of operation after 1670. What a shocking and hostile place it must have seemed to men coming from the temperate British Isles. James Isham, a trader for the Hudson's Bay Company in the early eighteenth century, graphically described the dangerous realities of winter on the bay:

abt the Last of august...the No. Wt. [north-west] and Nn winds begins to sett in, with unsufferable Cold weather, with hard snow, & great Drifts for 8 month's togeather,...itt oft'n happens we shall have fine moderate weather, in a winter morning w'n before night approches, a sudden gale will spring up with Drift & snow to that Degree, that if men happen's to be out, and drest for warm weather, they Run a great Resque of their Lives,— Several having perrishd, by such sudden Storm....I'have known men to stand at the saw for only 20 minuets when their face & hands has been froze so, they have been obligh'd to Retire to the Surgeon to have Such Cur'd or Cutt off &c.

Around Hudson Bay, the traders, like the Native peoples, would have found browsing deer, woodland caribou, and moose which David Thompson described as the "pride of the forest." Other animals important to them for both food and fur included bear and fox, beaver, muskrat, marten, land otter, lynx, rabbit, and hare— animals that still abound there today. Among the many varieties of fish were lake trout, whitefish, sturgeon, and pike. Ducks and geese could be found in plenty in spring and autumn. The early accounts of fur traders make it clear that large barren-ground caribou roamed the Hudson Bay lowland as far east as James Bay. In season, Hudson and James bays are the nesting places of millions of snow geese and Canada geese. Far inland, between the lower Saskatchewan River and Lake of the Woods, was one of the greatest muskrat-producing areas in the world.

The northern forest merges into an area of mixed deciduous trees that extends all the way into New Brunswick and Nova Scotia. It was here that the canoe birch, prized by Native people for its bark, reached its greatest size—fifteen centimetres (6 inches) or more in diameter. Wild rice, a nutritious food for the Indians as well as the Europeans, still grows here, particularly along the Rainy River to Lake of the Woods, while the Gulf of St. Lawrence was rich in cod, mackerel, seal, eel, whale, porpoise, and shellfish.

Where the Canadian Shield and the plains of the western interior meet, there is a string of large, fish-rich lakes, the most famous being Lake of the Woods, Lake Winnipeg, Lake Athabasca, Great Slave Lake, and Great Bear Lake. The plains reach from the United States border to the Mackenzie River delta and westward from the Shield to the Rocky Mountains. This is gently rolling country rising in two distinctive steps, one in western Manitoba—the Manitoba escarpment—and the other, the Missouri Coteau, in central Saskatchewan. Parts of the region, most notably the Red River valley, are extremely flat. In fact, this valley is one of the flattest plains in North America. Formerly the bed of an ancient lake, it is prone to floods on an enormous scale whenever ice blocks the lower Red River during spring runoff—a disaster that happens frequently, because the headwaters of this north-flowing river thaw before the lower reaches do. Early European settlers learned of this hazard the hard way.

Beyond the North Saskatchewan and Saskatchewan rivers, the boreal forest extends as far as the Rocky Mountains and the Yukon. In this wooded region, the Peace River valley was one of the richest in game. "On either side of the river, though invisible from it," observed the explorer and trader Alexander Mackenzie, "are extensive plains, which abound in [wood] buffaloes, elkes, wolves, foxes, and bears." Impressed with its pastoral quality, Mackenzie called the Peace River valley one of the prettiest countries he had ever seen. South of the North Saskatchewan and Saskatchewan rivers the forests gradually yield to open grasslands—picturesquely described by the early fur traders as "islands of trees in a sea of grass." This borderland between forest and plain was known as the parklands, and also—with the grasslands beyond—as the "fire country" because immense prairie fires were commonplace. The parklands and prairies teemed with game, especially the grassland buffalo, the largest North American terrestrial animal, weighing up to 900 kilograms (2,000 pounds). The buffalo massed on the grasslands in the summer during the rutting season and retreated to the bordering woods in the autumn when there was a

Pictographs—paintings on cliffs and cave walls, using natural materials such as ochre—are one of the oldest surviving Native art forms. This pictograph illustrates an Ojibwa legend involving the horned creature Misshipeshu, Great King of the fishes, the Snake Manitou, and a canoe paddled by five men. Agawa Site, north shore of Lake Superior.

winter chill in the air. By all accounts the summer buffalo herds were truly enormous. "I saw more buffalo than I had ever dreamed of before," recounted one prairie resident, in July of 1865, when he encountered a herd in the Battle River country of eastern Alberta. "The woods and plains were full of them. During the afternoon we came to a large round plain, perhaps ten miles across, and as I sat on my horse on the summit of a knoll overlooking this plain, it did not seem possible to pack another buffalo into the space. The whole prairie was one dense mass...." The effect these huge herds had on the prairies was like that of a swarm of locusts; they stripped the grasslands bare as they passed, and bordering woodlands were trampled flat.

In the woods there were moose, elk or wapiti, pronghorn antelope, and mule deer. Beaver thrived on the aspen trees and large packs of wolves preyed on the buffalo herds, killing the young, aged, and infirm. To the west, the Rocky Mountains tower over the plains, extending down to what is now coastal British Columbia. Movement through this dramatically beautiful region of mountains, plateaux, and forests in the days of canoe travel was very hazardous. Most rivers include reaches where water plunges in torrents through narrow, steep-sided canyons, as at Hell's Gate on the lower Fraser River. Foot passage around these barriers was often highly risky, sometimes impossible. "[At] the place where we made our landing," wrote Alexander Mackenzie of the Peace River canyon, "the river is not more than fifty yards wide, and flows between stupendous rocks, from whence huge fragments sometimes tumble down, and falling from such an height, dash into small stones, with sharp points. . . . no alternative was left us . . . but the passage of the mountain over which we were to carry the canoe as well as the baggage. . . ."

Partly because of its rugged character, British Columbia exhibits more geographical diversity than any other region of Canada. Some of the country's wettest and driest climates are found here. The mountains along the coast, exposed to moisture-laden westerly winds, are blanketed by dense rainforest, while the high windward slopes of the Rocky Mountains are clad in evergreen forests of spruce, fir, and pine. In contrast, the plateaux leeward of the coast ranges are more sparsely covered with grass and sagebrush. Nearly all the wildlife found east of the Rocky Mountains was also found here, except for the prairie buffalo, but the mountain goat, sea lion, and sea otter were, and still are, distinct to British Columbia. Whales and seals were found in plenty along the coast, and during the spawning season all the major coastal rivers swarmed with salmon, and with great runs of candlefish, or eulachon, a species of smelt, every spring.

In the early years, the land and its animals were very new to the Europeans. Their exploration of Canada was like a guided tour conducted by Native people who were very much at home in their own land. In a similar way, Europeans were educated by the original inhabitants in the uses of the different animals, fish, and plants they found in the vast land they called the New World. Trade in furs may have been paramount to the intruders, but the means and methods of survival were just as important.

The Native World: Capturing an Image

Like Europe, Native Canada was a complex cultural mosaic. The Native people spoke twelve major languages and many more dialects. Probably numbering some three hundred thousand individuals, they inhabited all areas of present-day Canada but they were very unevenly scattered across the land. The majority lived in semi-permanent villages along the rivers and bays of coastal British Columbia, in southern Ontario, and in the St. Lawrence valley. Otherwise the country was thinly peopled by small groups who led highly mobile lives.

Native societies ranged in character from the highly stratified ones of the west coast to the bands of the northern forest and tundra regions where people lived together in small kinship groups. The village-dwellers of the Pacific coast were primarily fishermen; those of southern Ontario and the St. Lawrence valley depended heavily on the produce of their gardens for food, supplemented by fish and venison from the hunt, while the remaining groups relied on the chase. Generally speaking, for all Native people religion stressed their close relationship with a natural world infused with supernatural power. Most people believed in a great spirit, who had given the land to them, and a host of lesser spirits from whom they sought assistance, guidance, and protection, although the ways in which these beliefs were expressed and the ceremonies practised varied a great deal.

It is not easy to obtain a clear picture of aboriginal Canada on the eve of colonial expansion. Native societies were non-literate, and so have not left us the kinds of written records historians ordinarily rely on. We must turn to archaeology, Native oral traditions, and the documents of the early European intruders—all sources that have their limitations—to form a coherent picture of life.

Archaeology gives us a very incomplete image of this time. Potsherds, stone implements, and most of the other materials archaeologists have unearthed say nothing directly about the ways people organized their lives or what they thought about their world. From these we can only draw inferences, based on similar features of our own contemporary cultural traditions.

Kutchin Warrior and his Wife. The traditional dress is similar to that found among other Athapaskan-speaking people such as the Chipewyan. The tunics are pointed in the back, following the shape of the skins. The only article of European manufacture here is the kettle. This 1851 lithograph is after a drawing by A. H. Murray.

And many elements are missing in archaeological excavations, because organic remains do not survive for very long periods, except in waterlogged bog soils, in permafrost, and in the semi-arid regions of the prairies. Often we have little to draw on for information about the lives of the early Native peoples, other than a small sample of stone implements or a few ceramic remains in places where pottery was made.

Most groups had well-developed oral histories, traditions, and legends, and they provide revealing glimpses of life before the European intrusion. Unfortunately, however, many of these accounts were not recorded until long after the first contact with the newcomers, and, as a result, they are fragmented and sometimes blend experiences from both before and after contact. In spite of these difficulties many of the histories, traditions, and legends offer us crucial images of belief systems, world views, and the experiences of a few individuals and groups.

Given that so little is available to us, we must, wherever possible, draw on the accounts of the first explorers, traders, and missionaries. But here, too, we face difficulties because virtually all records of initial encounters were kept by men, most of whom were isolated from their families and from European women for long periods. The kind of information they recorded and the ways they interpreted what they saw were strongly coloured by their own immediate social situation, their cultural background, and the purpose of their visit. The duration of the visit was also critical. It was necessary, in order to truly understand a community, to live with it for a lengthy period of time. But most of the early explorers had only brief encounters as they pushed on in search of mineral riches, new sources of furs, and the elusive western sea. Even those who spent long periods with the Native people found there were barriers that prevented them from completely understanding many aspects of their life, particularly religion. "I must remark," David Thompson wrote, "that whatever other people may write as the creed of these natives, I have always found it very difficult to learn their real opinion on what may be termed religious subjects. Asking them questions on this head, is to no purpose, they will give the answer best adapted to avoid other questions, and please the enquirer."

The season of the year and the place where Europeans first met Native groups similarly had an important bearing on the idea they formed of the Native world. Most of their overland exploration was by river between late spring and early autumn. Generally they were looking for a water passage to Asia, or they were seeking new trading partners. For these reasons our first pictures of the interior of the country are essentially riverine views and our first maps are route maps. Given that

Keskarrah a Copper Indian Guide and his Daughter Green Stockings; both appear to be wearing caribou-hide robes. Note their "Europeanized" faces. An 1823 coloured lithograph after a drawing by Lieutenant Robert Hood.

many Native groups moved up to several hundred miles on their annual rounds and often depended upon very different resources as the seasons changed, a summer glimpse alone, or a winter one for that matter, provided an unbalanced picture. Today, this has sometimes led to conflicting conclusions about where many Native groups lived and on what resources they depended. No longer are debates on these points merely of academic interest; Aboriginal and treaty rights claims often hinge on interpretations of these early records.

Even more confusing is the fact that away from the coastal regions, the European presence in North America began to affect Native life long before Europeans and Natives actually met, primarily as a consequence of different tribes trading European goods among themselves, and the spread of European diseases. The fact that changes were taking place long before any actual contact with the intruders means that many of the earliest first-hand accounts do not give us an accurate idea of Aboriginal Canada in its undisturbed state, because the Native societies were already in transition. When Alexander Mackenzie made the first European trek across British Columbia in 1793, he met Indians in the upper Fraser River area who had European goods, even though Mackenzie was the first white man they had ever seen.

European drawings, paintings, and, later, photographs often provide important depictions of life in early times. But many are impressions made by artists who drew their own interpretations from the accounts of others. Even when artists actually visited the Native peoples, their drawings and paintings were strongly influenced by their own attitudes towards their subjects, their artistic training, and current fashion. Photographs too can be very misleading. A good example is the work of Edward

Kutchin Winter Lodges; these semi-subterranean, wood-framed, earth-covered dwellings provided warmth under the most extreme conditions. They were similar in many respects to the winter houses of the Inuit of the Mackenzie Delta and Labrador. An 1851 lithograph after a drawing by A. H. Murray.

Curtis, the famous photographer of the late nineteenth and early twentieth century who set out to record Native culture before it disappeared. To accomplish this, Curtis took with him into the field a collection of Native artefacts and clothing that he used to stage many of his poses. He also "doctored" some of his negatives so that the resulting prints would not feature articles of European origin in any prominent way. Although Curtis's photographs are recognized works of art, they are not a reliable record of Native life.

Clearly, capturing a reasonably accurate image of Native Canada is no easy task; we must consider many types of evidence drawn from many sources, from the later precontact era through the first century after contact.

Hunters of the Northern Forest

The boreal forest is vast. It stretches westward from the Labrador coast over three thousand miles to the lower Mackenzie River and the Yukon. Within this northern forest, people spoke different dialects of two major languages: Athapaskan (north-west of the Churchill River) and Algonquian (to the south and east of the Churchill). Despite their inability to understand one another, Athapaskan- and Algonquian-speakers faced similar environmental challenges and found similar solutions, and so shared many aspects of everyday life. These forest people adapted well to their environment. Tools, weapons, clothing, and ceremonial objects were fashioned from locally available materials rather than secured by long-distance trade. Life was organized around commonly learned skills and highly portable tools and equipment. Weapons for taking large and small game consisted of bows and stone-tipped arrows, stone-tipped lances, deadfall traps, and snares.

Snares were particularly effective. In the late eighteenth century, on his epic overland trip from the Churchill River to the Coppermine River, the explorer and fur trader Samuel Hearne described their use by the Chipewyan for hunting barren-ground caribou:

When the Indians design to impound deer, they look out for one of the paths in which a number of them have trod and which is observed to be still frequented by them....The pound is built by making a strong fence with brushy trees...the inside is so crowded with small counter-hedges as very much to resemble a maze; in every small opening of which they set a snare, made with thongs of parchment deer-skins...amazingly strong....

Lured or driven into the pound and caught in the snares, the caribou were then speared or shot with arrows. Hearne added that this was such a successful hunting method that Chipewyan bands could often spend most of the winter at just one or two locations. In a similar fashion, the Cree took caribou by building "deer hedges" across pathways, and placing snares in openings left in these barriers. Smaller game, hare and rabbit, were taken by the same means, while fish were caught with hook and line, dip nets, and weirs, or fences stretched across the rivers.

Men fashioned most of the weapons, although women made the snares and traps for small animals. Women also made most of the household equipment, including stone knives, bone or wooden scrapers for processing hides and pelts, stone burns to etch bone and wood, bone needles, wood and bark containers, and, among the Algonquians, pottery. Vessels generally were of poor quality so it was not possible to cook in them over an open fire. Most food was therefore either boiled by placing hot stones in water or roasted on sticks or spits. With obvious relish Samuel Hearne described Chipewyan cooking methods as consisting

...chiefly in boiling, broiling, and roasting: but of all the dishes...a *beeatee*, as it is called in their language, is certainly the most delicious, at least for a change, that can be prepared from a deer only, without any other ingredient. It is a kind of haggis, made with the blood, a good quantity of fat shred small, some of the tenderest of the flesh, together with the heart and lungs cut, or more commonly torn into small shivers; all which is put into the stomach, and roasted, by being suspended before the fire by a string. Care must be taken that it does not get too much heat at first, as the bag would thereby be liable to be burnt, and the contents be let out....

The women also fashioned the clothing, from hides and pelts, and decorated it with porcupine quills, moose hair, and perhaps painting. Tailoring involved a minimal amount of cutting, relying instead on the natural shape of the hides; "Chipewyan" in fact means "pointed skins," referring to the animal tails left on the clothing. For most of the year, outerwear consisted of a long shirt or tunic worn by men and women alike, along with leggings and moccasins. Underneath, men wore breech-cloths and women culottes. Winter wear included a warm, durable beaver coat worn with the fur side inward and used for two or three years before it wore out. Towards the Mackenzie valley, women commonly made coats from strips of rabbit skin. For bedding, these Native people used deer and moose hides, hare blankets, and bear skins. Women usually made lodge coverings from moose or deer hides, bark, or brush, arranged over a conical framework of poles. Up to fifteen people could be accommodated in one of these dwellings.

Probably the best-known article of Native culture is the bark canoe—light in weight, of shallow draft, and easy to repair. It was these craft that made it possible for Europeans to explore the northern half of the continent so swiftly, because they were easy to portage over difficult terrain and to navigate over unexpected rapids and along the rivers. Although there were some minor variations in design between tribal groups, traditional northern Indian canoes were able to carry only two adults, one or two children, and a cargo of 115 to 135 kilograms (250 to 300 pounds).

In winter, snowshoes, dogsleds, and toboggans were all essential for moving over deep snow. Wherever possible, people travelled over river ice on leeward shorelines to avoid rough terrain and wind. Dogsleds were usually pulled by only one or two dogs, because hunters were rarely able to feed more. As a result, the northern Aboriginal people, particularly the women, carried many of their possessions on their backs when moving from one hunting ground to another. Such dependence on human and dog power meant it was impossible to accumulate possessions, given the mobile lives of these northern hunters. It also discouraged acquisitive behaviour and wanton exploitation of the environment.

Northern Native groups had what anthropologists call "small-scale" societies, in which daily contacts are ordinarily limited to close kin. The smallest group was the winter band, which usually consisted of a few closely related families. Its size was controlled by two factors, safety and efficiency. Moose and caribou, the primary winter game, were not herd animals and so were most effectively taken by hunters working in pairs or in small parties. Hunting and living in kinship groups also increased the chances of survival. If the male head of a family sickened or died, starvation could still be avoided, because the family would be supported by the band.

Marriages took place with little fanfare and, when necessary, were easily dissolved. Of this aspect of Cree life, the explorer David Thompson observed:

Nothing is requisite but the consent of the parties, and Parents: the riches of a man consists solely in his ability as a Hunter, and the portion of the woman is good health, and a

This 1880 oil painting by Thomas Mower Martin, *Encampment of Woodland Indians*, shows the blending of European and Indian cultures. The women are wearing European dresses and are using a trade kettle, but the lodges and canoes are still made of birchbark.

willingness to relieve her husband from all domestic duties. . . . When contrariety of disposition prevails, so that they cannot live peaceably together, they separate with as little ceremony as they came together . . . without any stain on their characters. . . .

Native people clearly did not have the same double standard about marital and pre-marital sexual relations as the European males who left us their accounts. Chastity was not considered an essential virtue, though Thompson reported that "sometimes it was found to a high degree." Samuel Hearne, speaking of the Cree, said that "no accomplishment whatever in a man, is sufficient to conciliate the affections, or pre-serve the chastity of a southern Indian woman." Hearne's remark reveals his sexism: it says nothing about the traders who often encouraged debauchery. Indeed, by Hearne's own account, traders were not averse to using force to win sexual favours. He noted that the Hudson's Bay Company trader Moses Norton, himself the son of a mixed marriage, kept several wives and a box of poison. The latter was employed against Indian men who refused him their wives or daughters.

Another Aboriginal social custom which many newcomers saw as scandalous was that of spouse exchange. Here Hearne exhibited more understanding:

I should acknowledge that it is a very common custom among the men of this country to exchange a night's lodging with each other's wives. But this is so far from being considered as an act which is criminal, that it is esteemed by them as one of the strongest ties of friendship between two families; and in case of the death of either man, the other considers himself bound to support the children of the deceased. Those people are so far from viewing this engagement as a mere ceremony, like most of our Christian god-fathers and god-mothers, who, notwithstanding their vows . . . scarcely ever afterward remember what they have promised, that there is not an instance of a Northern Indian having once neglected the duty which he is supposed to have taken upon himself to perform.

Perhaps reflecting the male perspective of the time, Hearne does not tell us whether Indian men had to seek the consent of their wives for these arrangements. Similarly, he does not consider the possibility that sometimes women may have initiated these bonds. It is clear from the commentary of other European observers that Indian women were not deferential to men.

Political organization was very flexible. The people tended to follow natural lead-ers. Usually, the headman of a winter band was a superior hunter, married, and a

Here the Indian is presented as a menacing savage armed with a traditional war club, a trade axe, and a musket. More puzzling are the undersized snowshoes the traveller is wearing with his summer dress. *Iroquois allant à la découverte*: etching by J. Laroque after a drawing by J. Grasset de St. Sauveur (Paris: 1796).

Iroquois allant a la Decouverte

skilled orator. The headman of the summer band was generally the most respected individual from among the leaders of the smaller winter bands. In contrast to European political organizations, these men held no power simply by virtue of their offices, and major economic and political decisions were made collectively. Nothing was done until a consensus was reached. Headmen operated by persuasion, not coercion. When dealing with the outside world, they were expected to be good spokesmen on behalf of their followers, and they were chosen in part because of their abilities as traditional orators.

One of the basic problems for Native peoples living in the northern forest was the periodic scarcity of game after forest fires, or from diseases and the normal fluctuations of animal populations. Generally these shortages were localized and of short duration. To cope with them, the Native peoples developed a number of effective strategies. Within bands, close kin felt obliged to help each other in times of need, sharing surpluses with their relatives without receiving an immediate return. "Those acts that pass between man and man for generous charity and kind compassion in civilized society," remarked David Thompson approvingly of the Cree, "are no more than what is every day practised by these Savages, as acts of common duty...." Because sharing was considered a duty, the hoarding of personal wealth was regarded as antisocial, and leaders were expected to exhibit great generosity. In direct contrast to the Europeans, a northern Native person gained status by giving rather than by accumulating. Sharing also took place between groups. If moose or caribou hunts failed in a band's territory, permission was normally granted to hunt on the range of neighbouring bands. Sometimes food shortages could be alleviated through trade, particularly for northern bands who lived adjacent to the Iroquoian area of southern Ontario. Generally, however, northern-forest people did not engage in extensive inter-tribal trade, simply because the forests lacked sufficient resources to make it practicable.

Individually through vision quests, and collectively through special feasts and rituals such as drumming, the peoples of the boreal forest sought the good will and assistance of the spirit world. Thompson, who exhibited great sympathy with Aboriginal religious beliefs, described those of the Cree:

They believe in the self existence of the Keeche Keeche Manito (The Great, great Spirit)… He is the master of life. … He leaves the human race to their own conduct, but has placed all other living things under the care of Manitos (or inferior Angels) all of whom are responsible to Him…each Manito has a separate command and care, as one has the Bison, another the Deer. … On this account the Indians, as much as possible, neither say, nor do anything to offend them, and the religious hunter, at the death of each animal, says, or does something, as thanks to the Manito of the species for being permitted to kill it.

Religion was a highly personal affair, but individuals who were thought to have special powers to commune with the spirit world became shamans. One important ceremonial rite that these visionaries performed among the Algonquian was that of the shaking-tent, in which the shaman conversed with the spirit world in a lodge specially constructed for the purpose. Among the Ojibwa, whom Thompson described as the "Great Religionists," these Native spiritual leaders formed a fraternity, the *midewiwin* or Grand Medicine Society, which was the most important religious institution in their traditional culture. Sacred symbols of the society were preserved on birchbark scrolls as mnemonic aids for its members.

Native people living in the maritime region of eastern Canada developed similar ways of life. The principal difference was that the Beothuk, Mi'kmaq, and Malecite inhabited both the seashore and the inland forests. And it was because they lived along the coast in the summer that they were the first to come in contact with European explorers and fishermen. Eventually the latter took control of marine resources and marginalized aboriginal people in the emerging commercial fishery.

Farmers of the North

Native societies elsewhere were substantially different. Two major groups dominated eastern Canada. The Iroquoian-speaking people who lived in what is now southern Ontario and around the St. Lawrence had well-developed farming methods that enabled thousands of people to live together in small areas and to develop complex political systems. The Iroquoians spoke various dialects and formed several separate and often mutually hostile nations, including the Five Nations or "Iroquois Confederacy" (consisting of the Seneca, Cayuga, Oneida, Onondaga, and Mohawk) and the Huron, the Erie, and the Neutral. These nations dealt with each other through networks of kinship, rivalry, war, and trade. The northern Iroquoians exchanged their surplus corn for the products of the Algonquians' hunting. The amounts were small, but the routes and methods of trade were well established, and goods and information were exchanged along them long before the Europeans and their goods entered the scene.

In sharp contrast to their Algonquian-speaking neighbours to the north and east, who had no permanent settlements and moved constantly from one hunting ground to the next, the Iroquoians were village dwellers who depended on the produce of their carefully tended fields. The Huron, for example, obtained as much as 75 per cent of their food by farming; they ate primarily corn, beans, squash, and sunflowers—supplemented with fish, particularly whitefish, and game, mostly venison. Before the arrival of the Europeans the Iroquoian-speaking Huron, Hochelagans, and Stadaconans were the northernmost farmers in North America, living as they did at the outer climatic limits of agriculture.

Iroquoian villages contained as many as two thousand inhabitants and were located close to the fields. A new village site was sought only when all the conveniently accessible land had been used up in the course of field rotation—a farming practice made necessary by the slash-and-burn method they used, best described in the first-hand account of Recollet lay brother Gabriel Sagard:

Clearing is very troublesome for [the Huron], since they have no proper tools. [The men] cut down the trees at the height of two or three feet from the ground, then they strip off all the branches, which they burn at the stump of the same trees in order to kill them, and in the course of time they remove the roots. Then the women clean up the ground between the trees thoroughly, and at distances a pace apart dig round holes or pits. In each of these they sow nine or ten grains of maize, which they have first picked out, sorted, and soaked in water for a few days, and so they keep on until they have sown enough to provide food for two or three years, either for fear that some bad season may visit them or else in order to trade it to other nations for furs and other things they need; and every year they sow their corn thus in the same holes and spots, which they freshen with their little wooden spade, shaped like an ear with a handle at the end. The rest of the land is not tilled, but only cleansed of noxious weeds, so that it seems as if it were all paths, so careful are they to keep it quite clean; and this made me, as I went alone sometimes from one village to another, lose my way usually in these corn-fields more than in the meadows and forests.

Fishing and hunting were largely male activities—fishing the more significant because fish provided the major source of protein. For the Huron, who occupied what is now northern Simcoe County in Ontario, the major fishing expedition was the month-long autumn one to Georgian Bay to obtain spawning whitefish. The Stadacona, who lived near present-day Quebec City, took mackerel, seal, eel, and porpoise from the Gulf of St. Lawrence. They differed from the other Iroquoians in that they developed a strong connection with the sea. Between planting and harvest they would venture as far as the Gaspé peninsula and the Strait of Belle Isle on fishing, sealing, and other food-collecting expeditions. Unlike the male-dominated autumn fishing trips of the Huron, men, women, and children all joined in these summer voyages.

Although the hunt provided less food than farming or fishing, it was important because hides and pelts were needed for clothing. Given the relatively close popula-tions in the settled areas of Iroquoian territory, game and fur were in short supply, so hunting parties were forced to travel considerable distances in search of their prey. The Huron, for example, mounted autumn and late-winter deer-hunting expeditions, usually of several hundred men, that took them on lengthy journeys south or east of their homes. Taking advantage of the fact that white-tailed deer gathered in herds in these seasons, the Huron men built V-shaped deer hedges 2.7 metres (9 feet) high and about half a mile long. Driven up against the hedges, the deer were slaughtered in con-siderable numbers. During the late-winter hunt, a few women would accompany the men to assist with the butchering and preparation of hides. Because venison did not preserve well (some was smoke-dried), most of the meat obtained on the deer hunts was eaten immediately. But the fat and the hides were brought home to the villages. Indeed, in order to stockpile provisions, the Iroquoians had developed various means of food preparation and storage. Women dried the produce of the fields and stored it in porches or hung it from the ceilings of their dwellings. They either sun-dried or smoked their fish and then packed them in bark containers.

Probably the most striking difference between the northern hunters and the more southerly farmers was the type of dwelling the Iroquoians lived in, for they were the people of the longhouses. A typical Huron house was up to 30 metres (100 feet) long and 7.5 to 9 metres (25 to 30 feet) wide. It was constructed on a frame of poles sunk into the ground around the outer perimeter, bent and tied together in the centre, and covered with bark, usually cedar. Enclosed porches were built at one or both ends of the longhouse to store food and firewood, and inside a raised platform was built around the walls. Near the centre, storage racks were lashed to large poles, and here the inhabitants placed pots, clothing, and other possessions. Also down the centre was a row of hearths about 6 metres (20 feet) apart. In the larger villages, the houses were surrounded by palisades of interwoven stakes for defence.

Besides building larger and more permanent dwellings than the northern hunters, the Iroquoians constructed more substantial canoes for trade, war, and fishing—craft capable of transporting five or six men and their possessions over the rough, deep waters of Georgian Bay and the larger rivers. It appears that such Iroquoian-speaking people as the Huron engaged in regular trade with their neighbours before the European intrusion. There was a solid basis for such exchange, because they produced sizeable surpluses of corn but fur and game were in short supply in the immediate vicinity of their villages. Their northern neighbours prized corn and usually had furs to exchange—pelts which were superior because of the harsher climate of the

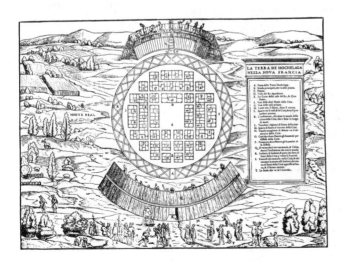

In the lower centre of *La Terra de Hochelaga nella Nova Francia* (1556), by Giovanni Battista Ramusio, Jacques Cartier and his men are being welcomed at the entrance of the Iroquois village of Hochelaga (Montreal) at the beginning of October 1535. The village is portrayed imaginatively. Iroquoian settlements lacked this geometric regularity.

northern forests. So it is not surprising that by the time the Europeans arrived among them a lively trade was already being conducted. Corn, tobacco, and nets figured prominently in the outbound traffic from Huronia, situated on the southern shores of Georgian Bay; furs, dried fish, meat, and winter clothing made their way in.

The Huron were also interested in trade for other reasons. They gathered around them more possessions than their Algonquian neighbours—partly as a result of their more sedentary lives—and although they discouraged acquisitive behaviour by individuals, each kinship group sought possessions collectively in order to maintain or elevate its status. This was done by redistributing wealth—obtained primarily through trade—to other members of the society at large. Understandably, such trading connections were jealously guarded by the kinsmen who had either developed or inherited them. Generally, the group whose members first developed a given trading route held the rights to it, but they could lease these rights or transfer them to other groups.

The longhouse society was complex and highly organized compared to the nuclear family of the Algonquian- and Athapaskan-speaking peoples. In the longhouse lived an extended family which consisted of a woman and her daughters, or a group of sisters, together with their husbands and their children. Descent was traced on the female side, and the family usually chose to remain in the mother's house.

Political life was organized around the clan, which was made up of all those extended families in a village who claimed descent from a common female ancestor. Depending upon the size of the village, one or

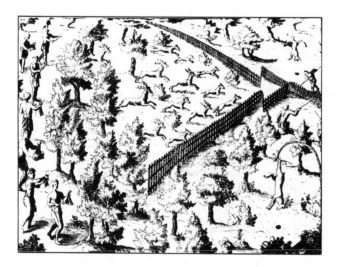

Huron Deer Hunt. Although the deer hedge is portrayed as it might look if a European farmer had built it, the engraving does indicate how the deer were killed with spears and snares near the opening of the hedge. After a drawing by Samuel de Champlain (Paris, 1632).

several different lineages might be present, and each lineage bore the name of one of the tribe's clans: Bear, Hawk, Turtle, etc. In the larger villages longhouses belonging to families of the same clan tended to be clustered together. Even people living in different villages but bearing the same clan name recognized a symbolic affinity towards each other, although marriage between clan members was prohibited.

Each clan had two headmen—a civil leader and a war leader. Of the two, the civil leader was considered the more important, and he dealt with all aspects of daily life. The war leader, or war chief, was held in high regard only in times of conflict. It was then his responsibility to organize raiding parties in the blood feuding that was common with villagers beyond Huronia to the south, particularly those living south of Lake Ontario. Generally, war parties made up of the fellows of fallen kinsmen would raid opposing villages to seek revenge. Conflict was more or less continuous, but relatively few deaths resulted from the fighting. Instead men, women, and children were taken captive, and the tendency was to torture the men and adopt the women and children to replace members from the captors' ranks. Certainly, annihilation of villages and groups was not normally the objective before the Europeans appeared.

Village councils made up of the civil heads of the various clans managed the daily affairs of the settlements. One of these councillors acted as the village spokesman but all the civil leaders were of equal rank, and they did not have to accept the decisions of their fellow councillors. Village administration was accomplished through consensus politics; besides civil leaders, old men who were respected for their wisdom attended village council meetings and took part in discussions. Councils arranged public functions, co-ordinated community building projects, and adjudicated disputes.

Each Huron village belonged to one of five different tribes, which together formed the Huron Confederacy. Each tribe controlled a portion of Huron territory, administered by a tribal council of civil leaders from the villages in that area. As with village councils, all tribal councillors were of equal rank, but only one acted as a spokesman for the group. Each tribal councillor had certain hereditary responsibilities, such as protecting the trade routes of his lineage. Tribal councils were chiefly concerned with inter-village and inter-tribal affairs. Overarching the tribal councils was the Confederacy, which apparently included all the members of the respective tribal councils. The Huron Confederacy attempted to maintain friendly relations among its five tribes, and co-ordinated trade and military affairs. Such diplomatic and political negotiations cannot have been easy, but clearly the organization of the Huron enabled them successfully to manage the affairs of a substantial population—

These two watercolours—*Dance for the Recovery of the Sick* and *Calumet Dance*—are from a series of sketches of Iroquoian dances and ceremonies by George Heriot, a Quebec-based painter, author, and postmaster (1766–1844). A calumet is a peace pipe.

some twenty-five thousand in the early seventeenth century—before Europeans caused extraordinary disruptions with which they were unable to cope.

Huron life was filled with public and private celebrations. The largest feasts were held at the time of the annual meeting of the Confederacy council and at the investiture of new leaders. Men and women also organized feasts to commemorate a variety of important personal events, and in general celebrations were a lively time of dancing, games, and eating. The most important of all Huron ceremonies was the Feast of the Dead, ten days of pomp and feasting held whenever a village changed location. Brother Sagard recorded this ceremony in great detail, though it is evident from the list of goods put into the common grave that European influence had already changed Huron life:

The other neighbouring tribes are notified in order that those persons who have chosen that town to be the burying place may bring [their dead] thither, and others who wish to come out of respect may honour the festival with their presence. For all are made welcome and feasted during the days that the ceremony lasts....

The grave is dug outside the town, very large and deep, capable of containing all the bodies, furniture, and skins offered for the dead. A high scaffolding is erected along the edge, to which all the bags containing bones are carried; then the grave is draped throughout, both the bottom and the sides, with new beaver skins and robes; then they lay in it a bed of tomahawks; next kettles, beads, necklaces, and bracelets of wampum, and other things given by the relations and friends. When this has been done the chiefs, from the top of the scaffold, empty and turn out all the bones from the bags into the grave upon the goods, and they cover them again with other new skins, then with tree-bark, and after that they put back the earth on top, and big pieces of wood.... Then they have a feast again, and take leave of one another, and return to the places whence they came, with great joy and satisfaction at having provided the souls of their relatives and friends with something that day to plunder and wherewith to become rich in the other life.

Sagard also grasped the fact that the Feast of the Dead played an important role in Huron society: "by means of these ceremonies and gatherings they contract new friendships and unions amongst themselves, saying that, just as the bones of their deceased relatives and friends are gathered together and united in one place, so also they themselves ought during their lives to live all together in the same unity and harmony."

A rich spiritual world infused life. Uppermost in the Huron pantheon was the sky spirit who controlled the weather and helped human beings when they were in need; lesser spirits, the Old, had the power to influence human beings. All Iroquoians called on this spirit world to assist them in their economic and military endeavours, but they were also very concerned with obtaining spiritual help to combat illness. The Huron, for example, believed there were three major reasons for sickness—natural causes, witchcraft, and the unfulfilled desires of a person's soul—and they turned to spiritual healers and curing societies to deal with these problems. Since dreams were regarded as the language of the soul, the shamans paid particular attention to them when treating patients—by taking appropriate ritual action, they were able to deal effectively with common emotional problems. The healing ceremonies were often, in essence, a kind of individual and group psychotherapy.

The Plains Buffalo Hunters

Probably none of the Aboriginal peoples of Canada has captured the popular imagination more than the nineteenth-century armed equestrian nomads of the prairies and bordering woodlands. These Native peoples, and their southern neighbours in what is now the United States, were a formidable military force in their short-lived heyday, and for many they symbolize the Canadian Native of historic times. But the lives of the Plains people were distinctively different from those of Aboriginal people elsewhere. Furthermore, the horse and the gun, which became an essential part of nineteenth-century Plains culture, were obtained from Europeans. Even today, it is hard to tell whether these two European elements fundamentally transformed Plains people's lives or simply intensified their older traditions.

Long before they had obtained horses and firearms, the Plains people were remarkable hunters and had devised various efficient means to pursue buffalo—to the near exclusion, indeed, of the other large game abundant in the region. The task of the hunters was made relatively easy by the fact that the buffalo gathered at the same winter and summer ranges every year and moved back and forth between them along well-established pathways. If the pattern changed, it was usually the result of a readily identifiable cause, such as an autumn fire that destroyed the forage for the ensuing winter, or unusually mild winter weather which encouraged the herds to remain out in the open prairies. In most instances, the Indians had forewarning and could take counter-measures to ward off food shortages.

A Buffalo Rift, an 1867 watercolour by Alfred Jacob Miller, shows the cliff-driving technique of slaughtering buffalo which was commonly used in the summer. Before the Indians obtained horses, they often used fire to help drive the herd forward.

The hunters had different strategies for taking large numbers of the summer and winter herds. In summer, the most effective was the cliff drive. This involved a large party of Native people, usually including women and older children, working together to stampede a herd over a drop-off; the height did not have to be great, just enough to cripple the animals in the plunge. The drovers fanned out in a V-shaped formation around the kill site. For protection, they often stood behind natural or man-made shelters of brush or stone. The most skilled hunters came up behind the herd and set it in motion towards the cliff, while those on the flanks created enough noise to keep the animals moving forward. The prairie grass was often set alight to drive the buffalo to their deaths, which is one reason fires were commonplace. Fire drives were efficient, but the hunters were unable to control the number of animals slain, and waste was the result.

Precontact cliff drive sites, known as buffalo jumps, are found widely scattered over the prairies. The reliability of these sites is graphically pointed out by archaeological evidence suggesting they were used repeatedly over thousands of years.

The individual who supervised the construction of the buffalo pound and distributed the returns was known as the poundmaker. Note that the use of horses to drive the animals into the pound was not traditional. *A Buffalo Pound*: engraving (1823) after a drawing by Lieutenant George Back (1796–1878).

The Gull Lake site in Saskatchewan, for example, is 4.5 metres (15 feet) deep in buffalo bones.

Plains hunters also used the "surround" technique, described in 1691 by Henry Kelsey of the Hudson's Bay Company, one of the first Europeans to visit the prairies: "when they see a great parcel of them together they surround them w[ith] men... they gather themselves into a smaller compass keeping y beasts still in the middle and so shooting ym till they break out at some place or other and get away." This technique was probably used most often when bands were *en route* to or from their summer camps; cliff drives were generally employed when the Native people were in their large summer camps.

In winter the hunters took advantage of the fact that the herds sought shelter. In those places known to be frequented by their quarry, they built fenced enclosures known as pounds. During a winter visit to the Assiniboine of Saskatchewan in 1776, the fur trader A. Henry observed a pound in use. His account is tinged with admiration because, like surround hunting, this strategy required both skill and bravery. The hunters risked being trampled if the herd was startled.

Arrived at the island [of trees], the women pitched a few tents, while the chief led his hunters to its southern end, where there was a pound, or enclosure. The fence was about four feet high, and formed of strong stakes of birch-wood, wattled with smaller branches of the same. The day was spent making repairs...by evening all was ready for the hunt.

At day-light, several of the more expert hunters were sent to decoy the animals into the pound. They were dressed in ox-skins, with hair and horns. Their faces were covered, and their gestures so closely resembled those of the animals themselves, that had I not been in the secret, I should have been as much deceived as the oxen....The part, played by the decoyers, was that of approaching them within hearing and then bellowing like themselves. ...This was reiterated till the leaders of the herd followed the decoyers in the jaws of the pound, which, though wide asunder toward the plain, terminated, like a funnel, in a small gateway....

No matter what the method, once the hunt was concluded the elder who had supervised it apportioned the kill. The women did the skinning, butchering, and meat preparation. In the summer, they put away a considerable quantity for later consumption: meat was dried and pounded to a powder; grease was rendered and placed in a buffalo-hide or rawhide container (or parfleche) to cool; powdered meat and heated grease were combined to make pemmican. Frequently, Saskatoon berries were added to flavour this highly concentrated, nutritious mixture.

Other game was pursued too, particularly red deer. These large deer (up to 500 kilograms/1,100 pounds) lived in the wooded margins of the grasslands, and the men hunted them during the winter whenever the buffalo failed to appear, using their skins to make clothing. Plains nations, including some of the Assiniboine, Blood, Cree, and Anishinabe (Ojibwa), who were recent immigrants from the woodlands, relished moose flesh. Prairie wolf, or coyote, and beaver were hunted for their skins and pelts to make winter clothing, as well as for food, and, in season, the waterfowl were always welcome. Besides hunting large and small game, some Plains people fished in the early spring and autumn. The Assiniboine and Cree, for example, took large quantities of sturgeon during the spring runs by building weirs at key locations along such major rivers as the Red and the Assiniboine. In contrast, older Plains tribes such as the Blackfoot had no taste for fish. In fact, their dislike was so pronounced that Matthew Cocking of the Hudson's Bay Company was told by the Blackfoot of southern Alberta that they would not accompany him to York Factory at Hudson Bay because they would have to travel by canoe and eat fish along the way.

Although the diet of the Plains people was very high in protein and fat, they did eat vegetables and fruit, particularly the wild prairie turnip and a variety of berries, the most important of which was the Saskatoon berry. Both were harvested in large quantities and dried for later use. Assiniboine and Cree living in southern Manitoba also obtained wild rice through trade: the lands east of the Red River marked the north-western limit of the wild-rice–growing area so they turned to the Mandan villagers, who lived in the upper Missouri River valley, for dried corn. The Mandan too were hunters, but they built a trade empire based on their surplus corn production.

But the buffalo remained the basis of wealth for the Plains people. As Henry remarked of the Assiniboine:

The wild ox alone supplies them with every thing which they are accustomed to want. The hide of this animal, when dressed, furnishes soft clothing for the women; and, dressed with the hair on, it clothes the men. The flesh feeds them; the sinews afford them bow-strings; and even the paunch…provides them with that important utensil, the kettle….This being hung in the smoke of a fire, was filled with snow; and, as the snow melted, more was added, till the paunch was full of water, and stopped with a plug and string….The amazing numbers of these animals prevent all fear of want….

Although the women of all the Plains tribes were skilled at dressing and painting buffalo hides, their more sedentary Mandan neighbours to the south excelled in the arts

and were renowned for their feathercraft and hair work. The Assiniboine and Plains Cree prized the products of the Mandan craftswomen, as well as the handicrafts that the Mandan obtained from tribes living to the west and south-west. So—along with the dried corn—painted

A painted buffalo robe. Prominent men often reminded the world of their heroic deeds by having pictures painted on their lodge coverings.

hides, buffalo robes, and feathered wear flowed northward from Mandan villages along well-established trading routes into the Canadian prairies. In return, the Plains Assiniboine and Cree carried unpainted hides, robes, and dried provisions southward to the Mandan. Very likely furs too were important in the southward-bound traffic, given that the Mandan lived outside the prime fur area.

Although the Assiniboine and Cree, relative newcomers to the prairies and parklands, used bark canoes, the bands which had settled the grasslands earlier and hunted buffalo did not build these craft. Instead, they used the so-called bull boat, an oval craft with a covering of buffalo hide stretched over a frame of small wooden poles. Bull boats were not intended for long-distance journeys; they were made for people who travelled primarily on foot and needed boats only for crossing rivers. On these pedestrian journeys, Plains travellers relied heavily upon dogs as beasts of burden. Linked to a travois, a single dog could carry 35 kilograms (75 pounds) of cargo, the equivalent of a buffalo-hide lodge cover.

Plains society was based on the family, but polygamy was practised, and men of high status usually had several wives, ordinarily sisters. Winter villages on the plains were approximately the same size as the summer camps of woodland bands, about one hundred to four hundred people, and they were pitched in the shelter of islands of trees. Today it is hard for us to imagine what it would be like to experience a winter storm while camping, with both man and buffalo desperate for shelter. Henry has left us a vivid account. While *en route* to the winter village of Chief Great Road, situated in central Saskatchewan, Henry and his Indian companions were hit by a blizzard as they stopped for the night:

The storm continued all the night, and part of the next day. Clouds of snow, raised by the wind, fell on the encampment, and almost buried it. I had no resource but in my buffalo-robe.

In the morning, we were alarmed by the approach of a herd of oxen, who came from the open ground to shelter themselves in the wood. Their numbers were so great, that we dreaded lest they should fairly trample down the camp; nor could it have happened otherwise, but for the dogs, almost as numerous as they, who were able to keep them in check. The Indians killed several, when close upon their tents; but, neither the fire of the Indians, nor the noise of the dogs, could soon drive them away. What ever were the terrors which filled the wood, they had no other escape from the terrors of the storm.

Big Snake, Chief of the Blackfoot Indians, Recounting his War Exploits to Five Subordinate Chiefs. This oil painting by Canada's famous artist-explorer, Paul Kane (1810–71), was done in the 1850s.

Once Henry reached the safety of Great Road's village, he found his host to be both generous and hospitable. The trader was treated to a succession of the feasts and entertainments that were a normal part of winter village life. Clearly, he thoroughly enjoyed his visit with Great Road's people:

...the chief came to our tent, bringing with him about twenty men, and as many women....They now brought musical instruments, and, soon after their arrival, began to play. The instruments consisted principally in a sort of tambourine, and a gourd filled with stones, which several persons accompanied by shaking two bones together; and others with bunches of deer hooves, fastened to the end of a stick....Another instrument was one that was no more than a piece of wood, of three feet, with notches cut on its edge. The performer drew a stick backward and forward, along the notches, keeping time. The

Indian Camp, Blackfoot Reserve, near Calgary, Northwest Territories, 1889. Lodge poles could also be used to make a travois; the uncovered poles shown in this photograph are several different sets of travois leaning against each other. This panorama is from two negatives by William Notman (1826–91).

women sung; and the sweetness of their voices exceeded whatever I had heard before.

The entertainment lasted upward of an hour; and when it was finished a dance commenced. The men formed themselves into a row on one side, and the women on the other; and each moved sidewise, first up, and then down the room. The sound of bells and other jingling materials, attached to the women's dresses, enabled them to keep time. The songs and dances were continued alternately, till near midnight, when all our visitors departed.

Village affairs in the winter were the responsibility of a chief and a council of elders, generally those considered to be the best suited to lead. As with the Iroquoians, council decisions were usually reached by consensus and implemented by persuasion, although sometimes force was used. During the summer the situation was somewhat different, because camps were often as large as the biggest Huron villages, numbering in excess of a thousand people. Clearly, social control and village security were needed then, particularly since mass buffalo hunts had to be carefully planned and tightly regulated to be successful; and also because a defensive posture had to be maintained constantly, summer being a time of widespread inter-tribal conflict. So

Blood Indian Sun Dance photographed by R. N. Wilson. The self-torture of boys of fifteen and sixteen by inserting ropes through their pectoral muscles was only a small part of the ceremony. The sundance was banned by the federal government in the 1890s, but continued in secret.

the tribal council, consisting of the elders of the winter bands, would call upon one of the men's military or police societies to enforce their rulings if necessary.

For both men and women, societies formed an important part of the Plains social life and helped to knit large groups together. Among the men, who were very status-conscious and competed strongly for social position, military or police societies were finely ranked in order of ascending status. Eligible men bought their membership, and only those who had the greatest wealth and highest personal status were able to gain entrance to the top-ranked society. Before the arrival of Europeans, one of the most important displays of wealth was the tipi lodge, made from ten to twelve buffalo hides; the best lodges were highly decorated. In the quest for wealth and status, it is clear that men were very dependent on their wives, who did most of the craft work. Although hunters killed bison in great numbers with relative ease, and therefore supplies of the most commonly used raw materials were readily available, making these materials into domestic articles was another matter. A hunter needed a wife, preferably more than one, and daughters for this work. Not surprisingly, the improved hunting that resulted from the acquisition of horses and guns was one factor that encouraged an increase in the number of polygamous marriages and the number of wives a man could have.

Today we would characterize Plains society as extremely "macho." Individual status was based to a large extent on the military prowess and boldness exhibited in daring raids. The introduction of the horse by the Spanish in the eighteenth century signalled a sharp increase in tribal raiding because forays were organized to capture the prize animals of others; given the range provided by the horse, and the acquisition of firearms beginning in the late seventeenth century, male mortality increased significantly. And fewer males were another reason for polygamous marriages.

The most important event in the religious life of the Plains people was the annual Sun Dance ceremony, which is also known as the Thirst Dance because participants avoid drinking. The people of the plains regarded the sun as the major manifestation of the Great Spirit. The ceremony generally took place in July or August, following a buffalo hunt which was specially undertaken to obtain the food needed for the elaborate feasts. The ceremony lasted three days, during which time the celebrants danced and the shamans displayed their conjuring skills. Great quantities of meat, particularly buffalo bosses (humps) and tongues, were consumed. Like the Iroquoian Feast of the Dead, the Plains peoples' Sun Dance was a great festival of renewal that brought families and related winter bands together at the height of summer.

Fishermen and Traders of the West Coast

The West Coast tribes were the great traders of aboriginal Canada. William Brown of the Hudson's Bay Company called one group, the Babine, "inveterate fishmongers." Brown's comment reflects both the frustration and the admiration that many traders felt, a dual attitude that characterized all European trade with West Coast people into the twentieth century. On the one hand, he knew that the Babine, like their neighbours, were tough, sophisticated, highly experienced traders—so much so, in fact, that at times Brown had to resort to strong-arm tactics. On the other hand, he had to admire their ability, and his comment is very much a trader's observation on other traders.

Brown quickly understood the situation when he told them the prices he was prepared to pay for their large salmon. In response, the Babine "gave us to understand we need not expect any large ones, they being accustomed when people were here *en derouin* to receive their own prices." The coast villagers were very much in control. It was they who dictated terms, and once Europeans had arrived on the west coast they struggled to maintain their traditional trading networks by playing one group of intruders off against another, whether the Hudson's Bay Company, the Russians, or the Americans.

Nowhere in Canada was the landscape more diverse or the culture more complex. Food was plentiful. Both trade and food hinged on salmon, although porpoise, seal, sea otter, and whale were taken along the coast, and halibut too. But while all five salmon species were found in abundance on the lower reaches of the rivers near the coast, only the sockeye travelled great distances inland to spawn in the headwaters of the large rivers. So while the coast fishers could usually obtain a catch sufficient to their needs, this was not the case near the headwaters of such major rivers as the Skeena and the Fraser, because the catch depended on the size of the sockeye run. And that uncertainty was compounded by random fluctuations of the fish runs, often caused by landslides that destroyed fishing sites and altered stream flows. As a result, the Native people of the interior had to rely more heavily on hunting than did their neighbours along the coast.

Salmon were caught in a variety of ways. Nets and fish weirs were the most efficient means where geography permitted; in the narrower canyons, long-handled gaff hooks and dip nets could be more effective. The women processed the fish, preserving large quantities for the winter season by smoking and drying. When, in 1793, Alexander Mackenzie crossed the continent from Lake Athabasca to reach the Pacific, he was welcomed by the Bella Coola. He watched the women preparing salmon, and noted that nothing was wasted:

I observed four heaps of salmon, each of which consisted of between three and four hundred fish. Sixteen women were employed in cleaning and preparing them. They first separate the head from the body, the former of which they boil; they then cut the latter down the back on each side of the bone, leaving one third of the fish adhering to it, and afterwards take out the guts. The bone is roasted for immediate use, and the other parts are dressed in the same manner, but with more attention, for future provision. While they are before the fire, troughs are placed under them to receive the oil. The roes are also carefully preserved, and form a favourite article of their food.

The fattier fish, sockeye, were best suited to smoking, and the leaner ones, chum, were better for drying. Once the processing was completed, the salmon was placed in cedar containers and stored in caches where the meat would be secure from predators.

The eulachon, or candlefish, is an extremely fatty species, and the oil obtained from it was used for both consumption and illumination. The Nass River was the site of the most famous eulachon fishery; West Coast people not only devised a means of extracting eulachon oil, they were also able to package it so well that it could be transported long distances. The result was a widespread oil trade into the interior over mountainous, sometimes treacherous routes that came to be known as grease trails.

The dense rainforest supported relatively little game, but hunting prospects were better inland. In the country bordering the middle and upper Skeena River, the Gitksan (Tsimshian-speakers) and Babine (Athapaskan-speakers) devoted considerable time to hunting the mountain goat, prized for its wool and horns, bear, and beaver, which they valued as a ceremonial food. Beaver, like groundhog, were also hunted for their fur in the Tsimshian area. Because the coastal mountains marked the western limits of the beaver's range, this was marginal beaver country, and the Indians carefully husbanded the precious resource.

Besides fish and game many varieties of berries were found west of the Rockies. Huckleberry cakes were particularly popular, and they were one of the leading commodities the inland people traded to the coastal villagers. The women made the cakes by drying and crushing the berries, then placing them in a cedar box and boiling them using red-hot stones. The cooked huckleberries were spread on a bed of cooked skunk cabbage or salmonberry leaves arranged over a fencelike cedar drying rack. A low fire burned continuously under the rack until all the berries were properly dried. The women then rolled the berries into a tube, a stick was passed through the centre, and the roll was hung in a warm place until all the berries were completely dry. The rolls were flattened, cut up, and packed in cedar boxes to be traded. When intended for home use, they were left intact.

Skidegate Indian Village, Haida Tribe, Skidegate Inlet, Queen Charlotte Islands, British Columbia, July 1878. By the time G. M. Dawson took this photograph, there were only twenty-five houses (several of them uninhabited) and fifty-three totem poles remaining at Skidegate.

West Coast villagers were the only Canadian Indians to develop the art of weaving—as shown in this monochrome wash and pencil, *Interior of a Communal House with Women Weaving, Nootka, April, 1778,* by John Webber (1751–92). Webber was a member of James Cook's crew on the latter's exploration of the Pacific.

The Aboriginal people of the west coast based their elaborate culture on finely crafted cedar. Certainly they were master woodworkers and their cedar-plank houses were the most substantial and permanent of all the dwellings built by Canadian Native people. Alexander Mackenzie admired the complexity and organization of the houses when he visited the Bella Coola village of Nooskulst (Great Village). The well-built houses were multiple-family dwellings similar to the longhouses of the Iroquois.

The village…consists of four elevated houses, and seven built on the ground, besides a considerable number of other buildings or sheds, which are used only as kitchens, and places for curing their fish. The former are constructed by fixing a certain number of posts in the earth, on some of which are laid, and to others are fastened, the supporters of the floor, at about twelve feet above the surface of the ground: their length is from an hundred to an hundred and twenty feet, and they are about forty feet in breadth. Along the centre are built three, four, or five hearths, for the two-fold purpose of giving warmth, and dressing their fish. The whole length of the building on either side is divided by cedar planks, into partitions or apartments of seven foot square, in the front of which there are boards, about three feet wide, over which, though they are not immovably fixed, inmates of these recesses generally pass, when they go to rest.…On the poles that run along the beams, hang roasted fish, and the whole building is well covered with boards and bark, except within a few inches of the ridge pole; where open spaces are left on each side to let in light and emit the smoke.

This coloured pen-and-ink drawing, *Interior of Habitation at Nootka Sound, April 1778*, is also by John Webber. Note the dried fish hanging from the ceiling, and the way food was roasted over an open fire.

For sea travel, these coastal people built the largest, most finely crafted, and most highly decorated canoes of any Indian group. Alexander Mackenzie described one canoe that he saw as "painted black and decorated with white figures of fish of different kinds. The gunwale, fore and aft, was inlaid with the teeth of the sea otter." Huge cedar trees were felled (quite an accomplishment considering they had no metal tools) and hollowed out to form canoes from 10.5 to 21 metres (35 to 70 feet) long, some slim and fast for war, some broad in the beam for trade. Packed with provisions and as many as seventy people, these ocean-going craft were capable of coastal trips of several hundred miles. War canoes could be as long as the visiting European sailing ships. Flotillas of these formidable craft full of Native fighters were a sight so daunting that trading vessels routinely dropped anti-boarding nets into place.

Men and women wore cloaks made from skins, strips of rabbit fur, or woven yellow cedar bark. Like their northern neighbours, the Tlingit of Alaska, the Tsimshian wove patterned blankets from the wool of the wild mountain goat, but since it was in relatively short supply and the intricate patterns very difficult and time-consuming to achieve, these blankets were possessed only by the most influential Native people. Indeed, they symbolized high status and became prized articles. For rainy weather, the

West Coast people wove ponchos and conical decorated hats from cedar bark. For cold weather, mittens and cloaks were fashioned from sea otter and other pelts (sea-otter cloaks, like the beaver coats of the northern-forest Native people, were coveted by early European visitors). It is hardly surprising that the most important piece of household furniture was the decorated bentwood box used for storage as well as seating.

As with the Iroquoians, the economic and social organization of West Coast villagers was based on kinship ties of clan and lineage. But the villages acted independently; there was no tribal organization to link one to another as in the case of the Iroquois. Sometimes neighbouring villages worked together or joined forces in battle, but these were purely voluntary joint ventures. Each village, however, contained one or several lineages; and each house within the village contained a lineage, that is, a number of related families. In the north, families traced descent through the female line; in the south, through the male line; and among the central coast Native people, through both lines. The house held the rights to certain fishing sites and hunting territories which were clearly defined, and access was carefully controlled by the head of the house or lineage. Partly for this reason, the first European traders to reach Gitksan and Wet'suwet'en thought of the heads of houses as "men of property." Indeed, the heads of households not only regulated outsiders' access to their territories, but also controlled the hunting and fishing activities of their own houses. Among the Babine, William Brown, the Hudson's Bay trader, estimated that one-half of the adult male population was excluded from beaver trapping by orders of the "men of property." In this way resources were carefully managed.

Probably the most striking way that their social life differed from that of all other Canadian Aboriginal people was that they had a system of inherited rank, divided into three groups. Chiefs came from the ranks of the nobility; beneath them were the commoners, making up the bulk of the population; and at the bottom were the slaves, who were generally captives or descendants of captives. Social position was determined by ancestry, except for the slaves, whose situation was usually a result of the misfortunes of war. Particular sets of privileges and obligations were associated with inherited titles and positions, and these included the right to use certain symbols in decorative art. Title transfers were publicly witnessed at one of the best known of all North American Native social institutions—the potlatch. Some of these ceremonial feasts were purely for pleasure. Through potlatching, rival chiefs also established new social hierarchies and gained new ranks. During a potlatch the new recipient of a title distributed presents, collected for that purpose with the help of his

Throughout Canada, Native people were fond of games of chance. Missionaries usually regarded these games as the work of the devil, however, and attempted to ban them. This watercolour, *The Game of Bones* (1861), is by W. G. R. Hind (1833–88). Hind, who travelled widely in Canada and produced hundreds of paintings and sketches, was the brother of the prolific scientific writer Henry Youle Hind.

kinfolk, to all the invited guests. The acceptance of gifts by these witnesses to the ceremony was symbolic of their acceptance of the new order; this was particularly necessary in the passing of rights and duties from one generation to another.

Besides playing a central role in maintaining the social order, potlatches served an important economic function. The West Coast people ardently sought wealth to maintain and enhance their social rank. Like the Huron and Plains nations, they used trade as one means to wealth. Possessions obtained through trade, as well as those made locally, were redistributed through the community at the potlatch. Sometimes, too, potlatches were held by members of one village for a neighbouring village which had suffered some economic misfortune, such as a fishery failure.

In the nineteenth century, potlatch ceremonies gained notoriety among the European immigrants, because Native leaders sometimes competed with one another for status through so-called potlatch wars in which one rival attempted to give away or destroy more wealth than his challenger. There is good reason to suppose that potlatch wars were more common after the Europeans arrived, a consequence of the disruption to the Indians' lives. A "war" could be set off when a village resettled to be closer to a trading post, or as the result of a fatal epidemic, or

Paul Kane made an expedition from Toronto to Fort Victoria in 1846–48; he based this oil painting, *Medicine Mask Dance*, on sketches done during that trip. Kane recorded in *Wanderings of an Artist* that the menfolk of the Clallum "wear no clothing in summer, and nothing but a blanket in winter, made either of dog's hair alone, or dog's hair and goosedown mixed...." Their mask dance was "performed both before and after any important action of the tribe...."

the increased circulation of European and American goods. Through potlatching, the Native peoples attempted to establish a new social hierarchy.

Along with their love for feasts, coastal people had a great fondness for gambling. Indeed, most of Canada's Native people had games of chance that they liked to play. According to Hudson's Bay Company traders, among the Carrier the "game which is most universal consists of about 50 small sticks, neatly polished...of the size of a quill. A certain number of these sticks have red lines around them and as many of them as one player finds convenient are rolled up in dry grasses and according to the judgement of his antagonist respecting their number and mark he loses or wins." Difficulties often arose when these games were played: "They are addicted to gambling. Umpires are chosen to observe that the parties play fair, but it is seldom terminated amicably." The stakes of robes, shoes, bows, and arrows, and other possessions were high, and large teams would back the players.

The religious life of the West Coast people was dominated by ceremonies that took place during the winter months. Indeed, among the Kwakwaka'wakw (Kwakiutl) winter was regarded as the sacred or "secret" season and the rest of the year was considered "profane." Winter ceremonies were sponsored by the many secret societies—eighteen existed among the Kwakwaka'wakw alone. These societies had strong hierarchies, and members of a given society tended to be of the same gender and social rank. Each society had a mythical ancestor, and its members carefully guarded its secrets. New members, who inherited their positions, were initiated at religious winter dances organized under the careful supervision of a master of ceremonies. Entire villages were invited to watch the dancers performing in elaborate costumes, including carved wooden masks, with a great sense of drama and theatre. These collective rites were unlike the individualistic spirit quests of most Native groups elsewhere in Canada but the goals were similar—to secure the protection of guardian spirits for the individual being initiated.

Besides the elaborate ceremonial aspect of their spiritual life, West Coast people, in a manner similar to Native peoples elsewhere in Canada, engaged in a variety of more simple daily practices and rituals that were intended to show deep respect and appreciation to the spirit world for providing for their basic welfare. Understandably, salmon were particularly revered. When Alexander Mackenzie visited the Bella Coola he was unaware of many of the taboos that had to be rigidly observed. Inadvertently his men violated some of them.

These people indulge in extreme superstition respecting their fish, as it is apparently their only animal food. [Animal] Flesh they never taste, and one of their dogs having picked and swallowed part of a bone which we had left, was beaten by his master till he disgorged it. One of my people also having thrown a bone of the deer into the river, a native, who had observed the circumstance, immediately dived and brought it up, and, having consigned it to the fire, instantly proceeded to wash his polluted hands.

When Mackenzie wanted to obtain a canoe to continue his voyage down the river to the coast, the Bella Coola man he approached kept making excuses. "I at length comprehended that his only objection was to the embarking venison in a canoe on their river, as the fish would instantly smell it and abandon them, so that he, his friends, and relations, must starve." Once the trader disposed of the venison, he easily obtained the canoe he wanted.

In west coast society, culture, art, and spiritual belief were closely linked. Decoration, whether on the plank prow of a canoe or on such smaller items as tools, household utensils, or containers, served a function beyond the aesthetic. Many decorative motifs were "house" crests, or belonged to a particular lineage that controlled their use. In this, as in so much else that characterized west coast life, the primary intent was the benefit of all members of a lineage.

Arctic Hunters

In some ways, the dilemma of West Coast Aboriginal people was how to dispose of so much food, so much wealth. The Inuit of the Arctic faced a very different problem: survival. Of all of the regions of Canada, the Arctic undoubtedly was the most difficult and challenging for the aboriginal peoples to occupy. It has long, dark winters of intense cold and blowing snow, and its ecosystem is very fragile and sparse.

The Inuit had come from Siberia some four thousand years before and had occupied the coasts of the Arctic islands and the mainland of Canada, north of the treeline. They were highly successful in developing hunting technologies and strategies to kill marine animals and those found inland on the treeless tundra lying between the Arctic shoreline and the northern boundary of the boreal forest. They were primarily big-game hunters, although they supplemented their diets seasonally with birds and fish. The most sought-after marine mammals were polar bear, ringed and bearded seal, walrus, narwhal, and beluga whale. On the tundra they hunted barren-ground caribou, and grizzly bear and the shaggy muskox in a few scattered locations. Wolf, wolverine, arctic hare, and arctic fox provided them with warm furs, as did beaver and muskrat in the Mackenzie River delta. They caught arctic char, a fresh water–salt water fish, and lake trout in large quantities.

In order to feed themselves throughout the year from this array of game and fish, most Inuit migrated on a seasonal basis. Summer was the main whaling season, especially the months of July and August, when bands camped on the coast. In the autumn most moved inland to catch arctic char as the fish swam upriver from the sea, and to hunt the caribou that were crucial to them for food, bone, and the skins that made up much of their winter clothing. Caribou skins made perfect winter wear because the hides were light and the hairs hollow, trapping body heat. The original survival parka, such clothes are still carried today by Arctic bush pilots as emergency

When the explorer Martin Frobisher (1539–94) returned to England from his 1577 voyage to Baffin Island, he took this Inuit man, woman, and child with him. John White may have done this watercolour on board ship during the trip home.

clothing. From late autumn and early winter until spring most Inuit gathered in fixed base-camps near the coastline or on the sea ice. From these settlements small hunting parties made regular excursions in search of seal and walrus, and—after contact with Europeans—on traplines for fur-bearing animals. With the increasing daylight of spring, the people moved to fishing camps where they dug through the ice to take advantage of the spring runs of arctic char as the fish returned to the sea.

The Inuit were adept and resourceful at fashioning weapons, transport, and shelter from antler, bone, ivory, wood, skins, fur, snow, and ice. For hunting, the men made several types of toggling harpoons (harpoons with detachable bone points), throwing boards (for harpoons and bird spears), spears, lances, and simple and double recurved sinew-backed bone bows. In the west-central Arctic, pure copper found on the surface of the ground was used for making knife blades. Fishing equipment included unbarbed bone fish hooks, jigs and lures, nets, fish rakes, and spears; stone or woven willow weirs were built along the lower reaches of coastal rivers to trap arctic char. Among the more useful tools for women were the stone and copper curve-bladed knives backed with bone and antler and known as *ulus*, scrapers for working hides, and sewing kits that included bone needles and thimbles. Men's tools included double-edged daggers made of bone, ivory, stone, and copper. Household equipment included containers made from wood and easily worked soapstone; long, shallow soapstone seal-oil cooking and lighting lamps; and bow drills used to make fires and to manufacture equipment.

One of the best-known features of Inuit life is the winter snow house or igloo that was commonly used in the central and eastern Arctic. Two types of igloo were

This 1824 engraving, *Esquimaux Building a Snow-hut*, is after a drawing by Captain G. F. Lyon.

constructed, using bone or wood snow knives and snow shovels. A small hut about 1.5 metres (5 feet) in height and 2.1 metres (7 feet) in diameter was built for temporary shelter during winter hunting expeditions or journeys. The main winter dwelling was much larger; 3 to 3.7 metres (10 to 12 feet) high and 3.7 to 4.5 metres (12 to 15 feet) in diameter, these igloos usually housed two or more families. On the basis of a small igloo constructed by his Inuit guide, Augustus, the Arctic explorer Captain John Franklin remarked in 1820 that:

They are very comfortable buildings. . . . The purity of the material . . . the elegance of its construction, and the translucency of its walls, which transmitted a very pleasant light, gave it the appearance far superior to a marble building, and one might survey it with feelings somewhat akin to those produced by the contemplation of a Grecian temple . . . both are triumphs of art, inimitable in their kinds.

In the drier western part of the North around the Mackenzie delta, as well as on the southern coast of Labrador, a semi-subterranean wood-frame structure covered with planks and ice-glazed sod was the typical family winter house. In the Mackenzie region, such dwellings had an open central area surrounded by three living chambers, each occupied by a family. During the warmer months of the year, Inuit bands lived in tents—either conical or dome-shaped—covered with seal or caribou skins. Besides dwellings, some groups also built larger snow or skin-covered structures called *kashims* for sporting and ceremonial activities.

Clothing, with some regional variations in style, was basically the same for all Inuit people. Winter outerwear consisted of parkas for both men and women, with pants for men or culottes for women, usually made from caribou skins, and knee-length boots fashioned from a variety of materials, including seal, beluga, and caribou skins. Women decorated clothes with hides of contrasting colours in ways that indicated the gender and age of the wearer. Undergarments were made from pelts and such warm, soft materials as eider-duck skins. In winter, these undergarments were worn with the hair turned inward; summer clothing largely consisted of the winter underwear worn with the hair side turned outward.

During the course of their migration with the seasons, the Inuit used several means of transportation. They used two crafts for open-water travel—the well-known kayak and the less familiar umiak. Most bands built the wood-framed, skin-covered kayak for single hunters to pursue their quarry along the edge of ice floes or to spear caribou swimming across lakes and rivers. The umiak, a flat-bottomed, wood-framed, and skin-covered boat that could carry ten people and up to four tons of cargo, was for transportation and for hunting large marine mammals. Designed for hunting among the ice floes, these craft were relatively light and puncture-resistant due to the tough beluga- or walrus-hide covering, and they could be pulled onto a floe quickly when shifting ice or a wounded animal threatened. Umiaks were also used to move camp, and in northern Quebec dogs sometimes helped pull these boats against the current, two men remaining in the umiak to steer it while others drove the dog teams along the shore.

Winter travel was mainly by sled. The runners were commonly made from wood, bone, or antler covered with a smooth layer of mud and ice for ease of movement; at the beginning of the day the runners were made even slicker by a fresh coat of urine. The dog teams that pulled the sleds varied in size, but most groups could not afford to support more than a few hungry animals. Among the Copper Inuit, for example, a husband and wife would use only two dogs to help pull the sled. Dogs were also valuable as pack animals—fully loaded, they could carry 14 to 18 kilograms (30 to 40 pounds) and drag the tent poles.

Winter Houses of Esquimaux; this engraving is after a watercolour by George Back. Back's journal
entry for July 11, 1826, records that these huts were "built of driftwood, with the roots upwards—
without windows—low and destitute of every comfort...." Back accompanied several major Arctic
expeditions, including Franklin's to the Coppermine River; a lake and river in the Northwest
Territories bear his name.

In several respects Inuit society was similar to that of the Indians of the Subarctic,
being based around a small family—mother, father, children, and grandparents.
However, a family alone could not be self-sufficient. Because of the exceedingly harsh
climate and the scarcity of food, families clustered together in small bands to make
co-operative hunting, fishing, and the collection of other foods easier. For example,
to hunt barren-ground caribou the Inuit used many of the same techniques that the
Athapaskans did. By collective effort, hunting parties drove herds either into lakes
and rivers where they were speared by men in kayaks, or towards converging stone
fences where hunters waited with bows and arrows. In winter, people living in the
central and eastern Arctic hunted seals on the ice using the breathing-hole technique,
and usually a small number of hunters and their dogs were involved. The dogs
sniffed out the breathing holes, many of which were then blocked to force the seals
to a hole where one of the hunters waited, standing on a piece of caribou hide and

A Labrador Eskimo in his Canoe (watercolour, 1821) by fifteen-year-old Peter Rindisbacher. Note the sealskin float in this drawing.

behind a wall of snow blocks to deflect the icy arctic wind. In spring, seals were decoyed onto the ice by a hunter lying on his side and mimicking seal movements.

Whaling required the co-operation of many hunters. Large whales were hunted by harpoon, but one of the most important species in the central and eastern Arctic was the small, white beluga whale that appeared on the edge of the sea-ice in late spring and generally stayed in the shallow waters of bays and estuaries. Hunting parties took advantage of the beluga's habits to trap and spear entire herds. Collective effort was also required to take large numbers of arctic char during the big autumn runs, and most bands maintained one or two stone barricades that extended across rivers leading to the sea.

When hunting or collecting food, the participants rallied around whichever leader was best suited to oversee the enterprise. The principal exception to this practice of temporary leadership was the village headman, whose primary responsibility was the organization of whaling-boat crews. These positions were inherited through the father in the Mackenzie delta, and in Quebec were held by men who owned an umiak, were great hunters, and had kinship status that gave them control over a number of male relatives. Otherwise there was generally no formalized leadership beyond the family.

In Inuit society, lifelong partnerships were established between men. Partners

The Migration, a 1964 sculpture in grey stone, bone, and skin, by Povungnituk sculptor Joe Talirunili (b. 1899), commemorates a tribal migration in a sealskin-covered umiak, traditionally rowed by women.

shared resources and sometimes wives and guaranteed each other mutual support and protection. Writing about the marriage practices of the Caribou Inuit of the western Arctic in 1821, John Franklin recorded that "The Esquimaux [Inuit] seem to follow the eastern custom respecting marriage. As soon as a girl is born, the young lad who wishes to have her for a wife goes to her father's tent, and proffers himself. If accepted, a promise is given which is considered binding, and the girl is delivered to her betrothed husband at the proper age." Beyond these alliances, sharing was a prominent feature of Inuit society generally, and there were many formal and informal means of making certain that it took place. There were rules for dividing the spoils of collective hunting and fishing, while ceremonial activities also ensured that scarce resources were distributed among the band.

Before the intrusion of the Europeans, the Inuit had a very active ceremonial life and usually constructed special areas or igloos for celebrations and rituals. Most common was the drum-dance feast, in which the men danced in turn while beating a large, tambourine-like drum and singing a personal song. The songs might deal with aspects of the singer's life, or they might be satirical of others; in part, they provided an outlet for hostile feelings in a public forum. During drum dances and on other occasions the Inuit engaged in games and sporting contests, for which they had a great fondness—particularly wrestling and boxing matches, and demonstrations of strength.

They shared the belief, common among Native groups, that everything was inhabited by a soul or spirit. So as not to offend the souls of animals and fish taken, rituals and taboos were observed both before and after the hunt. Shamans acted as intermediaries between the community and the spirit world, but in contrast to other areas of Native Canada, the priests were not organized into fraternities, and there were no elaborate religious ceremonies equivalent to the Feast of the Dead, the Sun Dance, or the winter dances of the West Coast Indians.

From the Arctic to the west coast to the east coast, Canada on the eve of contact with Europeans was a world in which the people had developed close material and spiritual bonds to the land, strongly influenced by the broad variations in climate and geography. Although there were profound differences in the lifestyles adopted by Native people in the core areas of the various regions, at the boundaries those differences tended to blur into one another. Such mixing and blurring was the result of continuous migrations of people, seasonal activities that required groups to move to new locations, and trade between regions. The fact that the people of different regions blended into one another along their borders greatly facilitated European exploration and the initial exploitation of the country. It meant that the Europeans could move easily across boundaries, and they soon discovered that within each area they could rely on the Native people to be very familiar with the terrain and very adept at harvesting what the land had to offer.

The European Invasion

The disruption of the Native world that resulted from European expansion into the North American continent took place on four frontiers, and the intruders were many: there were the French anchored on the St. Lawrence; the English centred on Hudson Bay and James Bay; the Spanish in northern Mexico and the American south-west; and the Spanish, English, Russians, and Americans on the west coast. Each frontier was significantly different. All the same, contact was made in similar, recognizable stages right across the continent.

On the east coast, the Native peoples' earliest encounters were fleeting ones with mariners, and sustained meetings only began at the very end of the fifteenth century with the explorations of John Cabot. Such meetings did not take place in Hudson Bay and James Bay until a century and a half later, starting with the voyages of Henry Hudson in 1610. They did not commence on the west coast until almost three centuries later, in 1774, when the Spaniard Juan Pérez probed northward from California as far as the Queen Charlotte Islands.

Masks were central to Native ceremonies throughout Canada, and were used to portray mythical beings and to represent spirits. The nineteenth-century Iroquois False Face mask (far left) represents a crooked-nosed giant who challenged the power of the Creator. Such masks were carved directly into tree trunks from which they were subsequently "freed." The wooden Dorset Inuit mask (below) is over one thousand years old, and was probably used in religious-magic ceremonies. The matched stone masks (top) were likely intended to be worn one over the other by a single performer in the winter rituals known as *halait* (sacred), and secretly switched to demonstrate the magical powers of the dancer. The unsighted "twin" was collected at the Tsimshian village of Kitkatla in 1879, and the sighted one on the Nass River or at Metlakatla.

A period of time—barely a decade on the west coast, as much as fifty years in the Hudson Bay and James Bay region—usually elapsed between these initial meetings and the beginning of regular contact along the coast. Once regular contact was established, either from ships or as the newcomers built settlements for themselves, European influence expanded rapidly into the interior. Throughout North America, explorers' accounts make it clear that news of their arrival spread swiftly over long distances. Even remote tribes soon became aware of the presence of the intruders. When the English and French first set themselves up on the western shores of Hudson Bay in the late seventeenth century, for instance, their Indian informants gave them accounts of the Spanish, who were described as bearded men with great canoes located several months' march to the west–south-west, even though none of

"Ceremony of the Pipe," from the Hudson's Bay Company's 1921 calendar. In this highly romanticized picture, the artist has attempted to portray an Aboriginal diplomatic institution that was a central feature of the early fur trade through which economic and political relationships were established and renewed annually. Subsequently, this tradition was continued in the treaty relationships between Aboriginal people and Canada.

these Indians had ever presumably travelled there. Through this information network, Indians living inland quickly learned, too, about exotic European items, and in a relatively short time Native routes were established for long-distance trade. In this way, European trade was carried inland from the coast by the Native peoples themselves well in advance of explorers or traders.

Soon after John Cabot's voyage to Newfoundland in 1497, Native people throughout the Maritimes would have begun to encounter Europeans fairly frequently. Many of the people of the eastern coast must have concluded between 1500 and 1550 that these seaborne newcomers were transient and unthreatening, yet eager to acquire furs and able to pay for them with attractive new items: iron axes, copper pots, cloth, and decorative beads. By the 1550s, small amounts of European goods had penetrated the whole Algonquian-Iroquoian system of eastern Canada, and people on Lake Huron or Michigan who would never in their lives see a European (or even salt water) had handled the remarkable novelties arriving from the east. The first interest of these strange items may have been symbolic and spiritual; beads, coppers, and ironwares were frequently buried in sixteenth-century cemeteries. Native societies, however, soon discerned the practical value of iron axes and copper pots, and the advantages of metal arrowheads and spear points in both hunting and Native

A Métis buffalo hunter photographed by Humphrey Lloyd Hime, 1858. The prairie Métis developed an economy and society that was very different from that of their relatives who lived in the forest regions of Canada. Buffalo-hunting, farming, trading, the freighting business using Red River carts, and wage labour were all important components of the Prairie Métis economy.

wars. During the mid-1500s, their growing interest in these goods made it possible for the Europeans to secure a foothold in the local networks of diplomacy and trade. When Alexander Mackenzie made his famous expedition across British Columbia, he learned from the Sekani, who had had no direct contact with the intruders, that "Their [European] ironwork they obtained from the people who inhabit the bank of that river, and an adjacent lake, in exchange for beaver skins, and dressed moose skins. They represented the latter as travelling, during a moon, to get to the country of other tribes, who live in houses, with whom they traffic for the same commodities...."

Disastrously for the Native people, these trading routes also carried European diseases, and measles and smallpox wreaked havoc. The exact tolls of these early epidemics will never be known, but losses of 50 per cent or more occurred during documented outbreaks of disease such as the one that hit the Huron in 1639.

Following in the wake of Native traders who carried their goods far inland came the European overland explorers, sometimes accompanied by missionaries. Because these first explorers only obtained limited glimpses of the country as they were conducted through it by their Native guides, for all practical purposes much of the changing Native world would lie beyond the view of the intruders for some time to come.

Sustained local contact between Europeans and Aboriginal people began with the establishment of trading posts. And trading posts brought settlements with them. Once again, there were considerable variations in the amount of time that elapsed between the arrival of the first explorers and the establishment of the first trading posts or missions. Some explorers built posts as they travelled, others did not—in British Columbia, for example, settlements did not follow for more than twenty years; in northern Ontario, for roughly eighty years.

The establishment of trading posts and missions in what is now Quebec changed the relationship between Aboriginal people and Europeans. It meant that there was much more social interaction between the groups, which not only resulted in increasing economic exchanges, but encouraged the rapid growth of a population of mixed ancestry and, eventually, the emergence of a distinct people—the Métis. In many respects the offspring of mixed ancestry became the new brokers between the Europeans and those Native groups that continued to maintain some physical and cultural distance from the intruders. The arrival of missionaries was an added complication, because these men had as their explicit goal the transformation of Native culture into something resembling the Christian European model.

All the same, the role of missionaries was minor before 1821—mainly because of the intensely commercial nature of the early Europeans' activities. Indeed, except for New France, and the Labrador coast, the missionary incursion happened quite separately from that of the fur traders. In most of central and western Canada, missionaries arrived long after the traders had set themselves up. Most were well intentioned by their own standards, and apparently attempted to shield the Aboriginal people from the worst aspects of European culture. Nevertheless, they believed European culture to be the proper, acceptable way of life, and their arrival marked the beginning of a systematic assault on Native religion and beliefs and many traditional social customs, an assault that would be intensified later when governments assumed responsibility for Native affairs.

Codfish and Furs

This was the general course of development; but particular events in different parts of Canada bring into focus the actual impact of the European on the Native world.

Probably we will never know the extent or nature of the encounters that took place between European fishermen and Native people west and south-west of Newfoundland before 1534. The first extended commentary we have is that written by Cartier on his first two voyages in 1534 and 1535–36. After examining the

Labrador coast in the Strait of Belle Isle area and making his famous "land God gave to Cain" observation, he sailed to the south-west, passing by the western shore of Newfoundland, the Magdalen Islands, and the western end of Prince Edward Island before reaching the eastern shore of New Brunswick near Miramichi Bay. He then proceeded to Chaleur Bay, where he encountered a large party of Mi'kmaq. It is unclear from his account of this meeting whether the Mi'kmaq were already accustomed to trading with Europeans, but his journal certainly indicates they were eager:

…we caught sight of two fleets of Indian canoes…which numbered in all some forty or fifty canoes. Upon one of the fleets reaching this point, there sprang out and landed a large number of Indians, who set up a great clamour and made frequent signs to us to come on shore, holding up to us some furs on sticks. But as we were only one [long]boat we did not care to go, so we rowed towards the other fleet which was on the water. And they [on shore], seeing we were rowing away, made ready two of their largest canoes in order to follow us. These were joined by five more of those that were coming in from the sea, and all came after our long-boat, dancing and showing many signs of joy, and of their desire to be friends.…

Despite these friendly gestures, Cartier, greatly outnumbered, felt threatened and fired two warning cannon shots over their heads. The next day he and his men got up their courage and went ashore to meet the Mi'kmaq. A brisk trade ensued:

As soon as they saw us they began to run away, making signs to us that they had come to barter with us; and held up some furs of small value, with which they clothe themselves. We likewise made signs to them that we wished them no harm, and sent two men on shore, to offer them some knives and other iron goods, and a red cap to give to their chief.…The savages showed a marvellously great pleasure in possessing and obtaining these iron wares and other commodities, dancing and going through many ceremonies.…They bartered all they had to such an extent that all went back naked without anything on them.…

Shortly after he left the Mi'kmaq, Cartier encountered a party of three hundred Stadacona who were camped on the Gaspé coast where they were fishing for mackerel:

We gave them knives, glass beads, combs and other trinkets of small value, at which they showed many signs of joy.…This people may well be called savage; for they are the sorriest folk there can be in the world, and the whole lot of them had not anything above the value of five *sous*, their canoes and fishing-nets excepted. They go quite naked, except for a small skin, with which they cover their privy parts, and for a few old furs which they throw over their shoulders.... They have no other dwelling [when travelling] but their canoes, which they turn upside down and sleep on the ground underneath.

As he prepared to leave for home, Cartier claimed the land for France. His account gives us an idea of how the Native people reacted to one of the first European land grabs:

...We had a cross made thirty feet high, which was put together in the presence of a number of the [Stadacona] Indians on the point [opposite Sandy Beach] at the entrance to this harbour, under the cross-bar of which we fixed a shield with three *fleurs-de-lys* in relief, and above it a wooden board, engraved in large Gothic characters, where was written, LONG LIVE THE KING OF FRANCE. We erected this cross on the point in their presence and they watched it being put together and set up. And when it had been raised in the air, we all knelt down with our hands joined, worshipping it before them....

When we had returned to our ships, the chief, dressed in an old black bear-skin, arrived in a canoe with three of his sons and his brother.... And pointing to the cross he made us a long harangue, making the sign of the cross with two of his fingers; and then he pointed to the land all around about, as if he wished to say that all this region belonged to him, and that we ought not to have set up this cross without his permission....

At this point Cartier ordered his men to seize the Stadacona and bring them aboard. They were given every sign of affection, as well as food and drink, "And then we explained to them by signs that the cross had been set up to serve as a landmark and guide-post on coming into the harbour, and that we would soon come back...." Cartier doubtless realized that the Stadacona were fully aware of the actual significance of the cross, and hence his baldly spurious explanation. He never did, in fact, return to this bay.

Just before he left for France, Cartier seized two young Iroquoian men, sons of Chief Donnacona, saying he would bring them back to the chief's village the following summer. He honoured this promise; in 1535 he visited Stadacona, near present-day Quebec City, and returned the men to their father. From there he travelled inland to the Iroquoians' substantial palisaded town of Hochelaga, at the present site of Montreal, to pursue his search for a water passage to the Pacific. He was impressed by the St. Lawrence valley and its people. Talking—mostly by signs—with the Hochelagans, Cartier gained the impression that beyond the rapids of Montreal, the rivers led inland to several large lakes and even to a land called Saguenay, the source of gold, silver, and copper. The hope that gold lay not far west of Hochelaga prompted Cartier's third and largest expedition in 1541, which was authorized to take control of these foreign lands "by friendly means or by force of arms." But sickness and the Native peoples' increasing readiness to ward off the intruders brought this venture to an inglorious end in 1543. There was no rich, hierarchical society here that might be conquered by a show of force, as there had been in the Spanish conquest. Nevertheless, in addition to furs and territory, this quest for a route to the Orient was to continue to be one of the driving forces behind overland exploration for the next two hundred years.

Cartier failed in his major objective, which he realized when he sighted the Lachine Rapids and understood that they marked the head of navigation on the St. Lawrence. But during the course of these voyages he learned a great deal about the geography of Maritime Canada, the Gulf of St. Lawrence, and the St. Lawrence valley. He noted that the waters teemed with fish and whales; there were excellent stands of timber in the Gaspé area; there was considerable agricultural potential on the New Brunswick coast and in the St. Lawrence valley; and furs were abundant. His voyages did much to establish the geography and place names of eastern Canada, and he also gave the country a name. The Iroquoians with whom he talked used the name "Canada" (the word seems to mean "village"), and Cartier took the name back to the mapmakers of Europe. By the late 1500s sailors spoke routinely of Terre-Neuve or Canada as a trading and fishing destination.

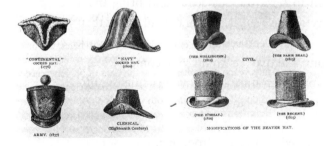

Modifications of the Beaver Hat. The fashion for the beaver hat was the driving force behind the early fur trade, as the under-wool from beaver pelts was used to make the high-grade felt that quality hatmakers demanded. Engraving in H. T. Martin's *Castorologia* (Montreal and London, 1892).

But, with the exception of fish and whales, the time was not right to make the capital investment needed to develop the resources in the New World. So for the next fifty years, the Aboriginal people along the Gulf of St. Lawrence would be disturbed only by fishermen and whalers who welcomed the chance to earn some additional income by trading for a few furs with the Native people who visited them on the coast during the summer.

Along the south shore of Nova Scotia, the fishermen set up primarily off-shore operations in which the cod was salted on the ships, so they had little, if any, contact with Mi'kmaq on the coast. The northern fishery was different. Drying stations were established on the Newfoundland coast, particularly on the Avalon peninsula, at good harbour sites which were often also favoured camping places of the Beothuk. In the early sixteenth century, fishermen had little interest in trading with them. The Beothuk did not welcome the fishermen because they occupied Native campsites and destroyed the surrounding forests with their clearing and reckless burning. Conversely, the fishermen disliked the fact that during the winter the Beothuk frequently plundered the drying stations to obtain nails and other metal scraps. Thus relations between the Beothuk and European fishermen were strained from the outset. The Beothuk suffered severely in the ensuing hostilities, and by the early nineteenth century became one of the few Native groups in Canada to be totally annihilated.

In the second half of the sixteenth century the economic climate in Europe changed, and conditions developed that encouraged the rapid development of the fur trade as a major industry. Beginning about mid-century, the felt hat became very fashionable in Europe, and it remained so until it was displaced by the silk hat in the middle of the nineteenth century. Hatters wanted beaver pelts only so they could shave off the hair; the skins could then be discarded. The most luxurious, durable felt was made from the short inner layers of shaven hair or under-wool of beaver pelts. Beaver had been nearly exterminated in western Europe by the sixteenth century, but they abounded in North America and could be obtained relatively cheaply.

Two types of beaver pelts were bought from Indians—coat beaver, called *castor gras* by the French, and parchment beaver, or *castor sec*. In the sixteenth century, only the Russians had mastered the technique of extracting the long guard hairs from parchment beaver pelts so the under-wool could be separated from the skin. But sending parchment pelts to Russia for processing substantially increased the cost of felt-making. Coat beaver, on the other hand, was second-hand, already worn by the Native people as winter coats. In the course of wearing the furs with the hair side turned inward, and scraping and rubbing them with animal marrow to oil and soften them, the Aboriginal people had worn off the guard hairs. The under-wool could now be easily removed from the skins, which meant the pelts could be processed directly by western European feltmakers. As a result, coat beaver became much sought after in the sixteenth and seventeenth centuries. For the Native people it meant a gratifying trade—indeed, in 1634, Father Le Jeune, the superior of the Jesuits at Quebec, reported that the Montagnais thought the European desire for beaver skins was foolishly extravagant:

The Savages say it is the animal well-beloved by the French, English and Basques,—in a word, by the Europeans. I heard my [Indian] host say one day, jokingly, *Missi picoutau amiscou*, "The Beaver does everything perfectly well, it makes kettles, hatchets, swords, knives, bread; and in short, it makes everything." He was making sport of us Europeans, who have such a fondness for the skin of this animal and who fight to see who will get it; they carry this to such an extent that my host said to me one day, showing me a beautiful knife, "The English have no sense; they give us twenty knives like this for one Beaver skin."

Father Le Jeune undoubtedly took some liberties in recounting this interview to make a point about the behaviour of European traders, but it is clear that early trade was very favourable to the Aboriginal people. Unfortunately for them, this situation did not last. By the end of the eighteenth century, western European feltmakers learned the Russian secret and parchment beaver became the preferred pelt because it was of more even quality than coat beaver. By the middle of the nineteenth century coat beaver was no longer in much demand—the result was that Native trappers had to trap more beaver if they wanted European goods.

While it lasted, the strong market for beaver pelts had other implications. For the first time it became possible for European merchants to specialize in the fur trade, so that by the 1580s it had ceased to be merely a small adjunct to the fishing and whaling industries. This change set in motion new economic forces that served to propel the industry across the continent over the next two centuries, upsetting the old order of aboriginal Canada in the process.

From the outset, a key problem for the fur industry was the high cost of transportation, given the great distance between Canada and the European markets. This encouraged merchants to try to monopolize the trade, to set prices highly favourable to themselves and at the same time capture a supply of furs sufficient to sustain profitable operations. In 1588 the King of France granted the first trading monopoly in Canada to Jacques Noel. Other French merchants immediately challenged it and it was hastily withdrawn by the Crown. This was but the first episode in a struggle that was to continue into this century. At best, merchants managed to enforce monopolies for only short periods of time before they were successfully challenged by fellow citizens or foreign traders.

Aboriginal people responded in a similar fashion. With the establishment of regular trade in a given area, Native trading specialists, or middlemen, promptly emerged. These entrepreneurs handled the traffic in furs and European goods between the trading stations and the Native groups living in the remote interior who supplied the bulk of the furs. Like other traders around the world, the Native middlemen sharply marked up the price of all the commodities they carried before passing them on. Understandably, these middlemen jealously guarded their lucrative trading routes, blocking access to all Native groups who did not have their permission to pass—a permission not readily obtained, and usually granted only after the payment of rather hefty toll charges.

Both Native peoples and Europeans struggled for economic control. This instability was, in fact, one of the driving forces behind the expansion of the industry. Repeatedly the Europeans sought to displace the middlemen in the hope that they could buy furs more cheaply, but they met with repeated failure as successive groups of Native people assumed the role of traders, thereby cashing in on their temporary strategic advantage. As trading routes reached deeper into the continent, transportation and storage costs mounted further, increasing the pressure on the Europeans to secure a high volume of fur. Invariably this meant, in turn, that the fur trade encouraged Native people to hunt and trap local animal populations at a level that could not long be maintained. The circular process set in motion would fuel the transcontinental expansion of the fur industry between 1580 and 1793.

The first Aboriginal trading specialists to emerge were the Montagnais who lived in the vicinity of the Saguenay River. The lower Saguenay is a deep fjord of stark and legendary beauty, and the mouth of the river had been an important whaling site since the middle of the sixteenth century, because the beluga whales breed there, and porpoises and fin, humpback, pilot, and even great blue whales are attracted to the area. Some fur trading had probably taken place there since that time too, and by the end of the century the lower Saguenay had become a major fur-trading centre, with merchant ships from European nations stopping there regularly. The Montagnais responded in two ways: they intensified their trapping and extended their trading connections northward and westward from Lac St-Jean towards Lac Mistassini and the upper Ottawa River; and they learned how to take advantage of a competitive market by playing off rival European traders against one another. By the turn of the century Frenchmen complained that the Montagnais had transformed the summer trade into an auction, driving prices up to the point that it was difficult for Europeans to make any profit.

Partly for this reason, the French, led by the explorer and cartographer Samuel de Champlain, pushed south-westward into the St. Lawrence River valley and established a post at the site of present-day Quebec City in 1608. Between Cartier's voyage in 1535 and Champlain's of 1608, the Stadaconans and Hochelagans disappeared. To this day historians debate what happened to them. What is clear is that at the time of Champlain's arrival the St. Lawrence valley had become a no man's land that separated two hostile Aboriginal groups—the New York Iroquois to the south of Lake Ontario, and the Algonquians of the Ottawa River valley and eastward as well as their Huron allies. Given the local political climate, it is not surprising that Champlain and his followers were quickly drawn into the conflict. In 1609 he accepted a request to join a party of Ottawa valley Algonquian and Huron on a raid into Mohawk country, where they attacked a Mohawk village on Lake Champlain. An escalation of the violence soon followed.

Although they were allied with some of their Algonquian-speaking neighbours to the east, the Huron were also eager to break the trading monopoly of two Algonquin groups, the Allumette and Petite Nation, of the middle and lower Ottawa valley, and to establish direct trading and military links with the French. With these objectives in view, the Huron invited Champlain to visit their country, and he accepted and set out for Huronia in 1613. However, his party was stopped *en route* by the Allumette, who wanted to protect their position in the trading system. They refused to let him pass. Champlain had little choice but to abandon his trip, although before leaving he presented gifts to the Allumette and promised to assist them in their struggles with the Iroquoians. This diplomacy would enable him to pass through their territory two years later, and in 1615 he finally reached Huronia; he himself was greeted warmly, but the missionaries who accompanied him were regarded with suspicion. The Huron believed, not without foundation, that these men were traders in disguise who had come to spy on them in order to learn their trading secrets. They were anxious not to reveal who their trading partners were. So the French priests got off to a shaky start; they did not establish permanent missions until the 1620s.

By the late 1630s, Huronia had become central to the French fur trade and a primary focus of missionary activity. But the area was still extremely unstable politically: by this time the New York Iroquois were beginning to be well armed with

European weapons, and they were making increasingly devastating raids on the lower Ottawa River and on Huronia in the hope of gaining access to the fur trade north of the Great Lakes. The Iroquoian attacks were no longer intended merely to obtain a few captives, as they had been before the European arrival—they were aimed at annihilating the opposing forces. As the conflict intensified, epidemics of smallpox ravaged the Huron, demoralizing them. The missionaries added to their problems by creating internal divisions between the converted and the unconverted. As a consequence Huronia was overrun by the Iroquois and collapsed in 1649.

After the fall of Huronia, traffic along the lower Ottawa River became intermittent because parties travelling there were often attacked by the Iroquois. Many of the old trading partners of the Huron withdrew to the west and north-west, out of range of the Iroquois war parties. This was a problem for the French traders, who were eager to retain contact with these groups. So, in 1656, French exploration into the upper Great Lakes was spearheaded by Médard Chouart Des Groseilliers. His brother-in-law Pierre-Esprit Radisson joined him in 1659, and by 1663 they had travelled as far as the Lake Superior country and possibly beyond to James Bay. In any event, the Cree, who at the time were fur suppliers to the Ottawa and Ojibwa, made it clear to the two Frenchmen that the prime fur country lay to the north of Lake Superior. The Native people also spoke of a northern "frozen" sea, and the two traders concluded that this was the one named for Henry Hudson, the hapless explorer left to die there in 1611 by his mutinous crew. Mindful of the mounting expenses involved in expanding the fur trade overland north-westward from the St. Lawrence River (Montreal and Trois Rivières), the brothers-in-law decided that an attempt should be made to establish a trading base on this northern sea. Then it would be possible to sail into the heart of the best fur country thereby eliminating burdensome overland transportation costs and, because access would be direct, outflanking another group of Native traders.

Radisson and Des Groseilliers failed to obtain French backing for their plans. It simply was the wrong time to approach French officials: in 1663 Jean-Baptiste Colbert, the new Secretary of State, had taken over direction of colonial affairs, and he opposed western expansion. He was more interested in promoting farming in the colony in order to establish the economy on a sounder footing. He did not want the local population drawn away from the settlements on trading or other ventures.

But Radisson and Des Groseilliers were not to be denied. After abortive attempts to gain support for their idea in Boston and France, they travelled to England. There they obtained a favourable hearing in the court of King Charles II, from a small, close-knit group of courtiers who were deeply concerned with establishing a balanced imperial economy. Included in the group were Anthony Cooper, later first Earl of Shaftesbury; Sir Peter Colleton; Sir George Carteret; and the first Duke of Albemarle, George Monk. This was an entrepreneurial, highly placed group of men who undertook the planting of Carolina in 1666 and were granted the Bahamas in 1670. They had the patronage of the King's brother, James, Duke of York, and his dashing cousin, Prince Rupert. After a bungled attempt to dispatch an expedition in 1667 (good summer weather passed before they were ready), one was finally launched on June 5, 1668, when the *Eaglet* and the *Nonsuch* weighed anchor in the Thames. These were small ships, ketches. Both weighed less than forty-four tons, and were approximately 5 metres (16 feet) in the beam and under 12 metres (40 feet) in length. The *Eaglet*, with Radisson on board, was forced to turn back, but the *Nonsuch*, carrying Des Groseilliers, reached southern James Bay on September 29. The crew wintered there and conducted a very successful trade with the Cree. The *Nonsuch* returned with such a large cargo of prime winter beaver and other furs that the press reported that it "made them some recompense for their cold confinement." Flushed with success, the English investors dispatched another ship in 1669 with Radisson on board, and took steps to establish the trade on a permanent basis. Accordingly, in the spring of 1670 the Hudson's Bay Company charter was drawn up, and it was signed by Charles II on May 2, 1670. The King gave "Governor and Company of Adventurers" monopoly trading privileges and the right to colonize all the lands drained by waters flowing into Hudson Strait. This vast estate (in modern geographical terms it included northern Quebec, northern Ontario, all of Manitoba, most of Saskatchewan, southern Alberta, and a portion of the Northwest Territories) was called Rupert's Land, in honour of Prince Rupert; in all, it was fifteen times larger than the present United Kingdom and five times larger than France. In several respects, the chartering of the Hudson's Bay Company (HBC) is one of the great ironies of Canadian history. The company was the conception of two Frenchmen; they helped guide it in the first critical years; yet it became one of the most successful English colonial ventures in Canada, and certainly the most lasting.

In 1671 the new company started erecting trading posts at the outlets of the major rivers. Within ten years forts were established on the Rupert, Moose, Albany, and Hayes rivers, and they had a major impact on trade. Between 1650 and 1670, Assiniboine and Cree bands living as far away as eastern Manitoba had been supplying Ottawa and

Ojibwa traders with furs in exchange for French goods. But with the establishment of the bayside posts, the Cree and Assiniboine no longer had to depend on Ottawa and Ojibwa middlemen, and were able to trade directly with the English. They became the sixth generation of important Aboriginal middlemen operating in the century-old land-based fur trade. Even more significant, they were well placed strategically to assume a merchant role themselves. Quickly they seized the opportunity and within a decade of the founding of the HBC, its Canadian governor, John Nixon, reported:

I am informed, there is a nation of Indians called the poyets [Dakota Sioux] who have had no trade with any cristian nation....It would be greatly to the advance of our trade if we could gaine correspondence with them....For they would faine have a trade with us but are affrayed to break through our neighbouring Indians for want of armes...our Indians [Assiniboine and Cree] are affrayed that they [the Dakota] will breake doune to trade with us, for by their good-will, they would be the only brokers between all strange Indians and us....

Given the crucial roles that Radisson and Des Groseilliers played in helping the HBC establish its commercial ties with the Indians, it is not surprising that many of the trading practices developed by the French were incorporated into the new company. Early HBC accounts give us a useful insight into the general character of the fur trade in the late seventeenth and eighteenth century. One of its most celebrated features was the pre-trade ceremony in which gifts of equal value were exchanged. This was a Native institution; in Native society, trade between groups who had no kinship ties did not commence until bonds of friendship were established or reconfirmed by the leaders of the respective parties. At the same time, peace pipes were smoked and formal speeches were delivered.

In the HBC's early days the pre-trade gift ceremony became central to the company's relationship with those groups who lived long distances from the bayside posts and only came to trade once a year. According to company accounts, Aboriginal trading parties rallied behind leaders who were skilled orators, knew the routes to the posts, and were astute traders. The English called these men "trading captains." The headmen who followed them were termed "lieutenants." Just prior to their arrival at the post, the trading parties would put ashore to dress in their finest clothing. Properly attired, they continued their journey. When they came in sight of the fort, the HBC post commander, known as the chief factor, would fire a round of cannon or musket in salute to the Native people, who replied in similar fashion with their muskets.

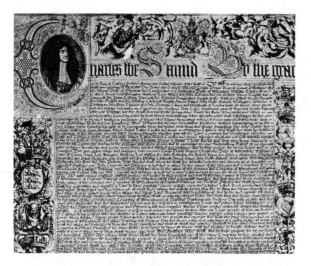

One of the most important documents in Canadian history is the charter granted to the Hudson's Bay Company by Charles II at Westminster on May 2, 1670; this is its first page. In 1870 Canada paid the HBC $1.5 million in cash to buy back its chartered territorial rights; the company also received land concessions amounting to one-twentieth of the prairie region, and retained the developed land around its trading posts.

As soon as the Native people arrived at the post they made camp at a clearing set aside for that purpose. While the camp was being set up, the trading captain and his lieutenants proceeded into the fort to greet the chief factor and his officers. Andrew Graham, chief factor at York Factory in the late eighteenth century, described a typical visit:

The Governor being informed what Leaders are arrived, sends the Trader to introduce them singly, or two or three together with their lieutenants, which are usually eldest sons or nighest relations. Chairs are placed in the room, and pipes with smoking materials produced on the table. The captains place themselves on each side of the Governor.... The silence is then broken by degrees by the most venerable Indian.... He tells how many canoes he has brought, what kind of winter they have had, what natives he has seen, are coming, or stay behind, asks how the Englishmen do, and says he is glad to see them. After which the Governor bids him welcome, tells them he has good goods and plenty; and that he loves the Indians and will be kind to them. The pipe is by this time renewed and the conversation becomes free, easy and general.

While these pleasantries were being exchanged, the company outfitted the trading captains and their lieutenants with new clothes:

A coarse cloth coat, either red or blue, lined with baize with regimental cuffs and collar. The waistcoat and breeches are of baize; the suit ornamented with broad and narrow orris lace of different colours; a white or checked shirt; a pair of yarn stockings tied below the knee with worsted garters; a pair of English shoes. The hat is laced and ornamented with feathers of different colours. A worsted sash tied round the crown, an end hanging out on each side down to the shoulders. A silk handkerchief is tucked by a corner into the loops behind; with these decorations it is put on the captain's head and completes his dress. The lieutenant is also presented with an inferior suit.

Dressed in new outfits, the trading captains paraded out of the fort in company with the chief factor and his officers, followed by servants carrying gifts for the other Native people, mostly food, tobacco, and brandy. After another round of speech-making in the camp, these additional gifts were presented to the chief, who ordered them distributed to his followers. At this juncture the company men departed and the Aboriginal people held a celebration in which they consumed most of what they had been given. Once the feasting was concluded, the trading party assembled behind the captain and his lieutenants and proceeded back into the fort to offer a return gift to the chief factor: one or two pelts from each follower were collected by the trading captain and presented to the chief factor on their behalf. While making the present, the captain delivered a lengthy speech reconfirming his people's friendship towards the company. The trading captain also took this opportunity to mention any troubles his followers might have had with last year's supply of goods; he detailed any hardships they had experienced over the winter; and he politely demanded that his people receive fair treatment. After a suitable reply, the Native people retired to their camp and trade was ready to begin. In the case of large trading parties, pre-trade formalities took several days to complete.

Such elaborate ceremonies were staged only for inland Natives. Local bands were treated less lavishly. These people, who came to be known as the "home guard" in recognition of their close ties to the posts, visited frequently. In addition to trapping, the home guard provided meat for the forts and worked as casual labourers in the summer assisting with maintenance of the post, collecting firewood, and doing other chores. Despite a company ban to the contrary, employees developed liaisons with home-guard women. Most of these were not casual relationships, they were marriages according to the custom of the country, or common-law marriages if viewed from a European perspective, and they drew home-guard people into the social orbit of the trading post. In the late eighteenth century the company bowed to the inevitable and lifted the ban, but by then a sizeable population of Indian-Europeans

Captain Bulgar, Governor of Assiniboia, and the Chiefs and Warriors of the Chippewa Tribe of Red Lake. Trading blended Native and European traditions of exchange. Key aspects of these ceremonies, such as gift-giving, were carried over into treaty negotiation procedures and the annual annuity-payment ceremonies. Watercolour (1823) by Peter Rindisbacher.

already existed, referred to as mixed-bloods or "citizens of Hudson Bay." Mixed marriages were commonplace at French posts also, and those offspring of French and Indian marriages later emerged as the Métis of Canada.

The trade itself was a matter of barter in which relative values were expressed in terms of the staple of the day—beaver. Furs and goods were said to be worth so many "made beaver." A "made beaver" was equal to the value of a prime winter coat or parchment beaver-skin. The directors of the company, known as the Governor and Committee, established the official price lists, or standards of trade, but the men in Canada deviated from these lists according to local conditions. When they were firmly in control, they charged Indians more for goods than the standards specified. Conversely, if competing traders were present, HBC factors sometimes paid the Indians more for their furs than the official price lists specified.

"Outfitting" Native clients was another important feature of the company's earliest trade, undoubtedly another carry-over from the French. Outfitting involved extending credit to Native hunters in the form of staple goods—the amount depended on local economic conditions—and it served several purposes. It assured the hunters that they would be supplied essential items even if their hunts were poor in the short term. This became an increasing concern in later years, as the hunters grew to depend on European guns, ammunition, hatchets, knives, traps, and even food. Also, by investing in future returns, Europeans were staking claims on those returns. This was a major consideration whenever there was competition. Though competing traders encouraged Native customers not to honour debts owed to the opposition, the majority of them resisted and repaid their creditors. Given the extent to which outfitting was practised, the fur trade is best described as credit barter, or truck trade. It was not until well after Confederation that cash fur-buying began to spread into the North, and as late as the First World War credit barter still accounted for most of the traffic in wild furs.

Guns, Cloth, and Kettles

The account books of the Hudson's Bay Company posts reveal that, contrary to popular belief, Native people did not part with their furs frivolously for cheap trinkets. Even as early as the eighteenth century the Native people spent most of their trapping income on firearms, ammunition, metal goods, cloth, blankets, tobacco, and brandy—only the last two articles are clearly luxuries. They were replacing their traditional technology with an exotic one, and they quickly learned to be discriminating consumers. Besides demanding quality merchandise, they had very specific design requirements: hunting and trapping demand lightweight, durable equipment. This proved a real challenge for European manufacturers when it came to making arms and metal goods of all types. Under the extreme winter temperatures of the North, any design deficiencies, casting flaws, or poorly soldered joints caused metal objects to fail. In the case of firearms, such failures unfortunately too often led to death or disabling injury.

Partly for these reasons, Native traders became harsh critics of English and French merchandise. The Governor and Committee directed their men in the bay to monitor Native reactions to the company's goods closely, and, when asked, the Native people only too willingly gave them an earful of complaints. The Native people also learned the advantages of comparison shopping as a trading ploy. In 1728 the chief factor at York Factory, Thomas McCliesh, wrote the Governor and Committee complaining bitterly:

Never was any man so upbraided with our powder, kettles and hatchets, than we have been this summer by all the natives, especially by those that borders near the French.... The natives are grown so politic in their way in trade, so as they are not to be dealt by as formerly...now is the time to oblige the natives, before the French draws them to their settlement...for here came at least forty canoes of Indians this summer, most of them clothed in French clothing that they traded with the French last summer. They likewise brought several strong French kettles and some French powder in their horns, with which they upbraided us with, by comparing with ours.

By taking advantage of competitive situations, Aboriginal traders played a critical role in forcing Europeans to adapt their technology to the climate and environment of northern Canada. All the same, in the late nineteenth century Native consumers still routinely complained about the quality of trading goods. HBC trader Walter Trail, who was stationed in Manitoba in the 1860s, makes this clear in a humorous account of how he passed long winter evenings with local people:

I have great fun with some of the old Indians when I get them telling yarns. They firmly believe that Queen Victoria selects for them, and personally supervises, the sending out of all the Company's goods. Nor do they doubt that all the shirts, trousers, capotes and other articles are made by her own hands. Many a rough blessing she gets from being a bad seamstress. Were she to know how bravely I fight her battles she would certainly raise me to peerage.

The trade goods clearly benefited Native women as much as the men—and the kettle probably had the greatest impact on their daily lives. For the first time they had a durable, transportable vessel that could be used over an open fire; no longer did they have to resort to the arduous procedure of boiling water by placing heated stones in it, and stews and soups became central to their diet. Although it was not until much later that men and women bought European clothing in large quantities, blankets and cotton and woollen yard goods were in demand early on. Woven cloth was not as warm as fur but it dried more quickly, and wool provided warmth even when wet.

Nicholas Vincent Isawanhoni. This Huron chief, shown wearing the regimental coat commonly awarded to Native "trading captains" and their "lieutenants," holds a wampum belt on which is marked the tomahawk given to him by King George III. Lithograph (1825) after a painting by Edward Chatfield.

And for fashioning hides, pelts, and yard goods into clothing, metal awls, knives, needles, and scissors made women's tasks much easier. Although the Aboriginal consumers spent a relatively small portion of their total incomes on European trade beads, the fact that these could be obtained cheaply encouraged the use of ornamented beadwork on clothing, and in time trade beads largely replaced traditional quill and shell work on Native garments.

Undoubtedly firearms had the most impact on the lives of woodland men. Traditionally they stalked and killed game at close range with bows and arrows or lances. The problem was that often the animals did not die immediately, and they might move considerable distances before bleeding to death. With firearms death was usually instantaneous, and so the hunters found they could be far more efficient using the smooth-bore flintlock musket, however inferior it was to the repeating rifle of the late nineteenth century.

In the late seventeenth and early eighteenth centuries, the Assiniboine and Cree used the arms they obtained from the HBC not only to hunt, but also to cordon off Hudson Bay and James Bay from rival trading groups, and expand their spheres of influence to the west and north-west. Considerable bloodshed was the result in some areas, and was one of the primary causes of the major population upheaval that took place in the heart of the continent just before European explorers arrived there. Most notably, the Chipewyan were displaced to the north, the Beaver and Sekani to the west, and the Gros Ventre to the south.

In the early days, European hatchets and ice chisels quickly became invaluable. Native trappers used these tools in the winter to open frozen beaver lodges, and they were essential components of a hunter's equipment until baited steel-spring traps became the usual method of taking beaver in the late eighteenth century. After that, traps and traplines became crucial. Men, like the women, quickly adopted the European metal knife too. One of the more interesting knives was the canoe knife, or crooked knife, that was used in canoe construction or in any operation where paring of complex wooden shapes was required.

Of all the commodities that the Native people obtained in trade, none was more disruptive to the fabric of their societies than alcohol. James Isham, who was favourably impressed by the kindness and generosity Aboriginal people commonly showed towards close friends and kin, pointed out that they often behaved in a very hostile manner when drinking liquor:

These Natives are given very much to Quarrellg. when in liquor having Known two Brothers when in liquor to Quarrell after such a manner, that they have Bitt one anothr. nose, Ears, and finger's off, Biting being common with them when in Liquor.—they also are Very Sulky and sullen, and if at any time one has a Resentment against another, they never show itt, till the Spiritious Liquor's work's in their Brains, then they Speak their mind freely.

This kind of behaviour undoubtedly reflected the fact that Native people had no prior experience with drugs as powerful as brandy or rum. Also, living most of the year in small, closely knit groups where survival depended on conformity and co-operative behaviour, they had few outlets for the personal resentments that inevitably arose. Alcohol reduced their good judgement and facilitated the expression of these feelings.

Unfortunately, the manner in which Aboriginal people and Europeans interacted in the fur trade encouraged the widespread use of alcohol. Under competitive circumstances, rival traders attempted to woo Native people to their side by being more generous with their gifts. This set off an upward spiral in gift-giving expenses—and one way to offset this trend was to give away larger quantities of relatively cheap, watered-down rum or brandy. That Native producers tended to harvest only enough furs for their immediate short-term needs was another problem; there was a limit to how much barter they could carry away, particularly when the posts were distant. So during highly competitive periods, when their furs fetched a higher price, they naturally curtailed their efforts. Since alcohol was cheap to obtain, could be consumed on the spot, and was addictive, the European traders had very strong economic incentives to trade and give away large quantities of liquor. In fact, the only thing that prevented widespread consumption of alcohol before 1763 was the fact that most Native consumers visited a trading post only once a year. Between 1763 and 1821, when competition reached a fever pitch and posts were built throughout the northern forest, the Europeans' abusive use of alcohol in trade led to the widespread demoralization of the Native peoples of central Canada.

"Sleeping by the Frozen Sea"

The Hudson's Bay Company posts placed the English on the northern flank of the French Empire and represented a threat that could not go unchallenged.

Furthermore, it was clear from the early results of HBC operations that the best furs were to be found to the north of the Great Lakes, and not to the south-west in the Ohio and upper Mississippi country. The French responded to the English advance in a series of armed skirmishes in both Hudson Bay and James Bay between 1682 and 1712. Although they were more successful in these clashes than the English, managing to capture and hold most of the posts, they were never able to dislodge the HBC completely. In the end French military successes in the two bays did not matter; the Treaty of Utrecht of 1713, ending the War of the Spanish Succession, awarded the HBC complete control over the northern maritime approach, and the French had to withdraw from the shores of Hudson Bay.

More important to the Aboriginal people, while naval battles were being fought in the bay, the French set up a few small French trading posts in the Lake Superior country, at Lake Nipigon in 1684 and on Rainy Lake in 1688. This was but a prelude to a major thrust overland by the French after 1713. Although the Treaty of Utrecht gave the HBC a monopoly on bayside trade, it left the interior open to both the English and the French. The two groups responded very differently. Rather than taking on the added costs of developing inland trade, the Governor and Committee of the HBC decided to leave it in the hands of Native middlemen. Critics who wanted the company to take aggressive action against the French sarcastically called this the policy of "sleeping by the frozen sea." In contrast, the French began to build a string of posts to encircle the bay and cut the English posts off from their surrounding hinterlands.

French expansion began under the leadership of Zachary Robutel, Sieur de La Noue, who had re-established an old French post on Rainy Lake in 1717. However, it was Pierre Gaultier de Varennes et de La Vérendrye, who carried the trading forward. In 1727 he devised a plan that linked the development of inland trade, and the profits it would generate, with the continued search for the western sea. La Vérendrye hoped that such a strategy would enlist the support of colonial officials who opposed expansion but were still interested in exploration. He was successful, but he placed himself in a difficult position. He was expected to pay the exploration costs out of his own fur-trading profits; but if he paused to develop the trade he was subject to criticism for not promoting exploration, while if he failed to generate enough income he was placed in an awkward financial situation. Thus La Vérendrye's position was not unlike that of the HBC, and in the end he was less successful in dealing with his critics than the company directors were with theirs. Despite these difficulties, he pushed

The inset above Philip Bauche's 1754 map is a copy of the map that Auchagah, a Cree guide, drew for La Vérendrye some twenty years earlier, to show him the way from Lake Superior to Lake Winnipeg.

exploration and the fur trade into new areas, beginning in 1732 with the establishment of a post on Lake-of-the-Woods.

As was customary, La Vérendrye was guided on his explorations by Aboriginal people:

…the man I have chosen is one named Auchagah [a Cree], a savage of my post, greatly attached to the French nation, the man most capable of guiding a party, and with whom there would be no fear of our being abandoned on the way. When I proposed to him to guide me to the great river of the West he replied that he was at my service and would start whenever I wished. I gave him a collar [necklace] by which, after their manner of speaking, I took possession of his will, telling him that he was to hold himself in readiness for such time as I might have need of him.…

According to La Vérendrye's journals, Auchagah, also known as Ocliagach, traced a map for him showing the route between Lake Superior and Lake Winnipeg. To the modern observer, the map appears odd; in fact, it is a reasonable rendering of the canoe route which shows most of the pertinent information a traveller needed. It is not unlike a modern subway or bus route map. Equipped with this map, his guides, and a fund of geographical information obtained by interviewing a number of other Native people, La Vérendrye was able to move on to explore the area that is now Manitoba.

By the early 1740s, French posts reached across southern Manitoba into central Saskatchewan near the forks of the Saskatchewan River. The only European known to have visited the area and left an account before this was young Henry Kelsey of the

Tlingit miniature mask of wood, paint, shell, and human hair (*c.* 1850), from the north-west coast of
British Columbia. The native people in each region developed distinctive art forms utilizing local raw
materials, and the result was a rich cultural mosaic.

Top to bottom:

1. Charm: Plains

2. Blanket and pattern board: Chilkat, Northwest Coast

3. Bow and arrow kit: Copper Inuit

4. Painted coat (back): Naskapi (Eastern Subarctic)

9. Pipes and pipe bags: Plains

10. Snowshoes: Eastern Woodland, Subarctic, and Inuit

11. Bow drill: Inuit

12. Spoon and cedar box: Tsimshian, Northwest Coast

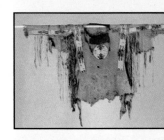

5. Birchbark basket: Slavey (Western Subarctic)

6. War shirt: Plains

7. Conical basketry hat: Northwest Coast

8. *Ulus*: Inuit

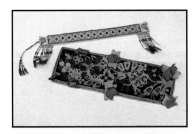

Facing page: Traditional clothing, tools, and art from the early-contact period. With the exception of some of the beadwork on the pipe bag, and the metal blades on the *ulus*, the materials are of local origin.

Above: Post-contact decorative art. The ready availability of beads led to a flowering of beadwork; basketry was applied to trade pipes; west-coast blanket-makers added European cloth and buttons to their repertoire; cloth was used to make traditional garments until European clothes were adopted: and even jewellery-making benefited from the exotic new items.

13. Armbands or garters: Cree
14. Button blanket: Nass River, British Columbia
15. Clay pipe: Woodland
16. Shirt, leggings: Plains Cree

17. Necklace of Russian trade beads: British Columbia Indian
18. Earrings: Inuit

Scene in Indian Tent: The artist has portrayed the domestic life of the Plains Indians under ideal conditions; their life in winter was much more miserable. Watercolour (*c.* 1829–34) by Peter Rindisbacher.

Facing page: *Portrait of Sa Ga Yeath Qua Pieth Tow (called Brant).* In their struggles for control of the new continent, Europeans sought strategic alliances with native peoples. This oil (1710) by John Verelst (*c.* 1648–1734) was painted during the visit to London of the "Four Indian Kings." Some of the Iroquois chief Brant's descendants remained loyal to the British during the American Revolution, and were awarded a reserve near Brantford, Ontario.

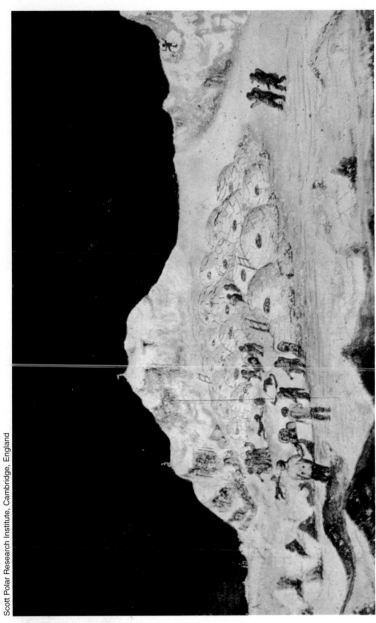

Facing page: *Return of the War Party*. Paul Kane probably never saw the event he depicted in this 1847 oil painting; he has the lead canoe being paddled backwards, stern-first. To the right is a *munka*, a Nootkan war canoe, and in the left foreground is a Salish canoe.

Above: *Snow Cottages of the Boothians*. This watercolour by Sir John Ross (1777–1856) shows an encounter during his second voyage in search of a Northwest Passage (1829–33), at an Inuit village known as North Hendon, near Felix Harbour on the Boothia Peninsula. The placenames honour Felix Booth, the distiller who funded the expedition.

Canoes in a Fog, Lake Superior. Frances Ann Hopkins (1838–1918)—married to the private secretary of Sir George Simpson, governor-in-chief of the Hudson's Bay Company—accompanied her husband on numerous company journeys. She included herself in this 1869 oil, seated in the mid-section of the birchbark freighter canoe in the foreground.

A North West View of Prince of Wales' Fort in Hudson's Bay, North America. This magnificent stone fort was in fact a "white elephant"; although built to protect the company's interests against a French assault, it was completely unsuited to the environment. The scant tree-cover of the surrounding land was burnt as firewood in a vain attempt to heat the fort in winter. Engraving (*c.* 1797) after a drawing by Samuel Hearne (1745–92).

HBC. In 1690 "boy Kelsey," as he was then called, had travelled as far as the border of eastern Saskatchewan, guided there by a party of Assiniboine who traded regularly at York Factory. But the precise route Kelsey and his party took remains a mystery, and unfortunately his account is cryptic and does not reveal a great deal. So for all practical purposes French records, beginning with those of La Vérendrye, are the earliest useful first-hand accounts of Native life in the western interior.

La Vérendrye and his followers arrived in the northern plains just before the horse did. His journals make it clear that inter-tribal raiding and trading had spread horses from the Spanish colonial frontier north-eastward as far as the Mandan villages of the upper Missouri River, but no farther. The Plains Assiniboine and Cree of south-eastern Saskatchewan and southern Manitoba did not obtain them until the second half of the eighteenth century. Their rapid acquisition of horses after that was doubtless made easier by their greater access to English and French goods, which they traded with the Mandan. Farther west, in what is now southern Alberta, horses had reached the western prairies by the early eighteenth century.

The horse was the single most important aspect of European culture to reach the prairie Aboriginal people before the post-Confederation reservation era. For one thing, it led them to abandon the traditional buffalo hunt in favour of headlong mounted pursuits. Although "running buffalo" on horseback was undoubtedly less risky than hunting them on foot, it was still dangerous. Managing a smooth-bore flintlock gun on a galloping horse in a blinding cloud of dust amid a thundering herd of buffalo was a real feat. Most Plain's hunters in fact continued to rely on lances or bows and arrows until repeating rifles began to replace flintlocks in the latter half of the nineteenth century. Using their traditional weapons on horseback a hunter was able to dispatch animals at the same rate as a Métis using a flintlock, with relative ease and without having to buy the equipment. So European weapons did not at first have the enormous impact on the prairie nations that they did on their woodland neighbours. As the primary symbol of wealth, however, the horse served to increase competition among Plains men. Firearms, ammunition, tobacco, kettles, knives, and hatchets obtained from the fur traders were valued also, but these too had less of an impact here than in the woodlands.

With the establishment of Fort à la Corne near the forks of the Saskatchewan River, the French push north-west of Lake Superior finally came to an end. Their system was strained to its limits, and without streamlining and reorganizing their transportation arrangements it is unlikely that they could have effectively extended themselves any farther. Given that the HBC did not respond in any major way to their expansion overland, there was little reason for the French to make the added investment other than to continue the search for the western sea. Similarly, the HBC had little incentive to abandon its policy of "sleeping by the frozen sea." Although the French apparently secured the largest share of the furs, Native traders were still bringing enough to HBC posts to enable the English to conduct a highly profitable trade. The only major new investment the company made during this period was the establishment of Fort Churchill in 1717—a move that had nothing to do with combating French activities, but was intended to outflank the Cree who were blocking the Chipewyan from visiting York Factory.

The fact that the English and French were content to compete at a distance worked to the advantage of Assiniboine and Cree traders. Although the French posts reached into the heart of Cree and Assiniboine territory, they lacked the transport capacity to bring in enough goods to satisfy Aboriginal demands. So the French tended to exchange lightweight, high-value goods for prime furs, while the more remote HBC posts, supplied by cheap ocean transport, were able to offer a full range of goods and to accept lower grade furs. This situation allowed Assiniboine and Cree middlemen to handle the important carrying trade, and it gave them the advantage of a competitive market.

The Nor'Westers

In the late 1750s the French abandoned their western posts. It was not until the mid-1760s, after the Conquest of New France, that political stability was re-established in the east and Montreal-based traders could reoccupy the old French trading territory in the West and begin to push outward beyond the old frontier. Initially these Montreal trading operations were organized as small partnerships between city merchants, who supplied the goods, and the actual traders who travelled inland and dealt with the Aboriginal people. Appropriately, these latter men came to be known as wintering partners.

In the beginning these new opponents of the Hudson's Bay Company faced two problems. Besides having to compete with a company that had more extensive financial reserves, they had to contend with one another. Furthermore, by the mid-1770s it was clear that the prime beaver country lay towards Athabasca in northern Saskatchewan and beyond. The HBC awoke from its slumber and, with the building of Cumberland House, a trading post on the Saskatchewan River, it began a program of expansion inland. In 1778 Peter Pond, the proud, impetuous, and intractable Yankee fur trader, demonstrated that Montreal-based traders could reach this new territory, difficult as the journey was; but it was clear that the small partnerships lacked the financial resources to exploit the new frontier on a large scale. Also, the unbridled competition among them led to violence and murder. To overcome these limitations and bring some order to the country, the Montreal traders began to join together, and in 1776 started to pool their resources into successively larger partnerships, the most famous of which was the North West Company (NWC). Among the early principals were Peter Pond and his second-in-command, Alexander Mackenzie (later Sir Alexander), both of whom played key roles in propelling the fur trade forward in the final surge to the Arctic and Pacific oceans.

Before a major invasion of the Athabasca-Mackenzie area could be carried out, however, the Nor'Westers, as they came to be called, had to resolve the logistical problems: financing was difficult; the region was too far from Montreal to be reached in a single canoeing season; the season was too short and game supplies too unpredictable to allow time for hunting and fishing *en route*; and, finally, the small, light woodland Native canoes could not carry sufficient quantities of food, trade goods, or furs over long distances. They overcame these obstacles in a number of ways. They divided the transport system into two components, one eastern and one northwestern; they adopted the *canot du maître* or Great Lakes canoe—11 metres (36 feet) long, 2 metres (6 feet) in beam, and able to carry three tons of cargo plus a crew—for the eastern leg of the trip; and for the route beyond Lake Superior, which had too much shoal and white water for the *canot du maître*, they developed the *canot du nord*—about 7.5 metres (25 feet) long, some 1.2 metres (4 feet) in beam, and carrying half the cargo. Thus the NWC extended Native technology to suit its own needs. In turn, some Native groups, particularly Anishinabe bands who had moved into the Lakehead area, specialized in building canoes for the company. The NWC also improved portage trails, and at Sault Ste. Marie constructed the first canal on the Great Lakes so its canoes could pass beside the Saint Mary's rapids; in later years, they also used small schooners on the Great Lakes.

To address the provision problem, the NWC drew upon local resources as much as possible. As a supplement to the pork and flour the *voyageurs* (canoe men) were given in Montreal, Indian corn was imported from the southern Great Lakes region and stored at Sault Ste. Marie for the passing brigades. Between the Lakehead and Lake Winnipeg the Nor'Westers canoe men, who were mostly Métis, depended on the local Ojibwa for corn, wild rice, and fish. Beyond the lower Winnipeg River they turned to the Plains bison hunters for food, and the prairies became the great pantry of the western fur trade. Pemmican was the ideal *voyageur* food; in fact, the western fur trade probably wouldn't have taken place without it. The daily calorie expenditures of the *voyageurs* were enormous, and pemmican provided calories in a portable, lightweight, highly compact form: a 40-kilogram (90-pound) bag, the standard size, was the equivalent of the dressed meat of two adult female buffalo (approximately nine hundred pounds). Besides pemmican, the *voyageurs* developed a taste for such Native delicacies as buffalo tongue, and these prairie provisions were forwarded to depots at Bas de la Rivière and Cumberland Lake. But even with these caches in the north-west, 25 to nearly 50 per cent of the cargo capacity of canoes leaving Fort William in 1814 was taken up by provisions.

The activities of the Nor'Westers adversely affected HBC operations much more

Sir Alexander Mackenzie. Mackenzie made two great efforts to find a route from Lake Athabasca to the Pacific. On the first, in 1789, the river that now bears his name led him to the Arctic; but on the second, in 1793, he reached Bella Coola and the long search for a westward route was over. Oil (1893) by René Emile Quentin.

than those of the French, and so these new opponents could not go unchallenged. The HBC faced many of the same problems but unlike the Nor'Westers it was not able to use enlarged canoes to carry its cargo because, except for Moose Factory and Rupert House, the bayside posts lay beyond the prime birch area. And it was impractical to buy canoes from inland Native groups. So the company men at Fort Albany began building shallow-draft boats for work on the rivers. In the nineteenth century these craft became the backbone of the HBC's transportation system, and they came to be known as York boats because of the vital role they played in the shipment of cargo to and from York Factory, certainly the company's most important depot for western Canada.

While the rival Nor'Westers and Hudson's Bay men were laying the groundwork for their overland trading empires, a new phase of exploration began. Although the Nor'Westers were first off the mark in the 1760s when they moved northward towards the middle Churchill River area, it was the HBC that made the first major probe beyond the old French frontier. In 1771, prompted by repeated Native reports of mineral wealth,

Moses Norton, chief factor at Fort Churchill (the same Norton that kept several wives and a box of poison for unhelpfully honourable Indian husbands), sent Samuel Hearne off on foot on a gruelling expedition that took him as far as the Coppermine River, about a thousand miles to the north-west, over very rough terrain.

Hearne had already attempted two such expeditions, which had taught him and Norton two crucial lessons. Expeditions were doomed to failure without first-class Native guides; those selected for the first two journeys had been totally unsuitable. Secondly, Hearne had learned that you did not lead these guides in their homeland; you followed them, at the pace they set for themselves. With these lessons in mind, they chose Matonabbee, a Chipewyan leader whom the English greatly respected, as a guide on Hearne's third attempt to reach the Coppermine. Matonabbee informed Hearne that he had failed previously for yet a third reason:

He attributed all our misfortunes to the misconduct of my guides, and the very plan we pursued, by the desire of the Governor [Norton], in not taking any women with us on this journey, was, he said, the principal thing that occasioned all our wants: "for," said he, "when all the men are heavy laden, they can neither hunt nor travel to any considerable distance; and in the case they meet with success in hunting, who is to carry the produce of their labour? Women," added he, "were made for labour; one of them can carry or haul, as much as two men can do. They also pitch our tents, make and mend our clothing, keep us warm at night; and, in fact, there is no such thing as travelling any considerable distance, or for any length of time…without their assistance."

In other words, given that economic roles were sharply defined by gender in Native society, a guiding party needed both women and men to function.

Most of the territory Hearne traversed with Matonabbee was within the trading sphere of the Chipewyan, who had dominated the north-western trade of Fort Churchill since the post was established. This land bordered on that of the Inuit—the Caribou Inuit on the south-east near the fort and the Copper Inuit on the north-west. This was a war zone where bloody conflicts took place whenever Chipewyan and Inuit met. No quarter was given. Hearne witnessed an attack on a camp of sleeping Inuit by Matonabbee's people in which all the men, women, and children were slain. The animosities between these groups seem to have been rooted in the distant past and their causes can only be a matter of conjecture. The HBC made efforts to end this violence, but it is likely that the company's very presence intensified the conflict in some quarters, as the Indians and the Inuit sought to limit each other's access to arms and goods.

Seven years after Hearne completed his trip, Peter Pond extended the frontier of trading posts to the Athabasca River when he built a small fort (Pond's Fort) only 65 kilograms (40 miles) from Lake Athabasca. While in the Athabasca country, he learned from the Chipewyan that the river was tributary to larger lakes and to the Slave River (later called the Mackenzie River). Then, during the winter of 1784–85, Captain James Cook published an account of his voyage to the Pacific coast in which he reported that there was a river flowing into the Pacific from the north-east. Apparently, Pond believed that the Slave River the Native guides had told him about might be the one Cook had mentioned—that the river flowed to the Pacific rather than to the Arctic Sea. This was an exciting prospect, for an extremely lucrative fur trade was rapidly developing on the west coast, and the Nor'Westers wanted access to it. Besides this, if a water route could be found leading from the beaver-rich Athabasca-Mackenzie area to the Pacific, the high costs of overland transportation from Montreal could be avoided.

Pond was not able to test his speculation before retiring in 1789. It was Alexander Mackenzie, who had served with Pond, who took up that great challenge. He called it the "favourite project of my own ambition." On June 3, 1789, Mackenzie set out from Fort Chipewyan. His party was guided by "English Chief," a Chipewyan who formerly had belonged to Matonabbee's band. In early July Mackenzie's expedition reached the delta of the river that now bears his name. There he discovered an abandoned Inuit winter camp. He had found the Arctic Ocean, not the Pacific. Understandably, he was very disappointed; indeed, he called the river that led him to the Arctic the "river of disappointment."

Despite his great frustrations, Mackenzie was not deterred. In the autumn of 1792 he set out from Fort Chipewyan once more, but this time headed westward up the Peace River. Near the confluence with the Smoky River he built a small trading post where he spent the winter before pressing on. Crossing interior British Columbia for the first time proved to be far more challenging than descending the Mackenzie River. The terrain was very rugged, most of the major rivers had vicious whitewater stretches, and frequently the explorer had to make major decisions about the route from among several alternatives. Mackenzie depended absolutely on the information his Native guides furnished him when making those choices, and judging from his account of the expedition, these guides were aware of their importance to him, teasing him about it and challenging his air of superiority. Mackenzie's journals make it abundantly clear that he was not comfortable with this situation. For example, on June 23, 1793, he called them together to determine whether it was better to follow the Fraser River all the way to the coast or to leave it and head westward via the West Road River:

> At the commencement of this conversation, I was very much surprised by the following question from one of the Indians: "What," demanded he, "can be the reason that you are so particular and anxious in your inquiries of us respecting a knowledge of this country: do not you white men know everything in the world?" This interrogatory was so very unexpected, that it occasioned some hesitation before I could answer it. At length, however, I replied, that we certainly were acquainted with the principal circumstances of every part of the world; that I knew where the sea is, and where I myself then was, but that I did not exactly understand what obstacles might interrupt me in getting to it; with which he and his relations must be well acquainted, as they had so frequently surmounted them. Thus I fortunately preserved the impression in their minds, of the superiority of white people over themselves.

Mackenzie then opted for the western route and abandoned the Fraser River, because his guides stressed the dangers of the latter and minimized the distance and difficulties of the former. Travelling partly by canoe and partly by foot, he reached the Bella Coola River at Friendly Village on July 17, 1793.

The two-hundred-year search for the Pacific begun by Cartier was over. Native people had guided the intruders from coast to coast. Most tribes had welcomed the newcomers to their territories; most let them pass beyond only reluctantly, seeing a golden economic opportunity going with them.

On to the Pacific

Alexander Mackenzie's remarkable journey extended the inland fur trade all the way to the Pacific. Simon Fraser and David Thompson, also of the North West Company, followed soon after, and they explored two of the four great coastal rivers of the Pacific north-west: Fraser descended the river that bears his name in 1808, while Thompson followed the Columbia from its source to the ocean in

1811. In their wake the trading frontiers expanded, and the NWC built several posts in east-central and central British Columbia—an area then known as New Caledonia. The coastal trade lay beyond their reach, however, because the distance from Montreal was simply too great given the problems of transportation and supply. New Caledonia remained the western margin of the territory the NWC was able to exploit effectively—and, needless to say, the Hudson's Bay Company was unable to gain entry.

By this time, however, the fur trade had been well established along the coast for nearly a decade, stimulated by Captain Cook's visit to the Nuu-chah-nulth (Nootka) of western Vancouver Island. James Cook, the greatest navigator of his time, had already charted part of the Gaspé and had helped James Wolfe's armada navigate the St. Lawrence River; he had served at the siege of Louisbourg, mapped the treacherous Newfoundland coast, and revealed the wonders of the South Pacific. In 1778 he sailed across the Pacific in search of the Northwest Passage and anchored in Nootka Sound. He obtained sea-otter pelts from the Nuu-chah-nulth for a very nominal expenditure of goods, and later sold them in China at a great profit. Word spread rapidly, and traders rushed to the coast.

The coastal trade of the late eighteenth century differed in some fundamental ways from the inland trade. Initially, four nations were involved: Spain, England, Russia, and America. With the exception of the Spanish, trading was conducted entirely from sailing ships until 1827. After 1795 the Spanish withdrew and English and American merchants became the major competition, although the Russians were active north of the Skeena River. Since the trade was largely restricted to the coast, lasting bonds were not established between the traders and the Aboriginal people and no pressures were exerted on the environment for food or timber.

Thanks to the large, ocean-going ships, the volume of goods traded on the coast was substantially greater than it was in the western interior. As many as twenty ships were visiting the coast every year by the turn of the nineteenth century. (In contrast, the HBC and the NWC together managed to carry into the Canadian north-west no more than the equivalent of four shiploads every year.) This represented a bonanza to the trade-oriented and status-conscious Native peoples of the west coast. Not surprisingly, the highly prized European goods received in exchange for sea-otter pelts increased Native trade and gift exchanges along the coast, and control of key routes provided an added incentive for inter-village struggles as it had in the interior.

However, most of the items being traded on the coast were luxuries rather than necessities. This was because West Coast people did not need to rely on European goods; they continued to take the bulk of their food—fish—by traditional means. Indeed, they did so until federal and provincial conservation legislation passed in the late nineteenth and early twentieth centuries denied them that right. Instead, firearms (largely used in warfare) were valued, as were the metal chisels, cloth, clothing, and blankets that became symbolic of wealth, and iron collars and copper bracelets.

Sea otters were ruthlessly hunted in this highly competitive atmosphere. By the turn of the nineteenth century, their numbers had declined sharply, and the trade was headed for trouble; by the late 1820s it was in its final stages of collapse. This posed a serious problem to groups living on the offshore islands, who had few alternative fur-bearing animals to exchange. The Haida of the Queen Charlotte Islands addressed the difficulty by creating artefacts specially designed for European visitors. On the mainland, the pelts of land animals—particularly beaver, and marten with its soft, lustrous fur—were increasingly sought. Inland trading connections along the major rivers now became essential and so inter-village conflicts increased.

The Shifting Balance of Power

An important milestone in the history of Aboriginal people was marked in 1821. By that date the fur trade had linked the Native world to that of the European in all areas of Canada except for the more remote sections of the lower Mackenzie valley and the Yukon. In 1821, a half-century of ruthless competition was brought to an end by the merger of the Hudson's Bay Company and the North West Company. The English Parliament gave the new concern, still called the Hudson's Bay Company despite the merger, monopoly control over the trade of Rupert's Land, the north-west, and the Pacific slope, believing that the company would best serve the interests of the people of these areas by eliminating the evils of unbridled competition.

Competition had, in fact, already ruined the Native economies of much of the Subarctic between the Churchill River and James Bay. In Rainy River, to take one example, the HBC had to import leather from the prairies so local Native people could make moccasins. Even more disastrous, the wanton trade in alcohol was leading to widespread demoralization. English politicians were determined to bring an end to this traffic. Even the traders themselves were aware that the struggle could not be continued much longer.

At the same time, the fur traders had to face the fact that the only new areas left to develop—the Yukon, sections of the northern interior of British Columbia, and the Arctic—were remote and costly to reach. The time had come when an effort had to be made to limit the fur trade to a level the ecosystem could support. In the absence of a strong governmental authority, there was no way to impose conservation measures other than through a monopoly. A monopoly would also lower the costs of the industry because duplicate posts could be eliminated, as could many of the jobs.

Although the motives that led to the granting of the monopoly may generally have been well intended, centralized control signalled an abrupt shift in the relationship between the Native people and the intruders. What had begun as a mutually advantageous partnership of equals became one in which the Europeans increasingly called the shots. Except on the Great Lakes, prairies, and west coast, where competition continued from the Americans, the HBC completely dominated the trade, and created a social and economic order in which Aboriginal people were placed in a more and more subservient position.

For the Inuit the experience was very different, if equally destructive in the end. Prior to 1821 regular contact between Inuit and Europeans was largely limited to the Labrador coast, Hudson Strait, and western Hudson Bay. The whalers did not seriously move into the western and central Arctic until the closing decades of the nineteenth century. But on the Labrador coast the Inuit developed trading contacts with European whalers in the early eighteenth century, and by the middle of the century this trade was centred in the vicinity of Hamilton Inlet. There Inuit middlemen sold baleen—the stiff, flexible whalebone which hangs in long, curtain-like strips from the bowhead whale's mouth—which they obtained from groups located farther north. But in the late eighteenth century British traders established trading posts to the north of Hamilton Inlet at Hopedale, and in 1771 the Moravian Brethren moved into the area to do missionary and social work, and established missions at Nain, Okak, and Hopedale. The Moravians wanted to make their missions self-sufficient and to discourage Inuit from travelling south to meet whalers. To realize these goals, they operated trading stores—stores that until the 1860s were the most important source of European goods for the Labrador Inuit. By the time the rapid expansion of the cod-fishing industry into the region broke the Moravian monopoly, as fishermen began to trade extensively with the Natives, alcohol had become an important trading item here too, to the considerable detriment of the Inuit. And since a very large number of outsiders, up to thirty thousand fishermen, visited the area each year by the late

Portrait of Joseph Brant. Mohawk chief, military leader, and Loyalist, Brant (1742–1807) symbolizes the problems later Native leaders would face in reconciling Native and European ways. A man of two worlds—as his dress suggests—he was well versed in Iroquoian customs but also Christian and highly literate. Oil (*c.* 1807) by William Berczy, Sr.

nineteenth century, alien diseases were introduced—epidemics of measles, typhus, and scarlet
fever swept through the Inuit communities. These,
and a shift in the traditional diet, soon brought
about a sharp decline in the Inuit population.

In the Hudson Strait and around Hudson Bay,
Inuit only occasionally encountered and traded
with the yearly supply ships from the HBC. More
important was the trade the company conducted
with the Inuit at Fort Churchill after 1717. Initially,
it sent sloops northward from this post in search of
Inuit living inland from the west coast of Hudson
Bay—a necessary move because the Chipewyan
used armed force to prevent the Inuit from visiting
Fort Churchill on a regular basis. By the late eighteenth century the company had managed to
arrange a lasting peace between the Inuit and the
Chipewyan, making it possible finally for the
Caribou Inuit to visit Fort Churchill in safety, and
as a result the sloops no longer needed to be sent
out. Some Caribou Inuit traders were able to find

In 1825 Shawnawdithit was the last
Beothuk still living. Those who
had not died of new diseases
brought from Europe were killed
off. In 1829 she too succumbed to
tuberculosis and an entire race
vanished.

employment at Fort Churchill, hunting seal and whales for oil, until the whaling
industry collapsed in 1813. This contact was very important: the firearms, fish hooks,
and nets the Inuit acquired from the company made it possible for them to occupy
the inland tundra at all seasons of the year. After 1820 they expanded southward, displacing the Chipewyan, and by 1860 the Caribou Inuit had become the dominant
population in the southern Barren Grounds.

On the east side of Hudson Bay, Inuit contact with the company was more tenuous. Not until 1750 did the company build a small post—Fort Richmond—on the
southern edge of Inuit territory. It was intended to serve as a base for mineral exploration and the development of a fur trade, but it was a commercial failure, and closed
in 1756. Operations were moved to Little Whale River, where the company had been
conducting a small summer beluga-whaling enterprise for some time. However, it
soon became apparent that the local Inuit population was not sufficiently large to
support a profitable operation here either, and the new post too closed after three

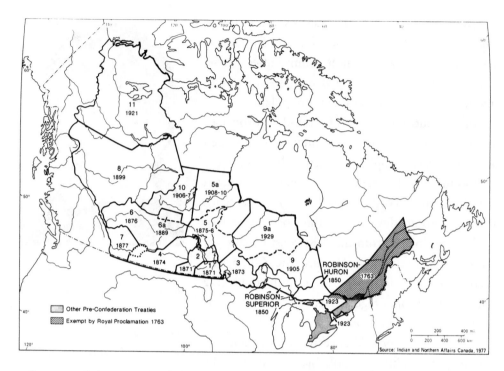

Indian treaties before 1930. These were generally prompted by a demand for land and mineral riches, and the dates of signing reflect that pressure in different areas. Since 1850, Indian treaties have included certain key provisions: an exchange of gifts during negotiations, once-and-for-all payments at the time of signing; annuities in perpetuity as deferred payment for the lands sold; and the rights to hunt and fish on undeveloped Crown lands. Government agents usually arrived with the treaty already drawn up. Indians forced them to negotiate, but many of the concessions were never written down. These "outside promises" are the focus of some Native claims today.

years. This time the company moved to Great Whale River where a trading post was operated intermittently until 1855 when it became permanent. But everywhere, the whalers and fishermen brought with them alcohol and diseases that devastated the Inuit. Looking back, it is clear that the Native peoples of Canada shared many common experiences in their early encounters with Europeans and their descendants. In the earliest years, the Native people usually held the whip hand. They outnumbered the intruders; they had the manpower and the skills to produce the materials the Europeans sought, at cheaper rates; and they were technologically self-sufficient in the difficult northern environment.

Métis fishermen at Sault Ste. Marie. By the early nineteenth century, there were over fifty Métis communities in the Great Lakes region. The mixed economies of these communities included commercial and subsistence fishing, hunting and trapping, farming, wage labour, and trading.

Unfortunately for the Native people, their superior position was quickly eroded. Their populations were decimated by imported diseases while the intruders increased steadily in number through immigration and natural growth. And when the Native people became involved in the fur trade, their economic way of life no longer revolved around local needs. Instead, they were drawn into international commodity marketing systems—systems that made demands on local resources far beyond what the ecosystems could bear. Depletion was the widespread result. Furthermore, the new technologies often improved the efficiency of the hunter and fisherman, thereby adding to the toll on local game and fish.

Making matters worse for Native people, their political power began to ebb also. Until the end of the War of 1812 they had been important military allies of the British. The desire to curry their favour had led the British government to issue the Royal Proclamation of 1763 which acknowledged the existence of Aboriginal title and established the Crown as protector of that title. Beyond the 1763 boundaries of Quebec, Aboriginal title could be transferred only to the Crown in public treaty-making ceremonies; the intention was to protect Native peoples from unscrupulous land speculators and so minimize the risk of alienating them.

After the War of 1812, colonial officials decided that the Native people were no longer needed as allies. They became more interested in the agricultural, timber, and mineral potential of Native lands than in the welfare of the people. Their prime concern now was to obtain access to the riches of the land as cheaply as possible and without bloodshed. In most areas of Canada covered by treaty, development pressures largely determined when agreements were concluded. (Lands not covered by treaty have experienced these development pressures only recently and in many of these areas negotiations are in process. The principal exception is British Columbia, where, in 1987, the provincial government still refuses to recognize Aboriginal title.)

Overwhelmed by the depletion of their resources, and by the adoption of new lifestyles, the Native peoples began to move from independence, through interdependence with the European traders, towards economic dependence. By 1821 this shift was well under way in most of Canada; only the most remote groups remained relatively unaffected.

Colonization and Conflict: New France and its Rivals 1600–1760

CHRISTOPHER MOORE

Published in 1632, three years before the explorer's death, this map by Samuel de Champlain is startlingly accurate. In just thirty years the essential geography of Canada from Newfoundland to the Great Lakes had been established—mostly by Champlain himself. Also indicated are the areas where the various Indian tribes of the period lived. Map printed from copperplate, in Samuel de Champlain, *Les Voyages de la Nouvelle France occidentale, dicte Canada*...(Paris: C. Collet, 1632).

S AMUEL DE CHAMPLAIN, FOUNDER and commander of New France, died on Christmas Day of 1635 at Quebec. Virtually the entire colony could attend his funeral, for after twenty-seven years of colonial settlement the European population of New France was barely three hundred people, many of them recent arrivals. At the end of his life, Champlain's achievement lay not in the size of his colony, which remained tiny, but in the fact that it had endured.

Since its founding in 1608, the settlement at Quebec had been constantly endangered: by starvation and scurvy, by commercial rivalries, by uncertain support from France, by the opposition of vastly more powerful Native nations, and by English military attack. Champlain was hardly the only backer the colony had, but his tenacious advocacy had played a vital role in keeping it in being. In Champlain's time, in fact, a decisive change had been engineered in European involvement with the lands and people of northeastern North America. Europeans had been crossing the Atlantic since 1000 AD, and there had been a century of regular visits to Canada before 1608. But Champlain had transformed transient contact into a permanent European presence in Canada.

Champlain's Colony

By 1600 whales and cod had been bringing Europeans to Canada for a century. It was beaver that gave them reason to stay. In the late decades of the 1500s, European hatmakers popularized a new style of headgear, the beaver hat. Hats made with beaver felt would remain firm, waterproof, and durable in any shape or style, and about 1600 the beaver-felt hat entered into two and a half centuries of prominence. Suddenly, the beaver pelts supplied by Canadian Native trappers and traders emerged from Europe's luxury fur market to become a staple of commerce. Of an appeal to the sartorial fancy of baroque-age European gentlemen, a great colonial empire was born.

French merchants, with their heightened interest in Canada as a source of beaver pelts, became more regular visitors to the Canadian coasts. Experimenting with permanent trading posts, they worked out the economics of settlement. The costs of colonization, they saw, would have to be borne by revenue from the fur trade, upon

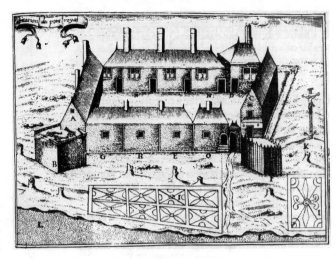

the Bay of Fundy to Hudson Bay, many of the
[Euro]peans' first outposts in Canada were something like
[the] spartan quarters in a small clearing, part fort and
[part] trading post. Established in 1604–05 on the north
[shore] of Nova Scotia's Annapolis Basin, the Habitation at
[Port]-Royal was abandoned, reclaimed, and fought over,
[event]ually becoming the nucleus of Acadia. It was recon-
[struct]ed near its original site in 1939–40. Copperplate
[engr]aving after a drawing by Champlain in *Les Voyages
[du Si]eur de Champlain*…(Paris: J. Berjon, 1613).

which a monopoly would have to be imposed. It was during these experiments that one of the merchants, François Gravé Du Pont, introduced to Canada the man who would eclipse them all, Samuel de Champlain. A commoner from the southwestern French town of Brouage, Champlain was probably about twenty-three (his birthdate, traditionally 1567, is now thought to be about 1580). He may have had some training in mapping and surveying, but he had no official title or standing in 1603, when he accompanied Gravé Du Pont up the St. Lawrence to Montreal Island, or in 1604–07, when he was one of the participants in a three-year settlement at Ile Ste-Croix and Port-Royal on the Bay of Fundy. Champlain gradually established himself as an explorer and geographer, but it is mainly from his published accounts of these voyages that we know of his presence on them.

In 1607 the settlement at Port-Royal was abandoned, but Champlain took a decisive step forward, recommending and being chosen to lead a new colonization venture on the St. Lawrence. Champlain had grasped that while (in the words of historian Guy Frégault) "it would take an army of colonists to found a settlement on the Atlantic coast, a battalion would suffice farther inland." In Algonquian, "Quebec" means "the place where the river narrows," and settlers there might be able to secure the working monopoly of the inland fur trade that had eluded the backers of the Port Royal venture on the seacoast. Champlain had seized the moment. Interest in the fur trade was growing, while fishing and whaling enterprises in the Gulf of St. Lawrence were in temporary decline. In July 1608 Champlain and a party of workmen landed at the foot of Cap Diamant, the great rock that still dominates Quebec City, and there they built a cluster of fortified buildings, the Habitation of Quebec. Twenty of Champlain's twenty-eight men died during the first winter there. The survivors,

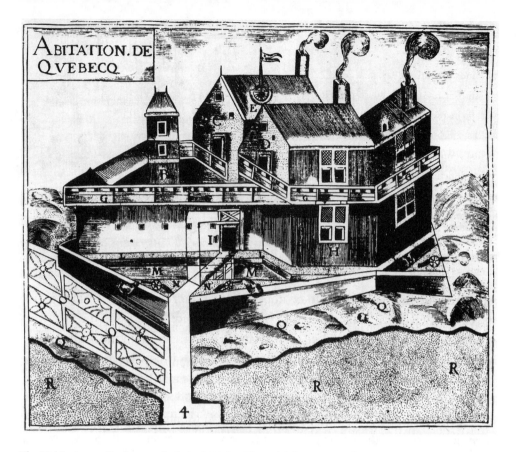

The Habitation at Quebec was built in 1608, by Champlain's twenty-eight-member wintering party, below the cliffs that define present-day Quebec City. It would be twenty-five years before a real town grew up around its site. Copperplate engraving after a drawing by Champlain in *Les Voyages du Sieur de Champlain*...(Paris: J. Berjon, 1613).

weak from malnutrition and scurvy when the ships returned from France in the spring of 1609, had established a permanent European presence on Canadian soil. "New France," the name that had symbolized all the French Crown's claims and interests in North America since Giovanni da Verrazano first used it in 1524, was becoming a reality. For a century and a half Quebec City, which grew up around the site of the Habitation, would be its centre.

In the spring Champlain took up the arduous diplomatic and military campaign that would turn his foothold into a colony. In 1609—and for decades afterward— New France was only a trading post and embassy, perched on the edge of a continent dominated by Native nations. Since the early 1500s, these nations had grown used to exchanging furs for iron axes, copper pots, cloth, and decorative beads brought by visiting fishermen and traders. For control of this trade, they had fought bloody wars, which by 1600 had made the St. Lawrence valley a no man's land hotly contested by two Native alliances. One of these alliances was built around the League of the Five Nations, or Iroquois Confederacy, a farming and trading society of perhaps thirty thousand people. The Iroquois homeland lay in the Mohawk valley and Finger Lakes district of what is today New York State, but a network of smaller tribes allied to them covered much of the territory south of the St. Lawrence River. The other Native alliance lay north of the St. Lawrence. Its most powerful element was the Huron Confederacy on the Georgian Bay shores of Lake Huron. The twenty thousand Huron (or Wendat, as they called themselves) were an Iroquoian people—that is, they resembled the Iroquois in their language, their extensive agriculture based on corn-growing, and their sophisticated political confederacies. But the Huron and Iroquois confederacies were longstanding rivals for power and influence. The Huron allies were hunting-and-gathering tribes, of whom the Montagnais, living on the north shore of the Gulf of St. Lawrence, were most familiar to the French. Because battles with the Iroquois alliance had almost closed the St. Lawrence River to trade, these northern allies took their furs to the coast by other routes. Tadoussac, a Montagnais village at the mouth of the Saguenay River, had been the centre of trade between the Native people and the French until Champlain arrived at Quebec.

The Native alliances and rivalries meant that Champlain's aim to control the exchange of furs from his base at Quebec entailed much more than simply setting up shop and offering to trade. Native Canadians welcomed European traders for the goods they brought, but ships that came and went every summer could supply the goods just as well. The French acquired their territorial foothold on the St. Lawrence, not through the altruism or weakness of the Native peoples, but by persuading some of them that a permanent French presence would be a bulwark against their rivals. Although Champlain fully intended to see his foothold grow in size and strength, his colony's survival in its early years depended on his ability to demonstrate its usefulness to his Native allies. It was not up to Champlain to choose his allies. Earlier French traders had made that choice by their trading agreements with the Montagnais. So, in 1609, Champlain set forth to aid the Montagnais and their inland allies—by making war on the Iroquois.

Warriors from three allied nations—Montagnais from east and north of Quebec, Algonquin from the Ottawa River region, and Huron from Georgian Bay—joined the French at the Habitation in the spring of 1609. "They celebrated for five or six

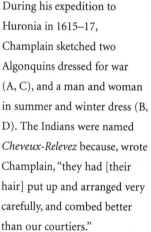

During his expedition to Huronia in 1615–17, Champlain sketched two Algonquins dressed for war (A, C), and a man and woman in summer and winter dress (B, D). The Indians were named *Cheveux-Relevez* because, wrote Champlain, "they had [their hair] put up and arranged very carefully, and combed better than our courtiers."

Two Huron women (F and H) are here gathering and grinding the corn that was basic to their agricultural society. The slatted wooden armour worn by the Huron warrior (E) was made obsolete by metal arrowheads and musket balls.

Engravings from drawings by Champlain in *Les Voyages de la Nouvelle France occidentale, dicte Canada*... (Paris: P. Le-Mur, 1632).

days," wrote Champlain, "which were spent in dancing and feasting." Trade goods were exchanged as gifts to cement the friendship, but what was being confirmed was a grimly practical political alliance, one that each partner hoped to turn to its own advantage. As soon as the feasting was done, the military campaign began. The allies travelled together up the St. Lawrence and Richelieu rivers to Lake Champlain, and in July 1609 they encountered an Iroquois war party. Champlain's European weapons gave the allies a decisive advantage—his first shot killed three Iroquois leaders and the battle quickly became a rout. That victory, and the continuing presence of French firepower based at Quebec, began to establish security of trade on the St. Lawrence. In the next six years Champlain would participate in several more battles against the Iroquois. The Five Nations would never again be taken so completely by surprise, but when a Dutch settlement on the Hudson River offered them an alternate trade route, a temporary truce developed. The northern allies were left in control of the lower St. Lawrence. Trade at the Habitation prospered.

The events of 1609 marked the beginning of the six-year period that would confirm the fateful alliance of French and Huron and establish Champlain's standing as an explorer. Until 1609 the Huron had never encountered the French, although they had been receiving European goods via the Montagnais and the Algonquin for fifty years or more. Indeed, the word "Huron" comes from a French root that indicates the French at first considered them backward rustics. In reality, the Huron Confederacy was larger, richer, and more powerful than any of the other tribes in the alliance. By trading the abundance of food they grew, the Huron amassed large stocks of fur. They became the middlemen between the French merchants and the woodland hunting peoples who actually trapped the beaver. Despite the displeasure of the Montagnais and the Algonquin, who would have preferred to see trade take place on their own territory, direct dealings between French and Huron grew rapidly, and the French and Huron became close partners.

In 1615 Champlain himself was permitted to accompany a Huron party on the month-long voyage from Montreal Island up the Ottawa River, via Lake Nipissing to Lake Huron, and south to the Huron homeland. That summer they went raiding into Iroquois country, and Champlain suffered a wound that forced him to spend the winter with the Huron. From his hosts, from his own travels, and from other Frenchmen, notably Etienne Brûlé, already living there, Champlain compiled a remarkably clear geography of the Great Lakes watershed. After a century of contacts that had never taken Europeans farther inland than Montreal, the Huron alliance enabled Champlain to extend European knowledge of the country as far inland as Lake Superior in less than twenty years. Champlain's 1632 map, which incorporates all these findings, is one of the masterworks of Canadian cartography.

"The great love I have always had for making discoveries in New France made me more and more eager to travel this country so as to have a perfect knowledge of it," wrote Champlain to introduce the book in which he described his year among the

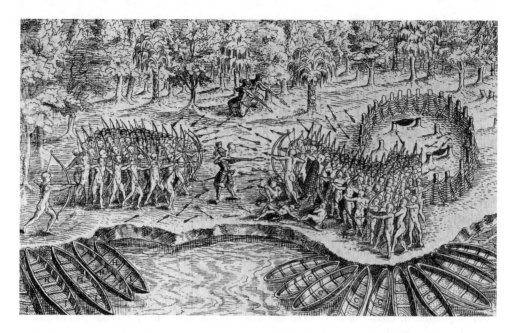

European weapons at first seemed to spell disaster for the aboriginal armies that had to face them. With a few shots from their arquebuses, Champlain and his companions routed an Iroquois army in this skirmish by Lake Champlain in 1609. Native tactics were soon revised, however, and the Iroquois were never again caught in the open like this—or defeated so decisively. Copperplate engraving after a drawing by Champlain in *Les Voyages du Sieur de Champlain*...(Paris: J. Berjon, 1613).

Huron. Yet for all his explorations and his mapmaking achievements, Champlain seems never to have sought knowledge for its own sake. His writings show less interest than others displayed in the world of the Native peoples, and his remark that the Huron were a people "without any religion or law" was a stunningly obtuse statement from a man who had spent a year living with them. After he returned to the Habitation early in 1616, he made no more voyages of discovery, and he left daily contact with the Native people to such traders as Etienne Brûlé.

Brûlé had been sent to live among them in 1610 in exchange for a young Huron who stayed with Champlain, and he spent much of the rest of his life among the Native people. The first time he returned to the Habitation, men there were shocked to realize that this young man—travelling with a Native trade party, eating their food, wearing their clothes, and speaking their language—was in fact a Frenchman. Brûlé remained a fur trader—indeed, his attempt to arrange a trade agreement against the interests of his Huron hosts seems to be what got him killed in 1633—but he adapted to Native ways much more fully than Champlain ever did. Champlain's writings often suggest the grim single-mindedness of a man who assessed things by their utility to his own projects, and by 1616, if not before, the foremost among those projects was the colonization of Canada.

Champlain was no longer simply the local agent of a fur-trading company. He was breaking away from the traders who had brought him to Canada. In France royal support for Champlain's colony was growing, and since 1612 Champlain had held the title of lieutenant of the King's viceroy for New France. In a plan for the colonization of Canada that he presented to Louis XIII in 1618, Champlain expressed his own vision for the colony centred on Quebec. Where the traders, French and Aboriginal, could have been satisfied with a small post to serve the fur trade, Champlain proposed the Christianization of the Native peoples and the establishment of substantial towns. He foresaw fisheries, mining, forestry, and agriculture in New France, as well as the trade in furs. He even predicted that the colony would open a route beyond the Great Lakes to the Orient, "whence great riches could be drawn."

For its first decade, the Habitation had been an outpost of young, transient workmen, but to build the colony he had described, Champlain needed both missionaries and families. The first priests arrived in 1615. In 1617 Louis Hébert, his wife Marie Rollet, and their three children came to settle, and in 1620 one of their daughters bore the first surviving child of the community. Hébert has been called "Canada's first farmer," and though the designation is ludicrous in light of the vast agricultural output of the Iroquoian nations of that time, the gradual appearance of occupations other than fur trading was vital to Champlain's plans for a permanent community. Yet by 1627 Quebec still had under a hundred people, fewer than a dozen of whom were women, and the settlement still depended on the Native people who brought in the furs and on the supply ships from France.

The colony might have received a significant boost that year, when Louis XIII's chief minister, Cardinal Richelieu, organized the Compagnie des Cent-Associés, a group of one hundred merchants and aristocrats committed to developing New France. The Cent-Associés was a private company, like others that had previously held the fur-trade monopoly in exchange for underwriting colonization efforts, but it was much wealthier and better connected than its predecessors and seemed much more likely to fulfil France's ambitions for its colony. In 1628 the Cent-Associés dispatched four hundred settlers from France to Quebec. But just as they sailed, war broke out with England, and an English company eager to replace the French in the trade of the St. Lawrence seized the opportunity. A fleet under David Kirke blockaded the St. Lawrence that summer and forced the Cent-Associés' ships back to

France. In 1629 Kirke and his brothers returned to capture the starving Habitation at Quebec and expel Champlain and most of his colonists.

The Anglo-French war had actually ended before the Kirkes captured Quebec, and during their occupation the English seem to have had difficulty maintaining the complex alliances needed to keep the fur trade going. France finally recovered New France by diplomatic negotiation in 1632, but the colony had to begin almost from nothing, and after several years of heavy losses and no fur-trade revenue, even the well-funded Cent-Associés was near bankruptcy. Despite these obstacles, the influx of settlers was steady, and the colony grew more rapidly in the 1630s than before. A new trading post took shape upriver at Trois-Rivières. At Quebec new farming lands were opened, the first streets of a town were surveyed, and the church had to be enlarged. The Jesuit Paul Le Jeune could report that to one who had known the place in the 1620s, Quebec in 1636 seemed "like a different country. It is no more that little corner tucked away at the end of the world." When he wrote this, the population of all of New France was barely four hundred, and Champlain had been dead for a year.

Samuel de Champlain's standing as the architect of lasting European settlement in Canada has often been inflated to make him the father and prophet of every aspect of French civilization in North America. He was hardly alone in his endeavours, for he came supported by trading companies and remained as the agent of royal policy. When he arrived at Quebec, traders had already forged the French-Native alliance that remained fundamental to New France long after his death. Moreover, Champlain's determination to claim, settle, and evangelize Canada ran directly counter to the interests of his Native allies, who were only persuaded to tolerate his outpost at Quebec because of the protection it gave to the fur trade.

But Champlain's aim was a colony, not a trading post. For him, pleasing the traders and Native peoples became a tactic, not a goal. Neither a merchant nor an aristocratic royal confidant, Champlain had adopted the Canadian colony as his own project, and for twenty-seven years he promoted it with an intensity that was probably crucial to its survival. Without a broadly based colony growing around it, a fur-trade outpost at Quebec would always have been hostage to commercial fluctuations and to military attack from either Native powers or seaborne raiders like the Kirkes. Over more than a quarter-century, Champlain's emphasis on settlement had engineered a decisive change in European involvement with the lands and peoples of Canada, producing a permanent community out of transient contacts. If he had not persisted, writes historian Marcel Trudel, "there would not have been a New France."

Missions, Traders, a Few Farmers:
Canada under the Cent-Associés

Champlain left no heir to his cause. In 1610 he had married twelve-year-old Hélène Boullé in Paris (he himself seems to have been about thirty). Though the marriage agreement had to stipulate that the bride would not live with her husband until she was fourteen, it was not too unusual a marriage for its time. Essentially it was intended to seal an association between the well-connected Boullé family and Champlain, and there is little to suggest that the couple grew close. Hélène Boullé did spend the years 1620–24 at Quebec, but she stayed in Paris most of her life. When Champlain returned to Canada in 1632, he left her all his property in France and never saw her again; she eventually became a nun. Nor did Champlain have a protégé at Quebec. To replace him, the King appointed Charles Huault de Montmagny, a military aristocrat from France who spent twelve years as Governor General (a title never conferred on Champlain but borne by all his successors down to the present).

The growth the colony had seen in Champlain's last years continued under Montmagny. Still, by comparison with other New World colonies that had been founded by then, New France began to fall behind. French and English colonies in the Caribbean had begun to prosper growing sugar, England's Virginia colony had discovered tobacco, and New England was developing fishing and trading enterprises. All of them were attracting thousands of settlers. When the Cent-Associés' mandate in New France ended in 1663, there were one hundred thousand settlers in the English colonies in North America and ten thousand in New Holland, the Dutch colony on the Hudson River. New France had barely three thousand people, and the fur trade, still the only commercial incentive that could draw settlers there, remained largely a Native enterprise. The French fur trade merchants needed to bring only handfuls of French workers to run their business at Quebec, and rather than take to farming when their term of service was over, many of those returned to France. Champlain's vision of a large diversified community around his Habitation remained unfulfilled.

The Cent-Associés became the scapegoat for the slow pace of development in New France, but the company can hardly be blamed for conditions that precluded a massive influx of settlers. Despite the disasters of the company's first few years and continuing troubles with its fur trade, the Cent-Associés actually met its colonizing commitments, underwriting a steady, if small, flow of migrants. Each year of its tenure a few more families acquired land and took up permanent residence, and more of the institutions of a society were established. Still, the colony remained mostly male, dominated by commerce, and rooted in the trading alliance run by the Huron and the other Native allies.

A motive other than commerce was growing, however. Protestants had been at least as prominent as Catholics among the first backers of Quebec, and the colony got along without priests for its first seven years. But in France, Catholic enthusiasm for the new colony grew as the settlement endured, and the drive to carry the Catholic message throughout the newly discovered world extended to Canada. The missionaries who came to New France were not primarily drawn by spiritual needs of the few traders and farmers of the colony. What drew them was the opportunity to convert North America's Native peoples. The Recollets, the first priests to come to the colony, brought this ambition with them in 1615, and they departed almost at once on *le grand voyage* by canoe along the Ottawa River route to the Huron country. The same aim inspired the Jesuits, who arrived in 1625. Their *Jesuit Relations*, the annual published account of their mission activities, soon became an important instrument for promoting the colony among the well-to-do and literate in France.

It was religious impulse, rather than the Cent-Associés or the fur trade, which led to the creation of Montreal in 1642. Its founders, a group of religious mystics in France who were moved by visions to build a missionary city in the wilderness, were led by a devout soldier, Paul de Chomedey de Maisonneuve, and inspired by a dynamic and devout laywoman, Jeanne Mance. They intended to convert the Native peoples by persuading them to live among the French and, in effect, to become French in their dress, work, and outlook. The Native peoples, however, proved largely indifferent. Despite the idealism and courage of many of Montreal's founders, the missionary society collapsed in debt and disillusion in the 1650s, by which time settlement and commerce were becoming Montreal's *raison d'être*.

The Jesuits chose a different mission strategy. They preferred to live among the Native people, learning their languages and studying their society in order to convert them more effectively. Jesuits went out to all the Native allies, but they focused on the Huron nation, as the largest, most settled, and most influential group within the French alliance. In 1634 Father Jean de Brébeuf led a party of three missionaries to the Huron country, and in a few years the Jesuit community there included missionaries, lay brothers, servants, and soldiers—more than fifty Frenchmen in all. In 1639 Father Jérôme Lalemant began the construction of Ste-Marie, a fortified mission on a riverbank close by the shore of Georgian Bay. The Ste-Marie mission, which included a chapel, a hospital, stables for animals, and residences for the French and for Huron

This supposedly Huron scene was published in 1683, some thirty years after the destruction of the Huron nation in the Iroquois wars. Though Champlain, the Jesuits, and many others had described this Iroquoian nation as a settled people living in large palisaded towns surrounded by cornfields, the European notion of Canadian Natives as small bands of woodland hunters endured. Engraving in A. Mallet, *Description de l'Univers* (Paris, 1683).

converts, offered the Jesuits and their assistants a corner of Europe in the midst of the Native nation.

The Jesuits in New France were taking on an enormous challenge. Intellectuals trained in theology and sciences, they confronted the crushing physical hardships of living in what seemed to them a wilderness inhabited by barbarians. Huron attitudes were equally daunting. From child-rearing through marriage to burial of the dead, all the normal customs of Huron society either horrified or disoriented the missionaries. There were few successes to encourage them, for despite conversion efforts that had started in 1615, virtually no Huron had made a sincere conversion by the end of the 1630s. Yet the missionaries persevered. Some found personal and intellectual challenge in the effort to understand their audience without losing their own faith, but what most strongly sustained them was a profound religious fervour. Welcoming whatever was God's will, they strove to accept all their hardships and told one another that martyrdom would be a sign of God's favour. The missionaries' acceptance of—often eagerness for—martyrdom was deep and sincerely spiritual, but it was also appropriate to their situation. No less than Champlain or the traders, the missionaries would be part of

The twentieth-century reconstruction of Ste. Marie among the Hurons, on the Wye River near Midland, Ontario, strongly evokes the Jesuit attempt to create a piece of Europe in the midst of the Huron nation. The missionaries' Indian hosts erected their longhouses (inset) in the narrow end of the palisaded village. Founded in 1639, this was Ontario's first European community. Five Jesuits died when the Iroquois attacked nearby Huron villages in 1648–49, so in 1649 the mission was withdrawn and the church burned to prevent desecration.

brutal wars, devastating epidemics, and all the wrenching violence of one civilization colliding with another. Few of them shrank from that reality.

As Jean de Brébeuf, Jérôme Lalemant, and other priests and brothers mastered the language and began to know the society, they wrote many vivid descriptions of Huron ways. Yet although they adapted to many aspects of Huron life and acquired a deep familiarity with Huron customs and beliefs, they continued to be unable to convert their hosts, some of whom were openly hostile to this foreign

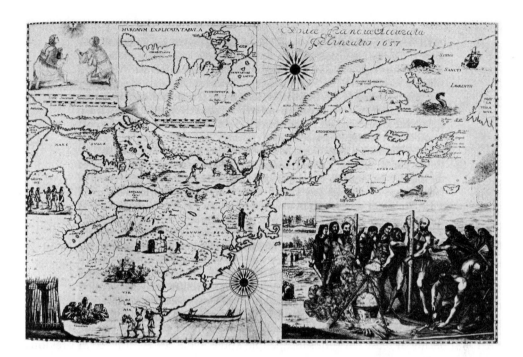

Attributed to the Jesuit François-Joseph Bressani, this map of New France, with its engraved vignette depicting the martyrdom of Jean de Brébeuf and Gabriel Lalemant at the hands of the Iroquois in 1649, shows the location of the Jesuit missions on Lake Huron's Georgian Bay. Map printed from copperplate (Rome, 1657).

presence. Those most opposed to the Jesuits had strong arguments to offer. Not only were the missionaries seeking to disrupt all the fundamental practices of Huron society, they were also sowing death wherever they went for, as they and their helpers moved among the Huron, they unwittingly spread new diseases to which the Native peoples had never developed any resistance. During the 1630s, smallpox and measles ravaged the allied Native nations, and thousands died. By the 1640s the Huron population had been halved, and many of the allied tribes suffered similarly. Still the Jesuits remained among the Huron, tending the sick, praying for the dead, and preaching their message. Strongly supported by the French Crown and the authorities in New France, the Jesuits could make their presence among the Huron a condition of the French-Huron alliance. In the 1630s and 1640s, it was still the Huron who gathered the beaver pelts (largely by their own trade with other Native peoples) and transported them to Quebec. As their numbers fell, this trade—and the military alliance based on it—remained important enough to them that they continued to accept the Jesuits' presence among them, despite the hostility many of them felt.

The Iroquoian Wars

Champlain's Iroquois war of 1609–15 had gradually subsided into an armed peace, but in the 1640s new Iroquoian wars—which remain among the bloodiest ever fought in Canada—destroyed the Native alliances that had been central to New France's existence since 1608. Rivalries between the Native nations were longstanding, but the coming of European alliances, European goods, and European weapons had greatly raised the stakes. Each now saw its rivals as threats to its survival and obstacles to its prosperity and prestige. As a result, the powerful Five Nations Iroquois confederacy sent its warriors, now familiar with European weapons, on a wide-ranging and astonishingly successful military campaign. Between 1645 and 1655, they destroyed all their Iroquoian rivals. In ten years, the Huron, the Petun, the Neutral, and the Erie nations, each numbering at least ten thousand people and each a powerful force in previous wars and skirmishes, were all destroyed. In the aftermath of these conflicts, the survival of the French community in the St. Lawrence valley was itself placed in question.

It was 1648 when the Iroquois invaded the Huron country itself. Under their attack the Huron nation, already weakened by its terrible losses to disease, was further beset by internal disagreements. Some Huron saw in Catholicism, the missionaries, and the French alliance the only hope of survival, and for the first time many of them began to accept baptism. Others blamed the French for the epidemics and the dissension among them. Unable to muster an effective defence, the Huron were overrun in 1648 and 1649. Father Antoine Daniel died in the attack; Jean de Brébeuf and Jérôme Lalemant's nephew Gabriel, along with many Huron, suffered the terrible death by torture that was a standard part of Iroquoian warfare. The priests had won the martyrdom they sought, but the Jesuits' most important Canadian missionary enterprise collapsed. One small remnant of exiles founded a Catholic Huron community at Lorette near Quebec, but the once strong Huron confederacy ceased to exist, its people killed, dispersed among allies, or absorbed into the victorious Iroquois population. The warriors of the Five Nations moved on to attack other rivals. New France, with both its missionary endeavours and its commercial alliances in ruins, was reduced to the position of an impotent spectator as the confederacy destroyed one nation after another. Finally, the French colonists felt the power of the Iroquois armies directly, as they turned their attack from the defeated Native nations to the French settlers in the St. Lawrence valley.

In 1660 and 1661, Iroquois raiding parties struck at every part of New France. They put Montreal under siege, pillaged the Ile d'Orléans near Quebec, and continued downriver as far as remote Tadoussac. The colony's farm families, terrorized by war parties that lay in ambush at the edge of their fields, had to retreat into palisaded forts. Workers headed back to France in greater numbers than ever, and the fur trade remained dangerous and unprofitable. Still, the Iroquois probably never threatened the total destruction of New France, although two hundred settlers may have died at their hands. Weakened by their own losses and seeking less to destroy the French than to make them pliable, the Iroquois never mounted a full-scale invasion against Montreal or any of the other settlements. Even the fur trade did not collapse completely. The loss of the Huron middlemen created an opportunity for Algonquian tribes to become traders. Indeed, the exploit of Adam Dollard des Ormeaux, a soldier who died with all his men in 1660 during a futile attempt to seize furs directly from the Iroquois, indicated that the French themselves were ready to go in search of furs.

Yet if the Iroquois did not intend to destroy the colony, they certainly played a crucial role in bringing down the Cent-Associés. The company had been in financial difficulties ever since its losses to the Kirkes in 1628 and 1629. In the crisis of the Iroquoian wars, the colony's inability to pay its way or even defend itself became plain. In 1663 Louis XIV—king since 1643 and now, at twenty-five, emerging from the shadow of his advisers to begin the personal rule that would last until 1715— ordained a new start for New France. He dissolved the Cent-Associés. No longer would the colony depend on a company constrained by the profit-and-loss columns of a commercial balance sheet. New France would be a royal colony under the direct authority of royal ministers and the Sun King himself. Champlain's colony, a settlement uneasily wedded to a commercial enterprise, became Louis XIV's royal province.

New France under the Sun King's Rule

From 1663 to 1763 the King of France ruled New France. Both Louis XIV and his great-grandson after him, Louis XV, actively shaped colonial policy, and their Ministers of Marine (the Marine department administered the navy and the colonies) were remarkably consistent in giving close attention to colonial matters. Successful ministers stayed in office for decades, and they left the margins of thousands of pages of reports, proposals, and requests marked with their handwritten verdicts: "*Bon*," "*Non*," "*Non absolument*," and with succinct policy directives that their clerks would expand into detailed instructions. The great palace at Versailles, just beginning to be built at the start of royal government in New France, was the real centre of colonial government. In the colony, the King's authority passed down through two officials. The Governor General, usually a military aristocrat, represented royal power both symbolically and directly. He commanded the armed forces, directed "foreign relations" with the British colonies and the Aboriginal nations, and presided as the vice-regal representative at state and public occasions.

No commander ever filled the office more strikingly than Louis de Buade de Frontenac, a bold commander with a flair for dramatic gestures who was Governor General from 1672 to 1682 and again from 1689 to his death, aged seventy-six, in 1698. Frontenac was an inspiring leader in the colony's wars, but his imperious rule and constant efforts to find fur-trade income to pay the debts of his extravagant style of life alienated many. Frontenac was not the only governor to resent limits on his freedom of action, for much of the daily administration of the royal colony was actually the responsibility of another official, the Intendant. The Intendant, usually from the minor, administrative nobility, handled military pay and provisioning and was New France's civil administrator as well. His responsibilities included finances, justice, and police—this latter being a catch-all for the order and well-being of the colony.

Governor and Intendant were aided by a council, the Conseil Souverain (later Conseil Supérieur), which became the colony's highest court and was supported by a series of lower royal courts. Under royal government, a colonial military establishment gradually developed. With the royal treasury supporting New France, the governing institutions of the colony could grow far beyond what the Cent-Associés had provided. Clerks, storekeepers, bailiffs, local agents, and port and road officials were gradually added to the Intendant's staff. Even the church felt the organizing influence of the new royal power. Native resistance, the disaster in the Huron mission, and the growing needs of the colonial population helped tame the missionary fervour that had typified the church's early years. Bishop François de Laval, who had come to the colony under the Cent-Associés, continued to wield great influence, but the coming of royal government generally meant the fading of clerical dominance over the affairs of the colony. On the other hand, royal authority aided the clergy in shaping a diocese, a parish structure, and a system of tithes to support the colony's priests. New France had been reserved for Catholic settlers since 1627, and although the presence of a few Protestants was tolerated, Protestant marriages and religious ceremonies were always forbidden in the colony.

For the people of New France, the first great consequence of royal government was the end of the Iroquoian wars. Louis XIV was prepared to defend his colony, and the Régiment de Carignan-Salières, more than a thousand, reinforced the colonial militia that had been resisting the Iroquois onslaught strong. It arrived at Quebec in 1665 with orders to invade the Iroquois country. Though the troops were unable to inflict much damage on the Iroquois, their intervention proved decisive. Already struggling with terrible losses from war and epidemics, the Iroquois made peace with New France and its Native allies. In 1667 a comprehensive treaty ushered in twenty years of peace. Small groups of Catholic Mohawks even moved north to found Kahnawake and other Mohawk communities near Montreal. The King's colony could now concentrate on its own development.

By the 1660s, as the French colony in the St. Lawrence valley began to grow again, European settlements were taking shape in other parts of what is now Canada. In 1608 Champlain had rejected Port-Royal as a colonization site because of the

François de Laval (1623–1708) came to New France in 1659, when the colony had barely two-thousand people; in 1674, after a long power struggle between the Pope and Louis XIV, he became the first Bishop of Quebec. Although a stern and determined cleric, he carried out his duties with charity and practicality, retiring in 1685 into spiritual retreat at the Séminaire de Québec, which he had founded in 1663. Bishop Laval also established a school of arts and crafts in which sculpture and painting were taught. Portrait in oils attributed to Laval's protégé, Claude François *dit* Frère Luc (1614–85), painted *c.* 1672.

difficulty of asserting control over the long, indented coast of Acadia. (The name may come from an Algonquian root, though "Arcadia," a reference to the classical image of rural contentment, which the explorer Verrazano had applied to part of the American coast, also influenced its adoption.) The events of half a century confirmed Champlain's insight. Although French fur traders and missionaries had soon reoccupied the abandoned colony at Port-Royal, the rival colonizing efforts of Jean de Biencourt de Poutrincourt, Nicolas Denys, Charles de St-Etienne de La Tour, and Charles de Menou d'Aulnay mostly generated fruitless skirmishes. One British venture was particularly short-lived. In the 1620s, Sir William Alexander, a Scottish poet and courtier to the Stuart kings of England, made elaborate plans for a Scottish colony north of New England. His expedition produced little beyond an enduring name—Nova Scotia.

The outposts these colonizers struggled for years to build and maintain in Acadia were chronically subject to attacks from one another and from New England, Virginia, and other English colonies to the south. Yet, if maintaining a coherent colony was impossible in Acadia, settlement was not. Gradually, starting in the 1630s, a small French population took root, particularly around the trading post of Port-Royal on the Bay of Fundy. The Mi'kmaq, rapidly integrating Christianity into their own culture and with their numbers seriously reduced by epidemics, accepted the colonists' presence, and the Acadian society was born, less from colonization projects than from the efforts of handfuls of individuals (there were Scots, Irish, Basque, and Mi'kmaq as well as the French) to find lives for themselves in the new Acadian community.

The settlers of Acadia confronted the mighty tides of the Bay of Fundy, which can rise and fall fifty feet at the head of the bay, and they soon began diking to create fertile new land from the tidal flats. The first dikes were simple sod ramps laid between high points, but over the decades they became more elaborate, enclosing an increasing acreage and equipped with sluices to drain away rainwater without letting in the salt tides. Gradually the sheltered parts of the Bay of Fundy shore were ringed with grassy, 1.5-metres (5-foot) dikes enclosing fertile fields where the Acadians raised wheat and livestock. The Acadians were French in origin and language, but the colonies of New England to the south were far closer and easier to reach than Quebec. Trading with the English in peacetime and often controlled by them when wars broke out, the Acadians began to refer to their New England neighbours as "*nos amis l'ennemi.*" Although the coming of royal government to New France eventually brought French governors, garrisons, and institutions to Acadia, the shaping of Acadian neutrality had begun.

Farther east, settlements were also forming out of the Newfoundland cod-fishing industry. The cod trade, of course, had long preceded settlement. There may have been more fishermen visiting Newfoundland during the obscure sixteenth century than during the early seventeenth-century years when Samuel de Champlain's colony was being founded. Through both these centuries, fishing remained mostly a transient industry despite some attempts to promote settlement. Fishing fleets came each

Whaling and fishing were European industrial processes transported to the coves and bays of Atlantic Canada. Fishermen caught the cod and delivered them to the wharf, where shore crews split, cleaned, and washed the fish, collected the cod-liver oil, and finally laid out the fish to dry. This engraving, inset in Herman Moll, *Map of North America*, 1718, is based on a vignette entitled *La Pesche des Morues*...in Nicolas de Fer's 1698 map of North and South America.

Dutch-born painter Gerard van Edema (1652–1700) travelled to Newfoundland and the American colonies under English auspices around 1690, but if the title of this oil is correct in locating the scene in Placentia Bay, the picture must represent one of the fishing stations of the French colony established on Newfoundland's south coast from the 1660s to 1713.

spring from England, France, Spain, or Portugal, and they took their dried or brine-soaked catch back home in the autumn. Although they might spend most of the summers of their lives in Newfoundland, most fishermen never established residence or spent a winter there. The European ports that invested in the cod fishery preferred it that way, fearing that colonial fishing ports would become their competitors.

Cod was at least as expensive as beef, and Europe lacked the means to transport it far inland, so only a minority of Europe's people ever ate Newfoundland cod, yet the cod trade was always much larger and more valuable than the fur trade. Along the English Channel, the preference was for "green" cod, lightly pickled in brine, but most Newfoundland cod was split, salted, and exposed to sun and air until it was perfectly hard and dry. Dried cod could be preserved for months or years, and it was this dried product from North America that opened a market for cod on the hot southern coasts of Europe. French and English fishermen competed for this market in Portugal, Spain, and into the Mediterranean.

To dry the cod, fishermen occupied the shores of Newfoundland from spring to fall, displacing the Beothuk people of the island, who were forced to the inhospitable interior of the island. By the end of the sixteenth century, Spain and Portugal had withdrawn from the fishery, so it was England and France that competed for fish and territory in Newfoundland, and a few permanent settlements began to appear. In 1610 John Guy of Bristol led a party of settlers to Conception Bay, and in the next decade Lord Baltimore began a short-lived settlement of English Catholics at Ferryland on the Avalon Peninsula. Baltimore soon shifted his interests south to Maryland on Chesapeake Bay. For most of the seventeenth century the fleets of fishermen who came and went from Europe had overshadowed the handful of settlers in Newfoundland.

By the late 1600s, English Newfoundland meant the eastern shore of the island, from Trinity Bay and Conception Bay to Ferryland and Renews south of St. John's. Here barely a thousand men—with a few women and children—might winter every year. They were joined every summer by thousands of fishermen from England. St. John's, a rendezvous of fishermen since the 1500s, was already the largest settlement, but people were scattered among a score of outports, wherever there was a harbour and an adequate supply of fish. French fishermen, travelling back and forth from Basque, Breton, and Norman ports, fished each summer on the northern coast of Newfoundland. About 1660 a small French settlement colony called Plaisance, complete with governor, garrison, fortifications, and a few hundred people, was formed on the south coast of the island.

The Peopling of New France

With peace and royal support assured in the late 1660s, New France began to fulfil the promise of population made by Champlain and kept alive by the Cent-Associés. In 1663 a third of the three thousand settlers of New France were children under fifteen, who would become the parents of many future colonists of Louis XIV. Still, after fifty years, three thousand seemed a pitifully small basis for a great royal colony, and the King embarked on a vigorous recruiting program to people New France.

One source of new settlers was the Régiment de Carignan-Salières, the force sent in 1665 to defend the settlers from the Iroquois. With peace secured, the regiment was disbanded, and the King made it plain to the officers that he wanted to see them settle in New France. Many of the officers and about four hundred of the men complied. Soon after, New France acquired a permanent military establishment, the Compagnies Franches de la Marine. These were infantry companies raised for colonial service by the Ministry of Marine rather than by the French regular army. Enlisted men for these Marine troops were always recruited in France, but their officers would come from the colonial aristocracy—which meant, in effect, the Carignan officers and their sons along with the sons of the most successful colonists and a few highborn immigrants.

New France also recruited civilian labourers—as many as five hundred in some years—and in the new conditions of peaceful expansion more of them began to stay on and settle. For these men the path to New France, under the royal government as under the Cent-Associés, began with a hiring contract, an *engagement*. This contract bound the hired man, or *engagé*, to do three years' service for his employer or anyone to whom the employer sold his contract. In return, the *engagé* would receive passage to New France, room and board, and a small annual wage. After his three years' labour, he was entitled to passage back to France if he chose. *Engagés* were under no obligation to remain longer in New France—and fewer than half did.

The men recruited to New France in these years were mostly young workers or soldiers. They rarely brought wives or children with them, and only a handful of Aboriginal women ever came to live and marry amongst the French colonists. In 1663 men outnumbered women almost two to one in the colony. So began one of the most famous episodes in the peopling of New France: the recruiting of the *filles du roi* ("the King's daughters"). Between 1663 and 1673, about 775 women accepted royal offers of transportation to New France. It was a straightforward arrangement: the Crown wanted the single men of the colony to have wives, and the *filles du roi* needed husbands. With the assistance of a royal dowry—usually fifty *livres*, or two-thirds of an *engagé*'s annual cash earnings—90 per cent of the women found husbands, often within weeks of their arrival. According to Marie de l'Incarnation, the founder of the Ursuline convent at Quebec City, who helped house the new arrivals, the women understood clearly that men who had already begun their farms were the best prospects. "This is the first thing the girls inform themselves about," she wrote, "and they are wise to do so."

The first Ursuline convent in Quebec was built in 1642, when the town had only a few hundred people; it burned down in 1650. This reminiscent view dated 1850, by painter and *patriote* Joseph Légaré (1795–1855), captures the rugged surroundings of what is now Quebec's *vieille ville*; notice the wigwams in the lower right foreground.

Who were these women? Every *fille du roi* had her own story, but typical enough is that of Nicole Saulnier, an eighteen-year-old fatherless girl from Paris. She arrived at Quebec in the summer of 1669 and in October she married an *engagé* who had settled several years earlier on the nearby Ile d'Orléans. She lived there with a growing family for more than forty years. Probably she and most of the others had become *filles du roi* because some accident had left them orphaned or otherwise unsupported. In a society with strict rules for female conduct, young, unprotected women were vulnerable, and that dangerous situation itself may have encouraged many *filles du roi* to seize the chance of a state-sponsored marriage in the distant colony. For a decade, as many as 130 women a year abandoned the hazards of life in France for New France and marriage.

The *filles du roi* became the future of New France, for by the mid-1670s the female population had almost doubled, and the tide of subsidized immigration, both male and female, was ending. By 1681, when the colonial population was nearly ten thousand, large-scale immigration had ceased. A few soldiers would settle in the colony, a few *engagés* would be recruited, and a few convicts would be sent there, but most of the colony's growth would be by natural increase.

Those ten thousand settlers of 1681 would produce most of the Francophone population of Canada. The majority of the civilian immigrants came from western France. Normandy at first provided many of the settlers, and the small adjacent region of Perche was a major source simply because of the efforts of one or two recruiters there. In 1663 a third of the colonists had roots in those two regions. But as La Rochelle replaced Rouen in Normandy as the main port of departure, the number of immigrants from the south increased, and more than half the seventeenth-century immigrants came from south of the Loire River, the traditional border of northern and southern France. Both northerners and southerners tended to come from provinces near the Atlantic, the exception being that many of the *filles du roi* and the soldiers were from Paris. In the end, half the immigrant population was city-born. Cities were the centres of crafts and industry, and so—although the vast majority of the French populace were rural peasants—half the male immigrants to New France claimed a trade. More than a third may have been literate, probably because they had learned some reading and writing "on the job" in a skilled trade.

As a group, the immigrants were poor (like most people of their time), but they surely were not among the most destitute of French society. They were more skilled, more literate, more urban, and more likely to come from the coastal provinces or towns than most of their contemporaries. In New France such skills and literacy would soon be lost in a colony fast becoming rural and agricultural. New accents and speech patterns would evolve from the mix of regional dialects, and new customs and traditions would be forged out of a varied inheritance.

Demographers—those who study population—used to consider a birth rate of somewhere above forty births per thousand people per year a "natural" rate of increase in a population without artificial restraints on reproduction. Today, there is a greater awareness that demography is never "natural": it is always linked in complex ways to a society's particular circumstances. Yet the birth rate of early Canada continues to impress. Over most of the century from 1663 to 1763—and beyond—the people of New France produced offspring at a rate of fifty-five or even sixty-five births per year per thousand people. (In modern Canada the birth rate is about fifteen per thousand, and even at the height of the mid-twentieth-century "baby boom" it never exceeded thirty per thousand.) Their annual death rate was kept to a relatively happy twenty-five to thirty per thousand, and the ten thousand settlers of 1681 expanded their numbers at a remarkable rate, almost unassisted by new immigration.

In the healthy environment of the New World, spared the grinding poverty and crowding of Europe, the colonists lived longer. Even newborns had a higher survival rate—perhaps three-quarters could expect to survive to adulthood. The high birth rate, which was the key to rapid increase in the population, has a simple explanation: women married young and they remarried quickly if widowed. Before 1680 half of New France's brides were married before they were twenty. Couples began families as soon as they married (premarital conceptions were less than 5 per cent of all births), and they kept having children as long as they could. As a result a child often had six or seven siblings, and more than half grew up in households of ten children or more. The children repeated the early-marriage, large-family experience of their parents, and so the population grew. This easy explanation is deceptive, however. It misses the real question. Early marriage was the secret to a high birth rate, in New France as in most North American colonies, but why did people choose to marry early?

Families and Land

Early marriages were a result of the way people lived in New France. Into the 1650s, New France's handful of settlers depended for their survival on the annual arrival of supply ships from France, but in that decade the reliance on imported food abruptly ended. As immigrants continued to arrive and take up land, New France began to produce more than enough to feed itself. The price of bread went into a decline that would last almost seventy-five years. Farming in New France became a subsistence occupation, in which people grew enough to feed themselves rather than producing mostly for commercial sale. Land was abundant. Even in the narrow St. Lawrence valley, there was never a shortage of adequate farming land. As a result, the *engagé* and his wife who decided to stay in New France, or the children they raised, could always acquire sufficient land to support a family. A family, in fact, was what a settler needed, for it was almost impossible to run a farm without many hands. Large families, often a burden in the land-scarce Old World, were a blessing and a key to success in the New.

The seventeenth-century *engagé* who decided to stay after his three years' labour usually planned to become an *habitant*, the tenant-proprietor of a family farm. He began with some small savings from his hired service and a concession, or conditional lease, to perhaps sixty *arpents* (an *arpent* is about one-third of a hectare, or slightly less than an acre) of primeval forest. His first task was not to plant but to clear: simply to attack the woods with an axe and let in the sunlight. As the clearing slowly progressed, he had to build a shelter and begin assembling the elements of a farm. He could pause to work for wages or go into debt, but to have a worthwhile farm he had to keep clearing an *arpent* or so every year. He might start this work alone—at least as long as men outnumbered women, some progress towards self-sufficiency was almost a prerequisite to marriage—but sustained effort was always a family enterprise. If he married the daughter of settlers, her family might assist them. If the couple had savings, they might buy the lease of someone who had already cleared some land, for there were always leases available as *habitants* turned to the fur trade or town life, returned to France, or simply sought new locations. Whatever the case, clearing and building became a couple's lifework. As historian Louise Dechêne writes of the pioneer *habitant*, "At his death, thirty years after he received the concession, he possesses thirty *arpents* of arable land, a bit of meadow, a barn, a stable, a slightly more spacious house, a road by the door, neighbours, and a pew in the church. His life has passed in clearing and building." For those who endured, the later years might be eased as the farm became productive and a growing family shared the burden. This arduous progress, as heroic in its way as any of the epic battles of New France, was the essential element in creating a permanent settled population along the St. Lawrence.

Far from any markets that would bid up the price of their produce, the *habitants*

L'Atre, a comfortable eighteenth-century stone farmhouse (now a restaurant) on the Ile d'Orléans, reflects the traditional style of New France's domestic architecture: steep bellcast roof covered with thatch (later, as here, with cedar shingles), dormer windows, thick walls, sloping gable ends derived from northern France, and centrally positioned parlour chimney.

grew what they needed. Bread was the staple of their diet, so wheat was New France's basic crop, although there might be a little corn, oats, barley, and a bit of tobacco. Most farms had a vegetable garden. There would be just enough livestock to support a family, and with even a little meat, dairy products, and eggs, the *habitants* were better fed than most European peasants or urban poor. Self-sufficiency extended to most of what the farmers used and wore: simple tools, woollens from their sheep, linen from homegrown flax, shoes from hand-cured leather. Since the work of the farm required the labour of every member of the family, there was barely a separate "domestic" sphere. Women tended the farm along with the men and could take over its management when widowed. Children were unlikely to receive much education beyond a rudimentary catechism (rural illiteracy rapidly rose towards 90 per cent), and they were soon working in the fields beside their parents.

The form of the standard farmhouse evolved early, particularly the steep roof to shed snow. Most farmhouses were built of wood, in *pièce-sur-pièce* construction: a timber frame filled with smaller, horizontal, squared logs. Sometimes plastered or whitewashed, the houses were roofed with thatch or boards. Inside there would be a single room or perhaps two, divided by a central chimney and fireplace. In the seventeenth century, few farmhouses had stoves, and most used the fireplace for both heat and cooking. The furnishings were spartan: the minimum in furniture, mostly homemade, and almost no decoration. In these rooms and a narrow attic lived the large *habitant* families.

Were the *habitants* good farmers? Many of the immigrants did not have farming backgrounds, and lack of education, participation in non-farm work (such as the fur trade), and isolation from markets probably kept *habitant* farming methods simple and resistant to change. The little farms arduously hacked out of the surrounding forest certainly looked primitive, though there is evidence of crop rotation and other techniques broadly comparable to those used elsewhere at the time. The key to *habitant* agriculture is probably not skill or ignorance but adaptation to local conditions. With land abundant and labour scarce, there was no need to learn or adopt the intensive farming practised in parts of Europe where the conditions were reversed.

Landlords and Tenants: The Seigneurial Regime

Families going out in the 1660s and 1670s to clear farms from the forests along the river did so within a system of land ownership known as the seigneurial regime, a system that shaped New France and continues to shape the historical image of it. In France, the tradition of *nulle terre sans seigneur* (no land without its lord) went back to medieval times, when a lord with his castle and retinue controlled and protected a territory, and its people supported him by their labour. Even as the political and military aspects of feudalism receded, a society of landlords and tenants remained the common one in France and most of Europe, and its transfer from France to New France went almost without debate. France simply took for granted that the land of the colony belonged to the King (and in any case the wars in the St. Lawrence valley had left only a small Native population there), and *seigneuries* were the natural way for the King to grant land, through his representatives, to his subjects.

The seigneurial regime granted lands of two essential kinds: *seigneuries* and *rotures*. Whether their land was granted directly by the King or from another *seigneur*, holders of *seigneuries* owed fealty to their lord, but they paid no rent. Those who held *rotures*, on the other hand, were tenants. On the land they received from a *seigneur*, they would pay rent forever. Tenancy also imposed a range of duties, notably to patronize the *seigneur's* gristmill and to pay a fee on the sale of land leases. A *seigneurie* was normally large enough to include dozens of *rotures*, but a *roture* was rarely larger than a single family farm.

Because the Cent-Associés wanted help in recruiting settlers when it was administering New France, the company granted *seigneuries* to anyone who seemed likely to bring them. Robert Giffard, a surgeon who had visited New France in the 1620s, became one of the first to participate in this system. In 1634 he received the *seigneurie* of Beauport just east of Quebec. Giffard came from the town of Mortagne in Perche, and it was he and a couple of friends who recruited the early rush of Perche settlers to the colony. Few *seigneurs* imitated Giffard's efforts, and most *seigneuries* developed slowly, but by the 1650s there were three distinct clusters of active *seigneuries* around Quebec, Montreal, and Trois-Rivières. Already the characteristic look of the land of New France was being established. Nearly all *seigneuries* were long, narrow blocks set almost at right angles to the riverfront, and the *rotures* in them were also long and narrow. Settlers wanted to be close to neighbours, and river access was precious to all because it was essential for travel and trade.

The *seigneurs* were not necessarily aristocrats: one did not need to be a nobleman to acquire a *seigneurie*, and getting one did not confer noble status. But the colonial aristocracy took the lead in landholding. In 1663 half the *seigneurs* were noblemen (or noblewomen, usually widows who had acquired their husbands' estates), and they held three-quarters of all the land the King had granted. The proportion of *seigneuries* held by aristocrats would grow as officers of the Régiment de Carignan and later the Ministry of Marine companies acquired the lands that helped bind them to the New World. Pierre de Saurel, for instance, came to New France as a captain in the Carignan regiment. To defend the colony against Iroquois raiders, Saurel's troops built a fort where the Richelieu River joins the St. Lawrence near Montreal. When the regiment was disbanded, the outpost became the *seigneurie* of Saurel (later Sorel), and many of Pierre de Saurel's soldiers became his first tenants there. For the seigneurial elite to be a military caste seemed natural, for the aristocracy had always defined itself as "those who command," and as leaders they expected to be supported by their lands and tenants.

"Those who pray," the clergy, also expected to be supported by the third estate, "those who labour," and the church was a leading landlord throughout the history of New France. Granting *seigneuries* to orders of priests and nuns was not simply a charitable gesture, for many of the religious orders had the money and skill to develop their estates. Perhaps the most successful example was the *seigneurie* of Montreal Island, where the Sulpician order had replaced the faltering missionary society that had founded the community with such high ideals. A wealthy and well-connected order, the Sulpicians appointed able managers and spent money developing their lands. They were rewarded with rapid growth and expansion, and they would own much of Montreal Island well into the nineteenth century. Not all church *seigneuries* were held by religious orders. Bishop François de Laval, an aristocrat as well as a clergyman, was personally the *seigneur* of the Ile d'Orléans near Quebec. Like the aristocracy, the church would expand its landholdings over the years.

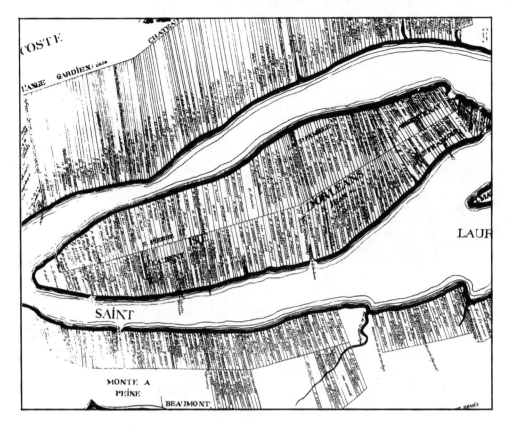

The familiar seigneurial landscape of narrow farms running back from the riverfront took shape with the earliest rural settlements in the St. Lawrence River valley. Gédéon de Catalogne and Jean-Baptiste de Couagne's 1709 map of the densely populated Quebec City region charts the system's early development.

The scarcity of aristocrats in New France's early years encouraged social mobility, and many commoners had a chance to become *seigneurs*. Charles Le Moyne, a Dieppe innkeeper's son, came to New France in 1641 as a fifteen-year-old *engagé* to serve the Jesuits among the Huron. The experience he gained there would help him grow wealthy in the fur trade, but his first *seigneurie*, Longueuil, across the river from Montreal, was a reward for bravery against the Iroquois in the wars of the 1650s. Later, securely established as one of the leading men of Montreal, Le Moyne was ennobled by the King. By the time he died in 1685, the innkeeper's son was Charles Le Moyne, Sieur de Longueuil et de Châteauguay, and he left a fortune and several *seigneuries* to his family of fourteen, several of whom would become even more distinguished. Similar progress was achieved by others of obscure birth and background

Labours d'automne à Saint-Hilaire, by Ozias Leduc (1864–1955); though painted in 1901, this canvas evokes the unchanging endurance of the three-century-old strip-farming pattern. In the interim, however, husbandmen had switched from oxen to draft horses—Percherons for preference—to pull their ploughs.

who distinguished themselves in the Iroquois wars or in commerce, and acquiring *seigneuries* was just one sign of their success. A few *seigneurs* began and remained commoners, but their estates were small and their numbers shrank over the years. On the whole, landholding, power, and social standing were closely linked.

In theory, a *seigneur* was not just a landlord but also the leader of his community. As a soldier, he would organize and command its defences. He would be patron of the parish church, which he personally might have had built. As owner of the land, as builder of the mill, and as the richest man around, he would be the economic power of the community. His imposing manor house would reflect and confirm his status as the head of his people, the rural squire around whom the *seigneurie* revolved. Later historians of New France took this image to be the truth of the seigneurial regime. Whether they saw the regime as benevolent, paternal, and co-operative, or backward, oppressive, and stifling, they assumed it to be the pillar of New France's essentially feudal social system.

Close attention to the actual workings of the seigneurial system has shattered that view. After Robert Giffard's day, at least, *seigneurs* learned there was little to be earned collecting rents from subsistence farmers, and so they did little to recruit tenants. They did not develop their estates into cohesive economic communities, they rarely lived on them, and they mostly drew an insignificant income from their rents. Tenant farmers moved frequently from one *seigneurie* to another and showed little deference or attachment to their supposed leaders. In many ways the typical farm, and the rural landscape, would have looked little different had the seigneurial regime never existed.

Nevertheless, the central reality of the system—the *seigneurs*' property rights—made the seigneurial regime important, not as a social system, but simply as a

Few New World subjects gave European artists more difficulty than the indispensable *Castor canadensis*, whose pelts long remained the basis of Canadian exports. In the corner of Nicolas de Fer's 1698 map of the Americas, an accurate sketch by Nicolas Guérard of the recently discovered Niagara Falls, copied from the famous drawing by missionary Louis Hennepin published in 1697, becomes the backdrop for scores of doglike and oddly unaquatic beavers.

financial burden on the tenant farmers. In early New France, when populations were small and tenants scarce, *seigneurs* may have earned little money from their tenants and paid little attention to their estates, but they still demanded their rents and services, and they awaited better returns as the tenant population grew. Seigneurial revenues rarely made the clerical orders or military aristocrats who received them much richer, but they surely made the *habitants* poorer. In the Sulpicians' Montreal *seigneurie*, 10 to 14 per cent of farm revenue passed from the tenants to their landlord. For most farmers in the lower Richelieu valley, payments to *seigneurs* took half or more of whatever surplus they produced. Little of this money ever returned to the land. It was sent off to the clerical orders in France or spent maintaining the aristocratic style of life in the towns. *Seigneurs* may have been distant and uninvolved in the life of their *seigneuries*, but for the *habitants* the consequence was not independence. They not only owed these rents but were also obliged to tithe (that is, to pay one twenty-sixth of their crop) to support the parish priest, to do militia service in wartime, and to give unpaid labour to the Crown when roads, fortifications, and other public works were undertaken.

The Fur Trade Frontier

When Louis XIV assumed personal rule of his North American domain, the fur trade needed rebuilding as urgently as the colony on the St. Lawrence needed soldiers and settlers. The trade of Champlain's day, when the Huron and their allies brought their pelts down to the trading posts on the St. Lawrence, had collapsed in the disaster of the Iroquoian wars, and the growth of agriculture scarcely relieved the need for a trade in furs. As long as farming was no more than a subsistence enterprise, the export of furs continued to be the only way for New France to justify France's investment in it, for royal efforts to develop timber trades, ship building, and other industries were unsuccessful and largely impractical.

In 1667 the comprehensive peace newly arranged with the Iroquois seemed mostly to benefit the victorious Native nation. The Five Nations already controlled the supply of pelts to the Hudson River, where the English had replaced the Dutch in 1664. With their Huron rivals destroyed, they seemed ready to control New France's hinterland as well and to play the two European powers against each other. Only with the help of the surviving Algonquian nations of the old trading alliance did New France avoid becoming a client state of the Iroquois. These hunting-gathering tribes had resisted both the war parties and the offers of alliance of the Iroquois. When the Huron were removed from the scene, several Algonquian groups, notably the Ottawa and Ojibwa, seized the opportunity to become traders and middlemen themselves. They quickly proved to be both resilient and adaptable. Nor were the French waiting passively for furs to reach them at Montreal. Whether war made pelts scarce or peace made them abundant, competition among Montreal's fur traders was always fierce, and some of them began to venture westward to seek out the Native trappers on their own ground. The *coureur de bois* was being born.

Coureur de bois was not a complimentary term—it meant an illicit trader, a smuggler in the woods. Established merchants, Montreal authorities, and royal officials right up to the Minister of Marine did not want to see colonists abandoning the tight little agricultural colony on the St. Lawrence to trade in Native territory. They all preferred to leave the transportation work to the Native people and to keep the trade focused on Montreal. But despite repeated prohibitions, young Frenchmen were soon ranging through the *pays d'en haut*, the "upper country" west and north of Montreal. Eventually there would be as many as a thousand of them. The exchange of French goods for beaver pelts began to move west of the settled territory of New France.

The colonists also returned to exploits of travel and exploration unseen since Champlain's day. First the Huron allies and then the Iroquois had controlled access to the *pays d'en haut*. A few missionaries and traders had gone to the upper country, but there had been no significant extension of geographic knowledge beyond that recorded by Champlain. Now, as trading alliances were reorganized, explorers both clerical and commercial expanded the frontier of New France. Among the pioneers of the western surge were Médard Chouart des Groseilliers and his younger brother-in-law, Pierre-Esprit Radisson. In his youth Groseilliers had been one of the Jesuits' *engagés* at the Huron missions, where he had learned Native languages and established ties to many of the Huron allies. Des Groseilliers made his first independent western voyage in 1654 and became one of the first *coureurs de bois*. In 1659–60 he and Radisson made a long and successful trading voyage to western Lake Superior, where both men became keenly aware of the rich beaver stocks awaiting exploitation north and west of the Great Lakes.

Others followed their explorations. In 1673 Louis Jolliet and Father Jacques Marquette explored the northern Mississippi. In 1679 René-Robert Cavelier de La Salle explored the lower Great Lakes and launched *Griffon*, the first sailing vessel above Niagara Falls. La Salle's ambition to find a route across North America to the Orient was so strong that his *seigneurie* and starting point on Montreal Island was given the name "Lachine"—China. In pursuit of his goal La Salle followed the Mississippi to the Gulf of Mexico in 1682. Three years later, on a sea voyage to the Gulf coast, the stormy, irascible explorer was killed by his own men. All these voyages, which vastly increased the French reach in North America, were official explorations sanctioned by Intendant Talon, Governor Frontenac, and their successors. But there were as many unofficial venturers, such as the obscure twenty-year-old *coureur de bois* Jacques de

truce in the Iroquoian wars of the seventeenth cen-
permitted new voyages of trade and exploration.
es remained the essential means of transportation,
he French soon built sailing vessels on the Great
s as well. In 1679 René-Robert Cavelier de La Salle
3–87) built the ship *Griffon* to open navigation on
Erie, Huron, and Michigan, but the ship was lost
all hands in its first season. The fantastic landscape
tropical trees in this illustration in Louis Hennepin's
*velle découverte d'un très grand pays situé dans
érique* (Utrecht, 1697) may be attributed to the
gination of the engraver, though some of Hennepin's
unts of his travels were no less fanciful.

Noyon, who pushed west almost to Manitoba in 1688. Many of them, like de Noyon, would eventually return to live in Montreal or on a rural farm, but some adopted the life of the Native people wholeheartedly and remained among them.

Official or not, all the voyages were linked to the trade in furs. To acquire guides, and even to cross the tribal territories they entered, explorers had to engage in diplomatic relations with the Native nations, and trade always mediated their agreements. The pelts that came back to Montreal provided the funding, when they were not the sole incentive, for the explorations. Governor Frontenac, always in debt, was himself deeply involved in trade. His Fort Frontenac, founded in 1673 (at the future site of Kingston on Lake Ontario), was as much a fur-trade venture as a military post, and trade profits helped inspire his vigorous support of La Salle's explorations. Through the late seventeenth century, trading posts sprang up all around the Great Lakes and the Upper Mississippi. The most important of these was Michilimackinac, on the strait between Lake Michigan and Lake Huron.

By the 1680s the *coureurs de bois*, the Native traders, and the explorers were bringing a flood of pelts into Montreal. In 1681 the royal officials acknowledged that this traffic had successfully undermined Montreal's role as the place where French and Native traders would exchange beaver pelts for garments, muskets, copper pots, and other trade goods. Offering amnesty to the *coureurs de bois*, the authorities established a system of permits, called *congés*, for these trade voyages. This legitimization of the *coureur de bois* created another figure in the trade: the *voyageur*. Holding a *congé*, or allied to a Montreal merchant who had one, the *voyageur* made the western trade into a profession. Recent immigrants, failing merchants, and even *habitant* farmers headed west to try making a living carrying trade goods over the canoe route to the Great Lakes and bringing beaver pelts back. Far from being threatened by this development, Montreal prospered. It was the Montreal merchants who supplied the *voyageurs* with trading goods—as they had, less openly, the *coureurs de bois*—and so the furs still came to them. The city founded as a saintly community was now firmly committed to a commercial vocation.

The transformation of *coureurs de bois* into recognized *voyageurs* did not remove all forms of illicit fur trading. Because the requirement for *congés* limited access to the trade, some traders began to seek alternate routes to market. One of these routes led south to the English merchants of the colony of New York. Merchants at Albany, New York, offered good prices for pelts, and a clandestine exchange between Montreal, Albany, and the western posts was born. It gave the *voyageurs* and their Native suppliers a useful outlet whenever the Compagnie des Indes Occidentales, the royally chartered trading company that bought and shipped New France's furs to France, sought to limit quantities or prices. New York's traders and their Iroquois allies would remain a tempting alternative, always ready to challenge New France's control of the trade. But a larger and stronger rival had appeared at Hudson Bay.

The Hudson's Bay Challenge

When Samuel de Champlain yielded Quebec to the Kirke brothers in 1629, some of the traders in the colony showed little compunction about changing sides. For Etienne Brûlé and others, the new lives they made in the North American fur trade had outweighed national loyalties, and they had worked under English control until the French returned to Quebec. Half a century later, the origins of the British fur trade in northern and western Canada were established by two colonists of New France who also found the logic of the trade more persuasive than national or even familial ties. Médard Chouart des Groseilliers and Pierre-Esprit Radisson had met at best a mixed reception in New France when they returned from the north-west in 1660. They felt they had saved the colony from commercial collapse with the furs they brought in at the height of the Iroquois onslaught, but the governor disciplined and fined them for their unauthorized venture. Their proposal for a fundamental reorganization of the fur trade was no better received.

New France had sound reasons to dislike what Groseilliers and Radisson proposed. It was most likely the desire of the northern Cree and Ojibwa to open a trade route safe from their Iroquois rivals, and not the strategic thinking of European merchants, which was turning European eyes toward Hudson Bay. Groseilliers and Radisson supported their Native allies, but the authorities in New France understood that a trade based on Hudson Bay would bypass Montreal and New France completely. Already concerned to see the trade moving westward, they were understandably unenthusiastic about losing it altogether. Rejected in New France, Radisson and Groseilliers eventually went to England. England and France were not then at war (indeed, they were allied against the still-dominant maritime power, Holland). Radisson and Groseilliers may have seen the move as a strictly commercial venture, but the enterprise soon became a national cause. In 1670 King Charles II's royal charter to the Company of Adventurers Trading into Hudson's Bay staked an English claim to New France's commercial hinterland.

The Hudson's Bay Company became what New France might have been had a policy of colonial settlement not persisted there. Like the Quebec Habitation in its early years, the Hudson's Bay posts were small, all-male establishments dependent on Europe for supplies and on the Native nations for furs. The intermediaries between Native trappers and company buyers were all Native people, and each post soon had its complement of "Home Guard" people living nearby as suppliers, hunters, guides, and surrogate families for the company's employees. Radisson and Groseilliers were correct in their estimation that a great commerce could be tapped from Hudson Bay. They were wrong, however, if they imagined that Montreal's trade would collapse under such competition. Instead, the arrival of the Hudson's Bay Company stimulated the expansion of New France's upper-country posts farther into the west and north. Throughout the French regime in Canada and even after the British conquest of New France, Montreal would outstrip the Hudson's Bay posts and New York as a source of Europe's furs.

The beneficiaries of this imperial contest included the Native peoples. Far from giving away pelts to exploitative traders, Native fur traders themselves assessed market values and demanded better terms of trade when they could. In the growing competition between French and English traders, the Native people could play one side against the other and assert their own demands in the exchange. Contact with Europeans had forced enormous changes upon the Native peoples, but the fur trade still created opportunities for Native participation and power. Though the French travelled far beyond the St. Lawrence and even built permanent posts, they did so only with Native consent won through substantial diplomatic negotiation. It had been Native hostility, for instance, that had prevented Louis Jolliet from reaching the Gulf of Mexico in 1673, and it was La Salle's success in making a treaty with the same Aboriginal people that permitted him to complete the trip nine years later.

The Renewal of War

By the 1680s, the Iroquois confederacy found the peace going against it, despite its wartime victories. Far from falling into dependency, the French had built new trading alliances that bypassed the Iroquois. French traders, English traders, and a widening network of Native traders were driving the fur trade westward across the continent. The Iroquois nation returned to war. At first the targets were the Native allies of the French, but these attacks failed to close the trade route to Montreal. Instead, the late seventeenth century produced a sharp setback for the Five Nations. They lost control of the southern Ontario territories they had taken from the Huron and the other destroyed nations. The war that effected this change was fought entirely among Native armies and went largely unobserved and unreported by Europeans, but Native traditions tell of many battles, from ambushes at portages to assaults on palisaded towns. The Iroquois and their northern rivals could each muster a thousand warriors and more, and both sides now used European muskets as well as their bows and hatchets. The outcome of the war, fought on rivers and lakeshores from Sault Ste. Marie south to Lake Erie, was clear: the Iroquois had to withdraw to their original territory south of Lake Ontario. By 1700 the Mississauga nation had moved down from the northern shore of Lake Huron to establish itself in southern Ontario. The Mississauga were never so numerous as the Iroquoian nations which had peopled southern Ontario before the seventeenth-century wars, but by the opening of the eighteenth century their claim to southern Ontario was unchallenged.

In 1689 the war entered a new phase, when William III of England and Louis XIV of France declared war on each other. The Iroquois, drawing on strong backing from the English colony of New York, opened an offensive against the populated heartland of New France. The French colony learned how this campaign would be fought on August 5, 1689, at Lachine, the *voyageurs'* departure point just west of Montreal. When fifteen hundred Iroquois warriors struck Lachine at dawn, they burned fifty of the eighty houses there, killed twenty-four people, and dragged perhaps ninety prisoners away. It was the start of another campaign against the farming settlements of New France, and for several years Iroquois war parties killed *habitants* and livestock and burned buildings and crops. Time and again they forced the colonists into the fortified retreats that once more became an essential part of every community. More than a hundred settlers were killed in 1691. In 1692 a raid at Verchères created one of New France's heroines. When the *seigneur's* fifteen-year-old daughter, Marie-Madeleine Jarret de Verchères, and her family's tenants defended their fort until relief arrived from Montreal, the seed was planted for a legend that would preserve the image of the embattled *habitants*.

In this long campaign, however, the survival of the colony was hardly put in question by the hit-and-run raids of the Iroquois. Although New France grew very little during the 1690s—the only sustained period of slow growth in its history—the colony now had a standing army of fourteen hundred, a chain of garrisoned western posts, and a thousand colonists with wilderness experience. New France could carry the war back to its enemies.

Louis de Buade de Frontenac (1622–98), Governor General of New France from 1672 to 1682 and from 1689 to 1698, was seventy-four when he commanded the last French invasion of the Iroquois territories, in 1695, so there was no shame in his being carried part of the way—yet the image of French power being borne on the shoulders of the Native allies is ironic in ways the artist surely never intended. Line engraving, c. 1710.

When the French, their Native allies, and the Iroquoian Five Nations reached a long-lasting peace in 1701, each Indian leader affixed a sketch of his clan totem as a signature to this treaty. The French used a different symbolism: a Roman soldier and toga clad aborigine represented the French–Indian alliance on the obverse of this Louis XV medal, struck in 1740 and distributed to chiefs for services rendered.

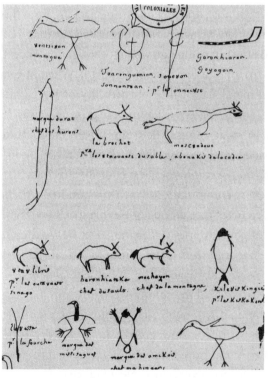

In 1697, during the battle for Hudson Bay, Pierre Le Moyne, Sieur d'Iberville (1661–1706), sank two English warships and drove off a third, then had to abandon his own damaged vessel at the mouth of the Nelson River. After reaching shore, d'Iberville and his crew went on to besiege and capture York Factory, the most valuable fur-trading station of the Hudson's Bay Company. Engraving in C. C. LeRoy Bacqueville de la Potherie, *Histoire de l'Amérique Septentrionale*... (Paris: J.-L. Nion and F. Didot, 1722).

New France's growing prowess in the wilderness fighting it called *petite guerre* was first demonstrated in 1686, when Pierre de Troyes led a war party of soldiers and *voyageurs* overland from Montreal to seize the Hudson's Bay posts on James Bay. In 1689 Governor Frontenac, seeking to restore morale and avenge Lachine, sent his troops and their Native allies to raid colonial towns on the New York and New England frontiers. Though colonial military officers led them, these attacks depended on Native tactics. The war parties travelled through the forests, often in winter, to launch surprise attacks on small English outposts and undefended towns. They killed and burned and fled with their prisoners before counter-attacks could be organized. Even Iroquois towns and war parties came under attack.

In 1690 New France repelled an English attempt to seize Quebec itself. The attack came from a fleet sent from New England under the command of Sir William Phips, but the besiegers found Quebec's defences too strong. They soon retreated, their demand for Quebec's surrender having provoked Governor Frontenac's memorable phrase, "I have no reply to make to your general other than from the mouths of my cannon." For the remainder of the war New France attacked as often as it defended, contesting control of Hudson Bay, striking at the English colonies, and raiding—not very successfully—into the Iroquois lands. In 1697 the English and French made peace. Soon after the Iroquois also began to seek an end to the conflict. The home territories of the Iroquois had never been effectively attacked, but war and epidemics were sapping their numbers, and the only beneficiaries of their struggle seemed to be their English allies and suppliers in New York.

Seeking to escape this trap, the Iroquois began to negotiate with the French, and in 1701 they achieved a great change in North American affairs. The Five Nations of the Iroquois confederacy made a comprehensive peace with New France and its Native allies and declared they would be neutral in the colonial wars of England and France. The Iroquois had not been defeated. In fact, they had fought the French to a standstill, and they would endure as an independent power in their own land until well after the passing of New France. But the peace treaty meant that no Native power would again threaten the fundamental interests of the French colony. During most of the seventeenth century, while New France had slowly been building its strength and numbers, all the Native societies had been suffering catastrophic losses from the diseases introduced from Europe. Most of them had adjusted and endured, but the balance of power was shifting. Native control of the fur trade and the entire territory north and west of Montreal would continue, but New France, with its homeland secure, was more than ever able to project its power and influence west.

At about the same time, a royal decree from the palace at Versailles started another transformation in New France's affairs. Despite the wars, the flow of beaver pelts through Montreal had continued unabated. The *voyageurs'* westward expansion had proved too successful: their furs were reaching France in quantities far larger than the market could absorb. Under pressure from the Compagnie des Indes Occidentales, which had to try to sell the furs, the Crown decided simply to shut down the fur trade temporarily. No more *congés* would be issued. The company would purchase no more pelts. Military posts in the *pays d'en haut* would be closed.

So drastic a change proved impossible to impose on the colony. The Minister of Marine was soon forced to compromise. A colonially based company emerged to market the beaver pelts, and some of the western forts were maintained. But the problem was real, for the market for beaver was glutted. Soon, however, the fur traders' problems were overshadowed by the declaration of the War of the Spanish Succession in 1702, which launched another decade of Anglo-French war. For New France, and particularly for the military aristocracy hardened in the Iroquois wars of the 1680s and 1690s, this became the last great conflict of the colony's embattled seventeenth century. Its great hero was Pierre Le Moyne d'Iberville.

D'Iberville had been born in Montreal in 1661, the son of Charles Le Moyne de Longueuil, the *engagé* who had become a nobleman, a *seigneur*, and the wealthiest of the colonists. D'Iberville first saw action in 1686. That year he was part of Pierre de Troyes's force of soldiers and *voyageurs* who made the exhausting two-month canoe voyage from Montreal to James Bay and then attacked all the Hudson's Bay posts there. Almost every year for the next two decades, d'Iberville fought in desperate land and sea actions. Before he died in the Caribbean in 1706, d'Iberville served in Hudson Bay, the New York frontier, Acadia, Newfoundland, and Louisiana, winning a fortune in plunder and losing three of his brothers in action. Like many of New France's seventeenth-century leaders, d'Iberville was brave, brutal, energetic—and short-lived. His career harked back to the violent times of men like Champlain and Brébeuf, but his death coincided with the end of an era. Even in the midst of this war a more peaceful eighteenth century was taking shape.

A Distinct Society: Eighteenth-Century New France

If the career of Pierre Le Moyne d'Iberville marked the culmination of New France's heroic seventeenth century, then the symbol of the new priorities of the eighteenth century may have been Philippe de Rigaud de Vaudreuil, Governor General from 1703 to 1725. According to his biographer, Vaudreuil had "one of the most remarkable careers in the history of New France but...one totally devoid of glitter and panache." During Vaudreuil's tenure, in fact, New France finally reached a time when even its governors could permit warlike panache to yield to more workaday virtues.

Vaudreuil was a younger son from the provincial aristocracy of France. He had come to New France as a senior military commander in 1687 and soon married into the colonial nobility. He became governor soon after the start of the War of the Spanish Succession, when Louis XIV's dynastic ambitions united nearly all the powers of Europe against him. New France could not avoid the war (which provided d'Iberville and other colonial soldiers with such opportunities for heroic exploits), but Vaudreuil grasped that with the Iroquois peace newly achieved, and with the overextended fur trade in full retreat, his colony had little to gain by war in North America. To support his threatened Mi'kmaq and Abenaki allies, he authorized *petite guerre* against the encroaching settlements of New England, but he spared the New York frontiers to avoid antagonizing the Iroquois out of their neutrality. Hudson Bay, which the peace treaty of 1697 had left partly in British hands, partly in French, saw no further conflict. The Atlantic seaboard saw the most campaigning: the French scourged English Newfoundland in 1706 and 1709, and the New Englanders captured Acadia in 1710. A British plan to attack Quebec City foundered when seven ships of Admiral Hovenden Walker's naval fleet were shipwrecked on the north shore of the Gulf of St. Lawrence in August 1711. In celebration, a Quebec City church, named Notre-Dame de la Victoire in honour of Frontenac's defence of the city in 1690, was renamed Notre-Dame des Victoires. When events in Europe ended the imperial war in 1713, Vaudreuil was ready to lead New France into a peace that would last until 1744. It was the longest peace in all New France's history, and even then there were clashes on the frontiers.

The War of the Spanish Succession had left France bankrupt and beaten, and for the sake of peace Louis XIV made colonial concessions. By the Treaty of Utrecht in 1713, France ceded all of French Newfoundland to Britain, and acknowledged British title to occupied Acadia. France withdrew from the forts it had captured on Hudson Bay and accepted British title to the bay and its entire watershed. France even recognized British title to the lands of the Iroquois confederacy. These were not France's to yield nor Britain's to hold, but Britain claimed that the alliance, or covenant, that New York traders had long maintained with the Iroquois actually constituted a transfer of land title, and France now accepted this pretence. The Iroquois, however, had no intention of being displaced by the terms of a treaty between the French and British. They remained where they were and even increased their strength. In these years the Tuscarora tribe moved north to become part of the confederacy. The Five Nations of the Iroquois became the Six Nations, as they have been since.

New France received some compensation for what it lost by the Treaty of Utrecht. Newfoundland had been yielded to the British, but French fishermen (who still vastly outnumbered the settled population) retained the right to fish and dry their catch on the island's north coast, which became known as "the French shore." France acquired clear title to Cape Breton Island and Ile St-Jean, the future Prince Edward Island. By forcing France to yield all claims to Hudson Bay, the treaty confirmed Montreal as the unchallenged centre of the French fur trade and reinforced the commercial contest between the rival trading empires. But for the colonists of New France, the prospect of peace was probably the greatest benefit of the treaty. The size and influence of the colony's military establishment would not shrink, but peace more than war would shape the affairs of northern North America in the first half of the eighteenth century.

New Colonies Arising

Samuel de Champlain's decision to make the St. Lawrence valley the focus of New France had been sustained for a century. Except for a few trading posts on Hudson Bay and the fragile colonies in Newfoundland and Acadia, the community that had arisen from Champlain's Habitation at Quebec remained the only European society in northern North America. By 1700 about fifteen thousand colonists lived in Quebec City, Montreal, Trois-Rivières, and on the steadily expanding farms that formed an almost continuous band of settlement between them. French traders and explorers had followed Native canoe routes almost as far west as the Great Plains, but outside the narrow St. Lawrence valley the vast northern half of the continent remained almost without European settlement. Shortly thereafter, other French communities in different parts of the continent buttressed the St. Lawrence region of New France, the part that in the eighteenth century came to be specifically referred to as "Canada." The French territorial claims in North America would grow rapidly, and they would confront an ever-larger British presence, as New England, New York, Virginia, and the other colonies pushed inland from the Atlantic seaboard. As colonial populations and territorial claims expanded, relations with other colonies would begin to loom as large for New France as its relations with the Native nations.

After 1713, British settlement in Newfoundland began to grow. During the war the outports and their vital sea links to Europe had been under constant threat. The lifting of this threat enabled more fishermen to become year-round settlers, and by the mid-eighteenth century Newfoundland had 7,500 settlers, including a growing number of women and children. They were still outnumbered by transient fishermen who came each summer from Europe, but they were becoming a permanent and vigorous community. Most Newfoundlanders were outport settlers, building their homes around scores of tiny, rocky harbours along the eastern coast. Climate and landscape made farming almost impossible, and even the forests grew so slowly that the settlers' woodcutting soon made the Avalon Peninsula and the northern coast a treeless barren. So the settlers imported most of their food and supplies, and by the mid-eighteenth century these came from New England more than from Europe. They caught salmon and seals and, above all, cod, and shipped it primarily to southern Europe and the Caribbean rather than to Britain. Though Newfoundland still had no official colonial institutions, St. John's began to develop as a trading port and the home of a number of merchants. As late as 1750, the Newfoundlanders were still

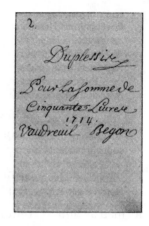

In 1720 the builders of Louisbourg placed a commemorative medal beneath the foundations of one of the town's bastions, where archaeologists discovered it again in the 1960s. The medal shows the fortress and the fishing boats that were the basis of its prosperity.

In 1684, Intendant Jacques de Meulles found he was short of coins to pay his soldiers; he resolved the problem by signing and distributing playing cards that could be redeemed when the king's pay-ship arrived in New France. Thereafter, printed forms were used for the colony's credit needs, but the name *monnaie de carte* endured. This modern watercolour-and-ink copy, attributed to Henri Beau, shows an example bearing the date 1714 and the signature of Intendant Michel Bégon.

mostly West Country English in origin, but the flood of Catholic Irish settlers who would create the Irish traditions of the island had already begun.

France had been forced by the Treaty of Utrecht to evacuate its fishing outpost of Plaisance on the south coast of Newfoundland. (It would not acquire the nearby islands of St-Pierre and Miquelon until another peace treaty produced further changes in 1763.) It turned to Cape Breton Island, which it renamed Ile Royale. To make Ile Royale a centre of power on the seaboard, France installed a full colonial administration and a garrison of troops. Louisbourg, founded on the east coast of the island in 1713, became Ile Royale's capital, and twenty-five years of labour gave the town the most elaborate fortifications in New France. By the 1740s Louisbourg was one of New France's principal towns. Fully two thousand of Ile Royale's five thousand people lived behind the town's encircling stone-and-mortar ramparts.

Ile Royale quickly developed a fishing industry similar to that which the British settlers were creating in Newfoundland. Its resident fishermen and those of the fleets that came annually from France to join them may have produced as much as a third of the French New World catch. This generated a busy shipping trade in Louisbourg, and in barely a decade the town began to rival Quebec City as a seaport. Although it was part of New France, Ile Royale lay several days' sail from the older community that was now referred to as Canada, and it grew into a distinct, and strongly commercial, society. The merchants of Louisbourg shipped cod to Europe and to French islands in the Caribbean such as St-Domingue (Haiti) and Martinique. They received sugar, coffee, and rum from the Caribbean, textiles, food, and manufactured goods from France. They passed these on, partly to Canada in trade for foodstuffs, but also to the New England colonies in exchange for ships, building materials, and livestock. Despite the growing commercial rivalry between the British and French empires, the French Crown grudgingly accepted this New England trade, too practical to be forgone. Under the same dispensation, Louisbourg also traded with the Acadians, now living under British rule in mainland Nova Scotia.

Although they had been thrust from French to British rule in 1710, the Acadians thrived in the peace of the early eighteenth century. The small community was so interrelated that half the marriages at Annapolis Royal (formerly Port-Royal) required a dispensation from the usual limits on marriages between relatives. Nevertheless the population grew from barely two thousand in 1700 to more than ten thousand by the late 1740s. Served by French priests but untrammelled by seigneurial exactions or military demands, and with few British settlers to disturb them, the Acadians were left to reap substantial harvests from the rich land that their dikes protected from the Fundy tides. Dealing with both sides but feeling dependent on neither, the Acadians worked out a complicated neutrality. The isolated British commanders in Acadia learned that their subjects would acknowledge British rule but asserted a right not to bear arms against the French. In peacetime the compromise demanded by "the neutral French" seemed tolerable to all, and the Acadians seemed able to live successfully under alien rule, the first French population in North America to do so.

A Search for the Western Ocean

On the western frontiers in the seventeenth century, it had been *coureurs de bois* and *voyageurs* who had pushed westward, leaving the governors scrambling to keep up. In the eighteenth century, official imperial policy increasingly guided the spread of French posts across central North America. In 1701, in the midst of the glut of furs, Versailles had initiated a clear challenge to English interests in North America by authorizing the foundation of the settlement of Detroit (from *détroit*, "the strait") on the Great Lakes and the colony of Louisiana at the mouth of the Mississippi. No longer would New France be restrained to a small community on the St. Lawrence with some westward trading interests. Instead, it became French policy that New France and its Native allies would hold a line from the St. Lawrence through the Great Lakes and down the Mississippi to the Gulf of Mexico, confining English colonists to the coastal strip east of the Appalachian Mountains. At the same time French forts would extend west and north to encircle the Hudson's Bay Company, perhaps even to open a route all the way to the Pacific.

This continent-spanning policy required a renewal of the fur trade. The long disruption caused by oversupply and war had not in itself exhausted the stockpile in Europe, but mice and other vermin had. What remained of the stored pelts had finally become unusable. Demand for beaver pelts revived, and markets opened for other furs. During the eighteenth century, moose, deer, bear, mink, and other pelts used for making robes and for trimming garments would become almost as important as the trade in beaver skins for the hatmakers, and with this boost New France's fur trade grew larger than ever. Expansion required a great many western posts, which became military bases, trading shops, embassies, and missions to the Native peoples—and springboards for exploration. Intricate Native alliances remained essential to the trade as it moved farther west. To support New France's Native allies, Governor Vaudreuil authorized his commander in the west, Constant Le Marchand de Lignery, to initiate a long war against their enemies, the Mesquatie, or Fox, nation west of Lake Michigan. The royal expenditure on forts in the west subsidized Montreal's fur trade, but it also increased the domination of the trade by military officers like de Lignery.

One military officer with a great influence on the trade was Pierre Gaultier de Varennes et de La Vérendrye. While commanding the *postes du nord* north-west of Lake Superior, La Vérendrye became convinced that with the help of his Native allies he could reach a river flowing west or south to the Pacific. He and his sons devoted fifteen years to the task, fighting, on one hand, to retain the support of royal officials and Montreal merchants, and, on the other, to persuade mutually hostile Native nations to permit this western movement. The La Vérendryes never reached the Pacific (where, about this time, Russian fur traders were just reaching Alaska), but they crossed the plains almost to the foothills of the Rockies, and they greatly advanced geographical knowledge. The chain of posts they left on the Manitoba lakes ensured that the Hudson's Bay Company could not monopolize the far-western fur

La France Apportant la Foi aux Indiens de la Nouvelle France: oil on canvas, *c.* 1675. This great idealization of France's mission to the New World is attributed to Frère Luc (1614–85). In 1644 Claude François abandoned a promising career as a court painter and associate of Vouet, Poussin, and Claude to join the Recollet order; as Frère Luc he spent 15 months in New France in 1670–71, designing and decorating many of the colony's churches. Returning to France with his patron, Bishop Laval, he continued to paint pictures for Canadian churches. The female figure on the left of this canvas—a portrait of Anne of Austria, mother of the Queen of France—represents France; in the background is the St. Lawrence River.

This remarkably imaginative bird's-e
view of the countryside around Quel
City (foreground) about 1664 accura
records how 30 years of labour had
cleared the forest to create the rural
landscape of New France. The Ile
d'Orléans (centre) and the Beaupré
shore (left) were among the first
seigneurial lands to be cleared, settle
and farmed.

Few of New France's small corps of trained artists left a record of daily life in the colony. It is better covered in the works of amateurs, such as this charming sketch in brown ink and watercolour by the Jesuit Louis Nicolas, illustrating a description of native fishing techniques in the *Codex canadensis* (*c.* 1700), the Abbé's manuscript of New World peoples, flora, and fauna.

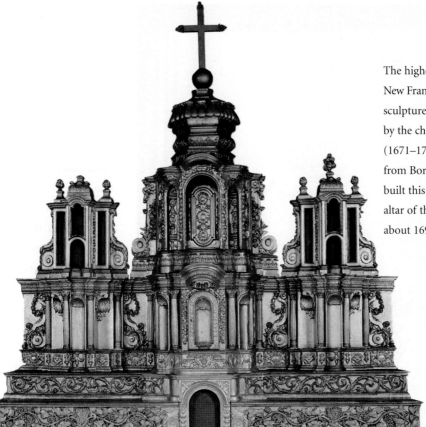

The highest artistic accomplishments of New France were the paintings, architect sculpture, and silverwork commissione by the church. Jacques Leblond de Lato (1671–1715), a painter and woodcarve from Bordeaux who later became a pri built this gilded wooden tabernacle for altar of the parish church of Ange-Gard about 1695.

Chalice, ciborium, and monstrance, dating from 1810 to 1812, by François Ranvoyzé (1739–1819). These three gold vessels from the church of L'Islet together constitute the most celebrated examples of Quebec *orfèvrerie* at its peak. Normally such articles were wrought in silver. This suite testifies to the continued flourishing of certain of Quebec's material arts decades after the Conquest.

Merchant and royal administrator Denis Riverin may have commissioned this *ex voto*, attributed to Michel Dessailliant de Richeterre (active *c.* 1700–23), and presented to the church at Ste-Anne-de-Beaupré in 1703 to express Riverin's gratitude for his family's survival of the epidemics that scourged the colony in the early 18th century. (A more usual motivation for such commissions was the donor's survival of shipwreck.) In New France, elaborate dress was the fundamental outward sign of status; even the Riverin children display the costly fabrics and adornments imported from France for members of the élite.

Marguerite Bourgeoys (1620–1700)—founder of the Congrégation de Notre-Dame de Montréal, a religious community dedicated to the education of young girls—personifies the ascetic zeal of the 17th-century missionaries of New France in this stark commemorative portrait by Pierre Le Ber (1669–1707), painted after the subject's death in 1700. The artist's sister Jeanne, a friend of Marguerite Bourgeoys, shared that spirit and spent most of her life as a religious recluse.

Though painted in 1786, nearly three decades after the end of the French regime, this work reflects one of the accepted but rarely depicted realities of New France's hierarchical society: slavery. The artist, François Beaucourt (1740–94), who studied painting in Bordeaux and became associated with pupils of Fragonard in Paris before returning to Quebec around 1786, was the first native-born Canadian to achieve real distinction as a painter. The model for this portrait is said to have been Beaucourt's servant, and possibly his mistress.

The Death of Wolfe, by American-born artist Benjamin West (1738–1820), became an icon of the British imperial triumph in the Seven Years War. It also created the genre of historical painting in contemporary dress, breaking the tradition of painting only classical scenes. The setting, scenery, and witnesses are almost entirely symbolic—Wolfe died during the battle, with about four aides present. Completed in 1776 and retouched in 1810, this version was either the third or the fourth of West's six renderings of the subject.

trade. The British company, however, was probably receiving all the furs it needed and may not have felt threatened by the advance of the French.

As western posts proliferated, fur-trade careers changed. To defray some of the costs of expansion, the French Crown increasingly yielded control of the trade to its military commanders in the west. A western command became a financial opportunity for ambitious young aristocrats willing to serve in the distant outposts. They could now make partnerships with merchants and *voyageurs* who would pay a fee or a share of their profits in exchange for access to the officers' local trade monopoly. These new arrangements sapped the independence of the *voyageurs* who had formerly run the trade. More and more, the men who portaged and paddled the goods over the ever-longer routes between Montreal and the trading posts became hired labourers earning a wage from the merchants and their military partners. On the main routes, bigger canoes were introduced. Some were 10 metres (33 feet) long and were paddled by eight men. By the 1730s, even a man's place in the canoe was specified, with the more demanding bow and stern positions being the most highly paid.

Brigades of these canoes left Montreal Island every spring. The shortest journeys—to Michilimackinac or Detroit—would bring the men back by fall. Longer voyages—half of all the departures from Montreal—demanded a longer commitment from the men, who often left in the fall and spent two winters in the *pays d'en haut*. As western trade and posts expanded in the 1720s and 1730s, some *voyageurs* began settling in the west. Bringing wives from home or marrying Native women, they started families at Detroit, Michilimackinac, and the Upper Mississippi region known as the Illinois country. Other *voyageurs* still kept homes in Montreal, returning for a season or two every few years to households that must largely have been run by their wives alone.

These years probably created much of the colourful tradition of the *voyageurs*, their cult of strength and endurance, and the rivalry between *hommes du nord*, who wintered in the far west and lived on Native food and pemmican, and *mangeurs de lard*, who returned to eat salt pork in Montreal each fall. *Voyageurs* were celebrated in songs and folktales such as the Chasse-Galerie, in which the devil would offer to fly a canoe full of *voyageurs* home in a single night. Reality was less romantic. As their manpower needs grew, fur-trade merchants began to recruit beyond Montreal Island, once the source of most *voyageurs*. After 1730, half of those who signed contracts to work in the fur trade described themselves as *habitants*—that is, as farmers. For most of these, a western voyage was temporary work, undertaken for the money and soon abandoned in favour of full-time farming. There were still *voyageurs* who followed their fathers

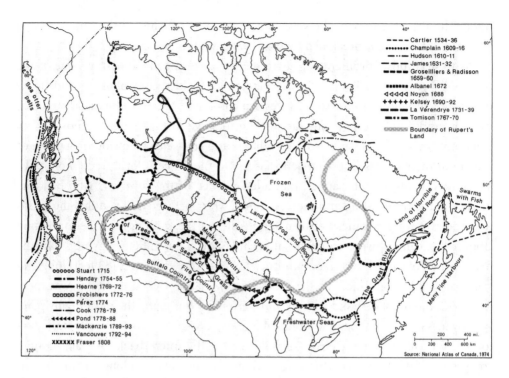

European Explorers and European Perceptions of Canada. From Cartier's time to the twentieth century European explorers, usually guided by Native allies, mapped routes across the continent—and struggled to build a mental geography of Canada, as a way to describe the diversity they found.

into the trade and made a career of it, but expansion evidently drew in an increasing number of less skilled and less enthusiastic participants from the countryside.

The *voyageur* era also saw the emergence of the Métis, "a people between" the colonists and the Aboriginals. Back to the time of Etienne Brûlé, there had always been Frenchmen who joined Native communities and made "country marriages" with Native women; indeed, such partnerships were a vital part of the fur trade alliances. Early on, the children of such marriages would have become part of Native society. Later, as fur trade posts proliferated around the Great Lakes, permanent communities, part-French, part-Native, grew up around them (just as Scots-Native communities did around Hudson's Bay posts). From these family networks evolved the Métis, the mixed-blood people, who developed a role in the fur trade distinct from both Native and colonial society. As the fur trade expanded into the North-West, the Métis moved with it, and on the plains they would become farmers and buffalo-hunters as well as traders and *voyageurs*. Gradually they developed their own dialect, called "Michif," and established their own Métis customs and identity as part of the cultural mix of the fur-trading world.

Society in the Eighteenth Century

The international peace that prevailed into the 1740s benefited all of France's North American possessions. The French Caribbean colonies exploited a rapidly growing slave population to produce huge amounts of sugar for Europe, and the labour of slaves also provided a modest prosperity for the planters in the struggling new colony of Louisiana. The fisheries of the Atlantic coast and the fur trade of Canada did well, and an expanding commerce began to link the colonies together. At last there was a demand—from Ile Royale's fishermen and the Caribbean slave plantations—for New France's abundant wheat, vegetables, and timber. Shipping in and out of Quebec City began to grow, river traffic increased as colonists expanded their activities towards Gaspé and the St. Lawrence north shore, and the price of the *habitants'* wheat finally began to rise as markets appeared for what had always been subsistence crops.

Along the St. Lawrence a population ravaged by epidemics and war resumed its rapid growth. From fifteen thousand in 1700 and eighteen thousand at the peace of 1713, it had doubled to thirty-five thousand by the 1730s and would almost double again by the 1750s. Immigration remained slight; by now most of the people were descended from generations of Canadian-born colonists. This increasingly rural population expanded most rapidly on the flat, fertile lands around Montreal, but land remained available even in the Quebec City region, still home to more than half the people. Population growth at last made *seigneuries* valuable to at least a few of their owners, and the Crown granted new *seigneuries* in areas of new settlement, such as the Beauce region south of Quebec City. Only after the *seigneuries* had been allocated were settlers permitted to move in from the crowded lands along the St. Lawrence.

From the beginning, land had been cleared and put to use in New France only about as fast as the population grew. In the early decades of the 1700s, however, Canada's farm output grew nearly twice as fast as the rural population. This meant, in part, that the *habitants* simply grew more in order to feed and clothe themselves better, but the expanding market for wheat and other farm products exported from Quebec City also encouraged greater productivity. As production increased and prices finally began to rise, there was a chance for prosperity to reach the country-side. If farmers could sell more, their land would become more valuable, farming would be less a vocation and more a business, and the interest of both *seigneurs* and merchants in the countryside would be revitalized. In the transformation from sub-sistence farming to commercial agriculture, everything in rural New France—from the look of the land to the size of the farm family—could have been transformed.

In fact, no transformation on this scale took place in New France. Traditional ways changed very slowly, and the market for wheat was both new and risky. A crop fail-ure—there were several in the 1730s and 1740s—a crisis in shipping, or a disaster in the market regions (as when Ile Royale fell to the British in 1745) could wreck the trade in wheat. Even without knowing that in advance, *habitant* farmers would not gamble on the possible benefits of selling off the crops that were also their family's food supply and seed bank. Although wheat was exported and the prosperity of the eigh-teenth century slowly worked its way down to the *habitants*, the changes

As seaport, religious centre, and capital of New France, Quebec was always the colony's largest and most sophisticated city. Attacked four times during the French regime, the city was protected chiefly by its geography; only in the 1740s was a wall finally built around it. Engraving in A. Mallet, *Description de l'Univers* (Paris, 1683).

With stark realism, some unknown artist, painting around 1700, has impressively conveyed the care offered to the sick by the religious orders who founded hospitals in New France's major towns—in this instance, in the Hôtel-Dieu, Montreal.

were not fundamental. Subsistence farming remained the vocation of the countryside, while commerce and diversity were mostly limited to the towns of New France.

The Life of the Towns

Trading centres had preceded farms in New France, and at the beginning of royal government in 1663, more than a third of the colonists lived in towns. This proportion fell slowly, but to the end of the French regime more than one in five of New France's people were urban dwellers. Montreal and Quebec City grew more slowly than rural New France, but in the eighteenth century they—along with newly founded Louisbourg—became substantial towns.

The Compagnies Franches de la Marine garrisoned the towns of New France with officers of the Canadian aristocracy and recruits from France, and built the fur-trade forts that carried French power as far west as the Canadian prairies. This water-colour drawing of a captain of the force is dated *c.* 1718.

In the last years of the French regime, the Marquis de Montcalm, no unrestrained admirer of the colony, said that in Quebec City one could live "*à la mode de Paris.*" There was, if anything, too much urban luxury and dissipation there for Montcalm's taste. The colonial capital, which grew from 2,500 people in about 1715 to 6,000 or more in the 1750s, was the most imposing city in the colony and the oldest—Champlain's landmarks and even his gravesite had already been lost. "Like one of the hilltowns of Italy," said an admirer, it crowned a cliff surrounded by water, and natural ramparts remained its main defences even after a line of bastions was laid across its landward side between 1746 and 1749. Atop the cliffs stood the great buildings of the colony. Military officers, haughty royal officials, priests, and nuns walked, rode, or were carried in coaches between the Governor General's Château St-Louis and the Intendant's palace, the cathedral, the seminary and convents, and the Hôtel-Dieu hospital. In the lower town, where the ships anchored and the barges docked, merchants, clerks and sailors crowded around the quay and the warehouses of the merchant community, unloading and storing the cargoes imported to the colony, all of which were landed at Quebec. Substantial two- and three-storey stone buildings,

LE THEATRE
DE NEPTVNE EN LA
NOVVELLE-FRANCE

Repreſenté ſur les flots du Port Royal le quator-ziéme de Novembre mille ſix céns ſix, au retour du Sieur de Poutrincourt du païs des Armouchiquois.

Neptune commence revetu d'vn voile de couleur bleuë, & de brodequins, ayant la chevelure & la barbe longues & chenuës, tenant ſon Trident en main, aſſis ſur ſon chariot paré de ſes couleurs : ledit chariot trainé ſur les ondes par ſix Tritons juſques à l'abord de la chaloupe où s'eſtoit mis ledit Sieur de Poutrincourt & ſes gens ſortant de la barque pour venir à terre. Lors ladite chaloupe accrochée, Neptune commence ainſi.

NEPTVNE.

ARRÊTE, Sagamos, * arrête toy ici, Et écoutes vn Dieu qui a de toy ſouci. Si tu ne me conois, Saturne fut mon pere, Ie ſuis de Iupiter & de Pluton le frere.

*C'eſt vn mot de Sauvage, qui ſigniſie Capitaine.

DEVXIEME SAVVAGE.

Le deuziéme Sauvage tenant ſon arc & ſa fleche en main peaux de Caſto

Poet and lawyer Marc Lescarbot (*c.* 1570–1642) spent a year at Port-Royal in 1606–07. After his return to France, he published a history of New France and this play, *Le Théâtre de Neptune*, which had been performed at Port-Royal during his stay there. C. W. Jefferys' pen-and-ink "reconstruction" of *c.* 1934, *The First Play in Canada*, depicts the canoe-borne pageant being presented to welcome the Baron de Poutrincourt on his return to his colony on November 14, 1606.

C.W.JEFFERYS

separated by distinctive high endwalls that served as firebreaks, lined narrow streets that were busy with wagons, with well-to-do ladies visiting the artisans' shops, and with servants and slaves doing their menial tasks.

Montreal, with about four thousand people, had neither the size nor the situation of Quebec. As the centre of the fur trade, Montreal retained a frontier air, frequently receiving parties of *voyageurs* and Native traders and warriors. But by 1750 it too had a stone rampart and had grown well beyond its trading-post origins. Its buildings were less impressive than the capital's, but more than half of them, like Quebec's, were built of masonry rather than wood. Serious fires in Montreal in 1721 and 1734 had helped establish this trend. Neither city had running water, paved streets, or public lighting, but both displayed a strongly commercial air. Nevertheless, royal preferences and economic realities ensured that manufacturing would be done in France, not in the colonies, and without industry the towns of New France had no pool of jobs for urban labourers. Montreal and Quebec City existed to serve trade and government and grew only as fast as these permitted.

As centres of government, the towns were the home of royal officials, military officers, and members of the religious orders. This elite, which dominated the whole colony, was particularly visible in the towns, where their families may have amounted to 40 per cent of the population. A few senior administrators came out from France to advance their careers by a term of office in the colonies. Educated, prosperous, and well connected to the ruling circles of Versailles, they added to the sophistication of town life, particularly in Quebec. But most of the colonial elite was Canadian, for by the eighteenth century a distinctly Canadian aristocracy had been defined.

The bulwark of this colonial aristocracy was New France's military establishment. Most colonial aristocrats had *seigneuries* in the family, but few received much income from them or gave them much time. Instead, they relied on commissions in the colony's troops, the Compagnies Franches de la Marine. By the end of the French regime over two hundred men were serving as officers in the Marine companies or holding *expectatives*—that is, waiting amid a growing crowd of officers' sons for a vacancy to occur. They formed an increasingly tightly knit and interrelated elite, following their fathers and uncles into the service, marrying one another's sisters and nieces, and finding in military command both a livelihood and a vocation. Commissions in the Marine companies were no sinecure, and even after 1700, when the King ceased to confer noble status on successful commoners, the aristocracy of New France never became a simply decorative class. The nobles justified their privileges in the most traditional way: by military command. They had led the seventeenth-century campaigns against the English colonies, the Hudson's Bay posts, and the Iroquois. In the eighteenth century they built and ran the frontier garrisons, conducted Native diplomacy and war, explored the west, and supervised the fur trade. Their orders could send them back and forth between distant outposts of the French American empire, and even in peacetime the demands of the service were high.

Not unusual was the career of Paul Marin de La Malgue. The son of an officer and the brother of a fur trader, he was commissioned an ensign in 1722 at the age of thirty and served for the next twenty years in forts around Lake Superior. In 1743, finally promoted to lieutenant, he visited France. In 1745 he led a military expedition overland from Quebec City to Acadia and Ile Royale, and the next year he led a raid on Saratoga, New York. In 1748 he returned to the west, where as military commander at Green Bay on Lake Michigan he earned substantial fur-trade revenue. In 1753 Marin died, aged sixty-one, on active service in the Ohio Valley. Although the Governor commended him as a brave officer, "made for war," Marin had never achieved either high rank or great distinction, and there were many others like him. "The family of the Sieur de Villiers has always distinguished itself in the service," wrote the Governor upon the death of another military officer. "There is not one of them who has not died in action against the enemy." One was hardly a veteran of the Canadian officer corps, almost, until one had been killed in action.

The Canadian aristocracy was not rich, although its standard of living was far removed from anything experienced by the common people. By the eighteenth century few colonial aristocrats retained links to prosperous estates in France, and Canadian *seigneuries* could rarely support a life of ease. Hard-pressed Canadian aristocrats had taken to marrying late and bearing fewer children, ensuring that the colonial nobility remained a small, exclusive caste. Aristocrats in the colonies could practise any form of commerce, and they frequently did, either as investors or—as with their *seigneuries* and their trading-post commands—by seeking to levy a kind of tax on the efforts of others. Such practices extended even to their military commands: officers who controlled their men's pay and provisions often skimmed off a share for themselves. Still, commerce in New France offered few easy fortunes. All these activities probably testified less to the commercial aptitudes of the nobles than to their search for an income to support their way of life.

Military salaries and what could be squeezed from positions of authority were vital. The officers' careers depended on the Governor General, who as commander-

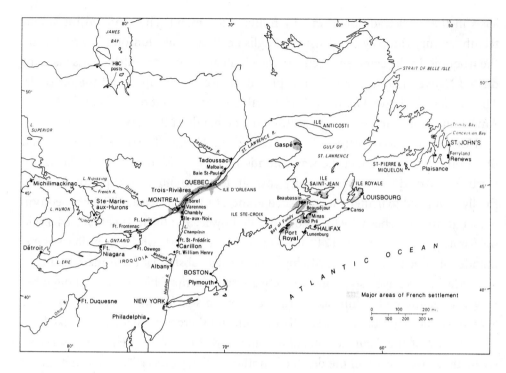

New France 1600–1763. French colonization in Canada began with wintering depots at Tadoussac and
Ile Ste-Croix around 1600. Forts and trade routes eventually commanded half the continent, but the
heartland of settlement always lay along the St. Lawrence between Montreal and Quebec. France
acquired the Atlantic islands St-Pierre and Miquelon in 1763, after the fall of New France.

in-chief dispensed patronage and promotion. His power helped create a courtier
society in Quebec that was a distant echo of the larger and vastly more splendid court
of Versailles. At Quebec, and to a lesser extent Montreal and Louisbourg, the colony's
leaders were entertained at balls, dinners, gambling parties, and elaborate festivities
with an elegance and luxury totally detached from the lives of most colonists.
Participation in the cliques around the high command could be vital to an officer's
advancement, and women could play a crucial role here. Convent schooling often
meant the women of the elite were better educated than the men. With their husbands or sons serving far from Quebec City, women who were skilful players in court
society could contribute greatly to the advancement of their families.

Display, in fact, was expected of the nobility. *Vivre noblement*, to live nobly, was
one of the obligations of noble status, though to do so usually meant debt. Nobles

Portrait of Père Emmanuel Crespel (1703–75), missionary, author, and provincial commissioner of the Recollet branch of the Franciscan order in Canada. The Recollets were the first religious order to send priests to New France. Though overshadowed by more powerful orders that arrived later, they were admired for their humble style, and served as military chaplains, parish priests, teachers, and missionaries. Painting by J.-M. Briekenmacher, who was also known as Père François (active 1732–56), a Recollet of the Montreal order.

Eustache Chartier de Lotbinière (1688–1749), seen here in this 1725 portrait, inherited the family *seigneurie* and followed his father into the high ranks of the colonial administration. After his wife died, leaving him five children, he turned to the priesthood and became in succession archdeacon, vicar-general, and dean of the chapter of the Quebec cathedral—one of the few native-born Canadians to hold a senior post within the ecclesiastical hierarchy. Artist unknown.

had to have grander homes than others, had to be dressed, coiffed, and powdered in the latest fashion, had to be attended by servants and slaves, and had to entertain and be entertained lavishly and often. Young male aristocrats, protected by their status, could fight duels, keep mistresses, and roister through the streets without much fear of retribution. Few of the colonial elite seem to have had intellectual or literary interests, and the education they sought for their children was largely military training for the sons and lessons in refined deportment for the daughters. After maintaining appearances all their lives, the military aristocrats often died in debt, counting on the king to provide a pension for their widows, while military rank or a marriage among the merchant class provided for their children.

The urban clergy was in some ways a branch of this aristocracy. From the time of the Cent-Associés, New France had been served by religious orders: Jesuits, Sulpicians, Ursuline nuns, and others. Initially attracted by the opportunity for mission service, these religious orders gradually became so rooted in the towns that at the beginning of the eighteenth century 80 per cent of the clergy lived in the towns, although 70 per cent of the people lived in the country. Many of the orders were aristocratic and educated. They recruited almost entirely from France and devoted themselves to prayer, theology, and religious observance at the cathedral in Quebec and the Sulpician church at Montreal.

For parish work throughout New France, however, the seminary at Quebec trained a less exclusive diocesan clergy. By the mid-eighteenth century, New France itself provided four-fifths of its parish clergy, but their numbers remained small, so that most parish priests ministered to widely dispersed flocks spread over several rural parishes. Orders of priests, brothers, and nuns devoted to charitable work provided almost all the colony's social services. The colony's schools and hospitals varied from the very refined to the rather humble. The Ursulines of Quebec ran a school for the daughters of the elite. The Sisters of the Congregation de Notre-Dame de Montréal, founded by Marguerite Bourgeoys in the town's early years, educated girls of all levels of society, and as far afield as Louisbourg on the Atlantic coast. Marguerite Dufrost, the widow d'Youville, had known poverty in her youth, even though she came from an old noble family. In the 1730s she founded the Sisters of Charity, or *Soeurs grises*, who served the poor of Montreal and ran a hospice, the Hopital-General.

The aristocrats may have dominated the towns, but they were also centres of trade and supported a core of mercantile families. In Montreal their trade was fur, in Quebec imports and exports, and in Louisbourg fish and shipping, but whatever their commodity, merchants defined themselves as a distinct group, the masters of credit, bookkeeping, and commercial negotiation. Merchants were also suppliers; they could provide the townspeople of eighteenth-century New France with rum and molasses and coffee from France's Caribbean colonies, with luxurious textiles and clothes, jewellery, wines, and spirits, even books and art from France—all commodities that were almost unknown outside the towns.

Merchant houses from the ports of France often sent a son or protégé to handle the cargoes they shipped to Quebec City. But outside of Quebec, few of the merchants who were settled in the colony had arrived with wealth, and their capital tended to be tied up and at risk. Merchant businesses were family businesses. In the smaller ones the merchant's wife usually helped run the shop, and even in large ones a widow could take over and run the business for years. Even minor merchant families had a standard of living above that of most colonists, and they had the potential to become wealthier than the aristocrats. In the aristocracy the merchants found clients and partners for both business and marital alliances, but bourgeois families seem to have been less inclined towards the ostentation that defined the elite.

The size and activity of this merchant bourgeoisie was always hampered by the colony's economic limitations. Control of the essential trade in furs ultimately lay with the Compagnie des Indes Occidentales, the French-based monopoly that bought and shipped each year's supply. Since metropolitan merchant houses dominated transatlantic shipping to and from Quebec, a few local agents in Quebec could handle most of the cargoes sent to the colony. Merchants could be shopkeepers to the townspeople and offer a range of commercial services, but as long as most of the colonists were largely self-sufficient farmers, opportunities to diversify were scarce.

Montreal was the town most constrained in its commerce. With few options beyond the fur trade, Montreal merchant families like the Gamelins handled the challenging business of organizing the *voyageur* brigades and their far-flung operations. It was the Gamelins who financed most of La Vérendrye's western explorations—and who took him to court when he could not repay his debt. Louisbourg had the best commercial opportunities. Its coastal location, diverse trade links, and active participation in the cod fishery supported lively enterprises in trade, fishing, and shipping. Quebec's merchants also benefited from the commercial expansion of the eighteenth century and the growing export market for wheat and wood. Two hundred ships were built around Quebec between 1720 and 1740, and local entrepreneurs began using them to haul cargoes to Ile Royale and the French Caribbean islands. As ship traffic in the river and gulf increased, some Quebec merchants began to invest in fishing and fur-trading establishments at Gaspé and along the north shore of the gulf as far off as Labrador. One of the most active in the 1750s was Marie-Anne Barbel, the widow Fornel. Widowed in 1745 after bearing fourteen children, she developed her husband's fishing and trading interests on the north coast into a thriving business, then put the profits into Quebec City real estate and retired to live comfortably to the age of ninety.

There was, in other words, a commercial climate, and entrepreneurial talent prepared to exploit whatever opportunities New France offered. But Canadian merchants laboured under a double domination. The subordination of the colony's fur trade to control from France and the difficulty of finding other profitable trades for the small,

Originally polychromed and gilded, this pine kneeling angel dated *c.* 1775, by Quebec craftsman François-Noel Lavasseur (1703–94), was designed for placement in a church niche. Its style reflects the enduring popularity of the baroque mode that flourished in Europe from the early 1600s to the late 1700s.

This rush-seated "salamander" armchair, dated *c.* 1720–40, is a superb example of a uniquely French-Canadian form. Typical of the furniture built towards the end of the French regime, it suggests the high level of craft achieved by colonial artisans, who generally eschewed the more ornate stylizations of their old-country counterparts. Only a member of the urban élite would have commissioned such a piece.

isolated colony left the colonials with only a limited sphere for commercial activity. At the same time, the aristocracy tightly held the positions and benefits of power that might otherwise have helped support the commercial class. New France seems to have possessed a merchant community as large and influential as the colonial circumstances permitted, but one never able to challenge the dominance of the aristocratic elite.

New France's towns were also home to a working class of artisans and a service population. At the core of the artisan community were the practical craftsmen:

This white-washed bedroom is stark by our standards, but in New France a family would have been proud of such quarters. With enough clothes to need an armoire, with time to make rugs and lathe-turned furniture, and with a fireplace to warm their bedroom, the people who lived here must have been considered well off.

housebuilders, carpenters, cabinetmakers, blacksmiths. The towns also supported butchers, bakers, innkeepers, and some suppliers of luxuries to the elite: wigmakers, dressmakers, and tailors. A few industries gradually emerged. The Saint-Maurice iron foundry, established near Trois-Rivières in the 1730s, bankrupted its founders, but it struggled on with royal subsidies and eventually produced many of the colonists' stoves and ploughshares. Late in the colony's existence a few potteries and other craft industries began to appear. The most important new industries were those linked to Quebec's shipbuilding enterprises, which supported many carpenters, coopers, and other tradesmen. Almost all the colonial artisans ran small, family operations—a master and his wife and one or two apprentices, who were most often the sons of other urban artisans. As in the merchant community, wives and daughters could be an active part of a working-class family enterprise, and the income they brought in could be essential. Frequently, artisans' wives ran small taverns, made clothes for sale, helped run the shop, and kept the family accounts.

A common-room of the period 1750–1820, typical of a prosperous urban household. Fine furniture in New France was first dominated by the Louis XIII influence (seen in the carved panels of the armoire), and later the simpler Louis XV style, until the British conquest in 1760, when direct contact with the mother country was cut off. The cast-iron six-plate heating stove, marked "F. St. M." (i.e., Forges Saint-Maurice), dates from *c.* 1810.

Despite the social distances between them, nobles, merchants, and artisans lived close together in the crowded towns, and the households of all three groups included domestic servants. Some male servants were recruited from France, but women outnumbered men in domestic service. Most of them were Canadian-born, for domestic service was a way for the community to provide for its dependent daughters. In the 1740s, more than half the servants at Quebec City were orphans or children of impoverished colonial families. Taken into a more fortunate household at an early age, these young servants were raised and fed in exchange for their labour until (as some servants' contracts put it) "married or otherwise provided for."

There were also slaves among the household servants of the towns. Slavery had been accepted in New France since Champlain's time, and about 3,600 slaves laboured there in the 1750s. Some were blacks brought to the colony from Africa via the plantation colonies of the Caribbean, but more were Aboriginal men and women acquired as war captives of New France and its Native allies. The aristocrats seem to have preferred these slaves called *panis*, Pawnee (although they came from many tribes and even the Inuit), who were thought to be exotic and decorative. In Canada, slavery never became essential in the way it did in the southern plantation economy. Most slaves were acquired only for domestic service. Some slaves were permitted to marry, and a few were granted freedom, but in general their lives were hard and often brief. Mathieu Léveillé was sickly throughout the decade he spent in Quebec City, where he had been brought to perform the ignominious role of hangman, and he died there in his early thirties. A Montreal slave, Marie-Joseph-Angélique, met a more spectacular end: she was executed for starting the fire that destroyed nearly fifty houses there in 1734. In the same year, Kiala of the Fox nation was shipped off to plantation slavery in Martinique as punishment for leading his nation's resistance to New France and its allies in the north-west.

Compared with European cities of the time, the towns of New France were too small to have a large number of destitute people. Lacking industries, they were never a magnet for the rural poor. The nearest thing to an urban under-class was the soldiery of the Marine infantry companies that garrisoned the towns. Recruited in France to serve in New France "at the King's pleasure"—that is, indefinitely—the soldiers were housed among the townspeople and with nearby farmers. In peacetime, they could hire out as labourers, and those who assimilated into the colony could seek a discharge to marry and settle. But the presence of several hundred single young men under loose military discipline could easily become disruptive. Soldiers were responsible for much of the petty theft and casual drunkenness of the towns. As the military population grew, illegitimacy rose sharply in areas where troops were billeted.

Seen against the background of rural society, the towns of New France seem almost another world. Trade, medicine, crafts, and learning were all urban enterprises. The royal law courts scarcely functioned beyond the edges of the towns (although *seigneurs* could and sometimes did settle their tenants' cases in their own courts). Cities were also the centres of artistic life. The aristocracy, though not highly cultured, supported silversmiths, portraitists, and other artists from whom some work of high standard survives. Silversmiths also profited from Native diplomacy, for "trade silver" made in the colony was frequently presented to Native leaders as a sign of friendship and alliance. The most important patron of the arts was the church. It not only had a near monopoly on education, science, and learning, but also commissioned substantial amounts of religious art. Most painting and sculpture in New France was ecclesiastical, providing saintly images, *ex voto* paintings, ornaments, and altarpieces for the churches and convents. Serious music, particularly organ and choral music, was almost entirely a clerical preserve. Marc Lescarbot, one of Champlain's companions in Acadia, had staged a play, *Le Théâtre de Neptune*, at Port-Royal in 1606, and in the 1690s Bishop St-Vallier complained about a performance of Molière's satire *Tartuffe* in Quebec City, but there was little literature and a very sparse tradition of non-utilitarian writing in the colony, which never had a printing press. Devotional literature and practical handbooks in business, sciences, or geography dominated the personal libraries even of the well-to-do. It seems fair to conclude that artistic and intellectual pursuits in New France were limited, conventional, and compatible with the established tastes of the ruling elite and the clergy.

The Life of the *Habitants*

The towns depended on the country for food supplies, at least the basic ones, and there was always some movement of people back and forth between towns and farms. *Habitants'* sons sometimes spent a few years as urban apprentices, and young men off the farms who spent a few seasons as *voyageurs* had some contact with urban commerce as well as with the woodland frontier. But the bond between town and country was tenuous: even the patterns of birth and death in the towns were different. Townspeople married later and bore fewer children than the farmers. Infant mortality was a greater risk in the towns, perhaps because of crowding and disease, but also because the urban well-to-do, like their counterparts in Europe, routinely sent their newborn children to wetnurses where a disproportionate number (fully half, among the colonial aristocracy of the eighteenth century) died.

If the eighteenth-century towns displayed complex relationships—prosperous merchants and working-class artisans deferring to the nobility, aristocrats seeking both ostentation and the money or credit to support it, and soldiers, servants, and slaves seeking secure niches—rural New France was still populated overwhelmingly by people who to the modern eye (as to most of their urban contemporaries) all seem the same. Beyond the towns there were few aristocrats, merchants, or craftsmen, no slaves, and not many servants. Rural New France meant farmstead after farmstead filled with families of peasants.

The rural people themselves did not see it quite that way. For one thing, they rejected the term "peasant" in favour of *habitant*. They took for granted their freedom to move, to sell or bequeath their land leases, and to organize their lives with little direct interference from *seigneurs*, merchants, or royal functionaries. In the early decades of the eighteenth century, the *habitants* still provided much of their own food, and the scarcity of rural craftsmen suggests they were still making many of their own tools and pottery pieces. Yet most were probably better off than their seventeenth-century parents, partly from the legacy of accomplishments handed them by the pioneers, partly from the general prosperity filtering down. As a result, some *habitants* had the time and opportunity to develop distinctive Canadian styles of woodcarving and furniture-making, so their homes were not only a little larger but also better furnished, and perhaps heated by a stove from the Saint Maurice foundry. In some areas rural prosperity even attracted merchants eager to exchange imported products for surplus grain; *habitants* might be wearing some imported fabrics, or consuming a little imported sugar or rum.

The arrival of merchants seems to have prompted the growth of the colony's first rural villages. Farms were usually strung along the road or river, but a few villages appeared late in the French regime, usually centred on a merchant or two. One remarkable example is François-Auguste Bailly de Messein, a Marine officer's son who abandoned his cadetship about 1730 to set up as a country trader at Varennes, downstream and across the river from Montreal. Buying grain, selling imported goods, and lending money, he became wealthy enough to give his sons an elite education that restored them to the status precariously held by their grandfather—one of them became associate Bishop of Quebec. Bailly, however, was a rare figure. The activities of a few rural merchants like him did not much alter traditional ways. In general the *habitants* of the eighteenth century seem to have absorbed a measure of commerce—with its chances of a better living standard and its deadly risks of mounting debt—without much changing their lives or behaviour. Some farmers, blessed with good land, strong sons, or just greater skill and ambition, nearly always had more wheat than the bare minimum they needed to cover their essential expenses. But prosperity could seem a dead end to less fortunate farmers, tempted to purchase more and then struggling under a growing debt. If grasping merchants, hungry townspeople, and demanding *seigneurs* seemed to be the main beneficiaries of their labour, *habitants* might simply reduce their production once they established a comfortable level. Intendant Gilles Hocquart accused them of doing just that in 1741.

Urban criticism of the rural *habitants* was common. "Canadians of the common sort are indocile, headstrong, and follow only their own will and fancy," reported a military officer in 1752. He was particularly offended to see them riding their own horses, "which they only use to go chasing their mistresses." Intendant Hocquart, who thought that the Canadians "do not have the rough and rustic air of our peasants in France," asserted that they "have too good an opinion of themselves, which prevents them from succeeding as they could." He blamed the long winters for encouraging their idleness.

Such abuse reflected the gulf that separated town from country; it ignored the skill with which the *habitants* met the enduring challenges of peasant life. Every family faced the stark annual obligation to produce enough to cover its rents and its tithes to the church, to feed itself, and to provide seed for the next planting. Failure could be staved off by debt, and debts could be passed on to the next generation, but each small setback made recovery more difficult. As a struggling family lost its few comforts and became poorer and sicklier, it would gradually be pushed towards smaller and less productive farms that would reinforce its poverty. Rural farming was a life-and-death game with little insurance, and despite their illiteracy and isolation, most farmers played it skilfully.

Farm families preserved a practical knowledge of the relevant sections of the colony's legal code, the Coutume de Paris, and the registers of notaries were filled with *habitant* transactions: the buying and selling of land leases, the rental of tools and livestock, and the *rentes constituées* by which indebted farmers, by promising their creditors 5 per cent annual interest, were spared all obligation to repay the debt itself—which in theory could endure for ever. The most important legal transactions concerned property and inheritance. To safeguard the family farm—the only asset of most rural families—farmers' wills were filled with rigorously defined property clauses. Marriage contracts, which were used by 90 per cent of Canadian couples, were equally specific in detailing what the families of the bride and groom would offer to help the new couple establish their own farm. The legal code called for estates to be shared equally among heirs, but it could not force generations of *habitants* into endless subdivisions of the vital family farm. Parents used donations and sales to transfer their land intact to a chosen child, who agreed in exchange to compensate the other siblings and to support the ageing parents for the rest of their lives.

Behind these legal agreements lay a great deal of mutual assistance. The family was the basis of peasant society, and most *habitant* plans were family strategies. The importance of the family in these plans is perhaps most clear in the way farm communities expanded into new areas. Once a rural district was fully occupied, it would not support a larger population, and the excess numbers of succeeding generations

Textiles and accessories were among New France's principal imports, but many of the *habitants* wore clothes of rough, homespun cloth, and made their own shoes and blanket coats. The Indian influence on French-Canadian dress is evidenced in the headgear, moccasins, sashes, and headgear-embroidery depicted in this watercolour (*c.* 1825–30) by the British army officer and amateur painter J. Crawford Young. Note the ubiquitous clay pipes and pigtails, common throughout and after the French regime.

A French Canadian Lady in her Winter dress and a Roman Catholic Priest: a hand-coloured aquatint illustration in *Travels through Lower Canada* (London: 1810), by John Lambers (*c.* 1775–?) Though sketched during Lambert's North American visit of 1806–08, this pair are attired in costumes essentially the same as those worn at the time of the Conquest.

had to find new land at the rear of the earlier riverfront farms or elsewhere in the colony. Yet the settlers of new districts were not single men going forth from the family farm to labour in isolation. In surprising proportions, new lands were settled by family groups. In one eighteenth-century group of new *seigneuries*, 40 per cent of the settlers were families led by couples who had been married for more than ten years. Almost certainly these families had mortgaged an established farm elsewhere and left it in the care of an elder child or sibling, so that the mature family could mobilize its resources for the greater task at the new settlement. Although the ease of individual members was being sacrificed, the family estate and the family future were enhanced. This pattern of ceaseless expansion, preserving the old family land while using it as a springboard for movement to new land, could continue as long as *habitant* agriculture survived and land remained abundant. It could be observed in rural Quebec into the twentieth century.

A Mature Society

The French revolutionaries of 1789 described all that they were sweeping away—the monarchy, the church, and the aristocracy—as "the old system," the *ancien régime*. Historians have borrowed the phrase to describe a whole way of life that disappeared in most of Europe with the rise of democracy, capitalism, and the industrial revolution. In the eighteenth century, New France had emerged from its stormy pioneering youth to become a mature society of the *ancien régime*. Like many European societies of its time, it was formed of a small and favoured elite and a vast mass of poor farmers. This social structure reinforced the political system in which an absolute government ruled without thought of representative institutions. Governors, intendants, and bishops all claimed a paternal authority over the colonists. They took for granted their right and duty, not only to rule in the King's name, but also to give or withhold favour as they thought fit and to impose their concepts of how their subjects ought to live. Perhaps it was inevitable that they found the people opinionated, for popular resistance to government was not unknown. When shortages drove up food prices in Montreal, women went into the streets, demanding royal action. Soldiers mutinied at Louisbourg in 1744, and rural *habitants* often resisted obligatory labour for the Crown or their *seigneur*. Nevertheless, popular protest rarely if ever called into question the structures of society or government. Agents of royal authority, from the Governor down to the militia captains in each parish, carried the King's will to his people, not vice versa. People might grumble at the results when the Governor drafted farmers for military construction labour, when the Intendant fixed the price of wheat, or when the clergy claimed its tithes, but there was little questioning of their authority to do so.

Catholicism was the basis of civil society. The colony closely restricted the rights of its few Protestants, and the teachings of the church hierarchy were strict and austere: even dancing was frowned upon. Of course, what the priests decreed, they could not always enforce. The governing authorities soon freed themselves from clerical dominance, and free-spirited aristocrats could disregard clerical dictates: in 1749 a group of them dared ask a Montreal *curé* to reschedule the Ash Wednesday morning service so they could more conveniently drop in on their way home from the Intendant's all-night

Mardi Gras ball. Even rural priests bemoaned the laxity, superstition—and resistance to tithes—of the *habitants*. Still, even when the church's temporal authority was weakest, there was a broad measure of popular faith and religious observance. The church participated in events of every kind: births and deaths and marriages, obviously, but also the celebration of military victories and public holidays, and the running of hospitals, schools, public charities, and craftsmen's associations. Both the parish mass and the gathering afterwards of the men of the parish were vital events in every community.

In a colony rapidly growing and building, there were always opportunities to change one's situation. Despite its inland location and scant immigration after the 1680s, the colony enjoyed a fair measure of outside contact and geographical mobility. Quebec maintained trade links with France and later with the Atlantic coast colonies. Louisbourg at one end of New France and Montreal at the other had regular, if barely legal, ties to coastal New England and the New York frontier, and a few people, as well as news and goods, passed back and forth. Within the colony, road and river traffic increased throughout the eighteenth century. The need to open new lands kept even farm families on the move, and a large minority of colonists married outside their local communities. The fur trade, of course, could always take young men into the west, where a few of them would merge into Native and Métis society or bring wives to the small settlements growing on the Great Lakes and the Upper Mississippi.

Nevertheless, any society where most people lived by subsistence farming was slow to change. Rural New France was massively illiterate, and even in the towns literacy was a skill acquired by the few for whom it was essential. Education was for religious indoctrination, or it was a path to refinement for the elite and practical training for the professions and trades. Commerce and trade existed and in places even flourished, but it was a commerce that fit comfortably into a non-commercial society, not a revolutionary capitalism spreading out to erode the traditional economy. Despite the New World's many opportunities for change, the eighteenth century saw the colony along the St. Lawrence maturing into a deeply stable and traditional society.

To be born on a farm meant an overwhelming likelihood of living one's life in (to our minds) intolerable plainness, ignorance, and toil. Within that fixed and demanding world it remained possible—by work, good fortune, or a shrewd marriage—for masons, *voyageurs*, *habitants*, or their children to improve their situations substantially. Still, society could be very hard on anyone who lost his or her niche. Most colonists remained close to the circumstances in which they were born, and found food, shelter, a livelihood, and a stake in their community.

The War of the Conquest

France's good fortune in the decades of peace helped spawn the conflicts that put an end to France's empire on the North American continent. In the first half of the century, the expansion of New France's fur trade, its agriculture, and its fisheries typified the successes of French commerce, both in Europe and in overseas trade as far off as India. A French commercial empire spanning the world seemed a realistic aspiration in these decades, but it was one certain to be challenged by British commercial interests pursuing the same goal. The ground was being cleared for a confrontation between the two great imperial and mercantile powers of eighteenth-century Europe.

The contest opened when Britain and France were drawn into a general European conflict in 1744. Despite the issues at stake, this war did not become a fully-fledged Anglo-French colonial struggle. Britain was caught up in a domestic crisis—Bonnie Prince Charlie's drive for the British throne in 1745–46—and old European alliances drew both powers into an inconclusive continental struggle that dissipated in 1748. In Canada, where the borders seemed secure, the Marquis de Beauharnois, an ageing naval officer who had been Governor since 1726, saw little need to add local struggles to the imperial war.

The only significant military events for New France focused on Louisbourg. In thirty years the French colony on Ile Royale had revived France's cod trade and its military presence on the Atlantic seaboard, and the outbreak of war created an opportunity to exert this power. In 1744 Louisbourg seized a New England fishing outpost at Canso in Nova Scotia, barely failed to capture Annapolis Royal and the only British garrison in Acadia, and unleashed its privateers against British shipping. Even in peacetime, the existence of Louisbourg had aroused resentment in the British American colonies, particularly Massachusetts. New Englanders had been willing to trade at Louisbourg, but the French presence in territory New England considered its own hinterland had never been accepted. Now the French military successes of 1744 generated a quick riposte—a New England invasion force aimed at Ile Royale itself.

Ile Royale was no easy target. France had fortified Louisbourg to a point where only a formal artillery siege could threaten it. Considering the lack of formal military organization in New England, France expected that a serious threat to Ile Royale could come only from Britain. As a result, Louisbourg had only its peacetime garrison and supplies when a hastily assembled New England militia army, supported by a British fleet from the Caribbean, arrived before the fortress in May 1745. The size of this siege force underlined the latent strength of the British colonies of North America. The little settlements that seventeenth-century English colonists had established along the Atlantic coast had grown large and powerful. The Thirteen Colonies had more than a million people, whose towns and farms had spread far inland from their coastal beginning. Canada, with its far-flung Native alliances and its military traditions, had always maintained the upper hand over the Americans in wilderness warfare, but on the seacoast the advantage was reversed. New England raised, equipped, and sent a four-thousand man army to Louisbourg with only a few months' preparation, but it proved sufficient. In six weeks of siege the besiegers pounded down the stone ramparts of the fortress, while their naval blockade cut off all relief from France. Louisbourg capitulated late in June 1745.

The colonists of Ile Royale were hastily deported to France, and with them went France's military power on the Atlantic coast. Since Ile Royale had handled much of Canada's exported grain, wheat prices in Quebec collapsed, and since Louisbourg had always been presented as the outer bastion of the St. Lawrence colony, an urgent building campaign began to provide the city of Quebec with some walls of its own. Neither Britain nor its American colonies, however, followed up New England's triumph in Ile Royale. Further military action in North America was slight, and the peace treaty of 1749 restored French possession of Ile Royale as part of a general return of conquests. Within a year Louisbourg was as busy, populated, and prosperous as ever, and some of the New Englanders who had besieged it in 1745 were returning to trade there. The first skirmish of the mid-century war had been inconclusive. Yet the collision of French and British interests was threatening conflict at several points in North America.

In Atlantic Canada the restoration of French control in Ile Royale did not restore the status quo. Partly to compensate for the return of Louisbourg to the French, Britain began to assert its control of mainland Nova Scotia. In 1749 two regiments and 2,500 settlers recruited in England arrived at Chebucto Bay to found the city of Halifax, and 1,500 "foreign Protestants" recruited from Germany and Switzerland established Lunenburg in 1753. At first the ill-equipped settlers, harassed by France's Mi'kmaq allies, suffered and died, but the new colony continued to grow, aided by the arrival of a few New Englanders, whose presence foreshadowed subsequent New England migration to the Nova Scotian coast. One of the New Englanders, John Bushell, began printing Canada's first newspaper, the *Halifax Gazette*, in 1752. By the end of the 1750s, Halifax had established itself in its enduring role as Britain's key

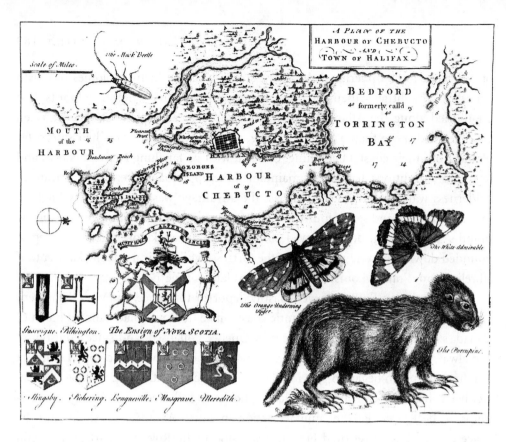

Natives and visiting fishermen had Chebucto's fine harbour to themselves until a fleet of British soldiers and colonists under Colonel Edward Cornwallis, newly appointed as Governor of Nova Scotia, arrived to found Halifax in 1749. Among them was eighteen-year-old Moses Harris, entomologist and engraver, whose *Plan of the Harbour of Chebucto and Town of Halifax* (with porcupine and butterflies), dated 1749 and published in the February 1850 issue of *The Gentleman's Magazine*, is considered to be the first graphic record of the new colony.

military base on the North Atlantic seaboard of America. The territory first claimed as New Scotland in the 1620s began to take shape as a British colony.

In response to the rise of Halifax, France posted a larger garrison to Louisbourg and fortified the southern limits of the territory it claimed along the Isthmus of Chignecto (the modern boundary of Nova Scotia and New Brunswick). Both developments threatened the isolation that had enabled the Acadians, now perhaps twelve thousand strong, to remain a neutral enclave within British territory. By the 1750s, some Acadians began to migrate to Ile Royale and Ile St-Jean. In Newfoundland, a less direct confrontation loomed between British and French. The growing British colony there was gradually expanding into territory reserved for French fishing stations, but the real competition concerned the market for cod in Europe. The control of Newfoundland that Britain had gained in 1713 was an important advantage, but French cod trades had recovered in peacetime. Military action in Atlantic Canada was one way to resolve this competition over an industry that was still far more valuable to the European powers than the fur trade.

Anglo-French interests also clashed on the frontier zone south of the Great Lakes, a region where Canada had felt secure since the Iroquois treaty of neutrality of 1701. By the 1750s, Pennsylvanians and Virginians were pushing west over the Appalachians towards the Ohio River, which would take them to the Mississippi. To stem this westward advance and to retain the trade and support of the Native nations south of Lake Erie, successive governors of New France established forts on the banks of the Ohio and its tributaries. At first fighting was confined to skirmishes between

By the mid-eighteenth century, British newspapers were actively shaping public opinion on many political issues. The domestic popularity of Britain's globe-spanning campaign against the French Empire spawned many anti-French propaganda cartoons, such as this engraving by John June after Louis-Pierre Boitard's drawing, printed in London in 1755. Note "Britannia attending to the complaints of her injur'd Americans" (lower left), and "The French overset at the fall of Niagara" (upper centre).

Native clients of the French and Americans, but as French troops and American militia expeditions asserted rival claims to the region, a direct clash became certain.

As these conflicts loomed, France reinforced its North American colony, doubling the complement of the Marine infantry companies, adding artillery companies, and strengthening the engineering corps. With garrisons expanding, expeditions being mounted, and new forts being built, the colony's expenditures soared. The expenses column of the colonial budget, kept below a half-million *livres* a year for most of the century, exceeded a million *livres* for the first time in 1744. By the first years of the 1750s New France's annual expenditures ranged between three million and six million *livres*. The colony was officially at peace, but military expenses accounted for virtually all the increase.

These expenditures—they would reach thirty million *livres* by the war years of the late 1750s—were supervised at Quebec City by François Bigot, Intendant of New France since 1748. Because of them, Bigot became one of the legendary figures of New France, supposedly a monster of corruption who diverted the colony's money into his own pockets at its time of greatest need and thereby became a principal cause of the colony's downfall. Bigot was certainly corrupt by twentieth-century standards. The year he was appointed Intendant, he joined a commercial venture to ship to Quebec City the goods he would purchase on the colony's behalf. Throughout his tenure, suppliers associated with him would profit greatly from the purchases he authorized. Bigot made money from his position, and he used his wealth and influence to acquire mistresses and to fund his prominent place in the scandal-fuelling luxury that typified the last years of Quebec's vice-regal society. Still, it was French imperial policy, not Bigot's profits, which caused royal expenditures to grow sixtyfold in barely a dozen years. The French Crown was not always prepared to accept the costs of its policies, and its endless demands for economy prompted the new Governor, the Marquis de La Galissonière, to reply tartly that wars are never made without spending. Military preparations were the main cause of New France's enormous debts. Versailles complained of the costs, but it continued the policies.

The use of public office for private gain was unique neither to Bigot nor to the French royal service. The eighteenth century tolerated a certain blurring of public and private interests among gentlemen, and little blame accrued as long as the books ultimately balanced. What earned Bigot imprisonment, exile, and infamy was less the profiteering itself than the fall of New France and the Crown's inability to pay its war debts, for both of which Bigot and his associates became scapegoats. In fact, Bigot's

Founded in 1713 to restore French power on the Atlantic seaboard, Louisbourg grew into a prosperous fishing port and trading centre. Twice besieged and captured by the British, it was left abandoned within a decade of the second siege, that of 1758—accurately recorded here in an engraving by P. Canot after a sketch "drawn on the spot" by Captain Ince of the 35th Regiment (London: Thomas Jefferys, 1762).

effort to profit by supplying goods to New France almost certainly strengthened the colony's preparations for war. Crop failures and increasing militia levies were eroding farm production during the 1750s, and New France became less able to feed itself as the Canadian garrison grew. Despite increased efforts to find supplies within the colony—particularly after a colonial, Joseph-Michel Cadet, took charge of supplying the forces in 1756—the gap between what the military needed and what the colony could supply had to be filled from Europe. Here a startling success was achieved. When war, the British naval threat, and skyrocketing insurance rates drove out most independent shippers, Bigot's associates were nearly alone in continuing to ship the vital supplies of food and equipment from France to the embattled colony. Yet shipping tonnages from France to Quebec City doubled and tripled under Bigot's administration.

In 1754 the border conflict finally brought the French and Americans to blows on the Ohio frontier. The experienced and well-organized Marine troops routed the British colonies' volunteer militias and their commander, a young Virginian named

George Washington, but the looming struggle prompted both empires to raise the stakes. Early in 1755 Britain dispatched two regiments of its regular army to the Thirteen Colonies. For the first time since the Iroquois wars of the 1660s, France sent regular army troops to support the Marine garrison of New France. War remained undeclared as both sides negotiated their European alliances, but the official state of peace prevented neither a British naval attack on the French troop convoy nor large-scale hostilities as soon as the regulars and their generals reached North America.

The campaigns of 1755 showed that the regular army regiments would not immediately transform North American warfare, for their training on the battlefields of Europe proved no advantage in the North American wilderness. The French army commander, Jean-Armand Dieskau, was wounded and captured in an inconclusive engagement south of Lake Champlain, and the British general, Edward Braddock, was killed and his army scattered by a small force of Marine troops and Native allies when he attempted to march on Fort Duquesne, the French Ohio River stronghold (where Pittsburgh now stands). Both sides fell back to rebuild, pending a formal declaration of war in 1756.

The Exile of the Acadians

More consequential than these frontier skirmishes was *le grand dérangement*, the deportation of the Acadians in the summer and fall of 1755. For Colonel Charles Lawrence, the acting Governor of Nova Scotia who initiated the deportation, this was simply a military act. His country was at war, in fact if not by declaration, and French forces along its borders and coasts threatened his colony. When Acadian spokesmen hedged over an unconditional oath of allegiance, Lawrence saw the removal of a potentially disloyal element from his colony as no more than a prudent precaution.

The deportation was done with astonishing speed. Once the decision had been passed—unanimously—by Nova Scotia's governing council in July 1755, Lawrence made full use of the forces Britain had amassed in Nova Scotia. A fleet of merchant ships was quickly hired and provisioned. Lawrence ordered his regiments to round up the Acadians and march them on to his ships with what baggage they could carry, and to burn the villages as soon as they were emptied. In a matter of months Acadia ceased to exist. Village by village, at Grand Pré, Minas, Beaubassin, all around the Fundy shore, at least seven thousand Acadians were seized and sent into exile before the end of 1755. Another few thousand would be exiled in the next few years. Perhaps two thousand fugitives and resisters would hold out in the woods.

The decision to deport the Acadians grew out of the changing circumstances of Nova Scotia. In 1713 Britain had left the Acadians in place through weakness as much as tolerance. In the peaceful 1720s and 1730s, British commanders, with scant resources and almost no non-French subjects, had to develop a delicate *modus vivendi* to secure their own position, even though it reinforced the Acadians' inclination to neutrality. By the 1750s, however, the founding of Halifax had brought British troops and settlers to Nova Scotia. Governors and commanders no longer needed to reach an understanding with the French subjects who occupied the best land of the colony. For their part, the Acadians sought more than ever to remain neutral. They could not help but be aware of the increasing British power around them, and they had become cautious about giving support to the French troops on their borders. But they were a people rooted in the Acadian land, ten thousand or twelve thousand strong, settled for generations on ground they had recovered from the Fundy tides. Despite Britain's growing power over them, they found the possibility of deportation unrealistic, inconceivable. Even under the guns of the gathering British forces, they felt able to bargain over the terms of their neutrality—until the day the deportation order was read.

For the Acadians, who saw themselves as powerless, unoffending, and unchallengeable in their right to their land and their way of life, the deportation meant the obliteration of their society, one established on lands they had tended for more than a century. Lawrence had ordered that they should be distributed "among the several colonies on the continent"—no American colony would have accepted them all—and so the ships discharged their passengers in seaports all along the Atlantic seaboard from New England to Georgia. Lawrence's officers had made no direct effort to divide families as they were herded aboard ship, but since Acadian families were extended, interrelated networks, all the exiles lost most of the people they considered their family. And although there was no plan to starve or infect the prisoners, in the stress and movement as many as a third of the exiles may have died of contagious diseases. In the continuing campaign of deportation between 1756 and 1762, some Acadians were shipped as far as Europe. In 1758 seven hundred died in a shipwreck on the way, and the survivors became refugees in France.

Some of the Acadians who found themselves unloaded in small groups in the American ports would remain there, a small unpopular minority in the heart of an alien society. Others began to move as soon as they could—towards the French

Caribbean, to Louisiana, to the St. Lawrence valley. After the war ended in 1763, a few began to return, by land or sea, to Acadia, in a slow, piecemeal, astonishingly persistent process that would take decades to complete. But the Acadia they were returning to no longer existed. New settlers had quickly appropriated the old diked lands, the best in Nova Scotia. Acadian families who avoided deportation or returned from exile had to find new homes in areas hitherto neglected. The heart of Acadia shifted westward into New Brunswick, where the shared memory of deportation and loss was the basic element in the gradual shaping of a new Acadian society.

The Path to the Plains of Abraham

The spring of 1756 brought the formal declaration of what became known (by its European dates 1756–63) as the Seven Years War. It also brought to the fore three key personalities of the conflict, two French and one British. Pierre de Rigaud de Vaudreuil, son of the governor who had led New France early in the century, had himself become Governor General in 1755. A Canadian by birth, Vaudreuil had been raised in New France's century-old tradition of carrying warfare to the enemy through frontier raids, and he knew the necessity for the colony to maintain its Native alliances. Vaudreuil came to resent the regular army officers' disdain for the colony's troops, who may have been less polished but were much more skilled in North American warfare. In 1756 Vaudreuil acquired a subordinate who would become a rival when Louis-Joseph de Montcalm, a veteran of European warfare, arrived to take command of the army troops in New France. Confident in his own abilities and given to sarcastic criticism of rival ideas, Montcalm found it difficult to defer to Governor Vaudreuil, whose colonial military experience he did not take seriously. In the growing professionalization of the colonial struggle Montcalm saw the need to keep his army intact, and he resisted Vaudreuil's emphasis on protecting widely scattered frontiers. Montcalm never shared the colonists' commitment to saving New France at all costs. He saw Canada as one of many French battlefields and speculated about the terms under which the King might agree to yield it. He and Vaudreuil were bound to clash.

The third figure to emerge in 1756 was William Pitt, the British politician who in that year overcame George II's opposition to him and became Prime Minister. Pitt was determined to fight France in a colonial rather than a European war. Despite the

King's concern that his German family lands and allies be defended, a series of diplomatic shifts in Europe that year gave Pitt's government a free hand. Unless Pitt was driven from office, British policy would emphasize a war on the French Empire, including not just the defeat but the conquest of New France. In previous conflicts, the French colony's military forces and its ability to organize for war had given it an advantage over the much larger British colonies in North America. Now Britain's growing command of the sea enabled it to dispatch troops and equipment to the colonies in far greater quantities than France could match. By the end of the war, more than 20,000 of Britain's 140,000-man army were serving in North America, supported by as many colonial troops and by the fleets of the Royal Nay.

Despite the British commitment to carry the war to North America, 1756 and 1757 mostly saw victories or successful defences for the French forces. The war was now being fought on the western frontiers, at the Atlantic bastion of Louisbourg, and on the Richelieu–Lake Champlain waterway that formed the frontier between Montreal and New York. Every part of the colony was becoming involved, and all New France's alliances were being used to rally Native support. Some Iroquois warriors (including a future leader of the Six Nations, Thayendanegea or Joseph Brant) joined the British cause, but most of the Iroquois confederacy stood by the treaty of neutrality, despite the persuasive efforts of the increasingly influential British agents among them.

"War enriches Canada," wrote a military officer who had observed the enormous royal investment in New France's military establishment. But he might also have noted how the war was eroding all peacetime enterprises as it made New France more than ever a society in arms. Males from sixteen to sixty had always been enrolled, parish by parish, in militia companies, and through these as much as a quarter of the population now went on active service each summer. The civilian militia not only fought alongside the frontier garrisons and the army troops, but also supported the far-flung campaigns by hauling supplies, maintaining depots, and building roads and forts. Casualties mounted steadily and, with so many men at war, agriculture and peacetime trades declined. "I do not know better people in all the world than these *Canadiens*," said Governor Duquesne, reviewing the heroic labours of his militias in 1754. "Their devotion and zeal delight me." But as early as 1755 his successor Vaudreuil was concerned about fields left uncultivated back at home, and the problem grew worse each year.

As scarcity drove prices rapidly upward, coinage disappeared and the paper currency signed by Bigot depreciated. Bigot imposed rationing, and royal officials

A capable commander and a savage critic of most of his colleagues, the Marquis de Montcalm (1712–59) spent four campaigning seasons trying to make the defence of New France conform to European styles of warfare. Wounded on the Plains of Abraham on the morning of September 13, 1759, he died the next day and was buried in the Ursuline convent in the city of Quebec, where his skull is preserved. Artist unknown, probably French, *c.* eighteenth century.

searched the rural districts to confiscate hoarded food and grain. The *habitants'* livestock—first cows, pigs, and sheep, then also horses, much to the public disgust—disappeared into the cooking pots. In the winter of 1757–58 there were serious shortages and a drastic cut in rations. In the streets of Montreal and Quebec City, women marched in protest against the government's failure to control the soaring prices of essential foods. There may not have been actual starvation, but smallpox ravaged colonists already weakened by malnutrition and an unusually cold winter.

Yet the morale of the colonists impressed even Montcalm, who was increasingly at odds with Governor General Vaudreuil. In 1757 Montcalm wrote that Canada would be no irreplaceable loss if France could hold onto its fisheries, but in the hungry fall of that year his second-in-command, François-Gaston de Lévis, praised the determination of the colonists and expressed New France's strategy for survival. "If the English are no more successful in their European ventures than in America," he wrote, "they will not long be able to sustain the immense expenditures that this war is costing them." If only New France's small garrison and mobilized population could continue holding off the armies massed against them, the colony might survive by enduring longer than the British taxpayers.

Late in 1757, Montcalm won royal authority to conduct his campaigns largely free of the supervision of Governor Vaudreuil, and 1758 saw the war turning towards the strategy he had always preferred. French control on the western frontier began to crumble with the loss of Fort Duquesne on the Ohio and the destruction of Fort Frontenac on Lake Ontario by a raiding party. At the other end of New France, Louisbourg also fell, this time the victim of a methodical siege undertaken by the new British commander-in-chief, Jeffery Amherst. The town held out until late in July 1758, and once more the colonists (about five thousand, with nearly as many troops) were shipped away to France by the victors. Louisbourg, its fisheries, and its sea trades would not be restored to France a second time. Its fortifications would be demolished and the town abandoned to decay. The crumbling of New France's outlying defences heightened the importance of the central campaign that had always preoccupied Montcalm. In August 1758 the French general won his greatest victory, smashing the British army that had advanced to Carillon (called Ticonderoga by the British) at the southern approaches to Lake Champlain. The defeat of one British army at Carillon and the weeks needed by another to besiege and capture Louisbourg ensured that neither would be able to move on the heartland of New France during 1758.

"This campaign will be critical," wrote François-Gaston de Lévis in April 1759. The French had just enough troops (perhaps 3,500 army regulars, 2,500 colonial marines, and 15,000 civilian militiamen) and just enough supplies (Bigot's organization brought more than twenty shiploads to Quebec that spring) to hope that with good fortune they could hold the St. Lawrence valley, Lake Champlain, and Lake Ontario, and give the British another costly year without victory. By the spring of 1759, however, Britain's colonial campaigns were beginning to bear fruit, making it unlikely that the struggle would be abandoned. That summer General Amherst took Carillon and Fort St-Frédéric in his deliberate, almost irresistible advance up Lake Champlain toward the Richelieu River and Montreal, while British and colonial troops took Fort Niagara and secured control of Lake Ontario. There was not much likelihood that this two-pronged advance could be stopped, in 1759 or 1760, whatever happened at Quebec City.

Quebec, however, saw the great confrontation. Samuel de Champlain had chosen the site of the city 150 years before for its natural defences and its command of the river. Now, in 1759, Montcalm's 2,200 regulars and 1,500 Marines, supported by as many as 10,000 civilian soldiers, would try to hold the city all summer against 8,000

British regulars, the naval fleet that brought them up the river, and Montcalm's newest adversary, thirty-two-year-old Brigadier-General James Wolfe.

"Montcalm is at the head of a great number of bad soldiers and I am at the head of a small number of good ones," wrote Wolfe during the siege of the city. Heavy casualties and sparse replacements had forced Montcalm to fill the ranks of his regular battalions with civilians from the militia, and against these forces Wolfe anticipated a decisive engagement in which his highly trained, well-disciplined soldiers would carry the day. Montcalm, however, had terrain in his favour and he drove back every attempt on his lines. When Wolfe ordered his first attack, at Montmorency Falls in July 1759, it was Canadian militia, to a professional soldier's eye the least "good" of Montcalm's troops, who turned back the British regulars.

Unable to get at the enemy, Wolfe ordered an artillery barrage that reduced much of the town of Quebec to rubble, and he dispatched troops to burn Baie-St-Paul and La Malbaie and every home along an 80-kilometre (50-mile) stretch of the densely populated south shore east of Quebec City. By September, Wolfe, plagued by ill health, was quarrelling with his officers and considering the mechanics of withdrawing his army from the siege. First, however, he tried one final effort, adapting a plan offered by his brigadiers for a surprise attack that might bring Montcalm to battle. The navy and the army worked together superbly on the night of September 12–13, 1759, and they took advantage of lapses by the defenders to seize a path up the cliffs west of Quebec. By morning Wolfe had about four thousand men and their field artillery on the Plains of Abraham. He had compelled Montcalm to give battle.

Wolfe's achievement in getting his army ashore might not have doomed New France. By delaying a confrontation while he brought up cannon and surrounded Wolfe's bridgehead with all the French forces east and west of it, Montcalm might have improved his chances of beating the British force, which had no way to retreat. Studying the situation from his camp east of the city, Montcalm apparently decided he could afford no delay that would give Wolfe's army more time to organize. He went into action that morning with only the troops he had at hand. On the Plains of Abraham, Wolfe's red-coated army formed one line, facing east towards the city. After some fierce skirmishing, Montcalm's troops in their white coats moved west towards them, drums beating, regimental banners flying, soldiers cheering. The two armies were roughly equal in numbers. These were precisely the conditions Wolfe had sought all summer. In a battle that lasted barely fifteen minutes, the close-range volleys of his skilled regulars tore the French army apart. Wolfe died on the battlefield.

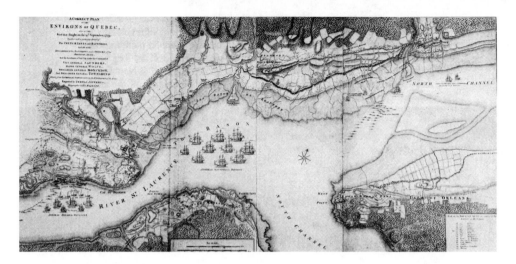

A Correct Plan of Quebec, And of the Battle fought on the 13th. September 1759. Skilfully charting the tortuous channels of the St. Lawrence, the Royal Navy carried Wolfe's army to Quebec and enabled it to move swiftly from its encampments on the south shore downstream to Montmorency (top right) and upstream to the Anse au Foulon, gateway to the Plains of Abraham. Engraved and published by Thomas Jefferys, London, 1759, from the original surveys taken by army engineers.

Montcalm was wounded in the retreat and died the next day. A few days later the capital of New France yielded to the British.

The war was not quite over. The French army retreated up the river to Montreal, to fight under Lévis's command for another year before Vaudreuil finally called a halt and signed the capitulation of New France. But for the Canadians, the battle on the Plains of Abraham seems to have been decisive. In 1759 the number of militiamen at Quebec City had exceeded all predictions: boys of thirteen and men of eighty had willingly turned out. In 1760 the militia in the territory still under French control had to be called out under pain of death, and Lévis was forced to adopt Wolfe's tactics and burn the homes of some reluctant militiamen. For five years a quarter of the Canadian population had been in arms, and finally they had seen war on their own soil. Every community had suffered, but devastation was particularly great in and around Quebec City. In the oldest and most populous part of the colony, many militiamen had gone home after the fall of the city to find their crops lost, the last of their livestock seized by the enemy, and their homes burned to the ground.

How many Canadians died during the conquest of their colony remains unknown. There had been heavy losses on all the battlefields and steady attrition behind the lines. In the towns and the countryside alike, everyone had faced recurrent hunger and epidemics. Invasion and economic devastation left the colonists

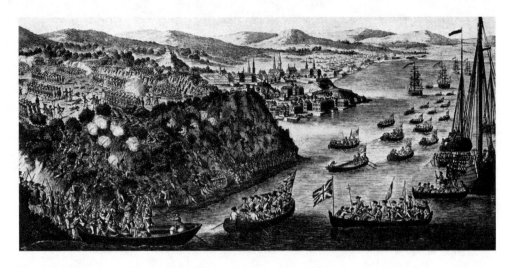

In an engraving based on a view prepared by Wolfe's aide-de-camp Hervey Smyth (1734–1811), who was severely wounded during the battle, the events of twelve hours are compressed into a single moment. Here the British forces move up the river, seize the path up the cliffs, and fight the battle of the Plains of Abraham as it transpired on the morning of September 13, 1759. Printed in London, 1759.

with an overwhelming uncertainty about the future. There may have been as many as six thousand or seven thousand Canadian casualties during the War of the Conquest—a tenth of the colonial population. Defeat meant risking the fate of the Acadians and the colonists of Ile Royale, but it also meant a chance for the society to revive. By the end of 1759 the Canadians badly needed a return to the more manageable hazards that *habitants*, traders, *voyageurs*, artisans, and the rest had been dealing with for a century and more. They went home, to scrape through the winters of 1759 and 1760 and to await developments in a society ruled by foreigners.

On the Margins of Empire
1760–1840

GRAEME WYNN

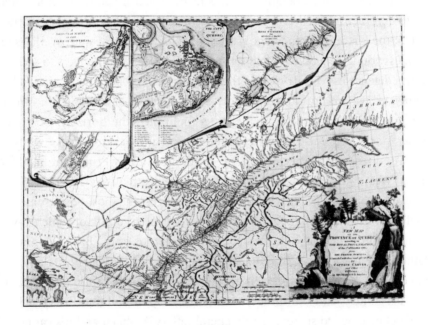

A fine example of the eighteenth-century map-maker's art, this illustration
includes the boundaries of Quebec established in 1763, plans of the colony's two
largest cities, and detailed depictions of its more densely settled rural areas. *A New
Map of the Province of Quebec*, by Thomas Jefferys and others (London, 1778),
based on explorations by Jonathan Carver.

A Land of Long and Barbarous Names

WHAT A SCENE!" wrote English essayist Horace Walpole on learning of the fall of Quebec in 1759. "An army in the night dragging itself up a precipice by stumps of trees to assault a town and attack an enemy strongly entrenched and double in numbers!" Coming so soon after earlier pessimistic dispatches from the St. Lawrence, and capping a "wonderful year of victories" for the British, the joyous news was tempered only by the pathos of Wolfe's death on the Plains of Abraham. Bonfires lit the English countryside; a medal was struck to commemorate the victory; the demoralizing defeat at Montmorency was forgotten; the fortunate coincidences that had allowed success were overlooked; and the ruthless young general who had set troops and American Rangers to sacking and burning a defenceless countryside in the summer of 1759 became a national hero. In New England, where Puritan conviction and a mistrust of Catholicism ran strong, and French claims to the continental interior limited the horizons of expansion, moral fervour lent point to laments for "the good and valiant" officer whose death demanded "a tear from every British eye, a sigh from every Protestant heart." When Benjamin West completed his interpretation of the death of Wolfe in 1771, the painting enjoyed enormous popularity. It remains, perhaps, the most powerful icon of an intensely symbolic triumph for British imperialism, accounts of which invariably make much of the tactical boldness and military genius of the British commander.

Although French resistance continued after the fall of Quebec, its end was not long in coming. When Montreal fell in September 1760, the capitulation was undramatic. Surrounded and outnumbered, Governor Vaudreuil and his French troops had little choice but to surrender to General Jeffery Amherst and his cannon. Thus concluded decades of bitter conflict between French and English in North America. The battle had run from Fort Duquesne on the Ohio, through the Hudson-Richelieu corridor, and beyond to Louisbourg and the north-eastern corner of the continent. Beauséjour, Oswego, Carillon, Louisbourg, and Quebec were its focuses; the Acadians were its most tragic and numerous civilian victims. But there would be no deportation for the inhabitants of New France; to them Amherst offered guarantees of religious freedom, property rights, and equality in trade.

But peace on the St. Lawrence failed to settle the fate of Canada. Through 1761, France and England continued the imperial struggle known as the Seven Years War, in India, the Caribbean, and Europe. When Spain entered the war, as an ally of France, the conflict spread to the East Indies. For a few months in 1762, French raiders held St. John's and most of the fishing stations of Newfoundland. But British power prevailed. Even before the conflict ended, popular debate in London turned to consider the spoils of victory. Britain could not keep all the territory its armies had occupied; what should be given up? Some urged retention of sugar-producing Guadeloupe: surely it held more profitable prospects than frigid Canada. And was not Jamaica a more important trading partner than all of New England? Many thought so; others not. When a group of journeymen tailors—several rousing toasts behind them—fell to discussing the issue one evening in London, an unfortunate supporter of Caribbean acquisitions "had his head broke with a gallon pot, and was kicked out of the company." Indeed there were good strategic reasons for keeping Canada. The exclusion of France from the St. Lawrence promised to end international competition for furs, as well as the Indian raids generated by that rivalry, while opening the prospect of westward expansion in trade and, eventually, settlement from New York.

So the map of North America was redrawn in 1763. By the Treaty of Paris, France withdrew from the mainland and the inhabitants of New France became formal subjects of the British Crown. Fishing rights on the northern coast of Newfoundland, and title to St-Pierre, Miquelon, Guiana, Martinique, St. Lucia, and Guadeloupe were the sole remnants of a once extensive French empire in the American hemisphere. East of the Mississippi River, Britain held sway from Hudson Bay to the Gulf of Mexico. Spain held the area south and west of the Mississippi, and laid claim to the northern Pacific Coast. Beyond the limits of European knowledge, Russian traders took sea-otter pelts from the remote north-western corner of the continent. In October 1763, a royal proclamation established the administrative framework of the new British territory. Quebec was created a colony, its boundaries very approximately encompassing the Gaspé peninsula and the St. Lawrence drainage basin from Anticosti Island to the Ottawa River. Nova Scotia included the mainland north of the Bay of Fundy, as well as the islands of St. John (Prince Edward Island) and Cape Breton. Labrador, Anticosti, and the Magdalen Islands were added to Newfoundland to unify control of the fisheries. Rupert's Land was confirmed to the Hudson's Bay Company. Settlement west of the Appalachian Mountains was prohibited as the rest

A view of the Bishop's House with the Ruins, as they Appear in Going up the Hill from the Lower to the Upper Town. This view of Quebec City after the British bombardment of 1759 is based on a sketch by a purser from the *Prince of Orange,* one of the ships supporting the assault on the Plains of Abraham. Engraving by Antoine Benoist after a sketch by Richard Short.

of continental British America—a great triangle of land encompassing the Great Lakes and stretching southward between the Appalachians and the Mississippi—was recognized as "Indian Territory."

The demise of French imperial power in North America opened a pivotal phase in the development of the territory that eventually became Canada. Between 1760 and 1840 new settlers spread their imprint across the north-eastern part of the continent, founding towns, clearing fields, and building roads, houses, fences, and barns. Many, many thousands of people—men and women and children of unexceptional backgrounds but remarkable resilience and fortitude—played an integral part in these developments. They endured the hardships of migration, the difficulties of bush settlement, the perils of ocean-fishing, and the dangers of work in the early forest industry to create the considerable colonial societies of 1840. But they did not do so without setback or restraint. Their fortunes were affected by weather and war. Their fates were conditioned by economic and political forces operating beyond their immediate ken. Their prospects were shaped by the decisions of colonial administrators. And in provincial societies whose people were drawn from many different backgrounds, their daily lives were coloured by the particular mix of ethnicity, language, and religion that prevailed where they settled.

These were the factors that affected the lives of ordinary British North Americans between the fall of New France and the eve of the railway age. In that three-quarters of a century of change, the colonies constituted a "diverse and fractured realm." Located on the margins of the British Empire, in "the Sun of England's Glory," they felt the great impact of imperial trade. They came into being within an imperial framework of administration intended to bring colonial societies under the authority of the British Parliament—but which also created a web of local authority that gave structure to life in the New World. The Rebellions of 1837 and the War of 1812 were, in some sense, consequences of Britain's imperial presence and of the shortcomings of its administrative system in North America. Between 1760 and 1840 hundreds of thousands of men and women came, individually or in families, to people the colonies. Often unhappily displaced by social, economic, and technological changes in Britain, they sought new chances in a New World. The circumstances in which they found themselves were both varied and challenging. Even the new towns, where all was "in a whirl and a fizz," added an unexpected element of diversity to colonial society.

Yet there were few early portents of these developments. The establishment of "Indian Territory" in the interior of North America by the proclamation of 1763 was a matter of necessity rather than generosity. In a desperate last effort to hold back European expansion, Native tribes had mounted a series of bloody, terrifying raids on interior trading posts during the summer of 1763. Brilliantly led by the Ottawa warrior Pontiac, they had killed more than two thousand people. Pacifying Native unrest was an urgent necessity. But the proclamation had other work to do. It was also shaped by the necessities of governing new subjects, securing new territory, and reconciling the interests of fur traders, settlers, and speculators in the West. To the young George Washington at least, it seemed clear that the prohibition of settlement west of the Appalachians was no more than "a temporary expedient to quiet the minds of the Indians." And events seemed to bear him out. To accommodate those who favoured the expansion of settlement from the seaboard colonies, land south of the Ohio River was removed from Indian territory in 1768. Six years later, when the Quebec Act expanded the bounds of that colony to include both the fur-trading domain of the interior (roughly the Great Lakes basin) and the seal fisheries of the Gulf of St. Lawrence, "Indian Territory" was removed from the map.

These adjustments failed to solve the difficulties and inefficiencies that bedevilled

Britain's administration of its increasingly fractious North American colonies after 1763. Although the Quebec Act was intended, in the long term, to anglicize the Canadiens, New Englanders were suspicious of the recognition it afforded French civil laws, the seigneurial system, and Roman Catholicism. They resented the new boundaries of the St. Lawrence colony as obstacles to their own westward expansion. And they objected to British taxes levied in the colonies to defray the costs of Britain's long war with France, and to meet the expense of administering the newly acquired territories. Protest had already flared in Massachusetts, when a shipment of tea on which the British were demanding customs duties was thrown into Boston harbour. When the Quebec Act was passed at Westminster alongside provisions intended to bring Massachusetts to heel, American discontent crystallized at Bunker Hill on the outskirts of Boston, where American militia men engaged British troops. That battle apart, an invasion of Canada was the main event in the first year of the American Revolution. St. John's, south-east of Montreal, fell to the invaders in the autumn of 1775, but an American attack on Quebec on the last day of the year was unsuccessful, and the rebels were driven back in the spring. When peace was finally reached, in 1783, the limits of British claims in North America were pushed back to the Great Lakes, to define the south-eastern boundary of the territory that became modern Canada. Known collectively as British North America between 1776 and 1867, the several colonies that made up this northern realm were very much the domain of Native peoples during the 1760s.

Across the northern half of the continent, indigenous peoples outnumbered Europeans by a ratio of at least two to one, and occupied a far more extensive area than the newcomers. Neither group formed a single community. Languages and traditions set Native peoples apart from each other. So too did the means by which they gained their livelihoods. Similarly, the European population of British North America—which numbered no more than 100,000—stemmed from diverse backgrounds, engaged in radically different economic activities, and lived in distinct and widely scattered settings. In broad terms European settlement was concentrated in two areas: on the Atlantic coast and along the St. Lawrence River. Beyond, in the eastern woodlands, across the extensive interior plains, and on the Pacific coast, Native peoples dominated, although small clusters of Europeans engaged in the fur trade occupied scattered posts in the interior and along the shore of Hudson Bay.

Strategic and economic factors had moulded settlement on the Atlantic coast. Traditionally regarded by British officials as "a great English ship moored near the

By 1830, St. John's, Newfoundland, was the very model of a colonial city, with its busy harbour, its dense cluster of wharfs and warehouses, and its garrison. The surrounding countryside is scattered with gentlemen's residences, as well as several hundred small farms which produced milk and vegetables for the city. *The Town and Harbour of St. John's*: aquatint by H. Pyall (London, 1831) after a drawing by William Eagar.

Banks" for the convenience of the fishery, cold, inhospitable Newfoundland was settled extremely slowly. Although European vessels had fished its neighbouring waters for centuries, they had done so seasonally, leaving Europe in the spring and returning in the fall. In Britain this migratory fishing industry was considered a vital nursery of seamen, turning "green men" into "salty dogs" who could man the navy in times of crisis. It was also a lucrative trade on which the fortune of many an English merchant was built. Settlement on the island, which seemed to threaten both the security and the profit of the English, was discouraged. But the disapproval of traders and politicians could not prevent a steady growth of population during the eighteenth century. When the fishing fleets left in the fall, crewmen who had contracted for two or three summers wintered over in Newfoundland to guard and maintain the shore-works required to cure and keep the summer's catch. Others preferred Newfoundland to the prospect of unemployment in Devon or starvation in Ireland.

Some found wives among the female domestics brought to the island by military officers and other officials, and sought permanent livings there. In the early 1760s, 8,000 or 9,000 people wintered in Newfoundland. Permanent residents, whose numbers probably included 850 to 900 women and about 2,000 children, accounted for slightly less than half of this total.

Each summer, migratory fishermen doubled the number of Europeans in Newfoundland. Their presence crowded coves and heightened activity, but it changed little the basic patterns of settlement. People concentrated where the fishing was best, between Bonavista and the southern Avalon peninsula. Along this deeply indented shore were scattered the small, strand-clinging clusters of dwellings, sheds, stages (or wharfs), and flakes (or drying racks) that tied sea to land and formed the focus of summer work. From each of them, day after arduous day, May through September, small boats with crews of three or occasionally four were rowed out to local fishing grounds and filled with cod taken on baited lines. Boats from English vessels, moored inshore and unrigged for the summer, worked alongside those of resident fishermen. Each evening the catch was split and salted; each morning it was spread and turned on the flakes to dry; until, in late summer or fall, it was shipped to market. Neither rhythm nor routine varied much. Storms broke the pattern. Here fifty boats might set out, there barely a dozen. But skills and circumstances were remarkably uniform. St. John's, with a garrison of two hundred or so and a cluster of merchants' stores, was the most important centre on the island. But there, as in the smallest settlements, cattle, sheep, and fowl wandered the rough paths that linked buildings, and foraged in the brush beyond. These were utilitarian places. The single-minded devotion of people to the business of fishing was everywhere apparent. "For dirt and filth of all kinds," wrote Joseph Banks, the botanist in Captain Cook's expedition to Newfoundland in the 1760s, "St. John's in my opinion may reign unequalled."

In Nova Scotia, the vacuum created by the Acadian expulsion of 1755 was already being filled. Entering its second decade, vigorous, even urbane, Halifax focused on its magnificent harbour and backed into forest, scrub, and rock. British investment, New England commerce, and preparations for the assault on Quebec had promoted its growth. Palisades bounded the town; an impressive Anglican church dominated the skyline; soldiers drilled on the Parade; and government officials were a significant leaven in the town's population of three thousand to four thousand. Although numbers fell as times worsened with the reduction of British spending after 1760, the town remained the most significant port between Boston and Quebec through the decade.

Beyond it, New Englanders began to establish agricultural settlements on the margins of the Bay of Fundy and fishing settlements along the Atlantic coast. Drawn from relatively few New England towns, they shared many ties of blood and marriage. They settled, for the most part, among migrants from neighbouring areas of New England. Among the 104 people who migrated from Chatham, Massachusetts, to Liverpool and Barrington, Nova Scotia, for example, more than half the husbands and wives shared five surnames. Official reports found some of the newcomers "Indigent…[and] Indolent"; others were "substantial…[and] laborious." By 1763 their tiny new settlements dotted the coast from the head of the Bay of Fundy to Liverpool, south-west of Halifax. Approximately nine thousand people lived in the colony. Yet with farms and fishing stations barely developed, and most of its settlers scrabbling to survive, Nova Scotia was heavily dependent on—indeed in many ways an outpost of—New England.

British officials found much to admire in the landscape of Quebec during the early 1760s. Viewing the St. Lawrence through the prism of their British background, they found there a version of the orderly, stable, essentially feudal agrarian society fondly recalled in the nostalgic dreams of England's eighteenth-century gentry. Whitewashed cottages, comfortable farms that ran back from the broad St. Lawrence to the rock and dark forest of the Canadian Shield, scores of church spires suggesting the importance of religion, small gristmills and sawmills, manor houses betokening a feudal order, and the robust prosperity of the *habitants*, who often seemed to combine "the language of the peasant" with some of "the unaffected courtesy and dignified bearing of the gentleman," all contributed to this view. And the long line of settlement that followed the river inspired many a sentimental description and romantic sketch.

Rarely did these views capture the full picture. There was an enormous difference between *habitant* life in North America and the reality and recollection of peasant circumstances in Europe. Although rural dwellers along the St. Lawrence were tenants, there was little disparity in wealth between *seigneur* and *habitant*, and agriculture was individual rather than collective. The power of the Catholic church was limited by the scattered settlements and a shortage of priests to attend them. By the mid-eighteenth century many *habitants* would have found France quite foreign. Indeed, one group of Acadians, who had been relocated there after the expulsion of 1755, soon crossed the Atlantic once again to settle in Spanish Louisiana and British Nova Scotia. After several generations in North America, they were no longer Europeans. Furthermore, almost a fifth of French Canadians lived in the towns of Quebec, Montreal, and Trois Rivières. Perhaps two thousand more lived beyond the

This is early Halifax at its best: the sun shines; the streets are clean; the buildings of church and state dominate the skyline. Full of life and detail, the painting conveys a wonderful sense of the mix of dwellings, activities, and people in this new, but in many ways striking, town. *Governor's House and Mather's Meeting House on Hollis Street, also looking up George Street*; oil (1765) by Dominique Serres after a drawing by Richard Short.

narrow bounds of the colony in the fur-trading country of the Great Lakes, where, with Native wives and Métis children, they formed a distinctive population often disparaged by British officials as lawless vagabonds.

For all these people, the early 1760s were years of adjustment: to the presence of British soldiers who marked the change of imperial authority; to the fact that English-speaking traders were quickly prominent in the commercial life of Montreal; and to the extension of English land-ownership, which by the end of the decade had left thirty *seigneuries* in English hands. Friction was generated by the transition from civilian to military authority. And the co-existence of French and English legal codes, which reflected different economic and social values, spawned animosities between merchants as well as administrative uncertainty. Adaptation was also necessary to the slow recovery of the fur trade; to the damage inflicted on the town of Quebec by the wars; and to the recession which followed the price inflation of the previous decade. But for most French Canadians, time-worn patterns of daily life continued in essentially familiar settings through the 1760s.

Beyond these few towns and settlements, European knowledge of the northern part of the continent remained limited. The explorers and traders who had crisscrossed the continent were commercial men, not scientists. Their knowledge of the waterways by which they generally travelled was utilitarian and correspondingly difficult to map. If not entirely forgotten, the information their journeys yielded was long neglected. Native peoples provided descriptions of territory they knew, but these too were difficult to systematize and synthesize. When English cartographer

Dated 1812, this watercolour of Montreal from the mountain was probably painted from earlier sketches; the artist, Thomas Davies, participated in the capture of the city in 1760, and returned to Canada as a lieutenant-general in the British army in 1786. Notice the line of houses, the thoroughly cleared land, and the wall of trees on the south bank of the St. Lawrence.

John Mitchell published his map of North America in 1755, he drew Hudson Bay, the Labrador and Atlantic coasts, and the lower St. Lawrence with some precision, but his Great Lakes only broadly resembled their counterparts on modern maps, and he filled open space south and west of Hudson Bay with the comment that, "The long and Barbarous Names lately given to some of these Northern Parts of Canada and the Lakes we have not inserted, as they are of no use and of uncertain Authority." At best, all that lay west of Hudson Bay, the Nelson River, and the forks of the Saskatchewan River remained *terra incognita* to Europeans in 1763.

This was not, of course, empty territory. Five distinct indigenous groups (broadly identified by language and culture) lived between the Great Lakes and the Rocky Mountains. The forested edge of the Canadian Shield was the territory of the Anishinabe (Ojibwa). Assiniboines and Western Cree occupied the area that is today southern Manitoba and Saskatchewan. Hunters and gatherers, they lived off the resources of this varied territory—according to well-established seasonal rhythms. Broadly, and traditionally, the Cree were people of the forest and parkland, the

Assiniboines of the parkland and prairie, but their economic systems overlapped and there was a good deal of economic and cultural exchange between them. South and west of the Assiniboine-Cree region lived members of the Blackfoot confederacy, plains hunters who neither fished nor built canoes, and depended heavily on the buffalo for food, clothing, shelter, and tools. Farther north, spread across the low Arctic between the western mountains and Hudson Bay, were Athapaskan speakers whose seasonal travels followed the migrations of the caribou, on which they depended for subsistence. All five of these groups had been affected by contact with Europeans. But their lives still revolved around traditional beliefs, skills, and patterns of seasonal movement. Continuity was more characteristic than change; the Native people had exercised a good deal of autonomy in their dealings with and borrowings from Europeans.

Still unknown to Europeans, a mosaic of Native worlds covered the Pacific slope. Except for ten thousand Athapaskans who occupied the northern area between the Rockies and the coastal mountains, these people spoke languages unfamiliar in the East. They were themselves divided linguistically; modern scholarship suggests that in a population estimated at hundred thousand there were probably thirty mutually unintelligible languages within half a dozen distinct linguistic families. Haida, Tsimshian, Nuu-chah-nulth (Nootka), Nuxulk (Bella Coola), Tlingit, Kwak-waka'wakw (Kwakiutl), and Salish had all elaborated complex, ceremonially rich cultures in the resource-rich environments of the coast. River, sea, and land yielded ample stores of food; houses, canoes, and containers were fashioned from western cedar; other plants and animals varied their diet and provided tools and clothing. Trade brought obsidian and jade if it was not available locally. Sedentary, free of the incessant food-quest, these peoples had developed rich traditions of ornamental carving and symbolic ritual. Backing on forest and fronting the sea, the lines of wooden houses and massive decorated poles that characterized their coastal villages formed striking landscapes, and reflected one of the most skilled and highly developed cultures of Native North America.

The small Inuit population of the high Arctic was scattered between the Mackenzie delta and Labrador. Like the Naskapi and Montagnais who lived east of Hudson Bay, they still remained largely beyond European influence in 1760. By contrast, in the Great Lakes–St. Lawrence drainage and on the eastern seaboard, Aboriginal life had been dramatically transformed by European contact. Here, Native numbers were a fraction of what they had once been. Smallpox and Iroquois guns (acquired from the Dutch) had decimated the Huron and their allies and largely

Winter View of Fort Franklin. Painted during a remarkable expedition led by Sir John Franklin that travelled overland from the Great Lakes, down the Mackenzie River, and westward and eastward along the Arctic coast in 1825–27, this view masterfully evokes the vast, remote, and harsh landscapes of the still little-known northern interior of British North America. Fort Franklin, north-east of Great Bear Lake, was a trading post for both the North West and Hudson's Bay companies. Watercolour (1825–26) by George Back.

depopulated the area that would become Upper Canada. Although a thousand or so Ojibwa from the north shore of Lake Huron had moved into the peninsula north of lakes Erie and Ontario, their total population was down; Nipissings, seven hundred or eight hundred strong in 1615, had barely forty warriors and no more than two hundred people a century and a half later. Once-marked differences between groups, reflected in dress and custom, had declined as travel, contact, and European goods worked to generalize the culture of the upper Great Lakes' peoples. Even more markedly, the never-numerous Mi'kmaq and Malecite of Nova Scotia had succumbed to disease and grown dependent on European goods; together disease and European trade had eroded spiritual as well as material traditions. In Newfoundland the Beothuk had been driven inland by Mi'kmaq migrants from Nova Scotia and by European fishermen, whose presence limited their access to essential coastal supplies. Their very existence was in jeopardy.

To Europeans of the late eighteenth century, the challenge of early British North America seemed clear. It was to encompass the unknown, exploit its resources, develop commerce, and settle the wilderness. It was met, magnificently. Historian Suzanne Zeller has usefully seen the scientific exploration of British North America during this period following two impulses, given form in the British imagination by *Gulliver's Travels* (1726) and *Robinson Crusoe* (1719). "Gullivers" (or explorers) sought to discover and observe, to improve the stock of geographical knowledge, and to make useful contributions. "Crusoes," by contrast, were settlers who sought, like their fictional namesake, to identify the characteristics of their new land and to take possession of it. Certainly traders and explorers expanded geographical knowledge with astonishing rapidity. Before the decade ended, Samuel Hearne had left the HBC post at Churchill on explorations of the Chipewyan barren grounds that took him down the Coppermine River to the Arctic as far west as Great Slave Lake. A few years later Matthew Cocking entered Blackfoot territory. Driving the artery of the St. Lawrence fur trade ever farther north and west, Alexander Mackenzie demonstrated his astonishing skill at penetrating the unknown by reaching the Arctic in 1789 and the Pacific in 1793. Early in the new century Simon Fraser and David Thompson pushed through the western mountains to reach tidewater at the mouths of the Fraser and Columbia rivers. Following the probes of Spaniards Bodega Quadra and Juan Josef Pérez, who explored the Queen Charlotte Islands, in 1778 the great English navigator James Cook sailed from Nootka on Vancouver Island into the Bering Strait; fourteen years later fellow-countryman George Vancouver began to explore the inner Pacific coast. In the 1820s British expeditions led by Sir William Parry, Sir John Franklin, Sir John Richardson, and others filled in charts of the western Arctic. These were epic and courageous achievements. By 1790 they had dispelled many of the uncertainties that had hindered the cartographer John Mitchell, and fifty years later only detail remained to be filled in.

Among others who contributed to expanding scientific knowledge of British North America, especially its eastern parts, were former British military officers and highly educated members of the professional and commercial classes in the colonies. Titus Smith Jr. in Nova Scotia, Abraham Gesner in New Brunswick, Phillip Gosse in Lower Canada, and Catharine Parr Traill in Upper Canada were but a few of the dozens who advanced knowledge of local botany, geology, and natural history before 1840. Indeed, Traill, well known for *The Backwoods of Canada* (1836) borrowed specifically from Daniel Defoe in titling her 1852 book *Canadian Crusoes*.

Through all of this, European attitudes towards the Native peoples were neither simple nor of a piece. The fur trade made Native people and Europeans interdependent. There were sincere efforts to "save" Native people by converting them to Christianity and agriculture. Yet the Beothuk were essentially ignored as they starved. Basically, few Europeans were troubled by the impact European exploration and the trade and settlement that followed in its wake were having on Native people. The dramatic decline of indigenous populations since 1500 was evidence enough of the impact, but officials and settlers were far too intent on pursuing the obvious challenge of this vast, newly acquired territory to heed such signs. For most Native peoples, the years after 1763 brought disease, starvation, and cultural destitution.

In "The Sun of England's Glory"

Flushed by the military and diplomatic successes of the 1750s, British politicians envisaged great things of their empire during the 1760s. Spanning the world, it seemed to offer endless possibilities of profit. Colonial products could meet British needs; colonial consumers could buy British goods; and colonial settlers could pay British taxes. In the Americas, thought the prominent English politician Lord Rockingham, Britain had a veritable "revenue mine." Canada occupied an important place in this scheme of things. Its fish and furs would yield great wealth. Whale oil for lighting, whalebone for corsets, and iron from the forge at Saint-Maurice would contribute to the trade of empire. Hemp and flax grown along the St. Lawrence would reduce British dependence on foreign countries for those commodities. And wood from Canadian forests would supply the West Indies. In addition, as Lord Shelburne of the Board of Trade happily pointed out, the Peace of 1763 had given Britain the opportunity to provide "the clothing of many Indian nations, besides 70,000 Acadians [he meant French Canadians], which in so cold a climate must annually consume full £200,000 value of British manufactures."

This grand mercantilist scheme, founded on the belief that self-sufficiency was the cornerstone of empire and designed according to regulations that gave a monopoly of imperial trade to British merchants, was severely shaken by the American Revolution. Recognizing the large contribution that the Thirteen Colonies had made to the trade of empire, Shelburne feared that with their loss "The Sun of England's glory... [had] set forever." The Scottish economist Adam Smith disagreed. Smith's *The Wealth of Nations*, published in 1776, challenged the very precepts of restriction and monopoly on which the prevailing views of empire depended. But Smith's endorsement of free trade among nations was not enough to set aside familiar doctrines. With the support of commercial men whose fortunes had been built under the old system, British politicians sought to make the empire that remained after 1783 as self-contained as its predecessor. The British North American colonies would replace New England, New York, and Pennsylvania as suppliers of the West Indies; naval stores—especially hemp for rope and white pine for masts—would come from New Brunswick and the St. Lawrence rather than from Maine and Massachusetts. Growing numbers of British North Americans would consume British manufactured goods, and foreign ships and merchants would be excluded from colonial ports.

This commercial edifice was easier to design than to build. British North America could not feed itself let alone supply the West Indies. By necessity, American grain, livestock, and lumber were allowed into New Brunswick and Nova Scotia, and the best policy-makers could do was limit the trade to British vessels. Similarly, American naval stores, lumber, livestock, flour, and grain were allowed into the British West Indies, and rum, sugar, molasses, coffee, and other commodities from those islands could be shipped—in British vessels—to the United States. Even this level of compromise was not without benefit to the northern colonies, however. Late in the eighteenth century, when West Indian ports were opened to American vessels, distressed Nova Scotian officials saw their "Capital stock...wasting,...[their] merchants removing as fast as they...[could] and...[their] interests suffering in every point...."

Smuggling opened another crack in the dike of the Empire's self-sufficiency. American fishermen, permitted to dry their catch on the long, indented coasts of Nova Scotia, Labrador, and the Magdalen Islands, conducted a lively illicit trade in such commodities as tea, rum, sugar, and wine. According to one aggrieved Nova Scotian merchant, there was scarcely a house without "an American package" in 1787. Twenty years later the Governor of Newfoundland estimated that 90 per cent of the molasses consumed in his colony came illegally from the French West Indies via the United States. Early in the nineteenth century this dark trade was helped along by Nova Scotian gypsum, which was exchanged for contraband in increasing quantities in the boundary waters among the islands of Passamaquoddy Bay. Officials attempted to "shut the [American] Rascalls" off the coast, but they were hamstrung by circumstances and by the readiness of contraband traders to consider themselves "one day British subjects and the next citizens of the United States, as it best suits their interests."

In England, the difficulties of maintaining a closed, self-sufficient Empire were becoming clearer. A rising population and increasing urbanization had raised doubts about the country's ability to feed itself. After 1795 a succession of bad harvests had driven up the price of bread. Famine seemed imminent unless grain could be acquired from abroad. But the colonies were not up to the task of producing it in sufficient quantity. Harvests, and thus prices, fluctuated wildly, and the high costs of transatlantic transportation generally offset the tariff advantages that the British gave to colonial grain.

Still, events conspired to maintain Britain's commitment to an essentially closed trading system. In 1803, the renewal of war between Britain and France led each side to blockade certain European ports. When American ships bound for Europe were seized by the British, President Thomas Jefferson sealed his country's harbours. This immediately eliminated the competition that had all but excluded British North American vessels from Caribbean harbours. With the schooners and the sledges of American dissidents carrying flour, potash, and other goods northward to fill the holds of British North American ships, merchants had few difficulties assembling cargoes. Their task was made even easier by the creation of a handful of British North American "Free Ports"—where British and American vessels could trade in certain goods—and business prospered in New Brunswick and Nova Scotia. Until these arrangements broke down in the early 1820s, the Maritime provinces reaped the economic benefits of their pivotal role in Atlantic commerce.

At the same time, Napoleon's European blockade seriously impeded the enormous trade in northern European (Baltic) wood on which Britain's expanding economy depended. Soaring prices quickly offset the high cost of shipping bulky timber across the Atlantic. Wood shipments from British North America increased a thousand-fold in five years after 1804. This was clearly a "hot-house" trade, called into existence by special circumstances. Not surprisingly, those engaged in it sought security for their enterprise. When they were successful in winning a tariff preference that gave colonial producers a substantial advantage over their foreign competitors, British North American wood sold in a thoroughly protected market. The consequences for the colonies were immense. From the St. Lawrence and New Brunswick, from Pictou and Prince Edward Island, hundreds of vessels sailed with cargoes of timber. Expansion and prosperity defined the times.

In England, however, rising support for free trade soon raised a cloud on the horizon of colonial optimism. The timber duties were especially opprobrious to those who followed Adam Smith in supporting a *laissez-faire* trade policy, and in 1821 their opposition led to a reduction in the preference afforded colonial timber.

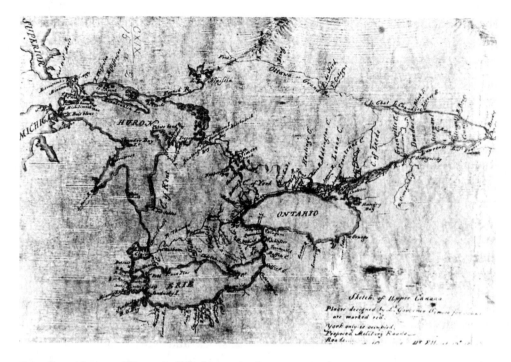

One of several maps of Upper Canada drawn—in this case on birchbark—by Elizabeth Simcoe (1766–1850), wife of Lieutenant-Governor John Graves Simcoe, and a talented amateur artist. Although several of these towns existed only in Colonel Simcoe's plans, the sketch suggests his vision of Upper Canada as the "vestibule of commerce" between Great Britain and the American interior.

Through the 1830s, as free-trade ideas gained momentum, old arguments for the duties were reiterated with new zeal: commerce was the link that bound Britain and its colonies together; without the duty preference, the timber trade would fail and colonial exports would be reduced to a few furs; to abandon the duties would orphan devoted colonial children and hurt the mother country. Together, invocations of patriotism, the arguments of vested interest, and inertia prevailed. The duty preference was again extended to colonial wood and with it the leaky, creaking structure of mercantilism survived into the 1840s.

For the colonies this was something of a Pyrrhic victory. Continuing uncertainty about the fate of the timber duties greatly exaggerated the volatility of a trade that was already highly susceptible to normal business-cycle fluctuations. Through the 1820s and 1830s bust followed boom in New Brunswick (and to a lesser degree in Upper and Lower Canada) as British market swings, rumours of tariff changes, and

Colonel John Graves Simcoe. Simcoe (1752–1806) was Upper Canada's first lieutenant-governor. "The most persistently energetic governor sent to British North America after the American Revolution, he had not only the most articulate faith in its imperial destiny but also the most sympathetic appreciation of the interests and aspirations of its inhabitants" (*The Dictionary of Canadian Biography*). Oil on ivory (undated) by unknown artist.

actual adjustments affected the heavily dependent colonial economies. So large did the question of the preference loom in New Brunswick that in 1831, when news of the defeat of a proposal to reduce the duties reached St. Andrews after five months of apprehension, citizens offered rousing toasts to the British MPs who had defended their interests and then engineered an elaborate celebration in the harbour. On the evening of St. George's Day,

A Boat said to be Baltic built, was filled with a cargo of combustibles and…towed into the harbour, where she was moored. The Effigy of a distinguished supporter of the Baltic interests was suspended from the mast with a paper in his hand bearing the superscription "Baltic Timber Bill"—several pounds of gunpowder were concealed under his waist coat, and there was a large quantity in the boat. The combustibles were set fire to, and in due seasons, poor —— was blown to atoms.

But no such fate stilled the free-trade cause in Britain. By mid-century, the colonial system that generations of British North Americans had considered "so eminently-prescribed by nature and society" as to be immutable had been dismantled. In retrospect it was less a coherent set of principles than a will-o'-the-wisp of piecemeal measures implemented to serve British interests. But such had been their effect on colonial economies and colonial lives that many feared their passing. From Montreal came a manifesto in favour of annexation to the United States, and to the alarm of local magistrates, the inhabitants of Chatham, New Brunswick, marched through the streets on July 4, 1849, firing pistols in the air and singing "Yankee Doodle." In the end, however, the impact of the commercial revolution of the 1840s was less catastrophic than anticipated. After decades of sheltered growth, the colonies were sufficiently robust to stand alone.

"Affairs...But a Bore"

On paper, at least, the diverse colonies of British North America were administered according to a simple pattern. Ultimate authority rested with the British Parliament. In each colony a governor served as the link between imperial authority and local interests, an Executive Council shared administrative and judicial responsibility with the governor, and (except in Quebec before 1791) an elected Assembly represented the interests of the colonists. Beyond this central hierarchy, justices of the peace—appointed by the governor but essentially autonomous—served as local magistrates, extending executive authority to far-flung communities and providing a degree of local control.

In practice, things were less straightforward. Westminster's role in the internal affairs of the colonies was a small one, especially in the last quarter of the eighteenth century. No British taxes were levied in the colonies after 1776. Until 1782 colonial affairs were overseen by the Board of Trade, which loosely co-ordinated the activities of individual departments (such as the Treasury, Customs, and the Admiralty) whose jurisdictions extended to overseas possessions of the Crown; then the Home Department assumed this responsibility. When colonial matters were assigned to the Secretary of State for War at the beginning of the nineteenth century, he was too preoccupied with the struggle against France to spend time on less pressing questions. Even the emergence of a full-fledged Colonial Office in 1815 yielded little real change. Broader moral and colonial issues—such as slavery or immigration—generated interest, but the individual colonies were rarely of much concern to British parliamentarians. New Brunswick's London agent was surely not alone in the rueful reflection that, "The Empire is so vast, and we are so distant, our affairs are but a *bore*."

In this context, governors were theoretically as powerful as Tudor monarchs. As representatives of the Crown and symbols of imperial control they stood high in colonial society, and their prestige carried a good deal of influence. In truth, though, their authority was constrained. Executive, judicial, and legislative powers were not exercised in a vacuum. Anxious about their futures, most governors contrived to act according to the mood of the Colonial Office. Given little specific guidance, they tended to choose the conservative path, implementing such policies as they were instructed to and ensuring that routine administrative responsibilities were met. Appointed executive councils played a significant role in government. They met approximately once a month to consider petitions for special favours, to issue regulations, and to approve grants and licences recommended by the departments to which they had been submitted. But because councillors generally treated these as routine functions, their initiatives were limited and their actions cautious.

Although governors could veto legislation or dissolve an elected assembly such action might be difficult, and would certainly be unwise, if popular support lay with the House. Most governors had few patronage appointments with which to oil the wheels of action, and they depended, by and large, upon the Assembly's assent to any expenditures beyond those already authorized. Assemblymen, as representatives of the people, were characteristically suspicious of "high-minded" proposals—for the relief of destitute immigrants, say—that threatened to consume the limited funds at their disposal. Allocations for local roads, bridges, and schools were an abiding preoccupation; other claims on the public purse generally received short shrift. Wise governors therefore recognized the limits of their power and worked with the drift of local sentiment, influencing and directing but rarely dictating. Those who attempted to do otherwise often found themselves at loggerheads with the Assembly, facing turmoil, and with few options for action.

Some governors had a significant impact upon the development of their colonies. The energetic and imaginative John Graves Simcoe, first lieutenant-governor of Upper Canada, provides a case in point. He sought to make the infant colony a model of effective British government. Although the large expenditures he considered necessary to realize this—by promoting development, providing for the education of the "superior classes," and endowing the Church of England—were not forthcoming, Simcoe set down firm foundations of conservatism and loyalty among the provincial population. He recognized the concerns of ordinary settlers and met their needs by creating an efficient land-granting system. Attracted to the idea of creating a hierarchial society in the wilderness, Simcoe made large tracts of land available to prominent individuals and others who were to encourage settlement and serve as local gentry. Although few followed this plan, they did form the nucleus of a colonial élite. By instituting the "Chequered Plan" of land survey—in which standard townships were 15 kilometres by 20 kilometres (9 miles by 12 miles) with fourteen rows of twenty-four 200-acre lots—

and by reserving two-sevenths of the land in a scattered pattern across each for support of church and state, Simcoe imposed a basic geometry on the landscape. And by pursuing a bold development plan in which London, on Upper Canada's own Thames River, was to be the permanent capital, and military roads running from there to York and from York to Lake Simcoe were to be the main arteries of overland movement, he channelled the course of settlement in the colony.

Over time, the balance of power in administration shifted. In the eighteenth century, lack of control, the slowness of communications, the smallness of colonial societies, and the opportunities for patronage that went with the development of new colonies allowed many governors a more dominant role than was generally available to their nineteenth-century successors. In the new century, executive authority was gradually narrowed by the expanding power of elected assemblies and the increasing efficiency of the Colonial Office in England. Of course, the pace of change varied from colony to colony. In late eighteenth-century Nova Scotia, American Loyalists successfully asserted the elected Assembly's exclusive right to introduce money bills. In the Canadas, in contrast, the Act of 1791, which established the upper and lower provinces, gave the Governor and his appointed Council control over the substantial revenues derived from Crown land reserves. With such fiscal independence, governors were able to pursue unpopular policies with little heed to opposition in the assemblies.

This was a recipe for resentment and confrontation—especially in Lower Canada, where an English governor and an English-dominated Council effectively ignored the French-dominated Assembly. When control of local revenues finally passed to the Canadian assemblies in 1831, the hostility and lack of co-operation between the elected and appointed branches of government led to one crisis after another. Despite attempts at conciliation political tensions persisted.

In 1837 there were rebellions in both Lower and Upper Canada. Their immediate causes were clear enough. In Lower Canada the insurrection was precipitated by the British government's refusal to alter the structure of colonial government, and its decision, in defiance of the Assembly's wishes, to allow the Governor to use provincial revenues without the consent of that body. In Upper Canada it hinged on the active role of Lieutenant-Governor Sir Francis Bond Head in the election of a Conservative majority to the Assembly. But the roots of unrest lay deeper. As the population of the Canadas grew in size and complexity, and provincial revenues increased, the old structures of government became more and more incongruous. In Upper Canada, where new immigrants from modest origins and of evangelical religious persuasion formed a growing proportion of the population, resentment focused on the reservation of one-seventh of the colony's land (the Clergy Reserves) for the benefit of the Church of England, and on the wealth and power of the "Family Compact," a small group of officials knit tight by marriage, patronage, and conservative conviction who dominated the government of the province in the 1820s and 1830s.

In Lower Canada the situation was more complex. English and Canadien parties had taken shape in the Assembly early in the century, but Lower Canadian society was not sharply polarized by language until 1809–10. Then the impulsive governor, Sir James Henry Craig, set in motion events which threw French and English into conflict. Mistakenly equating Canadien aspirations with those of Napoleon, and perceiving them as a threat to English authority, he imprisoned leaders of the Parti Canadien without trial, twice dissolved the Assembly, and attempted to stop publication of *Le Canadien*, founded four years earlier to defend French-Canadian interests.

Through the second and third decades of the century, as immigration and economic development recast Lower Canadian society, the cleavage between French and English deepened. "In the cities," wrote the visiting Frenchman Alexis de Tocqueville in 1831, "the English make display of great wealth. Among Canadians there are but fortunes of limited extent; hence jealousies and petty irritations...." Even in the countryside many felt that "the English race...[was] expanding about them in an alarming fashion...[and] that in the end they...[would] be absorbed." Under the masthead "Our religion, our language, and our laws," *Le Canadien* continued to rally nationalist feeling. "Anything which can inflame popular passions great and small against the English is raised in this paper," reported de Tocqueville. A proposal for unification of the Canadas, pressed forward by colonial officials and English merchants in 1822, had only heightened French-Canadian fears of being enveloped by the English. For Louis-Joseph Papineau, the eloquent spokesman of the Parti Canadien who led the resistance to amalgamation, Lower Canada was a distinct and important territory to be preserved as a French and Catholic home for the *habitant*.

With Papineau increasingly prominent at the head of the Patriote movement, which grew from the Parti Canadien in 1826, criticism of the English-speaking merchants who dominated the councils and judiciary of Lower Canada was stepped up. So too were demands for reform. The legislative council was a "putrid cadaver," its members drawn from "the aristocracy of bankruptcy." England must realize, urged Papineau, that the French-Canadian-dominated Assembly could not tolerate the "loathsome and insufferable" aristocracy, whose representatives appointed to both executive and legislative councils were but "twenty tyrants assured of impunity in all their excesses." Bolstered by a convincing electoral victory in 1834, Papineau pursued his republican and nationalist ideals ever more forcefully. Meanwhile, economic circumstances in the colony worsened. Harvests were poor, and in 1837 there was a financial and commercial crisis touched off by the collapse of English and American banks. Amid the distress, one troubled contemporary wrote that "shortage is great and hardship total in Canada."

In 1837, when Britain rejected the Patriotes' demand for control of provincial expenditures by the Assembly, Patriote leaders initiated a program of public rallies. At one, in Montreal, Papineau compared the situation of Lower Canadians with that of the Americans in 1775. The agitation continued through the summer. For a few fall weeks armed Patriotes controlled parts of the countryside near Montreal. In November there was street fighting in the city. British troops were called to restore order. Many Patriote leaders were arrested; others fled to the Richelieu. Late in the month, the rebels drove back a government attack on St-Denis. But they lacked the organization, equipment, and tactical leadership to triumph for long. They were defeated at St-Charles and then crushed after fierce resistance at St-Eustache. Several hundred Patriotes were killed or injured, there was a good deal of property damage, and over five hundred insurgents were imprisoned. Papineau and some others fled to the United States. A second, smaller uprising in November 1838 was quickly put down. A dozen of those involved were executed and fifty-eight others were shipped to the penal colonies of Australia.

In Upper Canada, William Lyon Mackenzie, a fiery critic of the Family Compact, and eight hundred followers emboldened by the dispatch of Upper Canadian troops to the lower province, marched on Toronto in early December 1837 in an attempt to overthrow the administration and establish democratic government on the American plan. Armed with pitchforks, staves, and guns, but untrained and undisciplined, this motley radical army was quickly dispersed by the local militia. Opposition to the powerful Compact was widespread but few wanted rebellion. After a second futile uprising near Brantford, the rebellion ended. Mackenzie fled to the United States; two of his lieutenants were hanged; several of his supporters were banished.

Neither uprising was a success, but together they had a significant impact on colonial administration. In 1838 the constitution of Lower Canada was suspended. The British government, perceiving the need for reassessment, sent John George Lambton, Earl of Durham, to British North America as Governor General, with the responsibility of deciding upon "the form and future government" of the Canadian

Painted almost forty years after the death of William Lyon Mackenzie, this 1903 portrait by
J. W. L. Forster (based on a daguerreotype by Eli J. Palmer) shows the Reformer and first Mayor of
Toronto with the 1835 Petition of Grievances of which he was the primary author. On his right is
Patriote and radical politician Louis-Joseph Papineau, who had retired to Montebello in the *seigneurie*
of Petite-Nation by the time Napoléon Bourassa did this painting in 1858.

provinces. "Radical Jack" Durham had a plan even as he set out: to create a union of
all the British North American colonies. But Nova Scotia and New Brunswick were
uninterested, and decisive action was essential. Moreover, Durham's belief—that the
rebellions reflected "a contest between a government and a people"—was soon
revised. Once in Lower Canada, he concluded that the struggle was "not of principles, but of races"; there were "two nations warring in the bosom of a single state."
His solution was the assimilation of French Canadians. Because they were "an old
and stationary society, in a new and progressive world," this seemed inevitable to
him; it might as well be expedited by unifying Upper and Lower Canada. If this were
done, representatives of the clear majority of English-speaking colonists (some 55
per cent of the combined populations of the two provinces) would legitimately
dominate the joint assembly, and French Canadians, reduced to a minority, would
abandon their nationalist aspirations.

Left: An incident from the 1837 Rebellion. Trapped "en chemise in the middle of a group of the most Robespierre-looking ruffians, all armed with guns, long knives, and pikes" in November 1838, Jane Ellice, wife of Lord Durham's private secretary, left this watercolour portrayal of her Patriote captors.

Below: "RADICALS *enjoying* their betting *profits* after the late Election." A Tory cartoon lampooning the 1836 defeat of Mackenzie and his Reformers.

There were other radical proposals in Durham's report. Critical of the "petty, corrupt, insolent Tory clique"—the Family Compact—that monopolized power in Upper Canada, he maintained that in domestic matters colonial governments should be responsible to their electorate, which was to say that the executive (or in modern terms the Cabinet) should be drawn from, and hold the support of, the elected majority in the Assembly. He urged the creation of municipal governments and a supreme court. He argued that Clergy Reserves, intended to endow the established church, should be abandoned; that land and emigration policies should be reformed; and that British

A fine example of Théophile Hamel's easy talent for portraiture, this oil (c. 1838) is sometimes described as *Three Indian chiefs leading a delegation to Quebec*. Durham family tradition identifies the figure on the right as Lord Durham, appointed Governor General of British North America in 1838.

North Americans should be encouraged in the development of a sense of identity to resist the powerful influence of the United States.

On such an array of provocative suggestions there could be no consensus. French Canadians were outraged by a policy designed, as Bishop Lartigue of Montreal saw it, "*pour nous anglifier, c'est-à-dire nous décatholiser...*" (to anglicize us, in other words to decatholicize us). English-speaking Tories questioned Durham's sanity and dismissed his report as "disgraceful and mischievous." Reformers rejoiced at the prospect of local self-government within the fortress of Empire. And British parliamentarians, ready to unify the provinces, balked at the idea of responsible government. As they struggled to cope with industrialization and the demise of mercantilism, they were unwilling to loosen the administrative ties on which they felt colonial allegiance to the mother country depended.

Through all of this, the vigour of British North America's southern neighbour was an important influence. The American Revolution had made British officials and North American Tories wary of democratic sentiments. At the turn of the century they were uneasy at the influx of Americans into Upper Canada, and at the "Republican Principles" invoked in opposition to colonial governments. Then, in June 1812, the United States declared war on Britain and attacked the Canadas. With many of its people relatively recent arrivals from the south, Upper Canada seemed to some "a compleat American colony." Convinced that settlers there would readily cast off the yoke of British authority, American president Thomas Jefferson had believed its conquest to be a "mere matter of marching." By 1812, barely 2,200 British soldiers remained in the Canadian garrison, and Native resistance to American movement in the western Great Lakes basin had been crushed at Tippecanoe on the Wabash River. But the apparently easy pickings were elusive. Early success built on the tactical skill of Major-General Isaac Brock of the 49th Regiment raised the confidence of the Canadian militia. Tecumseh, the Shawnee chief whose people had been beaten at Tippecanoe, took the British side; Tecumseh's supporters were crucial to British successes in the western peninsula in 1812 and 1813 before he fell at Moraviantown. All in all, the Americans

The Upper Canada Preserved medal (left), struck by the Loya[l] and Patriotic Society of Upper Canada for "extraordinary instances of personal courage and fidelity in defence of the Province" in the War of 1812, but never awarded, shows the British lion protecting the Canadian beaver from the Americ[an] eagle. Running between them is the Niagara River.

Fascinating though *The Battle of Queenston* (below) may [be,] it is as inaccurate as one would expect of something drawn fr[om] memory and seeking to capture as much action as possible. O[n] October 13, 1812, some 1,300 American troops crossed the Niagara River in thirteen boats and tried to take Queenston Heights. The defending commander, Isaac Brock, was killed i[n a] first charge against the invaders, but they were eventually dri[ven] back at bayonet-point. Lithograph after Major J. B. Dennis.

were surprisingly ineffective. One of their armies was led by a general too fat to ride a horse, and at Queenston Heights militia men stood on their constitutional guarantee and refused to advance into Upper Canada as ordered. The British had their share of luck—not least when Laura Secord heard American officers discussing their plans while eating at her house and carried word of them to the garrison. Most settlers wanted to be left in peace—farmers who had found cheap land and low taxes in the British colony were far from anxious to join the American republic.

At the start of the 1813 campaign, the invaders attempted to split the Canadas by taking Kingston. But first they attacked the easier target of York (Toronto), and occupied the town, burned public buildings, and seized naval supplies. There were skirmishes in the Niagara peninsula through the summer and fall of 1813. The Americans seized Fort George, but were repulsed at Stoney Creek and Beaver Dams. The burning of Newark (Niagara-on-the-Lake) by the Americans as they evacuated Fort George led to fierce British reprisals in Buffalo. On Lake Erie, naval victory by the Americans left the lake under their control for the rest of the war. The Americans again crossed the Niagara but failed to retake Fort George. In the dark night of July 25, the tired forces met at Lundy's Lane, within earshot of the Falls, in a bitter, confused skirmish which ended in a stalemate.

The conflict was also joined along Lake Champlain and the St. Lawrence, and on the seaboard. Troops from Halifax, led by the able military commander Sir John Sherbrooke, Lieutenant-Governor of Nova Scotia, invaded Maine to take Castine, and the British continued to hold much of Maine for the war's duration. In August 1814 they attacked and burned Washington, and the White House. But for most New Englanders and Nova Scotians the war was incidental; it barely affected coastal trade between the Americans and the British. Reflecting as much, the Treaty of Ghent signed in Belgium on Christmas Eve 1814 by British and American negotiators agreed to return to the status quo of 1811. Upper Canada, remarked some of those who lived there, had been "preserved" for Britain. In the 175 years since, many have found heroes and heroines—Brock and Secord and Tecumseh not least—among those who participated in the war. But in the end it was a local conflict.

Anglo-American agreements in 1817 and 1818 disarmed the Great Lakes and established the 49th parallel as the southern boundary of British territory between Lake of the Woods and the Rocky Mountains, but American ambitions and American influences remained a cause of concern to many British administrators. In the 1820s and 1830s vast sums were spent on fortifying Kingston and on building the

Rideau Canal between that city and Bytown (Ottawa) to provide a more secure, and alternative, water link between Montreal and the Great Lakes in case the Americans ever seized control of the St. Lawrence. Rising numbers of Methodists and Baptists in the pioneer communities of Upper Canada were considered an American threat to the Church of England. And both American schoolbooks—"in which Great Britain was not spoken of in the most respectful terms"—and American teachers—who would instill in children a "nasal twang," fanaticism in religion, and inveterate hatred of the British political system—were roundly criticized. If paranoia had the better of truth in these assertions, it fed on the perceived fragility of British institutions in the remote interior.

Such anxieties were only confirmed by the last throes of the 1837 rebellions. William Lyon Mackenzie received an enthusiastic welcome in Buffalo after his flight from Toronto, and in the northern states he and other refugees quickly found support for a campaign of border raids intended to generate fear and uncertainty in the British colonies. In 1838, some of the rebels formed a secret society called the Hunters' Lodges, with the aim of freeing Upper Canada from "British thraldom," and they made several small incursions into Upper Canada. The Lodges were quickly dominated by Americans. By some estimates their numbers exceeded forty thousand. Among the most provocative of their attempts to destabilize relations between Britain and the United States were the burning of the steamship *Sir Robert Peel* in the Thousand Islands and the blowing up of the Brock monument on Queenston Heights in 1840. Although Louis-Joseph Papineau refused to support such border raids into Lower Canada, and the first such effort in February 1838 was a humiliating failure, its leaders organized an impressive underground movement—Les Frères Chasseurs—in the colony. Late in 1838, several thousand insurgents mounted a second uprising. It was quickly put down, but bitterness about the events of 1837–38 lingered among both French and English.

Significantly, oft-repeated American entreaties to throw off the tyranny and oppression of Britain were never widely persuasive. Between 1760 and 1840, the colonies were irrevocably bound to the mother country by links of sentiment and fiscal dependence as well as by lines of authority and patterns of trade. French Canadians apart, most people in the colonies traced their roots back to Britain; considerable numbers of them had come north to British territory after the American Revolution; and by the standards of the day British expenditures in the colonies were enormous. Year by year these outlays for military construction and the maintenance of troops put money into circulation. Indeed, the garrison market for Upper

Canadian wheat was so large that merchant Richard Cartwright had concluded in 1792, "As long as the British government shall think proper to hire people to come over to eat our flour, we shall go on very well."

Peopling the Provinces: By Chance and Catastrophe

For those who came to the colonies, the process of occupying the land and pushing back the wilderness assumed epic proportions. Colonial societies were forged in the struggle for survival in new environments. Colonial economies depended upon the labour of men and women, as well as local resources, for their expansion. When Chief Justice Smith of Canada wrote, in 1787, "that *Men* not *Trees* constitute the wealth of a Country," he identified a basic equation: people equal power and prosperity. Size was the measure of success and progress. By this simple metric, the years between 1760 and 1840 saw remarkable growth. European population numbers—the only ones colonists counted—increased sixteen-fold; by 1841 there were over 1.5 million non-aboriginal people in British North America. Native peoples, whose numbers had shrunk through eighty years, were now outnumbered ten to one.

Between 1760 and 1800, immigration to British North America was largely a matter of chance. Britain had no coherent plan for the settlement of its transatlantic territories. Convinced that emigration would sap the strength of the nation, the English Parliament by and large opposed the movement of British citizens to the colonies. So British officials, anxious to secure Catholic, Acadian Nova Scotia after the foundation of Halifax in 1749, encouraged settlement by "Foreign Protestants" drawn in the main from the Rhine Valley. With defence in mind, they also encouraged soldiers whose regiments were disbanded in America to remain there, by grants of colonial land. But for fifteen years after 1760, it was assumed that Canada and Nova Scotia would be settled by pioneers moving northward from the older colonies of British America. Proclamations announced the availability of land in both areas to residents of Massachusetts, Connecticut, Pennsylvania, and New York. Only Nova Scotia lured significant numbers, and this only so long as lands west of the Appalachians remained closed to settlement. Settlers and fur traders gravitated to Quebec and Montreal, but their numbers were small. Few migrants, wrote Guy Carleton, the Governor of Quebec, would "prefer the long inhospitable winters of Canada to the more cheerful climate and more fruitful soil of His Majesty's southern

Encampment of the Loyalists at Johnstown, A New Settlement, on the Banks of the St. Lawrence, in Canada. Robert Hunter, a young Englishman on his way to see Niagara Falls, visited Johnstown (present-day Cornwall) in 1785. "The settling of the Loyalists," he concluded, "is one of the best things George III ever did. It does one's heart good to see how well they are all going on, and seem to be perfectly contented with their situation." Watercolour (1784) by British army topographer and surveyor James Peachey.

provinces"; barring a "catastrophe shocking to think of," the colony would remain the domain of Canadiens.

Individual initiatives brought some migrants across the Atlantic. In the 1770s, approximately 1,000 people were encouraged to leave farms and rising rents in Yorkshire for land on the estate of Michael Francklin, a leading Nova Scotian official. A decade earlier the energetic and persuasive speculator Alexander McNutt had brought 600 Irish folk to his enormous land grants in Nova Scotia. Such was the perceived "danger to Ireland of withdrawing so many of the population," however, that this practice was immediately proscribed. Ignoring regulations, a steady trickle of Irish went to Newfoundland with the fishery, and in the years after 1770 small numbers of Scots migrated from the Highlands to lands bordering the Gulf of St. Lawrence.

Far more consequential were the migrations precipitated by the American Revolution. In 1783 and 1784 vast numbers of troops and civilian refugees who had taken the British side in the American Revolution left the newly independent states for British North America. Approximately 35,000 of these "Loyalists" went to Nova Scotia and some 9,000 to Quebec. Their impact was immense. The population of peninsular Nova Scotia was doubled; north of the Bay of Fundy, where there had been fewer than 1,750 people of European descent in 1780, 14,000 or 15,000 Loyalists dominated the new colony of New Brunswick. Perhaps 1,000 more settled on the still sparsely peopled islands of Saint John (Prince Edward Island after 1798) and Cape Breton (which became a separate colony in 1784, and remained so until 1820). In the interior, approximately 7,000 Loyalists occupied hitherto almost empty territory at the head of Lake Erie, in the Niagara peninsula, around the Bay of Quinte, and along the north shore of the St. Lawrence. Another 1,000 or 2,000 settled near the mouth of the Richelieu River, beside Lake St. Francis, and on the lower Ottawa River.

As a group, the Loyalists shared little but the experience of relocation. Military and civilian; black, white, and Iroquois; educated and unlettered; rich and poor; they were drawn from old stock and recent immigrant families from all of the former colonies, and from all walks of life. If holders of Harvard degrees, former owners of abandoned plantations, people with substantial fortunes, and office-holders with pedigrees stretching back to the *Mayflower* loom large in the folk mythology that surrounds the Loyalists, they were indubitably a minority. Most Loyalists were ordinary people: small farmers, artisans, labourers, craftsmen, and their families. Among those who went to Nova Scotia were approximately 3,000 blacks, most of them runaway slaves, who clustered in separate settlements near Shelburne, Digby, and Chedabucto, as well as in Halifax. Rarely were their hopes of independence realized, and in 1792 almost 1,200 of them left Nova Scotia for Sierra Leone. Among those who moved north of the Great Lakes were almost 2,000 Native Americans, mainly Six Nations Iroquois under the leadership of the Mohawk chief Joseph Brant, who were granted land on the Grand River in return for their loyalty to the Crown and their losses in the war.

For all the Loyalists' passionate dec-

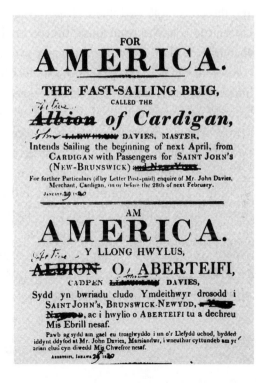

Among the thousands of migrants who came to British North America before 1840 were several hundred Welsh families. This poster from Wales, recycled after the wreck of the *Albion* in November 1819, is a reminder of the hazards of transatlantic sailing, and a good example of the information available to prospective migrants.

larations of loyalty—such as the epitaph, "He was known for his Loyalty to his King in 1775" on Thomas Gilbert's gravemarker in Gagetown, New Brunswick—few among them were ideologues. Caught up in a struggle that divided communities, many had reasoned that the insurgent Whigs could not succeed against British authority. Others likely chose the "Loyal" side for no better reason than the decisions of their friends (or enemies). In the event, their bets were on the wrong horse, and they left when their cause was lost. Still others came north simply because land and provisions were being handed out. Certainly, according to Governor John Parr of Nova Scotia, "the generality of those" who came to Shelburne, a major disembarkation point, were "not much burthened with Loyalty, a spacious name which they made use of."

Whatever their motives for migration, most Loyalists faced hardship in their new locations. Some complained almost as a matter of course, but for most the difficulties were real enough. Requesting medical aid, a group of Nova Scotian Loyalists summed up the plight of many in recounting their suffering from "hard labor, incommodious Lodging open Huts Long Fastings and Unwholesome Provisions." Discontent was a natural corollary of the conditions created by so massive an influx of population. Thousands had to be fed. Surveys and grants had to be made before the newcomers could take up their land. Demand for provisions, supplies, and accommodation drove up prices. And in the fluid social and economic conditions of the frontier there were tensions between Loyalists, between Loyalists and pre-Loyalists, and between Loyalists and those who followed them. "Late-Loyalists," so-called, were especially numerous in Upper Canada. Attracted there by the ready availability of good, cheap land, and encouraged, after 1791, by Lieutenant-Governor Simcoe, who admired the agricultural competence of American pioneers, settlers from New York and Pennsylvania surged into the colony. Among them were Quakers, Mennonites, and other pacifists unpopular at home for their neutrality in 1776–83. By 1812 approximately eighty thousand people lived in Upper Canada. Some 80 per cent of them were of American origin, but Loyalists and their descendants accounted for less than a quarter of the total.

Like most immigrants, those who came to the colonies were relatively young—in community after community, children and young adults were in the majority. Births were consistently more common than deaths, and women, who typically married in their early twenties, generally had several children. The result was a powerful dynamic, suggested by the experience of a New Brunswick missionary, who married 48 couples, baptized 295 infants, and buried 17 people between 1795 and 1800. Although there was little immigration to Quebec in the late eighteenth century, similar circumstances prevailed. The population of the colony actually doubled every twenty-five to twenty-seven years through the century—an increase of approximately 2.8 per cent a year, a rate similar to those now current in many African and Asian nations faced with a "population explosion."

The "sad result of passions and potatoes"?

With the turn of the nineteenth century, transatlantic migration to British North America quickened. Initially people came almost exclusively from the Highlands of Scotland; after 1815 they came from all parts of the British Isles but particularly from Ireland. The numbers involved were enormous. Official figures (which are probably low) counted a million migrants from the British Isles to the North American colonies in the first half of the century. Fully 60 per cent of them crossed the Atlantic before 1842, when the English novelist Charles Dickens, visiting Montreal, saw immigrants "grouped in hundreds on the public wharfs about their chests and boxes."

These migrations were largely the result of changing circumstances in Britain, where population was increasing significantly more quickly than in other European countries. No more than thirteen million in 1780, the population of the United Kingdom exceeded twenty-four million by 1831. Contemporaries generally attributed this, with the Reverend Thomas Malthus whose acclaimed *An Essay on the Principle of Population* was published in 1798, to a rise in the birthrate. At the same time, agricultural and industrial revolutions fractured traditional patterns of British life. In England, the enclosure movement replaced open fields, commons, and collective farming with compact individual holdings. In Scotland, English attempts to break down traditional clan society and develop the Highlands saw the glens turned into sheep pastures. And in Ireland, cultivation of the potato allowed a rapidly expanding rural population to survive by dividing and subdividing farms, to the point that by 1821 Ireland had the highest rural population density in Europe.

Everywhere the consequences were profoundly disruptive. By 1815, the Irish had become, according to French historian Eli Halévy, "a vast proletariat, ignorant, miserably poor, superstitious and disorderly." Initially, Scottish landlords endeavoured to resettle displaced crofters on the coast, to fish and to work in the kelp industry. When kelping declined after 1815, attempts to improve the efficiency of agriculture in the Highlands continued with the large-scale and often brutal evictions popularly known as the Clearances. With new crop rotations, scientific farming, and other agricultural improvements, the productivity of English farming soared. Deprived of grazing rights on open commons, squatters and small holders were forced to enter rural labour, to migrate to the growing towns, or to win a subsistence from an acre or two of ground and contract work at the handloom or knitting frame. These choices often led to poverty. The wages paid to rural labour were desperately low. For unskilled workers, life in the early industrial towns was generally harsh; factory discipline was unfamiliar; work was often arduous and sometimes dangerous; hours were long, pay was inadequate, and living conditions were difficult. In earlier years it had been possible to earn a reasonable living by spinning or weaving at home under contract, but in the early nineteenth century, technological improvements and the spread of factory production reduced both the opportunities and the remuneration of such work. Long hours yielded families but a penny or two a day, scarcely enough for a meagre diet of meal, buttermilk, and potatoes.

The destitution and unemployment were made worse after Wellington finally defeated Napoleon at Waterloo in 1815. Thousands and thousands of soldiers, sailors, and others engaged in the war in Europe came home to seek jobs in a country adjusting to the decline of wartime industries and the reduced price of wheat that came with peace. Respected observers estimated the number of indigents at almost 15 per cent of the population of England, and suggested that 120,000 pauper children—counterparts of Charles Dickens' Oliver Twist—ran the streets of London. Clergymen warned parishioners, as the Reverend Thomas Malthus had urged them to, of the "impropriety and even immorality of marrying" when they could not maintain their children, but this was hardly a solution to so vast a problem.

In the age of Britain's industrial supremacy, argued Patrick Colquhoun in 1814 in *A Treatise on the Population, Wealth, and Resources of the British Empire*, the answer lay in emigration. Overpopulation and economic stagnation could be alleviated by migration to the colonies, where people would consume British manufactured goods and provide raw materials for British factories. These were arguments whose time had come. By 1815 the benefits of emigration were widely acknowledged. In February of that year the first official notice on emigration since 1749 appeared in Edinburgh newspapers under the heading "Liberal Encouragement to Settlers." For the next twenty-five years (and more) emigration—described by Lord Byron in his poem *Don Juan* (1824) as "That sad result of passions and potatoes—/ Two weeds which pose our economic Catos"—was the focus of considerable interest in Britain. Government-

Not all the publicity about immigration was favourable. This anonymous lampoon, published in London around 1820, mocked those who set out for the colonies with visions of a genteel life, and warned readers of the dangers of dealing with land sharks.

assisted settlement schemes, initiatives of large landowners, select-committee inquiries, philanthropic ventures, regulations to control the "emigrant trade," and "colonization theories" shaped the flow of people. Still, migration from Britain to British North America during these years was, overwhelmingly, a movement of families and individuals from difficult conditions in their homeland to the most accessible of the colonies. Relocation was the pragmatic response of people whose lives had been disrupted; most of them were relatively poor (though not impoverished); their hopes—for modest comfort and security—were limited. There was little utopian dreaming in all of this.

Migrants often endured atrocious hardships in crossing the Atlantic. Many of the vessels engaged in the "emigrant trade" were poorly maintained. The passage was often stormy. Voyages might last eleven or twelve weeks; rarely was Quebec reached in fewer than thirty days. People were crowded, in astonishing numbers, into dark, unsanitary accommodations below decks. Not until 1835 were shipmasters required to provide essential supplies—usually no more than water, biscuits, and oatmeal. What this meant is sadly evident in the correspondence of emigrant agents and officials: "filthy beds"; "fetid stench"; "hundreds…huddled together." Vessels engaged in the timber trade generally carried emigrants on their westward voyages. To accommodate them, two tiers of rough bunks, each bunk 1.8 metres (6 feet) square, might be built along each side of the lower (cargo) deck. (In a 400-ton vessel this deck would be approximately 30 metres/100 feet long and 7.5 metres/25 feet wide.) In this space, with thirty-two bunks on each side and no light or ventilation save from the hatchways, 200 emigrants could be carried across the Atlantic under the regulations in force in 1803, and 300 under those of 1828 (when an additional central row of bunks would probably have been added). And many vessels carried more passengers than legally allowed. By the time the *James* arrived in Halifax in the 1820s, 5 of the 160 passengers who had embarked in Waterford had died at sea; 35 more had been put ashore in Newfoundland, too sick to continue; and the rest had typhus, which the Lieutenant-Governor attributed to "their scanty nourishment during the voyage…the crowded and filthy state of the ship, and…a want of medical assistance."

In 1832 cholera took a heavy toll in the close confines of the emigrant vessels. Through that summer, vessels reached British North American ports after harrowing voyages of death and affliction. Although emigrant ships were stopped at Grosse Ile, thirty miles downstream from Quebec, and quarantine regulations were strengthened, the disease reached both Quebec and Montreal in June. Within a week more than 250 people were ill, and for a black period in mid-month there were over 100 deaths a day in each city. Boards of health and quarantine sheds were established along the St. Lawrence, but panic was widespread. On June 19 the Jewish merchant Alexander Hart wrote from Montreal:

We none of us go into town, numbers are moving into the country. Yesterday 34 Corps passed our house, today till this hour 23—besides what goes to the old burial Ground and the Catholic ground 12 carts are employed by the Board of Health to carry away the dead who are interred without prayers.

Schools and shops were closed and the only business was in one-inch-thick boards for coffins. In September, when the epidemic ended, it had claimed almost 3,500 victims in Quebec, almost 2,000 in Montreal, and several hundred in Upper Canada and the eastern provinces. Two years later, a second epidemic killed 1,250 in Upper and Lower Canada, and others in Nova Scotia and New Brunswick.

Between 1801 and 1815 some 10,000 Scots drawn from many parts of the Highlands and islands arrived. One man—Thomas Douglas, Earl of Selkirk—played a pivotal role in this movement. Wealthy, energetic, deeply interested in the plight of the Highlanders, fascinated by the prospects of America, and attracted by the ideas of the early political economists, Selkirk committed himself to establishing a Scottish colony in British North America. In 1803, he accompanied 800 emigrants from the Hebrides to lands he had acquired in Prince Edward Island. The next year he was in Upper Canada, acquiring land near Lake St. Clair for a second venture to be called Baldoon. But the marshy site was unhealthy and with Upper Canadian officials luke-warm towards it, Selkirk's vision of a prosperous Gaelic community serving as a rampart against American expansion and influence in Upper Canada was stillborn. By 1812 Selkirk had concentrated his interests in the West after receiving an enor-mous land grant, centred on the Red and Assiniboine rivers, from the Hudson's Bay Company. Almost 350 Scots emigrated to the Red River before 1815, but the little colony suffered many difficulties, including resistance from the North-West Company, floods, and locust plagues. Expansion in the 1820s came not from the steady infusion of Scottish settlers Selkirk had envisaged, but from the retired HBC men who brought their Native wives to the settlement, and from the growing Catholic Métis population, linked to the Montreal fur trade by blood and by their role as buffalo hunters and provisioners. More important than any of these ventures, however, was Selkirk's book published in 1805—*Observations on the Present State of the Highlands of Scotland, with a View of the Causes and Probable Consequences of Emigration*. In this he challenged the arguments against emigration and defended the right of those who clung to their independence and created farms amid the forests of Nova Scotia, Prince Edward Island, and Upper Canada to maintain their traditional way of life; it had a major impact on public attitudes towards emigration in Britain.

For a decade after 1815 the British government—facing the domestic misery that followed peace with France, concerned that such emigration as there was tended to run to the recently hostile United States, and perceiving a need to encourage British settlement in American-dominated Upper Canada—fostered settlement in the colonies by offering assisted passages to qualified people. In all, approximately 6,500 disbanded soldiers, unemployed weavers and their families from the Scottish lowlands, Catholics from some of the poorest parts of Ireland, and others were car-ried across the Atlantic and given land in the Peterborough, Perth, and Rideau River areas of Upper Canada. Some described these efforts as "shovelling out paupers," but by and large they succeeded in providing immigrants with a new start. Moreover, the gratitude of those involved undoubtedly encouraged further emigration. But assisted-

Fumigation fires and a full moon behind ominous clouds cast an eerie light over the marketplace in front of Notre Dame Cathedral in Quebec's Upper Town during the cholera epidemic of 1832. Painter Joseph Légaré was a member of the city's Board of Health.

settlement schemes were also expensive and they were judged too costly to continue.

Corporate colonization ventures soon assumed some of the functions of the government schemes. Chartered in England in 1824, the Canada Company, for example, acquired almost 2.5 million acres of Upper Canadian land, including more than a million acres adjoining Lake Huron. By 1830, 50,000 acres of company land had been sold, Guelph was a comfortable little village, and development was proceeding in the vicinity of Goderich. Despite allegations that its officials often acted in a high-handed manner and the claim of one of its most colourful employees, William "Tiger" Dunlop, that the company neglected settlers' rights, many believed that its vigorous improvement program did much to stimulate growth in Upper Canada in the 1830s. The Canada Company had agents in all the major ports of Britain and Ireland, and along with other companies, such as the New Brunswick and Nova Scotia Land Company and the British American Land Company active in the Eastern Townships of Quebec, circulated maps, pamphlets, and advertisements through most of the cities, towns, and villages of Britain. Such publicity encouraged individuals and families to migrate to British North America during the 1820s and 1830s.

Faced with rural unrest in the early 1830s—the so-called "Captain Swing" disturbances manifest in barn-burnings and destruction of threshing machines by farm labourers demanding higher wages and winter work—many parishes in southern England sponsored emigration as a form of humanitarian aid for the poverty-stricken and unemployed. In total, some 20,000 migrants came to the Canadas this way before changing circumstances in Britain and the rebellions of 1837 put a stop to the process. Local, diffuse, short-lived, and poorly documented, these initiatives largely escaped the attentions of historians until Wendy Cameron and Mary McDougall Maude investigated the work of the Petworth Emigration Committee, which sent over 1,800 people from Sussex and neighbouring areas to Upper Canada in specially chartered vessels between 1832 and 1837. Most of those who crossed the Atlantic under this scheme, they conclude, adapted well, improved their circumstances, and made significant contributions to the development of some parts of the colony. Whether their leaving helped the parishes they left behind is less clear. On balance, the efforts and expenditures of the Petworth Committee likely aided the new world more than the old.

The basic point to remember is that people in Britain were on the move. Millions relocated during the early nineteenth century, moving from village to village, crossing parish lines, gravitating to growing cities, or taking ship to the colonies. Among those who opted to leave their homeland, the decision and destination was often swayed by pamphlets, guidebooks, and descriptions whose basic message of reassurance and advice hardly varied. Among the hundreds touting British North America were A. Picken's *The Canadas, as they at Present Commend Themselves to the Enterprize of Emigrants, Colonists and Capitalists*, and William Catermole's *Emigration: The Advantages of Emigration to Canada*. Agents combed areas notorious for their "redundant" population adding immediacy to the written pitch. Settlers already in the colonies sent cash or prepaid tickets to their relatives. Shipping agents travelled the British countryside recruiting passengers. Perhaps most influential of all, the letters of those who had come to the colonies before 1820 told of success and the potential of the new land: "Timber we have in abundance"; "we have plenty of good food and grog..."; "Malthus would not be understood here"; "Pray keep Anthony in the milling business... for by that in this country he may do well"; "the prospects for you here are ten to one above what they are in the old country"; "I do not like Canada so well as England; but in England there is too many men, and here there is not enough." Because pioneers rarely wrote of the hardships they faced or the doubts they bore, the message was compelling. By comparison with Britain, the new country offered high wages, cheap land, and good prospects. So tens of thousands decided to cross the Atlantic. Farms were sold, small savings scraped together, and new lives started.

Quite how these lives took shape depended in part on when and where they began. Because the fishing industry had created strong ties between English ports and specific settlements in Newfoundland, migrants from Somerset tended to concentrate in Trinity Bay while those from Devon clustered in Conception Bay. In similar fashion the Irish gravitated to St. John's and the southern Avalon peninsula. Because most came from relatively few parishes in south-western England and south-eastern Ireland, new arrivals were likely to settle among people who shared a familiar background. Their social conventions, their beliefs, even their traditional ways of speaking and singing were not dramatically out of place. And these tended to persist. Indeed, in Newfoundland—whose isolated and relatively remote settlements received few new-comers after mid-century—such distinct traits survived into the twentieth century.

In Upper Canada, in contrast, mixing was the norm. Although Scots clustered in some areas and the Irish, who were the majority of those arriving after 1815, commonly occupied poorer land back from the already-occupied lakefront north and east

John Galt

Far left: Scottish novelist John Galt, author of a life of Byron and several other works, came to Upper Canada on several occasions and was the Canada Company's superintendent there from 1826 to 1829; in 1827 he founded the town of Guelph. His writings show little Canadian influence.

Left: William "Tiger" Dunlop—journalist, surgeon, and politician—came to Canada with Galt in 1826 to administer the vast Huron Tract for the Canada Company; unlike Galt, he wrote several works based on his time in Canada. Both portraits are by Daniel Maclise.

This idyllic view—one of a series of illustrations designed to attract immigrants to the New Brunswick and Nova Scotia Land Company settlement—conveys an utterly unrealistic idea of the grinding labour settlers would face. *Process of Clearing the Town-Plot, at Stanley Octr 1834*: lithograph by S. Russell after a drawing by W. P. Kay, published in *Sketches in New Brunswick* (London, 1836).

of Kingston, both groups included Catholics and Protestants. Few Scots, Irish, and English settled in townships occupied exclusively by their countryfolk and even if they did so they were likely among people from very different parts of their home country. Thus settlers encountered practices and assumptions different from their own, and inevitably their old ways began to change. Furthermore, carving a farm from a hundred acres of Upper Canadian forest required skills vastly different from those necessary to feed a family from an acre of Irish ground or to meet the demands of an English tenancy. Most settlers developed broadly similar mixed farms to provide for their needs. The few items that had a ready market were widely grown, but kitchen gardens sometimes revealed traditional food and tastes. In some houses, furniture styles, fabric designs, and the use of space echoed the old country; here and there house façades reflected ideas carried across the Atlantic. But in general, the circumstances of New World life blunted the sharp edges of tradition. In Upper Canada more than in the Maritime colonies, and there more than in Newfoundland, the intricate variety of regional accents, beliefs, and practices that marked the Old World was submerged in a practical amalgam of North American ways that made the colonies new worlds indeed.

Work and Life

Consider four images. First the fisherman. Hardy, weatherbeaten, intimately familiar with the winds and tides of his local shore, capable of turning his hand to many things, squeezing a hard living from the treacherous sea—a figure rendered familiar by the words "Ise the bye who builds the boat / And ise the bye that sails her / Ise the bye who catches the fish / And takes them home to Liza." Next the fur-trader, represented by the strong-armed, free-spirited *voyageur*, his dress distinguished by bright sash and colourful toque, his life a mix of danger, hard work, and camaraderie; or by the "salty Orcadian," penny-pinching and docile, neither particularly imaginative nor reluctant to accept his place in the hierarchical structure of the Hudson's Bay Company. Thirdly, the lumberer, the settler who spends his winters "trivin away at all kinds of lumberin" to the detriment of his farm, according to some; the larger-than-life shantyman who ends months of isolation and dangerous work in the woods with an extended springtime bout of drunken carousing, according to others; one way or another he is a "character of spendthrift habits and villainous and vagabond principles" against whom more respectable settlers are advised to lock up their daughters. And finally the farmer, the sturdy yeoman whose life is "a pursuit of innocence and peace," who derives "his pedigree from the patriarchs," and is supported by nature's tribute; the man who settles each evening at the fireside of his snug cottage, to admire the virtue, health, and happiness of his family and be "charmed by the profitable humming of the spinning wheel."

These common perceptions of the men of early British North America create a colourful picture of the economic foundations on which settlement in the colonies rested. There were many other ways in which people made livings, of course. Small towns had their storekeepers, clergymen, shoemakers, carriage makers and so on; larger ones had their lawyers, merchants and businessmen. And none of this takes account of the vital work of women in town and countryside through this period. But fishing, fur-trading, lumbering and farming have become the standards upon which colonial economies are seen to have rested—in economists' terms they were the "staple trades" of British North America—and those engaged in these activities stand as recognizable "Canadian" types. Like most stereotypes, however, such popular images combine a few grains of truth with large measures of invention. They are the stuff of legends and moralistic tales, caricatures rather than portraits. Their continuing currency, in literature and in drama, and in museums that celebrate and replicate "more leisurely" colonial times, demands fuller consideration of the roles that these activities played in the lives of our predecessors.

"Who Ever Knew a Fisherman Thrive?"

Between 1760 and 1780 the "Newfoundland fishery" was essentially a seasonal enterprise conducted from Europe. It was disrupted by press gangs and privateers during the American Revolution, and when the trade resumed after 1783 there was a glut of dried cod. Prices fell and merchants suffered heavy losses. Several bankruptcies followed. With the resumption of war between Britain and France in 1793, the migratory fishery declined, and by 1800, permanent residents made up 90 per cent of Newfoundland's summer population and produced 95 per cent of its codfish exports. Suddenly, reported a British naval officer, the island had "more the appearance of a Colony than a fishery from the great number of People who have annually imperceptibly remained the Winter who have Houses, Land and Family's"—a transformation quickly consolidated by a dramatic increase in the proportion of women and children migrating there.

These developments revolutionized life in Newfoundland. Into the 1770s, the fishery had involved three distinct groups. Merchants, usually resident in England or Ireland, organized the trade, operated stores in Newfoundland, and participated in a far-flung network of international exchange. Boatkeepers (or planters), either resident or migratory, owned the boats and equipment of the inshore fishery, and acquired supplies from the merchants to whom they sold their catch. Servants (resident or migratory) made up the third group. They fished for the boatkeepers or those merchants who operated boats on their own account. But the shrinking pool of indentured or migratory labour, and rising equipment and food costs (which doubled while fish prices increased by half), squeezed the boatkeepers especially hard. More and more, they drew their crews from among their kin, while wives and children worked tending the catch on shore. In effect, the boatkeepers slid down the status ladder to become ordinary fishermen. As they did so, they fed themselves by cultivating potatoes and garden crops, keeping a sow or two, hunting, and perhaps gathering wild fruits and berries. Coincidentally, seal fishing increased, the returns from it usually providing small but valuable supplements to the fisherman's earnings. St. John's became the commercial centre of Newfoundland. Settlements along the coasts, known locally as outports, received supplies by sea from St. John's and forwarded their catch directly to that city's merchants. Barter replaced cash in these exchanges. Gradually the number of outport merchants fell, and the artisans who had built the boats and made the barrels for the fishery largely disappeared from the outlying settlements, as families themselves took up these crafts in their increasingly closed, self-sufficient communities.

So the scattered, isolated settlements of Newfoundland began to assume their typical nineteenth- and twentieth-century form. In essence, they simplified with time, as the differences in status and occupation among the settlers eroded. Gradually and paradoxically they became more egalitarian just as the specialization associated with modernity began to differentiate the world beyond the island. Life within these communities, dependent on the resources of a narrow band of land and sea, and centred around families closely linked by blood and marriage, was intensely local and highly traditional. Each family turned its energies to an enormous variety of tasks during the year, and each member of the household developed a wide range of skills, from mending nets to shearing sheep and from curing fish to barrelling pork. At busy times of the year the entire family would work together, but in general there was a clear division of labour between the sexes. Men fished, cut wood, did the heavy work in the fields, and hunted and trapped. They mended nets and repaired boats. Women were responsible for the gardens, the cows, and the poultry. They picked potatoes and berries, and helped to cure fish and make hay. They also looked after the interior of the house. From such a demanding routine people gained a living but little more. Dwellings were modest—many, said a visitor to Trinity Bay in 1819, "consist only of a ground floor"; although the best of them were clapboarded, most were "built of logs left rough and uneven on the inside and the outside," and they had "only one fireplace in a very large kitchen." Material comforts were few, and any decline in the price or the catch of fish was likely to produce "appalling poverty and misery." After the harsh winters, low catches, and poor seal fishery of 1816–17, Methodist preacher George Cubit wrote from St. John's that "Insurrection & Famine have been staring us in the face all the winter—I fear Sir that Newfoundland is almost ruined."

The fishing industry in the Gulf of St. Lawrence experienced similar hardships. The gulf fishery was a multi-faceted enterprise centred on a cluster of ports from Paspébiac on Chaleur Bay to Arichat and Chéticamp on Cape Breton, and employing "migrants" from the Channel Islands, skilled shore workers from Quebec, *engagés* (servants), and "operative fishermen" who owned their own boats. As in

Although many details are incorrect, and no place in British North America looked quite like this (those trees!), Duhamel Du Monceau's 1769 view illustrates the skills (gutting, splitting, and salting) and labour required for the production of dry cod.

Newfoundland, individual fishermen were crucial to the trade because their boats gave them ready access to the fishing grounds. But they depended on merchants to carry their catch to distant markets; almost invariably they required gear and provisions beyond those they could supply themselves; and, ever short of capital, they were vulnerable to the instabilities of the fishery: bad fish runs, inclement weather (which made it difficult to dry fish properly and produced a "poor cure"), and fluctuating prices were recurrent difficulties on these coasts. By supplying such fishermen in advance, against repayment in fish in the fall, merchants established a measure of control over a trade that was notoriously difficult to manage because of its scattered, unpredictable character. To do so involved them in some risk— fishermen might abscond; in poor seasons returns might not equal advances—and merchants kept a shrewd eye on both price margins and the character of "their" fishermen. But, more seriously, debt and dependency were the common lot of fishermen who relied, as most did, on credit. Answering his own question, "Who ever knew a Fisherman thrive?," Loyalist William Paine pointedly described those who lived by this hard trade as "ever... *poor* and *miserable*."

Wherever it operated—in Newfoundland, the Gulf, or the south shore of Nova

Scotia—the credit exchange ("truck") system left fishing families with meagre, if any, cash surpluses. They bought very few luxuries and kept purchases to a minimum. Those they did make—of molasses, or iron—were generally of goods from abroad. There was virtually no incentive for the development of local manufacturing, and the fishing communities neither needed roads nor demanded development of land back from the coast. Of ship- and boat-building there was some, but its scale and its opportunities for employment were small. Moreover, a number of factors—the continuing reliance on imported provisions, thin, acidic soils, a late, foggy spring, and the summer labour demands of the fishery itself—restricted local farming; nowhere on the fishing coasts was it more than a supplement to subsistence. Such profits as there were tended to concentrate in the trading centres that controlled the fishery—Jersey in the distant Channel Islands, St. John's, and Halifax—while harsh toil yielded a meagre day-to-day existence for the fishing families of the rugged Atlantic coast.

"Furs Picked Out and Traded"

Divided between the St. Lawrence and Hudson Bay, but heavily concentrated in Montreal, the fur trade was seriously disrupted by the Seven Years War. The hostilities actually began in the Ohio Valley, two years before France and England officially declared war in 1756. Cut off from the St. Lawrence, most French posts in the Saskatchewan country closed before the fall of Quebec, and by 1760 the English traders on Hudson Bay had a monopoly of western furs. But their pre-eminence was short-lived. With their impressive skills and experience, and with brandy and high-quality English goods to exchange, French-Canadian *voyageurs*, interpreters and traders soon, and again, became formidable competitors for the furs of the West. Early in the 1770s the Cree Wapinesiw, who had brought twenty or thirty canoes a year to York Factory between 1755 and 1770, conveyed, through an intermediary, his hope to Hudson's Bay Company factor Andrew Graham that "you will knot Be angre with him as has Drank So much Brandy this winter he canot Com." The willingness of the Montreal traders to mingle with the Native peoples, and their supplies of ammunition, tobacco, and liquor meant, concluded Graham, that "every inducement to visit the Company's Factories is forgot, and the prime furs are picked out and traded. The refuse is tied up and brought down to us."

Through most of these years of vigorous expansion, the Montreal-based trade

The original Fort Garry was built by the Hudson's Bay Company between 1817 and 1822, at the junction of the Red and Assiniboine rivers, and named after Nicholas Garry, who helped arrange the merger of the HBC and the North West Company in 1821. The stone-walled Upper Fort Garry seen in this view (c. 1884) by H. A. Strong was begun in 1835 at a site just to the west, and the following year it became the administrative centre of Assiniboia.

was a fragmented, highly competitive business. With the conquest the monopoly of New France gave way to a trade pursued by individuals, partnerships, and loose coalitions among them. Competition was often fierce—Peter Pond was twice implicated in the deaths of rival traders—but gradually firmer groupings emerged. Foremost among them was the North West Company (NWC), dominated by Scots who first combined their resources in 1776. In 1779 the company's sixteen shares were divided among nine partnerships, and a year later the group was expanded further. Competitors remained, but the most powerful of them were added to a new coalition in 1787 and allied to the company by co-operative agreements in the early 1790s. Then Jay's Treaty, signed by the United States and Britain in 1794, forced British traders out of American territory and the area south-west of the Great Lakes. Some of them joined the NWC in 1795, but others remained independent and began to challenge the Company in the interior. To strengthen their position, in 1798 the Forsythe–Richardson and Leith–James companies formed a New North West Company (also known as the XY Company after the identifying mark on its bales of furs). They were soon joined by Alexander Mackenzie and other wintering partners of the original NWC who were unhappy with their standing in that organization. Bitter and costly competition between the two Montreal groups ensued across the interior. It sorely tested the smaller XY Company, and with the death of Simon McTavish, the imperious "Marquis" of the original NWC, the competitors merged their operations in 1804.

Facing decline as the aggressive Montreal traders spread through the West, the HBC began to emulate and challenge its competitors by carrying its trade to the Native peoples. In its attempt to catch up to its rivals, it was characteristically methodical; rivers were mapped and posts were built. But the company was twenty years behind Peter Pond in reaching the "Eldorado" of the Athabasca, and was unable to exploit the riches of that area effectively until it recruited *voyageurs* into its service in 1815. The durable, roomy York boat formed the basis of the HBC transportation system into the interior; slow and cumbersome, but requiring less skill to operate than the canoe, it might stand as a metaphor for the company itself during these years.

For three decades, St. Lawrence and Hudson Bay interests jockeyed for position and advantage in the fur trade. Posts proliferated. By 1789 over 100 had been built, almost two-thirds of them by St. Lawrence traders. Through the next sixteen years another 323 posts were erected, some 40 per cent of them by the HBC. Such rivalry could not continue. The expense to the Montrealers of maintaining the interior posts was enormous. HBC costs also climbed, although it had fewer than five hundred permanent employees in the interior in 1805. Competition drove up prices and depleted fur stocks. And when European fur markets shrank during the Napoleonic Wars, the difficulties increased. HBC dividends, 8 per cent in the late eighteenth century, were nil between 1809 and 1814. By 1814 barely 100 posts (42 of them HBC establishments) were operating in the West. Still, competition jeopardized the trade, and in 1821 the Hudson's Bay Company and the North West Company amalgamated. By 1825 the Hudson's Bay monopoly operated a mere 45 posts.

For the Native peoples of the interior, who outnumbered Europeans by ten to one until they were decimated by smallpox in 1818–21, the consequences of the frantic European commercial penetration of their territory after 1760 were immense. By 1800 few inhabitants lived much more than 25 kilometres (15 miles) from a trading post. Relieved of the burden of travel to distant markets, and less constrained by the capacity of their canoes, the Native people were able to trap more intensively. Robbed of their strategic "middleman" position and the power it conveyed, Cree and Assiniboine had to find a new niche in the changing West as provisioners of the

European fur traders. So the Cree moved west from the interlake and Lake of the Woods area, and the Assiniboine migrated southward to the parkland-grassland margin, whence they pursued the buffalo of the plains. But these were the traditional resources of the Blackfoot and the Mandan, who now had horses from the south and guns directly from American, Hudson's Bay, or St. Lawrence fur traders. Conflict between the Cree-Assiniboine and their south-western neighbours escalated. By the 1830s the Blackfoot had assumed a new dominance on the plains, as suppliers of buffalo hides to the American Fur and Hudson's Bay companies. Profiting from a trade that yielded at least eighty thousand robes a year, they enjoyed a decade or two of cultural flowering that led all too quickly to disillusionment with the rapid depletion of once-vast buffalo herds after 1860.

For the Ojibwa who expanded into the territory vacated by the Cree, and the Chipewyans of the northern forest, the 1820s and 1830s brought a similar if less dramatic plight. Beaver, moose, and caribou, mercilessly hunted for trade and food, were increasingly scarce in these regions. Communal hunting over large areas in bands of twenty to thirty-five gave way, among the Ojibwa, to dependence on small, private, family hunting territories. As the Ojibwa's mobility declined, they hunted rabbits and other small animals more intensely. In the 1820s the people of Rainy River depended on buffalo hides, brought to them by the HBC, for moccasins and clothing. By 1840, the food and fur-bearing animals had been hunted to depletion and the ecological foundations on which traditional Aboriginal life rested were severely weakened. Many Native peoples were left dependent, at least intermittently, on European assistance, and their centuries-old autonomy was compromised.

Added to this were the effects of alcohol—over twenty-one thousand gallons reached the interior in the highly competitive year of 1803 alone—and disease. Smallpox devastated the Chipewyans in the 1780s; Samuel Hearne's estimate, though likely high, was that 90 per cent of the population died. It also took a heavy toll among the Ojibwa, Sioux, and Assiniboine. Between 1818 and 1820 measles and whooping cough may have killed half the Brandon Assiniboine, and a third of the Western Cree and other groups. In 1838 smallpox again carried off large numbers—possibly two-thirds or more of the Assiniboine, Blackfoot, and North Saskatchewan Cree—although the new vaccine administered by Hudson's Bay Company men reduced the death rate among the plains Cree and the woodland and parkland Native people of south-central Manitoba, southern Saskatchewan, and eastern Alberta areas. Ravaged, debauched, dislodged, and increasingly dispirited by their incorpo-

In *Wanderings of an Artist* Paul Kane noted that one evening in June 1848, after leaving The Pas, on the Saskatchewan River, he arrived at the place of encampment ahead of the rest of his party: "I got out my drawing materials and took a sketch of the brigade, as it was coming up with a fair breeze, crowding all sail to escape a thunder storm rolling fast after them." His *Brigade of Boats* shows the HBC's fur-laden York boats on their way to Lake Winnipeg. Oil, *c.* 1850.

ration into the periphery of the European commercial world, by 1840 the Native peoples of the interior were firmly embarked on a path that led to the reserves, unrest, and abject despair of the 1870s and 1880s.

As the fortunes and the mansions of the McGills, McKenzies, McTavishes, Frobishers, and Ellices of Montreal, and the stylish lives of HBC shareholders in Britain demonstrated, there were significant profits in this trade. But like those of the fishery, the profits from furs concentrated in the centres from which the trade was organized rather than in the areas from which the staple came. Because Native demands were met with goods from Europe, the trade generated little economic development locally. Its significance lay in its impact on the indigenous peoples and its consequences for the political and institutional development of British North America. The fur trade was the mould in which modern Canada was cast. Focused on the beaver of the northern woodlands, channelled through the two great north-

This late nineteenth century woodsman may be from Manitoba or north-west Ontario, yet his costume is much like that of his fellows in eastern Canada. *Lumberman Chopping Tree in Winter* (*c.* 1870), by W. G. R. Hind.

ern entries to the continent, and extending along the rivers that led into them, the fur trade ultimately defined the boundaries of the nation.

"Trivin away at all kinds of lumberin"

Vast as they were, the rich forests of British North America had little commercial importance until Napoleon's blockade of European ports drove English wood prices up and generated a transatlantic commerce that made wood the great export of early nineteenth-century British North America. Furs, which had dominated shipments from Lower Canada until 1790, constituted less than 10 per cent of the total by 1810, when wood products, including ships, accounted for three-quarters of the colony's exports by value. The trade was heavily concentrated until 1830 on the production of square timber—baulks, or "sticks" of wood hewn square with axes—but exports of sawn deals (7.5 centimetres/3 inches thick), boards (5 centimetres/2 inches), and planks (2.5 centimetres/1 inch) increased steadily thereafter. By 1840 they accounted for more than a third of British wood imports from the colonies.

By then there was barely a tributary of the Miramichi, St. John, and Ottawa rivers in which the forest had not felt the bite of the lumberman's axe. Wood (hewn timber and sawn lumber, as well as minor commodities such as barrel staves) came to the Quebec market from the Trent and Richelieu watersheds, and crossed the Atlantic from the Saguenay and many an inlet on the Gulf of St. Lawrence. Tied to the rivers, the trade first moved rapidly inland, removing the best pine trees from a relatively narrow band of the mixed hemlock–white pine–northern hardwood forest. Only as the supply of large, accessible trees dwindled and sawmill capacity increased were less impressive trees cut. Then operations pushed back up smaller streams in which lumberers sometimes needed to blast away obstructions, build dams from which water could be released to flush out the cut, or construct "canals" through swamps, and slides and flumes round rapids. So although extensive tracts denuded of timber were rare in the early nineteenth century, by 1840 large, heavily culled parts of the forest had been changed in character and in the mix of species they contained. And because fires were frequent—if rarely as notorious as the "Great Fire" of 1825 on the Miramichi, which ran over thousands of square miles—many burned and blackened areas scarred the landscape before mid-century.

Three factors—technology, climate, and regulations—shaped the early timber industry. Technology imposed a striking unity on the trade; whether producing timber or lumber, the industry depended upon the strength of men and beasts and the energy of wind and water. From Nova Scotia to the Canadian Shield, trees were felled with axes, hauled to riverside by oxen (or, increasingly, horses), and floated out on the spring freshet. All of this was hard work, and some of it was dangerous. The best trees in the forest towered roughly 46 metres (150 feet) and considerable skill and effort was needed to bring them down safely. The single bitted poll axe used to fell trees and lop branches from them weighed 2 kilograms (about 5 pounds). The broad-axe used to produce a smooth, square-hewn face was twice as heavy. Even after trees were bucked (cut into more manageable lengths) and squared (which wasted a quarter of the wood), sticks often measured 12 or 15 metres (40 or 50 feet) in length

Lumbering on the St. John River captures the annual flurry of activity on the river near St. John as rafts of timber and logs from the upper valley were sorted and sold. Watercolour (nineteenth century) by Lieutenant James Cummings Clarke.

and 60 centimetres (24 inches) a side. These were cumbersome to move and to load aboard sailing vessels. So the river drive, by which sticks and logs were brought to port or mill, was the most hazardous part of the lumberers' operation. Especially on narrow streams, crews were kept frantically busy using poles or "cant hooks" to guide their cut around snag and shoals. Men were often immersed in icy water; death and injury were constant risks.

Climate set the annual rhythm of the industry. Because trees fell to the axe more easily when their sap no longer ran, and the labour of hauling massive sticks was much reduced on snow and ice, lumbering was essentially a winter occupation. The downriver drive depended on the raised water levels of the spring snowmelt, and from Quebec, at least, shipping was limited to the summer and fall. Sawmills were also limited in season by their reliance on water power.

Regulations set the framework of the industry. Although there were important differences between the colonies, the tendency everywhere was to restrict and regulate the access of individual lumberers to the forest. Eighteenth-century imperial regulations that were intended to save masts for the King's navy proved anachronistic and ineffective in the face of expanding settlement and a rising market for wood, and by the mid-1820s licences were required to cut trees on ungranted (Crown) land. Payment of a low—but much resented—fee gave lumberers a short-term right to take a certain quantity of wood from specified tracts of the public domain.

When the trade began there was an expanding market for wood, good timber was readily available, and little capital was required to exploit it. Family groups and partnerships of three to six individuals, perhaps farmers attracted to work in the nearby forest during their off-season, dominated the trade. Often part-time operations, these ventures generally produced between twenty and two hundred tons of timber a year and sold it to a local storekeeper for cash or credit. They were frequently closely integrated with the other tasks of rural life, as the 1818 diary of William Dibblee, a New Brunswick farmer, neatly reveals. After several entries through January and March recording the activity of his boys, Jack and William, getting timber, Dibblee wrote:

April 1st All Fools Day...Too Cold for Sap—Boys geting Timber—Fredk [another son] & Ketchum [a young neighbour] at Sugar Camp—Afternoon Fredk Hawling Timber—Barked my Twine for Long Net.
April 3rd...It snowed last Night 3 Inches...Boys geting Timber—Bad Spring.
April 4th...Boys now Taping as fast as They can—The Sap now Runs a little...
April 30th Set out Some Onions. Sowed Some Lettuce and Pepper Grass. Wm. and Fredk. Hawling Timber. Boys fixing Meadow & Mending Fence.

This informal, easy-to-enter trade that linked settlers through storekeepers and merchants in provincial ports to commercial houses across the Atlantic was an important supplement to a farming life.

Changes began to be felt in the second quarter of the century, as large entrepreneurs increased their control of the trade. The changes they implemented had their roots in the growing capital requirements of the industry as it moved into remote and difficult areas and diversified into lumber production. At the same time, higher licence fees and tighter regulation of the Crown domain (which limited illegal cutting) increased the costs of forest exploitation. And the competition and the cyclical booms and busts that plagued the trade were especially detrimental to small, independent operators. Taken together, these forces squeezed small family ventures and opened the way to commercial integration and a few powerful companies.

The timber trade, unlike the trade in fish and furs, was a considerable stimulus to growth and investment in the colonies. It encouraged immigration to North America by making cheap transatlantic passages available on vessels that would otherwise have sailed westbound in ballast after delivering their wooden freights to Britain.

Ship building, which expanded in tandem with the timber trade and provided a large part of the fleet that carried wood across the Atlantic, employed over 3,300 people in Quebec during 1825 alone. Many thousands worked in the trade, in camps, on the drive, and in sorting and loading wood for shipment. The demand for hay and food in the lumber camps stimulated agriculture. Countless small contributions came from local farmers who hauled hay, oats, and other provisions into the forest during the winters. Larger quantities of oats, beef, pork, and livestock from the farms of Prince Edward Island supplied lumberers on the Miramichi; and fine flour, pork, quartered beef, butter, biscuits, and other supplies went from Quebec to feed "the great number of men in the Woods" of northern New Brunswick.

"A pursuit of innocence and peace?"

Colonial farmers were often considered slovenly by English visitors. Accustomed to the careful, increasingly "scientific" agriculture of their homeland, the English were dismayed to see stock browsing in the woods, manure lying uncollected, and wheat planted amid stumps. Many lamented the apparently widespread practice of alternating wheat and fallow ground in the same fields year after year, because it was bound to exhaust the soil. In fact, such rough and ready practices were far better fitted to the conditions that prevailed in much of British North America—where land was relatively cheap, capital was in short supply, and labour was scarce and expensive—than most visitors allowed.

Creating a colonial farm was no easy task. The land was a prisoner of the forest and could be liberated only by back-breaking toil. At best, an energetic settler could roughly clear four acres a year; as his little farm expanded, other tasks would occupy him and reduce the rate of his progress. And the aggressive growth of weeds and young trees on bare ground was a constant reminder that hard-won gains could quickly vanish. A tent, a primitive shelter of branches, or a rough windowless cabin was often the first home men and women had on their new land. When it was replaced by something better—most often a log cabin—that was likely to be small and simple. Many log cabins lacked foundations, had a dirt floor, and measured about 5 by 7 metres (16 by 25 feet). Heated by a fireplace on which meals were cooked, these single-storey dwellings were generally smoky, drafty, and dark. They were roughly furnished and offered no escape from the blackflies and mosquitoes

Some immigrants did maintain a genteel, civilized life in the New World. Anne Langton—seen here by the fire—came over in 1837 to join her brother at Sturgeon Lake, Upper Canada, where two-thirds of the male settlers were university graduates. Her journal and correspondence were published by her nephew in 1950, and titled *A Gentlewoman in Upper Canada*.

that abounded. Frame houses were more commodious, but they were five to ten times as expensive as well-made log cabins and were relatively rare in recently occupied areas of the colony.

The axe and the ox (favoured over the horse for the heavy work it could do) were the pioneer family's main instruments of improvement. Ploughs were of little use until fields were clear of stumps. Crops were sown by hand and harvested in the same way, using a scythe. Threshing was done with a flail, for there was no machine to do the job in Upper Canada until 1832; it was tiring, dusty work, carried out on the floor of the barn, with the doors open to admit the breeze that separated wheat from chaff. And there were countless challenges to the family's patience and ingenuity as they were forced to make do and repair broken equipment. One immigrant, an Irishman

View of Halifax Harbour. While carefully placed figures and objects decorate the foreground, the town itself is all but lost in a romantic haze. Oil (*c.* 1820) attributed to John Poad Drake.

Micmac Indians. The finely crafted canoes, the single-family wigwam, and the quillwork containers within it were made largely of birchbark sewn with spruce roots. Note the women's peaked and beaded head-dresses. Oil (*c.* 1850) by unknown artist.

Richer. A line of houses, eel traps, salt marshes, kitchen gardens; fields of wheat and peas; livestock and game; these were basic elements of the Lower Canadian landscape. Watercolour (1787) by Thomas Davies.

The Woolsey Family. A prosperous English merchant and his family carefully posed in their Quebec drawing-room. Elegantly dressed and comfortable in their fashionable neoclassical surroundings, they are a proper and self-confident group. Oil (1809) by William Berczy, Sr.

The Good Friends: a charming example of folk "animal portraiture," no doubt commissioned by a proud and prosperous farmer. Oil (after 1834) by Ebenezer Birrell.

La Procession de la Fête-Dieu à Québec. Corpus Christi was a major religious festival in Lower Canada. Here, the *curé* of Notre Dame leads his congregation along a route marked by young fir trees, symbols of death. Oil (1824) by Louis-Hubert Triaud.

The North West Part of the City of Quebec, taken from the St. Charles River. "What a scene!—Can the world produce such another?" exclaimed Susanna Moodie. "Rejoice and be worthy of her—for few, very few of the sons of men can point to such a spot as Quebec—and exclaim, 'She is ours!'" Oil (*c.* 1804–10) by George Heriot.

A Shot in the Dawn, Lake Scugog. Two men hope to bag a few ducks from the cover of a partly harvested wheatfield north-east of Toronto. Oil (1873) by John. A. Fraser.

more affluent, educated, and established than most, caught well the adaptability needed when he wrote to Dublin in 1832:

My time at home is occupied in shoeing horses, making gates, fences, chimney pieces, and furniture. Indeed my mechanical labours are so multifarious that I can hardly enumerate them, but you may form some idea of their versatility when I tell you that I made an ivory tooth for a very nice girl and an iron one for the harrow within the same day.

It was, concluded the remarkable pioneer gentlewoman Catharine Parr Traill in 1836 in her magnificent account of settlement, *The Backwoods of Canada*, a "Robinson Crusoe sort of existence."

Thousands of Upper Canadian farms began in much this way, and the young lives of countless men and women were absorbed by the labour they required. But with time small clearings devoted to oats, corn, pumpkins, potatoes, and turnips were expanded to include larger fields of wheat and rye. Buck and Bright ("the names of three-fourths of all the working oxen in Canada," claimed Mrs. Traill) were joined by the usual assembly of cows, calves, pigs, hens, and ducks. And a complex rural economy developed. Nine of every ten farms in Upper Canada grew some wheat, but unlike timber, before 1840 wheat was not a major export crop. Transportation costs, the restrictive British Corn Laws, and Canadian prices generally kept it from British ovens. Even in good export years, shipments from the colony averaged less than a modest four bushels a person. Significant quantities of flour went to supply the colony's growing urban population, and wheat generally yielded at least a fifth of farmers' incomes. But production fluctuated widely from year to year. It was also more important in some parts of the colony than in others. In eastern Ontario, pot and pearl ashes (from which came the lye to manufacture soap), and lumber, were often more important than wheat, while substantial quantities of pork were regularly taken in payment in the Lake Ontario region and, to the west, sales of rye, tobacco, and barley generally exceeded those of wheat. Although 40 to 50 per cent of the cleared land on the fringes of settlement was devoted to wheat, Upper Canadian farming as a whole rested on a broad mixed base.

Few colonial settlers were able or willing to divorce themselves from the market. If they had nothing to sell, the debts they incurred obtaining necessary supplies from country storekeepers bound them into the commercial system. Absolute self-sufficiency was not possible nor desirable. As they struggled to clear the land and make homes amid the forest, many of them saw their farms less as instruments of profit than as the means and focus of life in the new land. If the labour was available, and a market for their produce accessible, settlers anticipating good prices in the year ahead might plant a few acres more than necessary to supply the family, in hope that the surplus would yield a cash return or defray debts—in much the same way that others worked awhile in the woods to supplement their incomes. But surplus produce to take to market was as often the result of better-than-expected yields, or of a large and healthy litter, as of deliberate design. The essential purpose of many an early colonial farm was to provide for its inhabitants, whatever the vicissitudes of the market, and in general the farmer sold only what he and his family would not consume.

Of course, not all farms were like this. Especially in the lakeshore districts of Upper Canada which had been settled earlier, where markets were accessible, and where large farms existed by the first decades of the nineteenth century, farmers imbued with the spirit and the doctrines of improved English agriculture ran thoroughly commercial operations. Their fields were drained and manured; their crops were rotated according to approved ideas; and their mares and heifers were bred with imported stallions and bulls to improve bloodlines. But through much of Upper Canada before 1840, the connection between farm and market remained tenuous. Acerbic visitors complained at the "improper and wasteful profusion" of farmers who ate only the best ("roast beef almost every day"), and local enthusiasts of scientific farming, who formed poorly attended agricultural societies to spread their convictions, lamented the ignorance and apathy of those who refused to improve the quality of their stock and grain. But they would not see reform until the struggle to establish home and family was well won and improvements in transportation made reliable markets readily available.

There was much in the agricultural economy of early Upper Canada that was characteristic of rural life in the rest of British North America. In many parts of New Brunswick, Nova Scotia, and Prince Edward Island, credit, indebtedness, and exchange linked small farmers to a wider commercial world, but on the poorer soils and in the more difficult climate of these provinces surpluses were, if anything, smaller and more sporadic, and market connections less significant than in Upper Canada. "Enlightened" leaders of local agricultural societies tried in vain through the first half of the century to overcome the traditional "prejudices" of Scots and others notorious for their willingness to make do. The wants of the Highlanders, wrote Thomas Chandler Haliburton—distinguished but inveterate Nova Scotian Tory and creator of the fictional character Samuel Slick, in the late 1820s—"are comparatively few and their ambition is chiefly limited to the acquirement of the mere necessaries of life." Neither premiums to encourage higher yields and better stock nor the enormous effort spent in the 1820s "coying science to dignify the labours of the plough" realized the commercialization and improvement of agriculture that their proponents sought. "I never seed or heerd tell of a country that had so many natural priviliges as this," announced Slick the Yankee pedlar, while lamenting that its inhabitants, for whom he coined the name "Bluenoses," were "either asleep, or stone blind to them." Wanting three things—"Industry, Enterprise, Economy"—Nova Scotians, he continued, should have "An Owl... [for] their emblem" and "*He sleeps all the days of his life*" for a motto.

In Lower Canada too, early nineteenth-century commentators lamented the sluggishness of farming conducted according to old routines. But in this long-settled region, where farms had spread across the good agricultural land of the St. Lawrence lowland and run up against the thin soils of the Shield, the character and problems of rural life were different. In the last forty years of the eighteenth century, a growing population had cleared new land in the seigneurial lowlands at a striking rate. Access to West Indian markets and rising English prices in the 1790s stimulated agriculture, and Quebec traders sent out agents "to buy up all the grain which is not necessary for the farmer's subsistence." There was prosperity in the countryside, and many Canadiens, claimed deputy postmaster-general George Heriot, began "to lay aside their ancient costume and to acquire a relish for the manufactures of Europe." Although farming—which relied on a simple two- or three-course rotation in which wheat and pasture predominated—was as bad as it could be in the eyes of European visitors, by 1802 wheat exports rivalled those of furs in value. But then they declined precipitously. Soaring domestic consumption reduced the amount of wheat available for export, and to accommodate new families, old seigneurial lands were subdivided and subdivided again. Falling yields from fields so thick with thistles and weeds that the wheat from them made poor flour, and the growing pressure of people on the land, encouraged farmers to diversify. More and more potatoes were grown until, by the late 1820s, they made up almost half of the harvest. Pork assumed a new prominence in *habitant* diets, and by 1840, low-quality mixed farming was the norm in Lower Canada. *Habitants* of overpopulated *seigneuries*—from which a steady trickle of emigrants was already running to the United States in search of a better life—sought to provide for as many of their own needs as they could. Rural living standards were as low as at any time in the eighteenth and nineteenth centuries.

Contexts of Everyday Existence

Fishing, fur trading, lumbering, and farming each had their distinctive rhythms, routines, and practices and each left its mark on British North American life. But it is crucial to remember that people live in particular places, that communities rest upon distinct combinations of activities, and that the settings and circumstances of everyday lives are shaped by individuals and groups responding to diverse opportunities and challenges over time. Only by paying careful attention to local life can we grasp something of the rich and varied contexts in which British North America lived and loved, worked and played, hoped and despaired, struggled and triumphed. Only thus can we hope to bring the lives of otherwise unmarked British North Americans out of the shadows and into the comprehension of modern-day readers, whose experiences are, for the most part, worlds removed from the lives of those who contributed their varied pieces to early colonial development.

Habitant Life

In the early 1760s Théophile and Félicité Allaire lived in a modest house beside the Richelieu River in the parish and *seigneurie* of St-Ours. Their farm, relatively small by local standards, ran barely 100 metres (110 yards) along the river, but extended back fifteen times that distance to the west. Some 730 metres (800 yards) from the river, the Allaires' cleared land gave way to the forest and brush that provided them with firewood, fencing, and building materials and yielded their stock forage for much of the year. Rough fences divided the Allaires' 27 *arpents* (roughly 23 acres, or 9 hectares) of cleared land into a garden (0.6 *arpents*), a meadow (of approximately 7.4 *arpents*), and ploughed land (19 *arpents*), half of which lay fallow. Although Théophile varied the precise quantities he planted and harvested each year, wheat (two-thirds of the harvest), oats (perhaps a quarter), and peas were his main crops. In 1765 the census-taker found two horses, two cows, two sheep, and two pigs on his property. What this meant, in effect, was that the farm yielded barely enough to feed Théophile, Félicité, their small children (of whom there were three by 1767), and two older daughters from earlier marriages. By comparison with most of their neighbours, the Allaires' circumstances were difficult.

Slightly larger yet essentially similar farms lined both sides of the Richelieu above and below the Allaires' home. Downriver, the line of settlement ran beyond St-Ours through the low, sandy soils of the neighbouring parish of Sorel to the junction of the Richelieu with the St. Lawrence River; upstream it continued into the good land of the parish of St-Denis. In all, 1,750 people lived in these three parishes in 1765. Along much of the Lower Richelieu, settlement was sufficiently close that neighbours might have held shouted conversations from their front doors. Here and there were tiny villages, with six to twelve houses clustered around a church. Most dwellings resembled the one in which Théophile and Félicité lived although theirs was probably smaller than most, measuring only slightly more than 5 metres (16 feet) a side. Built of horizontal squared logs in the traditional *pièce-sur-pièce* style, the Allaires' home was no more than a simple cabin. A single room may have occupied its main floor; there Félicité cooked over an open fire, the family took meals, and she and Théophile slept. In the loft above food was stored, and in all likelihood the children slept there. Furnishings were few. Although most families probably had a pine table, the Allaires apparently did not. Apart from a large and rather elaborate bed, their house held a cast-iron box stove (worth more than the building itself), three old chairs, a pine chest, and a wooden sideboard. There were two goblets, two cups, and five forks, but no plates; meals were probably eaten straight from the cast-iron pots and frying pans, or from one of the several cups and bowls the couple possessed. Local tinsmiths and potters may have crafted the coffee-pot, the candlestick, the bowls and bottles used by the Allaires, but much of what they had was homemade. Théophile had a hammer and chisels as well as a few simple farming tools—axes, pickaxes, sickles, a scythe. Félicité likely made the family's quilts and bed linen.

Historian Allan Greer's vivid portrait of the Lower Richelieu in this period reveals that year by year the lives of men and women followed a cycle similar to that which the Allaires knew. Ploughing and planting began the agricultural year in April or early May. Following oxen or horses and the heavy wheeled plough of northern Europe (which prevailed until the adoption of the swing plough in the nineteenth century), Théophile prepared the fields for sowing; Félicité (with the help, perhaps, of the two older girls) set out squash, cabbage, onions, tobacco, and herbs in the garden that they would tend through the summer. Once the grain was planted, Théophile erected fences around the fields; house, barn, and equipment were repaired; drainage ditches were dug. To the incessant routine of feeding, washing, and cleaning the family, its clothes, and its house, Félicité added the tasks of milking the cows, making butter, and feeding the fowls. In midsummer the hay was cut and

"The whole of the Canadian inhabitants are remarkable fond of dancing, and frequently amuse themselves at all seasons with that agreeable exercise," observed George Heriot, in whose *Travels through the Canadas* (London, 1807) this illustration appeared. *La Danse Ronde; Circular Dance of the Canadians*: aquatint by J. C. Stadler after a watercolour by Heriot.

stored. And in September the grain harvest engaged almost everyone able to work in strenuous toil; on larger farms additional labour may have been hired, but the Allaires could not have afforded it. With the harvest in, fences were taken down to allow stock to graze on the stubble, and such fall ploughing was done as time and weather allowed. As winter came on, animals were killed to provide meat and to save fodder. Up and down the Richelieu women made cloth, spun wool, and produced apparel, rugs, and linen for their families. Through January and February Théophile and his neighbours threshed grain in the barn, cut firewood and fencing, and perhaps cleared a little more land. From the larger farms such surplus grain, meat, or butter as there was after tithes had been paid was taken to market. And then, up and down the valley, the early spring was given to maple-sugar production.

Fundamental demographic rhythms also gave shape to *habitant* life along the lower Richelieu. Most men married in their twenties, almost all women in their early twenties, and few of either sex remained unwed. The timing of weddings, concentrated in the late fall and winter months, reflected the agricultural calendar and the availability of supplies for the celebrations associated with them. Births were also

George Heriot's comments on Lower Canada's climate suggest that, like their peasant counterparts, the bourgeoisie and the seigneurial class warded off the winter chill on the dance floor. The two blacks in the upper left would have been slaves; slavery remained legal until 1834. *Minuets of the Canadians*: aquatint (1807) by J. C. Stadler after a watercolour by Heriot.

more common at some times of the year than others, because they mirrored the timing of weddings, and reflected the cycle of rural labour. Illegitimate children were uncommon, but birthrates were relatively high by modern standards (47 to 52 per thousand). Overall deathrates were low; rarely if ever did they approach birthrates. Although they reflected the incidence of smallpox, cholera, typhoid, and influenza as well as food shortages that came with poor harvests, Richelieu deathrates were never pushed terribly high by famines. Because women married young, most had large numbers of children. The first year of every infant life was precarious. In the late eighteenth century approximately a quarter of all children died before their first birthdays. But survival rates were relatively high after the age of one, and infant mortality declined somewhat in the nineteenth century.

Thus families were often large: to have eight or ten children was not unusual. In the six years that his first marriage to Amable Ménard lasted before her death, Théophile and his wife had five children. Only one survived infancy. When the widower Théophile hired the widow Félicité Audet as his housekeeper she also had a young daughter. Their marriage, the year after Amable's death, produced three children in six years, before

Théophile died in 1767. Félicité was soon married again, and bore her new husband at least three sons. In the 1770s, her third family included at least eight children.

For the Allaires, life unfolded within a traditional framework of obligation to *seigneur* and church. Although Théophile, his neighbours, and their successors could sell, deed, or mortgage their land, *seigneurs* retained the right to confiscate it in certain circumstances. They also exacted an annual payment—the *cens et rentes*—from every *censitaire* (broadly, *habitant*) on their *seigneurie*. Most *habitants* were also subject to other exactions—on the purchase of land, for use of the common pasture, for the right to fish, or on maple-sugar making. Payment by the poorer *habitants* was anything but prompt: by 1840 the *censitaires* of Sorel owed their *seigneur* at least 92,000 *livres*, those of St-Ours some 71,000 *livres*. Even so, the *seigneur*'s rights over land, and the obligations owed him by *habitants*, defined lines of authority in the community, and these were reinforced by the *seigneur*'s right to a pew at the front of the church and his position of honour in local ceremonies.

The Catholic church was also an important part of *habitant* life. Religious observance was the norm, the spiritual authority of the priest extended his influence through the community, and the church exacted a considerable tribute from its parishioners. Priests were entitled to the tithe, set by law at one twenty-sixth of the grain harvest, and *habitants* also contributed to collections each sabbath, paid annual pew rents, and were assessed periodically for repair of the church. Taken together with seigneurial dues these amounted to a significant levy—possibly half of all the produce that remained after the needs of *habitant* families had been met. Such payments limited the accumulation of wealth by the *habitants*, and maintained clergymen and *seigneurs* as the focus of economic power and social influence in the community. But their authority was far from absolute. *Seigneurs* neither specified the crops to be grown by their *censitaires* nor determined the conduct of their daily lives. *Habitants* resisted seigneurial power—by deferring payment of feudal dues, for example—and exercised a good deal of basic independence in running their affairs. So too, in their dealings with the church, *habitants* followed form in attending mass and having their infants baptized at birth, but they clung to traditional beliefs and used potions and incantations that religious authorities dismissed as superstition and magic. Time and again they also resisted clerical initiatives that threatened to increase the financial burden on them.

For all the constancy of life along the Lower Richelieu, the area saw substantial change in the years after 1760. Young men, living at home and depending on relatives to help clear land and build a house and barn, extended settlement back from the river until all the cultivable land in the three parishes was occupied. Early in the nineteenth century many farms were entirely under the plough, and the landscape was increasingly bare of trees. Tiny villages grew into small towns. Sorel prospered in the 1790s as a ship-building centre, and in the 1820s as a port of call for steamboats on the St. Lawrence. By 1815 St-Ours was a place "of about sixty houses, many of them substantially and well constructed of stone"; at its centre were "a handsome church and parsonage-house ... [and] at a little distance the manor-house"; and there were many persons "of considerable property," as well as traders and artisans among its inhabitants. Twenty-five years later, St-Denis had 123 houses, a distillery, and grist and sawmills. Its population, of more than six hundred, included merchants, notaries, millers, and such tradesmen as blacksmiths and carpenters. By 1825, eleven thousand people lived in the three parishes.

Well before this it had become impossible for most sons to develop new farms near their parental homes. On the poor soils of Sorel, *habitants* responded by subdividing their holdings and supplementing their incomes by sporadic seasonal work in the fur trade. The wages they earned brought relative prosperity to the *habitants* of Sorel during the 1790s. But the good times were short-lived. While the population of the parish more than quadrupled between 1790 and 1831, the demand for workers in the fur trade fell. With little to supplement the returns of small farms (few of which exceeded thirty-five acres, or fourteen hectares, by 1831) the community was impoverished.

In contrast, the farmers of St-Denis, who had an average of sixty-seven acres under the plough in 1831, were prosperous. By and large the farms of St-Denis (and neighbouring St-Ours) were worked to feed the families who lived on them, but they also produced a sizeable wheat surplus for the Montreal market. Realizing that this connection, and the rum and tea and pepper that it provided, depended on the cultivation of rather more land than was necessary for simple subsistence, the farmers of St-Denis modified the relatively democratic inheritance practices they had followed in the eighteenth century. As the population of the parish increased, only parents with unusually large holdings continued to divide them more or less equally among their offspring; others tended to convey their entire farms to one of their sons. The result was population decline, as young men and women left in search of opportunity elsewhere, some gravitating to the growing towns, to work as labourers or artisans. Of those who remained, a growing number were landless. By 1831 *habitant* proprietors (who headed nine in every ten Richelieu valley households in 1765) were a minority among the family heads of St-Denis. For the most part they lived relatively well, in larger houses and with more and better furniture than the Allaires knew. If not substantially bigger than Théophile's farm, their properties were more fully cultivated and carried far more stock. But one in seven of their fellows was a tenant and almost a quarter were day labourers. Most of these people lived poor and precarious lives, burdened by debt, and with little sense of the security that land ownership gave to even such families as the Allaires. When repeated failures of the grain crop created economic difficulty through much of St-Ours and St-Denis during the 1830s, many of them were left completely indigent.

Among Accomplished Gentlemen and Honest Sons of Poverty

Located on the north shore of Lake Ontario, midway between Kingston and Toronto, Hamilton Township rises from a flat, fertile, low-lying plain near the lake to an undulating ridge of glacial deposits in its centre. Northward it falls towards the steep bluffs that mark its northern boundary on Rice Lake. This is beautiful country. Late in the eighteenth century, a hardwood forest of maple covered most of the township. On the uplands grew oak and pine; ash, cedar, and hemlock thrived where the ground was moist. Here the growing season averages between 188 and 195 days, and the frost-free period varies from 140 days along the lake to 120 or so inland. With the fertile grey-brown soils that predominate, this is an environment well suited to farming.

Hamilton Township, situated on the main artery into western Upper Canada, was settled rapidly. Among those who came was Robert Wade, who migrated from County Durham in north-eastern England in 1819. He was forty-two, married, and the father of eight children. A relatively successful tenant farmer in England, he came to the New World with capital enough to buy a 200-acre (80-hectare) farm on the Hamilton lakefront. One of the seven hundred or so who entered the township in the decade after 1810, he quickly established himself. Settling his family into the two log houses that stood on his new property, he stocked it with six cows, eighteen sheep, ten pigs, two horses, and a foal, and began to cultivate and extend its 30 cleared acres, about half of which were in grass. Within a year he had also acquired land, by grant, in Otonabee Township, north of Rice Lake. In 1821 Robert Wade had one of the better mixed farms in Hamilton Township.

His fellow settlers were a diverse group. Members of Loyalist families who had settled elsewhere in the colony trickled into Hamilton through the first two decades of the nineteenth century. Americans crossed Lake Ontario to join relatives who had been among the first arrivals. Others came from Britain. At least eight were former naval officers whose half-pay pensions provided them with a steady and valuable income. Some, like Robert Wade, came with considerable sums of money. Many had little but the strength of their muscles and a willingness to work, and for most of them the road to success in the New World was far longer, more difficult, and more uncertain than that followed by Robert Wade.

Fewer than 200 families (1,250 people) lived in Hamilton in 1821. But no Crown land remained open for settlement there. Most of the Crown land set aside to endow the church and government—the reserve lands—was already under lease, and well over half of still heavily forested Hamilton was in the hands of speculators. Such speculative land-holding ensured that newcomers needed a good deal of capital to acquire property in this highly desirable location.

Compared with the cost of Crown land (available beyond Hamilton for about 5 pence an acre), farms in the township were expensive. Prices were highest near the lakeshore, and varied according to the extent and quality of improvements, but cleared land sold for an average of 15 shillings an acre in the early 1820s. Uncleared land could be had for half that price, but another £80 or £100 would then be needed to buy tools, stock, and seed, to build a house and barn, and to clear several acres. In short, settlers needed at least £150 to establish themselves on one hundred acres. Without such a sum they had to rent or accept wage labour. The consequences were clear. In 1821, a third of Hamilton's farmers leased reserve lands, and almost half of those who held land in the township were tenants. Well over a third of the assessed wealth in the township belonged to a tenth of its people.

By the 1840s, twenty years or so after Robert Wade's arrival, the average value of cleared land had almost tripled, that of uncleared land had more than doubled, and rents were five times the level of 1819. For those with land, such inflation brought large capital gains; in 1834 Robert Wade valued his property at £1,600. Farms were subdivided to realize the profits, and as new families established homes the forest was pushed farther and farther back. Many farms near the lakefront now had substantial houses and barns amid their fenced fields. Roads had improved and after 1842 stage-coaches connected Cobourg, a thriving commercial centre, with the back country. But the continuing influx of immigrants had flooded the local labour market, and as land prices rose wages fell. This quickly imparted a distinctive, divided cast to Hamilton society. For migrants of modest means, from the British Isles or elsewhere,

"Nothing can be more comfortless than some of these shanties, reeking with smoke and dirt, the common receptacle for children, pigs and fowls," commented Catharine Parr Traill, but she admitted that this was "the dark side of the picture." Note the characteristic snake-fence, and the "corduroy road" made of logs laid across the track in swampy places. *Bush Farm Near Chatham*: watercolour (*c.* 1838) by Philip J. Bainbrigge.

the township was a place to pause, to gain experience of the New World and make a little money, before moving on to continue the struggle for modest comfort and independence. On the other hand, for those with capital or connections or initial advantage enough to acquire their own properties, Hamilton was a place to settle and to develop the trappings of English country life. Before mid-century the township had an agricultural society, a lending library, an amateur theatrical society, a cricket club, and a hunt. Charles Butler, who emigrated from Middlesex in the 1830s with his wife and family and a stake of approximately £1,000, responded to just such attractions when he elected to live in the vicinity of Cobourg. To settle in Peterborough, barely 40 kilometres (25 miles) away across Rice Lake, he concluded, would be to "totally seclude myself and Family from Society...."

Rather sourly, Robert Wade looked on these newcomers as "broken down gentry." Quite typical of their sort were Dunbar and Susanna Moodie. Dunbar was an Orkneyman and soldier who had found his half-pay insufficient to keep him, in England, in the style to which he aspired. Susanna, the sister of Catharine Parr Traill and the author of two anti-slavery tracts before she left England, was the daughter of a well-to-do, articulate, literary family whose children were widely read and well schooled in the arts of poetry, painting, and nature study. For financial reasons the Moodies came to Canada after their marriage in 1831, and settled briefly on the fourth concession of Hamilton Township. Twenty years later, Susanna's *Roughing It in the Bush* undertook to portray "what the backwoods of Canada are to the industrious and ever to be honoured sons of honest poverty and what they are to the refined and accomplished gentleman." Drawn with rather more fictional latitude and dramatic vision than Susanna acknowledged, these sketches often border on the fanciful. Yet in them the gifted modern Canadian writer Margaret Atwood has discerned something of the obsessive compulsion, fear, tension, and toil that ran through the oft-repeated encounter of settlers and forest on the pioneer fringe of Upper Canada. No excerpt can do full justice to the insight of Atwood's sequence of poems *The Journals of Susanna Moodie*, but there is surely no more evocative an encapsulation of what pioneering meant to thousands of men and women than "The Planters":

They move between the jagged edge
of the forest and the jagged river
on a stumpy patch of cleared land

my husband, a neighbour, another man
weeding the few rows
of string beans and dusty potatoes.

They bend, straighten; the sun
lights up their faces and hands, candles
flickering in the wind against the

unbright earth. I see them; I know
none of them believe they are here.
They deny the ground they stand on,

pretend this dirt is the future.
And they are right. If they let go
of that illusion solid to them as a shovel,

It took half a century of unremitting work—clearing forest, maintaining fields, raising buildings, and tending stock—to create this serene landscape. The sense of achievement must have been tremendous. *View on the Road from Windsor to Horton by Avon Bridge at Gaspreaux river*: watercolour (1817) by J. E. Woolford, one of a series of Nova Scotia views painted for Lord Dalhousie.

open their eyes even for a moment
to these trees, to this particular sun
they would be surrounded, stormed, broken

in upon by branches, roots, tendrils, the dark
side of light
as I am.

"Through a Dreary Forest upon an Execrable Track"

When Lieutenant-Colonel Joseph Gubbins, his wife Charlotte Bathoe, three of their children, and nine servants arrived in New Brunswick in 1810, they entered a theatre of contrasts. Saint John was a closely built commercial centre with approximately three thousand inhabitants. Fredericton, the capital, was little more than a village with fewer than two hundred houses, "scattered," said one resident, "on a delightful common of the richest sheep pasture I ever saw." There were neat, convenient houses, valuable and "agreeable" farms, and pretty cottages with fine sloping lawns, but they were surrounded by forest and outnumbered by tiny, ill-built dwellings with warped boards that let in the draft, and smoky fires intended to keep out the mosquitoes. The colony's population of thirty thousand or so was made up of Acadians, Native people, Loyalists, Americans who had come before and after the influx of 1783–84, and several hundred migrants direct from the British Isles. Better than half of them lived in the Saint John valley; the remainder were thinly spread around the periphery of the province. Elite society turned around Government House, where there were levees and balls and sleighing parties, but in many a house on the Miramichi the rum bottle was "generally on the table from morning till night," and almost everywhere there were settlers who endured, or remembered, "the extreme of wretchedness."

Knowing nothing of this, Gubbins had come to the colony as Inspecting Field Officer of Militia, appointed to supervise training of the citizen army upon which the defence of New Brunswick would depend if the rising tension between Britain and the United States turned to war. Installed in the country estate of the recently deceased Loyalist and wealthy Chief Justice George Ludlow, the Lieutenant-Colonel and his wife were immediately embraced by Fredericton society. But Gubbins was forced by his commission to travel widely through the province, and his tours of inspection brought him into contact with the full spectrum of New Brunswick life. For the English Tory gentleman that he was, many of these encounters must have been disconcerting. But Gubbins was also an acute observer of the colonial scene.

Travel through this forested domain was not easy. The fine carriage that Gubbins had shipped to New Brunswick was virtually useless for want of decent roads. In winter the frozen rivers opened the way for visiting and carrying produce to market, because horses might draw sleighs 96 kilometres (60 miles) or more a day with ease. But making his inspections in the summer, Gubbins had no such easy conveyance. He rode where he could, but it was often "through a dreary forest upon an execrable track." Beyond the Saint John valley he frequently had recourse to canoes and open boats. When he travelled north from Shediac, through country about which little was known in Fredericton, military horses had to be exchanged for local "ponys" accustomed to the woods in which "they scarcely ever could take two equal steps in succession, but leaped from root to hillock and over trunks of trees at the rate of five or six miles an hour." Progress was unreliable, accommodation had to be taken where it was offered, and to compound the inconveniences, inns seldom had more than one sitting-room. Thus, recorded Gubbins, "had I taken a servant I must either have had him as a companion or have let him live in the stable. I therefore went without one."

The Mi'kmaq—whom he called Michilmackinac—were a source of considerable fascination to Gubbins. He visited the mission village at Aukpaque above Fredericton, where forty or fifty families congregated each summer, and described the construction of their birchbark-covered wigwams. Near Richibucto he discovered a group whose condition he considered much superior to that of others, who maintained themselves "principally by fishing," although they cultivated corn and potatoes and had also cut some timber for sale. Gubbins held the decline of moose and caribou herds responsible for reducing many of the Mi'kmaq "much against their inclinations to hew fire wood in winter, and in summer to till the ground in some degree for their support." And he reported on activities of the New England Company. This, the oldest of English missionary societies, based in London but administered in New Brunswick by several leading Anglicans, was dedicated to "civilizing" and Christianizing Native people. Funds to achieve these goals, paid to any settler who would take a Native child as an apprentice, had been "shamefully perverted" according to Gubbins. Young girls had been assigned "to most profligate persons," and money had gone to at least one settler with "a mulatto boy as a servant." To Gubbins it seemed all too clear that as the spread of settlement and agriculture reduced the availability of game and robbed the Native people of "the powerful stimulus of the chase" they became "inert, slothful and dependent." When heavy alcohol consumption was added to this equation, Native peoples were quickly brought "to a state in many cases disgraceful to human nature." In the end, he concluded pessimistically, "the aborigines…degenerate in proportion as they come in contact with Europeans."

Twenty-five years after the Loyalists arrived in New Brunswick its landscape still bore the marks of pioneering. No more than a quarter of one per cent of the colony's 28,000 square miles had been cleared by 1810. On some farms, trees were killed by girdling, or cutting out a large ring of the bark; although they might stand for years, they produced no leaves, and some cultivation could be carried on beneath them. More generally, because it was more immediately profitable, trees were felled, the brush fired, and the wood cut into manageable lengths for building, firewood, or more complete burning. Clearing in this way, observed Gubbins, was "an undertaking of infinite labour," yet "stumps and roots still cover and disfigure the ground and prevent a plough from being used for many years...." Time and again on his travels, Gubbins looked across land covered with burnt and fallen trees, and over fields divided by fences "made either with small trees or larger ones split into rails and put up in a zigzag direction," to houses and barns standing in the shadow of a wall of trees.

Gubbins was struck by the isolation of life in the colonies. At Shediac his party was greeted by curious Acadian women who "were in full dress of the Norman mode as it was perhaps a century before." Farther north he was surprised to encounter Acadian fishermen who had "not even heard of Bonaparte or of the war with France." And he could neither forget the curiosity with which his host on the Miramichi examined "some old London newspapers" from his baggage, nor leave unrecorded the settler's repeated exclamation: "What a bustle the world seems to be in!" The lax and inconsistent administration of provincial laws by local justices far from the scrutiny of the legal officers in Fredericton was a cause for more serious concern. So too was the poor quality of medical care in much of the province. One unprincipled pretender to knowledge, claimed Gubbins, prescribed "Cayenne pepper in large boluses as a specific for the cure of pulmonic complaints"; others, in their ignorance, committed "murders with impunity." Gubbins was even more outspoken about the popularity of evangelical religion among New Brunswickers in those rural areas that lacked established churches. An Anglican, the Colonel had little time for the "egregious fanatics" who propagated "their pernicious doctrines" among the people. A "want of morals" was hardly surprising, he reflected grimly, where converts believed they could not sin in spirit, and New Light preachers proclaimed that there was "no sin in man below his heart."

All in all, Gubbins found New Brunswickers decidedly American in habit and attitude. British customs—in "religion, neatness, frugality, husbandry...[and] cooking"—were little evident in the colony, even among the immediate descendants of the English. The poor were "not educated to respect the rich as in Europe." To make matters worse, servants insisted on dining "with the master and mistress whom they call Mr. or Mrs." Nothing was "more objectionable" than the American child's "want of attachment" to parents, a failing fully evident to Gubbins among the English-speaking children of New Brunswick. Paradoxically, the Acadians, whose loyalty to Britain was still suspect in official circles, were more respectful, orderly, and to Gubbins' liking than the rank and file of English New Brunswick. "Their behaviour towards their parents and friends as well as towards their superiors and even strangers," he noted, "is particularly conspicuous when contrasted with the ignorant self-sufficiency of the commonality of English extraction."

The reasons for all of this, Gubbins concluded, lay in the circumstances of New Brunswick life. Because uncleared land was cheap, newcomers to the province quickly moved into those remote, isolated areas in which it was readily available. There their circumstances were both "lonesome and extremely difficult." In families without the means or the opportunity of purchasing many necessary goods and utensils, "a little of everything [had to] be done to support life"; farmers were "their own weavers, dyers, tailors, shoemakers, and carpenters." Inexperience compounded the challenge they faced, and many degenerated "very rapidly to a state of barbarism"; at best, their "apprenticeship to hard fare" was certain to "wean...them from the habits of the mother country." With hired help scarce and expensive, even officers and gentlemen were forced "to undergo all the drudgery of farming." Few were the estates established by Loyalists of wealth and fortune that continued to prosper in the nineteenth century. In this country, wrote Gubbins, "children constitute the riches of parents and a widow with a large family is caught at as a fortune."

Much of this Gubbins deplored. He argued, for example, that the endless round of rural chores faced by almost everyone encroached upon education and left the youth of the colony "certainly inferior to their parents in every respect that relates to manners and good society." Even the older generation was not beyond reproach— nowhere, it seemed, were its failings more evident than in the Assembly, whose members appeared "poor and ignorant." Their stipend, he alleged, was "their greatest object of ambition," and in the business of the house "their private interests and popularity are more consulted than...the public good."

Although Gubbins was less forthright about it, even he found much to admire in New Brunswick society. Robbery was "almost unknown," and people were generous in assisting the victims of misfortune. Settlers joined in "frolics" (known as "bees" in Upper Canada) to assist newcomers in raising their houses and beginning their clearings, working for no more than meat and drink, the company, and the sense that help should be reciprocated. Wages were relatively high. The weakest and oldest could earn a living. If English manufactured goods were double the price in Britain, and Fredericton doctors were sometimes "embarrassed to get home...[their] fees of hay, salt fish, or banded pork," the timber trade had invigorated the local market and promoted a "general improvement in the appearance of the peasantry as well as in the comfort of their dwellings and in the number and value of their stock." Reflecting on the population of the province in general, Gubbins saw that "the necessaries of life...[were] produced upon their farms and a share of its luxuries they got by selling lumber."

Towns "All in a Whirl and a Fizz"

Relatively few British North Americans lived in cities and towns before 1840—urban dwellers accounted for no more than one in every six residents along the St. Lawrence in 1760, and for approximately 10 per cent of British North America's population in 1840. But however small in size, these places and their satellite communities were important centres of colonial life. They were the pivots by which the New World was most firmly attached to the Old. Ideas, immigrants, and commodities passed through them. Colonial officials concentrated in them. From commerce and government they derived wealth and status. Lines of trade and authority made them the core of their hinterlands. Their newspapers carried news of Britain and the Empire into the back country. To contemporaries they were, like Toronto in 1842, places where "all is in a whirl and a fizz, and one must be in the fashion."

The urban network of British North America grew substantially in size and complexity between 1760 and 1840. Early in the period, only Quebec, Montreal, and Halifax had more than three thousand inhabitants. By 1840 there were at least ten places of that size, and the number of smaller centres had grown even faster. By 1821, Quebec, with fifteen thousand residents, had ceded numerical and commercial superiority on the St. Lawrence to Montreal. By 1832 York, soon to be incorporated as the City of Toronto, had outgrown Kingston to become the largest urban community in Upper Canada with thirteen thousand souls. In the 1830s Saint John challenged Halifax in the eastern provinces. And by 1840, Montreal was the pre-eminent city of British North America with forty thousand residents—slightly fewer than the modern-day cities of Fredericton, Sorel and Welland, and only a trifle more populous than Belleville, Penticton or Prince Albert, Saskatchewan.

In settings where so much was new, settlers quickly recognized the importance of forwarding their interests. Growth was a universal ambition. Leading citizens of countless towns sought administrative functions and transport improvements in the hope of inducing the expansion of their centre. Small places competed with one another for the role of county seat or district town—both implied a quickening of town life by virtue of the official business conducted there. By 1840 judges, sheriffs, clerks of the peace, customs collectors, Crown land agents, district clerks, school superintendents, and licence inspectors might be numbered among the residents of important district centres. In the 1830s Kingstonians anticipated prosperity from the enlarged hinterland provided by construction of the Rideau and Trent canal systems, and early in the next decade they were enjoined to avoid the mistakes of New York, where Broadway, eighty feet wide and "originally deemed ample," was now crowded with traffic. *Their* "AVENUE ought to be a hundred feet wide; and straight as an arrow, should proceed onward to the Priest's Field—there, to terminate in a CIRCUS or SQUARE,—including the ancient pines, to remain as sacred memorials of the primeval forest."

The potent combination of vision and energy spawned imposing new buildings and impressive plans that ran streets through vacant land. Where mill-sites or other natural advantages added impetus to expansion, firm foundations for growth might be laid down. New names appeared on maps as crossroads settlements developed into villages and as villages grew into towns. City charters marked the rise of conspicuously successful places. In the end, though, trade set the urban pattern. The leading cities were commercial centres, located on sea lanes, and each served an extensive back country. For Montreal, at the head of navigation on the St. Lawrence, this hinterland encompassed Upper Canada until transport improvements such as the Erie Canal, canals on the St. Lawrence, and eventually the railroad quickened the rise of Toronto. But in the main each colony had its own principal commercial port. Although the French-language newspapers of Montreal maintained an interest in news from France, each of these major centres looked first and foremost to Britain. There were strikingly few links between the cities. In the 1840s very, very little of the commercial information appearing in the newspapers of Halifax, Saint John, and St. John's related to the Canadas. Such little Halifax information as appeared in the newspapers of Quebec and Montreal was generally ten days to two weeks old.

Spring and fall, the most active shipping seasons, were busy times. In Montreal and Saint John, the scene differed only in detail from that described in Halifax by the opinionated young army engineer Captain William Moorsom in the 1820s:

Signals are constantly flying at the citadel for vessels coming in; merchants are running about, in anticipation of their freights; officers of the garrison are seen striding down with a determined pace to welcome a detachment from the depot, or a pipe of Sneyd's claret for the mess; and ladies, tripping along on the tiptoe of expectation flock into two or three *soi disant* bazaars for the latest *à-la-mode* bonnets.

Beyond these major towns lay those of a lower order. Smaller in population, and in the volume of their trade, they served district markets with goods shipped from the regional centres, and, in some cases, with direct consignments from Britain and the West Indies. Each had its commercial district, whose shops—if neither very numerous nor very capacious by metropolitan standards—were generally "well filled, and some of them very neatly arranged."

Farther inland, storekeepers extended the trading network into even more remote locations. Clustered together with a blacksmith, a carriage works, a tavern, and a mill, general stores were integral parts of the "rising villages" scattered across the settled countryside. On their shelves, wrote the poet Oliver Goldsmith (Canadian grandnephew of his more accomplished Irish namesake) in *The Rising Village*, stood "all useful things and many more." Here "nails and blankets," there "horses collars and a large tureen":

Buttons and tumblers, fish hooks, spoons and knives,
Shawls for young damsels, flannel for old wives;
Woolcards and stockings, hats for men and boys,
Mill-saws and fenders, silks, and children's toys.

Collectors of country produce, providers of credit to neighbouring families, and suppliers of exotic necessities as well as occasional luxuries from abroad, storekeepers were the nuclei of rural communities. They were also the distant branches of a diffuse commercial and financial system whose roots led back, eventually, to the factories, banks, and trading houses of Britain.

In 1840 even the largest towns were strikingly different from the cities we know. In contrast to the sprawling urban spaces of our day, Montreal, Toronto, Quebec, Halifax, and Saint John were tight little centres. Each had its wharf and warehouse district, its retail area, and its fashionable streets, but they were small and few. If rich and poor, merchant and labourer, occupied different streets, they did so in most parts of the city. The juxtapositions were often striking. Imposing and gracious as Toronto's King Street appeared in the 1830s, oxen pulled carts along it; barely a block away there was an active lakeside fish market. In the old town site to the east, the splendid mansions of prosperous merchants were surrounded by dilapidated little cottages of immigrants and labourers that filled the back lanes of the district. To the west, public and private buildings in Georgian and early Gothic revival styles distinguished the lakefront but gave way to much humbler homes a short distance inland.

In Montreal, the commercial heart of the city was five blocks deep. Walking back from the waterfront a visitor saw, in sequence, relatively distinct concentrations of warehouses, boarding-houses, and taverns; the offices of brokers and lawyers; retail

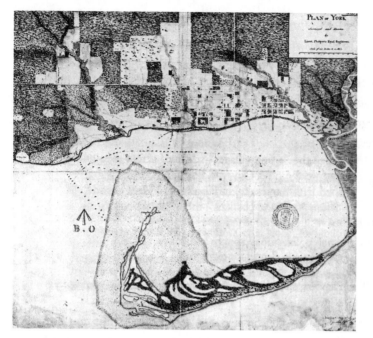

A fine example of early nineteenth-century military cartography, revealing much of the character of this village of perhaps one thousand people. Most houses and shops were within the original town; Yonge Street ran into forest half a mile from the lakeshore; other roads quickly diminished to paths. *Plan of York* (1818), by Lieutenant George Phillpotts.

stores, banks, and insurance companies; and light industry. Within these zones there was considerable diversity. Since important merchants, shippers, and commercial agents had offices amid the warehouses and hotels of the waterfront, some of them also lived on the upper floors of the three- and four-storey buildings in the area. Architects and other professionals were scattered through the central streets of the district. Brass foundries, carriageworks, candlemakers, and the shops of other artisans marked its inner edge. Large foundries and factories bounded it to west and east. Beyond, the southern slopes of Mount Royal remained in country estates laid out early in the century by some of those who had prospered from the fur trade: James McGill, Simon McTavish, and William McGillivray.

In Montreal and Quebec, ethnic areas began to divide the cities. In both places English-speakers were concentrated in disproportionate numbers in the central commercial section. Those areas in which most artisans, labourers, and small shopkeepers lived were predominantly French Canadian. These patterns clearly reflected the distribution of wealth and power. Although French-Canadian investors held significant concentrations of property in Montreal and Quebec, banking, insurance, and wholesale activities were almost exclusively in English hands. Banks, mansions, and official buildings (such as Customs Houses) proclaimed their British

Described as "a second Montreal in point of commercial and mercantile importance" early in the 1830s, York grew significantly over the next few decades. The court house, jail, and church added distinction to King Street. But the waterfront was the hub of the city. By 1838, Toronto's wharfs were accommodating heavy schooner traffic; hotels and warehouses lined Front Street, daily stagecoaches left the triangular "Coffin Block" for Holland's Landing, and a fish market added to the bustle. *King St. E., Yonge to Church Sts., looking e. from Toronto St.*: lithograph after a drawing by Thomas Young, published by Nathaniel Currier (New York, 1835). *The Fish Market, Below Front Street, Toronto*: sepia copy by an unknown artist after an engraving in *Canadian Scenery* (1842), illustrated by W. H. Bartlett.

domination by echoing metropolitan taste in their Georgian and classical architecture. So too, the Anglican cathedrals in both cities bore a close resemblance to the London church of St. Martin-in-the-Fields.

Smaller towns lacked the dense cluster of buildings that marked the central blocks of larger cities, and were even less distinctly set off from the surrounding countryside. Income, status, and religion set families and individuals apart, and people appreciated every nuance of these distinctions, but in such small places all faces were familiar and most residents felt themselves part of the community. Often this identification flowered into local pride. It was reflected in various ways in the newspapers, town halls, street improvements, and debating societies that sprang up in these places, the effect of which was to impart a vigorous localism to life. Lord Durham found this a particularly striking facet of Upper Canada. "The Province," he wrote in 1839, "has no great centre with which all the separate parts are connected, and which they are accustomed to follow in sentiment and action: nor is there that habitual intercourse between the inhabitants of different parts of the country, which…makes a people one and united….Instead of this, there are many petty local centres, the sentiments and the interests…of which, are distinct and perhaps opposed."

Cobourg, on Lake Ontario, well exemplifies the progressive character of such "petty local centres." Little more than a village in the 1820s, the town emerged during the 1830s as the commercial focus of a hinterland that extended beyond the bounds of Hamilton Township. By 1833 a steamboat linked the north shore of Rice Lake with the head of the stage line from Cobourg. Stagecoaches linked Cobourg to York and Kingston. At the end of the decade, packet steamers of the Royal Mail line connected the town to Rochester and other lake ports. In 1837 Cobourg was incorporated. Five years later it had grist and sawmills, fourteen general merchants, ten hotels and taverns, four carriage factories, and a cluster of tailors, tanners, cabinetmakers, and bakers. Five lawyers and four doctors practised alongside Cobourg's hairdresser and druggist. Agents of two banks and an insurance company had offices in the town. Because Cobourg was the administrative centre of Northumberland County, its population included several county officials. It also had a provincial postmaster and a collector of Customs. In a settlement of clapboarded frame houses, most of which were simple storey-and-a-half structures, Victoria College, built by the Methodist church, occupied a large and striking stone building back from the lake. A few prosperous commercial men built large houses; some of them were of brick and many were known by name: "New Lodge," "Beech Grove," "The Hill." One

The Launching of the ROYAL WILLIAM, Quebec, Apr. 29, 1831. Well-dressed crowds line the waterfront and look on from the cliff as the steamer leaves the floating dock at John S. Campbell's shipyard in Quebec. In 1833 she became the first Canadian vessel to cross the Atlantic under steam alone. Watercolour (1831) by J. P. Cockburn.

typical example, offered for sale in 1843, was a "delightfully situated cottage Residence" with five bedrooms, dining and drawing rooms, and a china closet; with garden lawn, stable yard, barn, and "three stable cowhouse," the whole comprised some two acres and commanded "a beautiful view of Lake and Harbour." In 1842 the Diocesan Theological Institute of the Church of England was established in Cobourg in association with St. Peter's Church. The town had a Mechanics Institute and a Loyal Orange Lodge. Yet its population barely exceeded one thousand.

As the towns grew into cities in the first half of the nineteenth century, they became crucibles of social change. Urban society became more complex, and the demand for goods and services rose. New crafts, trades, and occupations—such as furniture- and carriage-makers, carters, porters, butchers, and shoemakers—found their place in the urban fabric. Extremes of wealth and poverty were more noticeable, and society became more clearly divided. The concentration of people also threw ethnic and religious differences among them into sharper relief. Tensions rose as Protestants and Catholics, English, Irish, and French Canadians sensed their distinctiveness and competed to secure their own interests; they sometimes spilled over into

Imposing Victoria College set Cobourg apart from a score of other rising towns whose buildings huddled around a wharf or landing. Note the Customs House flying the white ensign, a reminder of the trade across Lake Ontario. Engraving after a watercolour by W. H. Bartlett in *Canadian Scenery* (London, 1842).

violence. Limbs were bruised and heads broken when Protestant Orangemen celebrating the victory of William of Orange over Irish Catholic forces at the Battle of the Boyne on July 12, 1690, dashed with "Green" Catholics in and around the Irish districts of several cities in the 1830s and 1840s. So too, Irish immigrants and French Canadians, who competed for jobs in the Ottawa valley timber trade, terrorized Bytown (Ottawa) with their brawling, drinking, springtime skirmishes.

Almost always, the frictions behind such ferment precipitated adjustment and accommodation. Older, intimate forms of urban administration which had integrated many people into the life of the community by distributing part-time jobs (in road work, the constabulary, and so on) among them gradually gave way to a more centralized and professional urban government. Responding to changing circumstances, and reflecting the rise of a new middle class drawn from expanding evangelical congregations, several reform groups sought remedies to the "problems" of these growing cities of strangers. Movements for the improvement of education developed momentum. Citizens sought better policing and improvements in such public utilities as sewers, water supplies, and street-lighting, as problems of waste and water contamination increased. There were also campaigns against theatres and tippling houses. From its beginnings in Montreal in the late 1820s, the temperance movement gained support across British North America. Orators proclaimed the virtues of the cause at noisy public meetings. Those who took the pledge forswore ardent spirits such as whisky or rum, or committed themselves to total abstinence. Sabbatarianism also took root during these years, as British North Americans were enjoined to put aside work and the "idle ramblings of recreation" each Sunday in favour of Bible study and worship. To be sure, most Anglicans and Roman Catholics preferred "the holy hilarity of the Lord's Day" to strict severity. Others regarded the "Damned Cold Water Drinking Societies" as potentially dangerous organizations, calculated to "impose upon and delude the simple and unwary." But pamphlets and newspapers such as *The Canada Temperance Advocate* and the *Christian Guardian* spread the reform message and eventually left their mark. Notorious for drinking and drunkenness in the 1840s, by 1890 the chief city of Ontario took pride in the evangelical righteousness celebrated in its reputation as "Toronto the Good."

A Diverse and Fractured Realm

In 1840, a quarter of a century before Canadians and Maritimers met in Charlottetown to pursue the vision of a transcontinental nation, British North America was a remarkably fragmented place. European settlement straggled over 2,500 kilometres (1,500 miles) between St. John's and the St. Clair River. A million and a half people lived, for the most part, in small, sharply separated pockets of territory. Fishing villages faced the sea from narrow beachheads in the isolated coves of the deeply indented Atlantic coast. Their foundations were, often as not, on rock. Spruce forest—"miserable spruce…fit only to be inhabited by wild beasts"—crowded their backs. Where agriculture was possible, its extent was generally bounded by rock, or by high land: the fertile Fundy marshlands were hemmed in by steep escarpments sufficiently forbidding to bear the name "mountain" despite their relatively slight elevations. The productive St. Lawrence lowlands gave way, often within a mile or two of the river, to the granite of the Canadian Shield and the acidic soils of the Appalachian highlands; the Shield swung down to the St. Lawrence below Kingston and presented its jagged southern boundary to colonists a few concessions north of Peterborough. Prince Edward Island offered a variant on the theme: much of its land was sand and swamp. And even where the land was tolerable, the climate limited its use. On Cape Breton, newly arrived Scots found vacant upland but a distressingly short growing season.

Ethnic divisions, language, and religion reinforced this fragmentation, especially along the St. Lawrence, where two tongues and two faiths reflected differences in the origins, outlook, and experiences of the people, and divided a population whose economic fortunes were tied together by the commercial importance of Montreal. But these factors also segmented the English-speaking society of Upper Canada, and created a mosaic of identities among the people of New Brunswick, Nova Scotia, Prince Edward Island, and Newfoundland. The Gaelic, the fiddle, and the pipes could be heard from Pictou to Inverness, but religion divided Nova Scotia's Scots even into the twentieth century. "Down-shore," in Catholic country, wrote Charles Bruce in *The Channel Shore*, a powerful evocation of life in eastern Nova Scotia between the two world wars, "there was dancing and card-playing and a church with a cross on a steeple....Upshore...[where Catholics were few and far between] there were box socials and strawberry festivals and small white box-like churches...." By clinging more or less tenaciously to their roots, the various groups—Acadians, Irish, German-speaking descendants of the Protestant migrants of the 1750s, those who were English, and those who were Yankees—added to the diversity of the eastern colonies. Largely a product of the settlement process which brought people at different times from particular source areas to one or another of the region's circumscribed pockets of habitable land, such distinctions lingered longest in those settlements which were most isolated.

Neither economic nor political interests unified this diverse domain. Similar techniques and technologies imposed similar patterns of settlement and production on the fishing coasts, and ensured that the lumberman's onslaught on the forest differed little from New Brunswick to the upper Ottawa valley. But the fishery, scattered along broken shores and focused on a resource to which it was difficult to control access, was a profoundly fragmented enterprise. And the timber trade, tied as it was to the drainage system, carved the colonies into a series of cantons focused on their major rivers. Each activity engaged people from a variety of backgrounds but neither obscured the cultural differences that set them apart. Links between these two most important export trades were virtually non-existent. Fishermen and lumberers shared little but the harsh and dangerous nature of their lives.

Most British North Americans were farmers whose energies went into the one hundred or two hundred acres of New World land that provided their subsistence and a sense of security and achievement. Where markets were weak, as they were in so much of the colonies, settlers' horizons were narrow. For some, they barely extended beyond the forest that bounded their clearings. For others, a small circle of neighbours defined the limits of everyday familiarity and concern. But for many, the major urban centres were remote and essentially unknown.

In some parts of New Brunswick and the Canadas, farming and lumbering intersected—settlers worked in the woods; farm surpluses found a market in the lumber camps. But by 1840 these activities began to occupy separate spheres. The St. Lawrence timber trade focused on the Ottawa River and its tributaries deep in the Shield and far beyond the main agriculture areas of Upper and Lower Canada. In New Brunswick, production centred more and more on the virtually unsettled northern and eastern interior of the province. There was no unity of political interest among the separate colonies, except in reaction to such external threats as the elimination of colonial tariff preferences in the British market. Even then, responses to common crises were more often individual and self-interested than collective and communal. So separate was life on the St. Lawrence and the Atlantic that a Canadian minister returning from Charlottetown in October 1864 was asked of those who lived in the eastern colonies, "What sort of people are they?"

Before the scruples of Victorian moralists took hold of colonial sensibilities, British North American society was rough, ready, vigorous, and violent. Life was hard and dangerous. Death was a frequent, unexpected, visitor. Sudden storms, crashing trees, unstable canoes, malfunctioning machinery, dysentery, disease, and the perils of childbirth ended many young lives. Wayward axe blows, falls, and other accidents maimed countless healthy bodies. Where life was so uncertain it was also regarded as cheap. Rum and whisky were ubiquitous sources of comfort, solace, and warmth among the masses, while imported claret and port were consumed in prodigious quantities by the better off, and as a result minor disputes frequently erupted into violent quarrels. Neighbours came to blows. Gentlemen duelled. Verbal abuse was common in political debate and between groups whose positions in the social fabric of the colonies provoked rivalry. Violent clashes between political factions at election time, and between Protestant and Catholic on July 12, were undoubtedly ceremonial skirmishes, enjoyed as a form of recreation as much as for the belligerence that marked them. But they hinted at a deeper anarchism. For all that local justices, appointed constables, and other officials appeared to extend the fabric of

Mothers and daughters of Lower and Upper Canada. Left: *Portrait of Mme Louis-Joseph Papineau et sa fille Ezilda*, an oil (1836) by Antoine Plamondon; right: *Mother and Child*, an oil (*c.* 1830–40) from Upper Canada by an unknown artist. Ezilda, daughter of the Patriote leader, became the mother of politician and journalist Henri Bourassa. The austerity of the Upper Canadians (possibly Mennonites from Waterloo County) is a striking contrast to the elaborate dress of their contemporaries in Lower Canada.

authority across the settled land, laws were widely honoured only in the breach. Squatters defied regulations and simply assumed rights to Crown land. Lumbermen regularly resorted to subterfuge to evade levies on the timber they had cut. Neither group was above violence, or the threat of violence, to ward off competitors and deter zealous inspectors. Taken together, such actions point to a significant independence of mind, individualism of spirit, and insouciance of character, in contrast to official longings for an ordered, deferential society.

Beyond the southern rim of the Canadian Shield life was very different. Europeans were a small minority in a vast, thinly settled area. By comparison with the East, Rupert's Land and New Caledonia bore few marks of European penetration. To the casual observer Aboriginal life might have seemed much as it had been half a century before. Most Native peoples maintained essentially traditional ways of life. Almost everywhere, fishing and hunting still provided a subsistence for small, widely scattered groups. Native bands moved as they wished, usually without European restriction, across the territory. Occasional fur-trading posts, tiny islands of English custom in an overwhelmingly Aboriginal land, were the only obvious indications that this area lay within the orbit of the British Empire. But change there had been. Significant numbers

Cheating the Toll. Intended as a commentary on the frequency of tollgates on the roads of Lower Canada, this lively scene offers a vivid reminder of how little authority was respected in much of early British North America. Oil (undated) by Cornelius Krieghoff (1815–72); one of a number of variants on this theme by the German-Canadian genre and landscape painter.

of the region's indigenous inhabitants were struggling to survive. Alcohol had lubricated their trade in furs and weakened their spirit. European demands and European guns had depleted the resources on which both trade and life depended. Some groups had occupied new territory, and a new people of mixed Native and European heritage had come into being. By 1840 there were 2,500 Métis at Red River, five times the number of 1821. Increasingly dependent on the buffalo hunt, which drew over 1,200 Red River carts to the plains in the summer of 1840, they played a large role in provisioning the Hudson's Bay Company. As they did so they forced further adjustment on the Native peoples of the plains and parkland fringe. For all its appearance of stability, the human geography of the continental interior was highly volatile.

Considered as a whole, British North America was a singularly incoherent realm. Its people hardly knew one another. Separated by origin and occupation, language and religion, they were also set apart by space and time. While Native peoples of the west lived by the seasons, followed the game, and maintained traditional beliefs in an animistic universe, eastern engineers celebrated the power and reliability of steam. Against the flexible rhythms of the countryside, the factories and foundries of

The Rebel Candidates. Before the secret ballot, when voters still had to declare their choices from a special platform, election campaigns such as this one in 1828, in Perth, Upper Canada, were rousing and often violent affairs. Vocal supporters tried to intimidate those likely to vote the other way, and competition for a position at the foot of the platform was fierce; more than a little alcohol was applied to help waverers to a decision. Watercolour (1830) by F. H. Consett.

Montreal raised the spectre of time-discipline and rigid routine. So too were the people divided by circumstances, aspirations, and style. Settlers bound to a crowded, earth-floored log cabin in an eye of the woods shared little with those whose coiffed heads, fine clothes, and witty conversation won them affection at fashionable official soirées. By the same token, Yankee manners regularly punctured Tory dreams. Gentle, proper Susanna Moodie, addressed as an equal by an "impertinent" young girl—a "creature…dressed in a ragged dirty purple stuff gown, cut very low in the neck…her uncombed tangled locks falling over her thin inquisitive face…"—was neither the first nor the last to express indignation at the casual familiarity of "lowly" neighbours.

Measured against the fractured patterns of 1840, Confederation was a bold idea indeed, and its realization, since 1867, has been a triumph of technology and commitment. But important foundations of the modern country were laid down between 1760 and 1840. The fur-trade link between the St. Lawrence and the West shaped settlement and kept open the possibility of a nation *a mari usque ad mare.* As settlements expanded, basic structures and patterns of rural life were established. The landscape was given form by the surveys and town foundations of these years. New means of transport followed corridors of movement entrenched before 1840. And attitudes forged in the process of colonization have shaped the outlook of later generations of Canadians.

So popular was *The Clockmaker; or the Sayings and Doings of Samuel Slick, of Slickville* that eighty editions of Thomas Chandler Haliburton's book were published in the nineteenth century. The vivid stories first appeared in Joseph Howe's Halifax newspaper, *The Novascotian*, during 1835.

"I am Sam Slick, says I."

In the middle decades of the nineteenth century, British North American society was less radical than that of the United States, less conservative than that of Britain. Upper Canadians were more "go ahead" than their English cousins. Nova Scotians, said the Yankee pedlar Sam Slick, were "etarnal lazy"; while we "go ahead," they "go astarn." Colonists were more egalitarian and, some claimed, more avaricious than English men and women, but their manners and ideas set them apart from Yankees. They were less expansive and more respectful of authority than their neighbours. One mid-century English visitor, recently arrived in Toronto from the United States, neatly if unconsciously summarized the drift of much contemporary opinion when she noticed that the people there did "not run *'hurry skurry'* along the streets" as they tended to do to the south, and that "there were no idlers to be observed."

These perceptions owed much to the circumstances of British North American development. By and large, English-speaking colonists were dislocated people. Displaced by industrialization, the pressures of overpopulation, or ideological conviction, they had come to environments in flux. Migration and mixing put tradition at a discount. Attachments to place were weakened by movement. Communities had to be formed anew. Where land was widely and relatively cheaply available, as it was before 1840, these communities were very different from those in densely populated, land-scarce Europe. Neither the very rich nor the very poor were as common in the New World, the former because there was little wealth to be gained from land *per se*, the latter because accessible land allowed most families some degree of security and at least a minimal subsistence. This was as true of Lower Canada as it was of the other colonies before 1840, and so it was too that Loyalist dreams of landed gentility faded quickly.

Economic and social differences existed, of course. Some immigrants came with capital, others with little or nothing at all. Local land markets were subject to inflation through population growth and speculation. As the price of land rose, those who possessed it profited, those without it generally found it harder to acquire. But, until 1840 at least, another migratory step could carry settlers who wanted land to a nearby settlement in which it was still relatively cheap. For those French Canadians for whom the Shield fringe was unappealing, jobs in the textile mills of New England were not far distant. In the colonies as in the United States, a reservoir of accessible land had a levelling effect on society, and led many a British North American "jack" to the comforting conclusion that in most things he was indeed "as good as his master."

Yet the belief in an individualistic, egalitarian way of life was never as pervasive in British North America as it was to the south. In an increasingly introverted French-Canadian society, family ties, the parish, and the close-knit settlements of the lowlands heightened a sense of community. Obligations and respect were due the priest and *seigneur*. Retrospection and an attachment to traditional institutions were strong. From all of this grew a sense of ethnic and regional distinctiveness that bound individual Canadiens into the web of an organic society. In the other colonies, liberal tendencies ran up, time and again, against the inherent conservatism of provincial politicians and the aspirations of colonial élites with strong attachments to British traditions. Loyalty was the cornerstone of English-speaking conservatism in British North America, and provincial conceptions of that term encompassed not only allegiance to the British Crown but also general approval of the established church, British liberties, and English imperialism—all of which, contemporary British North Americans hoped, would make their manners, politics, and social arrangements "different from, and superior to" those of the United States. Furthermore, a northern climate, acidic soils, and the scarcity of habitable land in Canada made it harder for people to envisage their territory as a boundless empire of virtuous yeomen. Such a poetic idea—as

Two architectural treasures of Upper Canada: Sharon Temple, at Sharon, north of Toronto (left), and Dundurn Castle, Hamilton (right). Built in 1830 by John and Ebenezer Doan after designs by David Wilson, leader of the Children of Peace, a dissident Quaker sect, the temple is highly symbolic: its four pillars represent Faith, Hope, Love, and Charity, while its four doors invite worshippers to gather from all quarters. Dundurn, the largest Regency house in Upper Canada when it was completed in 1835, was the home of Sir Allan MacNab, the first Queen's Counsel in the colony and Prime Minister of the Canadas between 1854 and 1856.

de Tocqueville called it—could hardly take hold of the Canadian imagination as it had seized the minds of Americans. Together, British ties and northern realities moderated the brash, aggressive individualism associated with the American frontier.

Still, the experience of British North American settlement engendered a growing sense of the importance and possibilities of progress among many colonial residents. Pushing back the wilderness to create farms was a pragmatic imperative. The forest was an obstacle. In the short term it likely seemed implacable, but year by year it fell back before the settlers' axe blades. And those engaged in this titanic struggle rarely counted the consequences of their advance as anything but success. Revealingly enough, the ungranted Crown domain was generally known as "waste land." Land was redeemed by settlement. Its resources, most specifically timber, were there for the taking. When regulations to control the plunder were drawn up they were intended to impose order on the exploitation, and to yield revenue from it—not to conserve the forest.

Ecological relationships were poorly understood, but by 1840 there were already signs of the damage wrought by the settlers' drive to dominate their environment. Many townships were well on the way to being laid bare of trees. The consequences were severe. When the sheltering foliage and extensive root systems of the forest were

Producing "deservedly celebrated" flour by means of "most expensive and complicated machinery," these water-powered mills—built in 1826 and possibly the largest in the colony—ground Canadian and American wheat into thirty thousand barrels of flour a year in the 1840s. Note the blockhouse to the far right; Gananoque was raided by American forces in September 1812. Watercolour (c. 1839) by H.F. Ainslie.

stripped away, sun baked and rain beat on the ground. Water sluiced away in surface run-off instead of soaking into the land. Rich topsoil was washed away, often to silt up streams. Lower ground-water levels desiccated crops and dried up wells. Water levels in streams became unpredictable and even dangerous, especially during spring run-off. Before long, mill-owners from Cape Breton to Canada West (Ontario) were petitioning for aid to overcome the detrimental effects of these changes on their dams and waterwheels. In New Brunswick, sawdust was already a nuisance—it clogged riverbanks and the gills of fish. And by 1850 mill dams at the head of tide on almost every important stream had seriously disrupted the spawning runs of Atlantic salmon. Populations of beaver and other fur-bearing animals had dwindled severely as a result of European demand. There were local scarcities of other once-common game animals in the Canadas. Passenger pigeons, once so numerous that they could be clubbed out of the air at dusk, were all but eliminated. Wild turkeys were also greatly reduced in abundance by 1849. Even Newfoundland fish stocks showed signs of depletion during this period. As British North American environments suffered

Illustrations of the Upper Canadian landscape in the mid-nineteenth century are often arresting for the over-clearing they reveal. Only remnants of a once magnificent forest remain in this view, by Thomas Burrowes, centred on one of the isolated churches that served the scattered population of the colony.

the onslaughts of settlement, new plants and animals—many of them, such as wheat, oats, sheep, and cattle of great economic value—were introduced into the colonies. With these, and others of more purely ornamental purposes (roses and daffodils), also came thistles, burdock, wild mustard, and other weeds of Europe. Together, they changed the face of the land.

Yet among British North Americans of 1840, none whose knowledge of a particular territory spanned a decade would have remained unimpressed by the progress men and women had wrought. By and large, the achievement and the prospects of further improvement seemed greatest in Upper Canada. To the east, land and climate were more niggardly, a modest subsistence was that much more difficult to secure, and hope rather than conviction underlay optimism about the future. So Thomas Haliburton's Sam Slick stressed the wealth of Nova Scotian resources to persuade dubious colonists of their province's potential. A few years later, many an Upper Canadian settler might have echoed the opinion that "nothing...but industry, and enterprise...[were] needed to change the waste and solitary places" of that territory into a "true land of Goshen." Others would have agreed with the apparently self-evident proposition that no country could "with safety be stationary." East or West, few would have denied the essential message of countless immigrant letters home: that in this new world, hard work and reasonable luck would bring independence and a modest comfort to ordinary men and women. From such conviction, English-speaking settlers, in particular, drew a strong sense of the importance of private property and individual interest. Experience instilled among them strong attachments to home, family, and independence. Mastery of the environment became the means to an important end: the achievement of material prosperity. With time, embryonic feelings became convictions. And these strong ideas—the basic tenets of liberal individualism—echoed through economic and political debates in the late nineteenth century, despite efforts to define Canada as a political nation in which ethnic and cultural differences could flourish, and group rights would be respected. Indeed, and for all that has changed in the years since, Canadians still struggle with the legacy of these events, as they strive to balance arguments for individual opportunity against claims for communal rights in shaping the country of the twenty-first century.

Between Three Oceans: Challenges of a Continental Destiny 1840–1900

PETER WAITE

The Canadian Pacific Railway, published in 1886 (the year of the CPR's completion) as part of a series of maps and pamphlets aimed at prospective migrants from Great Britain to the newly opened Canadian West.

From Sea to Distant Seas

APE SPEAR, PROJECTING OUT into the Atlantic at St. John's, Newfoundland, is the eastern tip of the North American continent. From there to the Queen Charlotte Islands on the north-western rim of British Columbia comprehends 80° of longitude, almost a quarter of the way round the earth. From the top of Ellesmere Island, at 83°N, where land ends and the mountains drop into the Arctic Ocean, to Point Pelee in Lake Erie at 42°N, is half the same distance. Canada's a big country. How we got that much of the earth's surface, put it together politically, continue to hold it (more or less), is in itself, without our quite realizing it, a major achievement.

In 1840 the total population of British North America—as present-day Canada was then called—was about 1.5 million, dispersed across seven colonies. Newfoundland had a population of 60,000, concentrated in the eastern, lobster-like Avalon peninsula, between Cape Pine in the south and Cape Bonavista in the north— the latter Cartier's North American landfall in 1534. Roughly, the populations of the other colonies were: Nova Scotia, 130,000; New Brunswick, 100,000; Prince Edward Island, 45,000; Lower Canada (Quebec), 650,000; and Upper Canada (Ontario), 450,000. (These last two colonies—"the Canadas"—were joined by a British law of 1841 into the Province of Canada.) West and north of Lake Superior was the chartered territory of the Hudson's Bay Company, the watershed of all the rivers flowing into Hudson Bay. Across the Rockies the HBC ("Here before Christ") had exclusive licence to trade in an area then called Oregon and New Caledonia, jointly occupied with the Americans, from 42°N, the border of Mexican California, on the south to where the coast met 54°40', the beginning of Russian Alaska. The total Native populations—east, west, and Arctic—would perhaps have been under 300,000.

The Arctic Ocean and its islands were one of the first major areas of Canada to be explored, as names such as Davis Strait and Frobisher Bay—honouring the sixteenth-century explorers Martin Frobisher and John Davis—suggest. About a 1,600 kilometres (1000 miles) of the northern Arctic coast was surveyed in 1825–27 by Lieutenant John Franklin of the British navy, east and west from the mouth of the Mackenzie River. In 1845 he set out on his expedition to find the Northwest Passage. He never returned. He died aboard H.M.S. *Erebus*, imprisoned in the ice west of King

William Island, in 1847. At the time, no one knew what had happened to him. Expeditions to find him and his men began in 1848 and continued until 1859, when written records were found. Then, in 1984, the first startling discovery of two frozen and remarkably well preserved bodies of crewmen was made.

The Arctic was and is fierce, majestic country, where survival depended upon adaptation, resourcefulness, courage, and luck (good or bad as the case might be). Native people, both north and south, had adapted marvellously to the demands of the Canadian environment over a period of several thousand years. It was necessary for the new white arrivals to do the same.

Sir John Franklin's Last Expedition, 1845–48. Franklin set out in 1845 to sail through the Northwest Passage. He never returned. Francis McClintock's Arctic expedition of 1857–59 discovered two skeletons, two guns, and a lifeboat at Point Victory on King William's Island. Watercolour (undated) by unknown artist.

In 1984 the body of Petty Officer John Torrington was found on Beechey Island, N.W.T., in an almost perfect state of preservation. Torrington was on Franklin's last expedition, and died in spring 1846. (The bindings were probably to fit him into the narrow coffin, and to prevent the grotesqueness of his jaw falling open.)

A Winter's Tale

Canada, even in the south, had a winter's tale as well as a summer's. In all of Canada, except for the coastal fringe of British Columbia, the freeze-up—*la prise des glaces*, French Canadians call it—was one of two decisive events in every Canadian's calendar. The spring break-up was the other. Between November and April winter struck dumb Canadian rivers and lakes, immobilized the boats, canoes, and barges that used them, shut down the farms, and partly numbed even business. By mid-November the working season was largely at an end in the country, and to some extent in the towns too. Power still came primarily from running water, though by the 1830s steam engines were beginning to change that. Most of the flour mills, and all the sawmills, were driven by water. Winter shut these down, and the millers and the lumber merchants with them. As the rivers froze, so did the canals; the steamboats were dragged up on shore; the raftsmen went home; construction stopped; workmen were paid off; farmers hibernated, partied, or did both. The main tasks that winter offered to this sprawled, dismantled labour force were in the lumber camps—on the Miramichi and Saint John rivers in New Brunswick, the St-Maurice, Gatineau, and Ottawa in Lower Canada—cutting trees in the winter woods for running downriver when the ice was out at the end of April.

Winter poverty was not uncommon, for the amount of work went down drastically and necessities—food, fuel, and clothing—became more important and expensive. In the towns this could produce hardship; on the farm you were apt to be prepared. You tried to fill your root cellar ahead of time with barrels of apples, potatoes, turnips, carrots, and cabbages. You stacked away wood and, as transport developed, put coal in the coal cellar. You put on the storm windows, and put sod or branches around exposed foundations. By December you had stored the wagons and carts and got out the sleighs and buffalo robes. Then you proceeded to enjoy winter!

It was a time of year that often enough seemed dismal in Europe or on the west coast, but for Canadians and Canadiens in eastern Canada it was often a time of delight: sun, snow, and the sound of sleigh bells. Winter was the time, wrote Anna Jameson, a visitor from Britain in 1838, "for balls in town, and dances in farmhouses and courtships and marriages...." From her window on a Toronto street she watched the sleighs go past—carriage sleighs, market sleighs, or handsome cutters mounted on high runners driven fast by young sporting bloods or by officers from the local garrison. What Mrs. Jameson liked best was the wood sleighs, hauling maple, birch, pine, and oak logs into town to stoke innumerable fireplaces. As she described it, the

Sleighing in the City...of Montreal and *Sleighing in the Country*; two sepia watercolours (*c.* 1842) by Henry James Warre (1819–98). Warre was very proud of his city sleigh that whisked around Montreal as fast as his horses could trot; he contrasts it to a heavy machine lurching through snowdrifts and bad roads in the country. Note the different ways the horses are harnessed for the city and the country.

logs would be piled six or seven feet high on the sleigh; on top of the woodpile might be a couple of deer, frozen stiff, their antlers projecting out over the sides, and, sitting on top of it all, the driver with his blanket wrapped around him, fur cap pulled down over his ears, a vast scarlet scarf adding a gay dash of colour. From this height the driver guided two stout oxen with "the clouds of vapour curling from their nostrils into the keen frosty air—the whole machine, in short, as wildly picturesque as the grape wagons in Italy...."

But winter was not a season merchants and businessmen relished. Think of the capital tied up uselessly, hopelessly, inevitably, expensively, in a frozen mill! Business, real business, required importation, shipping; yet bringing in woollens, china, engines, cottons, had to await spring. The St. Lawrence was frozen to below Quebec. Montreal was, commercially and literally, frozen in from November until May. Thomas C. Keefer, a civil engineer, wrote with passion about it:

...an embargo which no human power can remove is laid on all our ports. Around our deserted wharves and warehouses are huddled the naked spars—the blasted forest of trade—from which the sails have fallen like the leaves of autumn. The splashing wheels are silenced—the roar of steam is hushed—the gay saloon, so lately thronged with busy life, is now but an abandoned hall—and cold snow revels in solitary possession of the untrodden deck. The animation of business is suspended, the life blood of commerce is curdled and stagnant in the St. Lawrence—the great aorta of the North....blockaded and imprisoned by Ice and Apathy we have at least ample time for reflection—and if there be any comfort in Philosophy may we not profitably consider the PHILOSOPHY OF RAILROADS.

"The Ringing Grooves of Change"

Imagine a cold, rainy, late-November evening in a stagecoach on the road between Fredericton and Woodstock, New Brunswick. Your coach is being dragged up a long, mean, muddy hill. The horses are tired. It is messy and slow, at times only a mile an hour. But a railway train could easily do 50 to 65 kilometres (30 to 40 miles) per hour, and do it night and day, not stopping for mired wheels, for hay, oats, or changing horses. It is no wonder trains had an appeal nearly irresistible to Canadians: they just kept going. They released society from the bondage of dirt and mud; even more, from the bondage of winter. Motion no longer depended upon animals or weather. Regularity, control, speed, punctuality: these excellent bourgeois virtues of railways gave businessmen something of what they longed for: commercial certainty.

In British North America, with its forests, isolation, and vast distances, transport was the key to nearly everything. The canoe had made possible the range and versatility of the French Canadians; it had made possible the North West Company; the sturdy York boat was by 1840 the mainstay of the Hudson's Bay Company. Transport helped create commerce; in some ways it *was* commerce. "The iron civilizer," Thomas Keefer called railways. Steam, he said in a magical sentence, "exerted an influence which can only be compared to that which the discovery of printing had exercised upon the mind."

Technology and engineering had followed hard on the heels of invention. There were developments in many fields of human endeavour, biology and medicine not least, but the most visible effects on society were the steam engine and the telegraph. Change began slowly but accelerated through the second half of the century until by 1900 it had transformed Canada. Social historian Asa Briggs called this period in Great Britain the "age of improvement." What was merely "improvement" in Great Britain was revolutionary in Canada.

Moreover, railways were an economic factor of far-reaching significance. The investment was enormous. Railways soaked up colonial savings—capital is another word—but that investment alone was not enough. British North America also imported massive amounts of capital from Great Britain. It came in the form of railway stock, that is, ownership; it came as bonds, that is, various forms of railway indebtedness; and the colonial governments themselves could not resist the pressures to help build railways. Their support often came in the form of guarantees on railway bonds, like the guarantees offered, under certain conditions, in the Province of Canada's Railway Guarantee Act of 1849. Every municipality wanted a railway, preferably a trunk line passing right through town, and municipal bonds were used to persuade railway companies to bend the line in the right direction. The first step in building a railway was acquiring a legal charter, and shoals of railway charters were issued by colonial and, later, provincial legislatures. From 1850 onward, every year's statutes had, under private bills, a list of new companies, far more than would ever make a survey or lay a rail, let alone build a freight car or a locomotive. One railway engineer remarked, "The longest journey a railway can take is the one from charter to rolling stock."

The first Canadian railway line was the Champlain and St. Lawrence, built from La Prairie, opposite Montreal, to St-Jean on the Richelieu—all of fourteen miles. Completed in 1836, it was a ramshackle affair of wooden rails with strap iron on top, and it operated only from spring to autumn. Despite its hazards—the strapping had the bad habit of breaking free and snapping up into the cars above—it made money. John Molson, who had founded Molson's Brewery in 1786, provided 20 per cent of the capital, and in fact nearly all the capital was local. By 1851, the Champlain and St. Lawrence was a year-round, iron-railed line going down to the American border where it connected with the Vermont Central. By that time there was a serious competitor, the St. Lawrence and Atlantic, which ran from Montreal to the ice-free Atlantic port of Portland, Maine—the world's first international railway. It was built with American as well as Montreal capital; it also went through Sherbrooke and brought in the entrepreneurial talents of Alexander Galt, who lived there. On its completion in 1853, the St. Lawrence and Atlantic was swallowed up, partly at Galt's instigation, by a still bigger British project, the Grand Trunk Railway.

Britain's great boom in railway building in the 1840s had been made possible by huge accumulations of private savings engendered by the industrial revolution of the past fifty years. When it turned out that capital invested in railways could be profitable, new investment opportunities were sought abroad, in France, the United States, and, not least, British North America. Engineering was as exportable as capital. British engineers favoured a carefully surveyed, well-built right-of-way with minimum grades and curves. If this necessitated expensive bridges, grading, tunnels, so be it. It meant high initial costs, but ultimately, with a good roadbed, low running costs.

Few of the conditions that characterized British construction existed in Canada. Labour costs in England were based on nearly year-round work by gangs providing cheap labour. No one seems to have told the Grand Trunk that in Canada all work stopped in November; that all construction had to take account of heavy frost; that labour in Canada was both less productive and more expensive.

The Grand Trunk encountered most of these problems. It was a British-owned railway; both its major stockholders and the contractors were British. In fact, the railway was a creature of the contractors, who were looking for new worlds to conquer. It had the high initial costs of British railways, with some of the labour and construction problems of Canadian ones. But the railway was built. One still sees the handsome old stone stations between Montreal and Toronto, or Toronto and Guelph; the long, sweeping embankments east of Toronto, and the high bridges over deep valleys to the west. Still, within a few years the Grand Trunk Railway needed financial assistance from shareholders, bondholders, and, inevitably, the government of the Province of Canada. Governments that chartered such lines often had a tiger by the tail. Once the line was partly built, there was tremendous pressure to finish it, if necessary by bailing it out. Governments, and Assembly majorities, could be persuaded to authorize loans, sometimes by argument, sometimes by gifts of stock, sometimes by outright bribery. The story is not pretty. Sir Edmund Hornby, a British engineer, said ruefully, "Upon my word, I do not think that there is much to be said for Canadians over Turks when contracts, places, free tickets on railways or even cash is in question." Government and Opposition fought over Grand Trunk issues, but finally, in July 1862, the Grand Trunk Arrangements Act tidied things up. The new managing director, Sir Edward Watkin, ran his iron road with an iron hand. This was not the end of Grand Trunk difficulties, but by 1880, when the Grand Trunk reached Chicago, its future seemed assured.

British North American legislators were not—like those in London—gentlemen debating national issues while living mostly on private incomes. Gentlemen many colonial members of the Provincial Parliament were, no doubt, but most colonial legislators had businesses to look after; parliamentary life may have been, as in England, a duty to society, but for most it was an expensive duty. They were away from home, and their businesses were bound to suffer during the parliamentary session. As Lord Elgin, the Governor General, put it in 1848:

...political life is ruin to men in these Countries and the best will not remain in it a day longer than they can help. Landjobbers, swindlers, young men who wish to make a name... may find in public life here...a compensation for the sacrifices it entails, but with honest men who are doing well in their own line of business, and who have not private fortunes to fall back upon, it is otherwise.

In Nova Scotia and New Brunswick the pattern of railway building was different. Governments there could not persuade private capitalists to build because the population of both provinces was too small to provide prospects of sufficient revenue. But the people themselves were clamouring for railways, especially in politically powerful southern New Brunswick, with its concentration of population. So the New Brunswick government, in the absence of willing railway companies, contracted its own work. It built a government railway from Saint John to Shediac (about a hundred miles) with the delicious name European and North American Railway. Nova Scotia undertook the Halifax–Truro and the Halifax–Windsor lines, both built and run by the government.

The Nova Scotia Railway soon found, as did others, that the very existence of a railway created changes that could be neither stopped nor reversed. Railways, like highways later, generated their own traffic, with side effects that could not be

The "Stag Hotel" is kept by William Dear,
Outside, the House looks somewhat queer,
Only Look in, and there's no fear,
But you'll find Inside, the best of Cheer,
Brandy, Whiskey, Hop, Spruce, Ginger Beer,
Clean Beds, and food for Horses here;
Round about, both far and near,
Are Streams for Trout, and Woods for Deer,
To suit the Public taste, 'tis clear,
Bill Dear will Labour, so will his dearest dear

Signboard of the Stag Hotel. The hotel, ten miles east of Dartmouth, N.S., was popular with Halifax sportsmen for its hunting and fishing. On May 28, 1873, Joseph Howe—ex-Premier and new Lieutenant-Governor of the province—visited it for sentimental reasons. But the long drive was too much for his failing health, and he died three days later. Anonymous oil (mid-nineteenth century); words by Colonel William Charnley.

Grand Trunk Railway Station, Toronto. The Grand Trunk Railway was incorporated in 1852, and this watercolour by William Armstrong (1822–1914) was done around 1857–59. Note the Native woman on the left, and the car being shunted in the background.

predicted. The little taverns that had once existed on the old dirt road between Halifax and Truro, one every few miles, to provide oats for horses, beer for men, solace for both, began to disappear as people turned to the ease, speed, and comfort of railways. In cities—Halifax, Saint John, Quebec, Montreal, Toronto, Hamilton—access to railways shifted perspectives, and the pace of change speeded up. By 1872 George Brown's Toronto *Globe* sold half its copies outside Toronto; by 1876 special early-morning trains took it to Hamilton, where it competed with local newspapers. Railways created whole new markets and made available ranges of new products. Not without reason did Sir Alexander Campbell, the Postmaster-General, exclaim in 1885, thinking of the past forty years, "What a time! and what changes!"

By 1900 the world of travel, movement, and trade had changed markedly. As a result there came new ways of thinking, politically as well as economically. What could be linked by railways might, in the right circumstances, be united politically. The thinking behind the Italian union of 1859–60 and the German union of 1867 was a product of the railway age. The American Civil War was won by the Northern armies, true; but what made victory possible was the physical means of deploying the North's superiority in men and material: railways.

The thinking behind Canadian Confederation was generated partly by what railways so palpably could achieve. The Intercolonial Railway between Halifax and Quebec City, completed in 1876, was the price exacted by New Brunswick and Nova Scotia for Confederation. Prince Edward Island's 219-kilometres (136-mile) railway cost her colonial treasury so much money that she was forced by the debt to allow herself to be railroaded into Confederation! Newfoundland's 800-kilometres (500-mile) railway from St. John's on the east coast to Port-aux-Basques on the west just about broke the province and the builders with it in the 1890s. By then Canada's Canadian Pacific Railway, completed in 1885, was making money. It generated so much traffic that in 1903 Canada decided it needed not one new transcontinental railway but *two*. In short, by 1900 it was a world of railways and electric streetcars, both strengthening the octopus-like grasp of Halifax and Saint John, Montreal and Toronto, Winnipeg, Calgary, and Vancouver, over the growing metropolitan hinterlands.

Of Men, Power, and Patronage

In 1840 the colonies of British North America were still scattered and separated. Their individual status was symbolized by the first postage stamps of the 1850s, each colony having its own: Newfoundland, Prince Edward Island, Nova Scotia, New Brunswick, the Province of Canada, and, in 1858, both Vancouver Island and British Columbia. Each had its own governor, administration, customs houses. Each was concerned with its own relations with Great Britain. Nova Scotia had had representative government since 1758, Prince Edward Island since 1769 (when it was created a colony), New Brunswick since 1784, the Canadas since 1791, Newfoundland since 1832. During the early stages of colonial government the system had worked well enough, though some friction between an elected Assembly, and an appointed Council that in effect combined legislative and executive functions, was inevitable. As the colonies grew bigger, as assemblies began to criticize more openly the abuses they saw in executive power, the problems of governing such colonies became more difficult. This growing tension was something that the American colonies and Britain had failed to resolve in the 1760s. But in the British North America of the 1840s the problem was not so much tyranny by the British government as a stranglehold on colonial executive control exercised by a powerful few. Governors appointed from London could only do so much; their tenure was usually from five to seven years, so they came and went. Members of provincial executive councils were there a great deal longer. A governor, Joseph Howe of Nova Scotia pointed out forcefully in 1839,

…must carry on the government by and with the few officials whom he finds in possession when he arrives. He may flutter and struggle in the net, as some well-meaning Governors have done, but he must at last…like a snared bird, be content with the narrow limits assigned to him by his keepers. I have known a Governor bullied, sneered at, and almost shut out of society…but I never knew one, who, even with the best intentions…was able to contend, on anything like fair terms, with the small knot of functionaries who form the Councils, fill the offices, and wield the powers of the government.

In the 1830s the Executive Council of Nova Scotia was based upon four or five families and their intermarriages. The problem was not that such oligarchies were stupid or ineffective; they were generally all too efficient—at looking after friends and relations and using the government, when it suited them, for their own purposes. They had learned how to recruit able young men to their ranks by marrying off their daughters to bright aspirants on the prowl for place, preferment, and patronage. Only in New Brunswick did the Assembly have a semblance of control over the Executive Council, and that was owing to a quasi-American style of government the Loyalists, who had supported the British cause during the American Revolution, brought with them from the U.S. after 1782–83. Other colonial assemblies felt that they too should be able to control their Executive Councils, by forcing reliance on a majority in the elected Assembly. That way, if an Executive Council became too outrageous it could be dismissed. Governors, technically, always had the power to do this, but because of the difficulties described by Joseph Howe they rarely did.

Colonial reformers saw their struggle for a cabinet system—that is, "responsible government"—as a matter of high principle, as an attempt to apply the party system that had evolved in Britain in the 1830s to their own colonial circumstances in the 1840s and 1850s. The development of the British cabinet system had been closely watched by discerning observers in British North America, notably Joseph Howe in Halifax and Robert Baldwin in Toronto. It was no accident that Nova Scotia and the Province of Canada developed the main impetus for colonial cabinet government. The movement had its own drama, tensions, bitter arguments over principle. Tories said that Reformers who claimed to want responsible government were only after the spoils of power—control of purse strings and appointments—and that all talk of

The Province of Canada's first postage stamp, designed by railway surveyor Sandford Fleming (1827–1915) and issued in 1851, shows the industrious Canadian beaver on a field of trilliums (now Ontario's provincial flower), crowned by symbols of British rule.

Assembly control over the Executive was a mask to cover greed.

In Nova Scotia and in the Province of Canada the two long-established Tory regimes began to fall, in stages, and were finally defeated in two important general elections in 1847. Both governments resigned after want-of-confidence motions early in 1848. New governments, called Reform, now occupied the Executive Council chambers, made appointments, carried on the government. As Lord Elgin remarked:

That Ministers and oppositions should occasionally change places is of the very essence of our Constitutional system, & it is probably the most conservative element which it contains. By subjecting all sections of politicians in their turn to official responsibilities it obliges heated partizans to place some restraint on passion....

That was all very well. But a hard test of restraint came in 1849, when the Reform government of the Province of Canada passed the Rebellion Losses Bill. Supported by Reform majorities that included substantial numbers of French Canadians, the bill compensated those who had lost property in the Rebellion of 1837 owing to military action. But the government did not distinguish carefully enough between ordinary citizens and those actively involved in the Rebellion. Tories were furious: government ought *not* to pay citizens for rebelling. A Tory mob, English-speaking for the most part, rose up in anger in Montreal (at that time still the capital of the Province of Canada), assaulted Lord Elgin, the Governor who had signed the measure, and went on to burn down the Parliament Buildings with the help of its new gas

Robert Baldwin. Upper Canada's most perceptive political thinker, Baldwin (1904–58) was partly responsible for working out the alliance between the Reformers of Upper Canada and those of Lower Canada in 1840–41; he is remembered as the popularizer of responsible government, and one of the first advocates of a bicultural nation. Oil (1848) by Théophile Hamel (1817–70)

Louis-Hippolyte LaFontaine. LaFontaine (1807–64) was the leader of the French-Canadian reformers; he joined Robert Baldwin and Francis Hincks in the Reform alliance, and when the Province of Canada was granted responsible government he became the Reform premier—he was thus, in a sense, Canada's first prime minister. Oil (1848) by Théophile Hamel.

lighting. It was a world of direct action! The Rebellion Losses Bill remained law, but Montreal was never again the political capital of anything. In 1850 the seat of government was moved to Toronto, thence to Quebec City. Although the Losses Bill had triggered the action of the Tory mob in April 1849, the uprising was also partly the result of commercial frustration created by shifts of British economic policy. Within a year after the capital was moved westward to Toronto, business recovered, and the blackened walls of Montreal's old Parliament Buildings were just a memory.

The Province of Canada was an odd colony, put together out of Upper Canada and Lower Canada. It stretched 1600 kilometres from Gaspé to Sarnia, united by a common geography: by the St. Lawrence, its estuary, river, and Great Lakes hinterland; by its new canal system and even newer, and growing, railway systems. But it was also disunited. Lower Canada, the future Quebec, continued to retain its language, its civil law, its educational institutions tied closely to the Catholic church.

The Burning of Parliament. When the Baldwin–LaFontaine government passed the Rebellion Losses Bill in 1849, there was a storm of protest, and on April 25—after pelting the Governor's carriage with stones and rotten eggs—a Montreal mob invaded the Houses of Assembly and set fire to the building. Following this burst of violence the seat of government was removed from Montreal. Oil (1849) attributed to Joseph Légaré (1795–1855).

These were very different from the language, law, and education in Upper Canada, the future Ontario. Most of Lower Canada still held its land under old seigneurial rules, though that was changing; legislation for the system's abolition, devised with some skill, was laid down in 1854 and 1855. And the Province of Canada was a colony with the potential for federation built right into it: there was equal representation for both sections of the province in their common legislature. This was despite Lower Canada having nearly 50 per cent more people in 1841 than Upper Canada; equal representation was intended to negate this French-Canadian advantage. In the end that purpose was frustrated by the creation of the Reform party, when Robert Baldwin persuaded Louis LaFontaine that such an alliance would be in the interests of both French and English.

Despite their differences, the two Canadas had strong elements of potential common interest. These included commerce, transportation, and, not least, the development of a political system that might be compatible with shared colonial aspirations, a system centred on the new idea of cabinet government. And so a sense of common interests launched a colony that by the 1860s was much the most powerful and mature of all those in British North America.

A Decent Outfit: Settlement and Society

Most Canadians are either immigrants or their descendants. By 1840 French Canadians had been here over two hundred years, about seven generations, and their folk memories reached back to their beginnings. Robert de Roquebrune (1889–1978) remembered tales from his father and grandfather and other forebears; for example, the marriage of his seventeenth-century ancestor LaRoque de Roquebrune, a French army officer, to Suzanne-Catherine de St-Georges, a vivacious Montreal girl of fifteen in the 1690s. Robert's father would tell how they were married by Bishop Laval in Quebec, how they returned to Montreal, as they had come, by canoe, arriving at moonrise, the young bride sleeping, and how Roquebrune carried his tender burden home against his shoulder. It was a story young Robert, growing up in L'Assomption in the 1890s, always loved. *His* ancestors! There were many other stories: his grandfather's role in the Rebellion of 1837, and his subsequent marriage to the handsome young woman who had helped him escape British troops. Robert's father would pull out from a chest some piece of clothing, carefully preserved, and tell the family history associated with it. Much of French-Canadian life had this interior intimacy—language, memories, and family history all mixed together.

Other immigrants came from England, Scotland, and Ireland. Why did they choose to come to Canada? Usually it was for solid material reasons, rather than because of religious pressures. And as a rule it was a particular type of person who came, often to join a relative who had done well here already. The typical immigrant was young, ambitious, beset back home by an old-country society and economy too rigidly structured to allow success or a change of status. They were often men and women displaced by economic difficulties not so serious as to cause actual poverty, but serious enough to make the uprooting attractive. These immigrants had usually saved a little money, enough for the passage and to keep them going until the first crop was harvested. Those in the old country who were rich neither needed nor wanted to emigrate; the very poor could not, as a rule, afford it.

There was one celebrated exception here: the Irish famine migration of 1847–48. The westward passage across the Atlantic in creaky, ill-built timber ships—which would otherwise have been empty for the return voyage to Canada—was very cheap. Those Irish immigrants were so poor, so ill-fed, so ill-prepared, that they created horrendous social problems wherever they landed, whether New York, Boston, Saint John, Quebec, or Montreal. Theirs was a migration of desperation. But the majority of immigrants were capable, vigorous, and yearning for material improvement—bourgeois virtues. Don't go, said one adviser in Britain in 1821, if you can earn a comfortable even if homely living in Britain. Don't go if you dislike work. Don't go if you're a tradesman and know no farming. Do go—to Prince Edward Island, as was the advice in this instance—if you have, if not felt want, at least feared it.

Crossing the Atlantic in the mid-nineteenth century was not quite the experience of a century before. Auxiliary steam was not yet available on most vessels, and conditions were still primitive, but passages were improving. There was no denying, however, that even in the 1840s conditions for immigrants were anything but healthy. Hundreds of passengers, from children to people in their eighties, would be huddled together with little light or air, contagion rampant, food seldom sufficient (or sufficiently cooked). From a 700-ton vessel, the Atlantic can be both benign and malignant, cheerful and frightening. A winter passage was to be avoided at almost any price, but storms were always bad whatever the time of year, and sometimes dangerous. Vessels could simply disappear without trace. Many did. James Affleck, the father-in-law of Sir John Thompson, later Prime Minister, was a sea-captain out of Halifax; he, his crew, and his ship just vanished in the summer of 1870. So did regular passenger ships: the *City of Cork* went down that same summer. The *Hungarian*, a regular Allan Line ship with steam auxiliary travelling from Portland, Maine, to Liverpool, caught the south-western tip of Nova Scotia one wild February night in 1860 and drove aground on Cape Ledge with the loss of over a hundred lives. Atlantic travel was for the sturdy and the determined, who were willing to risk themselves and their children on a long and often perilous voyage.

Once across the ocean and past immigration and quarantine, the immigrant in the New World needed some money to get him where he wanted to go. (In the years before Canada's acquisition of the great West, land had to be purchased, except in special cases such as Loyalists and half-pay British officers. It only became generally free in the Dominion Lands Act of 1872.) He had also to support himself and family until the land produced a crop. It was, none of it, easy; but neither was it impossible. It could be done, given reasonable luck with the land, willingness and competence to do the work. Experience with axe or plough helped.

There are many stories of failure; but more important, because more pervasive, are the successes, which are told less often than they should be. James Croil was born in Glasgow in 1821 and came to Quebec early in the 1845 season with a wife and family, landing with seven sovereigns in his pocket. (A sovereign was worth £1, or twenty shillings.) Some of it he used to get his family to Glengarry County, Upper Canada, where his wife's brother lived. The brother-in-law lent Croil seed, stock, and implements, and with what was left of his seven sovereigns he laid in provisions for the summer. He started work with five shillings left over. He had a good crop in 1845, and returned his brother-in-law the seed and half the produce of the land. Croil's half of the produce bought him provisions for 1846. In the spring of that year he rented a small farm at £20 per annum, and by the end of the 1848 season, when his lease expired, he had implements and stock of his own. In 1849 he rented two adjoining farms at £33 per annum. In the autumn of 1851 the two properties were offered for sale. Croil had no savings yet, but the land looked good and his sons were growing healthy and strong. A family council was held; Croil told his boys that if they would

James Croil and Party. Croil, a Scottish immigrant who became the editor of the *Presbyterian Record*, was the author of several books. This 1888 photograph recreating the family's arrival in Canada in the 1840s is by William Notman & Sons; Notman (1826–91) was a prize-winning photographer with branch studios right across eastern Canada and the U.S.

Canadian Wedding. A dance at a Lower Canadian wedding; the fiddler is on the right. Note the metal stove in the middle of the room, a much more efficient mode of heating than a fireplace. Watercolour (*c.* 1845) by James Duncan (1806–82).

all work they could pay for it. After all, as one historian has noted, the main motive force on the family farm was the farm family. Accordingly, the double farm was bought for £300, to be paid off at £50 per annum, plus interest at about 4 or 5 per cent. Forty acres were already cleared, and Croil and his sons cleared six acres further per year. Thus, by 1861, sixteen years after their arrival in Canada, the debt was paid, a hundred acres (forty hectares) were cleared, and the farm itself was worth £1,000. (This was in colonial pounds—"Halifax currency"—although Canada had officially converted to a dollar currency around 1858.) The two older boys had left to set up farms for themselves, but with his two younger sons Croil still worked his land.

The economy he describes in his memoirs is fascinating. In summer the family lived on bacon, beef, and ham, smoked by themselves, supplemented by their own eggs, and cheese and butter homemade from their own cows. In October they killed a cow or a young bull; the blacksmith got a quarter, the shoemaker another, the tailor a third, and the family kept the fourth. Another beast was killed in December; it was cut up, frozen, and packed away in barrels with straw, where it would keep until the end of March. The hide of the second beast went to the tanner, who kept half,

Harvest Festival in Lower Canada. This watercolour (*c.* 1850) is attributed to William Berczy, Jr. (1791–1873). Of German-Swiss origin, Berczy followed his father, William Berczy, Sr., in pursuing a career as a portrait, landscape, and genre painter in Upper and Lower Canada.

returning the other half to Croil. Then, once a year, the shoemaker came to the farm and made shoes for all. The tallow from the beasts was rendered and made into candles, the refuse scraps boiled up with wood ashes to make soap. The women spun the wool and wove the cloth, sewed the quilts and counterpanes, made the feather beds. Whenever a son or daughter married, Croil would sell a pair of horses and a cow or two and give the young couple, as he put it, "a decent outfit." Best of all, he was none the poorer, for new calves and colts were always coming. The farm economy needed its calves, colts, *and* children!

The point about the farm economy, at least in the East, was that there was nearly always a crop of something. If it was too wet for the wheat, potatoes flourished and so did hay. For the farmers of eastern Canada the sheer diversity of their production meant that they could produce nearly everything they needed, and often in some abundance. Of course, Croil's account takes for granted everyday tasks that are now

Colonel Samuel Strickland (standing, right) and his family. Strickland—brother of authors Susanna Moodie and Catharine Parr Traill (third from left, holding child)—was sheriff of Belleville, Ontario, for thirty years, and wrote *Twenty-Seven Years in Canada West* (1853).

easy to forget. The sheer brute labour of clearing land—those six acres a year—cutting the trees, sawing them up, burning the slash, finally those heart- and back-breaking stumps! Even after they had rotted for a few years, they were terrible to get out. And then there were the normal farm routines. Even in winter there was no holiday from animals; cows had to be milked twice a day, every day; horses, chickens, pigs had to be fed and looked after. Wood for fires had to be cut and split. Fences had to be built or mended; barns repaired; the jam and pickles made; the spinning, weaving, and quilting done—and the thousand tasks which had been left until winter came and the outside work finally stopped.

Country recreation was dances, square dances usually, with fife and fiddles. There

Casimir Gzowski (1813–98) and family, photographed at their Toronto home, around 1857, by Armstrong, Beere, & Hime. Born in Russia, Gzowski came to Canada in the 1840s, and worked as an engineer. He became the Province of Canada's superintendent of public works, in charge of roads, parks, bridges, harbours, and waterways, but is most remembered for his railway construction and for the International Bridge from Fort Erie to Buffalo.

was a whole range of country dances, Scottish, Irish, American. Whisky was the universal drink in Ontario and Quebec, and rum in the Atlantic provinces, coming cheap off the vessels from the West Indies. Whisky could be made from almost anything—frosted rye, mouldy pumpkins, or proper malted barley—but it came strong and raw. It burned, inside and out, with a pale blue flame. At times drinking and farming did not consort well together. There were always bees, very popular in the countryside, a source of fun and frolic and often more. Bees for raising a barn or house required at least some modicum of sobriety; it was the logging-bees Susanna Moodie hated. "Noisy, riotous, drunken," was her description in *Roughing It in the Bush*. Mrs. Moodie—an English gentlewoman who moved to Canada with her husband in 1832—had good cause to know; she had to cope with the food and drink for thirty-two men for a three-day bee. Many social institutions could not have managed without punch. Choir practices in Halifax, and elsewhere no doubt, had to be lubricated, and there was usually someone who knew how to mix rum, lemon juice, and sugar for a little reinforcement at intermission. Singing was thirsty business!

Drink permeated male society. It was not unbecoming for gentlemen, so-called, to be drunk; it was an eighteenth-century style still holding on manfully into the nineteenth. There is a 1787 account by a twenty-two-year-old naval captain in Halifax who sat down to dinner with twenty other gentlemen at the Governor's. Sixty bottles of claret and a dozen or two beers later, those who were still able essayed walking up Citadel Hill to try their luck with the girls on Barrack Street.

But by the nineteenth century the teetotallers were fighting back. Beginning about the 1830s, there were temperance movements preaching the transcendent virtues of cold water. The Sons of Temperance actually succeeded in persuading the government of New Brunswick to try the experiment of prohibition; it was adopted in 1852, effective January 1, 1853, but repealed the following year as utterly unworkable. Another version was bravely brought in in 1855, effective January 1, 1856. It brought down the government and was repealed too. After that, New Brunswick governments left the whole question severely alone, as well they might. No other colony made such an attempt. Nevertheless, the colonies had a growing segment of Protestants who deplored sin and gin equally. Temperance movements were strong among the Methodists and Baptists, and also among Presbyterians; they were unobtrusive among Anglicans, and virtually non-existent with Roman Catholics. It was, after all, Saint Benedict who held that a pint of wine a day was neither sinful nor dangerous.

It should not be assumed that meetings of temperance societies were all preaching and piety. A young man or woman brought up under the aegis of a drunken father already knew what whisky could do, without hellfire lectures. Temperance societies were often of young, vigorous, enterprising types, anything but milk-and-water; they sponsored dances, picnics, suppers, and sleigh-riding parties in winter. On a sleigh ride there were ways of keeping warm at least as good as—if not better than—drinking whisky. As these societies developed and matured, they created such offshoots as building societies and insurance companies. Business collectivities were often the result of private ones.

However high-mindedly these rural delights may have begun, there was a kind of cultural Gresham's law on the frontier, whereby more primitive customs tended to drive out more civilized ones. The Protestant churches—indeed all churches—tried to hold onto civilization as best they could. But rural society in British North America could be narrow, intolerant, and occasionally brutal. For example, the charivari, a noisy serenade to a newly married couple, was often a harmless and cheerful social custom, but it could turn malicious, particularly if the couple were not popular.

The Orange and the Green sides of Irish life and politics, exported to Canada, made their own contribution to recreational violence and factional infelicities. It was fortunate, perhaps, that Irish Catholics tended to the towns, and Irish Protestants more to the countryside. Even so, an Orange march in Toronto or elsewhere could easily (and, after a few draughts of whisky, effortlessly) be translated into Protestant hooligans on the loose. Axe handles were especially valuable in any fracas.

Duelling was on the wane by the 1840s, but although illegal it was still around. It was difficult for a gentleman to refuse a duel and still retain his self-respect or, as important, the respect of his friends. Joseph Howe in Halifax illustrates the transition. On being challenged by John Halliburton, the son of Chief Justice Sir Brenton Halliburton, Howe—a newspaper editor in his thirties—said he had no option but to accept. He had either to hazard his life or to "blight all prospects of being useful."

So the duel was fought, early on the morning of Saturday, March 14, 1840, at the Martello tower in Point Pleasant. It was on the usual principles: pis-

An election day in Montreal in 1860 or 1861, near the Champs de Mars; open (public) voting was the rule until well after Confederation. Intimidation and rough-housing were common, and police were frequently called in to protect dissenting voters.

The majesty of the law, in Canada West—as seen from the Old Country. Top: A witness taking the oath at a country trial in Dufferin County in the 1850s. This would almost certainly be a minor case; important trials went to the County Court. Bottom: Only five "good men and true" deliberating the verdict in a nearby orchard. From *The Illustrated London News* (February 17, 1855).

tols for two, coffee for one. It is not known what the distance was; fifty paces was not uncommon, though Sir Lucius O'Trigger, the Irish duellist in Sheridan's play *The Rivals*, declares that "a pretty gentleman's distance" is twenty paces! John Halliburton fired first and missed. Howe, who was a good shot (having grown up in the woods along the North West Arm), fired into the air. He was not, he said afterward, going to deprive an old man of his only son. The best part of Howe's story, and the lesson in it, was that he was then free to duel or not, as he chose, for ever. He did not need to explain or apologize. A month and a half later he got a second challenge, from Sir Rupert George, the Provincial Secretary. Had Howe not been out with Halliburton, that challenge would have been impossible to refuse; now, however, Howe simply said no. He had no personal quarrel with Sir Rupert, and would not fire if he did go out; and he had no great fancy for being shot at whenever, as a newspaperman, he happened to contrast a man's capacities with his pay. The result in Halifax was that Sir Rupert was merely laughed at. It was much the best solution.

Inevitably, politics too was a struggle animated by local loyalties and passions. Small towns had their rival hotels; larger towns developed rival newspapers in which opponents were freely damned, painted as black as possible, and supporters made to look as white as snow. Families relished their political loyalties and passed them on to the next generation. In Antigonish County, Nova Scotia, it used to be said that a mixed marriage was not between Catholic and Protestant but between Conservative and Liberal.

Voting was then very different from what it is now. The hustings were a rowdy place, and voting was a public and social occasion. A man did not vote with a clandestine, secret ballot. He stood up openly and declared his choice. The crowds around the hustings cheered or derided, or both. This was called, rather euphemistically, the manly British system of open voting. It was occasionally followed by the less manly, but also British, system of knocking your opponent on the head.

This description of British North American society suggests a rough world. It could be that, sometimes, as in the 1840s Shiners' War in Ottawa between Irish and French-Canadian lumbermen. But it was only so at irregular intervals, when the passions of a group boiled over, when the social controls normally in place from church and community failed to work, as in the Rebellion Losses Bill riot of 1849, or the 1853 Gavazzi riots in Quebec and Montreal caused by Catholic fury over the maligning of their church by a renegade priest.

The system of law enforcement was rooted in the community too, but it was less casual than it might appear. As in Britain, colonial justice relied heavily on the unpaid Justice of the Peace. Appointed by colonial governments, the JP could be a man of almost any calling—farmer, tinsmith, fisherman, merchant—though usually a man of some standing in the community. He might or might not know much about law. As a rule, JPs were not lawyers; there was an old colonial saying that lawyers made more money defending criminals than arranging their prosecution. The JP was also in many ways a creature of the community he lived in: that was both the strength of the institution, and in some parts of British North America its weakness. What did one do about a JP so much under the thumb of local roughs that he was afraid to have them prosecuted, or to sentence them properly when they were convicted? And since JPs made their money from fees, some could be venal and treacherous. In *Sam Slick, the Clockmaker*, Thomas Chandler Haliburton's stories about Nova Scotian life in the 1830s, Justice Pettifog's horse carries more roguery than law. Justice Pettifog and his Constable Nabb are as precious a yoke of rascals as one would meet in a day's ride.

The diversity of *Behind Bonsecours Market, Montreal* is extraordinary: vegetables, adults, children, animals, and the sailing ships and steamboats of the St. Lawrence in the distance. The church, just visible here on the left, is Notre Dame de Bonsecours, founded by Marguerite Bourgeoys in 1657 and rebuilt in 1771. The oil (1866) is by German-born Jewish immigrant William Raphael (1833–1914).

The Canada Southern Railway. This line, running across the Niagara Peninsula of southern Ontario, was designed to tap American traffic between Detroit and Buffalo, and to steal business from Canada's Great Western. The International Bridge, built by Casimir Gzowski, was opened on November 5, 1873, and a Canada Southern train was the first over it twelve days later. Oil (*c.* 1873) by Robert Whale (1805–87).

Alexander Ross, a Red River settler, accompanied 400 Métis riders on a similar bison hunt around 1850; "the surface was rocky and full of badger holes," he observed. "Twenty-three horses and riders were at one moment all sprawling on the ground; one horse, gored by a bull, was killed on the spot; two more were disabled by the fall; one rider broke his shoulderblade; another burst his gun and lost three of his fingers by the accident; and a third was struck on the knee by an exhausted ball." Oil (*c.* 1850) by Paul Kane, *Métis Running Buffalo.*

Expedition to the Red River in 1870 under Sir Garnet Wolseley. Advance Guard Crossing a Portage.

This 1871 oil by Frances Ann Hopkins shows government troops on the Kaministiquia River below Kakabeka Falls, on their way west to put down Louis Riel's Red River Rebellion.

Sunrise on the Saguenay, an 1880 oil by Lucius R. O'Brien (1832–99), first president of the Royal Canadian Academy. This was O'Brien's diploma piece for the inaugural exhibition of the Academy, which opened in Ottawa in March 1880. The event is commemorated in a *Canadian Illustrated News* engraving (inset) depicting the Governor General, the Marquess of Lorne, declaring the exhibition open; note O'Brien's canvas on the wall behind him.

The Rogers Pass, an 1886 oil by John A. Fraser, was painted at the behest of Cornelius Van Horne, vice-president of the Canadian Pacific Railway. First opened up by the CPR in 1882, the Rogers Pass, at 4,340 feet (1,323 metres), is virtually the only route through the Selkirk Mountains.

The Covent Garden Market, London, Ontario. Markets were favourite themes of 19th-century artists, and Paul Peel (1860–92) painted this oil of his hometown market in 1883. Peel, who studied in Philadelphia and Paris, is famous for his luminous studies of pre-pubescent nudes, but his interest in light and shade in landscape and cityscape is obvious here.

This handsome *View of King Stree* *Toronto, showing the Jail and Cour House*, attributed to Thomas You▮ (d. 1860), shows the old Toronto market (later the site of St. Lawre▮ Hall) on the left, St. James Cathed on the right, and the view westwa▮ from Jarvis Street. Note the gas streetlamps, installed just three ye▮ before. Oil, *c.* 1844–45.

Lights of a City Street shows Toro▮ newsboys and pedestrians on a ra▮ evening at the corner of Queen a▮ Yonge streets, while bicycles and ▮ tric streetcars signal the approach▮ the 20th century. Oil (1894) by F. Bell-Smith (1846–1923).

Edges of Mortality

When Canada was 150 years younger than it is now, birth, life, illness, and death were closer to the bone. Light and dark, heat and cold, comfort and discomfort, repletion and hunger, had an immediacy we can now recover only distantly, from time to time, by an effort of imagination: after a cold day's skating on a frozen lake, the keenness of the delight in a fire and a mug of tea. The margins for living then were broad, but the margins for life were narrow. A mistake with an axe, a small cut with a knife, a bad chill—for these the results could be desperate. Lord Sydenham, Governor General of Canada, was out riding at Kingston one fine September day in 1841; his horse stumbled and fell, and his right leg was badly crushed. He was dead in two weeks from lockjaw. In 1880 George Brown, owner-editor of the Toronto *Globe*, was shot by a disgruntled ex-employee. It was only a minor flesh wound, but gangrene set in; Brown was dead in seven weeks. Remarking in Parliament on the sudden, unexplained death of a colleague, Sir John A. Macdonald quoted Burke: "What shadows we are, and what shadows we pursue."

It was worse for women. Giving birth to children could be horrendous. When things did not go right, anything could happen. An eccentricity of the pelvis formation, the baby turned the wrong way, any one of a dozen unhappy possibilities could kill baby or mother or both. Every family had its private tragedies. Infant mortality was staggering. Between 1871 and 1883 John and Annie Thompson had nine children: four died in infancy and a fifth became a cripple from polio. The stories of the deaths of children that one finds in the novels of Charles Dickens, mawkish as we now tend to think they are, reflect a reality few families could escape. Many popular songs concerned the deaths of children. The grim reaper's scythe had legends inscribed on it: diphtheria, whooping-cough, measles, typhoid, smallpox.

But the nature of this tragic harvest was changing, or beginning to. Smallpox inoculation had been known for some time, but it was risky, and most people resisted it. By the 1800s Edward Jenner had made his great discovery—vaccination using the milder form of the disease, cowpox. Ether was first used in Boston in 1846, and it and chloroform were adopted as anaesthetics in Great Britain and British North America. Dr. Edward Dagge Worthington pioneered the use of anaesthetic at Sherbrooke, Canada East, in 1847. Queen Victoria's son Leopold was born in 1853 with the help of chloroform. "That blessed chloroform," was the Queen's grateful reaction. She had some reason to know: it was her eighth child in thirteen years.

Victoria's example made the use of anaesthetics more acceptable among her subjects.

But between inventions and their practical application, to say nothing of popular acceptance, there was often a considerable time lag, and this was particularly true in medicine. While the use of anaesthetic became common quickly, the prejudice against smallpox vaccination lasted a long time. Compulsory vaccination produced riots in Montreal in the 1870s. There was a major smallpox epidemic in Montreal and Ottawa in 1885. It did not end there: smallpox devastated Galt, Ontario, in 1902 and Windsor in 1924.

Against Asian cholera the available defences were fewer. The disease was fast and it was deadly. You could be dead twenty-four hours after you felt the first twinges. Cholera had come to Europe in 1831; colonial authorities knew about it ahead of time and established quarantine stations at Grosse Ile in the St. Lawrence below Ile d'Orléans, and also in Halifax and Saint John harbours. In 1832 cholera came through anyway, into Quebec City and Montreal, and the Maritime ports. It struck again in the early 1850s, and sporadic outbreaks continued into the 1880s. Still endemic in India, it was, and is, spread through contaminated drinking water. Control and chlorination of drinking water was the answer, but it would take time for society to learn that, and more time to establish the public water systems that were essential to avoid contamination.

The doctors had to learn too. In British North America the attachment of medical schools to universities had begun early, with the formation of the McGill Medical School in 1829, and by the 1850s other medical schools had followed similar routes towards making medical education academic rather than merely a form of apprenticeship. It was at best an uneasy alliance; at Queen's in Kingston and Dalhousie in Halifax there were always stresses and strains between the universities and their medical schools. Their functions were different, but in the end they learned that they depended upon each other.

Perhaps the most startling development following the adoption of ether and chloroform was the whole range of medical operations that had not been possible before. Early operations with ether were often successful, but the patient died of infection. It took time to recognize one essential in an operating room: sterile conditions. Even in the 1870s doctors would carry out operations without gloves and with barely washed hands, holding their scalpels in their teeth when their hands were busy with something else. Joseph Lister's great discovery about antisepsis, that is, sterile conditions in surgery and the use of carbolic acid to disinfect wounds, was

McGill University was founded in 1821, with a legacy from Montreal's great fur-trading merchant James McGill, and was thriving by 1875, when this picture appeared in the *Canadian Illustrated News*. Much of its success was due to the driving genius of John William Dawson, a Nova Scotia geologist who was principal from 1855 till 1893.

The University of Toronto began in 1827, when John Strachan—later Bishop of Toronto—secured a royal charter for King's College, an Anglican university. In 1849 the college was secularized and renamed the University of Toronto. The architect W. G. Storm did this watercolour, *Design for the University of Toronto*.

A leading proponent of compulsory education was Methodist minister Egerton Ryerson, who became Canada West's superintendent of education in 1844 and held that position for over thirty years. Oil (*c.* 1850–51) by Théophile Hamel.

published in 1867. It took a decade to be accepted. By the 1890s operations were being performed successfully and safely.

Perhaps the most significant changes in Canada in the sixty years from 1840 to 1900 took place in medicine. Not least was the acceptance of women in hospitals, not only as nurses but as doctors. Emily Stowe, the first Canadian woman doctor, was refused admission to the Toronto School of Medicine in the 1860s. She studied medicine in New York and came back to practise in Toronto from 1867 to 1880 without a licence. Finally in 1880 she was allowed to qualify. In 1883 the Ontario Medical College for Women was opened, and finally the whole University of Toronto capitulated in 1886.

Medicine as seen in the newspapers was a very strange world. Every newspaper was filled with advertisements for marvellous medicines that were alleged to cure everything from the common cold to housemaid's knee or pneumonia. And if there was any left over in the bottle, it wasn't bad for horses either. For example, Radway's Ready Relief transformed the patient from a state of "pain, misery, weakness and decrepitude, to the delightful enjoyment of health and strength," and so swiftly was this effected that grateful patients ascribed it to enchantment. This was not a bad description; most patent medicines were 90 per cent alcohol.

Patent-medicine advertisements were notorious, but in other respects as well newspapers give a fascinating and doubtless misleading picture of nineteenth-century Canadian society. They could, and did, print almost anything they pleased. The reputation of the Toronto *Globe* was built on lively and often biased reporting; on its editorial page owner-editor George Brown enjoyed the freedom to pillory anyone he wanted to, usually his opposite numbers in politics. The public tolerated, indeed expected, newspapers to support friends and abuse opponents. They were like the cartoons of the present day; even when you know they exaggerate you are amused. And the laws of libel were light and easy. Newspapers in Victorian Canada were certainly not stuffy. Robbery, riot, murder, hangings, wrecks (by sea and land), war (European and North American), scandal, and vengeance were all there. A ball at Charlottetown in 1864 was described in terms that resemble the excesses of the Roman Empire:

Pleasure panoplied in lustful smiles meets and embraces exuberant Joy... the fascinating dance goes merrily, and the libidinous waltz with its lascivious entwinements whiles in growing excitement; the swelling bosom and the voluptuous eye tell the story of intemperate revel....

One Saint John newspaper commented on that delicious run of hyperbole, "There are some desperate fellows in the Prince Edward Island press."

Newspapers thrived on politics, and politicians needed newspapers. Newspapers had their principles, but newspapers, and principles, could be bought and sold. Sometimes they did not even need to be sold. They had occasionally to stand some stiff changes, in men and tactics. In 1854 John A. Macdonald wanted the Hamilton *Spectator* to support him through a sharp change of policy. It was, frankly, an outrageous demand, since it meant the *Spectator* would have to support a local politician it had denounced for years. "It's a damned sharp curve," the editor wrote back to Macdonald, but, he added loyally, "I think we can take it." Newspapers would have greater changes than that to urge, to oppose, or just to take, in the movement for Confederation that lay ahead.

Steam Packets and the Atlantic

By the late 1850s the Province of Canada and the four Maritime colonies had already achieved self-government and arrived at a coherent sense of themselves, and were developing ambitions about a possible place in the world. It was uncertain where the boundary lay between the jurisdiction of the Colonial Office in London and those of the greedy, anxious, volatile colonial governments in St. John's, Charlottetown, Halifax, Fredericton, and Toronto or Quebec City. What was certain was that colonial governments were developing a taste for more power. Nor did this appetite depend on size, but rather upon issues. Prince Edward Island was as vigorous in wanting jurisdiction over issues vital to its citizens as was the much larger and more powerful Province of Canada. Colonies were also beginning to write their own legislation, lightening old common-law rules about debt and debtors, dower rights, and the rights of women in general. There were colonial pressures to relieve women of common-law restrictions on control of movable property: that is, the money and securities that the common law had placed firmly under husbands' control. As colonies grew in population, prosperity, railways, and trade, so too did their confidence, not to say cockiness, about themselves and their wish to do things in ways that seemed proper to them.

But having risen to be, say, Premier of New Brunswick or Nova Scotia, where did one go from there? Retire to the Bench? Some provincial premiers did. But when

Loading a ship with squared-timber through the bow port, Quebec. The squared-timber trade in white pine had flourished during the Napoleonic years, but was beginning to decline by the time William Notman took this photograph in 1872.

Joseph Howe of Nova Scotia retired as defeated premier in 1853, he couldn't do that; he wasn't a lawyer. His successor, the Conservative Charles Tupper, couldn't do it either; he was a doctor. Samuel Leonard Tilley, Premier of New Brunswick, was a Saint John druggist. The Bench, however honourable a resting place after political labours, was not an answer for talented men who had reached the upper limit of colonial public office. Francis Hincks, a premier of the Province of Canada, was a banker; he was appointed by the British in 1855 as Governor of Barbados, and later of British Guiana. But by the 1860s the British government had decided it could not go on making colonial governors out of defeated colonial politicians, whatever their merits. Joseph Howe would have liked to be one in 1863; instead he got employment in the Imperial Fisheries Protection Service. It was thin pickings. Politicians chafed at the restrictions and impediments to achievement in colonial society. So did the newspapers and the public.

The restlessness of colonial politicians was directly related to developing political ambitions. But politicians were not the only unsatisfied ones. Sir Edward Watkin of the Grand Trunk Railway began to think that new political agglomerations would stimulate railway building; so did Sir Hugh Allan of the Allan Line and the Montreal Telegraph Company.

The twenty years since the 1840s had been replete with changes not just in railways but also in steamships. The *Royal William* had been the first ship to cross the Atlantic under auxiliary steam, in 1833, from Quebec and Pictou, Nova Scotia, to Gravesend, with seven passengers and a load of Pictou coal. The person who ultimately benefited

This poster can be dated to between 1875 and 1878, while William Annand was Agent-General of Canada in London. (In 1879 Sir John A. Macdonald converted the post to Canadian High Commissioner.) Note the Allan Line steamer, square-rigged on the main and foremasts, fore-and-aft rigged on the mizzen, with steam auxiliary.

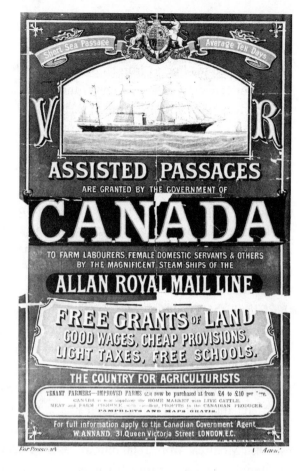

from that achievement was Samuel Cunard. He was born in Halifax in 1787, and had made some money in whaling, lumber, and coal, and he continued to reinvest his profits in shipping, warehouses, and the Halifax Banking Company, formed in 1825. Cunard grasped the central fact that the advent of auxiliary steam power in sailing ships meant that they could sail at least partly independent of wind or weather. Regularity, punctuality, speed, would not be achieved at once, for the sea was not so easily tamed; nor could human error be altogether avoided. Nevertheless, Cunard's famous steamship line was a considerable success and certainly was to be his most enduring monument.

In 1839 Cunard submitted a bid to the British government to undertake a regular mail service from Liverpool to Halifax and Boston. He won a ten-year subsidy of £55,000 a year; he continued to receive it after that partly because the Royal Navy liked his ships' design and speed. His line began operations at the same time as Britain launched the new penny postage. On July 17, 1840, at 2 a.m., the first scheduled steam packet, the *Britannia*, arrived in Halifax, twelve days out of Liverpool. Note the time; at that hour a sailing ship might well have hove to and waited for dawn. The *Britannia* did not wait for anything; she discharged her passengers and mail, and set off for Boston, where she docked at 10 p.m. on July 19. By 1855 Cunard had converted his line to iron ships; by the early 1860s he had abandoned paddle wheels for screw propellers. When Cunard died in 1865 he left a considerable fortune. As one Nova Scotian wrote to a Halifax friend in 1866, "I miss our old friend Sir Samuel C—I think he has left £600,000... a good large sum for him to have accumulated since the date that you and I remember him to have had little or nothing—so much for Steam in 20 years...." So much for steam, indeed!

The Allan Line is still more famous in the history of Canada. This Scottish-Canadian shipping line was founded in 1819. In 1854 the Allan consortium formed the Montreal Ocean Steamship Company, and in 1855 it too won an imperial mail contract. The Allan Line prospered, as had Cunard's, by using innovative design and engineering. Allan ships became the mainstay of Canadian travel from the 1850s until the line was finally sold to Canadian Pacific in 1909. The Allan ships—the *Canadian*, the *Indian*, the *Sarmatian*, the *Parisian*, the ill-fated *Hungarian*, the *Sardinian*, the *Buenos Ayrean* (the first steel liner to sail the Atlantic), and many others—were known to Canadians for sixty years, sailing out of Montreal in summer, out of Portland, Maine, in winter. And Hugh Allan's enterprise went much further than that; he launched into railways, banking, insurance, and manufacturing. In 1864 he founded the Merchants' Bank in Montreal; it was soon one of the most aggressive Canadian banks. Allan was the quintessential Montreal financier, and his great success helped to establish Montreal, from 1860 onward, as the financial capital of Canada.

Shipping and government worked together. The success of the Allan Line was made possible by the Canadian government's deepening of the main St. Lawrence channel through Lake St. Peter to sixteen feet in 1853. The government also made it a point to subsidize the erection and maintenance of certain lighthouses on the approaches to the Gulf of St. Lawrence, the most important of which was at Cape Race on the southern tip of Newfoundland.

Within twenty-five years of the first transatlantic steamship lines came the transatlantic cable. Telegraph companies had appeared in Canada within two years of Samuel Morse's first successful telegraph line between Washington and Baltimore in 1844; in 1847 Hugh Allan had founded the Montreal Telegraph Company, which soon connected Montreal with Portland, Toronto, and Detroit. The Atlantic cable was the natural outgrowth of shipping and the telegraph. The first cable was laid down on the sea-bed in 1858, from Ireland to Trinity Bay, Newfoundland. Queen Victoria used it to send a message to President James Buchanan before it ceased functioning owing to sea-water leaking through the insulation. A second cable was laid

Heart's Content, Newfoundland: Arrival of Transatlantic Cable, 1866. The first attempt at a transatlantic cable was a failure because water penetrated the insulation. But in July 1866 the *Great Eastern*, the largest steamship then afloat, landed the western end of a cable at Heart's Content, in Trinity Bay, Newfoundland; the eastern end was at Valentia, at the south-west corner of Ireland. Watercolour (1866) by Robert Dudley.

by a monster of a new iron ship, the *Great Eastern*, and was brought ashore at Heart's Content, Newfoundland, in July 1866. The transatlantic cable and steamships, like the railways, were symbols of how the world was being brought closer to Canadian shores, how distances were shrinking before the power of technology.

This marvellous new web of telegraph cables, transportation improvements, and innovations in ship design lay behind the political drive towards Confederation. British North American politicians were fully aware of these new techniques and used them; they travelled on Hugh Allan's and Cunard's ships, they banked at the Merchants' Bank, they used Allan's telegraphs. The Confederation movement was backed to the hilt by the Montreal business community, although quietly and behind the scenes. The Montreal *Gazette*, the business community's most characteristic spokesman, was enthusiastic about the new movement for Confederation—the union of all the British North American colonies.

The experience generated by new inventions, new technology, created expansionist political and social ideas. Not everyone shared such ideas, but anyone who read newspapers had to be aware that the world was changing rapidly. It was not surprising that as early as 1851 Joseph Howe spoke of the day when his younger listeners would hear the steam whistle of a locomotive in the passes of the Rocky Mountains. He tried and failed that same year to get them to hear it in the Cobequid Hills, to get the governments of Nova Scotia, New Brunswick, Canada, and Great Britain to agree to build the Intercolonial Railway from Halifax to Montreal. Given this failure, he cannot be blamed for thinking that the sea that lay at Nova Scotia's gates was an opportunity more inviting than the 1,000 kilometres (600 miles) of woods between Halifax and Montreal, and therefore basing his "federation of the empire" upon the technology of the steamship.

The High Adventure

Those 1,000 kilometres (600 miles) of woods would eventually be bridged by rail, after all. Confederation would soon establish a central legal and political structure, but it depended on the technology of railways for its ultimate material realization. Alexander Galt of Sherbrooke, the romantic, unstable financial genius of Confederation, was originally a railway man; George-Etienne Cartier, a pugnacious rebel back in 1837, had moved into law and to the right, and cut his political and legal teeth on Grand Trunk finance. So had his tractable, supple colleague, John A. Macdonald. Like them, most of the Fathers of Confederation were lawyers and businessmen, well versed in the new ways of the 1860s.

Confederation was, in many ways, a startling development. One can add up the causes of Confederation and still not get the sum of it. Like all political achievements, it was a matter of timing, luck, and the combination of a certain set of men and events. The men in this case were from several quite different and separated colonies.

There already had been a movement for Confederation that developed within the Province of Canada in 1858, partly the result of a New York stock-market crash in 1857 and the economic consequences of it, partly the result of internal problems in the Province of Canada itself. It was a policy adopted by the Cartier–Macdonald government (George Cartier was then premier) for want of something better, to get out from under a minor scandal occasioned by the government's committing itself to Ottawa as the new capital of the province. But the first Confederation movement of 1858 aroused little interest in the Atlantic colonies, who were minding their own business and doing well enough. The British government in London also treated it coolly, as if the political disequilibrium in the Province of Canada was bound to be temporary. The depression of 1857–58 eased, and the government of the Province of Canada survived, confirming Ottawa as the future capital. Nothing much was done about Confederation, but the possibility was publicized and talked about. That was, of course, something.

The Conservative party in the Province of Canada rather feared Confederation. It was a big step, for one thing, because even Conservatives grudgingly conceded that Confederation would have to include the North-West (the Hudson's Bay Company territory, called Rupert's Land). Conservatives, and even a few Reformers, thought of the North-West as nothing but a vast white elephant, a great lone land whose administration would do nothing but eat up good money. Settlement of it was, surely, decades away.

The Reform party was more aggressive about the North-West, not content with the status quo. The difficulties of living in political harness with the French Canadians were such that Reformers were quite certain the province could not go on as it was; they did not worry much about the Atlantic colonies, but they were very concerned about "French-Canadian dominance" of the Province of Canada. It was not that Reformers wanted a complete divorce from the French-Canadian region of Canada East; railways, canals, and the port of Montreal were too important for that. They were thinking of something like a common market between the two sections of the province, that would maintain the essential communications and transport tying the two sections of the province together, while divorcing cultural institutions already widely different. The Reform party met in a great conclave in Toronto in November 1859, and there the party's latent separatism was manifest.

It was George Brown's convention and George Brown's party. He was a tall, rather rough Scot, with a face as long as a bottle of Johnnie Walker, a Free Kirk Presbyterian with a strong anti-Catholic streak in his make-up and his politics. Using his paper, the Toronto *Globe*, Brown had created a political party from fundamentally Protestant farming communities in the western end of the province. The Reform party had two powerful urges, both becoming stronger as years went by.

First, Reformers demanded, give the western (Ontario) section of the Province of Canada the representation in the Assembly that its population warranted. End, Brown cried, the iniquitous system of having an equal number of members for both sections of the province: the western section now had half a million more people than the eastern (Quebec) section—in other words, half a million Protestants had as much representation in the Assembly as codfish off Gaspé. The principle of equal representation had worked against French Canadians back in the 1840s, when Canada East had a 50 per cent greater population than Canada West. Now, by the end of the 1850s, it was the other way around and what Brown and the Reform party wanted was representation by population. As the *Globe* put it, "Rep. by pop.!" And since the population of Canada West continued to grow more rapidly than Canada East's, the Reform party rallying cry grew steadily more powerful. Most political slogans quickly die a natural death; "Rep. by pop.!" was to keep getting stronger every year.

None of this might have been serious if George Brown's Reform party had not been so insistently Protestant. Canada West's Protestants had bitterly resented the separate-school system put in place in the 1850s, that allowed parents to send their children to state-aided schools that upheld the religion of their choice. The original 1840 constitution had allowed for such a system, but not many had worried about it. Separate schools, what few there were, were only loosely regulated, and were beginning to die out. But in 1850 a new act was passed that decisively arrested that easy-going system. In 1855 an extension of the powers of this Catholic-minority school system was passed by a government majority heavily dependent on French-Canadian votes. That, and the uproar in England over the papal establishment of new Catholic dioceses, sharpened Protestant fears of the Catholic church. If Catholic separate schools in Canada West were based on a wise and sensible principle, there were precious few Methodists or Presbyterians who could see anything but iniquity and tyranny in them. The new act sharpened Canada West's desire for separate government. In 1856 George Brown defined the conflict in the Canadian Assembly:

We have two countries, two languages, two religions, two habits of thought and action, and the question is can you possibly carry on the government of both with one Legislature and one executive. That is the question to be solved.

The Reform party's solution of 1859 was the federation of the Province of Canada—with an overall government for some functions and two local governments, east and west, for others. Even they recognized that because of economic interdependence, some degree of union, however decentralized, would have to be preserved.

The Reformers' second grievance was more long-run but no less urgent. Canada West's expanding population needed elbow room. By the middle of the 1850s it was clear that there was no more good land available at reasonable prices in that section of the province. Settlers were bumping into the Canadian Shield in the back country of Hastings, Victoria, Simcoe, Grey, and Bruce counties. Rock, birch, white pine, blueberries, and lakes make delicious country for summer cottages, as Muskoka, Lake of Bays, and Parry Sound still testify; but they don't make good farms. Brown and the Reform party looked hungrily beyond the rock of the Pre-Cambrian Shield, beyond Lake Superior, to the prairies of the Red River valley. Their view was: let the HBC's empty prairies be annexed. The North West Company had proved that the HBC charter was not worth much. Nor did Reform ambitions end at the Rocky Mountains. Beyond there were the new gold discoveries at Fraser River that produced the gold rush of '58. The Oregon Boundary Treaty of 1846 had carried the 49th parallel, the border between British North America and the United States, clear to the Pacific. By the end of 1858, there were established two west-coast colonies, Vancouver Island and British Columbia on the mainland. In the east the sense of nationality may not have been fully formed, but it was growing, and it had reached the Pacific. As the *Globe* had put it, back in 1854, "It is an empire we have in view...."

To both of these Reform party issues—their hostility to the separate-school system and their desire to annex the HBC's territories and the West—the Liberal-Conservative party of Cartier and Macdonald was opposed. The Liberal-Conservative party had been put together in 1854, as French Canadians shifted slowly to the right. This shift was inevitable, perhaps, as the sense of security of their language and national institutions increased with responsible government, and as the religious revival made their church stronger and more vigorous. English-speaking Conservatives in Canada East (and some French-speaking ones) tended to reflect the great business and communications interests of Montreal; Galt of Sherbrooke and Cartier of Montreal were by 1858 willing to consider and weigh the advantages of Confederation. Other Conservatives were more lukewarm and breathed a sigh of relief when prosperity eased the pressure for change after 1860. Macdonald himself had no driving interest in political change as such—what politician in power has?—but he always called his party Liberal-Conservative. Like many Conservatives he liked stability, but he also liked the Liberal willingness to take up new ideas whose time had come. Certainly as to "rep. by pop." Macdonald was quite clear; because French Canadians would not accept it he could not. The Liberal-Conservative party was heavily dependent on French-Canadian votes, and so it made some sense for Macdonald and his party to maintain the status quo, at least for the time being. And why should the Catholic French Canadians accept the eighty-two Protestant MPs from the western half of the province that "rep. by pop." would force upon them instead of the equal number of sixty-five that they presently faced?

Cutting out the 49th Parallel, on right bank of the Mooyie River, looking west. The 49th parallel constitutes Canada's "undefended border" with the U.S. from Lake of the Woods to the Strait of Georgia. This is what it looked like in 1860–61, on the west bank of the Mooyie River where it crosses from British Columbia into Idaho. North American Boundary Commission, Corps of Royal Engineers photo.

In April 1861, the first shots were fired in the American Civil War. Within a few months tensions rose, and both the British and the Yankees were suddenly at swords' points. With aggressive New York and Chicago papers telling British North Americans, "Just wait till this war is over, and then we'll fix you!," the British colonies, especially the large and vulnerable Province of Canada, sensed themselves more and more alone and isolated in a North American world becoming increasingly unfriendly.

Internally, political divisions within the Province of Canada deepened, the power divided so evenly between parties that it created a stalemate. The Conservative government fell in May 1862 over an appropriation to strengthen the Canadian militia. The governments that followed were little better. A shift of policy or an administrative slip was enough to precipitate their fall. The Taché–Macdonald government was forced to resign in June 1864 because of an unauthorized loan of $100,000 to the Grand Trunk by the Minister of Finance, Alexander Galt. Between 1861 and 1864 the Province of Canada had two elections and four different governments. On June 14, 1864, when the fourth government was defeated, the politicians in Quebec City—the capital had not yet moved to Ottawa—were wondering what to do next. A fifth government would have to be put in place, perhaps after another election. But the election in 1863 had changed little, and no one was confident that a further election would improve the narrow balance of parties.

This impasse, and the differences in policy between Conservatives and Reformers, were suddenly resolved by George Brown. In 1864 Brown offered a compromise better than federation of just the Province of Canada: he offered the co-operation of himself and his Reform party in the promotion of Confederation—the union of *all* of British North America, the Province of Canada included. The Province of Canada's own internal problems would then be solved by division of its two sections into two new provinces. It was bigger, better, and possibly even acceptable to Conservatives like John A. Macdonald and George-Etienne Cartier. Brown's about-face—his offer to form a coalition government in order to bring in Confederation—was so dramatic that some historians have suggested that the real originator of Confederation was not man but woman: Brown's new wife, Anne Nelson Brown.

She was the daughter of the Nelsons of Edinburgh, the still famous publishing house. She was well travelled and cultivated, fluent in German and French. Brown had met her in the summer of 1862, proposed in five weeks, been accepted, and married her in November. That was fast work! By June of 1864 Brown was the proud possessor of a new wife and baby, and hip-deep in love with both. Not a little of what we now know about Confederation is owing to Brown's enthusiastic letters from Quebec back home.

"Madame Quebec's Wild Boy."
Grip, August 12, 1882.

"Miss Canada Vaccinated."
Grip, February 25, 1882.

Confederation would give Canada West her "rep. by pop." in a central House of Commons, and a separate identity in a new and separate province. Both would be within the jurisdiction of a new British North American nationality that made far more patriotic sense than a federal system teased out of the Province of Canada. Federation of the Province of Canada alone launched nothing. With Confederation in place you could talk of launching a nation.

George Brown's great compromise was backed, and ultimately cemented into place, by means of a political coalition committed firmly to the principle. The Great Coalition, as it came to be called, included three of the four major political groups in the province: Cartier representing the French-Canadian Conservatives, Macdonald the English-Canadian Conservatives, and Brown the Reform party. (The fourth group, the "Rouges," was a French-Canadian left-of-centre party, rather at odds with the Catholic church.) The coalition cabinet that was put together that late June of 1864 was more cohesive, more powerful, than anything that had been seen in the Province of Canada for many a year, and its policy, Confederation, carried the support of about 92 of the 130 seats in the Assembly. There was now a real power, a driving force, behind the whole Confederation movement.

Confederation was thus brought into existence, fundamentally, by the political difficulties of the Province of Canada. It was the consciousness of the difficulty, perhaps the impossibility, of ever returning to the old state of things that drove the politicians of the Province of Canada resolutely onward. Behind the coalition—behind Brown, Macdonald, and Cartier—there was a strong public sense that the politicians were right in going for Confederation. A solution to Canadian political troubles Confederation undoubtedly was; but it was more than that: it was the formulation of *a mari usque ad mare*. From sea to sea. A Nova Scotian, travelling in Canada West, wrote in September, 1864:

All the newspapers discuss the proposed changes in every issue.... It is felt that the task to which these Provinces are called is no light or unimportant one;—they are now laying the foundations of Empire...whose bounds shall extend from...Newfoundland to the noble hills and peaceful havens of Vancouver's Island.... This is our destiny, and the Provinces from the least to the greatest should prove themselves worthy of it.

That argument was one that transcended all colonial borders.

Nevertheless, the internal wrangles of the Province of Canada could hardly be expected to have much effect on the four Atlantic colonies. They were doing quite well on their own; they had not had a tithe of the quarrels that had racked the Province of Canada, and they showed some disposition to mind their own business. That had been true in 1858; it was still partly true in 1864. The colony most reluctant to change was Prince Edward Island, comfortable with its farms, potatoes, lobsters, beaches, observing the mainland from across a stretch of sea. In 1864, many Prince Edward Islanders had never crossed Northumberland Strait. Nova Scotia was hesitant also, for different reasons. Prosperity had come in the wake of the Reciprocity Treaty of 1854, in which the U.S. gave the province certain import concessions in exchange for inshore fisheries. Nova Scotian ships sailed out of Yarmouth, Maitland, Avonport, Great Village, Maccan, Parrsboro; they were afloat on the seven oceans of the world; Yokohama, Canton, Barbados, and Falmouth were more familiar to many Nova Scotians than Ottawa. This was also true of Saint John, New Brunswick; but the latter had other visions as well—such as becoming the terminus of a railway from Montreal, becoming Montreal's winter port, taking over the role Portland, Maine, had assumed only a decade before. Newfoundland was more distant than all the others, in attitude and geography, and its population was at the farthest remove possible from the mainland; but in the 1860s inshore fishing was going badly, and economic difficulties were tempting Newfoundlanders to think about what had hitherto been unthinkable.

Behind all these reactions in the Atlantic colonies, there remained, half-dormant, what the Prince Edward Islanders called, irreverently, the glory argument. This was the idea that these several British North American colonies could, like the Americans a hundred years before, put together a country common to all of them, a nation that might take charge of the vast territories north of the American border and do something with them. Politicians and newspapers everywhere in the Atlantic provinces felt something of the force of this: it varied enormously from colony to colony. The Province of Canada had now given a mighty and realistic push to an idea that had been floating around for a generation and more.

Contributing powerfully to the move towards Confederation, and the changes it implied, were the enormous pressures generated by the American Civil War. There had been no war like it in the memory of North Americans. Not even the American Revolution, or the War of 1812, had created such havoc. If you wanted reasons for union, said orator and nationalist Thomas D'Arcy McGee in Montreal, on October 20, 1864, the answer was one word: *circumspice*. "Look around you, in this age of earthquake," he said, "to the valleys of Virginia, the mountains of Georgia, and you will find reasons as thick as blackberries." South of the border was a world of war, guns, and death. The colonies, who had once felt they could take their time with progress to emancipation, found their situation suddenly dangerous. "We were taught," said McGee in 1867, "that the days of the colonial comedy of Government were over and gone, and that politics had become stern, and almost tragic for the New World."

The Civil War proved to British North Americans that federations fell apart unless they were much more heavily centralized than ever the United States had been. It also suggested that when the Americans had done with hammering each other they might well turn their aggression outward.

A number of incidents in the course of the Civil War inflamed Yankee opinion. The case of a Confederate ship, the *Alabama*, was the worst. She was built in Liverpool under the very noses of the British government, ostensibly as a merchant ship, but her lines looked suspiciously warlike to the United States legation in London. The ship, not yet christened, got away on a weekend and the fitting-out was completed in France. So began the murderous two-year rampage of the *Alabama*. When she herself was finally sunk by Northern warships, in the Bay of Biscay in 1864, a $15 million bill had been run up for direct damages alone. The American State Department, and American newspapers, argued that the *Alabama* had prolonged the Civil War by two years; because the war had cost the American government $2 billion a year, indirect claims against Great Britain added up to two times $2 billion, or $4 billion. Yours sincerely!

A nice way of settling this bill, the Americans intimated not too delicately, could be British North America. And while Britain had no real intention of giving us over, it would be a different matter if we, the colonists, ourselves chose to go. The policy that animated Lord Palmerston's Liberal government in Britain during the Civil War was that while the British North American colonies had many disadvantages—they were expensive and awkward to administer just for a start—they could not be deliberately handed over to the Americans. They were an inheritance from the past and, damnably inconvenient though they were, Britain had a duty to them and to itself. But colonies, like children, did grow up. While the British could not let the Americans take them, there was nothing wrong, nothing against British pride, if the colonists themselves chose to take their future into their own hands. It would also be a lot cheaper.

The new Colonial Secretary in the Palmerston government was Edward Cardwell, a brilliant, quiet administrator, the toughness of whose mind was masked by his timidity in Parliament. When backed by colleagues in Cabinet and caucus, Cardwell had the ruthlessness of good administrators: once you have got your policy and believe in it, get it in place and keep it there. Cardwell certainly did this with Confederation between 1864 and 1866.

During 1864 the Confederation movement had prospered mightily. In the late summer of 1864, a conference on Maritime union was hastily called for Charlottetown. Maritime union was a pet project of the local governors, and in years gone by had had backing from the Colonial Office and desultory support from colonial premiers. The Province of Canada heard about the conference and asked if it could present more sweeping proposals for union of all the colonies. So on September 1, 1864, the Canadians came ashore from their ship, the *Queen Victoria*, anchored in Charlottetown harbour—feeling, as George Brown put it, a little like Christopher Columbus. The delegates from Nova Scotia and New Brunswick, and even a couple from the Island, were caught up in the sheer exhilaration of the Canadians' idea. To make a nation! The union proposals sketched out at Charlottetown were detailed further at the Quebec Conference a month later. At both places the delegates drank and danced as hard as they worked. What emerged at the end of October 1864 was the official proposals for British North American union.

The British government seized hold of them almost at once. With disconcerting speed Edward Cardwell took up Confederation just as it was, hot, so to speak, from the balls, parties, and conclaves of Charlottetown and Quebec. He made it into British government policy in late November 1864, the moment it became clear that it had sufficient local support. He announced British policy as early as December 1864; urged it upon his colonial governors in Charlottetown, St. John's, Fredericton, and Halifax; pushed it with dispatches; replaced a recalcitrant governor in Nova Scotia; bulldozed others in Prince Edward Island and Newfoundland; forced through a *coup d'état* in New Brunswick. If Cardwell had had his way there would have been Confederation in 1865, and with all the colonies in it.

What prevented him from getting his way was local elections on the issue in Newfoundland, Prince Edward Island, and New Brunswick, which led to postponement of Confederation in Newfoundland and rejection of it in Prince Edward Island and in New Brunswick. These results reflected great public unease at the speed with which Confederation was being rushed through. Strong local loyalties, and the entire absence of any railway connections with Quebec or Montreal, meant that an overwhelming distance still seemed to separate the Maritime provinces from the St. Lawrence valley. Maritime electorates also lacked the sense of urgency that animated the men from the Province of Canada. Whatever may have been the glitter of Confederation, careful consideration would have to be given to the means of effecting it. Many Maritimers did not like the look of the terms.

Nova Scotia was not exempt from such feelings either. The colony escaped without an election there because the Tupper government had just been elected in 1863, and so did not have to go to the polls again until 1867. Charles Tupper well knew that there was enough potential for defeat in Nova Scotia on Confederation that he dared not risk another election on the issue. He did the best he could: he bided his time. In April 1866, news came from Fredericton that on Cardwell's authority the Governor had turned out of office an anti-Confederation government and brought in a pro-Confederation one. Then Tupper acted. He got a Confederation resolution through both houses of the Nova Scotia legislature that same month. Two months later the New Brunswick electorate supported the pro-Confederation stance of its government. Even if Cardwell's pressure was not strong enough to force the issue in Newfoundland or Prince Edward Island, he reasoned that the mainland colonies were the important ones, and Confederation would go ahead.

Nova Scotia did not altogether like the terms of Confederation, but what it liked even less was the way Tupper had manipulated its consent without calling an election—constitutional though it was. An anti-Confederation delegation from Nova Scotia went to England in 1866 and stayed for nearly a year, trying to block passage in the British Parliament of what came to be called the British North America Act. They failed. The British government, Tupper, Macdonald, and others were convinced and adamant. With the magic of Westminster's sovereign power the three colonies— Canada, Nova Scotia, and New Brunswick—were made into a new entity, the Dominion of Canada, comprising four provinces: Ontario, Quebec, Nova Scotia, and New Brunswick.

The British North America Act was signed by Queen Victoria on March 29, 1867. It was proclaimed as of noon, July 1, 1867. Nova Scotians, and some New Brunswickers, despaired, kicked, objected; the British government was obdurate. What could the colonials do to fight a permanent political change resolved upon by London with the connivance of the local government? What Joseph Howe and his anti-Confederates could and did do was to punish at the polls those who had sold them down the river. In the Dominion and provincial elections of 1867,

The Charlottetown Conference, Prince Edward Island, September 1864. The Fathers of Confederation are posing on the veranda of Government House. Third from left, silhouetted against a pillar, is Charles Tupper (1821–1915) of Nova Scotia. Against the next pillar is Thomas D'Arcy McGee (1825–68), and immediately below him are George-Etienne Cartier (1814–73) and (seated) John A. Macdonald (1815–91).

Confederates in Nova Scotia went down to resounding defeat. Of the nineteen seats for Nova Scotia in the new Dominion House of Commons, eighteen went to the anti-Confederates; of the thirty-eight seats in the Nova Scotia House of Assembly, thirty-six went to anti-Confederates. That was decisive enough! Macdonald and others had been blinded by the confidence of Charles Tupper, the Nova Scotian premier, who was one of those people who believe you can carry anything through if you have enough brass. He had had his way, all right—but it rankled in Nova Scotia, and for many a year to come.

Sir John A. Macdonald—now knighted, now the Prime Minister of Canada—rarely showed greater ingenuity and skill than in negotiating his way out of the difficult position that the new Dominion of Canada and the former colony—new province—of Nova Scotia were in. Once Macdonald had been told by Samuel Leonard Tilley of New Brunswick, who went to Nova Scotia to see for himself, that there was no hope of blinking the issue away (as Charles Tupper seemed wont to do), and once Tilley had insisted that nothing at all could be gained, and much lost, in letting Nova Scotia go on festering, Macdonald took over and mastered the complexities of Nova Scotian politics from a thousand miles away with remarkable intuition. He sweetened up the terms of union and got Howe into the Dominion government as guarantee for them.

As for New Brunswick, the terms for its entering Confederation had been slightly better than Nova Scotia's; moreover, there had been two elections on the question, in 1865 and 1866, and the province thus took its place in the Dominion on the basis of a popular mandate. In August 1867 the federal elections gave the Macdonald government eight of fifteen New Brunswick seats.

French Canadians had been evenly divided over Confederation in 1865, when the main debate took place. In the 1867 election, with help from the bishops, the Macdonald government took forty-seven of the sixty-five Quebec seats. Many Quebecers began to like the idea of a provincial centre of power, and a provincial capital back once more in Quebec City. Ottawa, they reasoned, could remain a distant federal capital.

Ontario was the province that from the start had urged Confederation, and it was the driving force for its achievement. The government got fifty-two of Ontario's eighty-two seats.

Thus, in 1867 the new Sir John A. Macdonald government embarked upon its existence with a working majority of thirty-five seats in the House of Commons. It was enough for most purposes, not enough for complacency.

Westward to the Pacific

The constitution of 1867 was more Macdonald's doing than anyone else's. Charles Tupper and Leonard Tilley were local politicians, neither of them lawyers; Alexander Galt was a railway magnate and businessman; George-Etienne Cartier was a lawyer all right, but mainly connected with railways and civil law, which was of little use in the stern and thoughtful work of constitution-making; George Brown was a newspaperman. There was precious little real administrative and legal expertise among the thirty-three Fathers of Confederation. Nor was there much in the civil service. Macdonald told Judge Gowan of Barrie, Ontario, an old friend from the Rebellion days of 1837, that there was no one to help him, and he had to take it all on himself: "As it is I have no help. Not one man of the [Quebec] Conference (except Galt in Finance) has the slightest idea of constitution making. Whatever is good or ill in the Constitution is

George Brown (1818–80), above, founded the Toronto *Globe* in 1844, and although he was an active politician for many years, he never gave up control of the paper. Author and statesman Joseph Howe (1804–73), right, when he was Secretary of State for the Provinces in Sir John A. Macdonald's government. Note his trousers have no crease; that fashion came in after the turn of the century.

mine." In the end, the form of our constitution comes back to Macdonald's fertile, malleable mind.

One of the immediate, fundamental questions was what the balance of power should be between the federal and provincial governments. Macdonald must have realized at once, the moment the word "federal" was used, that it could cover a great deal of ground. There were many different kinds of "federal." At one end of the scale was a constitution like that of New Zealand in 1852, where the provinces were barely above municipalities; at the other, a constitution like the first American confederation of 1777–89, where the states had virtually all the power. Macdonald had one distinct and unequivocal aim—to combat that which the American Civil War had writ so large: the inherent tendency of federal systems to fly apart. It was the result of too much weakness at the centre. He therefore set out to centralize as much control in Ottawa as he could, save only the irreducible minimum which of necessity went to all the provinces.

The result was a very strong central government, with dominance over the provincial governments, and was clearly so intended. The central government's control over "peace, order and good government" was the biggest grant of power known to the Colonial Office drafters. It was a phrase that had been used for years—though more often in its other version, "peace, welfare and good government"—whenever the British Parliament wanted to bestow a plenary grant of power on any colonial government. Nor was that all. Ottawa appointed all the judges in the country, right down to and including the County Courts. It left the provinces with the power to appoint only the magistrates (the justices of the peace). And Ottawa appointed the official executive heads of all the provinces, the lieutenant-governors. Disallowance, the unfettered power given to the federal Cabinet to strike down any provincial law for whatever reason, be the law constitutional or not, was emphasized. In a famous memorandum in June 1868, just a year after Confederation, Macdonald told the provinces that in future they could expect to see disallowance, a weapon used infrequently by Great Britain against colonial legislation, employed much more often by Ottawa. Macdonald saw the Dominion government as the master, the provincial governments as subservient. He probably hoped that in the long run he might shake the provinces down into quasi-municipal governments, like those of New Zealand. Some of these perceptions also shaped his view of the role of the Dominion government in the new North-West whose future was being negotiated with the Hudson's Bay Company.

Within fifteen months of Confederation, while Macdonald was courting Joseph Howe and Nova Scotia, the Cabinet sent George-Etienne Cartier and William McDougall to London to negotiate the cession of the HBC's title to Rupert's Land. The two ministers came from radical political backgrounds; both were vigorous and opinionated. Cartier was French Canadian in style, manner, and beliefs; he had been rebel-minded in the 1830s, but had accommodated himself nicely to the tough new world of railways and investment portfolios, and to the role of politician in the mid-1850s. McDougall was a Reformer from Ontario, rather to the left of George Brown—radical, anti-Catholic, anti-French—who would have never been mixed up with Cartier at all but for the coalition that Brown had been instrumental in putting together in June 1864. McDougall was now, after Confederation, Macdonald's Minister of Public Works.

Cartier and McDougall agreed, each for different reasons, that Canada had now to take over the HBC title to Rupert's Land. Rupert's Land was big, very big; its boundaries, though quite precise, had never been run: Rupert's Land was the land comprehended by all the rivers that flowed into Hudson Bay. That meant, in present-day terms, part

Old Parliament Buildings, Ottawa. This pleasing and harmonious portrait of the Parliament Buildings of the Province of Canada was done in 1866, the year construction was completed; the next year the buildings became the home of the new Parliament of the Dominion of Canada. The principal architects were Thomas Fuller (1823–98) and Charles Baillairgé (1826–1906). Watercolour (1866) by Otto R. Jacobi.

of what is now western Quebec, most of north-west Ontario, all of Manitoba, most of Saskatchewan and Alberta, and part of the eastern Northwest Territories. The question for Canada was, at what price? The HBC wanted the best price it could get, and while it would prefer to sell to Canada, the price Canada seemed willing to offer was nowhere near what the company wanted, nor indeed remotely near its market value. The United States had paid a cool $7.2 million cash to the Russians for Alaska in 1867, hardly knowing what was up there—if anything. The HBC reasoned, not without justice, that if Alaska was worth $7 million, Rupert's Land, with seven hundred miles of common border with the United States, must be worth a lot more. There was talk of $40 million, and whispers that the HBC would like to sell to the Americans. But however tempted the company might be, the British government would never let that happen.

After six months of negotiation—the HBC reluctant, the British government insistent—Canada got a bargain. Canada paid $1.5 million for the whole of Rupert's Land, and gave back to the company one-twentieth of the fertile land; the HBC originally wanted one-tenth of the fertile land, but Canada refused. Bought by the Dominion government—paid for with the help of an imperial guarantee—this was Dominion land, and it was to remain so until alienated, sold, or given to subsidize railways. (What was left over in 1930 would be given to the three western provinces.) It was the biggest real-estate deal in our history, and Cartier and McDougall returned to Canada in the spring of 1869 with some reason to be pleased with themselves.

Louis Riel, Father of Manitoba

The negotiations in London obscured in the minds of the Canadian Cabinet some equally important problems at Red River. It was easy to assume in Ottawa that you just took the North-West over and administered it, with a modest lieutenant-governor in Council stepping in where the Hudson's Bay Company left off. That is probably what would have happened had it not been for Louis Riel, twenty-five years old, one-eighth Indian and seven-eighths French Canadian. Clever, ambitious, poetic, visionary, vain, Riel had been brought up in Red River and then educated in Montreal at the suggestion of the Archbishop of St-Boniface, Alexandre-Antonin Taché, who thought the boy had great potential for the priesthood. Potential he had indeed, but his power was put to the service not of the church but of his own Métis people, a group which few English Protestants quite understood, and which they frequently underestimated. The Métis lived in the winter and spring on river-lot farms along the Red and its tributaries, on deep, narrow lots in the French-Canadian style. In the summer and autumn they hunted buffalo. Like all hunting people they had evolved specific techniques. They were, in effect, a disciplined light cavalry. W. L. Morton, the great prairie historian who grew up in Manitoba, has this description of the Métis summer hunt:

Then the hunters, each mounted on his best horse, rode out under the captain and approached the herd up-wind behind any convenient fold in the rolling plain. When in position they charged in line at a signal from the captain. Every man carried his gun across the neck of his trained runner, and had a handful of powder loose in his pocket, his mouth full of balls. As the buffalo turned to run, each picked his animal, usually a young cow, and rode alongside. The gun was fired across the horse's neck, aim being taken by the angle. Up to fifty or even a hundred yards, the Red River hunter could bring down his prey, though usually the shot was fired from close range. Then a palmful of powder was poured down the barrel of the gun, a ball spat into the muzzle, and the whole shaken home by knocking the butt on the thigh or the saddle. The runner had meantime carried on at a gallop to overtake a new beast.... And so it went in the thunder of the hooves, the snorting and roaring of the herd, in the dust and glare of the summer plains....

The Métis did not like the obtrusiveness of the Canadians from the East. The ones in Red River were noisy and aggressive, and the Canadian government in Ottawa had already sent surveyors to run a survey—one very different from the old Métis river-lot farms. Although the Canadian government fully intended that Métis land titles should be respected, there were no assurances from anyone in authority that such would be the case.

Riel knew his people and what he might manage with them. He and Métis horse-men seized Upper Fort Garry, the main HBC centre at the forks of the Red and the Assiniboine, on November 2, 1869. They continued to hold it until they had forced the new Dominion of Canada to negotiate terms. The result was the minuscule Province of Manitoba, created in 1870, with special rights for the Métis and the French.

Riel can thus be regarded as the father of Manitoba, and in some ways he was. But he made mistakes—and he made one bad one. He knew his men, influenced and per-suaded them; they admired him; but he was unfamiliar with power and its use. Taking Fort Garry by *coup de main* created great tension and uncertainty. The Métis were not the only mixed-blood group; there were English-speaking mixed-bloods as well, whom Riel wanted to carry with him. But the Métis were the best organized and most cohesive, and they had moved first. They were resented by others, not least by Canadians from Ontario who had come to regard Red River as their natural, if future, possession. There were threats uttered—often more empty than real, but how could Riel know? He was upset at what he believed, rightly, were conspiracies against him. By late February 1870, after negotiations with Canada had been started and a delegation to Ottawa was arranged for the spring, and as the turmoil in Red River was just beginning to settle, there seemed to be another threat from some English-speaking Ontarians living out in Portage la Prairie. Riel's men caught them, armed, as they were passing by Fort Garry (though they were on their way home, as it turned out), put them in prison in the fort, and as an example had one of the most belliger-ent and noisy of them shot after trial by Métis court martial. This was an ill-judged move. Whatever Thomas Scott may have been—a Protestant recently from Northern Ireland who made trouble wherever he went—one did not shoot people, not even by court martial. Riel never really recovered from the disasters that the shooting of Thomas Scott brought in its train. The Manitoba delegates to Ottawa had to go through Toronto incognito, so inflamed had Ontario opinion become. When they got to Ottawa they were arrested on warrants sworn out in Toronto and Ottawa, much to Sir John A. Macdonald's embarrassment. They were freed, with Macdonald privately footing the bill for the lawyers, but the arrests were symptomatic of a bitter and hard Ontario-Protestant position that Macdonald had to take seriously.

In the end a postage-stamp-sized Manitoba, 225 kilometres (140 miles) wide and 175 kilometres (110 miles) deep, was brought into Confederation on July 15, 1870, pretty much on the terms originally negotiated with Riel. A military expedition was sent out west to show the flag, and it forced Riel into hiding; though this was not the official intent, the men of the Ontario militia would never have allowed Riel to escape had they found him. Riel was in time convicted of the murder of Scott. He was eventually given amnesty in 1875 by the Governor General, Lord Dufferin, on condition of five years' banishment from Canada.

Beyond Red River, in what had now officially become Canada's Northwest Territories, the great plains stretched westward into the arching distances, rising gradually to the vast swales of southern Alberta's grassland at 750 metres (2,500 feet). There, finally, the Rockies shouldered their height out of the foothills and fenced the whole western horizon. The western "plains," so-called, were inhabited by proud tribes, Assiniboine, Cree, Blackfoot, most of them with the horses that had spread north from Mexico and had reached the northern plains by the middle of the eighteenth century. The plains peoples hunted buffalo; they lived from, by, and because of, the buffalo. Already these tribes, especially the Blackfoot of southern Alberta, were being plied with rot-gut whisky by American traders operating out of Fort Benton, Montana. Canada would soon have to deal with that tragic problem.

The Gold Rush Colony

British Columbia was quite a different story. Bordered by the 49th parallel on one side and the American purchase of Alaska (in March 1867) on the other, British Columbia faced a difficult decision. The great Fraser River gold rush of 1858 had moved northward to the Cariboo country, to Barkerville, with its board sidewalks, board houses, and board cemetery, now a board monument to gold fever. As early as

1865 Barkerville's gold was starting to run out too; miners were leaving, colonial debt was accumulating, and the British government decided it did not need two west-coast colonies, Vancouver Island and British Columbia, each with its own stamps, officials, and capital. The two were joined together forcibly in November 1866, under the name of the mainland colony, but with the capital left in Victoria. This union did not end British Columbia's tribulations, and the American acquisition of Alaska made British Columbians distinctly uneasy.

The possibilities were few and awkward. The total white population was probably no more than eleven thousand, with twenty-six twenty Native people. British Columbians felt they were at the fag end of nowhere, a comfortable *cul-de-sac* on the benign shores of the Pacific. They were cut off from everything. If they wanted to send a letter from Victoria to Ottawa, they had to put an American stamp on it beside the British Columbian one; the American post office at San Francisco, some 800 kilometres (500

Above: Basilica, Quebec City, in a snowstorm, 1882.
Right: Richmond Street, London, Ontario, 1882.

Barkerville, B.C., is named for William Barker, a Cornish sailor who struck gold there in 1862. By 1865, when Charles Gentile took this picture, the gold rush was at its height; within ten years, though, the bonanza was over. Note the hillside of stumps; the trees had been used for buildings and boardwalks.

miles) to the south, would not accept it otherwise. It was humiliating and unfair. All things considered, why not *be* Americans? There were some British loyalties in Victoria, but in British Columbia annexation to the United States did not have the fierce, treasonous mien that history had given the idea in the East. It was coolly thought of as a legitimate possibility. However, representations from the Fraser valley were much more pro-Confederation than those from the Island; the mainland was at least contiguous with the Dominion of Canada, even if the distances were enormous and the territory hardly explored. The Sir John Palliser expedition of 1857–60 had explored southern Saskatchewan and Alberta, and had found a new pass, the Kicking Horse. Exploration does not make colonization; still, Canadian acquisition of the Hudson's Bay territory in 1869 did give the Canadianists in the British Columbia mainland a legitimate argument.

But what could the new Dominion of Canada offer to this vast, untamed world of mountains and sea coast? As it turned out, Canada offered quite a bit—and more than good sense might have suggested. British Columbia delegates went east to Ottawa in the summer of 1870. It was a long trip, from Victoria by steamer to San Francisco, then via a long, hot train journey on the very new Central Pacific–Union Pacific transcontinental railway, completed just the year before, to Omaha, Chicago, and Toronto. Macdonald himself was out of action; he had been struck down with a severe attack of gallstones early in May and was only now beginning to recover from what had seemed a mortal illness. For the time being the captain of the ship was George-Etienne Cartier. The British Columbians wanted a guarantee of at least a wagon road from Winnipeg to Burrard Inlet. Cartier was bolder than that. He knew something about railways, even about their use as machines for expansion. What

Americans could do, Canadians could do. In effect, Cartier said to the British Columbians, "What on earth do you want with a wagon road? It's no good at all in winter, and monumentally slow even in summer. Why don't you ask for a railway?" The British Columbians couldn't believe it. To have their own terms improved on by the very people they were negotiating with! The Canadian terms were enthusiastically accepted: a railway survey to be begun within two years of the date of union—July 20, 1871—and the railway itself to be completed within ten years. Thus Cartier committed the Canadian government to building and completing a railway to the west coast by July 20, 1881. The Conservative caucus in Ottawa blanched a bit at this but the British Columbia bill went through caucus, and later Parliament, on assurance from the British Columbians that they would not insist on the dates. After all, there wasn't even a railway survey in existence, and the nearest railway point to Burrard Inlet was probably Barrie, Ontario.

The Canadian union was taking on a more recognizable shape, Prince Edward Island being added on July 1, 1873. The Islanders were triumphant: after some fascinating manipulations they got their railway paid for, a guaranteed ferry service to the mainland, and a debt allowance double anyone else's. No wonder the Governor General reported, on his official visit to Charlottetown to celebrate July 1, 1873, that the Islanders were under the distinct impression that it was the Dominion of Canada that had been annexed to Prince Edward Island!

It was an audacious enterprise, that union put together between 1864 and 1873. But it had to be fastened down. The Intercolonial Railway from Halifax to Quebec, required by the British North America Act, was partly finished; the first through train was run in July 1876. Sandford Fleming, the engineer-in-chief, got his way and the railway ran over iron bridges, not wooden ones. At the other end of the country the railway was still at the survey stage. Sandford Fleming was put in charge there too, and a mighty work it was. The scale was enormous, and even now, a hundred years later, sufficiently daunting. The Americans had had a transcontinental railway by 1869; but there were formidable differences. The U.S. population in 1870 was 39 million, with the transcontinental railway serving a population of half a million in California alone; Canada in 1871 had a population of 3.7 million, and the future Pacific railway would serve 11,000 whites—given that the Native peoples were paid scant attention by British Columbia. Pulling Canada together with a railway system that would, by 1885, go from Halifax to Vancouver, was a considerable achievement for a young country that had, even in 1881, only 4.3 million souls.

Cartier's Pacific railway decision may have been unwise; lots of Ontario taxpayers had begun to think so. Still, the Macdonald government was struggling, not ineffectually, to master the enormous problems the Northwest Territories and British Columbia represented. One thing was abundantly visible: there could be no transcontinental nation without the physical means to administer it. *A mari usque ad mare* was our major problem of empire and communications.

At the House of Commons: Its Style and Character

Canada was a big country, awkward and difficult to govern; the internal brokerage of it was in party and in Parliament. The seats in the House of Commons were distributed on the principle that Quebec had sixty-five seats (as she had had before 1867 in the old Canadian Assembly) and these, divided into her population, gave a specific ratio that was applied to the other provinces. As for the rules of franchise, each province continued to apply its own pre-Confederation criteria until 1885, when a single Dominion franchise was established. All the provincial franchises, and the Dominion one, were based on some property qualification. It was not always very high, but all provinces took the view that owning property was a necessary condition of the vote. Women had not always been excluded—in colonial days women in certain circumstances could vote in Nova Scotia and Lower Canada—but that right had died out before Confederation.

However judiciously the House of Commons seats were apportioned, one fundamental fact could not be avoided: the West had little political power. Even as late as the election of 1900, only 17 of the 213 seats in the House of Commons were from west of Lake Superior. This was not an eastern conspiracy: it was elementary demography. Before 1885 the vast majority of MPs, Sir John A. Macdonald included, had never been west of Georgian Bay, on Lake Huron. Hector Langevin was unusual in that, as Minister of Public Works, he made an official trip to British Columbia in 1871 via the Union and Central Pacific.

In the general election of 1872 there were some difficult constituencies for the government of Macdonald and Cartier. Macdonald himself was probably safe in Kingston. Langevin in Dorchester was less certain; George-Etienne Cartier in Montreal East was definitely in danger. But it was not only personal seats that were in jeopardy; Macdonald, like the French-Canadian leaders, was also concerned about many other constituencies. Across Ontario, Conservative MPs worried about the Riel issue; the effect of the murder of Scott had not died away, and the Ontario government in 1871 put up a $5,000 reward for his murderer(s). The Pacific railway was bothersome as well, with Ontario taxes being thrown into the trackless mountains to run a railway to a negligible white population. With a new total of 88 available seats in Ontario, up from 82 in 1867, Macdonald did not like the look of things. So he told his followers in any doubtful constituencies to "spend money" persuading the electors to vote for them. After all, Macdonald said, "Our friends have been liberal with contributions." They had.

Most of the Conservative campaign money in 1872 came from Sir Hugh Allan, Montreal shipping magnate and president of the Canada Pacific Railway Company, who wanted the government contract to build the Pacific railway. His shipping line needed good railway connections that he could control. Allan needed the government, and the government needed Allan. A lot of money was dished out by Sir Hugh, about a third of a million to Macdonald, Cartier, and Langevin. (Multiply mid-century dollar figures by about twelve to get a contemporary equivalent.)

Macdonald did win the election of 1872 but not too comfortably, despite bribery of the electors. His 1867 lead had been substantially reduced. And he had been right about Ontario; of its 88 seats, the Liberal opposition won at least 46, perhaps more. His working majority in the House of Commons would depend on the nature of each particular issue.

After the election, Sir Hugh Allan was rewarded with the contract to build the Pacific railway, on the assumption that he would divest himself of American control on his board of directors. But since Allan, unknown to Macdonald, had used American money to persuade the government to award him the contract, this proved difficult, and finally resulted in blackmail. The Liberals broke the scandal on April 2, 1873. When, that same month, Macdonald, claiming that his hands were clean because he had not profited personally, moved for a committee to look into the scandal, his majority was 31. But party discipline was casual, and that majority certainly could not be counted on. It did not take long to whittle it down. Before long it was down to 8, in a House of 200. Macdonald may have hoped that Prince Edward Island's 6 new MPs would support him, but when they arrived in the autumn of 1873 the Pacific Scandal was in full swing. Macdonald's letters and telegrams of 1872 to Sir Hugh Allan were stolen by the Liberals and published. They made damning, juicy reading. "Must have another ten thousand. Do not fail me." These letters, printed in

I ADMIT I TOOK THE MONEY, AND BRIBED THE ELECTORS WITH IT. IS THERE ANYTHING WRONG ABOUT THAT?

Cartoonist J. W. Bengough (1851–1923) founded the satirical weekly *Grip*, which made its name by ridiculing Sir John A. Macdonald during the Pacific Scandal. The Liberal leader Alexander Mackenzie gazes skeptically up at Sir John A. Macdonald.

Liberal papers, forced even loyal Conservatives to wince or hope to heaven there wasn't a word of truth in it. But there was. And Macdonald's supporters were hardly mollified by his claim that he could simply not remember certain events and incidents. This may have been true—like many of his contemporaries, he was at times a heavy drinker—but that made things worse.

When Parliament met in October 1873, the new Prince Edward Island MPs kept their skirts clear of Macdonald and went mainly to the Liberals, lured by the promise of a Cabinet seat. The government thought it might survive by one vote, but even that failed, and it resigned on November 5, 1873. Lord Dufferin, the Governor General, called on the Leader of the Opposition to form a government.

Alexander Mackenzie did just that. He was a short, brisk, Scottish contractor from Sarnia, Ontario, who had begun his working life at the age of fourteen as a stonemason. He was not the dour figure he has sometimes been portrayed as; he had a sense of humour, but with little education, having come up the hard way by work and rugged honesty, he lacked quickness and was apt to be stubborn and intractable. The Liberal party, too, was rather a mixed bag of Ontario Reformers, Maritime Liberals, and Quebec "Rouges." As soon as Mackenzie got his feet under him, he called a general election for February 22, 1874, with the Pacific Scandal as the main item on the agenda. He and his Liberals proceeded to wipe the floor with the Tories. The Canadian electorate returned Mackenzie and the Liberals with a majority of 71 seats in a House of 206. It was devastating.

The House of Commons was not a place for the timid or the delicate. Charles Tupper, and others, were good at marshalling strong arguments for weak causes, but the House of Commons was apt to take its own debates with several grains of salt. It distrusted rhetoric or eloquence; emotion, if it did not grow out of the argument itself, was suspect. The new MP who tried to make a "memorable speech" frequently found the seats in the Commons emptying, and his fine periods and metaphors might become the joke of the smoking-rooms. It was a rough place, made more so perhaps by the two parliamentary bars. During night sittings in the 1870s, half the MPs would be under the weather, so Wilfrid Laurier observed.

Tall, slim, *soigné*, Laurier looked like the poet he was. He first came to the House of Commons in 1874, became a minister briefly in 1877–78,

Elevating the Standard—the Young Wilfrid Laurier. In 1877 Laurier (1841–1919) was made a minister in the cabinet of Alexander Mackenzie. He was defeated when he returned to his constituency for the statutory by-election, but was then offered a seat in Quebec (City) East. Here he is on the city's battlements, hoisting the Liberal flag in triumph, having won the new by-election. By Octave-Henri Julien, published in the *Canadian Illustrated News* (December 15, 1877).

and became Leader of the Opposition in 1887. Laurier had the grasp of Parliament from the start. He did not mind a good debate, for there was steel in him, but his natural fastidiousness abhorred dirt and wrangles and hurting people. He liked set occasions best, and seemed to manage those better than the casual cut and thrust across the floor of the House. Laurier was an actor really; he had a profound sense of theatre. It was sometimes said that the polish of his speeches came from their being well rehearsed.

Sir John A. Macdonald was in many ways the most intriguing figure of them all, always listened to in the House, though not a parliamentary orator in the usual sense. He rarely met argument with argument. His speeches were those of a man measuring his audience and his subject, feeling out his path, rather like a man working his way across the stones of a brook. Macdonald could pitch into the Opposition when he chose to, but his attacks usually took the form of insinuating a story that would amuse his followers, drawn from his great store culled from novels, biography, and history. He was certainly no beauty; his once thick, curly hair was clustered mainly at the back now, and his large nose seemed to have acquired ripeness as he went through years and whisky. He also had a rich, soft voice, a little gravelly, one of the more amiable legacies of years of drinking. He had a marvellous memory for names and faces, a memory that was legendary in his own time. All this was the stuff that kept his followers loyal to the end. Macdonald knew it; he never forgot that popularity was power, but his liking for human beings was genuine. He could not be pushed around too much, but the truth was that he had endless patience with the vagaries of the human animal. Still, when as a member of Cabinet young Charles Tupper (his father's son, indeed) wanted something from Macdonald in 1890, "Dear Charlie," Macdonald scribbled on the obtrusive letter from his young and bumptious colleague, "skin your own skunks."

Parliament was like that, too: abrupt, caustic, humorous, distinctly unrefined. Sometimes it could be tumultuous, and on certain occasions the throwing of blue books and papers across the House was authorized by tradition. Tupper once complained of being hit by some such formidable object; the Opposition replied that it was only the Supplementary Estimates! Mayhem also appeared in committee from time to time. During a standing vote the yeas would line up on one side and the nays on the other, the fun consisting of dragging or carrying an MP over to the opposite side. Alexander Mackenzie, although short, one day selected the larger Cartier as his prize, but the victim struggled with such energy that he escaped having to vote for the wrong side. Parliament sometimes proceeded amid the singing of songs, the mimicking of cats and roosters. In 1878, after the great parliamentary drunk of

February that year, the *Canadian Illustrated News* recommended that a special edition of the Hansard reports of parliamentary proceedings should be prepared for cab-drivers to teach them a proper stock of invective.

Sir Richard Cartwright, finance minister from 1873 to 1878, could denounce his Conservative opponents with vicious fluency. Cartwright loved finding things wrong, especially during the eighteen years (1878–96) when the Conservatives were in power. The magazine *Grip* had a cartoon of him in 1890 as a mounted knight, his shield bearing the legend, "Blue Ruin." Someone is asking him, "But can't you let us see the other side of the shield, Sir Richard?" "It hasn't any other side!" the Blue Knight replies.

The National Policy and Canada's Industrial Revolution

Alexander Mackenzie's government did not go well. It was not easy struggling with the "spoilt child of Confederation" (British Columbia), the Pacific railway, the finishing of the Intercolonial, and, not least, the depression of 1874–78. Losing one by-election after another, the Liberal majority sank from seventy-one to forty-two. What mainly brought about the Conservative resurgence, apart from Macdonald himself, was the failure of the Liberal government to do anything about the depression of the 1870s and its effects upon Canada. It may not have been possible to mitigate those effects: that was the position of the finance minister, Sir Richard Cartwright. But the fact that he said he couldn't ("We have as much power as a set of flies on a wheel and no more") and believed it did the Liberal party no good at the polls.

Sir John A. Macdonald had been persuaded by a group of Montreal manufacturers to accept the idea of a protective system of higher tariffs, and in the summers of 1876 and 1877 he pushed the idea where he was at his best—at political picnics. Fundamentally, the Liberal leaders were free traders who believed that governments could not tinker with economic laws—this despite the fact that the United States had been tinkering freely with them to protect their home industries; the American high tariff system had been in place since the Civil War. Mackenzie and Cartwright believed that tariffs were a necessity in Canada, not for protection but only because they were the main source of the Dominion government's revenue—77 per cent of such revenue came from them. (Even in 1900, 73 per cent of federal revenue would still come from tariffs.)

There was a spectrum of opinion across the Liberal party on tariffs. At one end were the free-trade leaders. Others reached towards what was called incidental protection—the point, say 20 per cent, where a tariff began to protect Canadian manufacturers from foreign (mostly American) competition; this position could be said to represent the more metropolitan opinions of the party, of Edward Blake, the Toronto lawyer who would be leader of the Liberal party from 1880 to 1887. But Blake was in and out of the government in the 1870s, and the counsels listened to were those of Mackenzie and Cartwright, who wanted only a revenue tariff—a tariff as low as possible consistent with the government's revenue needs.

What exacerbated the problem of the 1870s was slaughter selling (what we now call "dumping") by the Americans. American manufacturers were badly affected by the drying up of their own markets in the depression and found it helpful to sell their goods in Canada, often at less than cost, simply to clear inventory. Edward Gurney, who made stoves in Hamilton, told a House of Commons committee in 1876 that his Buffalo competitors were putting stoves into Canada at half the Canadian price. This was done not only to unload inventory; it also had the incidental purpose of driving Gurney out of business. There is a cartoon in *Grip* of February 1876 showing a Canadian factory closed down; in front Uncle Sam is beating Canadian industry, prostrate on the ground, with a large stick (the American protective tariff), while the Canadian's tariff stick is small, insignificant, and useless. Nearby is Prime Minister Mackenzie, dressed as a policeman, standing idly by with his government truncheon in his hand, ruminating, "Why do I hesitate?" The *Grip* cartoonist was quite definite as to what was needed. Underneath is written, in large letters, "WANTED—PROTECTION!!"

To Have a Country or None

Protection for fledgling Canadian industries—woollens, cottons, iron and steel, shoes, stoves—was not just an economic question, it was philosophical, debated then as now. It was one of the few issues that could be said to divide the two Canadian political parties. Macdonald himself had no philosophical axe to grind—if anything, he had been a free trader—but he had sensitive antennae, and he came to the idea of the protective tariff, slowly, even reluctantly. Perhaps he was convinced by Charles Tupper, who seems to have developed the idea from his Nova Scotian experience, calling it the National Policy. *Grip* in May 1877 summed it up:

...You this great truth should know,
Countries alone by manufactures grow...
Your tools, your arms, your raiment, make hard by.
Your farmers will your workmen all supply
With food, your workmen them with all they need,
Each helping each, and profits shall succeed...
Strength shall arise, and Canada be known
Not as a petty colony alone....
The present's here; the lazy past is done,
We'll have a country, or we will have none.

What had happened was that the conventional wisdom of the day had shifted over to protective tariffs (under whatever name). Macdonald shifted with it, but Mackenzie did not. Shifts like that are much easier when you are the Opposition and have nothing to lose. As a result, Macdonald was returned to power in the general election of September 1878 with as large a majority as he had been defeated by in 1874. The Liberals couldn't get over it. Some could not get over the new National Policy (NP) either, which through Macdonald was to become a permanent feature of economic and political

Women workers sorting ore in the Huntington copper mine near Bolton, Quebec, in 1867; a rare view of working conditions in Confederation-era Canada. Photo by William Notman.

Toronto Rolling Mills. This 1864 pastel by William Armstrong evokes the poem by Archibald Lampman (1861–99) "The City of the End of Things": "A flaming terrible and bright / Shakes all the stalking shadows there,… And only fire and night hold sway.…"

life in Canada. The basic idea of the National Policy was to encourage, by means of a tariff structure, the development of Canadian industry: allow raw materials in cheaply, such as cotton, wool, unrefined sugar or molasses; and put steep import duties (25 to 30 per cent) on goods that Canadian factories could now manufacture, such as cotton or woollen cloth, refined sugar, nails, screws, engines.

The other principle of the National Policy was that of permanence. No manufacturer was going to put $100,000 into a plant without some belief that tariff protection was going to stay in place for a while. Perhaps twenty-five years was long enough to establish a young industry. Whatever it was, Macdonald and the Conservative government insisted on the importance of "permanence." The Liberals who fought the NP with only indifferent results in Parliament and in three general elections (1882, 1887, and 1891) probably also fought the manufacturers who believed that business depended upon the re-election of the Conservative party. Whether that was true or not, it was true

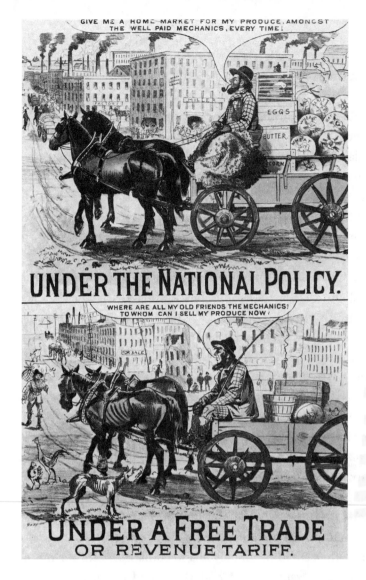

GIVE ME A HOME MARKET FOR MY PRODUCE, AMONGST THE WELL PAID MECHANICS, EVERY TIME!

UNDER THE NATIONAL POLICY.

WHERE ARE ALL MY OLD FRIENDS THE MECHANICS? TO WHOM CAN I SELL MY PRODUCE NOW!

UNDER A FREE TRADE OR REVENUE TARIFF.

Under the National Policy.... A colour lithograph (artist unknown) published in 1891 by the Industrial League for the Conservative Party, as part of a series of federal election posters attacking the Liberals' Reciprocity platform. In fact, the National Policy was always intended to benefit workers and farmers as well as manufacturers.

that the Liberal party only began to get real support from business after 1893, when Laurier and the Liberal party abandoned their free-trade stance and Sir John Thompson, for the Conservatives, came down a bit hard on the Masseys and others who were making too much money from tariff protection.

Factories, the intended beneficiaries of protection, had been in existence for some years, but it was with the National Policy that they became an important feature of Canadian life. To some contemporaries the Canadian industrial plant seemed to come almost at once, in the expansive years of the early 1880s. Whole new sets of industries appeared: cutlery, clocks, felts, tableware, woollen and cotton goods. The first piece of printed cotton in Canada was turned out in July 1884, from a factory with a capacity of 27,000 metres (30,000 yards) a day. Consumer demand rose; distribution networks expanded.

Stories of Life and Labour

This vast productivity undoubtedly promoted the prosperity and well-being of the country. Between 1840 and 1900 the standard of living went up, measured by the yardstick of what one dollar would buy; it probably bought about 25 per cent more in 1900. The dollars may have been slightly harder to come by in 1900; that is impossible to measure. Certainly the worker was less self-sufficient in the city than he had been on the farm. He had to buy goods and services from someone else. In the shift from farms to cities, the supposition was that the living was better. But it was probably an uneven process; city rents were high, and it is possible that, once having come, a family could be trapped in the city by bad times, unable to return to the farm. Still, there was no doubt that factories multiplied productivity enormously. Consider shoes, for example. A shoemaker of the 1840s could sew two pairs of shoes a day; in the 1880s, with the new sewing machine, a workman could, in effect, make a hundred. That is, he would make parts of a thousand pairs, and nine other workmen would make the other parts. Output rose steeply; prices fell.

There were also drastic changes in technique. The movement from the craftsman of the 1840s to the factory worker of the 1880s resulted in jobs that were much more routine. The pride of the craftsman was clearly diminished in the factory, for factories no longer required skilled and experienced workmen who had learned their trade over fifteen or twenty years. Most jobs could be mastered by unskilled labour—or by boys and girls. This kind of labour was much cheaper. Child labour, of boys under twelve and girls under fourteen, was prohibited in both Ontario and Quebec in the 1880s, but the law was impossible to enforce. In Nova Scotia boys had to be at least ten years of age before they could be employed and could not work for more than sixty hours a week until they were twelve! Child labour was not the creation of wicked capitalists alone: it was a conspiracy of parents and employers. The child needed training, the parents needed the money the child brought home, and the employers needed labour. This did not make child labour any less reprehensible, but the blame has to be apportioned. And the city family was an offshoot of the farm family; children worked long hours in both places.

Take the case of Théophile Carron, journeyman cigarmaker, age fourteen. He was apprenticed at eleven years of age, almost certainly by his father or mother, under a duly notarized indenture. After three years' work he became a journeyman, and in time he would be a full-fledged cigarmaker. Such young workers were hard to control,

Post Office and Parliament
Buildings, Ottawa, Ontario,
1901 (?).

and factory foremen were not always very nice about the rough-and-ready discipline they dispensed. Young apprentices who showed the least breach of factory discipline could be incarcerated in the factory's own prison. It could be suggested that if labourers did not want to submit to such conditions they did not have to. They had the option of getting out. But it was not as simple as that. You could store grain; you could store money; you could not store labour, any more than you could put hunger on the shelf and forget it. Labour and capital were not equal in bargaining force. Labourers had to work to eat. Capital just sat there, a bit devilish, seeming to spin money out of itself.

Sickness was worse. If you were ill on the farm, usually someone could take care of you and your work. In the city, if you were not well enough to work you earned no money. There was no safeguard against fate or bad luck. Despite this, workers continued to come into the city from the farms, exchanging the discipline of farm work, often long and ill-paid, for the tighter, more exigent discipline of the factory, but at least getting cash pay and a holiday on Sunday. The changes were not easy. In a factory town like Marysville, New Brunswick, north-east of Fredericton, workers rose by the whistle of the cotton factory. You went to work by it, ate your lunch and tea by it, and after a ten-hour day went home by it. On the farm, animals had their own routines, but within their constraints and those of the crops, you were to some degree your own boss. In a factory you were drilled into a routine that was not yours. The poet Archibald Lampman, raised in the countryside, came to hate many aspects of the new city of the 1880s:

And toil hath fear for neighbour,
Where singing lips are dumb,

An early example of the new (1889) snapshot, done with George Eastman's new roll film and a hand-held camera, speed being probably ⅟₂₅ of a second. With this new technique, instead of being stiff as a poker for several seconds or more, people could be photographed laughing, as in this family portrait of Sir John Thompson, Canadian Prime Minister, on holiday in Muskoka with his wife, family and friends, July 1894.

And life is one long labour,
Till death or freedom come.

One unhappy certainty was the reduction of wages in the winter. Winter was traditionally the slack season, on the farms and in the cities. Long after the railways came, workers continued to be laid off at the freeze-up. When more people sought work, employers were able to reduce wages. At the very time when you needed money the most, to buy clothing for your family, wood or coal for heating, your wages would be reduced. In the country winters were a social season; in the cities they could be brutal. And there was little protection for working classes, or middle classes either, against bad luck, misfortune, illness, or accident. A poor family in Montreal ran up a bill for $11 for groceries. (You paid your grocer every month or quarter-year in those days.) The wife became ill after only $7 had been paid off. The husband wanted time to pay the $4 remaining. Time was refused, perhaps by hard-bitten lawyers who sometimes took over accounts for collection on commission. A court judgment was got for the $4, plus $15 costs. The man's wages were garnisheed, and despair of it all drove him to suicide.

Labour unions tried to provide some kind of collective shelter against vicissitudes like wage cuts, or too long hours. Their success depended on their leverage. The strongest, the earliest, were among craftsmen whose skills either could survive mechanization or were part of it, such as, respectively, printers and train drivers. Less

Hamilton—Procession of Nine-Hour Movement Men. The Canadian labour movement has its roots in heavily industrialized "blue-collar" cities like Hamilton, Ontario, whose steelworkers are seen here marching for a nine-hour day. Note the painted trade-union processional banners. Engraving from a photograph in the *Canadian Illustrated News* (June 8, 1872).

strong were manual labourers; in fact there was a hierarchy in labour as in so much else. The skilled trade unions were not always anxious to pull chestnuts out of the fire for their less skilled brethren. One union organization tried, for a time successfully, to bridge this gap—The Noble and Holy Order of the Knights of Labour in North America. It included all kinds of labour in its ranks, even small businessmen. Many of the Order's struggles were over not only wages and hours, but basic union recognition. They had some real successes. One of their first encounters was with the Toronto Street Railway in 1886. Senator Frank Smith, the president, said no union man would be hired. There was a strike; the settlement that emerged was based upon the right of the men to belong to the union.

The issues of labour and unions, of toil in the city, were, one can safely say, the eastern, industrial side of Macdonald's National Policy: it was effective, busy, but carried with it concomitant social problems. Canadian cities were growing rapidly; Montreal's population doubled between 1871 and 1891. Doubling a city's population quadruples the strains on its institutions, fire protection, sewage, law and order, housing. On the western side the strains on Winnipeg were even more drastic: from 240 souls in 1871 the population soared to 25,000 in 1891. But then the West was in this, as in so many ways, quite a different story.

The Country of the Great Distances

It is difficult to understand the West without having been there; it was, and is, a special world. The very air is different: the wind, the distances, the winters, the summers. And the prairie West is far from being monotonous: overwhelming, perhaps, is the word, especially with that blinding light, transparent, without haze. Across the immense sky, as Wallace Stegner once put it, move whole navies of clouds, their bottoms scraped flat, it would seem, against the earth. Across the vast miles pours the wind, a grassy, clean wind, something you have almost to tighten into, the way a trout tightens into a fast river.

The West had its own exigencies; on the prairie farm you starved for fruit, and sometimes you ached for water and shade. In the pioneer days at least it was always meat, meat, from an eternal stew pot on the back of the kitchen stove, as eternal as the Newfoundland or Nova Scotian fisherman's fat teapot, which dispensed a liquid not dissimilar to stew, a tea of leather-like consistency. An easterner in Battleford, Saskatchewan, in the 1870s and 1880s would miss the pears, apples, cherries, peaches of Niagara, or the fat yellow Gravensteins of the Annapolis Valley—the sheer diversity of eastern farms. But then, the whole economy was different. Eastern farms were never completely self-sufficient, but they were not far from it. With thirty inches or more of rain a year in the East there was always a crop of something. But on the prairie there was that fundamental reliance on grain—on barley and oats where there was enough rain, and wheat everywhere.

In the West the harvest comes on with frightening urgency. Imagine 160 acres (65 hectares) of wheat dead ripe; it cannot wait, it has to be brought in at once, before rain, hail, or frost gets to it. That means rising before dawn and getting to sleep, half-dead, when the light has gone, and beginning again the next day. The women work as hard as the men: up at five a.m. getting a huge breakfast ready; in come the harvesters and clean out the food; there is just time after doing the dishes to get the potatoes started (and everything else) for the noon meal; and in the afternoon it is the same all over again for supper.

The urgency of the harvest also meant that your horses and, later, your machinery had to be as good as you could afford. A breakdown of the reaper or binder at harvest time was not to be contemplated. Massey, and Harris, and other Canadian manufacturers, made good machines, but their prices were protected by the 25 per cent National Policy tariff which prevented the cheaper American farm machinery (longer factory runs allowed them to put out similar machines more cheaply) from coming into the country; some western farmers began to think these eastern manufacturers were taking advantage of the fact. The whole point of the harvest was, however, the conversion of the 160 acres of grain into cash. The farmer was a businessman. He was converting his crop into clothing, harness, lumber, machinery, even some perhaps into savings. So he thought instinctively in terms of getting the product to market, about distances, freight rates, and prices in Winnipeg for Number 1 Northern wheat. There were success stories; had there not been more successes than failures, who would have come? John Fraser came out from Edinburgh, Scotland, to Brandon, Manitoba, in 1881 with $2,000 capital and bought a half-section of good black loam land from the Canadian Pacific Railway. Within two years it was worth $4,500, with forty acres (sixteen hectares) in wheat (at twenty to thirty bushels to the acre), twenty acres in oats, and twenty in barley. His cattle survived the winters on prairie hay.

John Fraser was luckier than some. To a large extent, he seems to have escaped the frost of September 1883 which affected Saskatchewan and Alberta. And the summer of 1884 was wet in Saskatchewan but not too bad in Manitoba. The prairie climates are not one! Some years there could be drought in southern Saskatchewan but bountiful crops in Manitoba and northern Alberta. Sometimes, an event like two bad years in a row (1883 and 1884) could produce, as it did in the Saskatchewan valley, conditions that nourished seeds of political and social discontent.

It has to be said at once that on balance the settlement of the Canadian prairies was peaceful: that in itself was a considerable achievement. We had not a tithe of the trouble the Americans had. This was largely because of the way we did it: we put the law and law enforcement in first, and the settlers afterward.

Louis Riel's Red River Rebellion of 1869–70 had shown Ottawa that the West would need something less than, and more than, a military presence. For one thing, Indian treaties were needed, and there was an important series of treaties between 1871 and 1877. But a concomitant of that was control, not so much of the Native peoples as of white settlers. They were, potentially, the more disruptive, by weight of numbers and influence—at least if American experience was anything to go on. When the Sioux ambushed General Custer at Little Big Horn in Montana on June 25, 1876—"Custer's last stand"—he was there because of an influx of white miners looking for gold. This was Sioux territory, and the miners had invaded it. In the year 1876 the Americans spent $20 million fighting the Native peoples. The whole Canadian federal budget was less than that; an Indian war would have been a disaster

Above: *Red River Cart Train* (*c.* 1862?) The carts were made wholly of wood, and could float if necessary. Below: *Civilization and Barbarism, Winnipeg, Manitoba* (*c.* 1871?) Both oils are by W. G .R. Hind, who participated in the cross-country trek of the "Overlanders" in 1862. Today we are less complacent about the "civilized" quality of modern society.

in not only human but financial terms. Canada had to have peace. The Canadian equivalent of Custer's last stand was Treaty No. 6, the Fort Carlton–Fort Pitt Treaty of August–September 1876 with the Plains and Woods Cree of the North Saskatchewan valley. When the Canadian Minister of the Interior, David Mills, went to Washington a year later, his American counterpart, Secretary of the Interior Carl Schurz, asked him, "How do you keep your whites in order?" Mills' response is unknown, but the answer was that the Canadian government got to the West first, with the Indian treaties, with a comprehensive and accurate survey, and with the North-West Mounted Police, in roughly that order. Each reinforced the others, and all of it was in place before the settlers really started to arrive.

The North-West Mounted Police were created in 1873 by Sir John A. Macdonald on strong recommendations from officials in the North-West, especially from Alexander Morris, Lieutenant-Governor of Manitoba and the Northwest Territories (1872–77). The NWMP was highly unusual in function and in organization, quite unlike anything in eastern Canadian experience. The eastern system—imported from England, the way the law was—worked reasonably well. It was local justice, very local, and the law was literally a common law. In times of real social crisis the militia could be called out, but those times were uncommon.

But this eastern law did not work well in the volatile and primitive communities west of Lake Superior. The Hudson's Bay Company had had its own legal system, but by 1869 that had really broken down, as Riel's seizure of Fort Garry showed. When there were British troops in Red River, as in 1846–48 and 1857–61, there was no problem. Once it was established as a province Manitoba would of course have to take on its own law enforcement, but that left Alexander Morris, and Macdonald, with the Northwest Territories to worry about.

Macdonald's NWMP was an inspired creation. The new force had powers and discipline unlike any British system of law enforcement except perhaps the Irish Constabulary. The brilliant idea of the scarlet Norfolk jacket was not original with Macdonald, but came from the adjutant-general of the Canadian militia, Colonel Robertson-Ross. (The colour was, of course, originally that of British army regulars.) Wallace Stegner was a boy of five in 1914 when he saw his first mounted policeman at Weyburn, Saskatchewan:

The important thing is the instant, compelling impressiveness of this man in the scarlet tunic. I believe I know, having felt it, the truest reason why the slim force of Mounted Police was so spectacularly successful.... Never was the dignity of the uniform more carefully cultivated, and rarely has the ceremonial quality of impartial law and order been more dramatically exploited.... One of the most visible aspects of the international boundary was that it was a colour line: blue below, red above, blue for treachery and unkept promises, red for protection and the straight tongue.

The NWMP were soldiers and police at the same time. They were more like the centrally controlled French *gendarmes* than the British police, but they were unlike French or British police in that they acted also as magistrates. The constables of the NWMP apprehended criminals; the officers tried them. Such formidable powers were

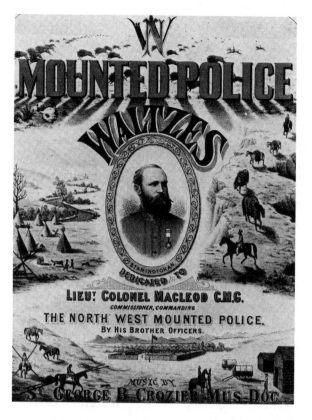

Sheet music for waltzes composed by George B. Crozier and dedicated to Lieutenant-Colonel J. F. Macleod, who founded Fort Macleod in southern Alberta in 1874 and became commissioner of the North-West Mounted Police in 1877. Crozier's son was also with the NWMP, and led their advance against the Métis at Duck Lake.

dangerous in combination: everything depended on the integrity and fairness of officers and men. Macdonald justified the radical departure from English legal traditions by the necessities of justice on a distant frontier. He also believed that the Mounted Police would be temporary, that as soon as provincial administrations were established they would no longer have any function. In fact, the Mounted Police were so successful that the two new provinces of 1905, Alberta and Saskatchewan, begged Laurier to keep the force on. Not only did they stay on, but they spread to all other provinces but two (Ontario and Quebec), although shorn of their judicial powers.

Even in the early 1880s, the disaffection in Saskatchewan—which would bring Louis Riel back to Canada and climax with the Saskatchewan rebellion of March–May, 1885—was not so much a reaction to the NWMP, but to long-distance government. It was a long way from Regina or Prince Albert to Ottawa. The grievances in the Saskatchewan valley were, some of them, minor. Could Métis claim land as homesteaders? They could and, as in the case of the popular Métis leader Gabriel Dumont, did, although not if they had had land in Manitoba. Could they have their land on the old Métis river-lot principle? This was awkward administratively and was generally discouraged. But neither the land claims nor the river-lot principle seemed at all minor to the Métis. Both were central to their way of life. Without effective representation in Ottawa, their only resort was memorials, letters, and petitions. Over the years these had come to Ottawa but the Department of the Interior was slow to respond, slower to act, leaving the Métis feeling much as they had a decade and a half before at Red River: a beleaguered, vulnerable people. Other substantial grievances remained, ones which the Canadian government could do very little about. The old life of the Métis as carriers and freighters for the HBC was mostly gone now that there were steamboats on the Saskatchewan River, and the new Canadian Pacific Railway (CPR); and they took ill to farming. With the buffalo largely gone too, there was hunger and restlessness in the Saskatchewan country by 1884.

But if the Métis had difficulties, the plains Indians had disaster. The buffalo herds had been disappearing since the late 1870s. The repeating rifle was the cause; the Native peoples, not knowing the ravages it could make, looked in vain for the great herds that once had been their whole livelihood. Nor were the treaties much help to them. Broadly, the treaties gave them reserve lands in proportion to population, at 128 acres (52 hectares) per capita, a token annual payment, medals and uniforms for the chiefs, farming and agricultural assistance, with rights to fishing and hunting to continue as before. The treaties took time to negotiate and then had to be translated into Native languages. The combination of

Gabriel Dumont (1837–1906), leader of the Métis bison hunt in Saskatchewan until 1881, was an able guerrilla tactician and a natural soldier. This famous photograph shows Riel's lieutenant after his flight from Batoche in May 1885. Failing to rescue Riel from execution, Dumont joined Buffalo Bill's Wild West Show as a crack marksman, returning to Canada in 1893 after the amnesty for rebels in 1886.

white perception of law and white language did not translate well. The Native person almost certainly had a different view of treaties than the white man. He thought he was agreeing to share land with the whites, as one shares the very air and sunshine. He had never seen a city, he had no notion that what the white man took by the treaties was the right to take over the land in fee simple. It was when he started seeing houses and farms and fences, and the CPR slowly coming onward in the summers of 1882 and 1883, that he began to understand what he had given up.

The whites in the Saskatchewan valley also had grievances. The CPR had changed route. The original line was to go north-west from Winnipeg to Edmonton; on this promise much land had been bought close to the projected line. Suddenly in 1882 the new CPR company changed all that and pulled the route drastically to the south, to go through Regina and Calgary. That dished the speculators and disappointed the farmers—often one and the same. With the bad frost of 1883 and the wet harvest of 1884 piled on top of all the rest, they kicked—or tried to. The trouble was that they had no voice in Ottawa, no MPs at all. Their only representative government was the North-West Territorial Council at Regina, while the very things that mattered most, land and its regulations, were wholly in the hands of the Department of the Interior and its officials in Ottawa and Winnipeg. That department was not well administered, especially after Macdonald gave it up in 1883. And too many of its officials, in Ottawa and in the field, were ineffective, inexperienced, or political appointees after a cushy job.

The English-speaking mixed-bloods and Métis of Saskatchewan combined to bring Louis Riel up from Montana to help them in the summer of 1884. Riel's political (and in the end military) support came mainly from the Métis, and to a lesser degree the Indians. But, his five-year banishment over, he was also welcomed by the whites of Prince Albert. He was brought in to help remedy the grievances, especially land claims, but his main weapon, a petition he prepared to the federal government, seemed to get nowhere. Within a few months he was being taunted by his friends for having accomplished nothing. A Riel so put on his mettle was dangerous. In January 1885, after being six months in the Saskatchewan valley, Riel shifted to more radical positions in both religion and political action. He lost the support of the Catholic church with the first—claiming that he was a "Prophet of the New World"—and that of the Prince Albert whites with the second—armed rebellion. On March 19, Riel, with armed followers, seized the parish church at Batoche, formed a provisional government, and demanded the surrender of Fort Carlton.

Riel believed that armed blackmail, which had worked so well in Manitoba

A RIEL UGLY POSITION.

A Riel Ugly Position: J. W. Bengough enjoys Macdonald's dilemma as French Canadians demand that Riel's death sentence be commuted. Macdonald held to the decision of the court. Anyone who had called up and led the Saskatchewan rebellion would probably have suffered the same fate, regardless of background. Engraving published in *Grip* (August 29, 1885).

in 1869–70, could be effective in Saskatchewan in 1885. But Sir John A. Macdonald was not having it, not a second time, especially not a second time from Louis Riel. And the CPR, almost finished now, was one solid reason why. Back in 1869 Riel had been master of Manitoba, and there had been no way Macdonald could get at him save by laborious negotiation. But in 1885 Macdonald and the Canadian government had troops unloading at Qu'Appelle station within eleven days of the first shooting at Duck Lake on March 26. Riel tried to carry the Native peoples with him, and after the abandonment of Fort Carlton it looked as if he might succeed. But although the loss of Fort Carlton was serious, unhinging as it did government control of northern Saskatchewan, Riel lacked the skill and communications for so delicate an operation as raising an Indian war.

The rebellion in Saskatchewan Territory did not much affect Assiniboia Territory or Alberta Territory, not in anything like the same degree. True, there was decided unease in Calgary early in April 1885 when news arrived of the rebellion in the Saskatchewan valley, but this fear was much relieved when the troops, French Canadians of the 65th Carabiniers regiment, arrived from Montreal. They were greeted at the Calgary train station with open arms:

Before the arrival of the troops the Canadian Government was freely sworn at. Many did not know there was a Government, and a number who were aware of it did not desire to cultivate its acquaintance; but the fact that it was sending troops here to protect the people…struck a responsive chord. The officers and men had come a long way…

Group of Rebel Leaders Taking a Prominent Part in the Armed Rising of 1585, In the North-West Territories of Canada. Left to right: Beardy, Big Bear, Louis Riel, White Cap, Gabriel Dumont. This romanticized image, by a French-Canadian illustrator working for an English-Canadian paper, conflicts with the Anglophone view of Riel and his cohorts as swarthy villains. At the time of the 1885 uprising, Riel—never a horseman—wore a full beard, but the portrait may be based on an earlier photograph. Lithograph by Octave-Henri Julien, published in *The Illustrated War News* (May 2, 1885).

The Calgarians were particularly worried about the Blackfoot tribes who lived 100 to 110 kilometres (60 to 70 miles) south-east. But the Blackfoot were kept quiet by promises and blandishments made in the name of the Dominion government by the missionary Father Lacombe, called by the Indians "The Man of the Good Heart."

Despite their small numbers, the Saskatchewan Métis put up a remarkable resistance to the militia. The Métis had an exceptionally able military leader in Gabriel Dumont. He read the prairie, its weather and its terrain, like a book, and had he had his way the Métis might have given the troops an even tougher time of it. Even so, the battle of Fish Creek, where he halted General Middleton's army, was bad enough.

At Frog Lake, Crees seized twelve whites and mixed-bloods. The Indian agent, a mixed-blood named Thomas Quinn, was too confident; he even sent away the Mounted Police detachment, believing he could command the respect of the local Natives. And on April 2, the Cree shot nine people including Quinn and two Roman

Catholic priests; only two women and the Hudson's Bay agent survived. As for Riel, he never fired a shot the whole time; he led his followers with a crucifix, saying, "Fire, in the name of the Father! Fire, in the name of the Son! Fire, in the name of the Holy Ghost!" When he was captured, the government had to decide what to charge him with. His Métis and Indian followers had certainly committed murder, but Riel had not murdered anyone. What he had done was raise a major insurrection. In the end he was charged with treason, under an ancient 1352 blunderbuss of a statute of Edward III. Macdonald knew the statute for it had been used by the Crown back when he was a young defence lawyer; he had thought then that it had a lot of holes in it.

But in 1885 Louis Riel was convicted and sentenced to death. Some said he was insane; he denied that himself, but there was doubt and the Macdonald government appointed a commission to decide. In the end they concluded he was sane. It was not surprising. Charles Guiteau had assassinated the American president, James Garfield, in 1881, and had been judged sane though his symptoms of insanity were much more obvious than Riel's. Both might have been held to be insane by twentieth-century definitions. The jury, in fact, recommended mercy for Riel. That was something the Cabinet would have to consider as they weighed his sentence. In the end Cabinet let the sentence stand. On November 16, 1885, Riel was hanged at Regina, as the Native people of the Frog Lake massacre would be eleven days later.

Riel's hanging created a furor in Quebec. The Quebec ministers in Macdonald's cabinet had given out hints that Riel would have his sentence commuted. The newspapers

Poundmaker, a Cree chief. During the North-West Rebellion his followers ransacked the abandoned village of Battleford, and subsequently routed a force led by Colonel W. D. Otter. Poundmaker had no part in the fight, and prevented his warriors from pursuing the retreating soldiers, but when he was later captured and tried he was sentenced to prison; he died soon after his release, his health and spirit broken.

tried to pressure Macdonald to step in, but Macdonald was not going to be pressured. Macdonald would have hanged anyone who did what Riel had done, whatever his name, whatever his origin. John Thompson of Nova Scotia, who was at this point Macdonald's new Minister of Justice, explained to Parliament that anyone who roused the Native peoples to war could not expect to get off with punishment less than that which the Native peoples themselves received.

Ranches and Railways

The West recovered quickly from the strains of the North-West Rebellion, especially in Alberta Territory, which had not been seriously affected. One dramatic symbol of this was the development of ranching. Ranching got under way in 1880 with the appearance on the North Atlantic of refrigerator ships, which allowed the export of frozen meat. But it was the export of live cattle to Britain, by 1884, that marked the real beginning of the age of Alberta ranching.

The North-West Mounted Police had come into southern Alberta in the fall of 1874, after an arduous trek overland from Manitoba. The NWMP threw out the American whisky traders (or rather, they simply melted away) who had debauched the Blackfoot. By the early 1880s the buffalo had disappeared, and cattle could now follow. Ottawa then made leases available, and ranching developed rapidly in the high-rolling range land west and south of Calgary. It was easy, with those big grazing leases. A good Hereford calf worth, say, $5 when born, could be fed on free, nourishing, sun-cured Alberta grass and in three to four years be worth ten times the price. In 1884 Canada exported fifty-four thousand head of live cattle to England. By 1900 it was double that, with heavy exports going also to the United States.

The men who managed the Alberta ranches were mainly easterners and not Americans as is sometimes suggested. They were educated professionals. As the western historian David Breen puts it, "Power in the Canadian West was exercised not by men carrying six-shooters but rather by men in well-tailored waistcoats who often knew the comfortable chairs in the St. James and Rideau Clubs." Some American foremen were brought in early on, but by 1880 the cowboys were Canadian or British. The law-and-order ethos of the Canadian range was strong, and the gun law of the American frontier was regarded as an unwanted (and unwarranted) import from south of the 49th parallel.

Harvesting on the Sandison farm with Massey Harris binders, Brandon, Manitoba, 1892. These workers are stooking wheat after it has been cut and bound in sheaves. Wheat harvested this way could be cut even before it was fully ripe, for it would then ripen stooked, and could be threshed as there was time. Note the number of people on hand needed for this harvest. Photo by J. A. Brock and Co.

Much of the ranching was made functional by the new Canadian Pacific Railway. Its achievement was a great adventure, and rightly have Canadians celebrated it; no one can travel from Calgary to Vancouver, even now, without being impressed. It was one of the great Canadian success stories, but like many such, it was a near thing. The principals of the CPR took big risks, not only financial but personal. The CPR had to be a first-class road, otherwise it could not have been run in winter, and Sir George Stephen, Sir Donald Smith, Sir William Van Horne, and others staked their money and their reputations on it. In the end, by 1900, the railway was making money for them and for its shareholders. Everyone knows about the driving of the last spike, November 7, 1885, on a misty day at Craigellachie, 80 kilometres (50 miles) west of Revelstoke. Perhaps more important was the first transcontinental passenger train: it left Montreal Monday evening, June 28, 1886, and arrived at Port Moody, B.C., at tidewater, at noon on Sunday, July 4. That was five and a half days.

As important, at least for the development of Vancouver, were the Empress ships that came in 1891 to bridge the Pacific. In October 1889 the Canadian Pacific placed on order three liners from Britain to establish a monthly service to Japan and China.

Cowboys on a cattle round-up near Cochrane, Alberta, *c.* 1900. Ranching expanded in southern Alberta and Saskatchewan until 1907, when a fierce winter killed much of the stock and wiped out hundreds of operators; many of them turned to wheat farming instead. Photo by Montgomery.

On April 28, 1891, the first of them, the *Empress of India*, docked in Vancouver. She was 6,000 tons, one of the largest then afloat on the Pacific service. She had left Liverpool on February 8 and come by way of the Suez Canal, with more than a hundred first-class passengers—the nearest approach to a world cruise yet offered. It was a major beginning for Canada on the Pacific; the Empresses' white hulls and long, elegant, clipper bows, their 16 knots and punctuality, dominated Vancouver's sense of itself and of the world for the next fourteen years.

British Columbia's history shifted dramatically, too. The province of the 1870s had been the "spoilt child of Confederation": but after 1886 her history is better called "the Great Potlatch." In the 1901 census British Columbia had 180,000 people, at least ten times what it had had in 1871. Vancouver was an international seaport, and there was a huge mineral production in the rest of the province: coal, silver, zinc, lead, and gold. Like all development it had some grim side effects: the great disparity of wealth between capital and labour and the bad working conditions in the mines would produce some devastating strikes in the next years and give British Columbia a long-lasting sense of class-consciousness. Indeed, British Columbia produced contrasts. It was a little like Vancouver itself, with the Empress liners docking at one end of Granville Street, at the other a bridge across False Creek leading first into a forest of stumps and after that into real forest.

The Trail of '98

And there was more to Pacific Canada than southern British Columbia. In 1892 Sir John Thompson—Prime Minister of Canada, 1892–94—was already concerned about the exact boundary with Alaska and raised the issue in Washington. The American Secretary of State, James G. Blaine, agreed to a joint survey, with a report to come in 1895. The Alaskan boundary posed no problem for the northern two-thirds of its length; that was simply a matter of running the line of 141° longitude. The difficulty lay where the boundary went south and east along the Panhandle, from Mt. St. Elias (Canada's second-highest mountain at 5,500 metres or 18,000 feet). Canada and the United States could not agree: did the Americans own the head of the 160-kilometres (100-mile) Lynn Canal or not? Canada claimed it but the Americans occupied it, as had the Russians before the Americans bought Alaska in 1867.

Within a year of that disagreement about the Panhandle, gold was found in the Yukon, in the summer of 1896. There was a big run of it, especially on Bonanza Creek, just off the Klondike River. By 1897 the news was out into the world, and by 1898 miners were pouring in, mostly through those *de facto* American ports at the head of the Lynn Canal, Dyea and Skagway, and by the respective passes that led northward, the Chilkoot and the White. By

A handsome CPR trestle bridge built on a horseshoe turn, west of Schreiber, Ontario, on the north shore of Lake Superior; *c.* 1890. A bridge like this could require two million board feet of lumber, and not a little skill and daring—which latter the company men are pleased to demonstrate, while the train waits in impressive proximity.

Through the Rocky Mountains, a Pass on the Canadian Highway. An 1887 watercolour by Lucius R. O'Brien (1832–99). A former civil engineer, O'Brien first visited the Rockies in 1882; he returned in 1886 to paint views for the CPR, and in 1888 painted on the Pacific coast. Many of his landscapes are notable for their sense of light.

1898, too, the North-West Mounted Police controlled entry to the Yukon from the summit of the passes, insisting that those who entered Canada have sufficient food, clothing, and gear to handle the rigours of the Yukon. The NWMP in fact policed the gold rush. Robert Service, a young bank clerk who worked in the Canadian Bank of Commerce in Whitehorse and Dawson City, watched the gold rush and amused himself and his friends by recalling it in ballads, "The Shooting of Dan McGrew," "The Cremation of Sam McGee," and "The Law of the Yukon," in *Songs of a Sourdough* (1907). His ballads were a heightened reality:

This is the Law of the Yukon, that only the Strong shall thrive; That surely the Weak shall perish, and only the fit survive. Dissolute, damned and despairful, crippled and palsied and slain, This is the Will of the Yukon,—Lo! how she makes it plain!

The Arctic offered more imposing challenges still. Canada's Arctic sovereignty was set out by a British Order-in-Council on September 1, 1880, and confirmed in a British statute in 1895. Canada became Britain's residuary legatee in the Arctic, as she had of so much else of British dominions in North America. Canada was not

Possibly the best-known Canadian photograph. Donald A. Smith, vice-president of the Bank of Montreal, is seen driving the last spike into the final rail of the CPR at Craigellachie, British Columbia, at 9:22 am. on November 7, 1885; general manager William Van Horne, chief engineer Sandford Fleming, and assorted officials and workers are looking on. Conspicuously absent are the immigrant Chinese labourers whose toil made possible the completion of the railway through the Rockies.

first transcontinental CPR paser train arrived at Port Moody, , on July 4, 1886. The CPR then ded to extend the line to :ouver, and this picture shows arrival of the first CPR passenger a in that city, May 23, 1887. (Just e months later the CP steamer ·sinia, from Hong Kong and)hama, tied up at the wharf on ieft, and became the first spacific liner to connect with ·ailway.)

prepared or able fully to shoulder the burden, but struck provisional districts of Ungava, Franklin, Mackenzie, and Yukon. It was the twentieth century that would test the limits of Canada's northern sovereignty.

By 1900 contact with the Inuit people was almost continuous. White men, whalers, had first appeared among them in the sixteenth century, but the real devastation of the Inuit dated from the early nineteenth century when the white man's diseases—smallpox the most virulent—claimed countless lives. The whalers and explorers brought their alien trade goods with them too, such as axes, knives, and guns, which displaced the Inuit's own brilliant technology based on local materials. Many Inuit devices are technological masterpieces: the domed snow house, the toggled (detachable) harpoon head, the kayak, and others. The

The ascent of Chilkoot Pass—3,500 feet (1,067 metres). North-West Mounted Police waited at the top to check that each prospector had all the required food and gear. Photo by E. A. Hegg.

Hudson Bay Expedition of 1884, looking south across Nachvak Inlet from Skynner's Cove, Labrador; H.M.S. *Neptune* in the foreground. Geologist A. P. Low initiated the exploration of interior Labrador and Ungava in 1884, for the Geological Survey of Canada, and with his co-worker Robert Bell—who took this picture—he carried out coastal reconnaissance work from ships of the Department of Marine and Fisheries.

disruption of the Inuit culture by the white man had already begun. But in 1900 it was still a long way from the igloos of treeless Baffin Island to the farms and forests of southern Canada.

Tall Ships and Telephones: The 1890s

In Vancouver the houses being built in the mid-1890s were supplied with running water and sewers; those were developments of the 1860s and 1870s. Even rocky old Halifax was putting sewer systems in during the late 1870s, and expensive going it was. But in neither Halifax nor Vancouver was there any principle of sewage disposal other than emptying it into the nearest large body of water, the tidal ocean. The new houses in Vancouver, in Halifax, and in points between were also getting such inventions as telephones and electricity. Canada had begun its long and happy love affair with Alexander Graham Bell's marvellous invention in the early 1880s. The telephone had been conceived in Brantford, Ontario, and although—as Bell admitted—the only place that had the technical and financial means to deliver it was the United States, the new arrival profited both sides of the border. Ottawa had its first telephone book (with two hundred subscribers) in 1882.

Electricity started to come in the 1880s. At first only railway stations and public buildings could afford it, but by 1900, in the cities and towns at least, it was more the rule than the exception. Not only were new middle- and upper-class houses getting it as a matter of course, but old houses were adding it. And as telephones and electricity proliferated, so did the clutter of wires and poles on the streets. Back in the 1860s Canadian streets had the clean-limbed look of Europe. The ground might be messy—muddy in spring, dusty in summer and fall, and smelling of horse manure all the time—but above that the view was uncluttered. By the 1890s much of that had changed. Telegraph wires were the first intrusion; when the poles first appeared in Halifax in the 1850s people came out with axes at night and cut them down. But as telephones and electricity spread, the poles multiplied; and by the 1890s downtown Toronto, Montreal, Vancouver, Halifax, were made hideous by mazes of cribbing and wires.

Bicycles were another symbol of change. The modern safety bicycle of the 1890s was the same as in the 1950s: it was fitted with Dunlop's new pneumatic tires, had two equal wheels, and could be managed by anybody. It made a social revolution in a few years. Unlike a horse, a bicycle could be stabled easily, and it left no manure. It

Main Street, Winnipeg, looking south, in 1879 (top) and 1897 (bottom), photographed by Robert Bell and William Notman, respectively. Main Street was, and is, 40 metres (132 feet) wide. Note the board-walks in the earlier picture—a small respite from the mud—and the complete absence of utility poles. Yet just 18 years later there are electric streetcars, and huge poles and cribbings for telephones and electricity. The monument is to the battles of Fish Creek and Batoche, in 1885.

was silent, comfortable, efficient, and cheaper than a horse. Young men and women and the not-so-young turned to it with enthusiasm. Though these critical steps were not always recognized by contemporaries—it is hard to catch society in the act of changing—the world would not be the same again.

It was like that with the passing of the tall ships, and the economy that went with them. You could still see the great square-riggers in Atlantic ports as late as the 1920s; but by then they had been relegated, by low freight rates and high insurance on their cargoes, to mean jobs in the mean places of the world. The great age of the tall, soft-wood square-riggers was the 1870s and 1880s; the biggest and best were being built as the 1890s came on, and the trade was already slipping then. Yarmouth, Saint John, and Halifax were often their working ports, but they were built in a score of shipyards around the Bay of Fundy, up Chignecto Bay or Minas Basin, in St. Martin's, Maccan, Parrsboro, Great Village, Maitland, Avonport, and then fitted out in the bigger places.

The old, tall ships were a splendid sight; even the iron men who worked so hard in them couldn't help but admire them. Imagine a grey day in deep southern latitudes, 50°S, with a chill wind blowing all the way around the world. Sailing east towards Cape Horn is a great three-masted ship, black-hulled, deep-laden, coming through the long blue-green seas with yards almost square. She is carrying a big press of sail, and as she passes a British vessel she sets out another royal and sheets it home

The interior construction of a large four-masted schooner, the *Cutty Sark*, being built at Saint John, N.B., in the 1880s; the view is looking forward. Her hull is clearly designed to carry a large cargo. Note the iron keelson bolted on top of the keel. The ship was named after the famous tea clipper built in Scotland in 1869 and now in drydock in Greenwich, England.

The *William D. Lawrence* was launched in Maitland, near the head of Minas Basin, in October, 1874. With a keel of 75 metres (245 feet), she was the largest sailing vessel ever built in Nova Scotia, constructed mainly of spruce and registered with Lloyd's at 2,500 tons. She is shown here in full sail on the starboard tack, driven a bit hard—as Nova Scotian ships normally were. She was sold to Norwegians in 1883.

in a manner reminiscent of a man-of-war. She is a Bluenose, spotlessly clean, well trimmed, and driven hard. An old signalman on the Britisher vouchsafed an opinion of life aboard the Bluenose ship. "For bums, hoboes, an' sojers, sir," said he to the master and mate, "they're a floatin' hell. One bit o' slack lip...and the mates'll have ye knocked stiff and lookin' forty ways for Sunday. But for a man what is a *sailor* an' knows his book there's nothin' better nor a Bluenose to sail aboard of. They works ye hard, but they feeds you good and treats you good if you does yer work." The ship he spoke of was the *William D. Lawrence*, built in Maitland and launched in 1874. She made money for her owners, but as she got older she was sold to the Norwegians in 1883, and was still going, more or less, in 1890.

The problem with the Bluenose softwood ships was that after a decade's hard work they began to leak, and by the 1890s they had as competition the iron-hulled sailing ships. The great barques with iron hulls did not need extensive repairs after a decade at sea, they did not leak, their insurance rates were lower, and they had bigger cargo capacity. Gradually fewer of the softwood ships were built. Nearly as big as the *William D. Lawrence*, the *Canada* was built at Kingsport, near Wolfville, in 1891, and she made a passage from Rio de Janeiro to Sydney, Australia, in fifty-four days in 1895. Within twenty-five years she was a barge carrying gypsum and being towed ignominiously from Minas Basin to New York. That was the fate of the softwood ships. All the wooden ships could do, like the sailors who once had sailed in them, was brood over past glories:

I can't help feelin' lonesome for the old ships that have gone,
For the sight o' tropic sunsets and the hour before the dawn,

And the white sails pullin' stoutly to a warm and steady draft,
And the smell o' roastin' coffee, and the watches must'rin' aft.

I'd like to ship off-shore again upon some Bluenose barque,
And shout a sailor chantey in the windy, starry dark,
Or fist a clewed-up tops'l in a black south-easter's roar,
But it ain't no use a-wishin', for them days will come no more.

Nova Scotia mourned the passing of these tall ships. But not all Nova Scotia suffered from the changes. Parts of the province prospered under the National Policy with its protective tariff system. In the 1880s Nova Scotian industries flourished in the new, growing towns created astride railways by the NP: Amherst, Truro, New Glasgow, Pictou, Sydney. But slowly, central Canadian competition in those industries began to make itself felt. A symbol of the beginning of the shift was the transfer in 1900 of the head office of the Bank of Nova Scotia from Halifax to Montreal—Nova Scotia had grown too confining. After the First World War there would be only a few industries left there.

Changes in political life in the 1890s were more obvious and dramatic. Sir John A. Macdonald died on June 6, 1891, having fought his last election in March of that year under the banner of the National Policy. He left the country sentimental about his charm, proud of his achievements, a bit rueful over the legacy of his methods. He was the father of his country, Sir John Thompson said; there wasn't a Conservative who hadn't lost his heart to the old man. Few could know how toilsome in detail was the life that seemed so full of projects and achievements. Fewer still could know, Thompson added, the gentleness and kindness of his nature. Still, the party was uncomfortable over evidence of his too great kindness, his habit of giving ministers their head once he trusted them. Sir Hector Langevin was by 1890 the senior minister, even once the heir apparent, but he was now under a gathering cloud of suspicion called the McGreevy–Langevin scandal. Langevin was Minister of Public Works, McGreevy a Quebec MP and friend who was a go-between with contractors. The latter were expected to make contributions to McGreevy's party slush fund in return for lucrative contracts. Sir John Thompson was now the obvious choice as Macdonald's successor, but he was a Roman Catholic, a convert at that; Canada had not yet had a Catholic prime minister. The party, worried about that, chose Sir John Abbott of the Senate as leader. Between them Abbott and Thompson were determined to scrub the Conservative party clean, whether the party liked the process or not. Langevin was forced to resign, and that helped the government survive the critical House of Commons vote on September 26, 1891, by 101 votes to 86. When Abbott retired a year later because of ill health, it was obvious that there was no alternative to Thompson as prime minister.

Slowly the Conservative ship began to regain trim. Its slim majority of 1891 was built up by a series of by-election wins in 1892, by-elections forced by the Liberals hoping, in vain as it turned out, to profit by the Langevin scandal. By 1893 Thompson and his Conservatives had a working majority of close to sixty. Despite the rancorous religious tensions between Catholic and Protestant so characteristic of the later 1880s and the 1890s, Thompson's patience, strong mind, and good sense helped to give the country a new sense of itself.

Then, in December 1894, Thompson was suddenly dead an hour after being sworn in by Queen Victoria, at Windsor Castle, as a member of the Imperial Privy Council. Within two weeks of his death came a decision from the Judicial Committee of the Privy Council in London that forced upon the new, uncertain government of Mackenzie Bowell that most unhappy of all decisions: the poisoned chalice of action. And it was action at once, in a tangled, difficult, emotional issue: the Manitoba school question.

There was no solution to the Manitoba school question, not at any rate one that was acceptable to both sides. On the one hand there was the provincial government of Manitoba—on something of a Protestant rampage—and on the other was the Roman Catholic church represented by the Archbishop of St-Boniface, Alexandre-Antonin Taché (Riel's old mentor), and his more extreme successor, Adélard Langevin. The issue itself was not difficult: did separate-school rights accorded to Catholic Manitobans in 1870 still obtain twenty years later? Were constitutional rights permanent, or could they be abrogated by a simple act of legislature later on? In 1890 Protestant Manitobans believed that a majority was entitled to overrule past decisions, that whatever rights might have been given in 1870, a majority in 1890 could abrogate them. Both sides had taken extremely hard positions. Like the square root of minus one, the question couldn't be solved, and will to compromise there was not. So the issue was joined; Canadian MPs on both sides of the House got it into the courts as soon as possible, which seemed much the best place for it. Unfortunately, in the long run the courts gave conflicting answers, especially so in the court of last resort, the Judicial Committee of the Privy Council in London. It said: one, Manitoba had the right to abolish Catholic school laws; two, the Manitoba Catholics had the right to appeal to the Dominion government to have the laws so abrogated restored. It was an astounding performance, as though deliberately designed to set two governments, Manitoba and Canada, at loggerheads. It would have been a hard helm for any prime minister to handle, but especially difficult for a weak, vain, decent old mediocrity like Sir Mackenzie Bowell. In the end the Dominion government was defeated, first by Manitoba, then by the people of Canada in the election of June 23, 1896. Bowell and company were also defeated by Wilfrid Laurier, who claimed he was like the traveller in Aesop's fable: he would get Manitoba to compromise by the sunny ways of sweet reason. As it turned out even Laurier had a rather difficult time getting sweet reason to prevail.

The views Canadians held in common were, and still are, as important as those on which they differed. As the Manitoba school question suggested, Canadians' sense of themselves came fundamentally in two quite different perceptions, French Canadian and English Canadian. Nothing could blink those differences away.

It was true that French Canadians were four or five generations away from the Conquest of 1760, but in folk memories that is not a long time. In the 1880s the poet and playwright Louis-Honoré Fréchette remembered standing with his father when he was fifteen years old, in 1855, watching *La Capricieuse*, the first French warship to come up the St. Lawrence in nearly a hundred years. His father pointed to the French flag flying from the gaff and said with tears in his eyes, "That's your flag, my son! That's where you came from!"

Ce jour-là, de nos bords—bonheur trop éphémère—
Montait un cri de joie immense et triomphant:
C'était l'enfant perdu qui retrouvait sa mère;
C'était la mère en pleurs embrassant son enfant!

(That day—too fleeting its happiness—
There rose from our shores an immense and triumphant cry of joy:
It was the lost child finding again its mother,
The mother in tears hugging her child.)

By the 1890s this sense of being French had grown and multiplied, as had the French-Canadian population itself. Calixa Lavallée's "O Canada" was written in 1880; it spoke of Canada as the land of their forefathers, of the glory of its history, of the nobility of its sacrifices, and of how both would protect French-Canadian hearths and rights.

English-Canadian nationalism was of a different order, less coherent, more diverse, but certainly not inchoate. Young Charles G. D. Roberts (already an admired poet), writing in 1890, was impatient; he could only chafe at the absence of any symbol, any obvious sense of being Canadian—as he did in his poem "Canada."

How long the ignoble sloth, how long
The trust in greatness not thine own?
Surely the lion's brood is strong
To front the world alone!

How long the indolence ere thou dare
Achieve thy destiny, seize thy fame?
Ere our proud eyes behold thee bear
A nation's franchise, nation's name?

The French-Canadian nationalists of "O Canada" and English-Canadian nationalists of "Canada" could not meet, not yet, for they came in two languages, from two different traditions, and with two different perceptions of what Canada should be. English Canadians could not quite believe that you could have a nation in two languages. Of course there *were* such countries; Switzerland, for example, had three

Cover illustration for *O Canada! Mon pays! Mes amours!* The young nationalist and future prime minister George-Etienne Cartier wrote this song in 1834, and sang it for the St-Jean Baptiste Society for its June 24th meeting that year. The first stanza reads:

L'étranger voit d'un oeil d'envie
Du St. Laurent le majestueux cours;
A son aspect, le Canadien s'écrie,
"O Canada, mon pays, mes amours."

(The stranger sees with envious eye
The St. Lawrence's majestic course;
At the sight, the Québécois cries out
"O Canada, my land, my loves!")

Lithograph (undated) by W. Leggo.

languages. But the idea of a country of two languages ran counter to the strong iden-tification in the late nineteenth century of race with language, and both with nationality. Canada was not thinking yet of bilingualism. Canadians did not yet know quite what they wanted or where they were going. Many were nationalists but they did not yet have a clear idea of how their patriotic urges should be directed.

There were a number of Canadians who extrapolated their nationalism into an identification with the glories of the British Empire. Canadian nationalism could thus be subsumed within a much broader perspective. This, one assumes, was the meaning of the large stamp issued by Canada, via Postmaster-General William Mulock of Toronto, in 1898. It had a large Mercator map of the world on it, the British Empire in red. Underneath was the rubric, "We hold a vaster Empire than has been." This identification was sentimental and tempting in the wake of Queen Victoria's Diamond Jubilee; few English Canadians could wholly avoid the appeal of it; but like many sentimentalities, it translated ill into practical terms.

Independence from Great Britain was also a possibility, but it looked an easier choice than it was. With the United States aggressive on most diplomatic issues, and opting so obviously for yet larger acquisitions, Canada still needed Great Britain, whatever views Canadians individually may have had of the British connection. No one denies, Sir John Thompson had said in 1893, that we will eventually become a great and independent people. But before we can do that we have to be stronger. With the United States so "immensely powerful even in peace, and intensively aggressive in pursuit of every inter-est," to talk of independence from Britain in 1893 was "to talk absurdity, if not treason."

This last was a cut directed at a small but noisy group of the Liberal party in Ontario and Quebec and elsewhere who spoke frankly of annexing Canada to the United States. They made rather a flurry in the period 1892–94. French Canadians had already moved to New England in the 1870s and 1880s, some half a million of them. In 1893, Honoré Mercier, leader of the Liberal opposition in the Quebec leg-islature, believed that Quebec would be better off as an American state than as a Canadian province. Most Quebec Liberals could not accept that. Judge Louis Jetté, of the Quebec Superior Court, was firmly of the opinion that French Canadians were safer being Canadians. As he put it, with some irony, "*Pour rester français, nous n'avons qu'une chose à faire: rester anglais.*" ("To remain French there is only one thing we can do: remain English.")

But there was no doubt that Americans, whenever they chose to think about Canada, still liked Walt Whitman's vision of the American flag flying over North

America from the Rio Grande to the North Pole. They had acquired some appetites by the 1890s, a taste for expansion. Sanford Dole effected a pineapple *coup d'état* in Hawaii in January 1893 which overthrew Queen Liliuokalani, and he presented Washington with Hawaii as the result. Grover Cleveland, the President as of March 1893, had the decency to turn the offer down flat. President McKinley (1897–1901) was not of such stern stuff and admitted Hawaii into the United States in 1898. In that year, too, came pressure to free Cuba from Spain, and the spineless president was pushed into a war no one needed or wanted, by a jingoistic American press.

Canada's main issues with the United States had been partly solved by arbitration, beginning with the landmark Treaty of Washington of 1871. There Sir John A. Macdonald had fought a skilful defence of Canada's interests against the Americans, who wanted all they could get, and also against the British, who seemed ready to present the Americans with as much of Canada as was needed to patch up British–American differences. *Grip* had a revealing dialogue between John Bull and Uncle Jonathan about Little Canada, a small boy evidently of not much account:

Little Canada—My pa is always forgiving. He has been for-giving my things away as long as I remember. I want to ask my pa if it would not be better to give me and all the farm to Uncle Jonathan at once...? perhaps if my Uncle Jonathan had me, he would not give my things away to any one who wanted them.

Mr. Jonathan—No! Omnipotent Snakes! I wouldn't. Say neow, J.B., couldn't yew let me have the little critter?

Mr. Bull—No, no! Disintegrate my Hempire? Never. (Aside—But say, hi couldn't let you 'ave him hopenly; happearances must be saved; but you are gittin' of 'im gradooal, you know.)

The American adventure in Cuba in 1898 put Canadians on the alert. Military adventures were regarded in those years as good for the national morale, good for the sinews of the body and the moral fibre of the nation. So when the South African war broke out in October 1899, many English Canadians itched for an adventure that would show the world what Canada could do. That was not the sentiment of French Canadians, where, not unexpectedly, sympathies ran more to the Boers, a pastoral, religious people, than to the noisy, aggressive English miners whom the Boers called Uitlander.

The Boer War split, and badly, the Cabinet of Sir Wilfrid Laurier, the elegant, courageous French Canadian. He had become prime minister—and head of Canada's first Liberal government since 1878—after defeating Sir Charles Tupper and the Conservative party in the general election of June 23, 1896, and had been knighted in London in 1897 at the Diamond Jubilee of Queen Victoria. The imperial glory of that marvellous occasion had now been translated into an imperial war.

Under the impress of the Toronto *Globe* and the *Montreal Daily Star*, English Canadians were off and running to fight in Africa. In the end, Laurier was forced to compromise about the English-Canadian demand for an official overseas contingent. There would be no official contingent, but volunteers could go overseas, transported at the expense of the Canadian government. They would then be paid and under the control of the British army. Sir John A. Macdonald had resisted such wild-eyed adventures in 1884; it was not so easy for Laurier fifteen years later. That was a measure of the change, of a world grown smaller through linked networks of transport, communication, electricity—and news. South Africa was closer in 1899 than Khartoum had been in 1884. It was a world growing vain with dreams of empire, with the glory of races: Russia with Panslavism; France and Britain rivals in, of all places, the Sudan, to say nothing of West Africa, Indo-China, and the South Pacific; Germany with its frantic, *nouveau riche* desire for an empire of its own. *Deutschland über alles* had its echo in every language. So English Canadians could sing, with the British,

We're the soldiers of the Queen, my lads,
Who've been, my lads, who've seen, my lads,
And who'll fight for England's glory, lads,
If we have to show them what we mean!

But that could hardly find an echo in French Canada. Some respect for the British flag there was; passion for England's glory there was not. The ambiguity is beautifully set out in Louis-Honoré Fréchette's "*Le Drapeau anglais,*" written in the 1880s:

—*Regarde, me disait mon père,*
Ce drapeau vaillamment porté;
Il a fait ton pays prospère,
Et respecte ta liberté....

—Mais, père, pardonnez si j'ose...
N'en est-il pas un autre, à nous?
—Ah, celui-là, c'est autre chose:
Il faut le baiser à genoux!

("Look at that flag, so bravely flown,"
My father said to me.
"It's made your country prosperous,
And respects your liberty."

"But Father, we've another flag,
Our own flag, haven't we?"
"That's different, son; that flag is to
Revere on bended knee!")

The Canadian achievement of the sixty years from 1840 to 1900 was this: to have made it possible to be Canadian, in an ambiguous way; to have, in fact, created Canada. There was still some way to go before the words "Canadian" and "Canada" could take on a meaning that had coherence and resonance. Being Canadian—and Canadien—was not too difficult for Wilfrid Laurier, who moved easily between the two languages, though even he was occasionally accused by French Canadians of being too English, and by English Canadians of being too French. It was a price he willingly paid to realize his dream—if not to make the twentieth century really Canada's, at least to create a real Canada in the twentieth century.

This remarkable stamp, with its decidedly imperial rubric, seems to have been the personal design of William Mulock of Toronto, Postmaster-General in the Laurier government. The stamp was issued to mark the inauguration of imperial penny postage, December 7, 1898.

The Triumph and Trials
of Materialism
1900–1945

RAMSAY COOK

In 1906, one year after Saskatchewan and Alberta were created from administrative districts of the Northwest Territories, this map was published in the *New Encyclopedic Atlas and Gazetteer*. Manitoba's boundaries were extended to include the southern part of the district of Keewatin in 1912; the British colony of Newfoundland did not join the Dominion until 1949.

Canada's Century

SARA JEANETTE DUNCAN'S NOVEL *The Imperialist* (1904) captured the spirit of the opening years of the twentieth century in Canada more tellingly than any other single document. In it idealism about the mission of the British Empire and Canada's place in it, and the materialism of an industrializing country, met in conflict. Materialism and what Canadians perceived as their self-interest triumphed, though lip-service continued to be paid to "imperialism." Less than a decade later Stephen Leacock, the country's greatest satirist, replayed that drama in his two finest works: *Sunshine Sketches of a Little Town* (1912) and *Arcadian Adventures with the Idle Rich* (1914). The first was a warm and witty exercise in nostalgia for the passing of rural and small-town life. The second was an acerbic dissection of the forces that dominated the new industrial cities and their principal institutions. Those forces were the drive for profit, power, and place.

In Quebec, the nationalist journalist and politician Henri Bourassa saw the same changes at work in his society. In response he preached a new nationalism that would not only act as a counterweight to imperialism, but also make the ideals of religion and culture the standard of social life. But all around him the transforming power of advancing capitalism was in the ascendant. In 1913, the French-born Louis Hémon published his famous hymn to the virtues of agriculture and Catholicism in his magnificent pastorale, *Maria Chapdelaine*. Movingly beautiful, it was already an anachronism. The industrial and urban age had arrived.

What some gloomily decried as materialism, others welcomed as growth, development, and prosperity, a turn-around from the depressed times of the nineties. Sir Wilfrid Laurier, the Prime Minister whose government presided over Canada's first great economic boom, caught the dominant spirit of the times when he claimed that as the nineteenth century had belonged to the United States, so the twentieth would be Canada's. John Hobson, a visiting British political economist, felt Canada's pulse in 1906 and reported that "a single decade has swept away all of her diffidence, and has replaced it by a spirit of boundless confidence and booming enterprise." Errol Bouchette, author of the highly provocative *L'Indépendance économique du Canada-français* (1906), fully agreed with Hobson's observations, as did other

On Pretoria Day—June 5, 1901—Torontonians celebrated victory in the South African War, flooding the streets on foot, on the ubiquitous bicycle, in horse-drawn carriages or the electric street railway. The bitter struggle between Britain and the Boers had aroused hostility between English and French Canada, but Canadian troops in Africa had distinguished themselves—and, once again, the Empire was triumphant.

French-Canadian writers. But most of them also underlined Bouchette's concern that French Canadians were being carried along with the economic currents, rather than directing them: "*Aujourd'hui c'est dans l'arène purement économique*," Bouchette wrote, "*que doit se décider la lutte de supériorité qui poursuit entre les différents éléments de notre population, puis entre les peuples du continent.*" (Today it is in the purely economic arena that the struggle for superiority going on between the different elements of our population, and among the peoples of the continent, must be decided.) It proved a prescient observation.

The history of the first half of the twentieth century in Canada, as in other industrializing countries, is the story of a society learning to live with and to control the forces of change released by economic expansion. Economic growth was accompanied by social tension and changed relations between classes, sexes, and ethnic groups. In Canada, new questions were raised about the integration of the regions into the nation, about the relations of French and English Canadians, and about the place that the hundreds of thousands of new immigrants should occupy. It was also a period that saw the gradual emergence of a new "modernist" sensibility in religion and culture and the halting growth of government involvement in the economic,

By the turn of the century Canada's *haute bourgeoisie* could aspire to aristocratic pretensions; when Governor General and Lady Minto came to Toronto in 1902, meatpacker Joseph Flavelle lent them his recently completed mansion, Holwood, on Queen's Park Crescent. The official couple are seen setting off for the races.

social, and cultural affairs of the country. The first half of the twentieth century that belonged to Canadians began with an imperial war, was punctuated by the First World War, and concluded with the Second. The optimism of the opening years was profoundly challenged by the social crisis created by the economic depression of the 1930s. But not even a war that witnessed the explosion of the first atomic bomb completely dispelled the belief that Canada's promise was still to be fulfilled.

Fleshing Out a National Economy

Between 1900 and 1912 the Canadian economy grew at an unprecedented rate. Although there was a brief downturn in 1907 and a more ominous one in 1913, the demands of the war revived economic activity, ensuring growth and prosperity until the beginning of the 1920s. The boom years before the war were financed by a combination of large-scale foreign investment and the successful overseas sale of wheat, Canada's newest staple. Indeed, it is not too much to say, while noting the irony, that the emerging industrial and urban society was founded on the success of the wheat economy. The prosperity of the Canadian economy as a whole was, of course, dependent upon a world economic environment that provided funds for investment and markets for exports.

The changes in the international economic climate from which Canada benefited were the increased interest of British investors in overseas capital exports, the expanding demand from industrialized countries for Canada's natural resources and food products, and the closing of the American agricultural frontier, which made Canada more appealing to prospective settlers. On the investment side, British and other foreign capital imports into Canada quadrupled between 1901 and 1921, reaching nearly five billion dollars. Since this investment, which made Canadian expansion possible, took place at a time when world prices, especially for agricultural produce, were rising and Canadian exports exceeded imports, the balance-of-payments problem remained under control, at least until 1913. After that date the drying up of overseas investment capital led to an economic downturn, the seriousness of which was evident in 1914 but the outbreak of war once again increased demands for Canadian goods. But the post-war years quickly revealed the weaknesses in Canada's economy, particularly its dependence upon foreign capital and foreign markets.

In the pre-war years increased foreign investment was accompanied by a rapid growth in overseas demand for Canadian products. And this demand coincided with technological and transportation changes—especially declining ocean-freight rates—which increased the availability of Canadian natural resources and agricultural products. A rapidly expanding railway system, new mining technology, improvements in farm machinery, and the development of hardier, high-yield grains, all ensured that Canadian products were available as demand grew. So, too, increased exploitation of such traditional energy sources as coal and, more significantly, the harnessing of the new and abundant source of hydroelectricity, gave manufacturers an opportunity to increase output and meet the demands of a growing, protected, domestic market. Population growth, fed by the large-scale influx of people from Great Britain, the continent, and the United States, provided a mobile, often cheap labour force, an army of agricultural pioneers, and a ready market for domestic production.

Perhaps the most striking fact about the growth of Canadian overseas trade was the changing character of exports. At the end of the nineteenth century Canadian

The McLaughlin carriagemakers first fought the challenge of the automobile with aggressive advertising. But the popularity of the auto, and the introduction of new technologies and the assembly line, meant that even McLaughlin finally had to turn to manufacturing the new vehicle. The company sold out to General Motors in 1918.

forests and sawmills provided the leading export goods. Ontario, Quebec, and New Brunswick were the principal sources of these products. Cheese from Ontario and fish from the Maritimes and British Columbia, followed by cattle, barley, nickel, coal, fruit, and furs, filled out the list. By 1900 this pattern was already changing as prairie wheat began to assume the leading place on the roster. The value of wheat and wheat-flour exports rose from $14 million in 1900 to $279 million in 1920. Britain and Europe were by far the largest customers. Export of pulp and paper, mainly for the U.S. market, developed more slowly but bounded forward after the United States abolished all duties in 1911. Wheat, lumber, and fish were now joined by a growing trade in base metals, mainly from British Columbia and northern Ontario. A new export, revealing the beginning of another innovation in transportation, was the automobile. By 1920 Canada was exporting $18 million worth of cars and trucks. The car, like such other manufactured exports as rubber products, leather goods, and farm machinery, came from Ontario.

Here was evidence that Confederation's promise of a national economy was coming to fruition. At its centre was the prairie West which not only produced the grain exports that fuelled the entire economy, but also provided much of the home market for industrial production. Moreover, the West's transportation requirements revealed the need for a vast extension of the country's railway network. After 1903, the Canadian Northern, the Grand Trunk, and the National Transcontinental were all given public financial support for new construction. Canadian railway lines grew from 29,000 kilometres (18,000 miles) in 1900 to 63,000 kilometres (39,000 miles) in 1920. As events were to prove, this expansion was excessive and ill-conceived. But during the boom years railway construction stimulated coal and iron mining, steel production, and the manufacture of rolling stock. All these activities encouraged spin-offs in harbour and canal improvements, expansion of such public utilities as street railways and electric-power facilities, roads, public buildings, and home construction. Whatever the social and economic costs of this largely unplanned and uncontrolled burst of economic expansion, it was what underlay the materialism, optimism, and nationalism of the first two decades of the century. And in this age wheat was king.

The successful exploitation of the agricultural potential of the Canadian West, and its ability to attract settlers eager to participate in the adventure, depended upon the success of scientific and technological developments. The relatively short growing season, shorter as the agricultural frontier moved north towards Peace River, required the development of improved, short-maturing varieties of wheat. Red Fife, introduced at the turn of the century, began a chain of developments that shortened the growing season and increased the yield. In 1911 Marquis became available, while Garnet and Reward were developed to meet the conditions of the northern prairies. Rust, limited rainfall, and grasshoppers remained difficulties for the future, ones which often exceeded the ingenuity of science.

From the earliest years of prairie settlement low and unreliable levels of rainfall had been recognized as a serious problem. The lands of the Palliser Triangle, on the south Saskatchewan-Alberta border, could be farmed profitably only in years of high precipitation. In Alberta, irrigation introduced by Mormon settlers from the United States solved part of the problem, while other lands were left for ranching. In the wheat-growing areas the technique of "dry farming," practised in the American West and improved by agricultural scientists at Indian Head, Saskatchewan, used fallowing, crop rotation, and shallow cultivation as means of conserving moisture. Such practices necessitated large-scale farming, with acreage far exceeding holdings in eastern Canada. These farms required improvements in agricultural machinery, many of which came from the United States, and also from such Canadian companies as Massey-Harris. Chilled-steel ploughs and mechanical reapers were followed by steam-driven threshing machines and, at the outbreak of the Great War, by the gasoline tractor. While increased mechanization reduced manpower requirements, agriculture continued to employ the largest percentage of workers of any industry: in 1921, 37 per cent of the labour force remained in agriculture, while only 19 per cent was employed in manufacturing.

Nevertheless, western wheat farming, even in the years before 1921, was at best precarious, at worst a gamble. Given the varieties of soil, extremes of temperature, and unreliability of rainfall, it is hardly surprising to find yields varying from nine bushels to twenty-five bushels per acre in Saskatchewan. While Number 1 Northern wheat, the top grade, fetched high prices, there were years when as much as 90 per cent of the crop was graded Number 3. To that were added the fluctuations of prices set on the so-called free market by speculation carried on through the Winnipeg Grain Exchange. The farmer also found himself subject to what appeared to him to be the arbitrary freight-rate structure, the whim of the railways, the power of the grain-buying companies, and, not least of all, a protective tariff which increased prices on everything from his ploughs to his children's clothing. What began as stoic complaints against the elements and the "Interests" gradually became the platform for an agrarian protest movement that would explode after the Great War.

Though economic growth was general between 1900 and 1921, it was far from evenly spread over all the regions. Ontario and Quebec, the most heavily populated areas and those where industrial development was already well under way when the century opened, received about 80 per cent of new investment in industry and hydro expansion. The smallest amount of industrial investment, not surprisingly, went to the prairie provinces. But the Maritimes, where such industries as ship building, textiles, and coal mining were already established, obtained only about 10 per cent of new industrial and hydro investment. Moreover, such established maritime industries as textiles and coal were increasingly drawn into the national economy, first by investments and then by takeovers by Montreal businesses. As national freight-rate structures came to be applied across the country, the maritime manufacturers, who were distant from their markets, found competition increasingly difficult. The economies of Nova Scotia and New Brunswick, which did not share fully in pre-war expansion, would find the post-war years even more difficult. As the difficulties of the coal and steel industries indicated, the maritime economy continued the decline that had begun in the mid-nineteenth century. By the 1920s maritimers, like westerners, began to express serious dissatisfaction with the manner in which national economic policies seemed to favour the central provinces over the regions.

Peopling the New Canada

The flourishing economy in the years before 1914 was both a cause and a consequence of a dramatic growth in the Canadian population. In 1901, 5,371,315 people lived in Canada; in the next ten years a 34 per cent increase brought the total to just over 7,200,000, and by 1921 the figure had jumped another 22 per cent, to almost 8,800,000. Like economic expansion, population growth was unevenly distributed. The Maritimes received only about 3 per cent of the increase, British Columbia 9 per cent, the prairies 49 per cent, and Ontario and Quebec 40 per cent. Though exact figures concerning the movement of people in and out prior to 1921 are impossible to ascertain (especially because of the relatively open Canada–U.S. border), it is clear that Canada benefited from a net inflow of about one million people, an extraordinary leap. But almost as striking was the varied ethnic character of this population.

The success of Canadian immigration policy after 1896 can be explained by changes both in Canada and elsewhere. With most of the cheap arable land in the United States occupied by the mid-1890s, the sparsely populated Canadian prairies became a magnet for people seeking a new life. That included a large number of Americans who sold their farms at a profit and headed north to take advantage of cheap lands for themselves and their children. About one-third of all the settlers in the pre-war years arrived from south of the border—many being Canadians who had moved south during the depression of the late nineteenth century. Their capital and machinery, the knowledge which they had of dry farming, and the ease with which they were assimilated into a fairly familiar cultural environment, ensured that these incoming Americans would be among the most successful agricultural settlers. But not all prospective settlers from the United States were welcomed. Blacks were vigorously and successfully discouraged from entering Canada.

Two international factors that contributed to the success of Canadian immigration policy were rising grain prices and falling ocean-freight rates, which together made agriculture more profitable. Moreover, the increase in Europe-bound grain ships made passage for immigrants as a return cargo readily available. Accommodation was less than luxurious, often not even comfortable or clean, but it was inexpensive. Since the recruitment of immigrants was, to a large extent, left in the hands of shipping companies, who received per-capita bonuses from the government, the availability of "unused capacity" was of major significance in the drive to populate the Canadian prairies and to create a labour force for mining, manufacturing, and construction industries. Into this changing international climate stepped Clifford Sifton, a westerner determined to turn the failures of the previous decades of immigration policy into a success story.

Though born in Ontario, Sifton had gone west as a youth. His father's success and his own convinced him that the West's potential was unlimited. But that potential

This lively poster advertising the precursor of Calgary's famous Stampede laments the changing shape of the West, when wheat farming was replacing cattle ranching. But Canada's "wild west" had been largely a romantic fiction. Colour lithograph.

could only be realized when the prairie grasslands were turned into cultivated grain fields. That change required people. Having served in the Manitoba government in the 1890s, Sifton moved to the federal Cabinet in 1896 to represent the West in Wilfrid Laurier's ministry of "all the talents." No one in that Cabinet was more energetic, strong-minded, or ambitious than Sifton, unless it was Laurier himself. When he left the government in 1905, after an unsuccessful test of wills with Laurier, Sifton could claim a record of achievement in several areas, but none more important than his administration of immigration. It was not so much that Sifton devised new policy, for he followed the general lines set by his predecessors. Rather, it was the energy and organizational skill he brought to the department that made the difference. Centralizing authority in his own hands, Sifton appointed a whole new group of officials—mostly identifiable Liberals from the West—who were convinced that Canada, and especially western Canada, was the land of promise. Using the Dominion Lands Act (1872), which offered new settlers 160 acres (65 hectares) of virtually free land, with pre-emption rights to another quarter section, in return for a ten-dollar registration fee, Sifton dispatched agents and a flood of propaganda to Great Britain, the United States, and Europe.

Great Britain had been the traditional source of immigrants and it remained so,

For newcomers from across the Atlantic, Quebec City was the principal point of entry. These arrivals from Great Britain include some Orthodox Jews who prefer not to be photographed.

sending more than a third of all those who arrived before 1914. British immigrants usually had much less farming experience than their U.S. or European counterparts. They ranged from the petty aristocrats of the Barr Colony in Saskatchewan, who attempted in 1902 to establish a little Britain, through the orphan children sponsored by Dr. Barnardo and other less famous agencies, to lower-middle- and working-class Englishmen eager to escape their class-ridden homeland. While the Barr Colony foundered on the unrealistic expectations of its leaders, many other British immigrants became successful farmers. Others found the new rural life too demanding and isolated, and the climate too ferocious. Some returned home; a few were deported for breaking the law; others drifted into towns and cities where they found work in industry or in domestic service. While signs reading "No Englishman Need Apply" occasionally appeared, suggesting that Englishmen had been found wanting—or too arrogant—by some employers, the majority fitted into the new society with relative ease. Like that of the newcomers from the United States, their cultural background made assimilation easy, and they were among the first to move into the mainstream of Canadian life.

The principal change in immigration policy initiated by Sifton was his concerted effort to attract European, and especially eastern European, settlers. While there had

A house of sod and mud-brick could be assembled quickly and cheaply by newly arrived settlers. The *boorday*, as Ukrainian settlers called such a house, would soon be replaced by a brighter, more commodious dwelling, but mud and straw often continued to substitute for lumber on the treeless prairies. Above: *Homesteading near Lloydminster, Alberta*: photo by Ernest Brown; left: *Galician Settlers. Theodosy Wachna and family, Stuartburn, Manitoba.*

been group settlements of small numbers of Mennonites and Icelanders before 1896, it was only after the turn of the century that large numbers of non-English-speaking people were sought out and directed to Canada. These included Germans, Scandinavians, Austrians, and a trickle of French-speaking settlers from Belgium and France. But most notable among these new groups were the people called "Ruthenians." These Slavic-speaking immigrants, mostly agricultural peasants known as "people in sheepskin coats," originated in the Polish part of the Austro-Hungarian Empire and in Russia. Eventually most of them would call themselves Ukrainians. Encouraged by Sifton's agents, who were instructed to find prospective settlers with farming experience, strong backs, and fecund wives, they settled in fairly homogeneous communities near Dauphin, Manitoba, and Yorkton, Saskatchewan, and in areas around Edmonton.

Vilni zemli, free land, attracted these people, and though the land they obtained was often chosen for its hills and wooded areas similar to their homelands, it was

The dream of every prairie settler was a comfortable house and a contented family. The reality was that getting the crop off before the first frost meant riding the binder from dawn till dark. *M. Seagart's Farmhouse*: photo by Ernest Brown.

sometimes poor and unproductive. The initial poverty of these immigrants frequently necessitated years of work in non-agricultural activities: mining, railway building, lumbering. Their lack of skills, their language problems, and, above all, their economic need meant that they often became the most exploited of the "bunkhouse men," working long hours for low wages, living far from their wives and families in cold, sometimes insect-infested shacks. Other men, sometimes alone, sometimes with their families, found insecure jobs in the burgeoning urban areas, especially in the West. There, in such places as north Winnipeg, on the other side of the tracks, families lived in tenements and slums, cheek by jowl with a mixture of new immigrants and traditional poor. They struggled to earn and save the capital necessary to pay for the equipment and domestic supplies required to begin farming. (One estimate suggested that $250 was necessary for even the most meagre beginning—a yoke of oxen, a milk cow, seed, a plough—and for those who wanted something better than a sod hut, the costs rose to between $600 and $1,000.) Conditions in these slums were hardly better than those in the bunkhouse: overcrowding, filth, unemployment, cheap alcohol, and prostitution were common. These conditions were only partly offset by the efforts of the city missions, and by the chance for their children to attend school.

Life in the rural settlements was more satisfactory, though just as arduous. There, the newcomers could rely on one another for aid in times of crisis. The loneliness of life in the new land was reduced by the presence of others who spoke the same language. Though the activities of the priests of the Russian Orthodox church could sometimes be a source of rancour and division, religion, or at least the church, nevertheless played an important role in easing the immigrant into his new surroundings. In many communities on the prairies, the onion-domed church stood

The herculean task of breaking prairie sod—once done with a horse-drawn single-furrow plough—was revolutionized by the steam tractor, which could weigh as much as 20 tons and pull a plough that could cut as many as fourteen furrows at once. The tractors could also be used to power threshing machines.

out against the prairie sky as the spiritual counterpart to the hard-edged, geometrical grain elevator, the symbol of prairie man's earthly ambitions.

While the foreign tongue and unfamiliar customs of the Ukrainians and other immigrants of European origin often caused French- and English-speaking Canadians to wonder what kind of a polyglot country Sifton's policies were producing, it was the Doukhobors, or at least a minority of them, who attracted some of the earliest and most vicious nativist reactions. In 1898, some 7,400 Doukhobors, under the auspices of Count Tolstoy and Professor James Mayor of the University of Toronto, negotiated an agreement with the Dominion government which gave them a block of some 40,000 acres (16,000 hectares) near Yorkton, Saskatchewan. This agreement included a recognition of the group's conscientious objection to military service. Though the majority of the Doukhobors were peaceful, hard-working settlers, a conflict took place in 1902 that led to the emergence of a radical sect. These believers in the coming of the millennium set out on a long trek towards Winnipeg apparently in an ecstatic search for the "Promised Land." But the Sons of Freedom trek collapsed in the cold prairie winter. Peace was restored between the factions of the community with the arrival of their leader, Peter Verigin, newly released from his Siberian exile. "Peter the Lordly," as he was called, could control his followers but he could not extinguish the suspicion and hostility that the wanderings of the Sons of Freedom had aroused in many western Canadians. As the prairies began to fill up, dissatisfaction against the Doukhobors grew, especially among those who coveted their extensive, community-owned lands. When in 1905 nearly half of these lands were confiscated after the Doukhobors refused, on religious grounds, to take the oath of

The Department of the Interior was run by Clifford Sifton, an aggressive promoter of immigration, from 1896 to 1905, and during that time it co-operated with private shipping companies to blitz Great Britain, the U.S., and Europe with pamphlets and posters extolling the future of the "last, best West." This poster showcases the government's experimental farms.

allegiance, the radicals once more demonstrated. But Verigin again proved equal to the challenge and brought the dissidents under control. He also decided that a new settlement should be established, this time on a large block of land in the Kootenay region of British Columbia. There, after Verigin died in the mid-twenties, the Sons of Freedom would cause new problems, but the majority of the community lived quietly and prospered.

The Doukhobors and Ukrainians were only the most distinctive groups among the numerous new ethnic communities that came to establish homes in Canada. When they began to arrive there was no settled policy about the future of their cultures, though it was generally assumed that they would assimilate into the dominant British mainstream. "We must see to it," one western Protestant leader declared, "that the civilization and ideals of Southeastern Europe are not transplanted to and perpetuated on our virgin soil." The process of assimilation was partly voluntary, partly enforced. The public educational system, outside of Quebec and those areas of other provinces where significant Francophone minorities lived, operated as the main vehicle of assimilation into the English-speaking world. Indeed, the influx of peoples of many different languages led to a stronger desire for linguistic uniformity, with results that were damaging to French-speaking groups outside Quebec. When

Saskatchewan and Alberta were created in 1905, only the most limited provisions for Roman Catholic schools and the use of the French language were included, and even those largely disappeared as a part of a series of school "reforms" in 1918. In both Manitoba, where multilingual teaching was permitted after 1897, and Ontario, where teaching in French had long been accepted in the early grades, the ethnic tensions of the war years ended these privileges. Outside of Quebec, Canada was to be an English-speaking country.

While the school system made the learning of English compulsory, something which most immigrants probably accepted as a key to social mobility, there were also voluntary agencies that assisted in the assimilation process. The missions established by the Protestant churches played an important role: Methodists, Presbyterians, Anglicans, and the Salvation Army all established special "home mission" branches to promote both Protestantism and Canadianism among the "foreigners." In 1908 the Methodist *Missionary Outlook* expressed a view which was common currency among English-Canadian Protestants:

If from this North American continent is to come a superior race, a race to be specially used of God in carrying on His work, what is our duty towards those who are now our fellow citizens? Many of them come to us nominal Christians, that is, they owe allegiance to the Greek or Roman Catholic Churches, but their moral standards and ideals are far below those of the Christian citizens of the Dominion. These people have come to this young, free country to make homes for themselves and their children. It is our duty to meet them with the open Bible, and to instill into their minds the principles and ideals of Anglo-Saxon civilization.

Near Bruderheim, Alberta, around 1910. These children attended a one-room school where reading, writing, and arithmetic were mixed with lessons on patriotism and loyalty to the British Empire.

Whether at Fred Victor in downtown Toronto, in All Peoples' in north-end Winnipeg, in McDougall Memorial Hospital in Pakan, Alberta, or at Frontier College, established to teach men in work camps, nationalist, Protestant, and humanitarian motives combined in an effort to Canadianize new immigrants. It was a difficult task and one that was far from complete before the outbreak of war in 1914. The simple truth was that the existing Canadian population was not large enough to absorb the waves of newcomers that arrived each year.

Whatever variety there was in the languages of early-twentieth-century Canada, colour uniformity was nearly complete. Native peoples were hived off on reservations; blacks, with the exception of small communities in Nova Scotia, Montreal, and southern Ontario, were excluded; while entry of Chinese, Japanese, and even fellow members of the British Empire who came from India was severely restricted. As the anti-Asiatic riots in Vancouver in 1907 revealed, even a tiny Asian presence created deep hostility. So, too, the southern European was unwelcome in a country built on the national self-image of the "true North, strong and free." Even such a sympathetic commentator on the Canadian ethnic mosaic as J. S. Woodsworth, the founder of All Peoples' Mission in Winnipeg, found it necessary to distinguish between desirable immigrants from northern Italy and the "diseased and criminal Italians from the south."

That a mosaic, not a melting pot, was the best description of the new Canada could not disguise the vertical character of ethnic relations. The English, and to a lesser extent the French, were the dominant groups. Edwin Bradwin, who carried out a careful study of the bunkhouse men in the early 1920s, discovered two distinct ethnic classes. The "whites," composed of Canadian-born French and English, English-speaking immigrants, and some Scandinavians, occupied the skilled, better-paid positions. The "foreigners" were those who "stolidly engage in mucking and heavier tasks." Class and ethnic divisions, then, frequently coincided, while in the growing cities the new immigrants were often separated, especially from the English-speaking middle and working classes. Most cities had a version of North Winnipeg, Toronto's "Ward," or Montreal's "City below the Hill"—ghettos for foreign workers and their families. One worker described a common situation in north-end Winnipeg:

Shack—one room and a lean to. Furniture—two beds, a bunk, stove, bench, two chairs, table, barrel of sauerkraut. Everything very dirty. Two families lived here. Women were dirty, unkempt, barefooted, half clothed. Children wore only print slips. The baby was in swaddling clothes, and was lying in a cradle made of sacking suspended from the ceiling by

In the early twentieth century, "bunkhouse men" formed a large, mobile labour pool for such industries as mining, logging, harvesting, and construction. They were often badly exploited, doing heavy work for low pay in hopes of earning enough to start a farm. This northern Ontario bunkhouse, owned by the National Transcontinental Railway, is better than average—some had bunks called "muzzle-loaders" which could only be entered head first.

ropes at the corners.... The supper was on the table—a bowl of warmed-over potatoes for each person, part of a loaf of brown bread, a bottle of beer.

For the newcomers life may have been better in Canada than in their homeland, but for many that was only because the future continued to look promising.

High City, Low City

The rapid settlement of the western agricultural plains overshadowed an even more striking feature of the Laurier years: the explosive growth of the country's major cities. It was this development rather than rural settlement that had the most profound long-run consequences for the shape of Canada. In 1901 about 60 per cent of the Canadian population was rural; this figure declined by 10 per cent over the next two decades. Even in the agricultural West the growth of cities was spectacular. Edmonton, Calgary, Regina, and Saskatoon were themselves creations of the period: in 1901 there were just over 4,000 people in Edmonton; by 1921 the number exceeded 58,000. Winnipeg, which jumped from a population of 42,000 to nearly 180,000, grew at a faster rate than that of the agricultural areas of Manitoba. Vancouver's population increased fivefold. Montreal and Toronto, the two largest cities, doubled in size. While the urbanization of the Maritimes was much slower, Halifax and Saint John experienced steady growth. People moved into the cities from two sources. Many, especially those who created the mush-rooming cities on the prairies, were recent immigrants. Urban growth in central Canada was also fed by new immigrants, but equally important was the move-ment of population from the countryside to the city. By 1911, Quebec and Ontario were predominantly urban provinces, and that trend was accelerated by the industrial expansion of the war years.

Rapid urban development created new opportunities for real-estate promoters, new demands on civic government, and new social problems. While the centre of older cities, such as Halifax and Montreal, combined affluent neighbourhoods and substandard working-class housing, the new population pressure led to the growth

of suburban areas, such as Maisonneuve in Montreal, and new subdivisions on the west and northern edges of Toronto. Verdun, a working-class suburb of Montreal, expanded from about 1,900 to 12,000 in the first ten years of the century. Transportation

Before the Second World War, the poor, the unemployed, and the underprivileged of large urban centres were largely dependent on voluntary charity.

between these outlying developments and the urban factories and offices was provided by electrically operated street railways. The increasing availability of cheap electricity led to widespread domestic and industrial lighting. So, too, the telephone became more common, contributing to commercial efficiency and domestic convenience. "All the modern conveniences of street railways, electric light, etc., are furnished in abundance," one visitor wrote of Winnipeg in 1906. "The brand new Manitoba Club, where the city magnates meet for lunch, leaves nothing to be desired in comfort or 'elegance', while the store set up by Eaton's of Toronto occupies a solid block...." Every city, and many small towns, were caught up in the spirit of boosterism that dominated the age. Claims about the finest civic facilities, the lowest taxes, the healthiest work force, and many other wonders were made in the most blatant fashion. Winnipeg boosters called their city "the Chicago of Canada," while their confrères in Maisonneuve, with even less discrimination, adopted for their city the title of "*le Pittsburgh du Canada*":

C'est dire que Maisonneuve avec ses trois chemins de fer nationaux, avec sa ligne électrique pour le transport des marchandises, opérant sous une franchise spéciale à travers les rues de la ville et faisant raccordement avec les chemins de fer, avec ses superbes installations maritimes, installations qui n'ont pas de rivales dans tout le Dominion, Maisonneuve, au point de vue de l'expédition, est unique dans son genre. (That is to say that Maisonneuve, with its three national railways—with its electric goods-transport system, operating through city streets under special franchise and connecting with the railroad—and with its superb maritime installations, unrivalled throughout the Dominion—Maisonneuve is, in terms of distribution, unique in its facilities.)

Progress meant growth, and communities were frequently willing to provide tax concessions and subsidies in the drive to attract new industries. For city politicians—some of whom benefited directly from the sale of unoccupied lands, factory construction, or real-estate development—cheap power, tram lines, and a growing work force were more important than housing, schools, and parks. Consequently, as cities grew, so did social problems. Housing, especially of the sort that working people could afford, was constantly in short supply. A public official reported in 1904 that in Toronto, "there is scarcely a vacant house fit to live in that is not inhabited, and in many cases by numerous families." Such conditions existed, in varying degrees, in virtually every urban centre despite the fact that about 400,000 new houses were built in Canada between 1901 and 1911. City priorities were explained this way in 1913:

In the mad scramble to secure the location of industries, our cities have appointed industrial commissioners to bring in factories with their hordes of workers and yet the problem of shelter for those poor people who will contribute so much to the ideal of industrial progress, which the towns have set up, receives scarcely a thought. There have been many unholy unions of city and industry.

Housing was not the only problem that plagued the crowded urban areas. Sanitation, clean water, public health, education, parks, and recreation facilities, all became matters requiring attention. The lack of proper sewage facilities, the consumption of unpasteurized milk, and the ineffectiveness of public-health programs contributed to a high mortality rate among children and astonishing numbers of deaths from communicable diseases. In 1911 in Toronto, eleven infants under one year of every thousand born died of a communicable disease, and forty-four died of a digestive problem. Figures like that led Dr. Helen McMurchy to state in a report on infant mortality that "...the Canadian city is still essentially uncivilized—it is neither properly paved nor drained, nor supplied with water fit to drink, nor equipped with any adequate public health organization."

These and other urban problems did not go unnoticed by those directly affected, though they were often denied the franchise and could do little to protest. A vocal group of middle-class Canadians, conscious of the human suffering and environmental ugliness that accompanied unregulated development, raised their voices in a demand for reform. These reformers, who insisted that changes be made in city government and urban social conditions, acted out of conflicting motives of self-interest and altruism. On the one hand, those same business and political leaders who led the campaign for growth soon came to recognize that cities without adequate sewage and sanitation, suitable housing, and accessible parks and schools would never produce the healthy and contented labour force that economic progress required. Consequently, businessmen often took the lead in demanding that civic politicians enact measures to improve the city. Attempts were also made to suppress prostitution and illegal alcohol sales, though, as with other reforms, success varied from city to city. So, too, there were campaigns to root out corruption in civic politics and to bring some privately owned utilities, such as street railways and electric generating plants,

By the turn of the century electricity was becoming a normal part of city life; on hot days Ottawa residents could escape to Britannia Bay on the electric railway. Life was changing in the country, too—in October 1908 the first free rural mail delivery began, between Hamilton and Ancaster, Ontario.

under public control. Stephen Leacock captured the spirit of businessman's reform in his wonderfully ironic chapter, "The Great Fight for Clean Government," in his *Arcadian Adventures with the Idle Rich*.

The greatest triumph of "civic populism" in these years was the successful campaign to create a publicly owned hydroelectric system in Ontario. The campaign's leader, a cigar-box manufacturer turned politician, Adam Beck, brought together a coalition of municipal leaders, businessmen, public-ownership advocates, labour leaders, and churchmen to argue that such a natural monopoly as electricity should belong to the community, not to private interests. If the wonder-working "white coal" was to be available to all Ontarians for industrial and domestic use on an equitable basis, government control was essential. The public campaign began to bear fruit in 1905 when Beck was included in a newly elected provincial Conservative government. Within the next five years public ownership was a reality. Though some business interests, pushed out of this lucrative area, denounced Ontario Hydro as socialism, most accepted it because it ensured the delivery of cheap power to the industries developing around the province.

Building God's Kingdom on Earth

If businessmen like Adam Beck acted out of mixed motives in advocating reform measures—"philanthropy plus five per cent," as Herbert Ames, a Montreal business-man-reformer candidly called it—there were others in the amorphous reform movement whose motivation was no less complicated. These were men and women, lay and clerical, whose reformist rhetoric was founded upon the conviction that society should be judged by the standards of Christian morality. Since the late nineteenth century, church leaders in Canada had been troubled by two particular developments. On the one hand, changes in scientific, philosophical, and historical attitudes—especially Darwinism and historical criticism of the Bible—had placed the churches on the defensive. At the same time, the social injustices accompanying industrialization seemed to demand that the church preach a more relevant social message if it wanted to retain its congregation, especially its working-class following. Faced with these challenges, many church leaders, especially Protestants, began to refashion Christian teaching into a "social gospel" which, in its most radical form, reduced Christianity to a formula designed to build the Kingdom of God on earth. In its more moderate versions it emphasized the primary need to regenerate society through social reforms. From these general concerns arose demands for industrial-safety and public-health legislation, prohibition of the manufacture and sale of alcoholic beverages, suppression of child labour and prostitution, "Canadianization" of immigrants, votes for women, and a myriad of other reform measures. Henry Harvey Stuart in New Brunswick, James Simpson in Toronto, the members of the Manitoba Political Equality League, and reformers in virtually every part of Protestant Canada were inspired by the ideals of social Christianity. Women like the suffragist Nellie McClung contended that once women could vote a whole new battalion would be enlisted in the army of righteousness. "The church has been dominated by men and religion has been given a masculine interpretation," McClung wrote, "and I believe the Protestant religion lost much when it lost the idea of the motherhood of God."

The spirit of Christian reformism sparked the women's movement from its beginnings in such late-nineteenth-century organizations as the Women's Christian Temperance Union, the Young Women's Christian Association, and the National Council of Women of Canada. Women like Dr. Emily Stowe, who had to study in the United States in order to become Canada's first woman doctor, and her daughter, Dr. Augusta Stowe-Gullen, had begun demanding votes for women and equal educational opportunities before the turn of the century. Flora MacDonald Denison, Toronto journalist and militant feminist; Cora Hind, western Canada's leading agricultural reporter; Lillian B. Thomas and her sister Francis Beynon, both Manitoba journalists; and the Alberta writer Emily Murphy, who in 1916 became the first woman police magistrate in the British Empire—all these believed that women had a special contribution to make towards uplifting Canadian society. While their reform program was capacious, the first goal was equal suffrage. That was achieved during the Great War, not least of all due to the number of women who entered the labour force to aid the war effort. Manitoba was the first province to grant women the vote, in 1916, and all the others, except Quebec, followed suit. Some women were enfranchised for the federal election of 1917, and that was broadened to include all women in the new electoral law of 1918.

The women's movement in French Canada was also inspired by Christianity, in this case social Catholicism, but the path it followed was somewhat different. Since the leadership of the Catholic church was stubbornly opposed to the suffragist movement (and French-Canadian nationalists condemned the movement as "Anglo-Saxon"), women like Marie Lacoste Gérin-Lajoie concentrated on improving the legal status and broadening the educational chances of women. In Quebec, where the church offered alternatives to women who preferred careers to marriage, nuns often worked in co-operation with their secular sisters in efforts to improve the condition of women's lives. It was not until the 1930s that French-Canadian women, under the leadership of Thérèse Casgrain, began a concentrated effort to gain the vote at the provincial level—a goal that was achieved in 1940—though they had been able to vote federally since 1917.

The Roman Catholic social conscience was aroused by many issues in addition to the problems faced by women. Since the 1890s the church had been struggling to develop a doctrine suitable to the needs of the emerging industrial order. In Quebec, and also among English-speaking Catholics after the turn of the century, the proclamations of Leo XIII, the "workers' Pope," had a growing impact. The ideals of Henri Bourassa's nationalist movement were rooted in those teachings, as were the efforts of parish priests in various industrial towns to encourage the formation of Catholic trade unions and credit unions. Christian reformism, the social gospel, and social Catholicism combined a genuine sympathy for the downtrodden with a concern to protect established institutions and beliefs. In the long run, business leaders were more successful than church leaders. But in the short run, the underprivileged benefited more from reforms advocated by Christian-inspired reformers than from those advanced by the economic élite.

Working-class Canadians were not willing to leave their fate solely in the hands of others. The principal means of self-protection was the trade union. While unions

Three early leaders of the women's movement. Far left, Marie Gérin-Lajoie—co-founder and president of the Fédération nationale Saint-Jean-Baptiste, which brought together women from different milieux—led French-Canadian women in their demand for more higher education, a fairer legal status, and laws to protect women and children. Middle: Nellie McClung lived in Manitoba, and later on the west coast, but made extensive speaking tours, using her sharp wit, strong will, and prolific pen to advance women's rights, Prohibition, and urban reform. Right: Toronto businesswoman Flora MacDonald Denison—journalist, spiritualist, and devoted follower of American poet Walt Whitman—was among the most outspoken and flamboyant advocates of women's rights before the First World War.

had existed in Canada since the early nineteenth century, it was not until the arrival of the Knights of Labour, in the 1880s and the American Federation of Labor unions in the 1890s that the movement began to develop on a national scale. By the turn of the century some 20,000 workers belonged to unions, more than 60 per cent with AFL affiliations. By 1902, when the AFL affiliates took over control of the Trades and Labor Congress of Canada, independent Canadian unions and the nascent Catholic unions in Quebec controlled only a small minority of workers. The dominance of AFL unions was the result of several factors: the return to Canada of men who had belonged to unions in the United States, the influx of U.S. capital and businesses into Canada, and the desire of Canadian workers to achieve conditions of equality with their counterparts south of the border. But the struggle to unionize Canadian workers—even skilled workers—was long and arduous, with the majority remaining non-unionized. Nevertheless, strikes were numerous and often bitter, touching nearly every industry: cotton workers in Valleyfield, Quebec, coal miners on Cape Breton and Vancouver islands, railway men on the Grand Trunk, and switchboard operators at Bell Telephone. Excuses were often found to use the militia to force workers back to work, and strike-breakers were common.

Government response was slow. In 1900 a Department of Labour was established, chiefly to collect information. The major piece of legislation came in 1907, after a strike in the Alberta coal fields had resulted in a serious fuel shortage the previous winter. The Industrial Disputes Investigation Act, devised by William Lyon Mackenzie King, the Deputy Minister of Labour, provided for a cooling-off period and conciliation proceedings as the best methods of encouraging industrial peace. Given the weakness of the union movement, the legislation probably helped some unions to win recognition. At the same time, however, by limiting the use of the strike, it may have hindered workers in their quest for wage increases and improved working conditions. The Combines Investigation Act of 1910 was designed to prevent the growing merger movement in business, but proved ineffective. The Laurier government only haltingly recognized the need for government to play an increased role in directing the social and economic transformation that was under way.

Thus, while the labour force grew rapidly during the first decade of the century, the unionized segment remained relatively small. Most working people lived on wages determined by employers alone and in conditions over which they had little control. Given the seasonal nature of many jobs and the lack of any safety net of unemployment insurance or Medicare, life was often lived on the margin. In 1913, a reasonably careful calculation was made of the budget required for a family of five. It totalled slightly more than $1,200 per year, a figure considerably higher than that earned by a year-round unskilled worker. That explains the large number of women and children who found it necessary to take up employment, working for wages even lower than those paid to men. Yet the availability of this "cheap" labour helped to keep men's wages down. It also meant that children left school early in order to supplement family income. That lack of education would condemn them to a lifetime of low-paying jobs.

Despite, or perhaps because of, these harsh conditions, working people were rarely susceptible to radical proposals for social change. Various forms of socialism, from revolutionary Marxist to gradualist Christian, found adherents in most Canadian cities. But these were small, sectarian groups often fighting as bitterly with one another as with the capitalist enemy. So, too, the more radical union groups— the Industrial Workers of the World and Western Federation of Miners, for example—made some impact on workers in the harshest circumstances, such as British Columbia miners. But, for the most part, working people improvised and endured. The Trades and Labor Congress frequently debated political questions but stopped short of direct political action. Instead, it took an annual list of demands to the federal government, was listened to politely, and retired to await another meeting. Dominated as it was by the representatives of the better-paid skilled trades, the TLC grew increasingly out of touch with the less-favoured majority of workers. But it was not until the end of the Great War that the slowly building frustrations of working people burst forth in radical action. And it was not until the 1930s that organization of the unskilled began seriously.

Laurier Liberalism

Sir Wilfrid Laurier (he had been knighted at the Queen's Diamond Jubilee in 1897), the man who voiced Canada's claim to the twentieth century, was the first French-speaking Canadian to become Prime Minister. His Liberal party, after decades of fruitless struggle in Quebec, had finally discovered a winning formula: the lustre of a native son, good organization, and moderation in policy. Laurier, bilingual, courtly, and handsome, won widespread admiration in English Canada, too. Where once he had seemed too French in defending Riel, he had grown into a "true" Canadian, willing to bask in the glow of the declining imperial sun, unwilling to press too hard for Roman Catholic and French-language school rights. But behind the charming and elegant exterior, more elegant as the silver of his shoulder-length hair grew to match his silver-tongued oratory, was a shrewd mind and a tough will.

In 1896 Laurier had formed a talented Cabinet, bringing in powerful representatives from each of the regions. He knew that talent and ambition went hand in hand, and was ready to ride herd with skill and firmness. The key to Laurier's success, as it had been with Macdonald before him, was his ability to bring men—since no woman voted, let alone sat at the Cabinet table, before 1917—representing different interests together and to make them work as a team. Of special importance to Laurier was harmonizing the interests and sentiments of French and English Canadians. And as the country grew, the task increased in complexity, because regional demands joined ethnic tensions, religious rivalries, and class conflict. For fifteen years Laurier proved himself the unrivalled master of a turbulent political scene. But by 1911 even he could no longer keep command.

During the early years of his term of office, Laurier's chief problems were associated with relations between French and English Canadians. Elected on a platform which promised that "sunny ways" could resolve the crisis over separate schools in Manitoba, Laurier hoped he had laid this matter to rest in 1897; the hope proved unfounded. In 1905, a new quarrel broke out over the extent to which the legislation establishing

Saskatchewan and Alberta should guarantee Roman Catholic and French-language rights. The outcome of the struggle was that the western minorities obtained only minimal protection, and Laurier lost Sifton and the trust of many English Canadians and even some French Canadians.

Prime Minister Wilfrid Laurier (1841–1919) in 1900. Laurier was renowned as a skilful compromiser and conciliator; one journalist wrote that he "had affinities with Machiavelli as well as with Sir Galahad." Sculptor Walter Allward was just twenty-five when he completed this bust.

More divisive than the issue of minority rights was the sensitive problem of Canada's responsibilities as a member of the British Empire. The Boer War and the controversy over Canada's participation in it had raised the storm signals. Henri Bourassa, grandson of Louis-Joseph Papineau, the rebel leader of 1837, though elected as a follower of Laurier in 1896, refused to support his leader's compromise policy on South Africa. Bourassa then set out to warn Canadians, especially French Canadians, of the dangers of imperialism. Equally dangerous, he believed, was Laurier's refusal to set out exactly the nature of Canada's relationship to Great Britain. Associating himself with a group of young nationalists in La Ligue Nationaliste Canadienne, Bourassa set himself up as the chief spokesman for French-

Surrounded by his wife and children, Henri Bourassa, the stern founding editor of *Le Devoir*, could forget the failings of Liberals and the schemes of imperialists. He is seen here celebrating his tenth wedding anniversary, on September 4, 1915, at his summer retreat at Ste-Adèle.

language minorities, for resistance to Canadian participation in imperial wars, and as a critic of what he thought was the excessive urban and industrial development of Quebec. He was a formidable foe, one both feared and admired by Laurier, who knew that, at least on imperial questions, Bourassa spoke for French Canadians. And Bourassa's close association with the leaders of the church in Quebec raised in Laurier's imagination the spectre of a revival of the clerico-nationalism that he had fought in the years before 1896.

While Quebecers sympathized with Bourassa's contention that Canada should not be called upon to fight the Empire's wars outside North America, English Canadians identified Canada's interests with the Empire. Many English Canadians were therefore eager to assert the country's nationhood through active participation in imperial affairs. "There is no doubt the age of Imperialism has come," a young Mackenzie King wrote at the height of the Boer War fever. "We will see (perhaps in twenty-five years) an Imperial Assembly of some kind at Westminster. The greatest of the world's known federations." Laurier, whose personal views were naturally those of a French Canadian, knew that the unity of the country, and the continued success of his party, depended on avoiding issues that would bring the French- and the English-Canadian views into direct conflict. Consequently, he devised a strategy that combined evasive rhetoric with a determination to avoid commitment to schemes that involved common imperial defence projects or any hint of centralized imperial policy-making. His critics at home were thus frustrated by the ambiguity of Laurier's policy. "Waffley Wilfy," Bourassa disparagingly called him; some English Canadians thought "Sir Won'tfrid" more appropriate.

The difficulty of achieving a consensus among Canadians about their country's place in the Empire only became fully evident when the tension between Great Britain and Germany intensified after 1909. As Great Britain, particularly in the sensitive area of naval supremacy, found itself seriously challenged by Kaiser Wilhelm's expanding fleet, pressure was put on the dominions to assume a larger role in imperial defence. That request was reasonable enough, since the dominions actually benefited from the defence system. For some Canadians, including most French Canadians, the proper response was simple: develop a united, economically strong Canada and, if necessary, increase Canada's domestic defences. Canada's contribution to the security of the Empire would be the defence of Canada. But many English Canadians disagreed. For them the best protection for the Empire would be a common imperial military system with each of the dominions making a direct contribution to it. To that was often added the assertion that Canada should have a voice in the determination of imperial policy.

In 1909 the crisis in Anglo-German relations made it impossible for Laurier to temporize any longer. Its hand forced by Opposition demands, the government brought forward a Naval Bill that provided for the establishment of a small Canadian navy which, in times of crisis, could become part of the imperial navy. This compromise satisfied almost no one. In Quebec, Henri Bourassa and his growing following denounced the scheme as a commitment of Canadian ships and men to automatic involvement in every imperial war. Conscription of Canadians would soon follow. In 1910, with some assistance from Quebec Conservatives, Bourassa established a daily newspaper, *Le Devoir*, for the explicit purpose of defeating Laurier's naval plans. In much of English Canada, the Laurier navy was denounced as too little and too late— a "tin pot" navy. If the Empire faced a crisis, the best policy would be a direct financial contribution to Britain for the construction of additional "dreadnoughts," a powerful new type of battleship. Robert Borden, the leader of the Conservative party, espoused this view, adding that these emergency measures should be followed by a permanent policy that would include a recognition of the right of the dominions to participate in the making of imperial policy. After an acrimonious debate, Laurier's Naval Bill was enacted, but the emotions aroused and the deep divisions created by the debate did not dissipate. Instead, they were carried over into the controversy that soon arose over relations with the United States.

Canadian–American relations in the early twentieth century moved from bad to better, and then to a crisis. The most difficult issue that had to be faced by the Laurier government was a long-standing dispute over the border between Canada and Alaska. In 1903, a commission composed of three Americans, two Canadians, and one representative of Great Britain was established to adjudicate the question. With President Theodore Roosevelt's "big stick" not very well hidden, the commission handed down a decision which favoured the U.S. claim, the British commissioner having sided with the United States. The result infuriated Canadians, their ire being directed against both the United States and Great Britain. Relations with the United States improved over the next few years, and several disputes, some dating back to the previous century, were settled. But there remained a lingering distrust that could be aroused on the appropriate occasion. That occasion came in 1911 when the Laurier government announced that an agreement had been reached on a reciprocal trade deal with the United States.

If the Liberal government's naval policy had left it open to the charge that it was insufficiently loyal to the Empire, the new trade agreement made the charge more plausible, especially to those whose economic interest seemed threatened. The initiative for another try at a freer trade arrangement had come from the United States, when President Taft was attempting to fend off growing protectionist sentiment. Taft's negotiators then proposed a broad free-trading arrangement. The Canadians, caught somewhat off guard by the proposal, agreed to it. Laurier and his ministers saw the new agreement, providing free trade in natural products, and lower tariffs on a broad range of manufactured goods, as a solution to several political problems and also an attractive economic offer. In the prairie West, farmers had grown increasingly unhappy with Ottawa's tariff policy, which benefited Canadian manufacturers at the farmer's expense. Reciprocity in natural products with the United States, while it did not greatly reduce the cost of manufactured goods, would at least give Canadian farmers easier access to the U.S. market. In this way, the Liberals hoped to undermine the farmers' complaints. So, too, the Liberals hoped that the heat of the naval debate would be dissipated by the introduction of the trade issue in a form which they believed would meet the approval of every region of the country.

At first this calculation seemed accurate. The trade agreement caught the Conservatives completely by surprise. But Borden soon recovered, after being prompted by several provincial premiers, notably James Whitney of Ontario. The trade proposals were now turned against the government as further evidence of "disloyalty" to the Empire. As the Opposition stalled the parliamentary debate, Laurier decided he had found a popular issue. A late-summer election was called.

As events proved, the new trade agreement, while welcomed in some parts of the West, was not the winning issue that Laurier had expected. The Conservatives played upon the fears aroused in the country's industrialized areas that the agreement was only a beginning. Once implemented, it would so alter the east-west pattern of trade that free trade in manufactured goods would be the next necessary step, and that would mean flooding the Canadian market with cheap American goods, the destruction of local industries, rising unemployment, and perhaps even annexation to the United States. When these threats were added to the attacks on the Liberals' naval policy, an issue that remained central to the campaign in Quebec, the Opposition gained the offensive. They were aided by the indiscretions of a few American politicians who spoke openly about the prospects of annexation, so that the Liberals found it increasingly difficult to focus on trade rather than on loyalty. "Shall we give up...

the glorious future which beckons us—the chance that we shall become the chief state in the British Empire and the most powerful nation in the world?" one Conservative newspaper asked emotionally. "Shall we bring the sacrifices of the Fathers [of Confederation] to naught?"

The Liberals collapsed under this barrage, one mounted by a powerful new Conservative-party organization composed in part of a group of dissident Toronto Liberal businessmen, led by Clifford Sifton, who denounced the trade proposal and its authors. These men, whose business interests had at last prospered under the protective policies that Laurier had inherited and strengthened, formed the hard core of the anti-Liberal campaign. And while this campaign plucked the strings of pro-Empire, anti-American sentiment in English Canada, Laurier's Quebec fortress was also brought under siege. There the Conservatives left most of the campaign in the hands of Henri Bourassa, who supported a group of *autonomistes* whose attack focused on the claim that Laurier's naval policy represented a betrayal of Canadian interests in favour of the Empire. "It is time for the people of the Province of Quebec to prove to M. Laurier that if they admired him when he served the interests of the country well, today he has prevaricated, today he has duped us," one nationalist claimed.

The walls of fortress Quebec were breached in the September vote. For the first time since 1891, the Opposition—the Borden–Bourassa alliance—won 40 per cent of the seats. In Ontario, the dispirited Liberal troops were utterly routed. Aided by defecting Liberals and Premier Whitney's powerful provincial organization, Borden carried 85 per cent of the seats. Reciprocity was dead; Laurier's Canadian navy mothballed. Robert Borden finally found himself called upon to form a government—and to solve the problems debated, but not resolved, in the election campaign.

Borden in Peace and War

Robert Borden, the new Prime Minister, was a marked contrast to Sir Wilfrid Laurier. A successful Halifax lawyer, he never seemed entirely comfortable in the rough and tumble of politics. He was formal, even stuffy, in manner, and though he could deliver an effective speech, his style was more suited to the courtroom than the hustings. His ten years as Leader of the Opposition had been difficult ones, characterized by defeat and internal party intrigue. But he had hung on, and in doing so he had provided his party with an electoral platform that called for modernization of the civil service,

Canadian Troops at the Front. The bleakness of the combat zone is captured in this post-impressionist painting of soldiers moving up under air cover—a new feature of modern warfare. James Wilson Morrice—one of the first Canadian artists to gain an international reputation—was commissioned to paint this oil by the Canadian War Memorials Fund in 1917.

increased state guidance of economic and social development, and an imperial policy that stressed Canada's right to a voice in the making of foreign policy.

His greatest weakness was Quebec. His French was elementary, and he had difficulty understanding the French-Canadian viewpoint. That problem was not eased by the rather motley collection of Quebec politicians who called themselves Conservatives. But he had to make a Cabinet out of the material at hand. Bourassa, who had not run in the 1911 election, was not available, so Borden was forced to rely on lesser men. The turbulent events of the next few years revealed how far Borden was from solving his party's weaknesses in Quebec.

From the outset Borden discovered, like Laurier before him, that governing was a delicate balancing act. But his problem was greater than that of his predecessor, for his party was an uneasy alliance of enthusiasts for Empire and anti-imperial French-Canadian nationalists. On some matters the potential division was unimportant.

Civil-service reform could be begun and patronage reduced. New immigrants continued to arrive, and an investigation into the failure to attract French-speaking immigrants was established. Efforts were also made to assist western farmers smarting over the defeat of freer trade. A Board of Grain Commissioners was established to supervise the grain trade, and new terminal elevators were erected to provide increased grain storage at the head of the Great Lakes. These and other measures such as extended rural mail delivery, additional financial assistance for railway construction, and subsidies for highway construction revealed the moderately progressive thrust of the new administration. But the most divisive problem remained to be resolved. What could be done about imperial defence—to meet the "crisis" the Conservatives insisted threatened the Empire?

After close consultation with the British Admiralty, Borden hit upon a plan which he believed would meet the needs of the Empire and ensure the unity of his party. The 1913 Naval Aid Bill, described as a temporary measure designed to meet a pressing crisis, provided for a $35 million contribution to Britain for the construction of three dreadnoughts. In addition, Borden insisted that no permanent policy would be decided upon until a method of allowing the dominions a voice in the making of imperial policy was devised. This compromise, if such it was, failed to preserve the unity of the party. English-Canadian Conservatives welcomed the new policy; in Quebec it was rejected. The bill passed the House of Commons after a bitter, partisan debate, only to be rejected by the Liberal-dominated Senate. As the last days of peace faded into the first days of war, Canadian defence policy remained in stalemate. The navy consisted of two aged light cruisers, *Rainbow* and *Niobe*, one of which saw action in 1914, preventing a shipload of Sikh immigrants from landing at Vancouver. It was hardly a famous victory.

The emergency about which so much had been said, and so little done, finally erupted into a European war in August 1914. It soon spread to virtually every part of the world, since the overseas empires of the European powers were both causes and prospective prizes of the conflict. Canada entered the war automatically as part of the British Empire. Though Canadians were free to determine the extent of their contribution to the war effort, few in English-speaking Canada doubted that it should be unstinting. It was natural, Sir Wilfrid Laurier said, for Canada to respond to the Empire's need with the firm resolve, "Ready, Aye, Ready." Even Henri Bourassa, stern critic of imperialism, agreed, though he thought there should be limits to Canada's contribution. Trade unions, whose leaders had spoken bravely about opposing war

On the morning of April 9, 1917, four divisions of the Canadian Corps storm the ridge at Vimy, France, capturing a previously impregnable German position. In this remarkable photograph by William Ryder-Ryder, the Canadians are slogging across no man's land under cover of a massive artillery barrage, while Germans overrun in the initial advance leave their dugouts and rush forward to surrender. The French called the victory "an Easter gift from Canada to France." The cost: 7,004 wounded and 3,598 dead.

The Vimy site was given to Canada by France, and is now a 250-acre memorial park marked by Walter Allward's towering monument, begun in 1926 and unveiled by Edward VIII ten years later.

with a general strike, were now swept along by the new patriotic fervour. The handful of farm leaders and assorted radicals who had previously warned of the threat of "militarism" were either mute or drowned out by the clatter of mobilization and recruitment.

Backed by a country that was at least superficially one in its determination to defeat Germany and the Central Powers, in what was widely expected to be a short war, the Borden government set about organizing the Canadian contribution. Sam Hughes, the Minister of the Militia, took charge of recruitment. More than 30,000 volunteers were assembled at Valcartier ready to set off for Britain by the beginning of October, only two months after the war's beginning. "Soldiers!" Hughes told them. "The world regards you as a marvel!" Perhaps so, but the troops were poorly equipped and inadequately trained, representing more enthusiasm than foresight. That weakness would characterize much of the war effort, especially the part directed by Hughes, and would lead in three years to a major manpower crisis.

Canadian troops, once in England, were given further training and sent to the front where they quickly proved their mettle. Unemployment at home, and a large body of recent British immigrants of military age, kept recruitment figures high throughout 1914–15, and soon two divisions at the front formed the Canadian Corps. Despite equipment problems—Hughes stuck obstinately with the faulty Ross rifle—the men fought gallantly. By 1916, with the short war moving into its third year, the casualty rates mounted. They fought at St-Eloi, Courcelette, and on into the bloody Somme, with a cost close to 35,000 men. Heavy shelling, miles of mud, and, eventually, deadly poison gas awaited the Canadians as they moved to Ypres and Vimy. Those latter victories led to the appointment of Brigadier-General Arthur Currie to command the Canadian Corps, which until then had fought under a British commander.

By the beginning of 1916 the government had committed Canada to a force of 500,000, all to be recruited, not conscripted. The commitment was to prove greater than the method could achieve. As the heavy casualties continued—15,464 Canadians lost at Passchendaele—the need for reinforcements became pressing. At home voluntary recruitment was falling off drastically as domestic employment absorbed every available man and woman. And now there were some Canadians, especially French Canadians, who had begun to think that Canada had done its share.

The war on the home front was fought energetically, though it sometimes seemed as difficult and chaotic as that on the military front. Certainly it required an unprecedented degree of government intervention in the lives of Canadians. Enemy aliens were required to register and were harassed by super-patriots. Indeed, as the war dragged on and the casualty lists lengthened, hostility to "foreigners" intensified, providing the right atmosphere for the politically opportune decision to strip them of the vote in 1917.

Much more demanding than internal security were the economic requirements of the war effort. At home and abroad, it had to be financed. Large amounts of new money—Dominion notes—were printed, new loans floated first in London and then in New York, and tariffs increased, the latter continuing to produce most of the government's revenue. In 1915, the government turned to Canadian investors, large and small, and launched the first of several successful campaigns for Victory Loans. In 1916, the Minister of Finance moved into the politically sensitive area of direct taxation, levying a modest business-profits tax and, the next year, income tax. The latter, it was stressed, was a temporary war tax, an example of the "conscription of wealth."

The demands of the war had an almost immediate inflationary impact on an economy that had been in the doldrums since 1913. Manufacturing, especially of shells and armaments, expanded rapidly. The War Purchasing Committee and the Shell Committee supervised the buying of supplies, though neither was entirely successful in preventing favouritism and corruption. The Imperial Munitions Board, under the chairmanship of the energetic meatpacker Joseph W. Flavelle, proved more effective. These organizations were only the first of several government interventions into the marketplace. Equally significant was the establishment in 1917 of the Board of Grain Supervisors, an action taken in response to the upward spiral of Canadian grain prices. Prices had to be stabilized and distribution supervised. Both were done in a manner that convinced many farmers that a wheat board organized to keep prices down in times of inflation might keep them up at other times. To these measures were added controls over fuel and food designed to promote careful use and conservation.

While hardly a new problem, the financial difficulties of the over-expanded railway system reached critical proportions during the war. Never, perhaps, were the railways more important for without them the transportation of men and equipment so crucial to the war effort was impossible. While this traffic increased revenues, costs also rose, especially expenditures on new rolling stock. By late 1915, the Canadian Northern and the Grand Trunk Pacific were literally faced with bankruptcy. This put the Borden government to a severe test, for the Conservatives had long been critics of these "Liberal" railways. Moreover, the government knew that the powerful Canadian Pacific Railway was strongly opposed to assistance being given its rivals. But the companies could not be allowed to collapse, for that would jeopardize such related institutions as the Bank of Commerce. Temporary financing and a commission of enquiry were put in place in 1916. But the problem was no nearer solution, and, faced with another crisis, the government moved towards public ownership, bringing the Grand Trunk Pacific, the Canadian Northern, and the National Transcontinental under a government-appointed board of trustees. Later that year government ownership became a fact, with shareholders receiving what many thought excessive compensation for property already heavily subsidized by taxpayers' money. While this was hardly the end of the country's perennial railway problems, it did lay the foundation for the Canadian National Railways system. The war had made this action necessary, though it was not welcomed by everyone and earned the Borden government more criticism than credit. The Montreal business community would not soon forget what could be represented as favouritism towards Toronto financial interests.

As the armed forces absorbed growing numbers of men, women were drawn into the workforce to fill the gap. Many found jobs in factories, but others, like these volunteers for the Ontario National Service, became farm harvest hands.

The wartime stimulation of the economy increased employment opportunities, though serious unemployment continued through the winter of 1914–15. But that had changed by the autumn of 1915, and wage rates began to rise, though the cost of living did too. As pressure on the labour force intensified, more and more women moved into industrial work—including thousands who worked in munitions factories in the later years of the war. Farms, offices, transportation, and many other industries found that women made effective substitutes for the scarce men who had dominated most industrial occupations before the war. The government only haltingly developed a manpower policy. Some effort was made to establish a fair-wages standard in government-funded contracts, though Flavelle resisted its application to those let out by the Imperial Munitions Board. Compulsory registration of the labour force was established, and in the summer of 1918 the right to organize and to bargain collectively was recognized, but strikes and lock-outs were banned. While working people benefited from the sellers' market created by the war, most of their gains were offset by inflation. The restrictions on strikes, added to the evidence that many employers were reaping huge profits from war contracts, created a restiveness among workers that would disturb many urban centres at the end of the war.

The Renewal of Cultural Conflict

Although Canada entered the war a unified and confident nation, the demands and emotions of war exacerbated the ethnic, class, and regional tensions that had been simmering during the pre-war years. Given the divisions created by the pre-war debates over minority schools and imperial relations, it was almost inevitable that the war years should witness a bitter quarrel between French and English Canadians, one which divided the country more deeply than at any time since the hanging of Louis Riel in 1885.

The source of the renewed conflict was twofold. Since 1913 a serious irritation had been developing over French-language educational rights in Ontario. In that year, the province's Department of Education had issued a circular, popularly known as "Regulation 17," which appeared to reduce the rights of Franco-Ontarians to an education in their mother tongue. In an effort to improve standards in Franco-Ontarian schools, and especially to raise the level of English taught, the Ontario government touched an area of great sensitivity. The rapid expansion of the Franco-

Ontarian population had raised the fears of Ontario Orangemen that their Protestant province was threatened. At the same time, ironically, English-speaking Catholics began expressing concern that French would soon be the dominant language in their church. Together, these normally hostile groups had pressed the Ontario government to limit the use of French in Ontario schools. Howard Ferguson, an Orangeman who would be premier of the province in the 1920s, spoke for these groups when he declared that "the bilingual system encourages the isolation of races. It impresses the mind of youth with the idea of race distinction and militates against the fusion of various elements that make up the population.... The experience of the United States where their national school system recognizes but one language simply proves the wisdom of the system." That view was angrily rejected by French Canadians in Ontario and in Quebec.

By itself, the quarrel over schools in Ontario would have been serious enough. But when it was placed within the overheated atmosphere of the war it became a tragedy. By 1915 relations between French and English were growing embittered over charges and counter-charges about enlistment that turned on the question of whether French Canadians were pulling their full weight. The rhetorical level reached dangerous heights when nationalists like Henri Bourassa claimed that the real war was not being fought in Europe, but in Ontario where the "Boches" were threatening minority rights. As the emotional temperature rose, federal politicians were drawn into the controversy. When Borden, resisting pressure from his Quebec supporters, refused to intervene with his fellow Conservatives in Ontario, the Liberals brought the matter before Parliament in early 1916. In a vote on a motion calling on Ontario to treat its minority justly, both political parties split along linguistic lines, Quebec Conservatives supporting the motion, western Liberals breaking with their party. Though the courts eventually ruled against the Franco-Ontarian claim and the Pope appealed to Canadian Catholics to cool the controversy, the damage was done. The country was divided and would soon be more so.

As the dispute over language grew muted, the controversy over enlistment rose to drown it out. By early 1916 voluntary-enlistment figures began a marked decline. The first flush of patriotic enthusiasm had passed. Domestic employment needs had risen and unemployment disappeared. Farmers' sons, always slower to enlist than their city cousins, were needed on the farm to produce the food so necessary to the Allied armies. But even taking these factors into account, there still appeared to be a greater lag in enlistments in Quebec. French Canadians had never shared the enthusiasm of their English-speaking compatriots for the war; they had no emotional attachment to Great Britain, and little to secular France. They accepted the need to fight as part of the Empire, but only if participation was voluntary. And then there was the matter of language. Not only was French under attack in Ontario, but it had only an inferior status in the armed forces where, apart from one hastily organized battalion, English was the dominant language. The same was true of military command levels, where French-speaking officers hardly existed. There were clearly fewer incentives for French Canadians to volunteer.

Whatever the causes of declining recruitment, the fact of increasing casualties was undeniable. What could the Borden government do? Reduction of the Canadian commitment was apparently out of the question. Throughout the war Borden had insisted that Canada was a full participant and that it should have a voice in determining policy. For this to be taken seriously, the military commitment had to be honoured. But Borden had also, repeatedly, promised that recruitment would be voluntary. By the spring of 1917, with the war apparently far from over, Borden had to resolve the dilemma posed by his obviously contradictory commitments.

The pressures of war made a new enlistment policy necessary; the pressures of domestic politics ensured that the new policy would be compulsory military service. The popularity of the Conservative government had reached a low ebb by 1916. There were charges of scandal and mismanagement, of "political colonels" in the organization of the war effort. There were the claims that central Canada, especially Ontario, had been favoured in the granting of munitions contracts. And, increasingly, there were critics who contended that the war had not been prosecuted with sufficient vigour. "Politics" seemed to take precedence over "patriotism." The resolution, for many, was a coalition government that would set politics aside and get on with winning the war. Such a government might also push through reforms like prohibition of alcoholic beverages, votes for women, and the abolition of patronage.

Growing Conservative unpopularity was patent: not one provincial Conservative government that faced the electorate after 1914 was returned. Since the Liberals, having accepted a one-year extension of the life of Parliament in 1916, were unwilling to agree to a second, a federal election in 1917 was a certainty. The Conservatives had little hope of winning unless drastic changes in personnel and policy were effected. By early 1917 Borden had come around to the opinion that a coalition could solve both his political and his recruitment problems. Conscription for overseas service was clearly necessary; a coalition would remove it from partisan debate, and the

Three cheers! In 1919 HRH the Prince of Wales (later, briefly, Edward VIII) was everywhere welcomed by enthusiastic crowds. In Ottawa he joined Prime Minister Borden (second from right) and the Governor General, the Duke of Devonshire (far right), in laying the cornerstone for the Peace Tower on Parliament Hill.

Conservatives could retain office on a shared basis with the Liberals. The stumbling block was Sir Wilfrid Laurier, who rejected the proposed coalition because he could not accept conscription. He was convinced that to do so would simply turn Quebec over to Bourassa. He was probably also convinced that if his Liberals stuck together they could return to power, given the unpopularity of the Conservatives. But his party did not stay together: many of his English-speaking colleagues were under great pressure to support conscription. Their willingness to support a coalition, without Laurier and without Quebec, was greatly increased by the passage of two new pieces of electoral legislation. The Military Voters Act made provision for troops at home and abroad to vote, and where soldiers could not identify their home riding they were allowed to vote "for" or "against" the government with their votes distributed by electoral officials. The Wartime Elections Act disfranchised a broadly defined group who came from "enemy" countries after 1902, and enfranchised the female relatives of enlisted men. The cards were heavily stacked in favour of candidates who supported conscription. English-speaking Liberals now rushed to the coalition colours, leaving Laurier and Quebec behind. As a final action designed to ensure the outcome of the election, the government promised exemption from military service to farmers' sons.

The result of the bitterly fought winter election was almost a foregone conclusion. The Unionists, as the coalition candidates were called, swept English-speaking Canada with the help of the soldiers' vote. Quebec remained loyal to Laurier, with even Bourassa urging support for his old foe. The country was split, even though the popular vote was less one-sided than the division of seats in Parliament. Sporadic rioting took place in Quebec in early 1918, and troops were moved into several areas of disaffection. An ambiguously worded secessionist resolution was debated in the Quebec legislature, but withdrawn before a vote was taken. Quiet was restored, but the bitterness remained as the war moved towards its conclusion. Then, in the spring of 1918, in response to a massive German offensive on the Western Front, the exemption for farmers' sons was cancelled—just when they were most needed for farm work. Yet another resentment awaited post-war revenge. In the end, almost the anticipated number of conscripts was obtained, though the Armistice in November 1918 meant that only a small number saw action. Consequently, the military benefits of conscription were slight, while the political consequences were great.

The year 1917 was one of cultural tension and political upheaval. There was something almost symbolic in the disaster that marked its end. On the morning of December 6 the Belgian relief ship *Imo* collided with the *Mont Blanc*, a French munitions vessel, in Halifax harbour. A mile-high explosion destroyed more than two and a quarter square miles of the industrial section of the city. An enormous tidal wave, then a raging fire, followed the explosion, engulfing office buildings, residential areas, and the transportation system. Approximately 1,600 Haligonians died, some 9,000 were injured, and more than 25,000 lost their homes or suffered serious property damage. Total losses were estimated at $35 million. The threat of further explosions in the munitions area of the main dockyard forced the evacuation of almost the entire city, and it was months before life settled down again.

This domestic disaster brought home to Canadians, as perhaps little else could, the destructive power of the weapons of modern warfare. Hugh MacLennan, a ten-year-old survivor of the explosion, gave those tragic events a permanent place in Canadian literary history in his first novel, *Barometer Rising* (1941).

The Fruits of War

The war years had proved Sir Robert Borden, knighted in 1914, an effective leader. His government had conducted a successful war effort, considering the magnitude of the war and the inexperience of Canadians in such matters. His Union government implemented a number of reforms long advocated, especially by English Canadians: prohibition, votes for women, and civil-service reforms. But Borden's major achievements were on the international front. Throughout the war years he had consistently pressed Britain to recognize the role played by Canada and the other dominions by allowing them to be included in wartime decision-making. At first the British stonewalled. But when Lloyd George became British Prime Minister in 1916, he had his own reasons for calling the dominions to London. There, in 1917, the Imperial War Cabinet met, including the dominion prime ministers. At the Imperial Conference of the same year a resolution drafted by Borden and Jan Christiaan Smuts of South Africa promised a post-war formula that would provide for "continuous consultation" in the formulation of imperial policies. Though vague, the resolution was a step towards an increased role for Canada in foreign policy-making. Another step was taken when Borden joined the British delegation to the Paris Peace Conference in 1919, and Canada signed the Versailles Treaty which ended the war with Germany. Membership in the new League of Nations followed logically, though no one quite knew how the unity of the Empire, "continuous consultation," and separate dominion representation could be reconciled.

Borden's long absence at the Peace Conference and his evidently declining interest in domestic politics meant that his colleagues had to devise plans for demobilization and post-war reconstruction. They had also to attempt to rebuild the Conservative party. The problems were awesome. Land-grant schemes for returning soldiers were implemented, pensions were established, and the soldiers gradually returned to private life, often displacing the women who had moved into industrial and other work during the war. The presence of these demobilized soldiers, often at loose ends, added to the widespread social unrest that touched many parts of the country in the months immediately after the Armistice.

Unrest and discontent were particularly notable among working people who, having heard the wartime rhetoric about the conflict leading to a better Canada, were now impatient for the fulfilment of the promise. Many workers believed that despite wartime wage increases their lot had hardly improved in an inflationary economy.

The idealism of the war years—"making the world safe for democracy"—ended in the bitterness of the Winnipeg general strike in May–June 1919. North Main Street was the scene of several clashes between the strikers and the police, and "Bloody Saturday," June 21, resulted in thirty casualties, including one death, and the effective end of the strike.

Others remembered the harshness of pre-war unemployment. Many resented the wartime ban on strikes. And workers, too, wanted to contribute to that brave new world which had been so much talked about by reformers of all stripes. Whatever the motives, and they were usually no more complicated than a desire for better wages and working conditions, workers across the country were determined to make their voices heard in the spring of 1919.

Though there were strikes from Vancouver to Halifax, and much radical talk about general strikes and even revolution in several centres, it was in Winnipeg between May 15 and June 25 that the most spectacular demonstration of workers' solidarity took place. There, virtually the whole labour force responded to the Winnipeg Trades and Labour Council's appeal for a general strike to support metal-trades workers whose employers refused to recognize their union and denied them a wage increase. With Winnipeg employers and their middle-class supporters organized behind the Citizens' Committee, and the workers led by the Strike Committee, the level of emotion and rhetoric reached a high pitch. The Russian Revolution provided a backdrop for strike leaders who spoke loosely of "revolution," and their opponents who muttered darkly about "Soviets and Bolsheviks," "bohunks," and foreign agitators. The drama worked itself slowly towards a brutal denouement.

Federal, provincial, and municipal governments agreed that the strike represented a threat to the established order. To end that threat police and troops were used to enforce the Riot Act and to disperse peaceful demonstrations. Inevitably, there were casualties, arrests, and a few "foreigners" deported. The strike collapsed. Though several strike leaders, including such active social reformers as J. S. Woodsworth and A. A. Heaps, spent time in jail, attempts to convict them of seditious and revolutionary activity failed. Even though the strike produced no concrete results, it did convince working people in Winnipeg of the need for political action, and in subsequent provincial and federal elections they sent their own representatives to Parliament. Their presence there testified to the profoundly altered shape of Canadian politics.

The Cultural Ambiguity of an Urban Age

If Stephen Leacock's satires caught the spirit of a country moving from a rural to an urban age, many other writers and artists reacted against these changes. In Quebec, fiction and poetry continued to explore the well-worn themes of rural virtue and the decadence of city life. The French writer Louis Hémon captured these best, but French-Canadian writers followed him in praise of rural and religious values at the very time that much was changing in the province of Quebec. Poetry in both French and English hardly emerged from the influences of nineteenth-century romanticism. Archibald Lampman, who had written of "The City of the End of Things," warning of the ills of industrialism, died prematurely in 1899. Of his successors, only Duncan Campbell Scott, especially in his poems focusing on the tragedy of Native people, was in tune with the new century. Bliss Carman and Sir Charles G. D. Roberts, whose romantic optimism often degenerated into sentimentalism, wrote popular verse, and the idylls of the half-Mohawk Pauline Johnson also attracted many readers and listeners. Nellie McClung's moralistic tales, Ernest Thompson Seton's animal stories, and, above all, the stories of muscular Christianity and patriotism written by "Ralph Connor" (the pen name of clergyman Charles W. Gordon) won widespread acclaim. Lucy Maude Montgomery's *Anne of Green Gables*, published in 1908, was an instant success, as were many of its seven sequels. In French, the poems of Jean Charbonneau and Albert Lozeau continued the romantic tradition. Only the tragic figure of Emile Nelligan, whose work evoked Baudelaire and Rimbaud, suggested the symbolism of modern poetry.

In painting, too, Canada seemed largely immune to the important trends that would soon nurture a modern art. The continued appeal of such bucolic painters as Horatio Walker, Homer Watson, Maurice Cullen, and Clarence Gagnon attested to the isolation of Canada from the new currents. The genius of Ozias Leduc, revealed both in church decoration and even more in still-life paintings, went largely unnoticed. And the post-impressionist floating world of J. W. Morrice, working in self-imposed exile in France, attracted only slight interest. After 1910, however, there were signs of the new developments that would dominate the post-war scene. Tom Thomson, A. Y. Jackson, and Lawren Harris found in Canadian nature a new image. Violence, in colour and form, replaced the pastoral romanticism of the previous generation. A bold and robust art based on the Canadian landscape was, they claimed, what a bold and robust new nation needed. Yet these artists concentrated

Stephen Leacock. Leacock (1869–1944) taught the "dismal science" of political economy at McGill University for over thirty years, but the world knew him as one of the finest humorists in the English language, and the author of over sixty books. Oil (1943) by Edwin Holgate.

Quebec writer Emile Nelligan (1879–1941), whose symbolist imagery and hallucinatory poetry won him many admirers by the time he was twenty; at that age he entered hospital, his nerves exhausted, and he remained there until his death. Retouched photograph by Charles Gill, *c.* 1904.

Yes Eutrope, if you wish I will marry you when the men come back from the woods for the sowing: egg-tempera illustration by Clarence Gagnon, painted 1928–33, for a deluxe edition of Louis Hémon's *Maria Chapdelaine* published in Paris in 1933.

primarily on parts of Canada far from the new urban-industrial heartland. Georgian Bay, Algonquin Park, and Algoma caught their attention. Like hundreds of prosperous, urban Canadians who every summer moved north to camps and cottages and took up hiking, mountaineering, and sailing as escapes from the tension of the city, these new artists identified the wilderness as the spirit of the new Canada. They found something deeply troubling and materialistic about the new society. A. Y. Jackson expressed the unease felt about the great transformation that was under way when he wrote in 1910:

Someday the farm hand will go to work, start the day by punching the clock on the Farm Products Company Ltd., and then set about turning levers and pressing buttons. Even now the romantic milk maid has faded away, and cows are being milked by machinery. The ploughman weary homeward plods his way no more—its nine furrows at once and run by gasoline. And how on earth the artist is to find any sentiment in that kind of thing beats me. The big round cumulus clouds that pile around the horizon in the summertime and look so majestic and calm—just imagine when the aeroplanes and dirigibles get busy at 90 miles an hour; won't we see poor old cumulus stirred up like custard, and flung all over the sky.

The painters who introduced an important aspect of modernism to Canada by turning away from literal representation were nevertheless both nostalgic and nationalistic. That, perhaps, explains why, after a brief struggle against conventional taste, they quickly came to dominate Canadian painting.

Above; Boardinghouse-keeper, monkey-fancier, naturalist, storyteller, and, above all, painter, Emily Carr in 1935 was still, she confessed, "an isolated old woman on the edge of nowhere." Yet she had created a new vision of earth and sky. Visible in this photo by Ira Dilworth is Carr's *Sunshine and Tumult*.

Top: *Above Lake Superior,* oil (*c.* 1922) by Lawren Harris.

Bottom: A year after first exhibiting together, six members of the Group of Seven and their champion around the Artists' Table at Toronto's Arts and Letters Club. Left to right, F. H. Varley, A. Y. Jackson, Lawren Harris, critic Barker Fairley, Frank Johnston, Arthur Lismer, and J. E. H. MacDonald. Absent is Franklin Carmichael.

Prior to the Great War, scientific, medical, and technological research, such as it was, was carried on mainly in universities. Agricultural research had been conducted at Experimental Stations since the 1880s, while the Conservation Commission, established in 1909, had overseen research in fields ranging from oyster breeding and reforestation to town planning. But the war convinced politicians that science and technology were of such significance that a more cen-

Dr. Charles Best and Dr. Frederick Banting, two of the four discovers of insulin, with an experimental subject on the roof of the University of Toronto's Medical Building. The picture was taken in 1921–22, around the time of the discovery.

tralized, co-ordinated approach was required. The result was the establishment, in 1916, of the National Research Council. This federal institution was given responsibility for developing an inventory of scientific research and for funding scientific activity in the universities. It was not until 1928 that Henry Marshall Tory, who presided over the NRC from 1923 to 1935, succeeded in establishing a national laboratory in Ottawa where scientists could conduct basic and applied research on a full-time basis.

Nevertheless it was not at the NRC but rather at the rudimentary laboratories of the University of Toronto's Faculty of Medicine that the most important Canadian scientific accomplishment took place. That was the discovery of insulin, in 1921–22, by a team of scientists which included Frederick Banting, Charles Best, James B. Collip, and J. J. R. Macleod. Banting, whose initial hunch began the work that eventually led to the discovery of a means of controlling diabetes, shared the Nobel Prize for Medicine in 1923 with Dr. Macleod. Since Banting had never recognized the contribution that Macleod and Collip had made, he chose to divide his prize money award with Best. It would be a long time before a Canadian would again achieve such international acclaim in science.

The Twenties: Decade of Illusions

The twenties in Canada, as elsewhere, were years of optimism and promise that ended in disillusionment and economic crisis. The roots of that crisis were embedded in the political instability and uneven economic development of the first post-war decade. Yet it was during this decade that the country acquired a new definition of itself on the international scene and gained a new confidence in cultural matters.

The heavy demands for Canadian products created by the war produced a boom that continued through most sectors into 1920. Relatively cheap credit in the immediate post-war years, and the consumers' rush to buy goods that had been in short supply during the war years, resulted in serious inflation. But the bubble burst quickly. By 1922 a rapid contraction of the economy had taken place and unemployment had risen dramatically. The collapse of prices was most serious in the agricultural sector, with wheat prices, for example, falling by 60 per cent between 1920 and 1922. Lumber, fish, iron, and steel also experienced steep drops in price. The hardest-hit regions were the Maritimes and the prairies.

Some parts of the Maritimes, notably Halifax, had experienced unprecedented prosperity during the war, but the whole region had benefited from a renewed export trade. Even the tragic Halifax explosion had its positive side, for it led to an increase in building activity. But after 1920 the value of virtually every type of production declined drastically, and the downward trend continued until 1925. Particularly hard hit were sales of coal and iron, which meant heavy unemployment in Cape Breton. Labour conflict, including strikes, lock-outs, and the repeated use of the militia to prevent violence and break strikes, was regular fare in Cape Breton in the twenties. More than any other region, the Atlantic provinces underwent difficult economic readjustments and enjoyed little of the intermittent prosperity that touched other parts of the country. The increase in freight rates on maritime routes, the integration of the Intercolonial Railway into the Canadian National, and the movement of some railway facilities from the Maritimes to central Canada all had detrimental effects on the eastern provinces. While overseas markets contracted, changes in transportation made access to central Canada more costly. It was these tough economic circumstances that underlay the "maritime rights" agitation central to the political life of the eastern provinces in the 1920s.

The prairie provinces, the heart of pre-war economic expansion, entered a period

ONTARIO RESORTS

CANADIAN NATIONAL RAILWAYS

By the 1920s and 1930s, as middle-class Canadians won shorter work weeks and bought family cars, they began flocking to resorts, national parks, and other tourist attractions. In Ontario one mecca was the Georgian Bay area, which the Group of Seven had popularized. This poster, possibly depicting Lake Muskoka, is by J. E. Sampson, head of Sampson-Matthews Ltd.—the commercial art firm that employed Group members Franklin Carmichael and A. J. Casson.

of marked instability in the early post-war years. Sharp declines in wheat prices, partially offset by increased yields, followed the war, while farm costs rose rapidly. The farmer's purchasing power dropped by about 50 per cent in the first half of the 1920s, though it bounded back and farming remained fairly prosperous until the crash in 1929. Throughout the period farmers carried large fixed costs which left them extremely vulnerable when the markets collapsed: heavy taxes required to finance roads, schools, and other necessities in undeveloped areas, rising land costs once homesteading ended, and the high price of tractors, separators, and threshing machines. Between 1926 and 1931, the number of tractors on prairie farms increased from 50,000 to 82,000, harvesters from zero to 9,000, and trucks from 6,000 to 22,000. These were not mere conveniences but rather necessities which made it possible to work larger farms and thus increase profits. New wheat varieties with higher yields did the same, while the opening of the Panama Canal shipping route provided cheaper transportation. But more mechanization and larger farms also often meant more expenditures and heavier debts.

These accumulating problems were disguised, to a degree, by the apparent prosperity of the last years of the twenties. Prairie agriculture shared in this turn-around as international demand for grain, and Canada's share of the market, increased, for Europe and the Soviet Union only slowly regained their pre-war agricultural out-put. During these years the area of grain farming expanded and immigration resumed, spreading out into the Peace River and other parts of northern Alberta and British Columbia. Some diversification also took place in the prairie economy: hydroelectric generation in Manitoba and British Columbia, and crude-oil production in Alberta. Railway construction resumed, including the completion of the controversial Hudson Bay route. Agriculture, nevertheless, remained the foundation of prairie life.

Ontario and Quebec, the urban-industrial heartland, had benefited greatly from wartime demand. The post-war years were a time of further growth. After wheat and flour, the country's leading exports were newsprint and wood pulp, base metals and gold, much of which came from the newly developed areas of the two central provinces, and also British Columbia. So, too, central Canadian manufacturing industries increased their output: pulp and paper, lumber, farm machinery, rolling mills, and steel furnaces were leaders, though by 1929 non-ferrous metals, smelting, and electrical goods were increasingly significant. The automobile industry, rubber manufacturing, and meat packing remained important. Cheap power prices were basic to the growing dominance of central Canadian industry, making possible the exploitation of aluminum in the Saguenay and nickel in Sudbury. Quebec remained heavily dependent on large-scale natural-resource industries and such traditional labour-intensive manufacturing as textiles and leather goods. Ontario, by contrast, grew more specialized and diversified, moving into automobiles and parts, electrical appliances, and tools.

The economic growth of the 1920s, especially during the second half of the decade, was once again accompanied by urban growth and concentration. The 1921 census recorded a population increase of nearly 22 per cent over the previous decade, the total reaching 8,787,749 Canadians. Ten years later, after another 18 per cent increase, the population finally broke 10 million. But once again the principal cities grew at an even faster pace: Montreal by 38 per cent, Toronto 32 per cent, Vancouver 48 per cent, and Winnipeg 24 per cent. That Winnipeg's rate of growth had fallen behind Vancouver's was highly significant. So was the spectacular growth of the southern Ontario automobile-manufacturing city of Windsor; its population increased by 56 per cent in the 1920s. Maritime cities, by contrast, remained virtu-ally stable, reflecting the economic stagnation of the area.

Although Ozias Leduc (1864–1955) earned his livelihood as a church decorator, he also created works of symbolic and lyrical power that remained largely unknown during his lifetime. *Erato (Muse in the Forest)*: oil, 1906.

Charles W. Jefferys (1861–1959) is perhaps best known as an illustrator of literary and historical subjects, but he was also one of the first Canadian painters to evoke that special relationship of earth, sky, and light so characteristic of the prairies. *A Prairie Trail*: oil, 1912.

Although contemporary with the Group of Seven, and at the time overshadowed by them, David B. Milne (1882–1953) followed his own modernist impulse, creating gentle landscapes and quiet interiors of exquisite beauty. *Interior with Paintings*: oil, 1914.

Above: Tom Thomson (1877–1917) died before the Group of Seven came into being, but his paint-ings of Ontario's rugged beauty and stunning colour had been a major influence on its members. *The Jack Pine*: oil, 1916–17.

Facing: The *art nouveau* technique and graphic-arts experience of J.E.H. MacDonald (1873–1932) lent themselves brilliantly to patriotic poster-making. After the war MacDonald was a founder of the Group of Seven. *Canada and the Call*: gouache, 1914.

ng: without stooping
here propaganda, the
sian-born Paraskeva Clark
8–1986) catches the Punch-
-Judy quality of the politi-
s' response to the social
s of the 1930s. *Petroushka*:
1937.

letter of 1941 or 1942,
y Carr (1871–1945) noted,
lay I have worked hard on a
erious little bit, little round
rella trees, spindly runts
grew up under forest giants
have been reduced to tim-
ong ago." *Trees in the Sky*:
. 1939.

No painter has more imaginatively captured the unique quality of French-Canadian life than Jean-Paul Lemieux (b. 1904). Here war and peace, complacency and the miraculous, are all brought together in a droll yet utterly serious fashion. *Lazare*: oil, 1941.

Smelter Stacks, Copper Cliff. Mining and smelting created whole new communities in the northern regions of most provinces. In this 1936 oil, artist Charles F. Comfort caught—perhaps unwittingly—both the majesty and the menace of the industry, in these pollutant-belching smokestacks near Sudbury.

The economy thus passed into the post-war years without any enormous dislocation, except in the maritime region. But there were serious problems in some sectors of an economy encumbered by heavy debt and dependent upon an often unpredictable international market. Indeed, it was the very openness of the economy that was both its strength and its weakness. Its openness and its changing nature were revealed when in 1926 the United States replaced Great Britain as the largest foreign investor in Canada. Less observed was the change from bonded debt in railways and manufacturing, to direct investment in mining, pulp and paper, petroleum, and other high-risk resource industries; bonded debt represented a repayable loan, direct investment meant ownership. Canada was not becoming less dependent on foreign money than in the past, but the altered terms under which the money was invested gradually drew the British Dominion more and more closely into the orbit of the United States.

Politics, Not as Usual

The end of the Great War brought substantial changes to Canadian political life. Both the Unionist and Liberal parties faced the necessity of regrouping and reorganizing their forces. Early in 1919, Sir Wilfrid Laurier died. He left a party fractured by wartime controversies and without an obvious successor. To find one, the Liberals called the first leadership convention in the country's history. The delegates gathered in Ottawa in August and chose young Mackenzie King over the veteran W. S. Fielding. King had remained loyal to Laurier on conscription; Fielding had not. The

Quebec delegates remembered. King appeared to be a man of the new age: a Ph.D. in political economy with a successful career as a civil servant, an expert in industrial relations. His political experience was limited to less than three years in Laurier's last Cabinet and a few years of organizational work. But his political sense was keen, his ambition unbounded, and his sense of mission powerful. He believed he had a divine calling to political leadership and he never forgot that he was the grandson of William Lyon Mackenzie, the rebel leader of 1837. Always cautious and moderate in outlook, King had learned from his Christian upbringing and from Sir Wilfrid that conciliation and compromise were the keys to success in Canadian politics. This labour expert would need all his talents for conciliation in the chaotic politics of the 1920s, when farmers, rather than workers, necessarily became his main concern.

The Unionists, too, acquired a new leader in the first years of peace. Once Borden, after a period of uncertainty, finally decided to retire, the Unionist caucus selected Arthur Meighen. He was a sharp contrast to the Liberal Mackenzie King. A Manitoba lawyer, he had served as Borden's most effective lieutenant, preparing and defending some of the Union government's most controversial policies. Meighen was a superb debater, a master of ridicule who hardly knew the meaning of conciliation. He too was ambitious, and no less self-righteous than King, though much less voluble about it. He despised the new leader of the Liberal party, whom he had known since student days at the University of Toronto. The feeling was mutual.

King and Meighen faced the same challenge: the growing militancy of the farmers' movement. Already in 1919, after the Union government had refused to implement certain tariff reductions, some western Unionists had broken with the government. This group was led by Thomas A. Crerar, a Manitoban who came from the Grain Growers' Grain Company to join the Union government in 1917. Crerar was not a radical, but he was convinced that the protective tariff weighed unjustly on the farmer, and that party politics had to be realigned along pro- and anti-tariff lines. The "New National Policy," which the Canadian Council of Agriculture had laid down in 1918, became the policy statement around which farmers were called to rally. It was an almost spontaneous revolt of farmers against both old parties that swept Crerar into the leadership of a new movement, the Progressive party. In 1919, with the aid of a number of members of the Independent Labour Party, the United Farmers of Ontario took office in their province. Alberta soon followed suit, while farmers in Saskatchewan and Manitoba effectively controlled their provincial governments. The balance of power in Ottawa was the next objective.

While not noted as an orator, William Lyon Mackenzie King was an effective campaigner; during the 1926 election he took advantage of this pause in the motorcade to denounce his "millionaire" opponent, Arthur Meighen. (King seems not to have noticed the misspelling of his own name.)

When the election of 1921 was called, three parties, rather than two, offered themselves to the voters. Prime Minister Meighen and Thomas Crerar hoped to fight the campaign on the tariff question. Mackenzie King, his Liberal party divided on the issue, chose to attack the government on its overall record, while at the same time wooing the farmers with ambiguous promises to look after their interests. King also told maritimers that the Liberals would deal with their growing economic problems if returned to office.

The outcome of the election was astonishing. That the Unionist government was defeated was clear. Not much else was. While the Liberals gained the largest number of seats, 116, the Progressives gained the most ground in electing 64 members, and the Unionists were reduced to a mere 50. The Progressive contingent included Agnes Macphail, the first woman to be elected to the federal Parliament. Two Labour members were also returned. For the next four years Mackenzie King's Liberals governed precariously, supported by most of the Progressives. A few concessions were made to the farmers' low-tariff views, and the preferential freight rates contained in the Crow's Nest Pass Agreement of 1897, which had been suspended during the war, were restored. But King's greatest advantage was Arthur Meighen's tactlessness, and the divisions that were emerging within the Progressive ranks. The Conservative leader was nearly as unrelenting in his attacks on the farmer politicians as he was on the Liberals, and that further weakened his party's standing in agricultural areas. At the same time, the Progressives revealed their own disunity and confusion about their role in politics. One wing, led by Crerar and centred in Manitoba, were "Liberals in a hurry," anxious to force their low-tariff views on the Liberals in Ottawa so that they could return to that party. A second wing, which looked to Henry Wise Wood of the United Farmers of Alberta, condemned Liberals and Conservatives equally and insisted that members of Parliament were only responsible to their constituents. These so-called Alberta Progressives rejected Crerar's leadership. These divisions made it possible for King to navigate the turbulent waters of parliamentary politics even without a clear majority.

But King's success in Parliament did not impress the electorate. Voters in the Maritimes had quickly grown disenchanted with King's Liberal government's failure to respond to their needs. The "Maritime Rights Movement," a bipartisan coalition of businessmen, politicians, and even some labour leaders, decided to throw its weight behind the Conservatives. Conservative fortunes were also improving in Ontario, where the Farmer-Labour government proved too inexperienced and too divided to govern effectively. Even in the West, where Progressive divisions and the revival of prosperity weakened the farmers' protest movement, Meighen's party benefited. Only in Quebec, where the Liberals constantly reminded French Canadians of Meighen's conscriptionist past, did King's party hold firm. Thus, in the 1925 election, the voters gave Meighen the largest number of seats—though not a majority.

At this point a deadly contest of political wills and strategies commenced. There could be only one victor. Though defeated at the polls, King, quite legitimately, chose to meet Parliament rather than to resign. He believed that with the support of the greatly reduced Progressive contingent he could continue to govern. Then convincing evidence of scandal and mismanagement in the Customs Department (Quebec Liberals had been receiving kick-backs from rum runners smuggling alcohol into the dry United States) was brought to light. The Progressives, who had long preached the need for political purity, could hardly support this corrupt government.

But before a motion of non-confidence was voted, King requested a dissolution and a new election. Lord Byng, the Governor General, declined the advice, insisting that Meighen, with the largest party, should be given a chance to form a government. King inaccurately declared that the Governor General's action was "unconstitutional." Meighen jumped at the opportunity to regain office. He acted correctly, but perhaps foolishly. Events soon proved that the Liberal King was a skilful strategist and that the Progressives could not be relied upon even to see the Conservative minority government through the session. But, in the end, it was bad luck as much as anything that destroyed the Meighen government: a sleepy Progressive cast a deciding vote against the government when he was paired with an absent Conservative and should not have voted, since pairing was an arrangement whereby both members agreed not to vote. In the inevitable election that now followed King made much of a trumped-up claim that a "constitutional crisis" had been caused by Byng and Meighen, and that the real issue was Canadian self-government. Meighen tried to ignore King's claims, and only too late did he realize that the almost complete collapse of the Progressives meant a Liberal victory. In the 1926 election King won his first majority; it was based on a solid Quebec, a sweeping triumph on the prairies, and important gains in Ontario and the Maritimes.

The Progressive revolt began with a bang and ended in a whimper. Few changes had been made in national economic policies, but the return of agricultural prosperity after 1925 dampened the anger of the farmers. Moreover, farmers continued to control their provincial governments and, through the co-operative movement, began to develop some of their own economic institutions. For a few years times were good on the prairies and the Liberals were given the credit. But westerners had tasted political insurgency, and some, at least, enjoyed the experience. Not everyone was reintegrated into the "old-line parties"; a "Ginger Group" of radicals remained after 1926, and they would form the nucleus of a new revolt once the illusory prosperity of the late twenties passed away.

The revolt of the Maritimes, never so spectacular as that of the farmers, was quelled with almost equal ease and at a minimal price. Rather than insurgency, maritimers had chosen to work through the existing parties, hoping to force a good bargain. Liberals and Conservatives both offered aid at election time, but once they were in office action rarely followed words. What the Maritimes wanted—protection for their steel industry and the restoration of preferential freight rates—ran counter to the interests of central and western Canada. Finally, in 1927, King's new Liberal government appointed a royal commission to examine maritime problems. Its report proposed some modest increases in federal subsidies to the Maritimes and some freight-rate reductions. It ducked the tariff issue. King acted on some of the recommendations, including minor freight-rate changes, increased subsidies, and federal aid to port development. It was not much and could hardly be expected to solve the fundamental structural problems of the maritime economy. But it was apparently sufficient to becalm the maritime revolt. "Anaesthetic has been administered in the form of the Report of the Royal Commission," a Nova Scotia newspaper commented acidly and accurately.

By the late 1920s Mackenzie King had completed his political apprenticeship successfully. He had combined ambition and skill with luck and a loyal Quebec to vanquish all comers. In 1927, Arthur Meighen stepped down. The tiny Independent Labour party, led by J. S. Woodsworth, with its roots in post-war labour unrest, had been contained. Even the women's movement, so full of hope at the war's end, had come to much less than its leaders hoped. The occasional woman elected to public office was hardly more than a token. Some of the old activists battled on, especially against the constitutional provision that barred the way to appointment to the Senate. When the courts finally decided in 1929 that women too were "persons," and therefore eligible for membership in the Senate, King moved to make sure his party reaped the rewards. It was not Nellie McClung or Emily Murphy, seasoned warriors of the suffragist battle, who went to the comfort of the Red Chamber. (Murphy, King thought, was "rather too masculine and possibly a bit too sensational.") He chose a loyal and worthy Liberal woman, Cairine Wilson.

Religion New and Old

If the protest movements of class, region, and gender that enlivened the early post-war years seemed exhausted by the end of the decade, one of the great wartime reforms, prohibition, had also collapsed. Born out of a combination of puritanical moralism, a genuine concern about the problems created by excessive drinking, the Anglo-Saxon desire to Canadianize foreigners, employers' need for a disciplined work force, and, finally, the belief that only a sober country could win the war, prohibition had not been a great success. Quebec, never very firmly on the wagon, slipped off first and quickly experienced an increase in tourist dollars. British Columbia soon followed suit. Prohibition lasted longer elsewhere, but illicit outlets flourished, and doctors found a growing clientele whose ailments required prescription alcohol. Gradually the anti-dry forces gained strength in every province by advancing the simple, demonstrable claim that prohibition did not work. "So much liquor is now smuggled and distributed throughout the province," a Nova Scotia inspector reported in 1925, "in motor cars and by bootleggers that the closing of bars and of blind pigs does not have much effect on the total consumption." But the alternative to prohibition was not a return to the free market. Instead, both wets and drys agreed on the virtue of government regulation and sale, a solution that promised increased revenue for the state. By 1930, only Prince Edward Island remained dry. Whether dependence on alcohol increased under the new regime is debatable. Certainly the dependence of provincial governments on revenue from liquor did. Ironically, those reformers who had advocated the suppression of the liquor traffic as one of a number of social reforms now realized that liquor sales financed those other reforms. Thus evil was turned to good.

Those earnest Protestant reformers who had enthusiastically advocated prohibition and other panaceas as steps towards the establishment of the Kingdom of God on earth must have been dismayed at evidence of backsliding among their countrymen. But by the 1920s many liberal Protestants could rejoice in the success of another of their causes: church union. In June 1925, the Methodists, Congregationalists, and most Presbyterians founded the United Church of Canada. For over two decades church people had argued that if the religious needs of this new country were to be met, scattered congregations served, immigrants Canadianized, and society cleansed, then Protestants, at least, would have to form a common front. When agreement was finally reached there were some Presbyterians who believed that haste had triumphed over good sense, and the desire for large membership rolls over sound doctrine. They stayed out. Nevertheless, the new church, led by Dr. George Pidgeon, came into existence with a following of about two million, compared to about four million Roman Catholics. The Church of England and continuing Presbyterians formed the next largest denominations. Like much else in the 1920s, the new church was more a summing of the past than a new beginning.

In Quebec, too, the old and the new, the religious and the secular, mixed together somewhat uneasily in the social and intellectual ferment of the 1920s. And, as elsewhere, the ferment subsided as the decade progressed. In 1917 Quebec had seemed utterly alienated. The clearest expression of that mood came from a small but influential group of young priests, lawyers, and journalists—the traditional Quebec élite—who founded the monthly journal *L'Action Française* in 1917. Their leader was Abbé Lionel Groulx, a priest-historian who viewed historical study almost as theology: history he saw as the source of a doctrine that would guide French Canadians to an earthly paradise where they would be free of English domination. This was the

After raiding a "blind pig" (illegal bar) at Elk Lake, Ontario, government agents dump 160 kegs of home-brew, under the disconsolate gaze of the townsfolk. But by the 1920s, when this picture was taken, the "noble experiment" was losing ground, and by 1927 almost all the provinces had abandoned prohibition.

theme of a special issue of their magazine entitled *Notre Avenir Politique*, and it formed the plot of a novel, *L'Appel de la Race*, which Groulx published under a pseudonym in 1922. While denying that they actively advocated separation from Canada, Groulx and his companions argued that French Canadians should be prepared—educated—for the eventuality that would become real some day as part of God's unfolding plan. Groulx, once Bourassa's protégé, soon found himself at odds with the editor of *Le Devoir*. Though deeply disenchanted by the events of the war, Bourassa never lost hope that his vision of a bicultural, autonomous Canada would one day be a reality. He condemned the supporters of *L'Action Française* for confusing religion and nationalism and appealed to his compatriots to reject "extreme" nationalism in favour of a pan-Canadian campaign to ensure that Canada was never again dragged into a British war.

Groulx's message never spread much beyond a segment of Montreal's clerical and intellectual community. It was difficult to convince French Canadians that their future was in jeopardy when their politicians, led by Ernest Lapointe, wielded such obvious influence in the governing Liberal party of Ottawa. When the sixtieth anniversary of Confederation arrived in 1927, Groulx had to confess that though Canada was an "anaemic giant" infected with "many germs of dissolution," it might still be revived and reformed. His nationalist movement, at least temporarily, was running out of steam. Prosperity was one reason. But almost as important was the fact that Mackenzie King had taken up part of Bourassa's nationalist program, a part approved by virtually every French Canadian, and had set about implementing it.

"The People of the Twilight"

The material wealth that grew so spectacularly during the early twentieth century was far from equally distributed. The Native people were left out almost completely. If anything their share declined as they were increasingly marginalized, a people without a future. When the century opened, those groups of Native people who lived in the southern regions of the country had already been subdued, brought under treaties, and placed on reservations as wards of the Indian Affairs Branch of the Department of the Interior. The major policy goal of the officials of that bureaucracy was the assimilation of Native peoples into white society—when they were ready. The preparation for that future involved education and agricultural or other settled employment. Education was left largely in the hands of missionaries, who also had a crucial role in the assimilation process: the replacement of traditional religious beliefs and practices by Christianity. The spirit of this policy was plain in a directive sent by the Superintendent-General of Indian Affairs to his agents in 1921: "I have... to direct you to use your utmost endeavours to dissuade the Indians from excessive indulgence in the practice of dancing. You should suppress any dances which cause waste of time, interfere with the occupations of the Indians, unsettle them for serious work, injure their health, or encourage them to sloth or idleness...."

Such traditional ceremonies as the Sun Dance, practised by some prairie tribes, were suppressed, as was the colourful and joyous gift-giving feast known as the potlatch on the north-west coast. Children were separated from their families and sent off to mission schools in utterly unfamiliar surroundings. Men were pressed to give up trapping and hunting in favour of farming, which many Native groups viewed as

On his first western tour, Lord Byng of Vimy—Governor General from 1921 to 1926—met with some of His Majesty's Cree subjects in Edmonton. Everyone turned out for the occasion in full ceremonial style.

women's work. Demoralization and alienation followed. Those who drifted off the reserves into the cities rarely escaped the traps of alcohol and prostitution.

Government policies met with very limited success, though some groups made the transition to modernity. As Indian Affairs Branch budgets were always small, and subject to frequent cuts, the meagre services which Native peoples had been promised in the treaties were stretched very thin. Disease, especially tuberculosis, continued to decimate the population. Alcohol, which Native people were forbidden to buy, continued to be consumed in lethal quantities. Poverty reigned on most reserves. "The new mode of life on the Reserve," a missionary reported at the beginning of the century, "dwelling in filthy houses, badly ventilated, has induced disease; the idle manner of living, being fed by the Government, and having little to do; the poor clothing worn in the winter; badly cooked food, the consciousness that as a race they are fading away." Thirty years later so sympathetic a student of the Native people as Diamond Jenness, chief anthropologist of the National Museum, predicted that they would soon disappear. "Some will endure only a few years longer," he wrote in his classic *The Indians of Canada*, "others, like the Eskimo, may last for several centuries."

With their population in steady decline, pessimism about the future of the Amerindians was well founded. Jenness's tempered optimism about the Inuit, on the other hand, was founded on personal observation. He and Vilhjálmur Stefansson were among the first white men ever seen by the inhabitants of Coronation Gulf in the Canadian Arctic, when they arrived there in 1914 on a scientific expedition. That expedition recorded the survival of the traditional Inuit way of life, unaffected by European values. In 1928 Jenness published his moving account of the long, frigid months that he spent among those gentle northern people. His humane reminiscences, *The People of the Twilight*, concluded with a question whose answer he obviously feared. "Were we the harbingers of a brighter dawn, or only the messengers of ill-omen, portending disaster?"

Yet, by the 1920s there were signs that some leaders of the Native peoples were awakening to the threat their people faced. At the end of the Great War, Lieutenant F. O. Loft, an Ontario Mohawk chief who had served in the Canadian Expeditionary Force like many of his fellows, travelled to London in an attempt to bring the grievances of his people to the attention of the British government. Rebuffed, he returned home to begin organizing the League of Indians of Canada. It was frustrating and often thankless work, but it was continued in subsequent decades by men like the Reverend Edward Ahenakew, a Saskatchewan Cree and ordained Anglican clergyman, Chief Joe Taylor, also from Saskatchewan, and others. Similarly, Northwest Coast groups organized for self-protection and protest in a province where Native peoples' lands seemed to shrink at every whim of the provincial government. Here, too, missionaries and converts to Christianity led the Native peoples' cause. The Reverend Peter Kelly, a Methodist Haida, and Andrew Paull, a Squamish brought up under the influence of the Oblate Fathers, were the most effective leaders of the Native Brotherhood of British Columbia. That organization's main concern was to defend the Native peoples' lands and fishing and hunting rights against the encroachments of white settlers, miners, and loggers.

These new organizations were signs of a resurgence of life among the Native peoples. But it was only a beginning, a small glimmer of light on a dark landscape of disease, deprivation, humiliation, and hostility. Earle Birney, in his 1952 radio play, *The Damnation of Vancouver*, put words into the mouth of his Salish chief that eloquently summed up the Native peoples' fate:

When the strangers came to build in our village
I had two sons.
One died black and gasping with smallpox.
To the other a trader sold a flintlock.
My son gave the gun's height in otter skins.
He could shoot deer now my arrows fainted to reach.
One day he walked into the new whiskey-house
Your fathers built for us.
He drank its madness, he had the gun,
He killed his cousin, my brother's firstborn. . . .
The strangers choked my son with a rope.
From that day there was no growing in my nation.

Canadian Nationalism and the British Commonwealth

By November 11, 1918, most Canadians had had more than enough of involvement in foreign wars. That was doubly true of French Canadians. Yet, at the war's end, Canada had assumed new obligations as a member of the international community. There was, as the prime example, the League of Nations in which Canada had been granted full membership. It very soon became evident that, for successive Canadian governments, membership was almost totally a matter of status. First Robert Borden in 1919 and then Senator Raoul Dandurand, speaking for the Liberal King government in 1922, made it plain that Canada lived "in a fireproof house far from inflammable materials" and felt no automatic obligation to the principle of collective security. High-sounding sentiments, even ambiguously phrased declarations of virtue were permissible; agreement to concrete action was something else. Like their southern neighbours, slumbering in isolation, most Canadians appeared to want a return to "normalcy."

This same mood of withdrawal lay behind Canada's pursuit of autonomy within the British Empire–Commonwealth. The terms of Canada's membership in the Empire remained almost as confused in 1919 as they had been in 1914, and almost no one in Canada was satisfied with that situation. The old pre-war divisions about the road to definition remained. But where Laurier had temporized, King was forced by events to decide. Meighen, as befitted a Conservative, attempted to follow Borden's path: a common imperial foreign policy formulated by a process of "continuous consultation." It worked well enough at the Washington Naval Disarmament Conference of 1921–22, but only because Britain accepted the Canadian view and terminated the Anglo-Japanese Alliance against the advice of the Pacific dominions. The United States wanted the alliance ended, and Meighen placed good relations with the United States at the top of his priority list. But Washington marked an end, not a beginning.

For Mackenzie King domestic harmony, rather than imperial unity, was the main goal to be pursued in foreign and domestic affairs. His strategy was evident during his first term of office. In 1922 the revolutionary government of Turkey denounced the peace treaty signed by its predecessor and threatened to invade Greek-held territory, a place called Chanak in Asia Minor. The British Prime Minister, David Lloyd George, appealed to Canada for assistance in enforcing the peace settlement. King was outraged because the appeal was made publicly. His reply was that he could make no commitment without the approval of Parliament, and that Parliament was in recess. In 1923 King further consolidated his position by insisting at an Imperial Conference that no resolutions were binding unless approved by each dominion parliament. After that there remained only legal details to be cleared up: a fisheries treaty with the United States was signed by Canada without British participation, and plans for a Canadian embassy in Washington were set afoot. In 1926 the Balfour Declaration described Britain and the dominions as equals in a Commonwealth partnership. The final constitutional definition came in the Statute of Westminster in 1931, when King was out of office. Canada's control over its foreign and domestic policy was made complete, though a procedure to amend the British North America Act in Canada had still to be devised, and appeals of Supreme Court decisions to the Judicial Committee of the Privy Council in Britain continued until 1949.

Most of this was mere icing on the cake of parliamentary sovereignty. The essence of King's imperial and foreign policy was his rejection of prior commitments and his repeated insistence that "parliament will decide in the light of existing circumstances." He believed that most Canadians were tired of foreign involvements. He

John W. Dafoe, editor of the *Winnipeg Free Press* from 1901 to 1944, chronicled the foibles, failings, and occasionally, successes of Canadian public leaders. Arch Dale, the paper's brilliant cartoonist, created this composite for Dafoe's sixtieth anniversary as a journalist.

knew, too, that foreign-policy issues divided Canadians deeply. A divided Canada meant a weakened Liberal party, perhaps even a repetition of the 1917 defeat. So he moved cautiously, but determinedly, towards a position of near isolation. Continuing to express his genuine attachment to the British Commonwealth, he manoeuvred Canada into a position of being able to decide alone and completely its obligations to that institution. While the result was hailed by nationalists in Canada, it had the effect of reducing the Commonwealth to virtual powerlessness as an instrument of collective security. That was what most Canadians, especially French Canadians, wanted. Ernest Lapointe, King's powerful Quebec lieutenant, believed that this policy would ensure the Liberals unbroken success in his province.

In following the road to full Canadian autonomy within the Commonwealth, Mackenzie King had adopted the platform designed by Henri Bourassa two decades earlier. No wonder the nationalist movement in Quebec lapsed into near silence by the end of the 1920s. But, equally interesting, the King–Bourassa policy satisfied most English Canadians, too. There were occasional cries from Ontario Conservatives that King had betrayed the Empire, or from isolated internationalists, like John W. Dafoe of the *Winnipeg Free Press*, that withdrawal and isolation would not preserve world peace. But most Canadians preferred to believe that those who lived in fireproof houses had no need for insurance.

Culture and Nationalism

If Abbé Groulx's cultural nationalism, as expressed in the novels, poetry, and historical writing of his followers, had political implications, the same was true of much of
the cultural production of English Canada. The work of the Group of Seven expressed
an increasingly dominant national sentiment. What the Group and its propagandists
contended was that Canada was a North American nation whose art should reflect
that environment and not be governed by inherited traditions. "For Canada to find a
complete racial expression of herself through art a complete break with European traditions was necessary," one of the Group's supporters wrote. He went on to assert that
what was necessary was "a deep-rooted love for the country's natural environment."

Though the mythology of the movement emphasized the Group's struggle for
recognition, success actually came early. By the time of the prestigious 1924 Wembley
exhibition in England, where the Group's work dominated the Canadian collection, the
new painting had been adopted by the National Gallery as "national" art. Here was a
"North American" art that suited the mood of a country weary of European war and
turned in upon itself. That such other artists as David Milne and Ozias Leduc were just
as talented did not win them the attention attracted by the Group of Seven. Jackson
and Harris and the others who presented the Canadian environment in bold strokes
and brilliant colours apparently touched the right nerve and, probably for the first
time, gave painting a leading place in the country's culture. When Emily Carr associated herself with them in the 1930s, even she, who had rarely tasted success, benefited
from the new national aesthetic. Milne may have been a little envious, but he was close
to the mark when he wrote of his countrymen's enthusiasm for the Group of Seven:

Tom Thomson isn't popular for what aesthetic qualities he shows, but because his work is
close enough to representation to get by the average man; besides his subjects are the ones
that have pleasant associations for most of us, holidays, rest, recreation. Pleasant associations,
beautiful subjects, good painting. Then in Canada we like to have our heavens made to order
and in our own image. They mustn't be too good, and above all not too different.

The patriotic promotions of the newly founded Canadian Authors' Association, the
self-conscious Canadianism of *Maclean's* and the *Canadian Forum*, and the Group of
Seven were all part of Mackenzie King's Canada. To some degree they all shared in
the illusory optimism of the last years of the 1920s. Changes in popular culture,

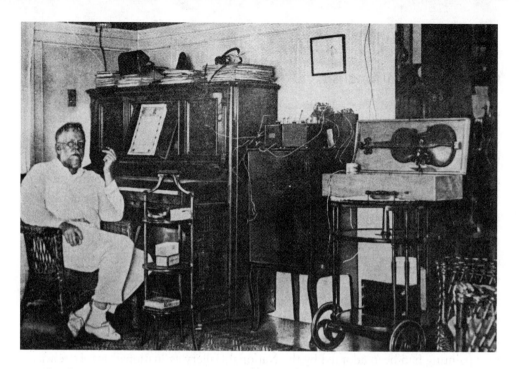

Canadian-born inventor Reginald A. Fessenden (1866–1932). While serving as a wireless expert for the U.S. Weather Service, Fessenden developed the principle of amplitude modulation (AM), the basis of all modern radio and television broadcasting. He made the first public broadcast of voice and music from Brant Rock, Massachusetts, on Christmas Eve 1906. In 1928 the U.S. Radio Trust paid him $2.5 million in recognition of his contributions to radio technology.

based on new technology, also contributed to the relaxed mood of the 1920s, and to Canada's integration in North America.

During the 1920s the automobile, the radio, and the moving picture began to make a profound impact on Canadian lives. The automobile, first as a curiosity, then as a status symbol for the wealthy, was already in use before the war. But in the 1920s mass production and declining prices made it more widely available, both as a means of transportation and for recreation. From about 20,000 registered motor vehicles in 1911, the number rose to nearly 400,000 in 1920 and exceeded 1,000,000 by 1930. In the immediate post-war years many of these cars were manufactured in Canada by such companies as McLaughlin's of Oshawa, but by the end of the decade the industry, by then employing some 13,000 workers, had been almost totally integrated into the U.S. industry—Ford, General Motors, and Chrysler. Not the least important aspect of the impact of the auto on society was the development of a system of good roads at taxpayer expense. The Canada Highways Act of 1919 pointed to the future:

by 1930 the country had built nearly 130,000 kilometres (80,000 miles) of hard-surfaced roads and hundreds of thousands of gravel and dirt.

Radio, too, came into its own after the war. In 1913 the first legislation governing transmission had been passed, and in 1920 the first program was broadcast from Montreal. Soon a number of private stations were established, often in association with newspapers, but sometimes with religious affiliations. Yet most Canadians, by the end of the 1920s, listened to programs that originated in the United States. That problem, and the question of the role of religiously oriented stations, forced the government, in 1928, to establish a royal commission to examine the whole issue of ownership and licensing. Its report, in 1930, surprised many by its strong advocacy of a publicly owned system that would not follow the U.S. dependence on commercials and would encourage the development of Canadian programming.

By the time the problem of radio was examined, the Canadian film industry had virtually disappeared. First accepted as a form of popular entertainment in the United States, the industry had begun to take root in Canada by the early twenties. Yet it had disappeared by the middle of the decade. Plagued by a lack of financing, a small local box office, and difficulties in gaining access to theatres dominated by the U.S. chains, the industry never grew beyond infancy. Consequently, successful and aspiring Canadian actors and actresses and filmmakers rapidly made their way to Hollywood, and Canadians became part of the audience for the flood of films that emerged from California. Attempts were made by both the federal government and some provinces to counteract what was seen by some as a dangerous threat to Canadian culture. But the efforts were feeble attempts to use films for the promotion of patriotism. It was not until the establishment of the National Film Board in 1939 that more systematic policies were developed to create Canadian films. But the NFB's work was confined mainly to documentary films, and almost nothing was done to encourage a feature-film industry.

Thus, in the new areas of popular culture, where expensive technology required either government assistance or enormous markets, Canadians fell increasingly under the influence of the United States. Radio alone was a partial exception, but even the Canadian Broadcasting Corporation, when it was established in 1936, still allowed for commercial programming, including feeds from the United States. It was not until late in the 1930s that the significant impact of radio on Canadian life, especially in politics, became fully evident.

The Thirties: The Bubble Bursts

The collapse of the New York stock market in October 1929 dramatically signalled the end of the shaky prosperity of the post-war years. The Canadian economy began its downward descent into the worst depression in the country's history, one that would indelibly mark two generations of Canadians. In Canada, as elsewhere, the crash was assumed to be temporary, merely another abrupt readjustment in the complicated mechanism of modern capitalism. Both company presidents and politicians alike, and doubtless most other Canadians, agreed with Edward Beatty, the president of the CPR, who, after reviewing the economic problems of 1929, concluded, "It is probably a fact that, when the temporary adverse effects of each shall have run its course, Canadian economic conditions will be that much more soundly based, and it will be found that the way has been cleared for a more vigorous and better bal-

The prairie dustbowl of the 1930s. The drought began in 1929 and continued, on and off, until 1937. Each summer the hot, dry winds carried off more of the rich topsoil, turning the breadbasket of Canada into a land of desolation, and destroying the hopes of those who had arrived in the promised land only a generation earlier.

anced forward movement than has been experienced in the past…." What seemed "temporary" in 1930 became unremitting by 1935. The simple, tragic fact was that no one realized the extent of the crisis that Canada, along with the rest of the industrialized world, faced. What made the crisis in Canada so desperate was that both industrial and agricultural sectors of the economy were hit: the first by the decline in investment and demand, the second by the shrinkage of markets and the ravages of nature. One blow would have been serious; together they amounted to a knock-out.

On the agricultural front the main problem of the early Depression years was the contraction of overseas markets for Canadian grain, especially wheat. During the war and early post-war years, North American grain farmers had increased their share of the European market. By the late 1920s, however, most European countries, in an effort to save their farmers, began to raise tariffs. And by 1928–29 the Soviet Union began to export wheat again. Once the protective trend began and wheat prices fell into decline, markets for Canadian grain contracted.

Nor was the trend towards protection limited to agricultural products. As virtually every country attempted to fight the economic crisis by protecting the home market, exporting countries like Canada suffered severely. The enactment of the Hawley–Smoot tariff in the United States in 1930 was just one of several measures that led to a drastic decline in Canadian exports which, prior to the crash, accounted for more than a third of the country's national income. With the shrinking of export markets for grain, pulp and paper, minerals, and manufactured goods, employment disappeared and farming became nearly futile. A bushel of Number 1 Northern, which sold for $1.03 in 1928, dipped to $0.29 four years later. The gross value of pulp-and-paper and base-metal production was more than halved in the same period. While manufacturing was less dependent on overseas buyers, the shrinkage of purchasing power at home meant that these industries, too, slowed down. Farm-machinery manufacturers, the automobile industry, and steel producers all retrenched by withholding new investment and laying off workers. By the summer of 1930 more than 390,000 workers were reported jobless. That represented nearly 13 per cent of the labour force; by 1933 the percentage of unemployed had doubled (26 per cent), and it fell back to the 1930 level only once before the outbreak of war in 1939.

And these figures do not include agricultural labour; a further measure of the destructive impact of the Great Depression can be seen in the decline of incomes. Between 1928 and 1933 annual per-capita income in Canada declined by 48 per cent, from $471 to $247. Saskatchewan led with a drop of 72 per cent, from $478 to $135;

For young, unemployed men, riding the rods became a familiar activity during the Depression. In the summer of 1935, men in the government's relief camps rebelled and organized an "On to Ottawa" trek to protest their lot; here a group of trekkers change trains at Kamloops. The excursion ended in riot and bloodshed in Regina.

Alberta followed with a 61 per cent fall, Manitoba 49 per cent and B.C. 47 per cent. Ontario, where the highest per-capita incomes were enjoyed, declined by 44 per cent, with Prince Edward Island, Quebec, New Brunswick, and Nova Scotia always at the lower end of the scale, falling between 49 per cent and 36 per cent. By every economic yardstick these were years of desperation for the jobless and for most prairie farmers, though there were marked regional variations.

Hardest hit was the prairie wheat belt. There market declines were followed by natural disaster. With wheat prices down near the thirty-cent-per-bushel mark, farmers discovered that the debt burdens assumed in the previous decades were unbearable. A University of Saskatchewan study reported in 1934 that, "To pay the interest on the present farm debt of Saskatchewan would have required about 4/5 of all the wheat available for sale from the 1933 crop, and for payment of farm taxes 2/3 of this wheat." Even when there was a crop, the market prices were too low to cover production costs.

In 1937, there was virtually no crop in Saskatchewan, two-thirds of the province's rural population was forced to seek public assistance—"relief," as it was called—and more than 95 per cent of rural municipalities were at the brink of bankruptcy. Indeed, by that year the solvency of the entire province was in serious doubt.

Sun, wind, and grasshoppers produced crop failure. The drought that struck the prairies in the mid-thirties was unprecedented. Years of adequate rainfall had disguised the unsuitability of some prairie land for grain growing. Now those lands, or at least the fertile top soil, blew away, piling up against fences and buildings, mixing with this- tles and tumbleweeds, about all that the parched earth produced. When the wind relented and the red-rimmed sun blazed through, it was often only to be obscured by the clouds of grasshoppers that swept over the plains in search of the last blade of wheat or grass. These locusts were especially devastating in 1937, a crop year that also experienced hail and dust. As one journalist recalled the last weeks before the harvest:

The grasshoppers came in clouds, curiously from the north, in concentrations never before experienced in Canada. Huge swarms appeared over Saskatoon and Regina in late July. They devoured everything in their paths as they ate their way out of sight. They travelled in narrow paths, but only the broken straw of what had promised to be a bumper crop was left behind. Then, seemingly from nowhere, came a second and even greater invasion.

Reduced to relief, the costs of which the province could not afford, prairie farmers lined up for a monthly food allowance of ten dollars and a ninety-eight-pound bag of flour for a family of five. Though the amount increased slightly in the late thirties, so too did the severity of granting conditions. Nor did relief meet unforeseen needs and tragedies. That, and the humiliation felt by those who had helped open up a new country and now faced disaster, was revealed in one of hundreds of letters received by R. B. Bennett, Conservative Prime Minister from 1930 to 1935, in those desperate years. An Alberta farmer wrote in 1933:

My crop is entirely gone,... and my wife is very sick... she has a tumor and as she has some terrible homorrhages which made her very anemic, an operation as inadvisable.... As you are aware the past three years have been very trying for farmers and ranchers. The price of products being below the costs of production, so with sickness also I have no money. Last week I enquired about relief.... I have been humiliated and sent from pillar to post, just as if I were a criminal or something. I have lived on my farm, or ranch in the old days for over 30 years, 31 years next March to be exact....Have paid taxes all the time, have helped several hundred people and yet, when I am frantic with despair what happens?...For my wife's sake I am asking you to help me....Only the most dire necessity would have induced me to apply for it. There is also the children, two of whom are of school age, 12 and 14 years of age. My wife has been ordered milk, beefsteak, orange juice, etc., and some certain medicines. She must build her strength up. I don't want to see her die by inches before my eyes.

With almost no protective social-security measures—a small old-age-pension scheme had been started in 1927, but nothing for the unemployed, the sick, or the destitute—farm and urban workers were thrown on the charity of private and public institutions. Many men took to "riding the rods," hitching rides on freight cars moving across the country in search of work, food, or relief from the boredom of idleness. The Bennett government, in an effort to provide some work and to control these moving gangs of men, established work camps in British Columbia. By early 1935 deep dissatisfaction had developed and some 1,800 men, organized by the Communist-sponsored Relief Camp Workers' Union, set off on a trek to Ottawa to demonstrate against a government that seemed unwilling to deal with the unemployment problem. They reached Regina before Prime Minister Bennett agreed to meet their leaders. And that meeting was little more than an acrimonious exchange of abuse. Then, on July 1, the RCMP moved in and arrested the leaders. In the ensuing riot one policeman was killed and many others were injured. The trek was halted. The problem remained.

Virtually every urban centre experienced unrest and disturbances, usually less serious than the Regina Riot. The Toronto city police were especially assiduous in checking every sign of suspected subversion, especially if university professors were involved. Uneasy public authorities often acted hastily, claiming the need to control a growing Communist menace. The arrest and imprisonment of the principal Communist party leaders in 1931, and the subsequent attempt on party chief Tim Buck's life in Kingston penitentiary, only encouraged the suspicion that what Prime Minister Bennett called the "iron heel" was the only answer the government had for the social discontent which the Depression nurtured.

Nor was it only supposed Communist-inspired activities that governments met with hostility during these troubled years. In almost every province, efforts to organize workers, especially the unskilled, or strikes by organized workers, were resisted by employers often supported by governments. The Cape Breton coal fields continued to be the scene of brutal conflict. A strike in the coal mines in Estevan, Saskatchewan, led to bloodshed in 1931 when the RCMP fired on a strikers' march. There were almost equally bitter struggles in the mines of British Columbia, the textile factories of Quebec, and the New Brunswick lumber camps and mills. But perhaps the most publicized conflict took place in one of the new industries where a new union attempted to gain a foothold. It was in the automobile industry in Oshawa, Ontario, where the American-based Congress of Industrial Organizations began its campaign to unionize non-skilled workers in 1937. The reputation of the CIO and its leader, John L. Lewis, preceded it to Ontario—especially the use of the so-called "sit-down" strike. Ontario business leaders, and their friend Premier Mitchell Hepburn, were determined to keep the CIO out of the province. Though Hepburn had been elected as a reformer in 1934, he had only hostility for the new unionism. When the United Automobile Workers, a CIO affiliate, began signing up General Motors' workers and then called a strike for union recognition, Hepburn declared that the CIO had no place in Ontario. When Ottawa rejected his appeal for the use of the RCMP to break the strike, he organized his own police force, "the sons of Mitches." But the company saw that a compromise was a better way out than a violent struggle, and an agreement was signed. In the short run, however, Hepburn had strengthened his hold on office by his vociferous opposition to the CIO.

Yet despite labour unrest and the hostility of business and government to unions, the 1930s was not a period that witnessed a large number of strikes and lock-outs. There was simply too much unemployment and too much insecurity to allow workers to take radical actions that might jeopardize their ill-paid jobs. Nor were workers much attracted to radical political movements, such as Communism. Some of the disenchanted on farms and in factories expressed their discontent at the polls, either by voting against the government in office, or by throwing their support behind one or another of the new political parties that sprang up. The very appearance of these groups was evidence that the economic and constitutional orthodoxy of the old parties no longer satisfied a significant portion of the voters.

The Politics of Unrest

As the Depression settled in, late in 1929, Mackenzie King's Liberals appeared to have a firm hold on office. Neither the Government nor the Conservative Opposition, led by R. B. Bennett, believed that the economic downturn called for any unusual measures. Both proposed tariff changes. In keeping with their traditions, the Liberals proposed tariff adjustments designed to reduce duties on a few items while raising them on others. Beyond that Charles Dunning, the Minister of Finance, budgeted for a surplus. The provinces were left to deal with the social problems created by the economic collapse. Bennett, also in keeping with his party's traditions, argued that higher levels of protection were needed to preserve the Canadian market for Canadians until other countries, notably the United States, lowered their tariffs.

King thought that the tariff issue was a good one on which to face the country. The election of 1930 was fought largely on the tariff, though King's ill-considered remark that his government would not give five cents to a provincial Conservative administration was effectively used by the Opposition. R. B. Bennett, to the astonishment of most Canadians, emerged from the election as the clear victor.

The new Conservative Prime Minister, a New Brunswicker who had made his fortune as a corporation lawyer in western Canada, was a man of enormous energy. A large, stern, Methodist bachelor, Bennett had little ability to delegate authority and slight respect for those who dissented from his views. Though a kindly and charitable man in private life—he often sent personal donations to those who appealed directly to him—he had the self-made man's attitude to social distress: self-help was better than public assistance. His roaring denunciations of real and imagined radicals soon earned him the dislike of those Canadians who needed more than sermons to deal with their distress. Bennett's wing collar and top hat, together with his ample form, came to symbolize the bloated capitalist in many a caricature.

During the first four years of his term, Bennett sought to restore prosperity with traditional economic policies. He raised the tariff to an unprecedented level, claiming that this was a necessary step in "blasting" open the markets of the world. Then, in 1932, an Imperial Economic Conference was called at his suggestion in Ottawa. He hoped that Britain and the dominions would agree to the establishment of an imperial free trading area, protected against the rest of the world. Britain, in particular, had trading interests that reached far beyond the Empire, and found this proposal quite unacceptable and Bennett's bluster offensive. Though some tariff changes were accepted, the conference was largely a failure, especially since it contributed to the protectionist trends that were strangling international trade. As the Depression deepened, Bennett, without departing from his free-enterprise view of the role of government in the economy, did increase payments to the provinces for the relief of unemployment. So, too, his government sponsored legislation establishing the Bank of Canada, adding an important weapon to the central government's fiscal and mon-

J. S. Woodsworth, posing with his daughter at their Winnipeg home. In 1904, Woodsworth moved from the regular Methodist ministry to social work among western Canada's new immigrants and the poor. An adamant pacifist and labour supporter, he was the first leader of the CCF.

etary arsenal. The work camps in British Columbia were a further attempt by the Conservatives to deal with unemployment. But by 1934, with growing unrest in the country, evidence of the government's declining popularity, and no sign that the Depression was lifting, Bennett was forced to begin rethinking his approach to economic and social policy.

Discontent with the Bennett government took a variety of forms. One, very close to home, was an attack on the spread between wholesale prices charged to large and small firms, which led to huge profits for some large companies and serious hardship for many small businesses. That attack was led by H. H. Stevens, a member of Bennett's own cabinet. In 1934 Stevens was made chairman of a royal commission authorized to investigate the price-spread issue. Much of the evidence it heard was damaging to the country's leading retailers and manufacturers. Stevens soon became recklessly outspoken in his criticisms of these firms. An angry Prime Minister forced his resignation from Cabinet in response to pressure from businessmen. This was only one sign of the growing disarray of the Conservative party, which was already evident from a series of party defeats at the provincial level.

Then there was the emergence of new, unorthodox political movements. One was the Co-operative Commonwealth Federation, soon known as the CCF. Founded at Calgary in 1932, this coalition of farmers, labour leaders, and intellectuals provided itself with an ominous-sounding program the following year. The "Regina Manifesto," prepared by a group of radical university professors, called for the implementation of a number of measures that would make government responsible for social and economic planning. It promised unemployment and health insurance, public housing, agricultural price supports, and laws to protect farmers against their creditors. But the new party's socialism was most clearly revealed in its advocacy of public ownership of leading industries and financial institutions. As its first leader the party chose the veteran radical and parliamentarian J. S. Woodsworth, who, since 1921, had been the member for Winnipeg North. The party's founders hoped to build widespread popular support by affiliating with farm and labour groups, but the latter proved very cautious. The beginnings were solid, but growth proved slow.

The mushroom growth of the Social Credit movement provided a startling contrast. Unlike the CCF, which had support in both central Canada and the West, Social Credit's origins were entirely western, almost entirely Albertan. The doctrine itself had been devised by an English engineer, Major C. H. Douglas, who argued that economic depressions did not result from over-production, but rather from under-consumption—the result of currency and credit shortages. That deficiency could be overcome by issuing a "social dividend" which, by increasing purchasing power, would lead to economic revival. Such an inflationary doctrine had a natural attraction for farmers, whose heavy debt load convinced them of the need for an increase in the money supply. In the early thirties Social Credit ideas began to circulate among members of the United Farmers of Alberta, but their political leaders, who had held office since 1921, remained faithful to the same monetary orthodoxy as the old parties.

What the UFA government rejected was accepted by the Calgary schoolteacher turned radio evangelist, William Aberhart. Since the early thirties, "Bible Bill" Aberhart had been using the new technology of radio to broadcast his fundamentalist Protestant message to a widening circle of prairie listeners. The misery the Depression created around him, especially the plight of his unemployed high-school graduates, turned his mind to social and economic questions. The essential simplicity of Social Credit economics appeared to offer a solution almost as apocalyptic as his biblical messages. His Sunday broadcasts soon began to mix religion with economics, something that social-gospel ministers had been doing for decades on the prairies. By 1935 the UFA government found itself facing a growing popular movement led by a political neophyte, who himself refused to run for the legislature, claiming his ideas were non-partisan. In the provincial election of that year, Aberhart's followers triumphed easily on the promise to abolish poverty in the midst of plenty by the application of Social Credit policies. Aberhart was called upon to form a government, and he later won a seat in the legislature in a by-election.

Once in office, the new premier found it difficult to transform the generalities of his message into concrete measures. Not the least of his problems was the constitutional one: the federal government controlled the fiscal and monetary powers that would be necessary to implement Social Credit ideas. At first Aberhart temporized. Then he had several measures enacted providing for a social dividend, restricting banking activities and debt collection, and regulating the press. Nearly all these measures were found unconstitutional by the Supreme Court in 1938. Aberhart now urged Social Crediters to work to win office in Ottawa, while he set about providing honest, efficient, and generally rather conservative government in Alberta. With the discovery of rich petroleum deposits at Leduc in the 1940s, Albertans were provided with a social dividend that promised even greater abundance than Major Douglas's doctrine—and one that Aberhart's successors found much easier to administer.

Finally, there was the emergence of a new political party in Quebec. The Union Nationale was a coalition of Conservatives and a number of young Liberals who were disenchanted with the conservatism of the Taschereau Liberals. Maurice Duplessis, a long-time Conservative, was an effective organizer and orator. The young Liberals, calling themselves L'Action Libérale Nationale, provided a program that was at once progressive and nationalist, focusing on the needs of urban dwellers and calling for provincial control of the electricity "trust." Duplessis chose instead to concentrate on the evidence of extensive corruption in the forty-year-old Liberal administration. His effective use of this evidence, combined with the discontent created by the economic crisis, brought Duplessis and his coalition to power in 1936. He rapidly clipped the wings of his reformist allies, introduced a series of measures which assisted hard-pressed farmers, and consolidated his political base. He ingratiated himself with Catholic church authorities by enacting a "Padlock Law" that allowed him to close buildings that he judged were being used for "subversive" activities. He won the support of nationalists by loudly defending Quebec's autonomy against real

During the Depression, Alberta preacher-evangelist William Aberhart denounced the "Fifty Big Shots" who controlled the banking system; his Social Credit government promised every adult Albertan a $25-a-month "social dividend." The Social Crediters swept to power in 1935.

and imagined federal infringements. His Union Nationale party had become conservative in everything but name.

By 1935, the irrefutable evidence that the Depression was not going to disappear, combined with the declining fortunes of the federal Conservatives, convinced Prime Minister Bennett of the need for a dramatic new departure. His model was Franklin Roosevelt's New Deal. Without consulting his Cabinet, the Prime Minister took to the air waves and in a series of addresses set out the general lines of his own "new deal." These reform measures, he claimed, were the necessary response to the "crash and thunder of toppling capitalism." His Cabinet, the Opposition parties, and the Canadian people were astounded at this conversion, one which many suspected had taken place at the death bed. Bennett now met Parliament and presented his hurriedly prepared legislation. It provided for unemployment insurance, minimum wages and maximum hours of work, and new fair-trade-practices legislation, and established a grain board to regulate wheat prices. These proposals met with little opposition from the other political parties, whose members were anxious to get on with the inevitable election. But the 1935 election revealed that Bennett's eleventh-hour reforms had been too late. The government was roundly defeated. The Liberals were re-elected with a comfortable majority, but the popular vote told a different story. The Liberals gained no larger a percentage of the vote in this victory than they had had in the 1930 defeat. Voters who deserted Bennett went, for the most part, to the new parties, as Social Credit, CCF, and even H. H. Stevens' Reconstruction party all gained seats. Though King was the official winner, his Liberal party was obviously on probation.

The new King government offered little to those who had voted for change. Bennett's "new deal" legislation was referred to the Supreme Court, which found its most important provisions unconstitutional. No new social policy initiatives were taken. A trade agreement with the United States, the negotiation of which had been begun by the Conservatives, was ratified. Beyond that the government seemed almost completely unwilling to challenge the bonds of fiscal orthodoxy or constitutional restraint. It was virtually helpless as a result. But as the economy again dipped in 1937, and the extent of personal suffering and institutional bankruptcy spread, King concluded that at least the appearance of action was necessary. He appointed a royal commission.

The Royal Commission on Dominion-Provincial Relations, or the Rowell–Sirois Commission as it was best known, had a mandate to examine the distribution of constitutional powers and the financial arrangements of the federal system. Judicial decisions since the 1920s had left the provinces with heavy responsibilities in social fields and the federal government with access to the largest sources of revenue. The commission's task was to find a new constitutional equilibrium that would distribute revenues and responsibilities in conformity with the needs of an industrial society. Its work was not welcomed everywhere: premiers Hepburn, Duplessis, and Aberhart were loud in their opposition, while other provincial premiers worried about the potential centralist thrust of the commission. In 1940, its major recommendations, which included federal responsibility for unemployment insurance and the establishment of a system of federal adjustment grants to the provinces, were rejected by the largest provinces, led by Ontario. But by that date the outbreak of another world war made a rearrangement of federal–provincial revenue sharing a necessity, at least on an *ad hoc* basis. Moreover, by then King had won the approval of the provinces for a constitutional amendment giving Ottawa the power to enact unemployment-insurance legislation.

The King government also moved cautiously towards a more interventionist approach to economic management. Leading members of the public service—O. D. Skelton, Clifford Clark, and some younger Liberals—insisted that the counter-cyclical doctrines of the British economist John Maynard Keynes were practical. That meant that the time-honoured goal of the balanced budget had to be jettisoned and deficit financing accepted as a means of "priming the pump." If consumer purchasing power was increased, the demand for goods and services would get the unemployed back to work. By 1938 the federal government was financing a variety of work projects, supporting a costly youth-training program, and contributing substantial subsidies to house building and other construction projects.

"In these days," the recently converted Minister of Finance stated in 1939, "if the people as a whole, and business in particular, will not spend, government must.... The old days of complete *laissez-faire*, and the-devil-take-the-hindmost, have gone for ever." Within months renewed world war brought unprecedented increases in government activities and expenditures. With it came an end to the years of deprivation, unemployment, and human despair.

The Return of International Anarchy

Canadians, like virtually every other people in the industrialized world, were almost exclusively preoccupied with domestic economic problems during the 1930s. The trend towards withdrawal from international commitments, already strong in the previous decade, simply accelerated, so that by the mid-thirties the supporters of collective security formed a small minority. For every John W. Dafoe, whose *Winnipeg Free Press* consistently called for support of the League of Nations, there were several J. S. Woodsworths or Henri Bourassas who favoured Canadian neutrality in any future European conflict. Bennett, perhaps, and King certainly, were closer to the neutralist position than to that of the supporters of collective security, and in that they read the mood of the country accurately. Consequently, Canada played a minor, unheroic role in the international conflicts that marked the drift towards a new world war.

Bennett's Conservative government, though its rhetoric was pro-imperial, followed the main foreign-policy lines laid down in the 1920s. It accepted the 1931 Statute of Westminster, which set the capping stone on the development of Canadian autonomy. At the League of Nations, in Geneva, Conservative-appointed delegates spoke the same non-committal phrases mouthed by their Liberal predecessors. Since O. D. Skelton, the Under-Secretary of State for External Affairs and a confirmed isolationist, remained the power behind the foreign-policy throne no matter which party was in power, that consistency was hardly surprising.

When Japan invaded Manchuria in 1931 Canada stated that it was unwilling to support any active resistance. The ominous rise of Hitler to power in 1933 hardly evoked a ripple of reaction. Nor was the new Liberal government prepared to act any differently. When the Canadian delegate at Geneva expressed support for oil sanctions against Mussolini's Italy, in retaliation against that country's invasion of Ethiopia, he was repudiated. King gave full support to the policy of appeasement adopted by the European powers in response to Hitler's increasing aggressiveness. When the Spanish Civil War broke out in the summer of 1936, King's government turned a blind eye to what was evidently a dress rehearsal for renewed world war. In Spain General Franco, supported by Hitler, challenged the legitimacy of the Communist-supported government of the republic. Despite their government's attitude of neutrality some 1,300 Canadians volunteered to fight for Spanish democracy, as members of the Mackenzie–Papineau battalion. Among them was the radical Montreal medical doctor Norman Bethune, who organized a mobile blood-transfusion service to assist the wounded in the failing republican cause. From Spain Bethune would move on to China, where he gave his services, and his life, to the forces of Mao Zedong struggling to overthrow the authoritarian government of General Chiang Kai-shek.

Mackenzie King's attitude during the Spanish Civil War reflected the sympathy of

Doctors Norman Bethune (right) and Richard Brown with soldiers of the Eighth Route Army, North China, probably in 1938. Inspired by a visit to the Soviet Union in 1935, Bethune became a dedicated Communist, and when the Spanish Civil War broke out he went to Spain to organize a mobile blood-transfusion service, the first of its kind. "Spain and China," he wrote, "are part of the same battle," and in 1938 he joined the rebel forces under Mao Zedong; he served as a surgeon, teacher, and propagandist until his death from septicemia in November 1939.

many Catholic Quebecers for Franco, as well as his own naïveté about Hitler's intentions. Believing that the Nazi dictator was just a "simple German peasant" who had only the well-being of his country at heart, King hoped that Germany's appetite could be quickly satiated. That self-delusion was increased by a visit he paid to Hitler in 1937.

Few dissented. When King, once a critic of a common imperial foreign policy, fell completely into line with Prime Minister Neville Chamberlain's efforts to appease Hitler at the expense of democratic Czechoslovakia, at Munich early in 1938, there were few critics. The lonely voice of the *Winnipeg Free Press* asked, "What's the Cheering For?"

King, and those who supported him, justified the policy of appeasement on two grounds. In the first place, it was argued, Germany had been punished too severely at the end of the Great War, and certain readjustments were necessary. Hitler's authoritarianism and aggressive tactics might be questionable, but a stable Germany was desirable as a counterweight to the power of Stalin's Soviet Union. Better the Nazis than the Communists. This argument was advanced with special enthusiasm in Catholic circles in Quebec. "More than two million Russians have already fallen victim to Lenin's work," *L'Action Catholique* declared in 1933, "and the Red oligarchy is not finished. Hitler and Mussolini say with a certain good sense: it is better to hammer than to be hammered; and they hammer."

National unity was the second ground on which King's government supported appeasement. Whatever attitude Québécois in particular but many other Canadians, too, adopted towards Fascism and Nazism—and the Canadian Fascist movement was very small—no one wanted another war. Quebecers especially believed that war would merely mean that Canada would again be tugged by Britain's apron strings. And that, as in the first war, would lead to conscription for overseas service. The spectre of 1917 had never been allowed to vanish in Quebec, especially since Liberal politicians found it a useful ghost to raise against the feeble Conservative party at election time.

Thus, as the almost inevitable collapse of the international order approached, King, like a good general, continued to fight the previous war. He would keep the country together—and he would avoid the troubles of 1917 and the near destruction of the Liberal party—by refusing to commit Canada to any action that could be interpreted as a willingness to fight again. His government even refused admission to those Jewish refugees who, fleeing the certain death of Nazi concentration camps, sought safety in Canada. Again and again the old formula, "Parliament will decide in the light of existing circumstances," was trotted out as a substitute for a foreign policy. Yet King never really doubted that should a European war again break out Canada would be involved once more. Hoping against hope for peace, he skilfully manoeuvred his country and his party into such a position that, when the dreaded day came in September 1939, it would enter the war united.

Hitler's invasion of Poland proved finally and conclusively that the German dictator could be neither appeased nor trusted. Britain declared war. True to his word, King called upon Parliament to decide, and, seven days after Britain entered the war, Canada signed up. But from the outset—in contrast to 1914—Canada's participation had a clearly specified limit. King, and even more emphatically, Ernest Lapointe, on behalf of the French-Canadian Liberals, stated that the war would be fought on the basis of voluntary enlistment. There would be no conscription for overseas service. That said, Canada entered a world war for the second time in twenty-five years.

Appeasement had kept the country united. It had not prevented war. That was what a solemn John W. Dafoe meant when he wrote towards the end of 1939:

I have postponed my departure for a day in order to see my son, Van, off to the wars. I met the troop train at Smiths Falls on Tuesday morning and accompanied it to Montreal. They were a fine lot of men, and I felt pretty sad seeing them going overseas to finish the job that we thought was finished twenty years ago if the achievements of the army had been properly seconded by the statesmen.

World War Again

Canadians entered the Hitler war in a more sombre mood than the one that had prevailed in 1914. They had been living with hard times that made the easy patriotism of an earlier generation difficult. They remembered the horrors of the earlier war. That mood translated into the limited war effort that the King government planned in the early months of hostilities, an effort that seemed appropriate for a "phony war" when nothing seemed to happen. But that complacency was shaken when the Battle of Britain opened in 1940, when France fell, and Dunkirk was evacuated. The real war had begun, and its outcome was highly uncertain.

Yet before the King administration could concentrate its undivided attention on the military war, it had first to settle certain issues on the home front. Some of King's political enemies saw the war as an opportunity to destroy him. He, in turn, saw it as a chance to settle once and for all the fate of his two provincial tormenters, Maurice Duplessis and Mitchell Hepburn.

In October 1939, Duplessis dissolved his province's legislature and called an election. The issue, he contended, was Quebec's autonomy and the threat to it from Ottawa in the name of the war effort. Led by Ernest Lapointe, the federal Liberals entered the provincial campaign at full speed. The goal was to defeat Duplessis; their weapon, in addition to a full campaign war chest, was Lapointe's threat that if Duplessis was returned he and the other Quebec ministers would resign. French Canadians would then be left unprotected in Ottawa. Once again Lapointe repeated his "no conscription" pledge. The Quebec voters responded sympathetically to Lapointe's appeal, rejecting the Union Nationale, temporarily as events proved, in favour of the provincial Liberals. Ernest Lapointe, who had only a short time to live, had won a decisive victory.

Bomb Aimer, C. Charlie, Battle of the Ruhr: a watercolour (1943) by Carl Fellman Schaefer. In peacetime a painter of haunting rural landscapes, Schaefer served as an official war artist from 1943 to 1946. An RCAF flight lieutenant, he experienced the fury of aerial bombardment at first hand.

The next engagement on the domestic front was in Ontario. There, in early 1940, King's nemesis, Mitchell Hepburn, won the approval of the provincial Conservatives for a resolution declaring that the federal government was not prosecuting the war effort with sufficient vigour. That was a code word for a conscription call—or so Mackenzie King chose to interpret it. With uncharacteristic decisiveness King struck back, dissolved Parliament, and called a wartime election. With the Tories advocating "national government," harking back to the Unionist coalition of 1917, the Liberals responded with the national-unity theme and, especially in Quebec, repeated the pledge of "no conscription." Once again King was victorious and the Opposition parties were humbled. The Liberal Prime Minister was never in a stronger position than the one in which he found himself in December 1940. Politics could now be set aside in favour of organizing the country for war. Or so it seemed.

Recruiting and the planning of wartime production were the first orders of the day. Once again Canadian factories began to hum, and unemployment quickly disappeared. Able-bodied men and women were soon in short supply as previously idle factories turned to the production of Bren guns, military aircraft, tanks, and ships. A deflated economy rapidly reinflated, and commodities that had once glutted the market fell into short supply. Rationing of sugar, meat, and gasoline was introduced, wages and prices frozen. Most striking, perhaps, was the enormous increase in the number of women who entered the labour force—as they had done in the earlier war. "Rosie the Riveter" in the munitions plants was joined by her sisters in virtually every area of the manufacturing and service industries, earning higher wages than ever before. Union organization, which had stagnated in the 1930s, now flourished both because of labour shortages and because new labour legislation recognized collective-bargaining rights. By 1945 the number of unionized workers in Canada had doubled, and a substantial proportion of the increase was among women.

By 1941 more than 250,000 men and some 2,000 women had joined the army. When victory finally came in 1945, over a million Canadians had seen service in the armed forces. Nearly 750,000 men and women had enrolled in the army, more than 230,000 men and 17,000 women in the Royal Canadian Air Force, and almost 100,000 men and 6,500 women in the Royal Canadian Navy. Casualties were very heavy, especially in the army and the RCAF. Though there were fewer fatal casualties than in the First World War, still 42,042 Canadians lost their lives in the Hitler war.

From the outset of the war the importance of the neutral United States to the outcome of the conflict was obvious. Prior to the Japanese attack on Pearl Harbor on December 7, 1941, Canada devoted much diplomatic energy to winning its southern neighbour to the sympathetic support of the Allies. President Roosevelt and his closest advisers never doubted that the Allied cause was the American cause, and that the defence of North America required Canadian co-operation. This belief led to the Ogdensburg Agreement of 1940 establishing the Permanent Joint Board of Defence, followed early in 1941 by the Hyde Park Declaration, whereby financial arrangements were made that allowed Canada to finance the war materials that were being provided for Great Britain under the lend-lease agreement between the United States and Britain. Both these steps were important for the success of the war effort. Both also marked Canada's passage from the British to the U.S. sphere of influence.

During the first years of the war, the Canadian army remained in Britain, prepared to defend that island against threatened invasion. Once that threat passed the "real" action, for which Canadians on the home front yearned, began. First there was the tragedy of Hong Kong, where Canadian troops had been sent in a futile attempt to defend the territory against the Japanese. (At home Canadian citizens of Japanese origin were evicted from their west-coast homes, their properties confiscated, and the community sent to camps in the interior soon after Pearl Harbor.) In the autumn

Early in 1942, when Japan had joined the war, the Canadian government moved to dispossess and relocate all British Columbians of Japanese origin, even those who were Canadian citizens; families were split up and whatever property they could not carry was disposed of by the government. This was the culmination of decades of anti-Asiatic feeling on the Pacific coast.

of 1942, the Second Canadian Infantry Division suffered devastating casualties in the ill-fated raid on Dieppe. Next came Sicily and the hard slogging up the boot of Italy, leading to the fall of Rome in the summer of 1944. At last the invasion of France was undertaken, with the First Canadian Army, commanded by General H. D. G. Crerar, playing a major role. But the cost was unexpectedly high. As the casualty lists lengthened and the call for reinforcements grew more insistent, the ghost of conscription returned to haunt Mackenzie King, and to revive the political wars.

Conscription by Halves

Mackenzie King thought, or at least hoped, that the conscription issue had been buried in an all-party agreement, at the war's outset, that voluntary enlistment was the best policy. But by early 1942 that consensus had disintegrated. Arthur Meighen had resigned from the Senate to resume the leadership of the Conservative party, relinquished fifteen years earlier. His policy was conscription, a policy with a growing appeal in English-speaking Canada. King decided that the only way to undercut Meighen was to hold a national plebiscite asking the people to release the government from its pledge not to introduce conscription. There was some resistance to the plan among his Quebec ministers, but Louis St. Laurent, who had replaced Ernest Lapointe, accepted the new policy. In English Canada the forces supporting an affirmative vote were overwhelming. Among French-speaking Canadians, who felt betrayed, opposition was even more powerful. The outcome of the first crisis was exactly what Mackenzie King had most feared: a country starkly divided along cultural lines. As he looked at the returns, he confided to his diary:

I thought of Durham's report on the state of Quebec when he arrived there after the Rebellion of 1837–38, and said he found two nations warring in the bosom of a single state. That would be the case in Canada, as applied to Canada as a whole, unless the whole question of conscription from now on is approached with the utmost care.

On D-Day—June 6, 1944—the 9th Canadian Infantry Brigade went ashore at Bernières-sur-Mer, Normandy, marking the long-awaited beginning of the liberation of Europe from Nazi Germany's domination. Photo by Gilbert A. Milne.

Tank Advance, Italy: an oil (1944) by Lawren P. Harris. The artist, son of Group of Seven founder Lawren Harris, served with the 5th Division in Italy as an official war artist. The inscription on the reverse reads, in part, "Tanks of the 3rd Cdn Regt (GGHG) moving into action...in the Melfa River area. Ruins of Abbe di Montecassino on Monastery Hill in background."

King, with his sense of history, had not yet played his final card. Though his government had been released from the no-conscription pledge, the Prime Minister contended that the time had not yet arrived to jettison the voluntary system. There were some rumblings in his cabinet: J. L. Ralston, the Minister of National Defence, offered his resignation, but it was not accepted. King prevailed with a policy that was a masterpiece of calculated ambiguity: "Not necessarily conscription, but conscription if necessary." The meaning of "necessary" was left undefined.

For some "necessary" meant the obvious: if the voluntary-recruitment system failed to produce the required reinforcements, compulsion would be adopted. By the autumn of 1944, the military was convinced that that point had been reached. The Minister of National Defence agreed. But for King "national unity"—and Liberal-party unity—was a prior necessity. If he accepted Ralston's advice, he would lose his Quebec following. King concluded that one last effort at voluntary recruitment should be made. Ralston disagreed, and King now, ruthlessly, accepted his resignation. Ralston was replaced by the popular General A. G. L. McNaughton who was not convinced that the voluntary system had been exhausted. He would try once more.

McNaughton failed too. If the men were there, they refused to volunteer. King now convinced himself that an about-face was necessary, for if conscription was not adopted, some of the army's leaders would challenge the authority of the civil government. He had shown his good faith to the French Canadians when he sacked Ralston, now he hoped that the French Canadians would support him. Louis St.

The "Bren Gun Girl," one of thousands of women who worked in the war industries during the Second World War, admires her handiwork during a cigarette break at the James Inglis plant in Toronto. Both the job and the cigarette reveal something of women's changing status in the 1940s. Still (May 1944) from a National Film Board documentary.

Laurent, who had never been committed to the no-conscription pledge, accepted his leader's position. The decision was made to dispatch men to the front who had been conscripted for home service. By the war's end only about 2,500 men had departed. But the second conscription crisis had been overcome, just as the first had been in 1942, by King's political skill and good luck. By administering the hated medicine in two doses, King had managed to so dilute it as to avoid a repetition of 1917. He had maintained the country's unity, though there were those who were disenchanted in both French and English Canada. His reward was re-election in 1945.

King's 1945 victory, however, was more than an endorsement of his wartime leadership. It was also, at least partly, due to his government's decision to prepare for the post-war years by the adoption of social and economic policies that would, it was hoped, prevent a renewal of the Depression. The cautious pre-war beginnings of Keynesian counter-cyclical policies were to be strengthened. In 1940 an unemployment-insurance scheme had been added to the Old Age Pension Plan of 1927. In 1944 a system of family allowances was introduced, giving mothers a monthly cheque earmarked for child care. A firm basis for the welfare state was thus laid. Policies to promote home building, to provide work for demobilized war veterans, and to increase federal aid to health care all indicated a turn towards a new involvement by the federal government in social and economic affairs.

There was more than new economic thinking behind the Liberals' new-found zeal for social security. There was also fear that the impressive increase in popular support for the CCF would result in a repetition of the party fragmentation that had followed the Great War. In 1943 the CCF had won enough seats to form the Opposition in Ontario. The following year the party in Saskatchewan, led by the

John Grierson came to Canada from Great Britain in 1939 and directed the founding of the National Film Board. His brilliance as a documentary filmmaker was soon put to use creating the "Canada Carries On" series, designed to stimulate wartime patriotism. He is seen here with poster designer Harry Mayerovitch.

dynamic and imaginative Reverend T. C. (Tommy) Douglas, formed the first socialist government in North America. The public-opinion polls revealed the party's rising strength at the federal level. King, and his party, moved to cut off the threat on the left by adopting some of the CCF's most popular policies. As the 1945 election results showed, the tactic was an effective one. King remained the master of Canadian politics as the country moved from war to peace.

Canadian Culture Comes of Age

The first half of the twentieth century witnessed a profound change in Canada's material and cultural conditions. What had become a dominantly urban society had begun to develop a culture that was both more North American in its flavour and more urban in its preoccupations. Frederick Philip Grove, whose novels written in the early decades of the century had mirrored the problems of a rural society, published *The Master of the Mill* in 1944. It was a story of class conflict familiar to those struggling for a living in the 1930s. Morley Callaghan's work dealt in a more sophisticated fashion with the social and spiritual tensions of urban living, while Hugh MacLennan, first in *Barometer Rising* (1941), in which he evoked the Halifax disaster

May 8, 1945, was VE Day, marking the victory in Europe. In Ottawa, as in other cities and towns, thousands turned out to express relief, joy, and thankfulness with cheers and ticker tape. Canada's third war in less than half a century was almost over; the A-bomb and victory in the Pacific were just four months away.

of 1917, and then in *Two Solitudes* (1945), a novel about French–English relations, sought to create a literature out of distinctly Canadian themes. So too in Quebec, the old hymns to rural values were gradually being set aside. Ringuet's *Trente arpents* (1938) exploded the arcadian myth, while Gabrielle Roy's magnificent *Bonheur d'occasion* (1945) revealed the human dimensions of French-Canadian urban life. New poets also emerged. The old patriotic romanticism of both English and French Canada was replaced by modernist writing. Saint-Denys Garneau led the way in Quebec, while such writers as E. J. Pratt, Earle Birney, and Dorothy Livesay represented the new trends in English Canada. In 1946, F. R. Scott's "Laurentian Shield" expressed the hopefulness of the new spirit this way:

But a deeper note is sounding, heard in the mines,
The scattered camps and mills, a language of life,
And what will be written in the full culture of occupation
Will come, presently, tomorrow,
From millions whose hands can turn this rock into children.

The dominance which the Group of Seven painters had established by the end of the twenties gradually gave way to new techniques and subjects in the next decade. Miller Brittain and Paraskeva Clark evoked the social distress of the Depression years. Lawren Harris moved on to abstraction, while John Lyman and Goodridge Roberts demonstrated that Canadian landscape and still life could be evoked in tones and shapes less harsh and more varied than in the work of the Group and its many imitators. LeMoine FitzGerald and Carl Shaefer turned to local and regional subjects and made no claim to express a national aesthetic.

It was among Quebec artists that the most radical new currents were running. There Paul-Emile Borduas, church decorator turned surrealist, gathered around him a group of young followers, including Jean-Paul Riopelle and Fernand Leduc, who were dubbed *automatistes*. These abstract artists faced the future and called for the erasure of the past. They brought the schools of Paris and New York together in an arresting and original fashion. In their manifesto of 1948, entitled *Refus global*, they demanded a complete remaking of French-Canadian society and full freedom for the creative imagination. But in a world where Canadians, and other peoples, had to come to terms with the annihilating power set loose by the split atom at Hiroshima and Nagasaki in August 1945, not even Borduas and his friends realized the full meaning of their assertion that "The frontiers of our dreams are no longer what they were."

Strains of Affluence
1945–2000

DESMOND MORTON

Eastern Canada: a mosaic of photographs taken from the LANDSAT-1 satellite, with provincial boundaries drawn in. Compare it with Samuel de Champlain's surprisingly accurate map of roughly the same area, at the beginning of Chapter 2. The great ring of water just left of centre is the site of two former crescent lakes, Manicouagan and Mushalagan, created when an asteroid collided with the earth 210 million years ago: they were flooded in 1964 following the construction of Manic 5, a Quebec Hydro dam.

Post-war Prosperity

PEACE CAME TO CANADA in instalments. Hitler's war ended on May 6, with enough notice to civic authorities that most of them put out bunting and Union Jacks and arranged celebrations. In Halifax, where they did not, servicemen and women made their own entertainment, looting a brewery and downtown stores to avenge wartime profiteering. VJ Day, less than four months later, was more spontaneous and less climactic: save to starving prisoners of war and their relatives, the Pacific War had never ranked with the war in Europe. Most Canadians still faced eastward to their origins.

In the post-war period, Canadians entered a time of prosperity that their forebears and, indeed, most of the fellow inhabitants of the world had never dreamed of. For most Canadians, the old rituals of scarcity, hard times, and sacrifice were soon forgotten. The largest cohort Canada had ever bred grew to maturity taking those benefits for granted, grumbling at the side-effects, transforming the life-styles of a wealthy few into the consumption patterns of a mass society.

The war years, a time of full employment, steady income, and the Liberal promise of a "New Social Order," were a foretaste of the decades to come. For the rest of the world, the war was at least twice as terrible as its predecessor; for most Canadians, it marked the end of the Great Depression. Canada emerged from the war with 42,000 dead—two-thirds the toll of the earlier war—the world's third largest navy, and the fourth largest air force. Much of Canada's war effort had been devoted to expanding an industrial base. The war debt was manageable, and the nation's vaults were stacked with foreign currency. For Canada, there were none of the costly colonial or overseas entanglements that trapped its larger allies. Africa, India, and the Caribbean had few Canadian connections. By the end of 1946, the last of its overseas forces were safely home and demobilized.

The government slogan for post-war reconstruction was "orderly decontrol." The presiding genius was the same curt, rumpled engineer who had managed wartime production, C. D. Howe. His wartime "dollar-a-year" executives returned to their peacetime empires, but they remained a powerful political network for the one man in government they respected. For the most part, the corps of professional civil servants bred and trained in the war stayed on to give peacetime Ottawa an administrative competence it had rarely boasted before. One reason was that the new "mandarins" felt needed to prevent a recurrence of the disastrous Depression.

The prospect of a renewed depression had made Canadians approach war's end with fear as well as joy. To judge from the public utterances of business leaders, they had learned nothing from the disaster of *laissez-faire* in the 1930s. As in 1919, peace meant freedom for old commercial habits. Within the government, a bitter struggle had raged between proponents of a reversion to free enterprise and those concerned about the costly, uncharted future of a welfare state. In the end, both views prevailed. Free enterprise would pay for social reform. It was the combination of social reform and free enterprise that allowed Mackenzie King his narrow election victory on June 11, 1945. By the end of the month, family-allowance cheques had reached most Canadian mothers. For families with enough wartime savings for a down payment, the National Housing Act guaranteed low-cost mortgages. No other belligerent, even the United States, offered its veterans such rich opportunities for education, training, and re-establishment. Unemployment insurance, which officially took effect in 1941 when the jobless rate was literally zero, helped make the transition from war production to peacetime industrial jobs virtually painless. Means-tested old-age pensions and provincially funded allowances for the blind and for abandoned mothers helped to create a welfare state that was utterly unprecedented for Canada.

Howe and his friends had scorned "the Security Brigade," as they called those who had put the welfare network in place, but he could draw on a much older Canadian tradition of "corporate welfare" to achieve his share of post-war reconstruction. The

From San Francisco, where Canada tested her new "helpful fixer" role in the first session of the United Nations, William Lyon Mackenzie King and Louis St. Laurent tell Canadians—on May 8, 1945—that the war in Europe is over.

rich incentives that persuaded industrialists to convert to war production were used again to prod them to "reconvert." Howe sold war plants at a tiny fraction of their cost to the taxpayers on condition that they be reopened for business. Faster write-offs—"accelerated depreciation"—and other tax devices worked as well in peacetime as during the war. Export insurance—with government underwriting the risks—encouraged businesses to sell abroad. Despite his contempt for socialism, Howe saw no irony in protecting the best and most innovative of his crown corporations, such as Eldorado Nuclear at Port Hope, Ontario, Polymer at Sarnia, Ontario, and his pre-war creation, Trans-Canada Airlines. Defence contracts helped guarantee that the wartime aircraft industry he had built would have an exciting and innovative future. And only government, Howe recognized, would have the strength to guarantee Canadians a future in science and technology. Otherwise, Howe believed if Americans wanted to invest in Canada, their money was more than welcome.

Industrial reconversion, enhanced by a burst of spending power, banished any threat of post-war depression. With a brief hesitation in 1945–46, industrial production soon climbed past the wartime peak. Veterans and former munitions workers found peacetime jobs and stayed in them. With post-war wages secure, Canadians could clamour for homes, cars, furniture, and the home appliances that had been beyond their means or unavailable for fifteen years. Organized labour, guaranteed a legal right to union recognition and collective bargaining by a wartime order-in-council, chose 1946 to prove to new members that they could win them a share in the new prosperity. A bitter strike at the Ford Motor Company in Windsor, Ontario, in 1945 had established a basis for compulsory check-off of dues, giving Canadian unions a financial security they had never known before. In turn, union militancy and prosperity combined to win workers high wages, paid vacations, and fringe benefits almost unknown in the pre-war years. By 1949, unions had become common in resource industries and manufacturing. By 1949, almost 30 per cent of industrial workers held union cards.

Without really admitting the fact, post-war Canada had evolved into a social democracy. Universal social programs, a strong union movement, and a state commitment to create jobs and eliminate regional disparities completed an evolution begun in the 1930s. Wartime experience and post-war prosperity had made it possible. Saskatchewan was rescued from bankruptcy and transformed into a laboratory for legislative innovation by the Co-operative Commonwealth Federation and its feisty young premier, Tommy Douglas. Other Canadian provinces were more

Only Saskatchewan followed the CCF banner after the war. The strength of the left-wing party was not in its slogans or the few billboards it could afford, but in the practical idealism of leaders like Tommy Douglas (centre), his provincial treasurer, Clarence Fines (left), and Clarie Gillis, the Cape Breton miner who held the only CCF seat east of Toronto.

traditional. Most spent their growing revenues on paving highways or adding schools and hospitals to serve an exploding population. The initiatives came from Ottawa.

Canadian prosperity depended, as always, on trade. Industrialization increased Canada's dependence on foreign capital, expertise, specialized products, and raw materials not available at home. In turn, the post-war world was eager for much that Canada could produce. Payment, of course, was another matter. Washington's wartime policy of Lend-Lease ended abruptly with peace. In 1945 Britain and other bankrupt, devastated Allies were faced with a blunt U.S. demand to pay up. In Washington, business was business. In an Ottawa desperate for markets, business was more complicated. It meant extending an immediate $2 billion credit to foreign buyers at a level—on a per-capita basis—far more generous than even the later American-sponsored Economic Recovery Plan of 1948.

Ottawa's credit scheme was a policy with acute limits. The more Canada produced for export—and for its own consumers—the more it had to import from the United States. Manufactured goods from Canadian factories were often heavy with American components. Favourable trade balances ranging from $250 million to $500 million dollars in the post-war years were cold comfort if Canada was selling on credit but paying in hard American dollars. By 1947, Canada's post-war reserve of $1.5 billion in U.S. currency had tumbled to only $500 million and it was vanishing at the rate of $100 million a month. Mackenzie King was in London for the wedding of Princess Elizabeth and it was unthinkable in his absence for his colleagues to summon Parliament. Instead, the finance minister simply imposed exchange controls and banned whatever imports Howe and his officials deemed non-essential.

Canadians who wanted fresh vegetables that winter would eat cabbage or turnips. People grumbled and conformed. Parliament would not decide.

The crisis passed. Soon the gathering cold war channelled U.S. investment dollars to Canada. Unnoticed in the developing exchange problem, Imperial Oil's 134th drilling attempt outside Edmonton delivered a gusher on February 13, 1947. Soon a new industry produced a rich export for Alberta and cut millions of dollars from Canada's import bill. In 1948, the U.S. Congress, as part of its new Marshall Plan for foreign aid, renewed for Canada most of the advantages of Canadian–American economic co-operation enjoyed under the 1941 Hyde Park agreement. If Europe was to be saved from Communism, business could not just be business. Canada also became the safest, closest source for the minerals, from nickel to uranium, that U.S. strategic planners wanted to stockpile in case the Cold War turned hot.

The 1947 economic crisis and its aftermath were a notification, if any was needed, that Canada's prosperity now depended utterly on the United States. John Deutsch, a Saskatchewan farmer's son and a gifted economist, persuaded fellow civil servants that it was time that theory became practice. If tariffs were evil, abolish them. Several Liberal ministers were impressed by Deutsch's case for Canada–U.S. free trade: their Prime Minister was more cautious. Defending Reciprocity—Laurier's version of free trade—had cost King his seat in the 1911 election. A long memory and growing concern about American domination finally led King to veto the project. Indeed, he went farther. On the eve of abandoning power in 1948, he warned

Joey Smallwood and the power of radio brought Newfoundland into Confederation in 1949. A former broadcaster, Smallwood used radio to force the Canadian option on the island leadership. His reward was almost twenty-three years of political domination of the new island-province.

The St. Lawrence Seaway, long promised, was another billion-dollar project by the time it was completed in 1959. These locks near Cornwall, Ontario, give some idea of the magnitude of the task of bringing ocean freighters to the heart of North America.

colleagues that he would come out of retirement to campaign against his own party if such a scheme was broached. Free trade went back to the freezer again.

Continental integration happened anyway. One symptom was the decision by Newfoundlanders to enter Confederation in 1949. Mainland prosperity, urged by Joey Smallwood, a popular broadcaster, won out against the proud penury of independence. The United States exercised a similar attraction on Canada. Trade barriers, proudly erected by politicians from Macdonald to Bennett, suffered a rapid erosion when Canada signed the post-war General Agreement on Tariffs and Trade, an attempt by the western powers to dissolve trade barriers, a major factor in the Great Depression. Even without a tariff wall to justify a branch plant in Canada, U.S. corporations could easily justify investment in a stable and increasingly affluent market. British capital had financed the east-west axis of Canadian transportation; U.S. money since the 1920s paid for links with the North. Bush pilots had opened the Canadian Shield to prospectors. Helicopters and remote-sensing techniques broadened the post-war assault. Two world wars had exhausted the rich red iron ore from

Minnesota's Mesabi Range. Since 1894, Canadian geologists had known of comparable reserves in the rugged interior of Quebec and Labrador but access could easily cost half a billion dollars. That was too much for Canadians, but by the late 1940s, U.S. steel producers had the money and the motive. Between 1951 and 1954, seven thousand men pushed a rail line north from Sept-Iles, on the St. Lawrence River, through two tunnels and across seventeen bridges to the boom town of Schefferville, 576 kilometres (358 miles) away, in the heart of the Quebec-Labrador peninsula.

For years, Canadians and Americans had debated the merits of a St. Lawrence Deep Waterway, but railway and Atlantic-coast lobbies feared competition and they ruled Congress; Canada could not yet afford to go it alone. Post-war prosperity and Labrador iron ore gave Canadians new confidence. In 1951, Ottawa declared that Canada would wait no longer. A year later, convinced that Canadians were in earnest and newly prodded by the Ohio steel lobby, eager for cheap Labrador iron ore, Congress finally agreed to joint development of both the Seaway and its hydroelectric potential. The deal was struck in 1954. A good many Canadians were unabashedly disappointed: they had finally found the courage to do it themselves.

Across Canada, in developments great and small, U.S. capital financed a resource and manufacturing boom. Between 1945 and 1955, U.S. capital in Canada doubled from $4.9 billion to $10.3 billion but direct investment tripled. Unlike British investors, who had generally lent their capital, Americans wanted to buy direct ownership and control. Critics, conservative and socialist, had long warned against U.S. "dollar diplomacy." A growing minority of Canadians in the 1950s shared their alarm. The CCF could point to an impoverished, misgoverned Central America for evidence of the cost of corporate imperialism. Conservatives insisted that U.S. investment weakened Canada's ties with Britain. In 1956, both parties finally united in resisting C.D. Howe's ultimate grand project, a trans-Canada gas pipeline, because he had turned to Texas developers for the capital and expertise.

Yet the pipeline debate of 1956 was political and partisan, not economic. No party doubted the need for a pipeline or for almost any other development accelerated by foreign capital. Most Canadians had known too little prosperity in the pre-war years to ask rude questions about its post-war source. The articulate professionals who guided the Liberal government had little patience with economic nationalism. Politicians knew that economic growth is the manure that sprouts votes. Workers claimed that U.S. employers often paid better wages than their Canadian counterparts. The 3,700-kilometre (2,300-mile) pipeline was quietly and profitably completed, from Burstall, Saskatchewan, to Montreal, Quebec, in October 1958.

The general prosperity deflected attention from regions and industries left out of the post-war boom. Crippled by a shift to oil and natural gas, coal mining on both coasts and in Alberta slid into a near-terminal decline. Europe could no longer afford to import Canadian cheese, cattle, bacon, or apples. There was no longer an Empire to serve as a protected market for Canadian-made cars, although a growing domestic market as a result of affluence at home concealed the loss of Canada's greatest industrial export. Distances and the lack of dollars overseas turned more and more Canadian export trade to the United States. U.S. tariff walls barred most manufactured goods but it was usually possible to bore a loophole into U.S. markets for Canadian newsprint, lumber, or nickel. After 1952, trade surpluses vanished, but a flood of U.S. investment dollars kept Canada seemingly solvent and certainly more comfortable than Canadians had ever been in their history.

A contented people knew whom to thank. On November 15, 1948, having carefully outstayed Sir Robert Walpole as the longest-serving prime minister in any British dominion, Mackenzie King finally retired. Chosen on August 7 by a Liberal convention, the new party leader, Louis St. Laurent, had waited three months in an awkward limbo. A leader at the Quebec bar, born in a French-Irish family of shopkeepers in Quebec's Eastern Townships, St. Laurent had brought intelligence, foresight, and a wholly unexpected world vision to Ottawa in 1941 when he was summoned as a raw replacement for King's *alter ego*, the late Ernest Lapointe. As Minister of Justice in 1942, he had braved the divisive English–French conscription issue and survived. Inveigled reluctantly into a post-war political career on the promise of running External Affairs, St. Laurent became the only logical successor to King. In turn eloquent, avuncular, cautious, and shrewd, St. Laurent managed Canada's business with the dignified restraint of a good lawyer. His qualities only strengthened a decision many Canadian voters had probably already made when they went to the polls in 1949. Instead of the grudging endorsement King had gained in 1945, St. Laurent won the most lopsided majority of any Parliament since Confederation: 193 Liberals to only 41 Tories, 13 CCF, and 10 Social Credit.

Four years later, there was no strong reason to revise the mandate. Post-war prosperity had easily absorbed the burdens of an impoverished province of Newfoundland, Cold War rearmament, and an unprecedented baby boom. Never had prosperity lasted so long and, had it stumbled, there was unemployment insurance, even for fishermen in their seasonal layoffs. With such Liberal accomplishments in place, what new promises were needed? For the Liberals in 1953 the loss of only twenty seats, neatly distributed among the opposition parties, was hardly more than a reaction against excess. Prosperity made a Liberal government seem immortal.

Living Prosperously

Post-war prosperity worked an almost unnoticed revolution in the lives of most Canadians. Until the 1940s, most people had been definably poor, unable to afford even a meanly calculated "minimum standard of decency." Working people endured seasonal layoffs, oversized families, crop failure, cyclical unemployment, and the certainty of an impoverished old age. After 1945, many of those hazards were alleviated by family allowances, unemployment insurance, and above all a booming economy. At a minimum of $5 per infant, the "baby bonus" was the equivalent of an extra week's wages each month for a big family. Full employment gave unions more bargaining power than conventional economists and most governments really wanted, but their influence helped double the average annual industrial income from $1,516 in 1946 to $3,136 in 1956. By 1948, men were earning an average hourly wage of one dollar; women would not reach that rate until 1956.

The poor certainly remained, among Native people, the elderly, and especially in the hinterland regions where traditional industries and occupations struggled at the margins of the economy. In the decade after the war, such exceptions to the new affluence were largely overlooked. The social issues that seemed to matter were the by-products of affluence: a pressure for decent housing, hospitals, schools, and municipal services neglected during a decade and a half of war and depression.

For the most part, the demands of the newly affluent were shaped by generations of cautious frugality. Canadians wanted a family, a home, a little land, and savings for those rainy days that had come so often in the past. The composite answer to most of those needs could be found in the suburbs. Outside every Canadian city, vast muddy tracts sprouted monotonous rows of houses. Scores of rural municipalities grudgingly came to terms with an invasion of people who now expected running water and sewer lines as well as schools and roads. Novice home-buyers learned to live with faulty fixtures, green lumber, and the tricks of fly-by-night contractors.

Beyond the cities, rural Canadians found their lives transformed by electrification, flush toilets, and paved roads which gave easier access to big-city shopping and

Don Mills, a Toronto suburb, was the country's first planned "new town," but its sprawl of homes, lots, and curved streets would be reproduced outside every major city. Canadians were finding a new lifestyle focused on a house, a car, and the neighbourhood shopping centre and school.

health services. Across the country, consolidated schools collected farm children in long, yellow school buses and graduated more of them with the skills and education that, in turn, drew them to the cities. Those who stayed increasingly practised scientific farming, creating an ecological time-bomb with new chemicals and seed strains, and increased yields. The greatest impact was on Canada's half-forgotten Native people. Improved health services sent birthrates soaring on the reserves; education gave young Native people an awareness of their poverty, frustration, and of a racism which seemed bound up in the Indian Act and the white officials who managed its terms. Residential schools, with their harsh discipline and cultural insensitivity, created new generations of victims.

After both world wars, there was pressure on Canadian women to make room for men by leaving the workforce. Simple financial need had steeled women to resist the pressure after 1918; rising income from 1945 onward is the best explanation of the only period in the century when the female workforce actually shrank. For the first time in generations, a single industrial wage could support a family. Moreover, in defiance of all the standard demographic assumptions that affluence and urbanization cut birthrates, those families grew to unprecedented size. By 1951, years of falling birthrates and rigid restrictions on immigration had made Canadians a middle-aged people. It was predictable that war's end and the veterans' return would produce a dramatic spurt in births. Children under five were 9.1 per cent of the population in 1941 and 12 per cent in 1951. What no one expected was that the post-war baby boom would continue all the way to the 1960s.

Canadians believed that education paid material dividends: jobs, income, opportunities. For most people, the costs of university and even secondary school had always formed a barrier that only the wealthy or the brightest and most ambitious of the poor could hope to cross. As one of the post-1945 veterans' benefits, men and women who had served could spend as much time in any university that would accept them as they had spent in uniformed service. By 1949 the veteran influx had almost tripled pre-war university enrolments. However poor the teaching, by ill-paid professors in shabby, neglected institutions, education became one of the advantages Canadians wanted in their newly affluent society.

The suburban migration and the baby boom compounded the problem of meeting the new demand for education. From 1917 to 1947, about a quarter-million youngsters annually came to school age; after 1947, that total rapidly doubled. Ugly, utilitarian buildings could be improvised from cinder brick and steel, but the overworked drudges who had taught Canada's young found themselves armed with new status and bargaining power. Between 1945 and 1961, both enrolment and the number of teachers in Canada's elementary and secondary schools more than doubled. Teachers' wages tripled; operating costs rose more than sevenfold; capital spending rose tenfold. Inside, of course, nothing changed. In most of Canada, the 1950s were years of rigid educational conservatism: straight lines, discipline, and an old-fashioned curriculum.

The suburban escape was impossible without cars and roads. The purchase of even a second-hand car was the beginning of many a family's flight from the high costs and

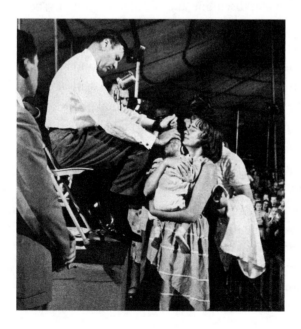

the restricted opportunities of an urban slum. Between 1945 and 1952, passenger-car registrations in Canada doubled, and they doubled again by 1962. The 39,600 kilometres (24,600 miles) of paved roads had grown to 112,700 kilometres (70,000 miles) by

In a scientific age, many Canadians still believed in miracles. If science failed, a desperate mother could turn to a faith-healer like Oral Roberts, shown here laying on hands in a tent near Hamilton in 1956.

1960. It was no longer an adventure to cross Canada by highway. One consequence of affluence was that most Canadians could enjoy paid holidays. Vacations, a luxury before the war, became a standard annual expectation. The edge of the Canadian Shield became "cottage country." So did the Maritimes and the Rockies. Tourism catered to Canadians, all the more urgently because of the powerful lure of the United States.

Almost no aspect of post-war affluence was unique to Canada. Americans, too, moved to the suburbs, demanded schools and a college education, cherished their equity in a shrinking mortgage, and ignored the intellectual puritans who deplored the crassness of mass materialism. Canadians certainly had larger families and, at least statistically, were more law-abiding and more faithful in religious affiliations than their neighbours. The chief distinction between a Toronto and a Philadelphia suburb, at least until 1950, would have been the absence of a forest of television aerials. It was not a distinction most Canadians enjoyed.

Canadians focused their new-found affluence on themselves and their families. A steady stream of new products, from tape-recorders to Tupperware, became tests of a family's ability to "keep up with the Joneses" next door. The image of post-war Vienna, turning first to rebuild its burned-out State Opera House, would have seemed impossibly alien. Outside the home, most Canadians found their entertainment at a local movie theatre or in sterile beverage rooms that often still segregated men and women. Only in Quebec did restaurants routinely serve wine with meals. As for orchestras, live theatre, and other performing arts, cultural life in Canada reached its nadir in the late 1940s. Without the French and English networks of the Canadian Broadcasting Corporation, actors and musicians would have starved or turned to what many of their fellow Canadians obviously regarded as "honest work." Financed by a small but unpopular licence fee on receivers, the CBC served its radio audiences with more variety and imagination than ever before. For their part, consumers showed a strong devotion to "Hockey Night in Canada"—with English audiences largely restricted to the exploits of the Toronto Maple Leafs—and the succession of soap operas, variety shows, and half-hour dramas purchased from the U.S. networks. CBC's "Wednesday Night" and its "Stage" series deliberately catered to a minority. Language barriers made Quebecers a more faithful audience for Radio Canada's programs, but outside Quebec little French could be heard.

Culture may always be a minority concern. The St. Laurent government consciously cultivated its élite supporters when it invited Vincent Massey, former High Commissioner to Great Britain, and Father Georges-Henri Lévesque of Laval

By the 1950s, painters had moved on from the bold landscapes of the Group of Seven. The Painters Eleven show in Toronto in 1957 included some of the stars of the next generation: from the left, Alexandra Luke, Tom Hodgson, Harold Town, Kazuo Nakamura, Jock MacDonald, Walter Yarwood, Hortense Gordon, Jack Bush, and Ray Mead. Photo by Peter Croydon.

One product of post-war prosperity was the teenager as independent consumer. Here a group of teens indulge their new spending power, in 1949.

University's controversial young faculty of social sciences to head a royal commission into the national development of the arts, letters, and sciences in Canada. The issues were urgent. How should Canada enter the television age? Would Canada's universities survive when the millions spent to educate veterans were gone? The commission's report in 1951 reflected an appropriate élite concern at the vulgarity of mass culture and its U.S. sponsors but it squarely backed federal spending on universities, CBC control of the costly new television medium, a national library, and a national endowment fund to support artists and writers, theatres and orchestras.

The Massey-Lévesque Report was not welcome in Ottawa. Universities were as provincial a matter as schools. Louis St. Laurent had recurring nightmares about voter reaction if taxes subsidized ballet dancers. Yet, in the 1950s, that was precisely what some Canadians seemed eager to see. In 1949, Winnipeg's ambitious dance company turned professional. So did younger ballet troupes in Toronto and Montreal. In 1951, three bold Montrealers launched the Théâtre du Nouveau Monde to present Molière in repertory. Two years later, an even bolder Stratford, Ontario, businessman, Tom Patterson, realized his impossible dream of a first-class annual Shakespeare festival. With Tyrone Guthrie as producer and Alec Guinness as star, *Richard III* opened in a circus tent. In the same year, Jack Bush, Harold Town, and others, who would unite as Painters Eleven, persuaded Simpsons, a Toronto department store, to stage a major exhibition of abstract art. If Paul-Emile Borduas and Jean-Paul Riopelle had taken their enormous talent abroad, some pioneers might make at least a slim living at home.

Perhaps the most significant cultural event of the decade came in September 1952, when the CBC entered the television era—with its logo upside down. Soon Toronto and Montreal had become major television production centres, though at a cost that no mere licence fee could sustain. Advertising, cheap imported shows—"I Love Lucy," "The Honeymooners," "The Howdy Doody Show"—drastic cuts in the quality of CBC radio, and growing parliamentary subsidies, undermined CBC autonomy, and betrayed the Massey–Lévesque Commission's refined expectations. On the other hand, a Massey goal was realized in 1957, after the opportune death of a trio of millionaires gave Ottawa a windfall in succession taxes. A Canada Council, largely free of partisan and civil-service control, spent the proceeds of its $100 million endowment on the arts and scholarship.

No one conscious of opinion polls and audience ratings in the 1950s could claim that Canadians suddenly embraced high culture. What affluence created was tolerance. As national income rose beyond expectations, subsidizing playwrights, composers, and even ballet dancers caused no pain, although some politicians drew the line at poets who indulged in obscenities or blank verse. Tolerance also contributed to a more culturally diverse and comfortable Canada: the influx of 2.5 million immigrants between 1946 and 1966 and the fading of legalized racism.

In the 1930s, mass unemployment had seemed reason enough to bar immigrants, even the desperate refugees from Hitler's Germany. Full employment was more than enough reason to open the gates, even to some who had shared in the crimes of the Third Reich. Inmates of refugee camps could easily be persuaded to exchange an ocean passage and an entry permit for work Canadians had never wanted to do— farm labour and domestic service. The "DPs" or "displaced persons" were forerunners

Between 1947 and 1967 more than 2.5 million immigrants came to Canada. While Mackenzie King had declared that the "fundamental character" of Canada's population would be preserved, traditional racial barriers gradually crumbled. They did not necessarily disappear.

of a flood of skilled and unskilled who helped open new resource frontiers and transform the drab, self-centred Canada they encountered. In 1947, Ontario met an acute shortage of skilled workers by launching its own airlift from Britain.

The war and the horrible evidence of the Nazi Holocaust finally persuaded many Canadians that racism was repugnant. Change came very slowly. In announcing a new immigration policy in 1948, Mackenzie King had pledged that the "fundamental character" of the Canadian population would be preserved. No one could pretend that government officials were colour-blind. What died were the old and vicious distinctions that found northern Europeans acceptable and southern Europeans not. A government that had interned Japanese Canadians in 1942, and tried to expel them in 1946 in deference to West Coast racism, belatedly extended full citizenship to all Asian Canadians in 1949. There was hardly a murmur of protest. Saskatchewan and Ontario passed human-rights codes that finally gave hope of redress for the insults and discrimination that Jews, Blacks, and Native people had routinely suffered for generations. Prejudice was not abolished or even dormant, but it was no longer publicly condoned. Toronto, as firmly British in its ethnicity in 1939 as Belfast or Birmingham, was transformed by Italians and Greeks, Ukrainians and Poles. By 1961, Protestants were in a minority in the Queen City, but there were no riots or protests. Instead, Toronto's citizens were persuaded that cosmopolitanism and better restaurants were among the rewards of prosperity.

Of course the old prejudices did not die. Opinion polls showed that a majority of Canadians were suspicious of the immigrant influx and most French Canadians were solidly opposed. What anaesthetized open protest was prosperity and full employment. As ever, there were jobs Canadians did not want to do. If newcomers would work in the mines and dusty construction sites, they were entitled to the wages. If Canadians preferred to educate their children for office and professional work, the products of Scottish or German apprenticeships were wanted for the skilled tasks that make an industrial economy possible. The savage competition for scarce jobs that had always underlain racial and religious conflict in Canada almost dissolved in the 1950s. Without an economic base, the old atavisms could only circle and wait.

Prosperity gave Canadians added confidence in their own identity. In turn, Canadians, new and old, began to make a contribution to the international community of science and literature. Canada's first two Nobel laureates in the sciences, Gerhard Herzberg and John Polanyi, began to establish their reputations in this period; Northrop Frye in Toronto and George Woodcock in Vancouver began their very different contributions to the world of letters. In his cross-grained fashion, Donald Creighton encouraged and enraged a generation of young historians who would, in time, give Canadians a new sense of themselves.

Money and confidence changed the Canada those historians would describe. In 1949, Newfoundlanders voted narrowly to complete the Confederation planned in 1865. The fiscal meanness which had frustrated earlier negotiations had become absurd in the 1940s; the lure of Canadian social programs proved irresistible to Newfoundland voters. In 1946, Canadians had established their own citizenship; in 1949, they had accepted the supremacy of their own Supreme Court; in 1952, they accepted a Canadian, Vincent Massey, as Governor General. If Canadians still refused to take full responsibility for their own constitution, a prosperous people could be excused a quirk or two.

Middle Power

On a hot September evening in 1945, Igor Gouzenko had slipped out of the Soviet embassy in Ottawa and brought Canada into the Cold War. Mackenzie King's first inclination was to deliver the Russian cipher clerk back to his masters. Canadians could not escape the post-war trauma so easily. Nor, in their unaccustomed prosperity, did they wish to do so. The war seems to have convinced most Canadians of the need to play a role in the world. The collective security Mackenzie King had so scorned between the wars might have stopped Hitler; the feeling was that it must certainly stop Stalin. Prosperity raised Canadian self-confidence and it made the costs of defence, diplomacy, and external aid vastly more bearable.

A return to isolationism would, in any case, have been impossible. Gouzenko's revelations that a Soviet spy ring was operating in Canada, extending even into the sacred sanctum of the Department of External Affairs, only renewed awareness of a struggle that had begun with the Bolshevik Revolution of 1917. Instead of its old geographical immunity, Canada found itself placed squarely between two hostile neighbours. Knowledgeable Canadians might argue that a war-ravaged Soviet Union would have all it could do to absorb its new European satrapies, but Canadians since 1940 were no longer sole judges of what they must do for their defence. Acutely aware that Washington had never acknowledged Canada's sovereignty in the Arctic— the vital geographical buffer between the U.S. and Russia—Ottawa officials confessed that they would have to do more in continental defence than any cool assessment of the risks might warrant. Otherwise, the U.S. might defend Canada out of her vast geographic future.

Not all Canadians agreed. Isolationism had survived the war, notably in French Canada and at the universities. In a Soviet–American conflict, only dreamers could believe in Canadian neutrality, but the prospect of a nuclear Armageddon would breed such dreamers by the thousands. Mackenzie King had been as dismayed as anyone by the drift of post-war power politics, but he and his caution were gone by 1949. In Louis St. Laurent, the able, ambitious officials in the Department of External Affairs had someone to fight their battles in the Cabinet and to give voice to their bold vision of Canada's place in the world. Whatever intellectuals, isolationists, and a tiny fringe of Communist apologists might wish, most Canadians were intrigued by their international stature and converted to the once-suspect doctrine of collective security.

In the wartime alliance, Canadian officials had insisted on a "functional principle": representation in United Nations' councils only when Canada could be a major actor. In allocating supplies or feeding refugees, Canadians must have a voice; on grand strategy, they would be silent. At San Francisco, in May 1945, Canadian delegates applied the same "functional principle" to Canada's role in the new United Nations. Between the great powers, bent on monopolizing decision-making, and a host of minor countries with voices but no leverage, Canada was a "middle power" with too little influence to claim a global voice but with too great a material strength to be ignored.

On the whole, "middle" was not a category that major powers deigned to notice. Canada was excluded from talks on a German peace treaty—pretext enough to

STRAINS OF AFFLUENCE 491

withdraw its occupation forces in 1946 and to send no more than good wishes to the Berlin airlift of 1948. Within the United Nations, deadlocked almost at once by stormy Cold War debates, Canada's pretensions of independence were brutally deflated by Andrei Gromyko: it was, claimed the Soviet delegate, only "the boring second fiddle in the American orchestra."

The charge was true enough to be deeply wounding. Canadian diplomats struggled to give their country options beyond the U.S. sphere. In the wake of the Brussels treaty of 1948, cobbled together by Britain, France, and the Low Countries after the Soviet take-over of Czechoslovakia, Ottawa had used an invitation to join the alliance as a lever to involve the United States. As promoted by Escott Reid, an ingenious official in External Affairs, a North Atlantic alliance was almost "a providential solution" to a host of Canadian concerns. It would prevent a new American isolationism, but it would also subject Washington policy-makers to the influence of more powerful allies than Canada. It might even create a broader economic community for a country searching desperately for alternatives to the U.S. commercial embrace. Among the twelve signatories in Washington in April 1949, there were many who claimed authorship of the North Atlantic Treaty Organization (NATO); a handful of Canadians could take discreet but honest pride in their creation. A prosperous middle power had shown its value.

NATO and the Marshall Plan of 1948 solidified the front lines of the Cold War in Europe. They did not affect the titanic civil war in China which ended in 1949 with a Communist triumph. Ottawa, with whatever misgivings, might well have recognized the new regime. For once, it followed the U.S. lead and did nothing. Suddenly, in June 1950, forces of the Soviet client-state of North Korea invaded the U.S.-backed republic to the south. A Soviet boycott, at the United Nations, allowed the Security Council to authorize UN assistance—although an outraged United States would have poured in its troops in any case. UN support made it easier for Ottawa to dispatch three destroyers and make an air-transport squadron available. Six weeks later, with UN forces beaten back to a narrow bridgehead, the St. Laurent government added a brigade of 5,000 troops to its commitment. Eight months later, when Canadian soldiers finally entered battle, the campaign had careered up and down the narrow peninsula and hundreds of thousands of Chinese troops had come to North Korea's aid. The Canadians joined in two more years of struggle along the 38th parallel until a 1953 armistice. For Canada, the cost included 312 soldiers' lives.

Hardly had the war in the Far East absorbed all available U.S. forces than the

René Lévesque interviews French-Canadian soldiers in Korea. If Quebecers, like other Canadians, were puzzled and surprised by their role in the post-war world, Lévesque made himself their guide and interpreter through his brilliant television program *Point de Mire*. In turn, his credibility as a commentator gave him powerful credentials as a politician.

horrifying implications struck NATO planners. Had the Russians deliberately sucked U.S. military power into a remote corner of Asia to leave Europe defenceless? Instead of a leisurely rearmament, NATO needed strength at once. The wartime allied commander, General Dwight Eisenhower, was summoned from retirement to become Supreme Allied Commander in Europe. Ottawa had to respond. A new brigade was recruited for Europe, with the balance of an infantry division, 15,000 men, in immediate reserve. Twelve squadrons of jet fighters would strengthen NATO's obsolete air forces. A crash program to build destroyer-escorts would meet a Soviet submarine threat in the Atlantic. Canadian defence spending, only $196 million in 1947, soared to $2 billion by 1952, two-fifths of all federal spending for the year. In the crisis, the original Canadian hope that NATO could also be an economic and even a cultural union faded fast. Even the unthinkable was possible: West Germany was rearmed and two bitterly antagonistic neighbours, Greece and Turkey, were added to "secure" NATO's southern flank.

NATO grew under a menace more dangerous than that of Korea. Far sooner than experts had predicted, the Soviet Union had tested its first atomic bomb in 1949. Thermonuclear weapons followed fast. So did huge bombers, able to deliver nuclear devastation to the heart of North America. Elected president in 1952, Eisenhower switched U.S. strategy to a policy of nuclear deterrence—"a bigger bang for a buck." A new world war might now begin in western Europe or with the mutual destruction of the superpowers. In either case, Canada would be involved. For the first time, the defence of its vast territory actually mattered. To protect the U.S. deterrent, three sets of radar stations, the Pinetree, Mid-Canada, and Distant Early Warning lines, sprouted across Canada's northern expanse. Squadrons of fighters practised interceptions. Hundreds of millions of dollars were poured into development of a supersonic intercepter, the Avro Arrow, powerful enough to cover Canada's distances.

Surprisingly few Canadians, French- or English-speaking, had condemned NATO, the Korean involvement, or the rearmament of the 1950s. Brooke Claxton, the defence minister who presided over the tripling of the armed forces, even believed that conscription had lost its political dangers. His faith was not tested: regions that prosperity had bypassed filled the ranks of the expanded forces with volunteers. The implications of the nuclear age were slowly absorbed. Rearmament had eased a slight recession in 1949, and it spread jobs and contracts. As part of the 1954 agreement to build the northernmost Distant Early Warning (DEW) radar line, Washington even recognized Canada's territorial sovereignty in the Arctic.

The Cold War also heightened Canada's bilateral involvement with the United States. After 1947, Canada's armed forces were systematically converted from British to U.S. equipment, tactics, and training. Canadian troops in NATO joined the British Army of the Rhine, but the RCAF air division was integrated with the U.S. Air Force. Air defences in Canada developed in close co-operation with the United States long before the North American Air Defence Command (NORAD) was formally established in 1957.

Rational, beneficial, even inescapable as Canada's Cold War arrangements might be, they could be frustrating for those who had imagined more creative and idealistic roles for a young and prosperous middle power. If NATO had proved less than a providential escape from the bilateral yoke, perhaps there was more hope in a Commonwealth association which, by definition, Americans could hardly join. Mackenzie King and St. Laurent deserved much of the credit for broadening a small club of white dominions into an organization dominated by third-world countries and their concerns. It was King—grandson of William Lyon Mackenzie, leader of the Rebellion of 1837—who helped persuade India's Jawaharlal Nehru that Commonwealth membership was compatible with a long and sometimes cruel struggle for independence. Louis St. Laurent's discomfort with much that was ostentatiously "British" gave him kinship with the Indian leader and the newer Commonwealth members. In turn, Commonwealth connections made Canada a logical source of military observers in Kashmir after the first India-Pakistan War of 1948. At Colombo, capital of Ceylon (Sri Lanka), in 1952, a Commonwealth conference committed Canada to its first significant program of external aid.

Yet, like NATO, the Commonwealth gave Canada only meagre options. No more than any other alumni association could the Commonwealth interfere with its members' careers and private lives. Only a few of the new members maintained the parliamentary institutions which symbolized a common British heritage. Nehru's conspicuous neutralism and the diverse and often conflicting policies of other members were reminders that the Commonwealth survived as a forum, not as an alliance. Not all Canadians understood the changes or welcomed them when they did.

After NATO and the Commonwealth, Canada's third multilateral forum was the United Nations. Canadians had welcomed the new world body in 1945 with an emotional idealism that somehow survived the worst years of Cold War deadlock. Perhaps it was the relative proximity of New York, or guilty memories of letting down the League of Nations, but ordinary Canadians, as well as their diplomats, showed a constant allegiance to a world body that more often frustrated than fulfilled its designers' hopes.

Canada's patient commitment to the United Nations was finally vindicated at Suez. Lester Pearson, one of O. D. Skelton's ablest appointees to the Department of External Affairs, had switched from civil servant to politician when he replaced St. Laurent in 1948. Pearson's prestige was valuable to Canada and to the UN's Security Council in 1956. It was a difficult year. Furious at American refusal to finance his Aswan dam project, on July 26 Egypt's Gamal Abdal Nasser seized the Suez Canal, connecting the Mediterranean and Red seas, from its British and French owners. The tolls from the vital shipping route would replace U.S. funds needed to finance the dam across the Nile at Aswan. In turn Britain, France, and the tiny, imperilled new state of Israel secretly plotted revenge. As planned, Israel struck first, at the end of October, driving an armoured wedge across the Sinai. As agreed with Israel beforehand, Britain and France commanded both Egypt and Israel to stay clear of the Canal and, as fast as their rusty war machines allowed, proceeded to intervene directly, bombing the Canal Zone.

Much of the world was outraged. Third-world countries instantly sympathized with Egypt. The Russians, who saw Nasser as a client, threatened to bomb Paris and London. The Americans were furious that they had not been consulted. Even St. Laurent's blood boiled at such apparent latter-day British imperialism. Not least, Whitehall's assumption that Nasser's regime would crumble proved absurdly wrong. To add to the crisis, the Suez affair coincided with the brutal Soviet repression of an uprising in Hungary.

For once, the United Nations abandoned posturing for peace-making, and the clearest reason was the work of Lester Pearson and the credit Canada had collected in a decade of middle-power diplomacy. By inserting a multinational peace-keeping force between the combatants, the UN helped to extricate British and French forces while Israelis returned to their borders. Appropriately, the Canadian who had been commanding the UN's truce supervisors on the Israeli frontier, Lieutenant-General E. L. M. Burns, took charge of the new United Nations Emergency Force. Among his first problems was softening Colonel Nasser's blunt rejection of the Queen's Own Rifles of Canada, not least because of their British-style uniforms and traditions. After wearying negotiations, Canada was allowed to supply administrative troops for the mundane but necessary support of the UN force.

In Canada, Pearson's achievements met mixed reviews. Opinion polls showed that most Canadians had sympathized with Britain and France. Voters resented their humiliation at the hands of an Egyptian leader who, in some bizarre fashion, had commanded both Soviet and U.S. backing. Few understood the intricacies of Pearson's diplomacy or the magnitude of his accomplishment. While the world might understand how Lester Pearson could win the 1957 Nobel Peace Prize, many of the people of a middle-power Canada could not, and their discontent would matter.

Regional Discontents

Post-war prosperity seemed to anaesthetize Canadians from politics. Maurice Duplessis, restored to power in Quebec in 1944, and Ontario's Tory premier, George Drew, led a ritual resistance to an all-powerful central government, but their voters backed the Liberals in federal elections. CCF supporters beat out the Communists for control of the new industrial unions, but only in British Columbia, Saskatchewan, and Manitoba did the CCF collect many votes. Oil wealth made Alberta safe for Social Credit.

The wartime tax-rental agreements showed how Ottawa could fulfil the Rowell–Sirois royal commission's 1940 proposal to redistribute revenue from rich to poor provinces. Premiers from the wealthier provinces made sure that no such schemes survived the wartime emergency. In the end, only Quebec insisted on collecting a separate income tax, but all demanded a growing share of Ottawa's richest revenue source. Provinces needed the money for the highways, hospitals, and schools suburban voters demanded. Rearmament, social programs, and some modest efforts at interprovincial equalization more than tripled Ottawa's spending between 1946 and 1961. In the same period, municipal expenditure rose by 580 per cent and provincial spending increased by 638 per cent. While federal finance ministers regularly boasted surpluses half as large as the entire Quebec or Ontario budget; their provincial colleagues squirmed under voter hostility to new sales taxes. Ottawa disposed of its regular surpluses by announcing a shared-cost program for university expansion, completion of a Trans-Canada Highway, and new technical schools. Rich provinces could benefit; poor ones scrambled desperately for their share. Paying only 25 cents to Ottawa's 75 cents, Ontario could build 196 vocational high schools in 1962; less favoured provinces could only look on. Quebec's Maurice Duplessis demanded financial compensation for federal development schemes he rejected: Ottawa ignored him.

Provincial politicians also felt the heat from the regions and groups post-war prosperity had bypassed. In an urbanizing Canada, legislatures were still dominated by the rural and small-town folk who had gained least from a changing economy. Eastern agriculture felt the loss of markets for bacon, apples, and cheese. An epidemic of hoof-and-mouth disease in 1952 devastated the prairie cattle industry. That year, the wheat farmers of the West harvested a 700-million-bushel bumper crop. European recovery and fierce competition from other grain suppliers made the harvest an economic disaster. Much of the world might be hungry but prairie wheat was piled in curling rinks and community halls to wait for buyers. Farmers wanted cash for their carry-over; Ottawa refused. Prices, artificially controlled during the war years, now sagged under market pressure.

By the 1950s, fiscal caution was becoming fashionable in Ottawa. The Korean War had sent inflation to 10 per cent a year. The CCF demanded price controls. James

John Diefenbaker on a whistlestop campaign tour in Saskatchewan in 1965, among the people who knew and loved him. Prairie farmers gained solid benefits from Diefenbaker's policies, and his image as outsider and underdog evoked instant recognition from western voters.

Coyne, the new governor of the Bank of Canada, lectured Canadians against living beyond their means and boosted interest rates. Official Ottawa had accepted the economic wisdom of John Maynard Keynes: spend in bad times, even if it means borrowing, and save in good times to pay off the debts. Coyne's "tight money" plus surpluses in the federal treasury fitted Keynes's "counter-cyclical" recipe for good times but the policy enraged farmers, merchants, and all who depended on cheap credit. The fatal flaw in the new economic wisdom was political: not *all* regions were prosperous but all regions had votes.

Provincial Liberals were the first to pay the price. In 1935, they had run all but two provinces. By 1956 only four Liberal regimes survived. That year, the Conservative Robert Stanfield destroyed the oldest of them, in Nova Scotia. In Ontario and Quebec, prosperity helped Tories and the Union Nationale hold power.

On the prairies, an ailing Liberal party would lose Manitoba in 1958. Depression memories and a grass-roots, reforming style kept Tommy Douglas's CCF in power in Saskatchewan. In 1952, Liberals and Conservatives in British Columbia agreed to a tricky transferable vote to keep out the CCF. The surprise beneficiary turned out to be a Tory-turned-Social-Crediter, W. A. C. Bennett. Only in Newfoundland was Liberalism safe, under the increasingly illiberal one-man rule of Joey Smallwood.

Canada's holiday from politics ended with the pipeline debate of 1956. A two-week debate should have sufficed for a project all parties and most Canadians wanted. By enforcing closure—cutting off debate—C. D. Howe looked like an arrogant old man in a hurry. St. Laurent, at seventy-four, simply looked too old. Had the Liberals held power too long? George Drew, Tory leader since 1948, might have crushed that questioning mood with his own starchy arrogance, but ill health suddenly removed him. To the dismay of the Tory establishment, a leadership convention chose John Diefenbaker, a lone Saskatchewan Conservative with a demagogic style and a record of backing underdog causes. Within months, election audiences were thrilled by an old-fashioned political passion they had not heard for years. For the first time, many Canadians saw their would-be leaders in the flickering black and white of television. Diefenbaker looked dynamic; St. Laurent was plainly weary and ill at ease. The images made a difference. On June 10, many Canadians voted Conservative, knowing that Diefenbaker could not win but hoping that he might. And he did.

In a Parliament of 112 Conservatives, 107 Liberals, 25 CCF, and 19 Social Credit, St. Laurent might have formed a coalition, but he was too depressed to try. He retired at once. Within weeks, a Diefenbaker government boosted old-age pensions from $40 to $56, paid farmers for their wheat, and showed the Commonwealth that a Tory Canada would support its first African member, Ghana, against white members of the club. The Liberals chose Lester Pearson, with his Nobel Prize prestige, as their new leader. Warned by pollsters not to risk a dissolution, the novice leader instead used evidence of a worsening economy to invite the Tories to hand power back to their more experienced predecessors. It was all Diefenbaker needed. Armed with a secret cabinet paper that had warned the Liberals of bad times, the Prime Minister roasted his enemies in rhetoric. Then he dissolved Parliament and repeated his campaign speech to scores of rapturous audiences. On March 31, 1958, there was simply no contest. The smaller parties were destroyed. Only 49 Liberals and 8 CCFers survived to face a phalanx of 208 Conservatives. Quebec, at Duplessis's direction, gave 50 of its 75 seats to the unilingual Baptist lawyer from Saskatchewan.

The victory was too great. The enormous mandate became a prize Diefenbaker refused to damage by hard decisions. Instead, it dissolved in indecision. The tiny Opposition found itself free to use all the old Tory tactics of obstruction to thwart the government's plans. Closure, made offensive by the Tories in opposition, seemed equally repugnant to Tories in power. Running a law office, and a generation in the Opposition, had not prepared Diefenbaker for power. Civil servants, eager to prove their professionalism by loyalty to the new government, were none the less treated as enemies. In a spur-of-the-moment policy, Diefenbaker announced that 15 per cent of Canada's imports would be shifted from the United States to Britain. When Britain responded by offering free trade, Diefenbaker was nonplussed and silent. When the British next proposed to join the European Economic Community, Diefenbaker insisted that the Commonwealth oppose the British initiative. External Affairs veterans winced. Among officials and journalists, confidence in the Prime Minister's consistency or competence crumbled.

In power, the Tories did much for the people who had elected them. New programs encouraged marginal farmers to leave the land and helped others to prosper. The government ignored U.S. pressure and its own ideology by opening China as a huge new market for Canadian wheat. Royal commissions, headed by loyal Tories, began studies that would lead to tax reform, Medicare, and armed-forces reorganization. The new National Energy Board made all of Canada west of the Ottawa River a safe market for Alberta oil. The new Board of Broadcast Governors granted prominent Tories a licence for the first commercial television network—the English-language Canadian Television Network. CTV and the CBC would now compete for advertising and U.S. network shows.

Diefenbaker and his ablest ministers gave western Canada a voice in Ottawa it had never enjoyed before. Quebec, in contrast, seethed over its feeble representation in government. As recession deepened across Canada in the late 1950s, each Quebec layoff was blamed on Ottawa. Business and finance were outraged at an ostensibly conservative government that outspent its predecessor. Donald Fleming, finance minister and Toronto's voice in government, proved helpless to curb mounting deficits. James Coyne's resolute insistence on tight money in the face of recession was an economic folly that earned him dismissal from the Bank of Canada in 1961. But by attacking Coyne for his retirement pension, not his principles, Diefenbaker managed the near-impossible: he made the banker into a popular martyr.

Even good decisions backfired. The re-elected Liberals would probably have cancelled the Avro Arrow, seeing it as hopelessly extravagant. Instead, Diefenbaker dithered for months. By the time the axe fell in February 1959, Avro had convinced most Canadians that the Arrow was a supersonic marvel; the company had also done absolutely nothing for the fourteen thousand men and women who were fired on "Black Friday." In days, every Arrow was hacked into scrap. Instead of telling the truth about a flawed plane and an inept corporation, Diefenbaker proclaimed that rockets had made manned fighters and bombers obsolete. Within months, Canada was dickering for a second-hand U.S. fighter, the F-101 Voodoo, and preparing sites for an anti-bomber missile, the Bomarc-B.

Diefenbaker took power in 1957 as a cold warrior, boasting to cheering audiences that he would roll back the Iron Curtain. Within weeks he had signed the NORAD agreement, putting Canada's air defences under U.S. control. Close to a billion dollars were devoted to new weapons that depended on nuclear warheads. Millions were spent on civil defence—officially rechristened "National Survival." As Canadians began to recoil at the prospect of thermonuclear immolation, Pearson's Liberals pledged to make Canada non-nuclear. So did the New Democratic Party (NDP), created in 1961 out of the old CCF with backing from the young Canadian Labour Congress founded in 1956. Letters and petitions poured into Diefenbaker's office from peace groups and individuals. Howard Green, a Great War veteran and passionate anti-American, brought his own anti-nuclear convictions to the Department of External Affairs in 1959. Diefenbaker read his mail, listened to Green, and felt his own resentment of the Americans fuelled by John F. Kennedy, the brash young

The Avro Arrow was already a dead duck when it rolled out to a welcoming crowd in 1958. A magnificent airplane, it was more expensive and problem-plagued than a government on the verge of recession could afford. The Arrow measured the extent—and limits—of Canada's bid to compete in high technology.

Democrat in the White House. Canadians were now told that they had no nuclear commitment in NATO or NORAD, and that their country would continue to set an example of military self-denial to the world.

Threats of nuclear holocaust probably mattered less to most Canadians than Canada's troubled economic performance. The warnings in the secret Liberal cabinet document had been well founded. The post-war era had ended. Europe had recovered. By 1957, Germany surpassed Canada as the world's third-largest trading nation. By 1959, unemployment reached 11.2 per cent, reminiscent of the 1930s, especially for workers who had exhausted their unemployment benefits. The government was not indifferent. Accidental or not, its budget deficits reflected the Keynesian economic wisdom. Winter works programs finally taught contractors that their industry did not have to be wholly seasonal. Big spending and large deficits horrified bankers and business executives, but they helped end five straight years of heavy trade deficits and paved the way for the prosperity of the mid-1960s.

That made little difference to voters, particularly in the cities and regions that had gained most from post-war prosperity. Businessmen now yearned for the ordered management of a C. D. Howe. Workers blamed Diefenbaker for the first long layoffs since the war. A sophisticated middle class ridiculed "The Chief" as a rustic anachronism. New Canadians,

By 1963—after years of demonstrations by anti-nuclear groups and an extensive letter-writing campaign—the majority of Canadians were opposed to acquiring nuclear weapons. This proved acutely embarrassing to the Diefenbaker government, which had recently ordered the Bomarc and other nuclear weapons systems.

who had initially identified with Diefenbaker as a fellow outsider, now associated his period in power with unemployment, reviving prejudices, and restrictions on immigration. The creators of the NDP had hoped to build on disillusionment with both old parties, but they had to battle the ancestral slogan that "Liberal Times Are Good Times." In opposition, the Liberals had rejuvenated their organization. By the 1960s, business had money for them again. Lester Pearson's past prestige was compensation for his awkwardness on a platform. So was the galaxy of ex-deputy ministers among his Liberal candidates.

What the Liberals and most Canadians forgot was how regional Canada had become in the years of post-war affluence. On election day, June 18, 1962, the prairie West stayed almost solidly Conservative. So did half the Maritimes and much of rural, small-town Ontario. In Quebec, utter disillusionment with the Conservatives in backwoods and working-class constituencies benefited not the Liberals but a passionate car dealer from Rouyn named Réal Caouette. Of 30 Social Crediters, 26 Créditistes came, like Caouette, from Quebec. With their help, 116 Conservatives could keep Diefenbaker in power against 99 Liberals and 19 New Democrats.

An early election was inevitable. No one could have predicted the reason: Diefenbaker's nuclear indecision. Late in October 1962, John Kennedy took the world to the brink of war to force Soviet missiles from Cuba. Alone among Washington's allies, Canada did not promptly co-operate. (Privately and probably unknown to the Prime Minister, the Defence department did all that could be asked.) Americans were angry. Canadians were dismayed, not so much at Kennedy as at their own government's mid-crisis failure to answer "Ready, Aye Ready" to their new imperial power. Polls showed Canadian opinion moving to support a full alliance role, nuclear weapons and all. On January 12, 1963, Pearson switched sides: Liberals would accept nuclear warheads and then negotiate for other alliance roles. In Parliament, Diefenbaker insisted that Canada's allies were entirely content with its performance. A blunt message from the U.S. State Department corrected the Prime Minister's more explicit untruths and succinctly concluded: "the Canadian government has not as yet proposed any arrangement sufficiently practical to contribute effectively to North American defense."

The American statement cracked a log-jam. Diefenbaker's defence minister resigned in disgust. For the first time since 1926, a government was defeated in the House of Commons. Across Canada, hardly a newspaper had a kind word to say about John Diefenbaker. Several Tory ministers fled politics before the certain débâcle. Their leader set out across Canada in the role he adored, the lonely, righteous prophet. The Liberals pursued him with a "truth squad," issued colouring books, and performed other meretricious media tricks as their support slowly sagged. On April 8, Pearson had his victory but it was no triumph: 128 Liberals, 95 Conservatives, 24 Social Credit and Créditistes, and 17 New Democrats. Across the West, only 10 Liberals had won in the region that had given Mackenzie King his majorities. In all of Quebec, only 8 Progressive Conservatives survived. Not only would Canada have a minority government as in 1921, but key regions would be ranged against each other.

The regions were back in Canadian politics. They might well make Canada almost ungovernable.

Unquiet Revolution

Canadians who voted Liberal in 1963 expected to restore the tranquil, prosperous era John Diefenbaker had interrupted. The prosperity had already returned; the tranquillity would not.

As a vigorous alternative to Diefenbaker's moody indecision, Liberals promised "Sixty Days of Decision." Lester Pearson rapidly patched up relations with the Kennedy White House. His finance minister, Walter Gordon, equally promptly produced a budget to penalize the foreign investors Gordon had earlier criticized in a 1957 report on Canada's economic prospects. To the government's embarrassment, the Gordon proposals were both so inept and so unpopular that they had to be withdrawn. It was the start of two years of retreats and embarrassments. Through much of 1964, Parliament was stalled while Pearson's determination to endow the country with a distinctive national flag tangled with Diefenbaker's fervent defence of the old red ensign. Memories of the nasty 1956 pipeline closure delayed the end of debate until December. In the intervals, Tories raised allegations of Liberal scandal that ranged from free furniture to cabinet-level intercessions for a notorious drug dealer, Lucien Rivard. A vengeful Diefenbaker was in his element; Pearson was not.

Amid the cacophony, few noted the achievements. By 1965 Canada had a new flag, a national contributory pension plan, a Canada Assistance Plan for the poor, and an unemployment rate of only 3.3 per cent. The integration of armed-forces command structures was complete and beneficial. A fairer system of locating constituency boundaries ended a venerable political abuse. Burgeoning revenues and the power of example allowed the government to imitate many of the policies of Kennedy's "New Frontier" and Lyndon Johnson's "War on Poverty." A short-lived "Company of Young Canadians," resembling the U.S. Volunteers in Service to America program, attempted to harness youthful activism. Consultants swarmed into Ottawa to give well-paid advice on the cure of poverty, regional underdevelopment, and the plight of Native people.

Such a flood of good works, insisted Liberal strategists, would earn the government a clear majority and freedom from its Tory and NDP tormentors. A reluctant Pearson called an election for November 8, 1965, and promptly unleashed Diefenbaker for another burst of shallow populism. English-speaking Tory audiences revelled in accounts of scandal that, somehow, always affected Pearson's French-speaking colleagues. "It was on a night like this," Diefenbaker told audiences on warm evenings, that Lucien Rivard had been allowed to make ice on the prison skating rink—and had used the hose to scale the wall. Pearson's limp performance and a floundering campaign even managed to leave the Liberals short of money by election eve. On November 8, voters chose a Parliament that was virtually a replica of its predecessor. Only the NDP gained strength, adding 50 per cent to its voting support. Unnoticed, exasperated Canadians had voted for social reform, not the old politics.

Almost nowhere in 1965 did Canadians debate the issue that now preoccupied their Prime Minister. Indeed, in most of the country, it was hard to believe that Confederation was in crisis. Since 1945, however, Pearson had witnessed the birth of dozens of new nations; he could now see the same symptoms in Quebec. He wondered if they could be reversed.

John Diefenbaker had had no such perceptions. Like

Cartoonist Duncan Macpherson captured the apparent confusion and weakness of the Pearson government, "all at sea" in the 1960s.

most Canadians outside Quebec (and many English-speaking Quebecers), his knowledge of French Canada had been shaped by obsolete myths of a priest-ridden, rural society intent on guarding a noble but archaic culture. In 1958, Maurice Duplessis's desire to be on the winning side had given the Conservatives a chance to build a Quebec base. It was an opportunity Diefenbaker fumbled. Like other western Canadians, Diefenbaker believed that his "unhyphenated Canadianism" was the only acceptable alternative to a Babel of conflicting languages and cultures. To be denied recognition as a "founding nation" was as insulting to Quebecers in the 1960s as it had been to Henri Bourassa in the 1900s. A very different version of history taught Quebecers that they were one of two founding nations, that Confederation was a "compact" between two equal peoples which could not be altered unilaterally without dissolving the union. It was an enchanting myth and a political weapon of great power.

In the 1960s, it was Quebec, not Saskatchewan, that set the political agenda. As elsewhere, affluence had transformed French Canada. Montreal and those communities that enjoyed American markets for their raw resources shared unprecedented wealth; rural Quebec fell behind. Prosperity and a new secularism mocked the old nationalist faith in Catholicism and poverty. In the 1950s, Duplessis's alliance of church, state, and *bien-pensant* Quebecers did their best to hold the line. For inspiring *Refus global*, a ringing appeal for freedom of expression, the painter Paul-Emile Borduas was fired from his teaching post in Montreal. His manifesto inspired a generation of younger artists and writers. A year later, in 1949, a strike by Catholic unionists at Asbestos pitted workers and a few young nationalists and church leaders against the Duplessis regime, most of the Catholic hierarchy, and the American-owned companies. After much violence the strike was settled. Prosperity and fresh battles with Ottawa restored Duplessis's popularity, but Asbestos was not forgotten by Jean Marchand, the union leader, and not by Pierre Elliott Trudeau, a wealthy young lawyer who espoused the union cause. By 1960, Marchand had helped convert the Catholic unions to a secular nationalism.

Prosperity and secularism seemed to draw Quebec closer to North American norms. An added pressure was television with its universal values and homogenized culture. Among the personalities who opened Quebecers' minds to the world was a balding, chain-smoking television commentator named René Lévesque. By the end of the 1950s, the major remaining barrier to Quebec's full modernization seemed to be Duplessis and his Union Nationale. The rest of Canada took heart when two Catholic priests boldly denounced the electoral corruption of the regime. In *Le*

This congenial gathering of Maurice Duplessis and Archbishop Joseph Charbonneau at Ste-Thérèse may have symbolized relations of church and state in Quebec in 1946, but they were not to last. In 1949 Charbonneau espoused the cause of the Asbestos strikers against their American employers, while Duplessis set out to frighten church leaders into submission.

Devoir, Pierre Laporte exposed scandal at the heart of the Union Nationale. *Cité libre*, a small magazine edited by Trudeau, even argued for lay control of education. Unexpectedly, in 1959, Duplessis died. An able young successor, Paul Sauvé, proclaimed his allegiance to reform: "*Désormais*" was his slogan—"from now on." But within months, Sauvé, too, was dead. His successor, Antonio Barrette, was a shopworn survivor from the old guard.

The 1958 Liberal defeat in Ottawa had released Jean Lesage, a St. Laurent minister, to become Quebec Liberal leader. Duplessis's decision to back Diefenbaker gave Lesage sweet revenge. No longer were Quebec Liberals the "travelling salesmen" for their Ottawa cousins; the Union Nationale could now be blamed for Diefenbaker's misdeeds. Powerful allies joined the Liberal cause, among them René Lévesque, angry that Ottawa had allowed the CBC to shut down its French network rather than settle a dispute with him and his fellow television producers. In June 1960, Lesage won a narrow victory. After sixteen years, the Liberals were back in Quebec.

"*Il faut que ça change!*" ("Things must change!") Lesage told cheering backers, but it was by no means clear that he himself wanted change. A courtly, old-fashioned politician, he preferred to speak of "the hour of restoration." But Lévesque and other new Liberal ministers had nothing to restore. At once they began creating a modern, professional—and high-salaried—bureaucracy. Lesage had sworn that there would never be a department of education. By 1964, a provincial ministry presided over a highly centralized, lay-controlled school system; within a few years, Quebec created secondary schools and a network of junior colleges and achieved dramatic increases in school attendance. At Lévesque's insistence, Quebec's private hydroelectricity industry was nationalized. In a snap 1962 election, provincial voters showed that they overwhelmingly approved.

So did most of Canada. Exciting changes in Quebec, promptly labelled the "Quiet Revolution," seemed to make the province more like the rest of the country. After all, most provinces ran the schools, controlled hydroelectricity, and, outside Atlantic Canada, had curbed the ugliest abuses of patronage. What outsiders were slower to recognize was that the prime motive for reform was not modernization but Quebec nationalism. The nationalists who set the pace for Lesage's government insisted that Catholicism and rural poverty were lamentable defences for French Canada. In a secular age, cultural and linguistic survival depended on a powerful government. Given the resources, there was nothing that a Quebec state could not do at home, from fostering the arts to creating a nuclear industry at Gentilly. What it could not do was defend the French-Canadian minorities beyond its borders. The rest of Confederation could concede the resources and powers Quebec needed or the world would soon have yet another sovereign nation—richer, larger, and more lavishly endowed than most. The logic was inescapable.

Outside Quebec, it also seemed invisible. At its creation in 1961, the NDP had endorsed the "two nations" theory and bilingualism, confident that the new Quebec would also endorse its vision of a nation-wide social democracy. Nothing was so simple. Having digested the "Quiet Revolution," Canadians were astonished, in 1962, by the popularity of Real Caouette's Créditistes: clearly, illiberal, old-fashioned, Catholic nationalism persisted outside the urban and middle-class glitter of the Quiet Revolution. For Pearson and the Liberals, utterly dependent on Quebec votes, the evolution of French Canada easily became their central national issue. It justified the weary 1964 struggle for a flag. It had already inspired the creation, in 1963, of the Royal Commission on Bilingualism and Biculturalism. Headed by André

Laurendeau, editor of *Le Devoir*, and A. Davidson Dunton, a former head of the CBC, the commission would do as much teaching as listening. Canadians would have to learn that French must be an equal national language. Canada's government could no longer speak only English. If Quebecers could not be persuaded that all Canada was their homeland, the country would break up.

Quebec might not even wait. By 1963, one Quebecer in six believed in separation. That year, a handful of youthful terrorists began bombing mailboxes and armouries in the name of "*Québec libre.*" When provincial premiers met in Quebec City to discuss the Canada Pension Plan, student mobs chanted outside. A flushed, angry Lesage raged at Ottawa's failure to hand over the money Duplessis himself had forfeited for refusing shared-cost programs in the 1950s. Quebec would go it alone on a pension plan, collecting a huge reserve fund for its own investment purposes instead of Ottawa's cheaper "pay-as-you-go" scheme. Other premiers, cash-starved as usual, demanded the Quebec plan and Pearson gave way. Ottawa's post-war fiscal pre-eminence had taken another battering. Whatever Quebec won, other provinces would have too.

For all his apparent ferocity, Lesage was a frightened man, pushed by forces he could not control. In 1963, he had insisted that Queen Elizabeth pay a visit to commemorate the Quebec Conference of 1864. When she arrived in October 1964, riot police held off thousands of jeering students; Lesage blamed the episode on Ottawa. Nationalizing the hydro companies had absorbed the surpluses Duplessis had squirreled away. Creating a modern education system sent Quebec deeper into debt. Abolishing the traditional patronage system enraged the thousands of local notables and rural workers any Quebec party needed, particularly to control a legislature in which small towns and country districts were lavishly over-represented. In June 1966, over-confident Liberals found themselves beaten by a man and a party they despised, Daniel Johnson of the Union Nationale.

Johnson, defeated in 1962, had modernized his party and attracted nationalists as fervent as any in Lesage's Cabinet. There was no dismantling of what the Liberals had done but neither was there money to do more. What the Johnson government *could* afford was a systematic challenge to every federal constraint on Quebec's autonomy. In France, President Charles de Gaulle was an eager ally. Canada he regarded as simply another of the Anglo-Saxon countries that had humiliated him during the war. Quebec would be a convenient surrogate for the new age of glory his Fifth Republic was creating for France. Johnson's representatives in France rose in status; Canada's

When Montreal's Expo '67 opened, critics and doubters fell silent, and Canadians celebrated their new-found sense of style, showmanship, and elegance. For once, protests over cost and practicality were forgotten.

ambassador was snubbed and a visit by the Governor General, Major-General Georges Vanier, was bluntly rejected. Pearson was angry, and helpless.

Of all the projects that symbolized the new Quebec, the most grandiose was not provincial at all. Montreal's Mayor Jean Drapeau had dreamed up the idea of a world's fair to celebrate the centennial of Confederation; he had sold it to the world and then bullied and blackmailed Ottawa and Quebec City into grudging co-operation. Despite all of Canada's open spaces, the fair had to be built on artificial islands in the St. Lawrence, shaped from the dirt excavated for a new subway system. Of all the absurdities of centennial year, Expo '67 took the prize. A city that could not afford to clear its slums or provide sewage treatment was spending millions on a show. Moreover, as the deadlines approached, strikes and disputes almost guaranteed that it would never be finished on time.

Yet, to national astonishment and then delight, Expo '67 did open on time. Then came a suffusing mood of pleasure and even smugness as Canadians came to believe that it was they who had sponsored an unmixed artistic and innovative delight. Suddenly, in the warm spring of 1967, it felt good to be a Canadian. The improbable Drapeau became a national hero, the logical successor if the Tories could rid themselves of John Diefenbaker. It was easy to forget that Quebec separatists had fashioned their own licence-plate tags for the year, proclaiming *"100 ans d'injustice."* This time, there were no angry mobs when the Queen came. If President Lyndon Johnson, resentful of Canadian criticism of his Vietnam policies, paid only a perfunctory visit, few Canadians felt repentant. There would be a warm welcome, too, for the aged President of France, a war hero most Canadians admired. Few knew of Ottawa's frustrations. Quebec's Daniel Johnson had monopolized the arrangements, almost excluding federal officials. A long triumphal procession up the St. Lawrence from Quebec produced a climax in a vast rally before Montreal's City Hall. There, on July 24, arms outstretched in a great V, De Gaulle cried out his greeting: "*Vive Montréal! Vive le Québec! Vive le Québec libre!*" The crowd roared in ecstasy.

De Gaulle's ringing endorsement of the separatist slogan and the echoing cheers provoked a sharp, undiplomatic rebuke from Pearson, indignation in most of Canada, and unrepentant glee in much of Quebec. At a Confederation of Tomorrow conference sponsored by Ontario's peace-seeking premier, John Robarts, Daniel Johnson proclaimed that henceforth the State of Quebec would deal as equal to equal with the rest of Canada. By the end of 1967, René Lévesque had broken with the Liberals, created a Mouvement Souveraineté-Association, and set out to unite quarrelsome separatists in a single independence movement.

A Time of Liberation

Political turmoil in Ottawa, an independence movement in Quebec, even Expo '67 itself, were symptoms of an age of liberation from old fears, constraints, and experiences. Canadians were finally coming to terms with the changes in post-war Canada. The 1948 message of Borduas's *Refus global* was finally in fashion. Twenty years of almost unbroken prosperity persuaded a generation that there was almost nothing that they could not have soon and without sacrifice. A generation whose parents had doubled their incomes and which itself could slip into comfortable middle-class jobs felt no fears for the future. If young Québécois believed that they could unload the incubus of Confederation, they unconsciously echoed counterparts in Toronto or Vancouver who demanded economic independence from the United States, or young Native people whose dreams of "Red Power" promised their own liberation.

In any age, wealth is the basis of freedom; in every age, youth seeks a separate identity. Never had so many Canadians come of age at a single time and never had they been so affluent. By the late 1960s, Canada was dominated, as never before, by its young. The long prosperity which still struck their elders as a lucky accident seemed to them a normal state of affairs. At the universities and colleges more and more of them attended, young Canadians were taught that economists had solved the old problem of recurring depressions: the swift departure of the Diefenbaker recession proved the point. The Economic Council of Canada, created in 1963, would provide even better guidance in the future. Limitless natural resources guaranteed that the Gross National Product would continue to grow at an effortless 5 per cent a year. The venerable disciplines of self-denial and hard work seemed as obsolete and tiresome as the bickering of Pearson and Diefenbaker.

Many Canadians in the 1960s believed that they could look forward to anything their hearts desired. Governments did their best to oblige. The bounty from the Canada Pension Plan Fund was poured into new universities and community colleges on the claim, echoed by educators, that education paid a better dividend than any other investment. Good times made for buoyant revenues. Federal-government income doubled between 1957 and 1967 but Ottawa's share of the GNP actually fell. Only the provinces, responsible for meeting most of the voters' demands, seemed greedy as their tax bite grew. The new money supported scores of programs, from student loans to the promotion of physical fitness and amateur sport. After eight lean years of living on its endowment, the Canada Council was granted millions to prepare for the Centennial in 1967. By the 1970s, public funds had created a large and powerfully articulate "cultural industry." Thousands of artists and actors, poets and playwrights, lived, albeit meagrely, on the bounty of the state. Another centennial event was Medicare, a federally funded, provincially run system of universal health insurance. Pioneered by Saskatchewan's CCF government in 1962, in the face of a doctors' strike and efforts to frighten voters with "socialized medicine," prepaid health care had become an irresistible national demand by 1967. Though the Liberals had promised such a system in 1919 and 1945, they needed pressure from the New Democrats, fast rising in the polls, to implement an old pledge. The resistance was not so much financial as professional: doctors went on fighting for total control of

In the 1960s, expanding universities struggled to reconcile staid academic tradition with the rising counter-cultures and protest movements. Here, two professors congratulate the winner of a Governor General's medal, at the University of Toronto's brand new Erindale campus.

"Topping off" the Toronto-Dominion Centre at the 56th floor, in April 1966, gave construction workers a chance to cheer. Most were new Canadians but some were aboriginals—Mohawks with a tradition of expertise in high steel. With office towers mushrooming in all the major cities, such skills were much in demand.

health care, including its price. In the mood of the liberation era, patients' rights now mattered more than those of a guild of affluent professionals.

If governments could afford almost anything, so could the governed. Winter holidays and foreign travel became routine experiences for the middle class. The first volunteers for the Canadian University Services Overseas went abroad in 1961. They became a vanguard for thousands of young Canadians who wandered the world, carefully distinguished from Americans by the maple-leaf flags sewn to their knapsacks. Canadians clamoured for new homes and then furnished them in the costly, ascetic style set by Scandinavian designers. In the post-war years, larger cities had been transformed into sterile collections of upturned glass and concrete bricks, symbolized by the B.C. Electric Building in Vancouver or the Toronto-Dominion Centre. In the mid-1960s, there were signs of revolt at such a bleakly utilitarian international style. Architects began showing a grudging concern for heritage and humanity. The first covered shopping malls admitted the extremes of Canada's climate; a conservationist movement insisted that communities could also afford to keep their old buildings. Politicians and publicists began talking of "people places." After two decades of building super-highways, the Ontario government won votes in 1971 by scrapping a billion-dollar Spadina Expressway that would have threatened Toronto neighbourhoods. Who cared about the money? Haligonians briefly struggled to protect their historic skyline from the usual monotonous clump of high-rise offices. Federal and provincial governments built historical parks and recruited college students to masquerade as pioneers or soldiers. Tourism was only part of the motive; pride mattered too.

In a country hitherto dominated by the middle-aged and elderly, the young forced the pace. Their styles, as usual, were borrowed from elsewhere: Liverpool's Beatles, Berkeley's Free Speech movement, the urban black culture of Memphis or Detroit. A Canadian, Marshall McLuhan, proclaimed the age of the global village. Young Canadians wanted to share in the American civil rights crusade, the opposition to the Vietnam war, and the environmental movement. They did so vicariously by applauding the Travellers, Gordon Lightfoot, Ian and Sylvia, or more obscure folksingers in smoky coffee-houses. They sometimes participated directly: travel to Selma, Woodstock, or Chicago was easily arranged. Parents who had dreamed of swooning to Frank Sinatra in the 1940s were disturbed at offspring who screamed at the Beatles, Mick Jagger, and other visiting rock stars.

Social passions eased into the individualist doctrine of "doing your own thing." A counter-culture borrowed largely from California sanctified liberation from almost every traditional constraint: clothing and language and human relations. A dependable and seemingly safe birth-control pill, devised in 1960, provided the material basis for a sexual revolution. Women could control their own fertility. In the decade from 1957 to 1967, Canada's birthrate tumbled from 29.2 per thousand women to 18.2; the fall was even more precipitous in a once-fecund and Catholic Quebec. The change in family size was not due solely to sexual inhibitions: between 1957 and 1967, Canada's illegitimate births doubled. Old taboos against public nudity, homosexuality, and pre-marital cohabitation faded.

Affluence inspired a vast expansion of spectator sports. The competitive elegance of the six-team National Hockey League dissolved as a welter of American and Canadian cities campaigned for franchises. Both available talent and the playing season were stretched beyond reason by the thirst for entertainment dollars. Canadian football

Edmonton in 1978. A hundred years before, it had been a fur-trading post with a few scattered houses. The Alberta capital flourished in the oil boom, and its championship football and hockey teams were among the signs of regional self-confidence. Photo by Egon Bork.

If anything dented Canadian pride in the 1960s, it was a succession of international hockey humiliations. But what if professionals from the NHL could match the best? In 1972 Canada and the U.S.S.R. face off in a tense series of eight games. In the last game, in the last minute of the last period, the series is tied. Paul Henderson shoots; the Soviet goalie stops it. Henderson shoots again—he scores! Canada 6, U.S.S.R. 5.

faded before the heavily tele-vised American alternative. By the 1970s, two American major-league baseball franchises were firmly established at Montreal and Toronto.

Yet affluence also inspired individual excellence and collective exertion. A jogging governor general, Roland Michener, led a sedentary and often overweight nation into a quest for personal fitness that soon pervaded all ages and classes. Canadian men and women achieved world-class standards in a seemingly endless variety of sports, from trap-shooting to lawn tennis. Steve Podborski won a world championship in downhill skiing as one of the "Crazy Canucks," Sylvie Bernier won Olympic gold as a high diver, and there were hundreds more. Few athletes caught the nation's imagi-nation more than Terry Fox, who, having lost one leg to cancer, crossed half of Canada in 1980 in his "Marathon of Hope." His physical collapse and early death from the disease created a drama not equalled when his feat was completed, two years later, by another one-legged runner, Steve Fonyo.

The liberation era undermined many of the institutions which once had bol-stered a socially conservative Canada. In the 1950s, most people went to church; in the 1960s, attendance fell by half. Divorces had averaged six thousand a year. In 1967, when the law was liberalized, the rate promptly doubled. By 1974, there was a divorce for every four Canadian marriages and by 1990 the rate had doubled again. City streets were still relatively safe, but drug use, one of the saddest enthusiasms of the counter-culture, transformed criminal statistics. In 1957, 354 Canadians were convicted of narcotics-related offences; in 1974, the total was 30,845.

The police struggle against the drug traffic was unpopular, largely unavailing, and unusual. Most of the pressures of the liberation era were met by at least a shuffling acquiescence. Rebels, often with "non-negotiable demands," pushed against open doors. Universities, expanded out of recognition in wealth and enrolments, accepted student demands for a share in their management and even in determining academic programs, although the rise in satisfaction, scholarship, or relevance was not discernible. Governments had traditionally refused civil servants the right to strike or even to negotiate collectively. Only Saskatchewan, thanks to the CCF, was an exception. Between 1964 and 1968, virtually all provincial and federal employees won bargaining rights and most were entitled to strike. Clergy, faced with empty pews, preached "situational ethics" and opened coffee-houses in church basements. Denominations promoted ecumenicism, like shaky corporations seeking a merger. Faced by the 1967 changes in the law on abortion, divorce, and homosexuality, Catholic bishops explained that they would not impose their views—though they

discreetly worried how the "health" of a woman seeking to terminate a pregnancy might be defined. Governments tried to outflank the drug culture by lowering the drinking age. A royal commission contemplated the legalization of marijuana.

Northrop Frye—biblical scholar, literary critic, and moral eminence—was an intellectual whose status in the firmament is broadly suggested by Douglas Martin's 1972 acrylic.

Wyndham Lewis's 1944 drawing of Marshall McLuhan cruelly leaves him without a cranium. While some wondered whether McLuhan's Delphic assertions about the media were part of a giant intellectual confidence, most were reassured once he had been given his due by American television and news magazines.

A Vancouver mayor and Toronto's police attracted national ridicule by well-publicized attempts to uphold traditional morality by closing art galleries and hip newspapers. In most provinces, censorship retreated to mere classification.

Pornography and drug addiction were ugly side-effects of a process that, on the whole, made Canada a more civilized, creative, and interesting place to live. The millions of dollars poured into the coffers of arts organizations, universities, orchestras, publishers, and the CBC generated far more talent than Canadians had ever believed they possessed. Most provinces created counterparts of the Canada Council to encourage the study and enjoyment of the arts, humanities, and social sciences, and burgeoning public patronage spread cultural activity beyond the great urban centres. In the spirit of the times, a robust regionalism pitted local virtues against the alleged pretensions of metropolitan centres; nationalism demanded safeguards against American invasions; governments and their granting agencies nervously obliged. Cultural and academic politics proved as nasty and self-serving as any other version of the form.

The bonanza of art, music, writing, and every other form of cultural expression included much that was mediocre, self-indulgent, and derivative, but what else could be expected from an adolescent growth? An older generation of authors, artists, and performers finally found the Canadian audience they had always deserved: Glenn Gould, Maureen Forrester, Lois Marshall, Oscar Peterson, Mavis Gallant, Antonine Maillet, to name only a few. The more talented newcomers disciplined themselves to the demands of excellence. Margaret Atwood's precise language and humane instincts made her the most respected young writer of her generation. Out of scores of new dramatists, Michel Tremblay stood out for the dynamism of his plays and their brilliant use of *joual*, the dialect of ordinary Quebecers. The value of regional-

Jazz pianist and composer Oscar Peterson, left, was performing on radio at the age of fifteen, and has been among the world's reigning jazz kings since the 1950s. His compositions include the *Canadiana Suite* and the *African Suite*.

Glenn Gould, right, was the world's greatest interpreter of Bach's keyboard music when he died in 1982 at the age of fifty. The eccentric musician was a true child of the electronic age, abandoning a concert career in 1964 in favour of the technical perfection possible only from recording studios. Photo by Walter Curtin.

ism could be illustrated in the Maritimes by the influence of Alex Colville's evocative realism on such brilliant Newfoundland disciples as Mary and Christopher Pratt.

For all the predictions of gloom, valid institutions survived the liberation experience with only their self-importance damaged. Churches were no weaker when their social conformists departed and only believers remained. Unions were more militant and more democratic in the hands of an educated and expectant membership. Even most schools and universities survived folly and timidity, although they found it harder to escape the consequences of ill-advised staffing decisions and over-expansion. New curricula helped change attitudes to women, Native people, minorities, and the environment. Social science added precision to business and government, as well as self-serving jargon and an appetite for data processing.

Mon Oncle Antoine, a powerful 1970 film about growing up in a modernizing Quebec, established Claude Jutras as a brilliant director. Seventeen years later, just after his tragic death by drowning, the film was judged Canada's best movie ever, by an international panel of film critics.

Norman McLaren (1914–87) was a leading innovator in animation and produced many prize-winning films for the National Film Board; *Pas de Deux*, left, was nominated for an Academy Award in 1967.

Left: In her novel *The Stone Angel*, Manitoban writer Margaret Laurence (1926–87) gave Canadians the unforgettable image of Hagar Shipley, an indomitable, uncompromising woman who both reflected and challenged the feminist age. Laurence is most remembered for her cycle of novels set in the imaginary town of Manawaka. Photo by Peter Esterhazy.

Right: Francophone writer Gabrielle Roy (1909–83) grew up in Manitoba, and was able to write about the hardships of Québécois life with a compassionate detachment that made her novels particularly accessible to English Canadians. "Even when her work described alienation and loneliness, it also reached out in hope." (*Maclean's*)

Improvements in the teaching of science and mathematics compensated for an alleged decline in the standards of literacy among the educated.

The wealthy are often scornful of the sources of their own riches: the liberation generation was no exception. Not since the very different context of the 1930s had corporate capitalism been under more savage and sustained assault. Disdain for mass-market affluence provided a foundation for the environmentalism of the 1970s. Young and old, conservative and radical, deplored what earlier generations had cheered: the exploitation of resources or the vanishing of Canada's finest farm-land under the relentless flow of suburbia. Part of liberation was a romantic back-to-the-land movement, supported by an emotional outcry against chemical pesticides and such traditional Canadian industries as the fur trade and the seal hunt. Native people, newly vocal in defence of aboriginal rights, found allies for their claims—and new enemies of their traditional livelihood as hunters and trappers.

Liberation was even more explicit when it turned to the condition of women. The earlier maternal feminism had fought to protect and enhance women's traditional nurturing role. Liberation meant an end to all predetermined roles. If, as social scientists began to claim, women had been conditioned by dominant males to accept an inferior place in society, it was evident that women must immediately occupy enough of the positions of power—in business, government, education, or the professions—to smash the old stereotypes. What was valid for women was as important for the other great collection of stereotypes—race. A nation which had begun the decade with self-satisfied condemnation of the racial policies of South Africa and the United States ended the 1960s with an embarrassed awareness of the bleak plight of Blacks and Native people in many parts of Canada.

Environmentalism, feminism, and awareness of racial discrimination came, like most of the other trends of the liberation era, from abroad. If Canadians grew more eager than ever to identify their own contribution to an international culture, it was not easy to find anything uniquely Canadian in a rock group like the Guess Who or a *chanteuse* like Monique Leyrac. Even the rhetoric of anti-Americanism which helped fuel Canadian nationalism at the end of the decade was to be derived from anti-Vietnam War protests in the United States. The war, and its effect on the U.S. economy and politics, helped Canadians feel a smug detachment from their neighbour. Prosperity, fed in part by U.S. war purchases, gave Canada an extra sense of well-being. Despite his humiliating misjudgements in the 1963 budget and the 1965 election, Walter Gordon was allowed by his prime minister to launch a fresh exploration of U.S. domination of Canada's economy. The resulting report, by Melville H. Watkins, with its statistics of corporate Americanization, inspired both Liberal and NDP policy-makers in the 1970s.

As ever in Canada, the liberation mood had to feed not one nationalism but two. If Canadians felt entitled to an overdue independence, so did Quebecers. The liberation era had dissolved old safeguards of nationalism—the church, the birthrate, an anxious conservatism. It created new ones. Why should young Québécois, surging in their thousands through new and expanded colleges and universities, have to master English as the price of mere acceptance in Ottawa or even in the corporate offices of their own province? A decade of the Quiet Revolution suggested that there was nothing the Québécois could not accomplish—unless they were barred by the rules of Confederation. If Canadians were encouraged by unending prosperity and excited by their cultural creativity, so were Québécois, and with more reason, for in the smaller Francophone culture Quebec's burgeoning community of authors, singers, and artists was all the more significant.

Nationalism, both Canadian and Québécois, posed challenges for politicians in Ottawa and Quebec City. In Ottawa, at least, the politicians were changing. In 1965, the Liberals had at last managed to elect overdue reinforcements for their Quebec contingent. Jean Marchand, the labour leader, and Gérard Pelletier, editor of *La Presse*, were wanted; a third, Pierre Trudeau, was accepted only because Marchand insisted. Within months, Trudeau's tough mind and flair for publicity made him the star of the trio. By the end of 1967, as Minister of Justice, he had forced Parliament to accept reforms on divorce, abortion, and the rights of homosexuals that no previous Quebec Catholic minister could even have considered. "The state," Trudeau declared, "has no business in the bedrooms of the nation." No phrase caught the values of the liberation era more precisely.

In September 1967, the Tories finally won their brutal struggle to dislodge Diefenbaker. Their reward for picking Robert Stanfield, the Premier of Nova Scotia, was a prompt surge in the opinion polls. A half-dozen Liberals manoeuvred for Pearson's mantle without perceptible national acclaim. In February 1968, buoyed by his triumphs in the year of Expo, Quebec's Daniel Johnson joined a well-televised federal–provincial conference with high spirits and fresh demands. As Minister of Justice, Trudeau was at Pearson's side. For the first time in memory, Canadians heard a federal minister talk back to Quebec in tough, eloquent French. Perhaps, as observers claimed, the outcome was a draw. But that was not how most Canadians saw it.

Trudeau's leadership campaign was launched. Weary after two unilingual prime ministers, Quebecers favoured the sole French-speaking candidate. Pearson, himself, endorsed the principle of an alternation of French and English leaders. Canadians in and outside the Liberal party perceived in Trudeau a man who broke the stereotypes of political leadership. His victory at the Liberal convention was not a foregone conclusion; his triumph in the ensuing election was. For a few warm spring months in 1968, Pierre Elliott Trudeau synthesized the dreams, achievements, and illusions of the liberation era. Beyond such flip promises as "no more free stuff" and the offer of a "Just Society," few admirers listened to Trudeau's words. They warmed to a brash defiance of convention, an elegance of style, a coolness under the jeers and stones of a separatist mob in Montreal, all mediated by television. On June 25, Trudeaumania helped achieve the Liberal majority Canadians had denied Pearson: 155 seats to 77 for the Stanfield Tories. Diefenbaker loyalists in the West helped the NDP's Tommy Douglas win 22 seats. Had the age of liberation come to Ottawa? Or was it over?

Political Realities

It was easy to forget that most Canadians in the 1960s and 1970s wanted children, stayed married, decried the drug culture, and, for that matter, never voted for Pierre Elliott Trudeau. American draft dodgers in Canada were far outnumbered by the young Canadians who joined U.S. forces to fight in Vietnam. Liberated life-styles were more visible in downtown Vancouver or Montreal than in Kamloops, Kirkland Lake, or Medicine Hat—or even in Burnaby, Mississauga, or Laval. As usual, the fashions that defined an age were set by the urban middle class. People who wore blue jeans because they were cheap, not chic, followed more slowly and sometimes not at all.

Television and the new recording tape kept people in touch with images of change but they could not always transcend actual experience. Outside the boutique culture of the big cities, plenty of Canadians did not believe that prosperity was permanent or even that it affected them. There had been no economic take-off in Atlantic Canada or in the small-town hinterland of Quebec. Prairie farmers ended the booming 1960s with falling prices, a new wheat glut, and their ineradicable memories of the Great Depression. Mining communities from Pine Point, Northwest Territories, to Buchans, Newfoundland, knew that world prices or a new technology could wipe them off the map.

Trudeau took power in 1968 to tackle the great French–English dialogue; he needed time to discover that there were many other divisions in Canada. At forty-nine, Trudeau was not Canada's youngest prime minister, but politically he was the least experienced. He ran his Cabinet as an academic seminar, built his staff as a buffer against political pressures, and set out to govern Canada on philosophical first principles. Economics and administration interested him little. Jean Marchand, in a new Department of Regional Economic Expansion, could spend whatever he liked to end the old disparities. Eric Kierans, the radical ex-stock-exchange president, was free to automate the post office. Eugene Whalen could fascinate or infuriate farmers with his marketing boards and subsidy schemes. The tax reforms which might have

Above: In 1971 Gerhard Herzberg, one of the few Jewish refugees from Hitler admitted by Canada in the 1930s, became the country's third Nobel laureate for his work in molecular spectroscopy.

Left: John Polanyi, professor of chemistry at the University of Toronto, won Canada's fourth Nobel Prize, in 1986, for his contributions concerning the dynamics of chemical processes—specifically, his work on chemical laser technology.

helped fulfil Trudeau's pledge of a "Just Society" were savaged and convoluted by Edgar Benson, the finance minister, until they chiefly enriched millionaires and chartered accountants. These were not the Prime Minister's concerns.

Nor, on the whole, was he preoccupied by Canada's place in the world. Vietnam and the new strategic doctrine of mutually assured destruction (MAD for short) had cooled the nuclear fears of the early 1960s. Like the NDP, whose cause he had briefly espoused, Trudeau believed in disarmament and disengagement. Canada's armed forces, painfully unified in 1968 by Paul Hellyer, Pearson's defence minister, found that their hated new green uniforms were only the beginning of humiliation. Canada's NATO contingent was cut in half in 1969 and armed-forces strength was chopped by a third. NATO allies were not pleased. Nor were diplomats in the Department of External Affairs, after Trudeau, claiming that he could learn all that

While Lester Pearson looks sombrely statesmanlike, Pierre Trudeau makes little attempt to hide a smile, as Quebec presents its usual non-negotiable demands to the 1968 federal–provincial conference. Trudeau's televised performance, standing up to fellow Quebecers, helped make him prime minister only weeks later.

he needed to know from *The New York Times*, closed some overseas missions. Though the world had changed since Trudeau travelled it in the post-war years, he did not feel that he needed to know very much.

One issue which he did understand and which gripped his attention was Quebec's role in Canada. Brilliantly bilingual and utterly self-confident, Trudeau urged young Quebecers to abandon the "ancestral wigwam" and join him in dominating the country their *voyageur* ancestors had helped create. Unlike Laurier and St. Laurent, who had carefully surrounded themselves with enough English-speaking ministers and advisers to reassure the majority, Trudeau promoted any Quebecers who matched his intellect and flair. An Official Languages Act, establishing the equality of French and English and making the central government and its agencies effectively bilingual, was the cornerstone of Trudeau's first term. With the exception of John Diefenbaker and a few Tory loyalists, Parliament gave ungrudging consent.

Trudeau had done nothing that he had not urged eloquently and in both languages during his 1968 campaign. Bilingualism would be the basis for a fundamental equality of citizenship. Special status for any province, group, or individual struck Trudeau as undemocratic. Having heard Native people denounce the Indian Act as an engine of oppression, he was astonished when its abolition, and the consequent removal of a special status for Indians, was denounced as genocide by the same people. Jean Chrétien, the ebullient young minister responsible, promptly corrected himself.

Canadians might have been more hospitable to Trudeau's recipe for national unity if they had understood the Quebec-Canada crisis and if their prime minister had shown equal sensitivity to other regional concerns. "Why should I sell your wheat?" Trudeau demanded of angry western farmers. The Wheat Board, of course, was a major federal agency. Grain growers would remember the Prime Minister's arrogant forgetfulness. Nor did Trudeau seem very sensitive to the economic chill that ended the soaring sixties. As early as 1966, inflation began to tarnish prosperity. From 1961 to 1965 the consumer price index had risen about 5 per cent; in the balance of the decade, it climbed 17 points. Since industrial wages climbed twice as fast, economists had an easy scapegoat: greedy unions, especially in the public sector. One of the last reforms of the Pearson era had been to grant the right to strike to many federal employees. Government workers had certainly done their best to improve their lagging wages. Inflation had other sources, too, from the high cost of Expo '67 to Washington's determination to finance its Vietnam war with borrowed money. Whatever the causes, inflation hurt. So did the tight-money cure promptly administered by the Bank of Canada. A stylish, sophisticated prime minister was as obvious a scapegoat as he had once been a hero.

The West got angry first. In 1968, Trudeau had carried a majority of the seats west of Lake Superior. That would not happen again. Instead of selling wheat, Ottawa told prairie farmers to cut their acreages. Those who obeyed suffered most when Soviet and Chinese crop failures sent demand and prices soaring. Provincial Liberals paid the price. A year after Trudeau's victory, a cautious, multilingual Ed Schreyer led the NDP to victory in Manitoba against an anti-Quebec, anti-Ottawa Tory. Next door, Ross Thatcher's Liberals had beaten the weary Saskatchewan CCF in 1964, after the lone social-democrat government had won its bruising fight for Canada's first Medicare scheme. By 1971, any kind of prairie Liberal was in trouble. Allan Blakeney of the NDP had his vengeance on Ross Thatcher's regime. A year later, Dave Barrett gleefully led his "socialist hordes" to power in British Columbia. In every case, defecting Liberal voters made up the NDP's winning margin and the Trudeau government deserved at least some of the blame. In Alberta, there was no great ideological shift in 1971 when Peter Lougheed's Progressive Conservatives crushed the thirty-six-

After Hawker Siddeley, the latest owner of Sydney's aged steelmill, announced its shutdown, Cape Breton sent Ottawa a sadly familiar message. The government's response to regional disparity and economic decline was subsidy, public ownership, and forced optimism.

year-old Social Credit regime, but Alberta's Liberals almost vanished. Ottawa would soon feel the change.

Atlantic Canada, more cautious and far more dependent on Ottawa's redistributed largesse, was more restrained in its resentment. In the vacuum left by Robert Stanfield's departure, Nova Scotia narrowly returned the Liberals in 1970, but New Brunswick elected the first Tory regime ever backed by the province's powerful Acadian minority. A year later, Joey Smallwood's hubris as well as his Trudeau ties allowed the Newfoundland Conservatives first a narrow and then a sweeping triumph, their first on the Rock since the 1920s.

Political upheaval in the West and East left Trudeau and his advisers unmoved. Alternation of identical governments with different labels was a norm in the Maritimes; the three NDP regimes were sufficiently embattled with corporate and conservative enemies to cause Ottawa no problem. Post-war population growth in the central provinces had only reinforced the fact that any party that held Quebec and much of Ontario could rule Canada. Prosperity and a capacity for opportune reform may have made Ontario's Tories unbeatable, but the federal Liberals co-existed comfortably, taking credit for the 1965 Auto Pact and claiming the allegiance of continuing waves of immigrants. Ontario's wealth fostered economic nationalism among academic élites, but few wanted to condemn a deal that spread dozens of auto-parts plants and thousands of jobs across the cities and towns of south-western Ontario.

Quebec was another matter. In the national balance of "have" and "have-not" provinces, Quebec was perched in the middle, a mixture of Ontario-style urban growth and the decrepit, subsidized industries and regional unemployment characteristic of the Maritimes. Daniel Johnson's political skill and nationalist grandstanding had forged a narrow victory in 1966, but his sudden death and a decent but colourless successor, Jean-Jacques Bertrand, left the Union Nationale floundering. By 1969, René Lévesque had inspired and bullied separatists into a single Parti Québécois (PQ). Bertrand's fumbling, and evidence from the Laurendeau–Dunton Royal Commission, gave the new party an issue. Like Toronto, Montreal had been flooded by hundreds of thousands of hard-working immigrants from southern Europe; as in Toronto, most of them sent their children to English-speaking schools in sensible recognition of the language that dominated the local economy.

Native children in Mistassini, in northern Quebec, use skipping rhymes that might be heard anywhere in Canada. In the 1970s Canadians began to realize what a bleak future the young people in northern communities were facing.

Laurendeau–Dunton statisticians only confirmed Québécois suspicions. While the English were top earners, the newcomers' average incomes surpassed even those of bilingual French Canadians. A post-Expo recession fuelled resentment and fed crowds into language riots in the predominantly Italian suburb of St-Léonard. Shocked by the threat to Quebec's traditional linguistic and educational pluralism, Bertrand temporized. Only Lévesque and the PQ could profit from an issue that threatened not only Quebec traditions but Trudeau's push for nation-wide bilingualism.

The language question posed a real problem for Quebec Liberals: they commanded the near-total allegiance of the province's English minority, but obviously they needed many more votes to win. Robert Bourassa, the youthful technocrat who now led the Liberals, chose to outflank the issue. Backed by Trudeau and his own credentials as an economist, Bourassa launched his 1970 campaign by promising a hundred thousand new jobs. Confederation, he proclaimed, would be made profitable. To most Quebecers, anxious about their own jobs and fed up with a succession of riots, demonstrations, and violent strikes, Bourassa's message was welcome. The Union Nationale vote split among competing Social Credit and Parti Québécois candidates. On April 29, 1970, Liberals won 72 of the 108 National Assembly constituencies. The PQ won 7 constituencies.

The victory was no prize. Quebec was deep in debt. Only subsidies and tariffs kept many local industries in business. Thousands of graduates demanded the kind of jobs a university degree had once promised. Quebec teachers now espoused Marxism, with an ardour they had once reserved for Catholicism. A succession of Montreal street riots seemed a herald of revolution. When Mayor Jean Drapeau warned of terrorism, opinion leaders sneered that he was merely trading on alarmism for his own re-election.

On October 5, 1970, James Cross, the British trade commissioner in Montreal, was kidnapped. Among the kidnappers' demands was the broadcast of a manifesto from the Front de Libération du Québec (FLQ), a romantic revolutionary movement with a terrorist core. The Bourassa government nervously agreed. Mass rallies of nationalist students shouted their contempt for the young government and their allegiance to the FLQ. On October 10, Pierre Laporte, Bourassa's Minister of Labour, was seized from his front lawn. There were more mass rallies. A self-proclaimed lawyer for the kidnappers held court for television and journalists. René Lévesque, Claude Ryan of *Le Devoir*, and other eminent nationalists mustered to give Bourassa their advice: don't involve Ottawa. It was too late. The Premier had asked Ottawa for help.

Auto workers enjoying a rest break, 1974. Thanks to the unionization of manufacturing, Canadian workers achieved a security and quality of working life that their ancestors could hardly have imagined.

Trudeau acted. Before dawn on October 16, he proclaimed the War Measures Act. As armed troops fanned out to guard key public figures, local police rounded up 468 people. A day later, Laporte's captors strangled him and left the body in a car trunk. The cheering was over. A search, slow and sometimes inept, finally located both the British diplomat and Laporte's killers. Those swept up in the police raids were released. Some were cases of mistaken identity; most had suffered brief imprisonment for the heady thrill of preaching revolution. They now wanted revenge. So did other Canadians who somehow resented Trudeau more than the terrorists.

The man elected as the embodiment of liberation had dissolved that image in October 1970. His reasons were utterly clear. The government, Trudeau insisted, had acted "to make clear to kidnappers and revolutionaries and assassins that in this country laws are made and changed by the elected representatives of all Canadians— not by a handful of self-selected dictators." Most Quebecers and most Canadians agreed. An articulate minority did not. Civil libertarians never forgave Trudeau for a blunt decisiveness that was at odds with the liberation era. Using the War Measures Act in a domestic crisis had created martyrs and an ugly precedent. It also ended the erosion of Bourassa's democratically elected government.

While the NDP and, belatedly, Robert Stanfield deplored Trudeau's assault on civil liberties, the "October Crisis" sent Liberal popularity soaring. Then, as other issues inevitably intruded, it sagged. Inflation kept climbing. So did unemployment. Ingenious schemes to target social programs to the poor at the expense of family allowances produced outrage: universal programs were now too hot to touch. When the government transformed unemployment insurance into a version of guaranteed

530 Desmond Morton

Montreal's traditional St-Jean Baptiste Parade turned ugly in 1968, when nationalist demonstrators used the occasion to attack the Prime Minister. Trudeau remained impassive in the face of their violence, and won by a landslide in the election the following week.

This soldier and military helicopter reflect Ottawa's reaction to the October Crisis of 1970. While the government's imposition of the War Measures Act and its massive deployment of troops shocked some Canadians, most people approved.

income, taxpayers bridled at the cost and alleged that armies of "welfare bums" abused the system. David Lewis, the CCF veteran who took over the NDP in 1971, raged at "corporate welfare bums," whose billions in deferred tax dollars could have lightened the burden on the lower-paid. Most Canadians preferred to condemn their poorer neighbours and a government that subsidized them without putting them to work.

Trudeau floated serenely above the sea of troubles. In the fall of 1972, he offered voters little more than the slogan, "The Land Is Strong." The voters were not impressed. By October 30, the 1968 Liberal coalition had dissolved. Only Quebec, rural and working-class Ontario, and New Brunswick's Acadians remained. In a House of 109 Liberals and 107 Tories, Lewis's 31 New Democrats would decide the government. "The universe," Trudeau recited to his anxious followers, "is unfolding as it should."

Western Challenge

In the 1970s, most of the post-war certainties collapsed. Twenty-seven years after the United Nations conference at Bretton Woods had settled the U.S. currency as the basis by which all money was measured, Washington suddenly devalued its dollar. Gold would no longer be worth U.S. $35 an ounce. Two years later, the United States accepted defeat in Vietnam, though the ultimate, humiliating fall of Saigon was deferred for two years. American prosperity slid away from the industrial north-east, leaving a residue of pollution, pensioners, and poverty. Asian nations of the Pacific Rim took over industries U.S. capital had abandoned. A business-backed research group, the Club of Rome, predicted the imminent depletion of most of the world's resources. In Europe and North America, a combination of unemployment and inflation—"stagflation"—seemed to defy the old Keynesian claim that economies could be "managed" into equilibrium. Once again economics had become "the dismal science"; some of its practitioners returned to worship older doctrines.

As a trading nation, Canada felt the instability of the U.S. dollar, the protectionism of American and European governments, and its own dependence on resource exports. Crop failure made the Soviet Union, as well as China, a customer for Canadian wheat but such markets were precarious. So was the boom in British Columbia coal and timber. On the whole, Canada's growth in the 1970s was as expansive as before, but there was no accompanying sense of confident well-being. As the baby boom came of age, three million extra Canadians joined the labour force, an increase of one-third. Among women, the increase in labour-force participation was double the rate for men. Not only could they now defer or avoid child-rearing, but inflation made two incomes necessary for the life-style most families demanded. The poverty of most single parents and the elderly, most of them women, made pension and family-law reform urgent priorities. At the same time, while Canadians demanded better homes and filled them with new electronic gadgets, governments no longer seemed to have the resources to cope with costly problems or even to maintain the health and educational institutions created in the 1960s.

Politicized by near-defeat in 1972, Trudeau's strategy was to hold power with NDP backing, put his philosophical principles in storage, and demonstrate that he would protect people from inflationary pressures. When food prices rose in the wake of huge Soviet grain purchases of 1972–73, the government offered bread and milk subsidies and a Food Prices Review Board to scold alleged profiteers. Since the Board's villains included the government's new marketing boards, farmers would at least know whom to thank for their higher prices. Economists condemned the meddling with free markets but David Lewis and his New Democrats did not.

Politics, not conventional economics, also dictated the Liberal effort to insulate Canadians from the 1973 oil-price shock. Angered by the falling value of the U.S. dollars that paid for their oil, and then by western backing for Israel in the Yom Kippur War, an Arab-dominated Organization of Petroleum Exporting Countries (OPEC) proceeded to quadruple the cost of a barrel of crude oil. As winter approached, the Trudeau government promptly provided subsidies for eastern Canadian oil imports, financed by a tax on western Canadian oil and gas exports to the United States. A longer-term government strategy extended western oil supplies to the Quebec market, created a government-run oil company, encouraged conservation, and promoted Arctic and offshore petroleum exploration. A 320-kilometre (200-mile) limit, claimed but hardly enforced by a tiny navy and coast guard, belatedly offered the off-shore fishery a chance to protect its stocks.

The success of OPEC reinforced the comforting lesson that inflation was beyond Canada's control. Instead, tying wages, pensions, and government payments to a rising consumer price index seemed a painless way to protect people from rising prices. In 1974 the finance minister, John Turner, even borrowed a Tory idea and indexed tax payments. While spending climbed, the government's revenues would not. It was a certain recipe for a huge deficit, but voters made no complaint. After two months of unwonted charm from Trudeau, bleak warnings from the Tories, and protests from the NDP, voters on July 8 gave 141 seats to the Liberals, 95 to the Tories, 11 to Créditistes, and a mere 16 to the NDP, half their 1972 contingent. David Lewis lost his seat.

Yet Trudeau had not reproduced his 1968 triumph. A solid Quebec and most of Ontario and New Brunswick could dominate Parliament, but across the West, Liberals won only 13 seats, 8 of them in British Columbia. Since 1968, Trudeau's support on the prairies had fallen from a third to only a quarter of the electorate. Though a Liberal victory had been predicted by the opinion polls, the vast majority of westerners had refused a lift on the bandwagon. Like René Lévesque's followers, western Canadians were fed up with their place in Confederation, though their concerns and their solutions were very different.

If Ottawa misunderstood the West, understanding was not easy. Dramatic changes in the region produced contradictory messages. Painful transformations are easier if someone else can be blamed: a distant federal government was a traditional prairie scapegoat. Often, it was western radicals who defended nostalgic visions of rural community life, while prairie right-wingers demanded sweeping changes. Nowhere were changes more apparent than in the West's basic industry, agriculture. If the family-owned farm remained the basis of production, machinery and prosperity had transformed it into a million-dollar enterprise, covering thousands of acres. Success depended on scientific and financial skill as well as on the traditional partnership of nature and hard work. While wheat remained the staple, wise farmers had diversified into canola, flax, and, when climate or irrigation permitted, vegetables. Huge farms meant depopulation: three-quarters of a million prairie people left the land after the war. The familiar infrastructure of a horse-drawn era—villages, rail lines, grain elevators—was obsolete. No longer was the landscape shaped by the fifteen-mile range of a loaded wagon and a team of horses. In 1933, 5,758 elevators had broken the prairie skyline; by 1978, almost half of them were gone. Between 1940 and 1980, the rural share of the prairie population fell from 60 per cent to 30 per cent.

By the 1970s, business had replaced farming as the dominant prairie preoccupation. Winnipeg, Regina, and Saskatoon more than doubled in population; buoyed by oil and gas revenues, Calgary and Edmonton grew sevenfold to 800,000 each. By 1981, both of them had surpassed Winnipeg to become competing regional metropolises. Over the mountains, western growth and Pacific markets helped make Vancouver a city of more than a million people. All of this was possible because of diversification far beyond agriculture and its related industries. Until 1947, Alberta had supplied about 10 per cent of Canada's oil and gas. The Leduc oil field discovery brought billions of dollars in investment and a swift takeover by the multinational corporations that dominated the western world's oil industry. By 1970, Alberta's production could have satisfied the Canadian market, although it made more economic sense in a continental industry to export to the United States. Alberta's neighbouring provinces strained to match its good fortune. Saskatoon proclaimed itself the potash capital of the world; Regina boasted a steel complex, serving the region's pipeline needs; nickel mines at Thompson and Lynn Lake gave Manitoba its own claim to diversification.

Prairie politics were tied to development strategies. The claim that Manitoba Tories had been swindled by foreign developers of a forest-products complex at The Pas helped win power for the NDP in 1969. So did resistance to ambitious

In the midst of the 1970s energy crisis, it seemed sensible to build a pipeline down the Mackenzie Valley to bring oil from proven and future finds—but not before Native people had been consulted. Their views, collected by Mr. Justice Thomas Berger in countless small communities, shelved the project. Local rights and Native claims were beginning to be taken seriously.

hydroelectricity developments on the Nelson River by Native and environmental groups. The continuing resource debate helped defeat the NDP in 1977 and, in turn, the resurrected Tories in 1982. In Saskatchewan, the statistics of rural depopulation had helped beat the CCF in 1964; a determination to control the province's potash industry helped restore the NDP to power in 1971. That year, Peter Lougheed annihilated Alberta's Social Credit regime by articulating a provincial concern about the long-term future when the oil and gas were gone. Wealth had not made prairie people forget the Depression or their vulnerability as primary producers.

Outsiders might find little in common between Lougheed, with his background in professional football and Calgary boardrooms, and the soft-spoken socialism of his Saskatchewan neighbour, Allan Blakeney. Certainly, oil magnates preferred the freewheeling style of Edmonton to the regulatory caution of Regina. What both provinces shared with most of the Canadian West was a determination to control their own natural resources and, so far as they could, their economic destiny. Nothing in their history had persuaded westerners that their interests were much safer in Ottawa and Toronto than in New York or Houston.

Trudeau's intervention in the 1973 oil-price shock made obvious sense in eastern Canada. Why should Canadians suffer from a foreign cartel when Canada had enough domestic oil to be free of OPEC machinations? Taxing energy exports to the United States to subsidize consumers temporarily dependent on OPEC supplies was no injustice to Americans or Albertans, though it was a splendid demonstration, particularly to Quebecers, of some of the practical benefits of Confederation. And why should Alberta expect the new world prices when these were the product of a monstrous international extortion? The entire country would benefit from oil policies which made Canada self-sufficient. Alberta itself would share in a billion-dollar project to extract usable fuel from the vast tar-sands deposits near Fort McMurray, as well as access to new Quebec markets. Promoting frontier oil exploration and a federally run oil corporation, Petro-Canada, should have made sense east and west.

It did not. Angry westerners argued that Ottawa had never intervened to save them from the world price of cars, overcoats, or anything else produced in Ontario or Quebec. Holding down prices for a depleting resource robbed future generations of money that otherwise would have poured into the Alberta and Saskatchewan Heritage funds. Without foreign investment, there would have been no energy industry in the West. As it was, production from proven sources had now passed its peak. Frontier oil would be an enormous gamble to find and a near-impossibility to deliver. The fatuity of Ottawa's dreams was underlined when plans for a Mackenzie Valley Pipeline to transport natural gas and later oil from the Arctic Ocean to Alberta were scuttled when a royal commission headed by Mr. Justice Thomas Berger endorsed the claims of northern Native groups and their southern sympathizers. Inuit and Dene—terms that now supplanted the older white names of "Eskimo" and "Indian"—suddenly found themselves with the leverage to stop northern development until their own rival political and territorial demands had been satisfied. While Native groups demanded control of resource policies in the North, prairie governments fought to retain the power they had won in 1930. Saskatchewan's government lined up with Alberta's Conservatives when the Trudeau government attempted to scuttle NDP plans to nationalize the provincial potash industry.

Claims of rich offshore oil deposits turned even impoverished consuming provinces, such as Newfoundland and Nova Scotia, into allies against Ottawa.

Newfoundland's brash Premier Brian Peckford borrowed Heritage Fund money from Alberta to sustain his fight against Ottawa's claim to the ocean shelf. British Columbia, with its own share of natural gas and its own offshore dreams, completed the hostile provincial phalanx.

Ottawa also found itself trapped by dilemmas westerners themselves hesitated to face. During the late 1970s, prairie farmers enjoyed some of the richest years in history, but they might have been richer still if prairie products had not been snarled in an overloaded, obsolete transportation system. Economists had an easy explanation: the obligation to ship wheat at 1897 prices, set by the Crow's Nest Pass Agreement, was all the argument railway managers needed against modernization. Yet farmers and their political representatives defended the "Crow rate" with all the passion owed to a sacred regional totem. Counter-arguments—that high freight rates would force farmers to sell their grain as feed for western cattle—were not designed to win farm votes. Federally purchased hopper cars did not smooth the steep Rocky Mountain grades or expand Vancouver's clogged grain terminals, though their manufacture did create some jobs in Nova Scotia.

Oil prices, freight rates, and business investment inflamed the West's view of Confederation. The truth was that a region with a sense of its own economic power wanted respect and influence. When corporate headquarters, fleeing Quebec nationalism, leaped over Toronto to erect their huge glass towers in Calgary, westerners were properly gleeful. Politicians and financiers wanted regional banks and stock exchanges. They rejoiced in local multimillionaires—Fred Mannix, Jim Pattison, Peter Pocklington, Murray Pezim—and accused eastern critics of jealousy.

Far from wanting out of Confederation, most westerners believed that they were excluded from their rightful influence. Constitutional reforms that would have given only Ontario and Quebec a veto on future amendments, proposed by Ottawa in 1971, symbolized an outdated Canadian political order. Alberta, Peter Lougheed insisted, had as much right to a veto as any of the central provinces: it was not his view alone. As for the bilingual, bicultural fixation of Trudeau's Ottawa, such ideas might be positively harmful to a region acutely conscious of its many competing linguistic and cultural groups.

By 1979, when Lougheed, Blakeney, and the West seemed to have reached some accommodation with Ottawa on energy costs, a fresh OPEC initiative virtually tripled prices. In an election year, the Trudeau government responded as it had in 1973, subsidizing the importing provinces at the expense of Alberta. That did not save the

Liberals, but it left a bitter legacy that Joe Clark's short-lived Tory government would not be able to overcome. Caught between Lougheed's intransigence and the obduracy of Ontario's Progressive Conservatives, not even an Alberta-born prime minister would be able to survive. When, on February 18, 1980, Quebec and Ontario made Pierre Trudeau prime minister again, the bitterness between West and East would be close to a political flashpoint.

Quebec and Constitutions

Because they had never been evenly distributed, even good times added to the strains of Confederation. In the quarter-century after the war, most of Canada could only envy the easy affluence of southern Ontario and Quebec. In the 1970s, that changed. The energy boom drew wealth westward until Alberta boasted the highest average income in the country. For Nova Scotia and Newfoundland, reports of rich offshore resources promised equal wealth in a matter of years. It was the central provinces that now faced anxious futures. Soaring energy costs, obsolete industrial technology, and foreign competition closed factories and wiped out tens of thousands of the well-paid jobs that once had sustained the consumer revolution. The American industries which had once devoured Ontario nickel and Quebec iron ore had been reduced to stark, silent landmarks in the rustbelt states. What did the Auto Pact matter if Canadians now preferred German or Japanese cars?

Provinces, forced to satisfy a voracious public appetite for education and health care from shrinking revenues, braved the defiance of militant teachers and angry health-care workers. In the spring of 1972, 200,000 Quebec public-sector workers spearheaded the largest general strike in Canadian history. The "Common Front" campaign ended in violence, defiance, and the jailing of labour leaders. Ontario hospital workers defied the government to arrest them. In 1975, resentful voters almost defeated an Ontario Tory regime that had lasted since 1943.

Having purchased a 1974 majority by lavish spending and subsidies, the federal Liberal government chose the resulting inflation as the culprit for an economic malaise and decided, after all, that it could be curbed by domestic policy. Having denounced wage and price controls as Tory folly, the Prime Minister proclaimed his own "restraints," on Thanksgiving weekend 1975. An Anti-Inflation Board froze union bargaining power for three years. Labour's rage, expressed in court battles, demonstrations, and a million-member walkout in October 1975, had no effect on a government sustained by the courts and most public opinion.

Yet inflation and strikes were symptoms of deeper problems. Economic nationalists renewed old charges that an economy based on foreign-owned branch plants was inherently inefficient and imitative. Critics from left and right demanded an industrial strategy for Canada, though it was never clear, amid the rancorous voices, what precise strategy would simultaneously satisfy labour, capital, environmentalists, and regional patriots. In Quebec, Robert Bourassa's bid for a "profitable federalism" struggled against inflation, nervous investors, an increasingly radical union movement, and media opinion-leaders who had long since espoused the captivating dream of independence. By 1973, Quebec was polarized between the increasingly business-oriented Liberals and a resolutely independentist Parti Québécois. In a two-party fight, almost a third of the votes gave the PQ just a handful of seats. The minority was unreconciled; the majority felt uncertain of its mandate.

In Ottawa and beyond, Bourassa's reputation as defender of federalism had been hurt by the October Crisis. A year later, when Trudeau summoned provincial premiers to Victoria to discuss the patriation and reform of the venerable British North America Act, Bourassa should have been jubilant. Forty years earlier, Quebec and Ontario had scuttled Ottawa arrangements to bring the constitution home from London because they would not have a veto on future amendments; at Victoria, Trudeau gave Bourassa and Ontario's Bill Davis that right plus most of Quebec's traditional demands. On the flight home, however, Bourassa learned of a waiting storm. In Montreal, Claude Ryan of Le Devoir had whipped up a nationalist furor because Bourassa had not won everything the powerful editor had demanded. Bourassa's self-confidence wilted, the Victoria Charter died, and so did Trudeau's respect for his former protégé.

That would have mattered less if Quebec had prospered. Bourassa's prize achievement was a vast hydroelectric development on James Bay. Critics denounced the financial risks, the environmental damage, even the financial settlement with the Native people, but it took a violent rampage by workers in the winter of 1975 to turn the project politically sour. An inquiry showed that the government had counted on union goons to keep labour peace. Montreal's staging of the 1976 Olympic games left as bitter a taste. Canadian athletes won few medals; an African boycott and tight security blighted any possible euphoria and Montrealers were left with an unfinished stadium, too many hotels, and mass unemployment. Mayor Jean Drapeau had boasted that there could no more be a deficit than he could have a baby. A cartoonist depicted

Triumphant young people on the night of November 15, 1976. For the first time, a party pledged to seek Quebec's independence had swept to power. Only four years later, Quebecers showed that while they wanted René Lévesque and the Parti Québécois, they also wanted Confederation. But by 1985 they did not even want the PQ. On May 20—referendum night in Montreal—the Quebec premier acknowledged defeat.

him phoning Henry Morgentaler, a well-known doctor specializing in abortions.

Economic difficulties intertwined with Quebec's unresolved language dispute. Nationalists claimed that it was English-run businesses that issued layoff notices or had no room for the swelling torrent of university-trained Québécois. Bourassa's compromise solution, Bill 22, satisfied no one. English-speaking parents were indignant that six-year-olds would be tested on their right to be educated in English; nationalists insisted that only a unilingual French-speaking Quebec would be tolerable. In the spring of 1976, a tiny dispute suddenly churned into a hurricane of emotion. Ottawa announced that French would join English as an official traffic-control language in Quebec skies. Then, faced with protests from English-Canadian pilots, controllers, and politicians, the government backed down: a year's delay was necessary. The interval gave nationalists the issue they wanted. When Bourassa led his battered government to the polls on November 15, 1976, Liberal support had evaporated. The Parti Québécois garnered only 41 per cent of the vote, but it was enough to grow from 7 to 71 seats. The Liberals kept 28. Nine years after his break with the Liberals, René Lévesque and his separatists had triumphed.

For a moment, Canadians were stunned. They had hardly imagined such an outcome. Ironically, a prime minister who had presided over regional disintegration now became Canada's saviour. "I say to you with all the certainty I can command," Trudeau told Canadians, "that Canada's unity will not be fractured." By February 1977, half the Canadian electorate would have voted for him. Then, slowly, the country relaxed. Once in power, René Lévesque postponed the independence referendum in favour of popular reforms more typical of an NDP government. The Parti Québécois ended the folly of examining toddlers, but its own language law, Bill 101, made French the only legal and also the only visible language of Quebec, from government forms to billboards and menus. If Anglo-Quebecers were squeezed out of their province, they made room for ambitious Québécois. If they stayed, they would work in French, whether in the stock exchange or on factory assembly lines. Children of newcomers, even from Alberta, would be taught only in French.

Outside Quebec, few Canadians worried about the harshness of Bill 101. The province's English minority had never commanded much sympathy. A task force was sent out to find a national response to Quebec's discontents. It returned, like the Laurendeau–Dunton Commission, dizzy from the myriad of grievance-mongers and eager to endorse constitutional schemes that satisfied no one. For the most part, Canadians soon felt free again to denounce a federal government that kept causing them more pain than pleasure. In the summer of 1978, Trudeau came home from a seven-nation economic summit at the West German capital of Bonn, primed for a fresh assault on inflation and a growing deficit. The restraint program was scrapped; its replacement was the new old-fashioned monetarism: high interest rates, cuts in public spending, the certainty of mounting unemployment. Few rejoiced.

Canadians had had almost enough of their philosopher-prince. They admired Trudeau in crises, sympathized with his dignified endurance of a collapsing marriage, but they resented his aloof disdain for their daily concerns. A government of power-hungry officials and mediocre ministers had been too long in power. All that remained to the Liberals was to spread the impression that the alternatives were worse. Canadians admired the dogged decency of the NDP's Ed Broadbent but only a stubborn fifth of the electorate ever endorsed his party. In 1976, the Tories had replaced Robert Stanfield with Joe Clark, a pleasant young Albertan whom no one disliked. After watching Clark lead his fractious party, few respected him either. Clark's weaknesses could, however, be disguised by image-makers; the Liberal record could not. On May 22, 1979, Quebec voters were solidly loyal to Trudeau; elsewhere Canadians remembered falling incomes, lost jobs, and a government that had forgotten them. The Tories emerged with 136 seats, 8 short of a majority. It was a frail mandate for change.

Voters soon had second thoughts. Clark took a leisurely summer to organize his government. Amid growing panic at an impending Quebec referendum, the Iranian oil-price shock, and interest rates soaring to 15 and 20 per cent, Clark's caution began to look like hapless indecision. Tory support tumbled. In November, Trudeau's resignation from public life seemed to promise the new government more time. A budget, tougher in rhetoric than substance, tried to satisfy Alberta oil magnates at the expense of Ontario energy consumers. Peter Lougheed was not appeased; Bill Davis, Ontario's Conservative premier, was furious. Liberals took courage from the polls and backed an NDP motion to reject the budget. Amazingly, the Conservatives did nothing to avert defeat. Canada faced an unexpected mid-winter election. Clark was confident that he would repeat Diefenbaker's 1958 feat. Leaderless Liberals felt a momentary chill. Then, suddenly, Trudeau was back, armed for his apotheosis. On February 18, Ontario, Quebec, and the Maritimes gave him back his majority: Liberals 147, Tories 103, NDPers 32.

There was much to do. The crisis of Quebec in Confederation had brought Trudeau to Ottawa in 1965, and it remained his unfinished business. At times, the world of summit conferences, arms races, and cruel North-South disparities had

In 1976 Ed Broadbent won the New Democratic Party leadership, and Rosemary Brown came second. The member of the B.C. legislature was the first woman and the first black to seek a party leadership. In the 1970s, it no longer seemed extraordinary.

deflected Trudeau's interest, but the bread-and-butter preoccupations of Canadian businessmen, unionists, and farmers had consistently bored him. Now, in his last mandate, Trudeau was finally free to do what he could and leave history to judge.

Lévesque had planned his referendum for May 20, 1980, with a question continuously market-tested until it could not fail: surely most Quebecers would approve a mandate to negotiate sovereignty-association—with a further chance to vote on the outcome? The "*Non*" side, led by Claude Ryan—once the austere nationalist editor who bedevilled Robert Bourassa and now, ironically, was his successor—was a feeble coalition, preoccupied by academic schemes for decentralizing federalism. Trudeau ignored Ryan. Instead, he sent Jean Chrétien, a popular minister and self-proclaimed "little guy from Shawinigan," to galvanize opposition to Lévesque. Barely aware that its own Bill 101 had taken the heat out of Quebecers' fears for survival, the PQ made error after error. It bored its own supporters, insulted opponents, and worried the undecided. In a heavy turnout the "*Nons*" triumphed, 60 per cent to 40 per cent.

In his referendum speeches, Trudeau had promised Quebec and Canada a new constitutional deal. Though he had once warned that constitutional reform would open a Pandora's box, Trudeau now believed that patriation and an entrenched Charter of Rights and Freedoms would be the enduring monument his political career had lacked. National relief at the referendum outcome and the embarrassment of a constitution that still had to be amended in Britain would help Trudeau to his goal. Through the summer of 1980, Jean Chrétien and Saskatchewan's Attorney-General, Roy Romanow, crossed Canada, urging a package of constitutional proposals on provincial premiers.

In September, when Trudeau and the premiers met in Ottawa in a televised spectacle, it was apparent that the premiers were not converted. Only Ontario's Bill Davis and New Brunswick's Richard Hatfield shared Trudeau's priority; their colleagues believed that provincial vetoes could stall proceedings until regional demands and personal priorities had been satisfied. A puckish Lévesque took pleasure from the renewed constitutional impasse.

He reckoned without Trudeau. Early in October, the Prime Minister sliced through half a century of constitutional dithering. Whether the provinces liked it or not, Ottawa would act alone to bring the constitution home, give it a made-in-Canada amending formula, and adopt a charter of basic rights and freedoms. Davis and Hatfield promptly approved. So did the NDP's Ed Broadbent, after he had persuaded Trudeau to add guarantees of a stronger charter and protection for the West's resources. For their part, Lévesque, Lougheed, and most other premiers were almost beside themselves at Trudeau's audacity. In Parliament, Joe Clark used the issue to rally his demoralized Tories. Lawyers and a host of experts, real or imputed, joined the fray. As the Canadian economy slid into its worst recession since the 1930s, Government, Opposition, and occasional ill-informed British parliamentarians belaboured each other on issues most Canadians found arcane and irrelevant. Provinces filed challenges in the courts. Clergy, feminists, Native leaders, the disabled, and a host of groups fought for their own special places in the emerging constitution. Dissenting premiers met at Vancouver to devise their own complex amending formula with vetoes for no province.

Beginning in the 1960s provincial social workers, guided by non-Indian views of child care, began to remove Native children from their reserves at an alarming rate. As the proportion of Native children in welfare care grew to five times the national average, Indians began to insist that they have jurisdiction over child care: "Young people are the hope and life-blood of our nations, and their removal strikes at the very heart of our culture and heritage." (Restigouche Band, 1983.)

Even Lévesque agreed, confident that the "Vancouver Charter" would go nowhere. In Ottawa, constitutional debate paralysed Parliament.

In September 1981, the Supreme Court of Canada ruled on the validity of Trudeau's initiative: what the government had done, most judges agreed, was legal but defied convention. Since there was no precedent for patriation and therefore no convention, the verdict was nonsense, as Chief Justice Bora Laskin politely advised his brethren, but the decision forced Trudeau to make another attempt at consensus. The premiers gathered again in Ottawa for another fruitless meeting. Then, after midnight on November 5, 1981, Chrétien, Romanow, and Ontario's attorney-general, Roy McMurtry, wrestled a compromise into shape. Trudeau's charter of rights would be combined with the premiers' Vancouver amending formula. Premiers were wakened and summoned to the former railway station that served as Ottawa's conference centre—all but Lévesque, sound asleep in Hull. When he awoke, the deed had been done. The midnight compromise, embellished with clauses covering provincial control of resources, fiscal sharing, and other small change of federal–provincial wrangling, had become a constitutional document. Quebec's historic veto, blithely sacrificed at Vancouver, was gone. So were many of the provisions women and Native people had painfully fought for. After frenzied lobbying, sexual equality and an undefined commitment to aboriginal rights reappeared: Quebec's veto did not. On a cold, rainy April 17, 1982, Queen Elizabeth gave her royal assent to a Constitution Act few Canadians had read and even fewer understood. Pierre Elliott Trudeau had made his mark on history. The lawyers and judges who would give meaning to the turgid phrasing of the Act and its Charter of Rights and Freedoms had acquired a vast new power. Only time would tell how much power remained to the elected members of Parliament and the provincial legislatures.

End of Affluence?

In retrospect, Pierre Elliott Trudeau should have left in the wake of the constitution-signing ceremony. The outcome of the Quebec referendum made him dispensable. The Constitution Act guaranteed him the historical niche his long career had otherwise failed to earn. The liberation era, which he had once personified, had degenerated into a selfish conservatism. Above all, by 1982, Canada was mired in the kind of economic crisis in which Trudeau showed to least advantage.

The stagflation of the 1970s had undermined a post-war faith in the government-as-economic-manager. Beginning in 1978, average real incomes in Canada began to decline, a phenomenon masked by a surge of double-income families. Such families grew scarcer as divorce rates rose, and mother-led families became almost synonymous with poverty. Long before American voters elected Ronald Reagan in 1980, "New Deal" reformism was in eclipse, even among Democrats. In 1979, British voters elected the most unabashedly right-wing government since the 1920s. Americans then followed suit with Reagan. In Canada, too, a mixture of anxiety and self-interest curdled the liberal optimism of the post-war years. The baby boomers, the "big generation," evolved into a self-interested consumerism. Personal fitness became an industry. As public opinion turned against smoking, cigarette manufacturers and tobacco farmers suffered. Middle-aged consumers switched to wine and exotic brands of beer. Drunk driving became a scandal. Pro- and anti-abortionists argued their cases without charity or concession. Conservatives demanded rigid school curricula and testing, curbs on unpopular opinions, and (unsuccessfully) a return to capital punishment (abolished in 1964). Feminists split on whether pornography or unfettered free speech mattered more. Students in the 1980s espoused conservative causes, competed for marks, and switched to career-oriented programs. Polls reported that Canadians considered "Big Government" their worst enemy, with "Big Labour" close behind. Rarely in the century had "Big Business" been more admired or less criticized. One of the few successful government initiatives of the 1970s spread across Canada by the 1980s. Initiated as a "voluntary tax" by Jean Drapeau to fund his Olympic ambitions, lotteries created effortless millionaires and political pin money for provincial governments. The post-war faith that hard work plus economic growth would fulfil any reasonable dream ended with prayers for luck in a nation-wide Lotto 6/49 draw and prizes of $10 million and more.

In Quebec, the 1980 referendum result seemed to bury nationalism. When Lévesque cried betrayal over Quebec's defeat in the constitutional negotiation, he encountered as much ridicule as sympathy. In truth, his own language law, Bill 101, had helped undermine the separatist cause. Who could worry about English domination when the language itself had virtually disappeared from sight and when the jobs of departing Anglophones were available for ambitious Québécois? The language of business in Montreal was now French, but the boardroom ideology was as conservative as ever. Having embraced secularism and democratic socialism, Quebec opinion-leaders now had "le gout des affaires." The PQ itself looked more and more like the old Union Nationale. Re-elected in 1981, after Quebecers again rejected the Liberals under an uncharismatic Claude Ryan, the PQ reacted to the economic recession by stripping public employees of their rich pre-referendum pay increases. Teachers and civil servants, once the militant core of separatism, could look for no relief from the Liberals.

In Ottawa, the re-elected Liberals initially ignored the rightward trend. Party insiders blamed their own 1979 defeat on the government's monetarism and cutbacks. While Trudeau had forged ahead with his constitutional plans, colleagues attempted to deliver on election promises of tax reform and a "made-in-Canada" energy policy. Allan MacEachen used his first budget to plug a long list of cherished tax loopholes. Joe Clark's blunders had included a threat to dismantle Petro-Canada, the government-owned oil company. To eastern voters, any Canadian-controlled agency that could protect them from Arabs, Albertans, and Esso was popular. When the National Energy Program, or NEP, was proclaimed by Trudeau late in 1981, Petro-Canada became the centrepiece of a drive for Canadian ownership, self-sufficiency, and an abolition of the tax concessions that had filled oil company coffers. From the Beaufort Sea to Newfoundland's offshore Hibernia deposits, the government itself would finance frontier oil exploration while taking a share of fresh discoveries.

Ten years earlier, both tax reform and the NEP might have succeeded. In 1981, they inspired outrage in the West and among business leaders. Under furious assault, the government promptly unplugged most of the tax loopholes and forgot about reform. On the NEP, Ottawa was firm. Still waiting for his cut after oil prices tripled in 1979, Alberta's Peter Lougheed shut down two giant oil-sands conversion projects and twice reduced supplies to eastern Canada. By the fall of 1982, Ottawa had settled with Edmonton, though the oil companies were left out. Executives cancelled investment plans, shifted capital to the more sympathetic environment of Reagan's America, and reminded Washington of their displeasure with folks up in Canada. Hundreds of Canadian companies, born or bred in the oil boom, either folded or took their drill rigs south in hope of American business. Floods of workers, drawn from the East by reports of Alberta riches, turned around and went home. Others stayed to join local hordes of unemployed. In 1979, Alberta had boasted virtual full employment—96.3 per cent. By 1983, one in ten of the province's workers was hunting for a job. The western boom had bust. Bitter Albertans knew whom to blame.

More than the NEP, it was the recession that punctured the resource boom, dragging down world oil prices despite all the OPEC cartel could do. The protectionism of new trading blocs, deepening third-world poverty, and panic by bankers, who had loaned not wisely but too well, contributed to the squeeze. For a time, high interest rates fed inflation: in Canada, they reached a post-war high of 22.5 per cent in 1981. Then, amid bankruptcies, mass unemployment, and crumpling national economies, rates fell. Few noticed. In 1979, 836,000 Canadians had been looking for work, with the greatest share in Quebec and the Atlantic provinces. By 1982, the monthly average was 1,314,000 and rising. A fifth of would-be workers under twenty-five had no job. The toll was highest in Newfoundland, New Brunswick, and Quebec, but the collapse of world markets for coal, lumber, and paper left one British Columbia worker in six unemployed. In constant dollars, Canada's GNP tumbled 4 per cent in 1982, the first such setback since the 1930s. A federal deficit that had been adding a worrying $12 billion to $13 billion a year to the national debt through the 1970s began a stratospheric climb as revenues stagnated and the costs of welfare soared. In 1982, the federal deficit was $23.99 billion; by 1984 it was $35.79 billion, higher, per capita, than anything the Reagan administration had imposed on Americans and the world. In response, the Canadian dollar slid gracelessly from 93 American cents in 1981 to an historic low of 70 cents by the end of 1985.

It was easy, in the prevailing mood, to pin the blame for economic disaster on Ottawa. Yet in the name of free-enterprise principles, British and American working people suffered comparable hardships. In Canada, bad luck and bad management dogged the NEP. The sinking of a huge oil rig, the *Ocean Ranger*, in a storm off Newfoundland, with the loss of all its crew, underlined the costly risks of offshore oil. Dome Petroleum, a joyous collector of NEP grants for its

In the recession of the 1980s more than a million Canadians, most of them young, lost their jobs. Resource industries, hit by falling world prices, were most affected. This young couple seeks assistance and advice from a union help centre in British Columbia.

For Native peoples the age of "space" is long past; they must fight to preserve their cultures in a technological world. From the North has come a new and distinctive style of sculpture and printmaking, bringing income, recognition, and a renewed sense of identity to the Inuit. Pudlo working on stone block at the Art Centre, Cape Dorset, N.W.T., August 1981.

Snowmobiles may be "recreational vehicles" in Southern Canada, but for the congregation of this Anglican church in Cape Dorset, some 240 kilometres (150 miles) below the Arctic Circle, they are just sensible transport.

The Raven and the First Men, a 1980 carving by Haida sculptor, printmaker, and goldsmith Bill Reid. This contemporary version of an ancient creation myth symbolizes the rebirth of North-West Coast Indian art in the last three decades. Photo by W. McLennan.

Beaufort Sea explorations, collapsed amidst soaring costs and tumbling oil prices. In 1983, when the government abolished the Crow's Nest rate, an historic subsidy for prairie grain exporters, it stoked the anger of western wheat farmers. Even the "6&5 plan," the Trudeau government's attempt to restrict all wages and prices it could control, made enemies without achieving its goal. The post-1981 recession made 6-and-5 per cent wage increases seem generous when millions of private-sector workers faced wage cuts and layoffs.

Good times had pushed Canadians deeper into the American orbit, bad times accelerated the pull. Japan had long since replaced Britain and even all of Europe as Canada's second trading partner. Japanese cars, cameras, television sets, tape recorders; South Korean jogging shoes and sweat pants; and much else that defined consumerism in the 1980s had long since supplanted goods that Canadians or even their neighbours had once produced. Corporations that struggled back from layoffs and near-bankruptcy looked to Japan for robotics, microchips, and management philosophy, but only after American head offices and business gurus approved. The United States was twelve times larger than Japan as a supplier to Canada and twenty times bigger as a Canadian market.

At the depth of the recession, in 1982, the Trudeau government appointed a Royal Commission on the Economic Union headed by his former finance minister and

Part of an international movement by popular musicians, *Tears Are Not Enough* was recorded to raise funds for victims of famine in Africa. Among those who sang on the record and performed on the popular video were (top row) Murray McLauchlan, Liberty Silver, Mike Reno, Robert Charlebois, Ronnie Hawkins, Corey Hart; (middle row) Burton Cummings, Véronique Beliveau, Bryan Adams, Claude Dubois; (front row) Gordon Lightfoot, Anne Murray, Carroll Baker, Geddy Lee, Joni Mitchell, and Neil Young.

potential successor, Donald S. Macdonald. Seemingly every prominent economist in the country was recruited to produce a study. Their influence and the mood of the times persuaded the Commission, perhaps to its own surprise, to emerge squarely in favour of closer economic links, even free trade, with the United States. And why not? A so-called "Third Option" of enhanced trade with Europe and the Pacific Rim had won little support from Canadian business, and virtually none from the branch-plant managers or their bosses. American markets beckoned. So did American culture. Satellites and VCRs outflanked the cultural nationalism of the Canadian Radio-television and Telecommunications Commission (CRTC) and fed a Canadian appetite for American mass entertainment.

Post-war Canadians had hoped for something more than a continental embrace. A handful of able officials and its own natural wealth had secured for Canada a visible measure of independence at a time when the United States dominated the world. Paradoxically, Canada's dependence seemed to grow as American economic stature and power worldwide diminished. External Affairs officialdom proliferated, but innovative genius had retreated to familiar platitudes about peace, collective security, and moderation. Becoming the junior member of the Group of Seven major industrialized countries in 1978 only added to the output of free-enterprise platitudes. External aid, expanded enormously since the 1952 Commonwealth Conference in Colombo, was a brave but lonely vestige of post-war idealism. Nowhere was the stasis in policy and inflation of bureaucracy more apparent than in defence. More generals and admirals than Canada had needed in 1945 presided over 82,000 men and women and a largely obsolete collection of ships, tanks, and aircraft. By the mid-1980s, Canada's most modern warships were four destroyers ordered in the Pearson years. While the forces and their effectiveness diminished, the host of commitments, from Kashmir to NATO's northern flank, seemed to grow.

Despite acknowledged brilliance and a veteran's longevity among world leaders, Trudeau gave little of the commitment to Canada's international role that he devoted to its internal conflicts of language, culture, and constitution. Trudeau had little respect for the mediocrities, from Nixon to Reagan, whom American voters sent to the White House during his career, and he received none in return. Trudeau had spurned NATO in 1969, discovered its usefulness in the 1970s, and finally, in a sudden bid to be acknowledged a peacemaker, denounced NATO's Cold War preoccupations. The Third World and "North-South dialogue" were remembered and forgotten with equal ease. Prime-ministerial caprice did not help Canada's influence in the world.

World status worried Canadians less than the state of the economy and their own livelihood. Within a year of his triumphant re-election, Trudeau's support was crumbling. Joe Clark's admirers credited the Tories' stout resistance to Trudeau's constitutional proposals; his Tory critics wondered whether voters could ever support someone they had rejected so contemptuously in 1980. By 1983, they had manoeuvred Clark into putting his leadership to a public challenge. At Ottawa, on June 11, Diefenbaker loyalists, right-wingers, and resentful patronage-seekers coalesced behind an affable, outgoing Montreal lawyer who had come surprisingly close in 1976. Brian Mulroney had never sought elected office but he was charming, Catholic, colloquial in both official languages, and comfortable with the power brokers of business or either political party. If Mulroney's major public achievement, as president of the Iron Ore Company of Canada, was turning Schefferville into a ghost town, he had merely obeyed his American employers. Moreover, the settlement was generous

Canada's newspapers used to claim to reserve their bias for the editorial pages, but would the *Globe and Mail* have portrayed their chosen candidate with forks playing the role of devil's horns? In the Trudeau years, John Turner had been a business hero. But by 1984, business leaders—and the publishers and editors who served them—favoured Brian Mulroney. Canadians got the message.

enough to satisfy local unions. In the 1980s, government, not business, was the public's preferred villain.

Tories had no illusions that Canadians wanted a Thatcher or a Reagan. When British Columbia's Bill Bennett celebrated his 1983 re-election with an unheralded assault on social services and public-sector unions, Mulroney solemnly proclaimed that, to him, universal social programs were "a sacred trust." When Manitoba Tories raised a public clamour about an NDP government attempt to provide bilingual services, Mulroney firmly disavowed them. Conservative support rose, even draining votes from the NDP. The Liberals were undismayed: they had their own saviour.

After a hurriedly improvised world-peace mission failed to raise his stock, Trudeau strode into a snowstorm on February 29, 1984, and made up his mind to resign. Most Liberal insiders promptly coalesced behind John Turner. In the ten years since he quit as finance minister, he had built business connections as a Toronto corporation lawyer. He had also made no secret of his distaste for Trudeau's policies and his contempt for Jean Chrétien, the NEP, and much else that had happened since his departure. With Turner in the race, Liberal fortunes rose. So did Chrétien's, campaigning as Trudeau's unofficial heir and as a populist hero. On June 16 the final Liberal convention ballot pitted two rival versions of Liberalism against each other. Turner prevailed and a honeymoon of favourable opinion polls enticed him into an immediate general election.

Never in Canadian history has a party or politician fallen faster. Trapped into rewarding a host of Trudeau cronies with patronage plums, a stuttering Turner had to confess, in a television debate with Mulroney, "I had no choice." Ill-informed and oddly awkward after his years with the business elite, he also had no organization, no policies and, after a few weeks, little money or support. Lavishly financed, furiously organized, and smoothly presented, Brian Mulroney coasted on an electoral landslide that seeped and then deluged across Quebec. So complete and certain was the Tory triumph even before election day that defecting supporters raced back to the NDP to save a likeable Ed Broadbent and his party from total eclipse. Mulroney's victory on September 4 matched Diefenbaker's in 1958: 211 Tories to a mere 40 Liberals and 30 New Democrats. Turner's election in a wealthy Vancouver constituency owed more to compassion than conviction.

Four times Conservatives won power in twentieth-century Canada only to fall victim to war or economic disaster. The fifth occasion gave Brian Mulroney the mandate for the unequivocal promise he had made in his campaign: to restore a sense of community to Canadians. With eight out of ten provinces under Progressive Conservative or sympathetic governments, it was a promise he seemed able to keep. There was more, of course, that he and his lieutenants and business backers wanted: an assault on the federal deficit, "privatization" of a host of federal activities and enterprises, a tax system that would provide incentives for the wealthy to get wealthier. Despite its massive mandate and overwhelming parliamentary majority, the new government found that some old political rules had not changed. Regions and provinces had been unanimous for Mulroney, but old differences soon resurfaced. The prosperity that slowly returned to Canada, even before the 1984 election, favoured the urban, industrial regions of central Canada, leaving the vast hinterland regions hurt and hurting. The sudden emergence of free trade offered some Canadians a panacea, but to a host of protected ventures, from brewing to publishing, it was a nightmare. Deficit-cutting was not much easier: outrage from the elderly killed a proposal in the government's first budget to end indexing for old age security. A prime minister too fond of his cronies and a party with a 31-year thirst for patronage helped make embarrassing headlines. Like the Liberals, the Conservatives rediscovered the painful trade-offs of regional politics. In 1986, a $1.8 billion contract to repair fighter aircraft went to Montreal, not to the low bidder in Winnipeg. Quebec had more leverage than Manitoba. Western voters, faithful to the Tories during the long Liberal years, felt betrayed.

At midterm, opinion polls showed the Mulroney government lagging even

A Canadian ice-breaker, the *John A. Macdonald*, ploughs through heavy ice in Eureka Sound. In the 1980s, as the U.S. challenged Canada's claim to the Arctic, some Canadians began to wonder whether they had left their sovereignty over the vast North a little too much to chance.

behind the NDP. Within two years of the Tory sweep, the provincial political pendulum had begun to swing back. The PQ's decision to put its independence plank into storage helped Robert Bourassa take Quebec for the Liberals on December 2, 1986, by 99 seats to 23. A host of issues, from a lurch to the right to a Conservative decision to allow full funding for Catholic schools, ended Ontario's forty-two-year Conservative regime in May 1985. A written agreement with Bob Rae to adopt NDP policies allowed David Peterson to form the first Liberal government in the province since 1943. Joe Ghiz, a lawyer of Lebanese origins, did the same in Prince Edward Island in April 1986. Only in the West did Tory premiers hold their provinces.

Yet Mulroney was shrewder than his critics imagined. To replace the Liberals as the natural majority party, he cultivated their old stronghold, Quebec, with contracts, patronage, and as much concern for language and culture as his caucus rednecks would allow. In the 1984 campaign, Mulroney had promised to succeed where Trudeau had failed: he would bring Quebec into the constitution "with honour and enthusiasm." Bourassa's return was his opportunity. After his government had substantially reduced its demands, two marathon bargaining sessions with all the provincial premiers, at Meech Lake on April 30 and in Ottawa on June 3, 1987, produced a unanimous accord. In future, provinces would submit lists of potential senators and Supreme Court justices for the prime minister to make his pick. Ottawa would share responsibility for immigration policy with the provinces and provide full compensation for provinces that opted out of federal programs. Above all,

Quebec would be recognized as a "distinct" society. Conscious of the achievement, both Turner and Broadbent promptly pledged their parties' support. Critics checked with the former prime minister and, encouraged by Trudeau's boiling rage, began to muster their forces. Soon after the Meech Lake Accord a swirling controversy over Premier Richard Hatfield's private life cost New Brunswick Conservatives every seat as Frank McKenna's Liberals swept the province on October 13, 1987. Howard Pawley, head of Manitoba's lonely NDP government, fell six months later, a victim of voter discontent at bilingualism and high premiums for government-run car insurance. McKenna and Manitoba's new Liberal opposition leader, Sharon Carstairs, condemned the Meech accord; as a minority premier, Manitoba's Gary Filmon would be prudent. Two signatories of the Meech Lake Accord were gone and, if the constitution had hardly been an issue in their downfall, it would not be unaffected.

An End to Confederation?

While Quebec preoccupied the prime minister and a large part of his caucus, many more Tories wanted a closer affinity with Ronald Reagan's free-enterprise America. The U.S. president joined Mulroney at Quebec City for their first official meeting, and shared a concluding duet of "When Irish Eyes are Smiling." "Good relations, super relations with the United States will be the cornerstone of our foreign policy," Mulroney assured the *Wall Street Journal*. This was frustrating for those Canadians who wanted action on acid rain, deplored U.S.-armed contras in Nicaragua, and worried about the implications of a hugely expensive U.S. anti-missile defence. American insistence on international access to the Northwest Passage, enforced by the transit of an American icebreaker, moved the government to promise a comparable Canadian ship—only to scrap the plans at the next convenient budget cut. In opposition, the Conservatives had promised that Canadian defence, meagre in the eyes of its NATO allies, would be strengthened. Hadn't Trudeau left Canada's warships to "rust out"? A 1987 defence white paper proposed a navy, army, and air force fit to meet the mighty Soviet military challenge—though a visionary proposal to achieve three-ocean capability with a squadron of nuclear-powered submarines was sunk by the joint firepower of the peace movement and the Pentagon. Still, twelve new frigates and a three-division "Total Force" army would have restored Canada to NATO's front line, if only the Warsaw Pact had not begun to crumble.

The prime minister and Mrs. Mulroney, the president of the United States and Mrs. Reagan, pose at the start of an evening which reached its climax when the two politicians sang "When Irish Eyes are Smiling." Did "good relations, super relations" with the United States have to go as far as the Free Trade Agreement of 1989?

The report of Donald Macdonald's Royal Commission, soon after the Conservatives took power, gave them a Liberal-inspired argument for urgent negotiation of a comprehensive free trade agreement with the United States. It would, Macdonald confessed, represent "a leap of faith," but how else could Canada hang on to the market for four-fifths of its exports? Mulroney in opposition had resisted free trade, reminding followers of the history lesson of 1911. In office his opinions proved flexible. Free trade gave Mulroney the ready-made economic policy he had lacked. Canada's major corporate lobby, the Business Council on National Issues, was strongly in favour. So was President Reagan and, in 1980, he had even campaigned for a North American free trade area. In the Canadian West, free trade was a traditional faith. Even in traditionally protectionist Quebec a new francophone business elite seemed wholly converted, and Robert Bourassa believed free trade was essential if he was to sell Quebec water and hydroelectricity to the Americans.

Opposition would be strong too, but a shrewd politician could see the weaknesses. Academic and cultural nationalists had few votes, and trade union and NDP opposition would toughen business support. What better than free trade and U.S. competition to wean Canadians from their socialist tendencies? Once business, industry, and finance were fully integrated, arguments for distinct social programs, industrial relations systems, and even cultural institutions would be overwhelmed. Three of the ten provincial premiers were opposed, but only Ontario's David Peterson had an important political base and, as Mackenzie King had discovered generations before, nothing was easier than uniting Canadians against the rich, comfortable central province. And what alternatives would the critics offer when faced with a protectionist U.S. Congress? Without a free trade deal, how many Canadian jobs would vanish as American politicians barred the door to Ontario steel and B.C. lumber?

By naming Simon Reisman, the outspoken negotiator of the 1965 Canada–U.S. Auto Pact, as its man at the table, the government persuaded itself and many Canadians that a good deal would result. At the same time, by his desperate campaigning for an agreement, Mulroney undermined Canada's bargaining power. After months of negotiation, Reisman was faced with the U.S. refusal to consider a binding disputes-resolution mechanism (a Canadian condition) and warnings that a long list of programs, from Medicare to relocation grants, might be considered unfair subsidies. On September 23, 1987, he walked. By October 4, after a talk with President Reagan, two cabinet ministers were in Washington to sign. Crucial issues were compromised or postponed for seven more years of bargaining.

The 1989 Free Trade Agreement went far beyond the "Unrestricted Reciprocity" Canadian voters had rejected almost a century before. In return for an early end to tariffs that were already minimal, and for help in negotiating non-tariff barriers, Canada agreed to share her natural resources, to allow unfettered access to Canadian banking, financial, and other service industries, and to award full compensation should any future government dare to interfere. Breweries and "cultural industries" were protected; wineries and just about everything else were "open for business." Confronted with a one-sided deal by an unpopular government, Canadians could be excused for thinking that Mulroney had overreached himself. Throughout most of 1987 the Tories plumbed new depths in the polls while the anti-free trade NDP surged into a commanding lead. Once the Tories were beaten, only six months notice would be needed to repudiate the deal.

But appearances were deceiving. Once protectionist, Canadian business had reversed itself. A handful of entrepreneurs, led by Robert Campeau, threw themselves into the high-stakes game of acquiring American companies. In Quebec, passions once absorbed by nationalism poured into entrepreneurial adventures. Separatists and federalists alike embraced free trade and denounced its critics as anti-Quebec. Under this torrent of conflicting arguments, Canadians were now split almost evenly on the deal, confessing more confusion than conviction. Mulroney spent the summer of 1988 delivering $14 billion in grants and pledges, ranging from Newfoundland's cherished Hibernia project to aid for multicultural newspapers. Private polls told him the tide was turning; so did a midsummer by-election when his friend Lucien Bouchard won easily. In Washington, Congress approved the deal by lopsided majorities. But in Ottawa, Mulroney had to use his majority to cut off debate. John Turner, galvanized by the struggle, threatened to use the Liberals' Senate majority to force an election. On October 1, Mulroney obliged him by dissolving Parliament.

The first election polls showed that what was unthinkable a year before had become almost inevitable: a Mulroney majority. Deep in debt and even more deeply divided, the Liberals had spent the previous year trying to depose Turner. The NDP, at 40 per cent early in 1987, had lost half its support, chiefly in Quebec. Combined, the two opposition parties might have concentrated the anti-free trade vote but that, too, was unthinkable. Still, for a moment in mid-campaign Mulroney was derailed. In 1984, a minute's interchange in a television debate helped Mulroney win his huge majority; in 1988, it was Turner's chance and he seized it, turning the free trade issue from cold economics to hot emotion. Liberal fortunes soared. But the Tories had foreseen the danger; scheduling debates early enough to allow for damage control. Business flooded the media to boost free trade. Reisman labelled Turner a traitor while nationalist cartoons made the same point about Mulroney. On November 21, the nastiest and most divisive campaign most Canadians could remember came to an end. The Liberals and NDP made gains—to 83 and 43 seats respectively—but, for the first time since 1891, the Conservatives had a renewed majority. As it had done so often for the Liberals, Quebec had given Mulroney his mandate, but even Ontario had split in favour of the deal. Only in Atlantic Canada did the Liberals make major gains. On January 2, 1989, the prime minister and his colleagues gathered in full formality to proclaim Canada's ratification of the Free Trade Agreement. In California, Reagan interrupted his ranching activity to scribble his signature.

The Tories saw their victory

Having been worsted in a well-choreographed confrontation in the 1984 leaders' debate, John Turner tried the same strategy in 1988. While the Liberal leader scored points, the Conservatives and their business allies had given themselves plenty of time to recover and win the election.

Sous le vent de l'île, by Paul-Emile Borduas, is an abstracted view of l'île d'Orléans; it reveals the expressive painterly philosophy which this leader of the Automatiste movement in modern Quebec art would take, in an increasingly non-objectivist direction, until his death in 1960. Oil, 1947.

Collection of Barry Callaghan, photo by T.E. Moore, Courtesy of the Isaacs Gallery, Toronto

William Kurelek's *Manitoba Mountain,* of children playing on a snow-covered haystack, typifies this self-taught artist's great interest in celebrating the experiences of the homesteading Eastern European immigrants between the two world wars. Oil, 1968.

The internationally renowned Nova Scotian painter Alex Colville was a founder of the Magic Realist school, identified with the Maritimes and with Newfoundland since the late 1950s. *Low Tide*, 1987.

View from Taber Hill III, by Glenn Priestly, is a reflection of the typical North American suburb—where more and more Canadians have sunk roots since the 1950s. Oil, 1987.

The late Clark McDougall's *A&A Music* pays homage to the pop-hues of the sixties—in this case of downtown Toronto's free-wheeling Yonge Street strip. Enamel and acrylic, 1969.

When the Stratford Festival staged *The Mikado*, in 1982, they called on one of the country's top illustrator's, Heather Cooper, to do this poster.

Untiled wall hanging (*c.* 1980) by Elizabeth Angonactuaq, a Baker Lake Inuit artist.

Elegy for an Island, by British Columbia painter Jack Shadbolt, uses a Southern Kwakiutl motif flying, phoenix-like, over a wasteland of stumps—a comment on the logging of Lyell and Moresby islands, unique wilderness environments claimed by the Haida Indians of the Queen Charlotte Islands. Acrylic on canvas, 1985.

Photo-realist painter and filmmaker Jack Chambers captures the unequal balance of sky and earth that is so characteristic of open Canadian countryside as seen from a modern superhighway—whether the Trans-Canada across the prairies or, as here, in rural southern Ontario. *401 towards London No.1*; oil, 1968–69.

Supernova Shelton 1987A is the brightest and nearest supernova to be found since the one Johannes Kepler recorded in 1604, a few years before the invention of the telescope. It was discovered on February 24, 1987, by Ian Shelton, at Las Campanas, at the University of Toronto's southern observatory in north-central Chile.

as a mandate not only for the Free Trade Agreement, but also for a conservative agenda that had been muted in 1984 and seldom discussed during the campaign. In the first post-election budget, Michael Wilson imposed drastic cuts on such national symbols as the CBC, Canada Post, and VIA Rail. Community post offices were closed, their services transferred to whatever store owner found them profitable. The elderly had defeated de-indexing of pensions in 1986; now they would lose the pensions altogether if their taxable incomes climbed over $50,000. Taxes on consumption, not income, could preserve incentives and eliminate an outdated tax on Canadian manufactured goods. The Goods and Services Tax, or GST, had more exemptions than a European-style value-added tax but it had a sweep, visibility, and cost (at 9 per cent, later reduced to 7 per cent) that shocked Canadians when, after the election, the government released the details.

The government had vaguely promised to shield Canadians during the transition to free trade. It made no such promise about the inevitable recessions in the business cycle or the routine industrial restructuring any free-enterprise economy should expect. In the next two years, an estimated one hundred thousand well-paid industrial jobs vanished in Ontario alone. Could anyone prove that free trade was the cause? Was free enterprise, glorified through the decade, a problem too? At its height, corporate empires turned to cannibalism. The huge Molson's company devoured its brewing rival, Carling O'Keefe. Wardair, on the brink of ruin, fell to Pacific Western, as did CP Air. There was no one to rescue Donald Cormie's Principal Group or his 67,000 trusting investors. Robert Campeau, whose acquisition of huge American retailers made him a free trade hero in 1988, had become a loser by 1990 as his empire collapsed. The Reichman family, Campeau's backers, were soon mired in their own British quagmire, London's Canary Wharf. Meanwhile, nature aggravated man-made disasters. Years of over-fishing by local and foreign trawlers led to the collapse of Atlantic fish stocks and the ruin of scores of coastal communities that made their living from the sea. In 1989, a hot summer and greedy management practices gave Canada its worst season of forest fires in decades. Any wheat the prairie farmers harvested from parched fields was hardly worth marketing while the subsidised growers of Europe and the United States pursued their trade war. The economic boom that helped the Tories through their first term was over. Within months of his historic victory, Brian Mulroney's popularity was plummeting again.

Other parties changed leaders. Ed Broadbent's successor, Audrey McLaughlin, was a two-term MP from the Yukon, convinced that her consensual style was a valid feminist approach to leadership. When John Turner followed Broadbent's lead, Liberal party managers stalled a leadership convention for more than a year, but there was no real alternative. At Calgary on June 23, Jean Chrétien avenged his 1984 defeat by a first-ballot sweep. For a decade, a procession of tiny right-wing protest parties had voiced Western grievances, collected a few votes and an occasional provincial seat, and then dissolved in their own bile. The Reform Party was built from the same roots and causes but its leader, Preston Manning, had grown up as the son of Alberta's most durable Social Credit premier and he understood politics and his region. He mobilized those who thought there was too much money in Ontario, too much influence in Quebec, and too much government in Ottawa. By the end of 1989, Reform had its first seat in the House of Commons and, in Stan Waters, the first senator ever to win an election, after Alberta included a vote for senator on municipal ballots.

Critics could do little about the GST, free trade, or Mulroney. They could, however, savage the constitutional deal he had nailed together at Meech Lake, but which had to be ratified by the federal government and all ten provinces if it was not to die by June 23, 1990. Canadians might not know what the Meech Lake Accord meant, but they knew they despised its author and, for many, that was argument enough. Under their new premiers, New Brunswick and Manitoba were shaky; a Newfoundland election toppled a Tory, Brian Peckford, and replaced him with Clyde Wells, a Liberal lawyer who had once worked on Trudeau's constitutional team. There was nothing shaky about his stand: Wells was opposed. So was a growing alliance. Feminists complained that the "distinct society" clause could rob Quebec women of their charter protection. Native leaders were angry that their claims went unresolved while Quebec was appeased. Would the Territories, where they dominated, ever become provinces if unanimity was required? English-speaking nationalists, normally sympathetic to Quebec, were furious at its support for the free trade deal. Their anger was fuelled when Bourassa, hard-pressed by Quebec nationalists, sharply restricted the right to display English signs in the province. Was this what a "distinct society" meant? Fifty Ontario communities used Bourassa's Bill 178 as a pretext to vote themselves English-only. In the 1989 election, Parti Québécois support rose to 40 per cent. In March 1990, Clyde Wells rescinded his predecessor's support for the Meech Lake Accord. When a House of Commons committee proposed compromises, Mulroney's former friend and Quebec lieutenant, Lucien Bouchard, abandoned the government and began collecting dissident MPs in a federal Bloc Québécois. The accord was in trouble; so was Canada.

Still, bargaining was Mulroney's chief political talent. Born in two all-night sessions, the accord would surely be saved by another marathon of bargaining. It began in Ottawa with a dinner on June 3, 1990, and lasted, hour by hour, for more than a week. At one point Bourassa walked out, at another Wells's departure was blocked by Alberta's Don Getty, a former footballer. Moods rose and fell. Reporters, experts, and a subdued crowd of spectators assumed that history was being made in the bowels of Ottawa's former railway station. Late on June 9, the prime minister and his provincial and territorial colleagues wearily took their seats and began a round of speeches unveiling the compromises of a "companion agreement" that somehow would save the accord and launch fresh rounds of constitutional reform. Canada was saved.

Then it all fell apart. Was it Mulroney's vulgar boasting to a newspaper that he had "rolled the dice"? Was it the outrage from Meech's opponents that "eleven middle-class white men" had dared to settle Canada's fate? Was Clyde Wells's pride bent by his last-minute concessions or had his convictions been revived? Certainly opponents of the accord wanted him as a hero, but he soon had a rival. When all three of Manitoba's party leaders returned from Ottawa pledging to support the latest compromise they found the province unconverted. A single NDP MLA, Elijah Harper, a Cree, solved their problem. Exploiting his legislature's rules, he stalled debate, and then a vote, until the normal recess on June 22. Ottawa's frantic efforts to force Wells to bring Newfoundland's House of Assembly to a vote also failed. So had the second attempt to give Quebec its place in Canada's new constitution.

Quebec failed to erupt in riots. Instead, commentators described a "serene

Brian Mulroney and ten provincial premiers display varying degrees of good cheer, unaware that they face more than seven days of marathon negotiations to save the Meech Lake Accord. Alberta's Don Getty avoids eye contact with Newfoundland's Clyde Wells at the end of the table.

A young soldier of the Royal 22e Regiment faces a Mohawk code-named "Lasagna" at the Oka confrontation in 1990. While a golf course was the pretext, the real issues included the Mohawk claim to a large area of rural Quebec and Cree claims to much of the province's huge resource hinterland.

When Canada dispatched two destroyers and a supply ship to help enforce the blockade of Iraq, was Ottawa responding to the United Nations resolution or to United States influence? Conveniently, both answers could be correct.

certainty" that independence was now inevitable. Convinced that his provincial part-ners had reneged on their 1987 commitments, Bourassa announced that never again would he share in their negotiations. A commission headed by two of Quebec's most respected financiers, Michel Bélanger and Jean Campeau, would make recommen-dations on the province's future. Support for independence soared to 70 per cent among Quebecers, and subsided only among those who believed the rest of Canada would now make concessions far greater than those envisaged in the Meech Lake Accord. Twice, Quebecers insisted, they had been humiliated in constitutional nego-tiations; there would be no third occasion. When the Bélanger-Campeau Commission reported in March 1991, it recommended an ultimatum: Canada would have until October 1992 to offer Quebec acceptable terms for a renewed Confederation. The choices would be made by Quebecers.

As a Native, Elijah Harper showed no dismay at his role in provoking such a cri-sis for Canada. Canadians, after all, had created a few crises for the Native peoples too. For 466,000 status Indians on 2,200 reserves, infant mortality was double the national average and life expectancy averaged eight years less. Birth rates on the reserves had soared and legislation under the Charter restored status to thousands of Indian women who had married whites. Already too small to support traditional lifestyles of hunting, fishing, and trapping, the reserves faced a population explosion. Prison and suicide were often the unhappy fate of young Native people. Poverty was a common condition, aggravated when huge hydroelectricity projects flooded their land or animal rights activists destroyed the market for Native fur trappers. For a million Métis, Inuit, and "non-status" Indians off reserves, life was not much better. Optimists could see signs of progress: land claims for 7,000 Yukon Indians, 13,000 Dene and Métis in the Mackenzie valley, and 17,000 Inuit in the eastern Arctic seemed close to resolution. Nova Scotia had finally granted almost a million dollars to Donald Marshall, a Mi'kmaq who spent eleven years in prison for a murder he did not commit. An enquiry into Manitoba's judicial treatment of Indians had provided the evidence to justify Native self-government and their own justice system.

For Native leaders, represented by an increasingly outspoken Assembly of First Nations, such progress was too meagre. Its leader, George Erasmus, dismissed argu-ments that the Meech Lake Accord was essential if Quebec was to get involved in defining the 1982 constitutional promise of aboriginal rights. If Native demands were separate, Erasmus reasoned, they would be ignored. He also knew that there were far more militant forces at play than the Assembly. Mohawks settled on reserves

Ontario's lieutenant governor, Lincoln Alexander, presides at the appointment of the province's first socialist premier, Bob Rae, on October 1, 1990. A decade of drastic changes for Canada began with the utterly unexpected: a socialist government in Canada's richest region.

in southern Ontario and Quebec, and straddling the American border, insisted they were still a sovereign people, allies at best of the descendants of George III and exempt from foreign laws. It was an ambiguous relationship. People at Akwesasne, a reserve situated on both sides of the border, complained that police had failed to intervene until two Mohawks were killed in an internal struggle over gambling. At Kanesatake, west of Montreal, armed Mohawks of the Warrior Society blocked roads in early 1990 to enforce claims to land around the Quebec village of Oka. After months of negotiations and court hearings, police stormed the barricade on July 9. In the ensuing fusillade, an officer was shot. Within hours, Mohawks from another reserve, Kahnawake, blocked a major bridge across the St. Lawrence between Montreal and Chateauguay. Across Canada, sympathizers blocked highways and railways. In Quebec, weeks passed as police surrounded the Mohawk communities and commuters grew angrier. Violence between Native people and their white neighbours persuaded the Bourassa government to resort to military aid of the civil power. Soldiers, perspiring in battle order, endured taunts and threats until, on August 29, they pushed the Native people back from their barricades without bloodshed. A defiant remnant surrendered on September 26.

For once in their history, Québécois felt grateful for military professionalism. Outside Quebec, the media encouraged most Canadians to sympathize with the Mohawks, further separating the two angry solitudes that emerged from the Meech breakdown. Erasmus warned that Oka might only be the beginning if Native claims were not met. Although it was clear under the law that Quebec had acted constitutionally, even in requisitioning troops, Mulroney's array of critics added Oka to his sins. Nor were they mollified when the government acted promptly in support of the United Nations after Iraq invaded neighbouring Kuwait on August 2. Within days, two aging destroyers and a supply ship were ordered to the Persian Gulf and a squadron of CF-18 fighters followed in October. New Democrats and even some Liberals protested that Canada's participation in a largely American build-up of forces was a sacrifice of a reputation for peace-keeping, rather than a necessary response to aggression. While the brief, victorious war in early 1991 converted many critics and persuaded some of them to demand condign punishment for the Iraqi leader, Saddam Hussein, few of the allies in the Gulf War seemed as removed from the harsh realities of *realpolitik* as Canadians.

Political and Economic Turmoil

Even in a changing world, there are always a few certainties. One dependable feature of Canadian politics was modern Ontario's unswerving loyalty to cautious, centrist politics. Yet on September 6, 1990, 38 per cent of the province's voters gave themselves a majority NDP government. Ontario's astonishment was matched only by the NDP's. Had voters punished their Liberal premier for his devotion to the Meech Lake Accord or for David Peterson's complacency about a deepening recession? And why had more voters gone left than right? And had the NDP promised more than it could deliver? As premier, Bob Rae found no magic to dispel the impact of a recession nor the power of business, but he could try to bring greater opportunities for women and for the visible minorities that had crowded into Ontario's major cities.

Cynics saw Ontario's choice as a brief aberration; others insisted that a pendulum had begun to swing, an impression confirmed when, in October 1991, the NDP's Roy Romanow defeated Saskatchewan's bankrupt and corrupt Conservative government in Saskatchewan and Mike Harcourt, the former Vancouver mayor, led the same party to power in British Columbia. However, as the recession deepened, with dwindling revenues and rising deficits, left-wing governments found themselves trapped by debt. Their own supporters opposed spending cuts, but business threatened to leave if taxes rose. Bob Rae utterly failed to persuade government workers to accept pay cuts in return for involvement in management. Public sector unions became his most vitriolic critics. Spared the worst of the recession, Harcourt's government was caught between environmentalist concern for the old-growth forests of Clayoquot Sound and loggers, who saw their livelihood vanishing. Overdue efforts to settle Native claims were similarly caught between sky-high demands and a widespread refusal to acknowledge any serious aboriginal rights.

Only Saskatchewan's NDP succeeded, perhaps because the previous government had been so bad and partly because Romanow's cuts seemed humane as well as necessary. Those who protested could soon look to Alberta. By 1992, the twenty-year Conservative regime seemed doomed. But when Don Getty stepped down, his surprise heir was Calgary's former mayor, a rumpled ex-broadcaster named Ralph Klein. His populist promises—to cut back government big shots, get tough with criminals, and give welfare bums a shovel—delighted a lot of people who wanted easy answers to tough problems. In June 1993, Klein annihilated the NDP opposition, humbled the Liberals, and swept Alberta with a program of drastic spending cuts and sweeping privatization. As administrators of universities, schools, and hospitals bemoaned shrunken budgets, Klein's public cheered. Why shouldn't drinkers buy booze in privately owned stores? If private medical clinics made a profit, Klein reasoned, they helped him slash the costs of Medicare. "Ralph," as admirers named him, was soon a hero far beyond Alberta. Ontario's Conservative leader, Mike Harris, in third place after Liberal and NDP victories, took note.

Canada in the 1990s found itself in a global economy where national governments had a diminishing power to enhance their country's prosperity or to protect their citizens from hard times. The Free Trade Agreement of 1989 was followed, with near inevitability in 1994, by a North American Free Trade Agreement (NAFTA), which extended much of the earlier agreement to Mexico. The immediate advantage to Canada was a presence in what, otherwise, would have been a series of bilateral agreements between the United States and other hemispheric neighbours. As one of the world's major exporters, Canada could only hope for the best in trade liberalization with Europe and, in 1995, with Asian countries. There were winners among firms that mastered new technologies and filled the international niches available to countries with a command of English and adequate public education; the losers were more audible. It was a strenuous time to do business and, for those who failed, the lowest common denominator of social security fell significantly through the decade.

The Canada Round

Beleaguered by the recession, its popularity plummeting, the Mulroney government had to keep the country together in the wake of the failure of the Meech Lake Accord. Quebec's post-Meech ultimatum gave Canada until October 1992 to find an alternative proposal. Otherwise, the province would vote on leaving Confederation. Meanwhile, a special commission headed by Michel Bélanger and Jean Campeau would tell Quebecers about its options, including sovereignty.

Since critics denounced the closed-door style of the Meech Lake negotiations, Ottawa and some provinces organized public forums, opinion polls, and hearings across the country. Special interest groups hurried to promote their views. As part of a "Canada Round," a host of issues got to the table, from creating a Triple-E (Equal, Elected, and Effective) Senate to giving Canadians a constitutional right to health care, education, a clean environment, and free collective bargaining. Natives demanded that the constitution recognize their "inherent right of self-government" and their consent to any constitutional amendment that affected them. Most Canadians seemed to agree to aboriginal demands that had seemed unacceptable when they were made by Quebec.

Not only would any future deal be far more complex, many more participants would be involved. While Quebec's Robert Bourassa boycotted constitutional negotiation, claiming that it was up to the rest of Canada to come up with an offer, Mulroney and his constitutional affairs minister, Joe Clark, decided to include first ministers of the Yukon and the Northwest Territories governments, leaders of organizations for status and non-status Indians, Métis, and Inuit, as well as the nine remaining premiers. The 1982 amending formula had helped kill the Meech Lake Accord; the process soon got even harder. Alberta and British Columbia passed laws requiring plebiscites before they ratified changes. By their presence, Native, Métis, and Territorial leaders would henceforth need to be placated. And Quebec's deadline forced the pace.

A year of consultation showed that recession-ridden Canadians resented their leaders, but produced little specific constitutional advice. Critics promptly denounced whatever ideas the government and Parliament generated. Slowly, the shape of a possible agreement emerged; the package included a cut-down version of the Meech Lake proposals, Aboriginal self-government, a limited social charter, and a Senate that would be elected, equal but only "equitable" in representation. When formal negotiations replaced consultation, weeks slipped by. For a month, negotiations stalled on the shape of a future Senate and opposition to Quebec's constitutional veto. A desperate government searched for a way to get past provincial premiers to Canadians at large. In June, the Mulroney government armed itself with the power to conduct a national referendum. Mulroney would offer Quebec a deal it would not refuse and dare other Canadians to break up the country. Instead, to his private dismay, the prime minister learned that his former rival, Joe Clark, had found a deal that nine English-speaking premiers had accepted. To get unanimity on Native rights, the NDP premiers from B.C. and Ontario had given way on Senate reform and a constitutional veto for all provinces.

Mulroney saw the danger: rights for everyone insulted a Quebec that insisted that it was unique. Montreal's *Le Devoir* ran a simple, one-word response: "NON!" Parti Québécois leader, Jacques Parizeau, demanded a sovereignty referendum. However, Bourassa returned to the table. While his advisors quarrelled and denounced him behind his back, Bourassa compromised. Saskatchewan's Romanow helped broker a deal: Quebec would accept a Senate with six members per province if her representation in both houses of Parliament became and remained a quarter of the total. (With a falling birthrate, Quebec would otherwise have a shrinking share of the members.) Ontario's Bob Rae accepted that his province would sacrifice seats in the House of Commons to make room for Quebec. In return, Quebec dropped its resistance to the Native peoples' "inherent right of self-government on Indian lands" subject to the "peace, order and good government" of Canada. Ottawa would abandon its role in housing, immigration, regional development, manpower training, forestry, and urban affairs; Quebec and other provinces would win old demands.

On August 28, the apparently impossible was done. At Charlottetown, Brian Mulroney, ten premiers, two Territorial leaders, and leaders of the First Nations, the Métis, and the Inuit were unanimous. A few days later, Brian Mulroney announced that, on October 26, all Canadians would have a chance to vote on the Charlottetown Accord in provincial or national referenda. The critics would have their turn. They were soon heard. As politicians tried to organize non-partisan "*Yes*" committees to sell the deal, Preston Manning of the Reform Party announced that he would campaign against "the Mulroney Deal." So would the former prime minister; by October 1, Trudeau had joined the battle. Quebec leaders, he declared, were no better than blackmailers. The Charlottetown Accord would create a hierarchy of people, with French Canadians at the top, Native people below them, and ethnic minorities next. The loudest protests predictably came from Quebec's nationalist parties, the Bloc Québécois and the Parti Québécois. Bourassa, wrote journalist Jean-François Lisée, was nothing but a *tricheur*, a cheat. Rival Native leaders denounced Ovide Mercredi, Erasmus's successor as grand chief of the Assembly of First Nations. Westerners complained that, despite their Triple-E Senate, the central provinces had as much power as ever.

Supporters had been sure that voters would accept the Charlottetown Accord as a true Canadian compromise. Their hopes slowly fell apart. On referendum day, Newfoundland, New Brunswick, Prince Edward Island, and Ontario (by a margin of only 28,000 of its eight million voters) voted "*Yes.*" The "*No*" side prevailed, taking 55 per cent in Quebec votes, a narrow margin in Nova Scotia, and lopsided victories from Manitoba to the Yukon. Analysts called it a repudiation of Canada's political and business leaders, a rejection of compromise, and an assertion of popular sovereignty. Sovereignists announced that Quebecers found the accord inadequate; the rest of Canada insisted it went too far. The only alternatives for Quebecers were sovereignty or an unacceptable federalism. Native leaders threatened fresh acts of defiance though their own ranks were deeply divided. The only certainty, after October 26, was that most Canadians were tired of constitutional arguments, and none of the old issues had been resolved.

Chrétien and Crises

The constitutional defeat terminated Brian Mulroney's usefulness. After a farewell tour of world capitals reminiscent of Trudeau's in 1984, he quit on February 24, 1993. Only two junior ministers, Vancouver's Kim Campbell and Sherbrooke's Jean Charest, sought the succession. Though some delegates had second thoughts, prior deals guaranteed Campbell's victory when the Progressive Conservatives met in Ottawa on June 11. A former minister of justice and defence minister, Campbell became Canada's first woman prime minister on June 25, 1993. Clever and well educated, with a sense of humour, she attracted support, and then repelled it with her brittle temper and evident inexperience. Like John Turner in 1984, she inherited a demoralized party and a political staff that aggravated her gaffes. There would be no Campbell miracle. When the votes were counted on October 25, she and all but two Tory candidates (Charest was one of the exceptions) had lost their seats. Never had a national party been so humiliated. The NDP almost shared its fate. Robbed of official party status in Parliament after winning a mere 9 seats, the party fell below its worst standing in its CCF phase. Seventy per cent of the seats in the House of Commons changed hands.

The winner was Trudeau's protégé, Jean Chrétien. He had sat out most of the Mulroney years, taken the Liberal leadership at Calgary in 1990, and built a victory from the Tory ruins. The Liberals held 177 seats, 99 of them from Ontario, a mere 19 from Quebec. There had been no such Parliament before, not even in 1921. The real upset came from West and East. From British Columbia to Manitoba, Preston Manning had inherited most of the old Conservative strength for his untried Reform Party—52 MPs, only one from Ontario—and not even a candidate in Quebec. Quebecers had given Lucien Bouchard's Bloc Québécois all but 21 of their 75 seats. Canada now had a Leader of Her Majesty's Loyal Opposition who insisted that Parliament would be no more than a new forum to struggle for Quebec sovereignty.

Mastering the Deficit

Never had a French-Canadian premier been so repudiated by his own province. Chrétien had always offended Quebec's intellectual élite, and nationalists would never forgive his role as Trudeau's bulldog in 1980 and 1982, or his opposition to the Meech Lake Accord in 1990. In the rest of Canada, however, these roles were seen as proof of his honesty and combativeness. Only the Liberals had elected MPs in every province and region. Chrétien was better tuned than most to the mood of Canada in the 1990s.

Chrétien had seen how an era of favours, kickbacks, backroom deals, and slush funds had become "the sleaze factor" that rotted public respect for Mulroney and his government. The Chrétiens immediately announced that used furniture was good enough for their official residence on Sussex Drive. Meanwhile the prime minister trimmed his new cabinet to 23 ministers, each with no more than a half-dozen aides. Mulroney had needed 38 to 40 ministers, each with a platoon of assistants. Chrétien also cancelled an allegedly gold-plated Tory deal to buy naval helicopters and sell Toronto's airport to wealthy pals. Both decisions would ultimately cost taxpayers heavily.

Chrétien's priority was cutting a deficit that had grown to $42 billion since 1974. Otherwise Canada risked losing its membership in the G-7 nations and intervention by the International Monetary Fund, humiliations intolerable to a First World nation.

Pre-election pledges to end the Goods and Services Tax (GST) and re-negotiate or quit Mulroney's 1989 Free Trade Agreement were forgotten. Chrétien's chief economic agent was Finance Minister Paul Martin, his leadership rival in 1990. The son of a major architect of Canada's welfare state, the younger Martin embodied Chrétien's less overt business ideology. The recession of the 1990s had changed Canadians' shrinking belief in a "common interest." Elected in 1992, former Calgary mayor Ralph Klein found Albertans spending far more on social programs than they wanted to pay for. Influenced by New Zealander Roger Douglas, a convert to small government, Klein persuaded voters to applaud cuts in health, education, and welfare. To national astonishment, Klein's popularity soared. Chrétien and Martin took their cue.

In his 1994 budget, Martin plugged some minor loopholes, froze federal taxes, made Unemployment Insurance harder to get, and forced major spending cuts, particularly in defence and the CBC. Critics were muted; most urged deeper cuts. He obliged. In 1995, Martin cut $2.3 billion in business subsidies and warned 45,000 civil servants to find other work. Federal transfers to the provinces for health, welfare, and post-secondary education were cunningly combined as a single Canada Social Transfer and drastically cut. Public investments—from Petro-Canada to Canadian National Railways to air traffic control—were ordered sold off. The 98-year-old Crow rate died—with a one-time $1.6 billion pay-off for prairie farmers. In 1996, Martin promised that the deficit would vanish by 1998. His main victims that year were future old age pensioners— higher premiums and lower benefits fell only on those under 60. Reform and conservatism were setting the Liberal agenda. Left-wingers had to be content with

Jean Chrétien, with his wife, Aline, arrives at Rideau Hall to accept the Governor General's invitation to form a government. The "little guy from Shawinigan" had risen to wealth, power, and Canada's highest political office at a time when his country was threatened as never before by its own internal disunity.

firearms control, a few concessions to gay rights, and earnest speeches about Medicare while the necessary funds were carved away. By the end of 1996, Liberals claimed 63 per cent in opinion polls.

Chrétien's ministers followed orders. New Brunswicker Doug Young handed over most of Canada's publicly-built airports to local operators. Users, not taxpayers, would foot the bill for air traffic control. Closing unprofitable rail lines saved $2.3 billion in subsidies. Ron Irwin pledged that Indian Affairs would vanish as responsibilities were transferred to bands. By 1995, 84,000 Manitoba Natives faced self-government with $4.8 million in start-up funds. Even the Chief Electoral Officer economised with a new permanent voters' list, scoffing at warnings that Canada's traditional high turnouts would fall.

As Human Resources minister, Lloyd Axworthy renamed Unemployment Insurance as Employment Insurance (EI). No longer a life-support for repeat users, benefits and entitlements were cut; retraining became obligatory. Business found a sideline. "Job-creation grants" spread billions of dollars: who measured results? Axworthy cut $7.8 billion from the deficit and turned EI premiums into a major revenue source.

Since the 1960s, Ottawa had helped provinces finance universities and colleges. The new focus was enticing banks to provide bigger student loans. Except in British Columbia and Quebec, universities sent fees soaring. Students now emerged with degrees, diplomas, and debts their parents had never known. Policy-makers spoke of "income-contingent" repayment. Those with no income stayed in debt. It was a far cry from the ideals of the sixties.

The 1995 Quebec Referendum

Most Canadians insisted that the deficit, jobs, housing, and the environment mattered more than the constitution and sovereignty. Yet their votes forced the "c" word back into the headlines. Undermined by the loss of the Meech Lake and Charlottetown Accords, Quebec federalists lost a cunning leader when skin cancer drove Robert Bourassa to retire in 1994. His successor, Daniel Johnson, was the son of one Quebec premier and brother of another, but his role as Bourassa's finance minister had earned him few friends. In the provincial election on September 15, 1994, Johnson took only 26 seats. Jacques Parizeau and his Parti Québécois won 88. The popular vote was almost a tie—44.3 per cent to 44.7. "Soft sovereignists" in the Action Démocratique won the balance, though only its leader, Mario Dumont, won a seat.

Tens of thousands of Canadians flooded into Montreal on the Friday before the 1995 referendum vote, eager to involve themselves in a campaign that was suddenly going very badly for Canada. A huge Canadian flag passed over the crowd. The rally raised federalist morale, but cost support. Some Québécois, angry that the support had come so long after the Meech Lake Accord, switched to the "*Yes*" side.

Parizeau promised voters "Another Way of Governing," but he made no secret of his real goal: an independent Quebec, achieved in an early referendum. But how? Every poll predicted defeat. PQ strategists softened their approach by substituting "sovereignty" for "independence." Still support lagged. In June 1995, Parizeau was forced to compromise. Pressured by Bouchard and Dumont, he agreed to allow Quebecers to vote for both sovereignty and a "partnership" with Canada. After sovereignty, Parizeau promised, Quebecers could still use Canadian money and passports. Support rose for a few weeks, then slumped again. In September, an impatient Parizeau finally launched his campaign. The question was not simple: "Do you agree that Quebec should become sovereign after having made a formal offer to Canada for a New Economic and Political Partnership within the scope of the Bill respecting the future of Quebec and of the agreement signed on June 12, 1995?"

What could federalists do? Quebecers wanted constitutional recognition of their uniqueness, yet even a hint of compromise provoked fury from other provinces. In Ottawa, Martin delayed the impact of his budget, and U.S. President Bill Clinton visited to praise a united Canada. It was little enough, compared to 1980, and the federalists' message of fearful consequences was losing effect.

A year earlier, Bouchard had lost a leg to a devastating bacterial infection. When he finally emerged in mid-October, he supercharged the sovereignist campaign with passion, credibility, and charisma. He appealed to the pride and identity which

Quebec premier Lucien Bouchard came to power in the wake of a 1995 referendum which his impassioned oratory had almost won for the "*Yes*" side. Faced with the problems of high taxes, a sagging economy, and a budget deficit, tough measures slowly drained his popularity and dynamism. By the end of the century, the challenge of a global economy undermined support for sovereignty, at least among Quebec's élite.

united Quebec as a nation. Voting "*Yes*," he claimed, would be like waving a magic wand. It would make all things possible. It would force even *les Anglais* to come begging for a new partnership with Quebec.

Suddenly, the federalists were losing the race. Desperate appeals from Johnson brought Chrétien to Montreal on October 25 to stand with the Conservatives' new leader, Jean Charest, and to promise changes he had refused before—recognition of Quebec as a "distinct society"; and a constitutional veto. Outside Quebec, other Canadians suddenly realized that their country might be lost. Tens of thousands of them poured into Montreal by car, bus, train, and plane for a rally on October 27.

Did the sudden outpouring of love for Canada alter the outcome? Did Chrétien's promises? The evidence is contradictory. What was apparent, on the night of October 30, was that 93 per cent of eligible voters had cast ballots—2,308,028 in favour, 2,361,526 opposed. The margin—62,498 votes—was smaller than the 86,676 spoiled ballots. Perhaps 60 per cent of French-speaking Quebecers had voted "*Yes*"; virtually all who spoke English or other languages had voted "*No.*" That morning, a confident Jacques Parizeau had promised unilateral independence if Ottawa dared to stall Quebec's freedom; that night, he blamed "ethnics and money" for the narrow defeat. The following day, he resigned.

In February 1996, Lucien Bouchard became Quebec's new premier. He promised that solving Quebec's desperate economic problems would be his first priority, but he put Canada on notice. There would be another referendum, and he would use all his skills, prestige, and opportunities to create the winning conditions. Meanwhile, Chrétien's critics blamed him for the outcome, though few showed any insight into Quebec's psyche or offered any promising strategies.

Was Canada now doomed? Evidence to support that gloomy conclusion was not hard to find. The unexpectedly narrow result persuaded many that Quebec independence was inevitable, perhaps by the end of the century. Voices across Canada insisted that it was time to forget Quebec and move on. A few others insisted that the country must be held together by law and force. Ottawa turned to a two-track strategy: Plan A sought compromises that would win back Quebec allegiance; Plan B developed the tougher tactics that would be necessary if Canada once again threatened to come apart. Neither option was easy. Even after the shock of October 30, Canadians—prone to lecture others about compromise—were rigidly opposed to any special recognition of Quebec. More confident than ever, sovereignists were eager for fresh rebuffs to strengthen their sense of grievance (a proven source of inspiration). Chrétien's proposal to use Ottawa's constitutional veto on Quebec's behalf had to be extended to Ontario, the East, and the West—and then to British Columbia, leaving all dissatisfied.

Seemingly more productive was the evolution of a Social Compact in 1997. With apparent provincial unanimity, Ottawa agreed that it would not introduce or significantly amend a social program—such as day-care—without the consent of at least seven provinces. Those that opted out or chose a different route to the same end would receive compensating funding. Once achieved, Bouchard found a pretext to opt out. Ottawa promptly reassured Quebecers that they would still get the benefits.

As for Plan B, English-speaking "No" voters insisted that, if Quebec could divide Canada, they could split Quebec. Some backed lawyer Guy Bertrand's bid to persuade the Supreme Court to rule on Quebec's right to secede. On August 25, 1997, the Court ruled on what it defined as a political question: Quebec had no right under Canadian or international law to unilateral secession. Federalists cheered. But the Court continued: if a clear question won a clear majority, the rest of Canada would be obliged to negotiate. It was the assurance Parizeau had lacked in 1995, and its absence had made voters nervous. Bouchard appreciated its value. If federalists celebrated, so too did leading sovereignists. Both sides had won—or lost.

Canada's Roles in the World

In 1993, External Affairs became Foreign Affairs and its new minister, André Ouellet, declared that his priority was to create jobs for Canadians. Quebec concerns helped shift the agenda. The FTA had been popular in Quebec: talk of its abandonment ended. Instead, Quebecers must be shown what a strong Canada could do for them in the world. High-profile trade promotion justified a series of "Team Canada" excursions in which the Prime Minister led provincial premiers and business executives on tours of Asia and Latin America.

Meanwhile, American sympathy for Ottawa in the Quebec-Canada debate must not be jeopardized by any needless national assertion. When they found the Americans planning bilateral trade deals with other Western Hemisphere countries, the Liberals promptly embraced a three-nation North American Free Trade Agreement (NAFTA) with Mexico. At Marrakech on April 15, 1994, Canada helped replace the post-war GATT treaty with a 131-member World Trade Organization (WTO), with expanded powers to end dumping and subsidies and enhance "fair trade." Canada promptly joined the United States in challenging a European Union ban on cattle raised with growth hormones. Better known were WTO rulings against Canada's protection of its domestic magazines, and a 1999 decision condemning the 1965 Canada–U.S. Auto Trade Pact.

Not all disputes went to formal tribunals. Faced with evidence of Spanish over-fishing on the Grand Banks, Fisheries Minister Brian Tobin had the trawler *Estai* seized and hauled into St. John's. Spain threatened gunboats; the European Union, sweeping trade sanctions. Tobin shipped the *Estai*'s nets to New York and displayed their illegal features to assembled media. A Canadian submarine went out to wait, discreetly, for Spain's armed intervention. However embarrassing to diplomats, Tobin's war "to save the last lonely turbot, clinging to the Grand Banks by its finger nails" gave unholy joy to Canada's Peaceable Kingdom.

But many Canadians envisioned a more idealistic role in the world. Canada, they insisted, had to be a moral leader—promoting human rights, gender equality, and social justice. Was this agenda compatible with sweatshop labour in China or Indonesia? In 1997, when Chrétien welcomed a cluster of dictators and democrats to the Asia Pacific Summit in Vancouver, protesters gathered. When the RCMP used pepper spray to drive away the crowd, Jean Chrétien felt the outrage. Had he ordered police violence to protect Suharto, Indonesia's brutal ruler?

Canada's most conspicuous role on the world stage was played by its UN peace-keeping contingents. The post-Cold War "peace" was more conflict-ridden and violent than the long armed truce that preceded it. Not since the 1940s had more civilians died in a decade, or fled their homes—many to find refuge in Canada. The Gulf War had been a harbinger of things to come. In 1992, the Yugoslav federation dissolved into murderous nationalism and "ethnic cleansing." Canadian troops arrived from German NATO bases to serve as UN peace-keepers and remained long after their bases were closed in 1993. Civil wars continued in South-East Asia and spread across Africa from Somalia to Liberia. Washington asked for help in Somalia. It became a disaster for the Americans and for Canadian peace-keepers. No one had dared admit that Canada no longer had suitable troops to send. On a hot January night in 1994, a few violent, frustrated Canadian troops beat a Somali thief to death. Over the next three years, the episode tarnished the Canadian brass, wiped out the Airborne Regiment, and reduced Canadian Forces morale to tatters. When a Canadian general, Roméo Dallaire, warned the UN of the imminent massacre of Tutsis in Rwanda, no help came. Dallaire's UN supervisor in New York, General Maurice Baril, became Chief of the Defence Staff in 1997. His own mission impossible was to ensure that, by 2000, women filled a quarter of the combat positions in the Canadian Forces.

After 1993, defence spending dropped from $13 billion to $9.6 billion and numbers of regulars from 83,000 to 59,000. Only the missions increased. Skills faded and equipment aged. Cancelling new helicopters left pilots flying worn-out aircrafts, older than they were, often on rescue missions across the Arctic or the oceans. When 1960s-vintage armoured carriers wore out, soldiers took Canadian-made training vehicles to Croatia and Bosnia. The armour really was make-believe. As service strength shrunk, more and more reservists were called up. Members spent months on difficult and sometimes dangerous peacekeeping assignments. After a few months at home, they were sent out again. The training and experience needed to produce specialized professionals became a luxury. If senior commanders protested, it was up a chain of command that had become political. Since the 1970s, civilians matched the military in the Defence Department. Like admirals and generals, their promotion depended on telling superiors what they wanted to hear. A Reform backbencher finally shocked Parliament into action with a report that showed how low salaries sometimes forced junior ranks to deliver pizza or turn to food banks to feed their families. The government ordered a pay raise, but Paul Martin found only a fraction of the amount. To meet the cost, defence officials promised fresh cuts and purchasing delays.

Transferred from Human Resources to Foreign Affairs in 1997, Lloyd Axworthy broadened Ouellet's dour mandate. Recognizing a Canadian appetite for doing good in the world, Axworthy spearheaded a multinational protocol against the manufacture and use of landmines. China, Russia, the United States, and other major users did not sign, but who could criticize Canada for trying? Axworthy found other noble goals—the abolition of child soldiers, the release of Cuban political prisoners. This served a more practical goal. When Cuba ignored the demand, relations cooled with the aging Castro and Washington was pleased.

Axworthy's human security agenda led Canada into more conflicts abroad. After UN peacekeepers failed to protect unarmed Bosnians from a Serb massacre at Srebrenica in 1993, they were replaced by NATO troops, largely committed to protecting neighbours from Serbia. When civil war broke out again in the Serb province of Kosovo at the end of 1998, Serb atrocities, publicised by Kosovar nationalists, once again encouraged NATO intervention. Canadian CF-18s were "interoperable" enough to join American and British jets in devastating Serb infrastructure. A month later, when Serbia pulled its forces from Kosovo, eight hundred Canadians joined NATO's occupying army. In September 1999, after Indonesia ended its occupation of East Timor with devastation and massacres, Ottawa sent aircraft, a supply ship, and a company of infantry to diversify a largely Australian security force.

Did human security agendas require more force in the support of righteousness than most Canadians wanted to pay for? It seemed so. Eighty-eight per cent of Canadians admired what their soldiers had done, but barely seven in ten wanted to pay for the necessary weapons and equipment.

A New Economic Paradigm

Most decades after the Second World War opened or closed with a recession. The 1990s recession was deeper and longer than any since the 1930s, and it affected many of its victims almost as cruelly. Mass lay-offs, plant and mine closures, and corporate "down-sizing" raised unemployment rates well into double digits by 1991. The young were shut out of jobs; older workers found that they wee too old to be hired again. Falling revenues deepened government deficits and cutbacks often targeted the victims of recession. Ontario, hard-hit when the Free Trade Agreement decimated its protected industries, suffered added losses when Ottawa cut transfers to richer provinces. For a time, links to Asia protected British Columbia's prosperity. Then, as the rest of Canada recovered, Asia's financial collapse in the mid-1990s made the West Coast a collateral victim. Markets for its wood, coal, and fish declined sharply.

The nineties were rich in ecological gloom. Newfoundland's ancient cod fishery finally collapsed after decades of over-fishing and the Pacific salmon was close behind. Billions of dollars were diverted to support families ruined by wholly predictable ecological disasters. Forest industries complained of competition from fast-growing trees closer to the tropics and cut back on reforestation. Environmentalists battled to save old-growth forests. Meanwhile, prairie grain farmers protested their vulnerability in a subsidy war only the European Union and the United States could afford and wheat prices plummeted. Farmers in Ontario and across the prairies who diversified into hog-rearing denied the threat to water supplies as waste products accumulated. The scandal exploded in the small Ontario town of Walkerton in the spring of 2000 when thousands fell ill and seven died from E. coli infection.

Economic recovery began in 1993, and accelerated as laid-off workers, jarred by the Liberals' tighter Employment Insurance rules, felt obliged to accept minimum-wage jobs without benefits, security, or overtime premiums. For the most part, union bargaining power faded and even when recovery began in mid-decade strikes remained scarce. Admirers and critics attributed Canada's changing economy to the 1989 Free Trade Agreement, reinforced by NAFTA and the newly powerful World Trade Organization (WTO). If North America was to be a "level playing field", economists predicted, American interests would prevail but Canadians, if liberated from high taxes and trade unions, could prosper in market niches. A Canadian dollar worth barely two-thirds of its American counterpart increased Canadian exports of goods and services, and the United States finally began to rival neighbouring provinces as a market. Growing sales brought growing dependence on a single foreign market. Traditional corporate names—Macmillan-Bloedel, Eaton's, Seagram's—vanished into bankruptcy or, more often, into multinational deals, to be replaced by Weyerhauser, Sears, Wal-Mart or The Gap. The merger plans of four of Canada's large chartered banks were halted only because of a rude lack of consultation with the finance minister, Paul Martin, and then by a public outcry.

Throughout the decade, Canada's economy moved away from resource industries and manufacturing and towards information management. A well-developed telephone system became the backbone for a wired world of facsimile transmission and networked computers. Huge sums were spent on communications infrastructure. In a single decade, the compact disc came and virtually left in favour of the still newer Internet. Canadians had never been more connected with each other and the world, though critics noted that the same citizens who had such limitless access to information and to each other had seldom professed to feel more isolated. Security in a job well done—a fundamental of Canadian middle-class life for much of the century—also faded, even in the public service. A decade of economic liberalism and shrinking general affluence stretched the divide between expectations and realistic possibilities. The 1980s had fostered a growing gulf between rich and poor and an apparent loss of faith in institutions and values that once distinguished Canadians from their neighbours. The trends continued in the 1990s. Canada, some citizens told pollsters, was worth keeping only if it gave them prosperity From that perspective, had Canada failed the First Nations, single mothers, the unemployed, and a growing army of homeless, some of them full-time workers who could not afford shelter on their minimum wages. The loudest protests came from the rich who could have made even more money if only they had been Americans.

The Biggest Change in the Nineties

Without the 1990 Oka Crisis, relations between the First Nations and later arrivals might have changed but only with some other catalyst. As the decade wore on, it became clear that Oka was not unique. In 1995, months of armed stand-off at British Columbia's Gustafson Lake and the deadly climax to a confrontation between provincial police and Natives occupying a former military camp near Grand Bend were reminders of the violence that could erupt between impoverished and impatient communities and a Canadian majority whose sympathies often seemed shallow and short-lived.

Oka's chief legacy was a $60 million Royal Commission on Aboriginal Peoples (RCAP) that reported at the end of 1996. Canadians acquired five volumes of information and advice on issues the country had buried for generations in the backwoods and in urban slums. Co-chaired by Mr. Justice René Dussault and former Grand Chief George Erasmus, the Commission provided Canadians with an uncompromised Native perspective, insisting that First Nations be given the powers and resources to manage their own lives. Without land, the Commissioners warned, there could be no basis for Native life.

Conscious that the commission's principles would transform Canada and cost billions without a guarantee of success, Ottawa moved slowly. One step was a formal apology for the earlier policy of educating Native children in harsh, underfunded residential schools, together with a $350 million "healing fund". Until 1994, British Columbia had none of the treaty settlements common in other parts of Canada. When the province's NDP government announced that it would negotiate treaties to secure a Native land base, First Nations promptly claimed 70 per cent of the province's territory. Canada's Supreme Court accelerated the process when it ruled that Delgamuukh, a member of the Gitskan and Wet'suwetan nation, had a claim to his ancestral lands. In July 1998, Ottawa and Victoria initialled a 500-page agreement that established Nis'ga ownership over 2,000 square kilometres (1,250 square miles) of the Nass Valley and surrounding territory, and recognized the band as a third order of government, with municipal-level powers. Furious that governments with little popular support in the province could make such sweeping decisions, both Reform and the B.C, Liberal parties pledged to overthrow the treaty if elected. Neighbouring bands claimed that they had been shut out by Nis'ga claims while other B.C. bands pledged to get even better settlements. On the other side of Canada, a Supreme Court decision threw long-established fishing and logging arrangements into question by restoring old treaties that gave a Mi'gmah Native the right to make "a moderate living" from traditional resources. The aftermath included painful encounters between Mi'gmah activists and local fishers, fearful of losing their livelihood.

With the proclamation of Nunavut on April 1, 1999, 25,000 people—21,000 of them Inuit—won control over half the Northwest Territories or a third of Canada. Nunavut's Tunnagavit, an Inuit-owned economic development corporation, was empowered to spend the $1.6 billion that Ottawa had paid the Inuit to settle land claims. The remainder of the Northwest Territories, with 40,000 people, evenly divided between Natives and whites, continued to govern themselves from Yellowknife. Exuberance in celebrating a young government briefly averted attention from average incomes of $11,000, 25 per cent unemployment, high living costs, severe drug and alcohol addiction problems, and the resulting family break-down. Some insisted that traditions of consensual government by local elders would solve problems that highly trained experts from the south had failed to alleviate. Others were bluntly sceptical that folkloric ways would overcome the impact of television and under-employment in small, isolated communities dominated by a few families. Only the future would tell.

Meanwhile, across Canada, close to a million Native, Inuit, Métis, and non-status Indians seek futures that all Canadians help to provide. Thousands of young Natives

One of the major historic developments of the 1990s was the changing status of Canada's Natives. Having denied aboriginal land claims for a century, courts, public opinion and an NDP govenment forced British Columbia to change. At New Aiyanish on August 4, 1998, federal Indian Affairs minister Jane Stewart, Nisga'a chief Joseph Gosnell, and BC premier Glen Clark culminated a century of negotiations with an historic treaty. Opponents still pledged to kill the deal.

have made unprecedented strides in post-secondary education and now provide their communities with lawyers, teachers, social workers, accountants, and health professionals.

Divided Country: The Chrétien Mandates

By 1997, Jean Chrétien was confident of a new mandate. His government was close to its goal of a balanced budget. Angry lobbies denounced gun control, gay rights, and abortion but most Canadians approved the government's cautious policies. Some Atlantic provinces had integrated their sales taxes with the GST. Since 1993, the prime minister and his party kept a safe lead in opinion polls. Only Reform had the same leader as in 1993, but a stylish makeover was not enough to make Preston Manning popular with moderate voters. Even sympathizers were troubled by the authoritarianism inherent in populist leadership. The Bloc's leadership had passed to Michel Gauthier and then to Gilles Duceppe, an ex-Communist union organizer and son of a great Quebec actor, but the sovereignty cause had lost steam since the 1995 referendum. Could Jean Charest raise Conservative support? The NDP's Audrey McLaughlin was replaced by another former social worker, Alexa McDonough, a former Nova Scotia leader. She found her party deeply unpopular in Ontario and British Columbia but, for once, attractive to Maritimers.

In Ontario, NDP idealism and inexperience soon eroded Bob Rae's majority. Initially, polls gave the Liberals a big lead but when Rae called a June 1995 election,

Attuned to the issues and language of conservative populism in Western Canada, Reform leader Preston Manning found it harder to speak the language of Ontario conservatism and impossible to win support in Quebec or the Maritimes. His United Alternative appeal to "Think Big" threatened to leave many of his western supporters behind while potential recruits wondered whether they were hearing the "real" Manning.

Mike Harris, a former golf pro, led Ontario Tories to an 86-seat victory with his "Common-Sense Revolution". Imitating Alberta's Ralph Klein, Harris's program seemed better suited to Texas or Arizona, with drastic deregulation, welfare-bashing, government-downsizing, major tax cuts—and immediate scrapping of photo radars because respectable speeders hated them. This was the common sense many rural and suburban Ontarians wanted and Harris had a team of young ideologues ready to deliver. Confusion, waste, and protest did not bother them. Would Mike Harris's conservatism help Charest or Manning? Harris wasn't saying. In the spring of 1997, Jean Chrétien decided to call an election before the Right got organized.

For a few weeks, it seemed like a big mistake. Chrétien had no good argument for a $200 million election with more than a year left in his mandate. Caught in a Red River flood, Manitobans were especially hard to convince. A new-style Manning drew crowds; so did Charest. The NDP focussed on Maritime discontent at Liberal cuts to Employment Insurance for seasonal workers. A Reform ad, denouncing the string of Quebec-based leaders, pleased Western voters and drove resentful Quebeckers to the Bloc.

Voter turnout was low on June 2: counting voters left off the new permanent list, barely 55 per cent of eligible Canadians voted. Chrétien took 38 per cent of the vote and 155 of 301 seats, 100 of Ontario's 101. Western solidarity made Reform the official opposition with 19 per cent of the vote and 63 of the West's 91 ridings. The Bloc and the NDP each took 11 per cent of the votes but Duceppe took 44 and McDonough 21 seats, eight of them in Nova Scotia and New Brunswick. Charest's 18 per cent almost matched Manning's 19, but it gained him only 20 seats, largely from Quebec and the Atlantic region. What if Reform and the Tories had united? It was now too obvious a thought.

Chrétien's Third Mandate

After the 1997 election, Preston Manning resumed his campaign to unite the right with the primary goal of breaking into Ontario. Newspaper magnate Conrad Black helped by buying half the country's major dailies for his Hollinger chain and launching the *National Post* as an organ of conservative views. Tory leader Jean Charest left for Quebec in a bid to unite federalists and defeat Lucien Bouchard's Parti Québécois. All that his former party could find for a leader was Joe Clark. Still, many conservatives were suspicious of Manning's regional bias and moral fundamentalism.

Meanwhile, the Chrétien government lived quietly with its narrow majority. By 1998, a surplus had replaced the deficit: Chrétien promised to split it between social reinvestment and debt repayment. Efforts at constitutional change were shelved, but a Canadian Social Union agreement with the provinces was offered as a renewed co-operative federalism. A cabinet newcomer, Stéphane Dion, designed a Clarity Bill to satisfy a Supreme Court ruling that Quebec could force the rest of Canada to negotiate over secession but only after a clear majority of Quebecers had voted on a clear question. Sovereignists reacted with fury but, as Dion and Chrétien had foreseen, Quebecers preferred clarity; many were now bored by the sovereignty issue.

By 2000, the longest boom in recent North American memory showed signs of weakness. As the prime minister reminded audiences, Canada (narrowly) ranked first in the UN's Social Development Index. Ottawa had money to restore battered health services and to restore unemployment benefits to people in Atlantic Canada. By 2000, only Newfoundland had a Liberal government. In 1998, Charest failed to defeat Bouchard. In June, an Alliance leadership convention denied Manning the chance to take his new party into the promised land. It preferred Stockwell Day, a brash and engaging 43-year-old former Pentecostal preacher who served as Alberta's provincial treasurer. Once in Parliament, Day demanded a general election; Chrétien gave him his wish. Each man felt buoyed by the national outpouring of admiration for Pierre Elliott Trudeau, who had died on September 28. Each felt himself the heir of Trudeau's leadership style.

As in 1997, critics and the media denounced Chrétien for calling an election for November 27, 2000, only forty months after his previous mandate. Even Liberals worried about Chrétien's age, costly favours to his constituents, and hints of scandal in government job-creation grants. Then, as he expected, they looked at the opposition. Alliance officials undermined Day's bland campaign by admitting plans to privatize much of Canada's health system and to allow referenda to determine sensitive policies like access to abortion. The Liberals left the West to the Alliance and focused on holding Ontario and winning back support in Quebec and the Maritimes. Despite an early slump, Liberal support rose again in the last days: NDP and Conservative voters switched to Chrétien to bar Day's uncompromising right-wing Alliance from power. More voters stayed home than in 1997. The Liberals won 172 seats; the Alliance 66, only two of them in Ontario. The three smaller parties all suffered: the Bloc fell to 38 seats and the NDP and Progressive Conservatives to 13 and 12, a minimum for official party status. Jean Chrétien had joined Macdonald, Laurier, and Mackenzie King as one of only four Canadian prime ministers to win three consecutive majorities. The "Little Guy from Shawinigan" had again outsmarted Canada's opinion-leaders and enraged those who saw a divided opposition as the key to permanent Liberal power. Alliance backbenchers turned out their callow leader and found his replacement in a Calgary-based ideologue, Stephen Harper.

On September 11, 2001, Al Qaeda terrorists used hijacked American airliners to demolish New York's World Trade Center and one side of the U.S. Defence Department headquarters in Washington. President George W. Bush declared war on terrorism and invoked the NATO alliance to assault Afghanistan, home of the Al Qaeda network. Chrétien invited John Manley to manage Canada's response. NATO membership brought Canada into Bush's war too. Canadians were soon reminded of who called the shots when Americans were frightened. After U.S. borders slammed shut on September 12, 80 per cent of Canada's foreign trade stopped, jeopardizing the livelihoods of millions of Canadians. Despite grumbling, Manley's efforts allowed Canada's economy to recover. By the time Americans began investigating their intelligence failures, earlier charges that Canada was overrun with terrorist cells and dangerous refugees had faded, though not before the RCMP had helped the CIA transfer some Muslim Canadians to Middle Eastern jails and torture chambers. The Chrétien government spent billions of dollars in programs to assure Americans that their northern frontier was as secure as technology and intelligence could make it. Exploiting "interoperability" with U.S. forces, Canada sent warships to the Arabian Sea. A new Joint Task Force helped U.S. Special Forces and rebel warlords to establish a more congenial government in Kabul. A Canadian battalion spent six months guarding the U.S. base at Kandahar. When their time was up (with four deaths from "friendly fire"), Canada's shrunken army had no troops to replace them.

Canada's "Ready, Aye, Ready" did not shelter it from U.S. protectionism. Eight

Canadians have learned to live with natural forces more powerful than themselves. Typical was the January 1998 Ice Storm—several days of freezing rain that coated trees and transmission lines with ice until they toppled from the weight. More than a million homes were left without electricity and heat. Troops, hydro crews, and relief workers rushed to help as much of Canada, from Eastern Ontario to New Brunswick, shivered and waited for power.

months into their war on terrorism, lobbyists persuaded Congress to close down Canada's softwood lumber industry. Congress also pledged huge new subsidies to U.S. producers of farm commodities Canadians had been exporting. President Bush would waste influence on persuading Congress to appease an insufficiently tractable neighbour. Urged by editors and politicians to be ready whenever embattled Americans called, Canadians began instead to be troubled by a colonial dependence on U.S. political priorities.

Having overthrown Afghanistan's Islamic regime, President Bush turned on Saddam Hussein. His father had left the Iraqi dictator in power in 1991 rather than assume the burden of running his bitterly divided country. The younger Bush insisted that Saddam had backed Al Qaeda and developed weapons of mass destruction (WMDs) for its terrorists. The United Nations was unconvinced—Saddam Hussein was one of the secular Muslims Al Qaeda regularly denounced; UN weapons inspectors politely insisted that American evidence of WMDs was bogus. Denied UN backing, President Bush created his own "Coalition of the Willing" and launched an invasion of Iraq in March 2003. Canada and most Canadians were among the unwilling.

Though White House relations with Ottawa turned frosty, Canada's warships in the Persian Gulf co-operated with U.S.-led invasion forces and Canada met UN and NATO commitments by sending a battalion-sized force to protect the Hamid Karzai government in Kabul.

The Paul Martin Interlude

Like William Lyon Mackenzie King, Jean Chrétien recognized that Canadians are nervous about change, welcome compromise, and support leaders who divide them least. Like other voters, they are also easily bored. The rivalry between the Prime Minister and his finance minister might have entertained them but, beyond Martin's claim that he had single-handedly defeated the federal deficit, his campaign was mostly hidden until the end of May 2002, when Chrétien dropped him from the cabinet, precipitating a power struggle within Liberal ranks that was as unusual as it was unseemly. After much searching, the prime minister chose John Manley as his preferred successor. Calm, intellectual, and a long-distance runner, Manley was as pro-business as Martin and a generation younger. His radicalism was limited to discreet criticism of the monarchy.

The 2000 election had taught supporters of right-wing politics the futility of a divided conservatism. To win the Progressive Conservative leadership, Peter MacKay pledged to a rival that he would never merge with the Alliance. His promise was a political fib. Stephen Harper found MacKay an eager recruit. In 2004, the two men proclaimed an unhyphenated and unabashed Conservative Party.

Though Canadians had rejected the compromises needed to make Quebecers more comfortable in Confederation, they blamed Chrétien for doing too little to avoid the cliffhanger referendum of 1995. While endorsing Dion's Clarity Act, Chrétien also set out on a cruder strategy to make Ottawa, Canada, and, inevitably, the Liberals more visible in Quebec. He left the details to his Quebec lieutenant, Alfonso Gagliano. Using his own staff, political agents, and the few advertising firms willing to forgo business with Quebec's PQ government, Gagliano could claim by the early 2000s that sovereignty now appealed to less than a third of Quebecers, and was fading fastest among the young. Under Lucien Bouchard, the PQ had been narrowly re-elected in 1998 but his successor, Bernard Landry, lost to Jean Charest in 2003.

Conservatism was more acceptable to Quebecers and perhaps to other Canadians too. One reason was disillusionment with an aging federal government. Outrage after a young man murdered thirteen female students at Montreal's École Polytechnique in 1989 led Liberals to propose a national gun registry. Resistance from rural areas and especially from western provinces so complicated the project that it ultimately cost a billion dollars to implement, with no apparent impact on violent crime. When Liberal deficit-cutting slashed their funding, colleges and universities raised tuition, leaving new graduates   with debt burdens their elders had never experienced. Advocates of universal health care had trusted in enhanced physical fitness to control costs. Instead millions of citizens, often self-indulged and overweight, denounced waiting times and physician shortages. Conservatives argued for private, for-profit services so that wealthier patients could get faster service. Invited to rule that a constitutional right was involved, the Supreme Court ordered provinces to solve the waiting-list problem.

Most Canadians entered the new millennium in a grumpy mood. Spared a widely predicted computer programming disaster called "Y2K," Canadians soon had plenty of other crises to worry about. New technologies linked them to work, family, and friends wherever they were. One result was a global awareness more likely to terrify than empower. After many lifetimes of grumbling about cold winters, Canadians learned that imminent global warming would flood coastal cities, devastate the Arctic ecology, and threaten their lives with global epidemics reminiscent of the Spanish flu of 1918-19. At Kyoto, the Chrétien government nervously signed an international agreement to reduce greenhouse gas emissions. Fast becoming the major foreign supplier of gas and oil to a non-signatory, the United States, Alberta refused to jeopardize its short-term prosperity to satisfy Ottawa Liberals. Didn't provinces control their own natural resources?

The Liberals' leadership struggle reached a crisis when the federal Auditor General claimed that millions of the dollars allotted for the Chrétien–Gagliano "sponsorship" program had simply vanished. Sending Gagliano to Denmark as ambassador only intensified public outrage. Isolated in his own party by Martin's restless jockeying for control, Chrétien finally announced his departure. On December 12, he was gone. Martin and his supporters turned the occasion into a virtual change of government. Ambitious backbenchers, denied power in the Chrétien years, took most of the portfolios. Gagliano was recalled from Copenhagen. John Gomery, an appeal judge of the Quebec Superior Court, agreed to be a royal commissioner with full power to investigate the sponsorship scandal. Perhaps convinced that Canadians were as delighted that he was prime minister as he was himself, Paul Martin called a general election for June 28, 2004.

Voters, in fact, felt otherwise. Most were sick of the Liberals and discouraged by politics. Chrétien supporters sat on their hands. Furious at the implication that their allegiance was for sale, the sponsorship scandal drove Quebecers to Gilles Duceppe's

Bloc; New Democrats backed their earnest new leader, Jack Layton, a Montrealer elected as an activist Toronto alderman. Stephen Harper's Conservative message was determinedly moderate but his campaign as a tightly-programmed policy wonk was undermined whenever the media found a veteran Reformer eager to speak his mind. On election day, confusion, apathy, or the flaws of an imperfect permanent voters' list kept almost half the voters at home. The rest gave the Conservatives 99 seats, the Bloc 54 and Layton's NDP 19, leaving Martin a parliamentary minority of 135. He swallowed his humiliation, reminded his party that it was still in power, and hunted for the tactics to win a majority.

Since medicare was the voters' top priority, Martin met the provincial premiers and gave them the federal surplus in return for abiding by the Canada Health Act. Since mothers wanted daycare, more money might persuade the premiers to create more spaces. Since everyone knew that the armed forces had worn-out aircraft and guns, boosting the defence budget by a few billion allowed a few new ones. Above all, Canadians watched a sardonic Judge Gomery expose a succession of shifty operators associated with the sponsorship scandal. Martin, as Jean Chrétien's former finance minister, had to insist that he was completely unaware of the entire affair and was as eager as anyone to impose full accountability on public officials.

Accountability was popular with Harper and rival party leaders too and, after so many Liberal years, the Opposition promises sounded more authentic. If good times continued to yield greater federal surpluses, all parties could promise more spending and tax cuts. To keep NDP backing, Martin cancelled some tax cuts for the wealthy. Still, only a party switch by Belinda Stronach, a former leadership candidate, and the vote of a former Reformer, forced by Harper to run as an independent, saved Martin's government in May 2005. During the summer Harper's handlers worked on his political skills until he had learned to smile, shake hands, and make small talk. Meanwhile, the media watched as Martin struggled with a host of inherited issues, from the environment to sponsorship. While the media labelled him Mr. Dithers, Martin proposed a curb on income trusts, the business world's latest scheme for tax avoidance, met with First Nations leaders at Kelowna to promise a generous settlement of outstanding issues, and agreed to shift Canadian solders from Kabul to a Taliban-infested Kandahar province. Gomery's first report exonerated Martin and loaded the full blame on Chrétien-era officials. By December, polls showed growth in Liberal support. Gomery's second report, proposing a cure, could be an excellent election send-off. First, Martin warned the NDP, there would be no more deals for

Prime Minister Stephen Harper tours Mayan ruins at Chichen Itza, Mexico, on Thursday, March 30, 2006, with President George Bush of the United States, left, and President Vincente Fox of Mexico, right, during one of the periodic meetings of the three partners in the North American Free Trade Agreement of 1994.

them or anyone else. Who would dare force an election over the Christmas holidays?

The NDP's Jack Layton, that's who. Liberals duly protested anyone daring to upset their election timetable. Their holiday plans disrupted, journalists grumbled too. Most voters saw no problem with voting on January 23, almost a month after Santa Claus had left town. This time, Stephen Harper was prepared. Announcing a policy a day, he seized the initiative and silenced party troublemakers. Liberals struggled with the Conservatives and waited angrily for Martin's platform. Auto union leader Buzz Hargrove told his members that the NDP had risked a Conservative government and urged them to vote Liberal. In Quebec, Duceppe boasted that Gomery had given the Bloc every seat. In fact, the campaign turned the sponsorship scandal into old news. When Martin announced that he had dropped plans to plug the income-trust loophole, the RCMP soon declared it was investigating a cabinet leak that allowed some Bay Street operators to reap windfall profits. Who needed Gomery when the Mounties poked at scandal at the heart of Martin's government? When Paul Martin said nothing, voters had heard enough. Moderate weather across Canada denied voters an excuse to stay home and they produced the result many had predicted: a Conservative minority with 124 seats, ten of them from the Quebec City region; 51 seats for Duceppe; and 29 for Layton, the obvious beneficiary of left-Liberal disenchantment. With 30.1 per cent of the vote, the Liberals collected 103 seats, almost all of them east of Manitoba.

That night, Paul Martin quit as prime minister and Liberal leader. On February 6, 2006, Stephen Harper became Canada's twenty-second prime minister. He announced that his election priorities would rule his government. Accountability regulations might cripple some operations of government but who, outside the

Newly elected Liberal Party leader, Stéphane Dion, with former Prime Ministers Jean Chrétien (left), John Turner (right), Paul Martin (second right) and interim-Liberal Party leader Bill Graham (second left) at the Liberal Convention in Montreal, December 2, 2006.

Senate, dared complain? Provinces gained money to cut hospital waiting lists. The 7 per cent federal goods and services tax (GST) dropped a single point. A week-long spending spree offered $17 billion in new ships, guns, and airplanes for the Canadian Forces if the Conservatives stayed in office. Photo opportunities with President Bush and a hurried settlement of the long-running softwood lumber dispute showed Washington that it had a good friend in Ottawa, though Harper, like Martin, opposed missile defence and sent no troops to Iraq. Instead, Canada's troops lost close to forty dead in Afghanistan in 2006 and Harper's enthusiasm for the mission allowed many to blame him, not the Liberals, for sending them there. As evidence accumulated of global warming and its devastating impact on the Arctic, Harper's Bush-like dismissal of the Kyoto Accord began to hurt him. By the end of his first year in office, Conservative support across Canada had slipped, and almost collapsed in Quebec. The environment and Afghanistan were obvious explanations. Could a cool pragmatist turn "green" without enraging his petro-dollar power base?

The Liberals took a year to find a new leader. Major figures from the Chrétien and Martin eras tested the water and dropped out. A field of nine candidates presented themselves to a convention in Montreal: their common feature was novelty. The two front-runners were covertly backed by the Martin and Chrétien camps respectively. Michael Ignatieff's grandfather had been the Russian Czar's last Minister of Education; he was a scholar-journalist who knew the world better than Canada. Bob Rae had switched from the NDP but Ontario Liberals let no one forget his troubled years as premier. Seemingly unaware of the rage mere words had provoked during the Meech Lake debate, Ignatieff ignored Trudeau doctrine and proclaimed that Quebec was a nation. Gleeful sovereignists jeered at Liberal divisions until Stephen Harper intervened to proclaim that Québec indeed formed "a nation within Canada." Eventually the Parti Québécois told the Bloc to shut up and vote for it. Verbal slips and old guard backing froze Ignatieff in his first ballot standing. He and Rae failed to grow. Stéphane Dion, cabinet workhorse and sole francophone in the running, was most delegates' second choice. On the third ballot, Dion won. But could an uncharismatic but straight-talking professor win Canada?

Canadians live with forces in nature, geography, and politics that are much greater than themselves. A half-century of affluence allowed most Canadians to learn the virtues of tolerance. A partial erosion of prosperity at the turn of the century reminded them of both the source and the limits of that most essential civil virtue. United in a sovereign state or divided in regional provinces, all the vast distances of our half of North America cannot allow us to ignore or betray each other. Only with tolerance can Canadians hope to live well.

What Canadians need to remember from their history is the power of community and the continuity of life in a great and generous land. A cautious people learns from its past; a sensible people can face their future. On the whole, Canadians have been both.

Further Readings

Further readings on the general themes and topics in *The Illustrated History of Canada* are suggested here. The authors of each of the chapters offer more suggested readings for people who wish to study a particular era or time period in greater detail.

The historical geography of Canada is beautifully illustrated in the three volumes of the *Historical Atlas of Canada*. Volume I, *From the Beginning to 1800* (1987) is edited by R. Cole Harris. The editor of Volume II, *The Land Transformed, 1800–1891* (1993) was R. Louis Gentilcore. Donald Kerr and Deryck W. Holdsworth are the editors of Volume III, *Addressing the Twentieth Century* (1990). R. Cole Harris and John Warkentin, *Canada Before Confederation: A Study in Historical Geography* (1974) is also valuable.

The *Dictionary of Canadian Biography, 14 Volumes* (1965–), a unique multi-volume project, organized chronologically by death dates, sketches the people who made our history, high and low, sacred and profane, rich and poor, in beautifully written accounts of their lives and times. To date the DCB covers our biographical history from aboriginal times to 1920.

The *Canadian Centennial Series* in 19 volumes (1963–1987) is a rich source of historical narrative and analysis. Among the volumes Hilda Neatby, *Quebec, 1760–1791* (1966); Gerald M. Craig, *Upper Canada: The Formative Years, 1784–1841* (1963); Fernand Ouellett, *Lower Canada, 1791–1840* (1980); W. Stewart MacNutt, *The Atlantic Provinces, 1712–1857* (1965); J. M. S. Careless, *The Union of the Canadas, 1841–1857* (1967); W. L. Morton, *The Critical Years, 1857–1873* (1964); P. B. Waite, *Canada, 1874–1896: Arduous Destiny* (1971); R. C. Brown and Ramsay Cook, *Canada, 1892–1921: A Nation Transformed* (1974); Morris Zaslow, *The Opening of the North, 1870–1914* (1971); John Herd Thompson and Allan Seager, *Canada, 1922–1939: Decades of Discord* (1985); and J. L. Granatstein, *Canada, 1957–1967: The Years of Uncertainty and Innovation* (1986) are most useful.

The definitive survey of the history of Canada's Native peoples is Olive Patricia Dickason, *Canada's First Nations: A History of Founding Peoples from Earliest Times* (1997). Arthur J. Ray, *I Have Lived Here Since the World Began: An Illustrated History of Canada's Native People* (1996) and J. R. Miller, *Skyscrapers Hide the Heavens: A History of Indian–White Relations in Canada* (2000) are also excellent.

The standard source on Canada's external relations through the Second World War is C. P. Stacey, *Canada in the Age of Conflict: A History of Canadian External Policies, Volume I, 1867–1921* and *Volume II, 1921–1948* (1977 and 1984). Nicholas Mansergh, *The Commonwealth Experience, Volume I, The Durham Report to the Anglo-Irish Treaty* and *Volume II, From British to Multi-Racial Commonwealth* (1983) is an excellent survey of Canada's Imperial and Commonwealth relations. Desmond Morton, *A Military History of Canada* (1999) and Donald J. Goodspeed, *The Armed Forces of Canada, 1867–1967: A Century of Achievement* (1967) review Canada's military history. Three modern perspectives on Canada's relations with the United States are Robert Bothwell, *Canada and the United States: the politics of partnership* (1992); J. L. Granatstein and Norman Hillmer, *For Better or For Worse: Canada and the United States to the 1990's* (1991); and John Herd Thompson and Stephen J. Randall, *Canada and the United States: Ambivalent Allies* (1994).

Roger Gibbins, *Conflict and Unity: An Introduction to Canadian Political Life* (1990) and William Christian and C. Campbell, *Political Parties and Ideologies in Canada* (1990) are general examinations of Canadian politics. W. T. Easterbrook and Hugh G. J. Aitken, *Canadian Economic History* (1988) is a standard source. More recent is K. H. Norrie and Doug Owram's excellent *A History of the Canadian Economy* (1991). A lively, insightful analysis of the history of Canadian business is Michael Bliss, *Northern Enterprise: Five Centuries of Canadian Business* (1987). Peter Baskerville and Graham Taylor, *A Concise History of Canadian Business* (1994) is also useful.

Craig Heron, *The Canadian Labour Movement: A Short History* (1989) and Gregory S. Kealey and Peter Warrian, eds., *Essays in Canadian Working Class History* (1979) are fine examples of recent analysis of the history of Canada's working women and men.

Important studies of Canada's social and women's histories are Margaret Conrad and Alvin Finkel, *History of the Canadian Peoples* (1998); Alison Prentice, et. al., *Canadian Women: A History* (1988); and Susan Mann Trofimenkoff and Alison Prentice, *The Neglected Majority: Essays in Canadian Women's History* (1977 and 1985). John Webster Grant, *The Church in the Canadian Era: The First Century of Confederation* (1972) and Mark G. McGowan and David B. Marshall, *Prophets, Priests, and Prodigals: Readings in Canadian Religious History, 1680–Present* (1992) are valuable accounts of aspects of our religious history. Carl Berger, *The Writing of Canadian History: Aspects of English-Canadian Historical Writing since 1900* (1986); A. B. McKillop, *Contours of Canadian Thought* (1987); and Serge Gagnon, *Quebec and its Historians* (1982 and 1985) are thoughtful accounts of our intellectual history and historical writing.

When Two Worlds Met

General histories of Canadian Aboriginal people include: Olive Patricia Dickason, *Canada's First Nations: A History of Founding Peoples from Earliest Times* (1997); J. R. Miller, *Skyscrapers Hide the Heavens: A History of Indian–White Relations in Canada* (2000); and Arthur J. Ray, *I Have Lived Here Since the World Began: An Illustrated History of Canada's Native People* (1996). An excellent historical geographical overview is available in R. Cole Harris (ed.), *Historical Atlas of Canada*, Volume 1 (1987).

Regional overviews are available in Bruce G. Trigger and Wilcomb E. Wasburn (editors), *The Cambridge History of the Native Peoples of the Americas*, Volume 1 (Part 2) (1996). Archaeological and ethnographic surveys for all of the major culture areas except the plains region are provided in William Sturtevant (general editor), *Smithsonian Handbook of North American Indians*, Volumes 3 (the Subarctic), 5 (the Northeast), 7 (the Northwest Coast), 12 (the Plateau), and 15 (the Arctic). For an historical geographical perspective of the Great Lakes area see, Helen H. Tanner (editor), *Atlas of Great Lakes Indian History* (1987). A good overview of the western interior is provided by Sarah Carter, *Aboriginal people and colonizers of Western Canada to 1900* (1999).

Insightful Aboriginal perspectives about aspects of the contact experience are available from Howard Adams, *Prison of Grass: Canada from a Native Point of View* (1989); Freda Ahenakew and H. C. Wolfart (editors), *Kôhkominawak Ota~cimowiniwa~wa—Our Grandmothers' Lives, As Told in Their Own Words* (1992); Keith Thor Carlson, *You Are Asked to Witness: the Stó:lo in Canada's Pacific Coast History* (1997); Ella Clark, *Indian Legends of Canada* (1960); Julie Cruickshank, *Life Lived Like a Story: Life Stories of Three Yukon Native Elders* (1990); Julie Cruickshank, *Reading Voices: Dan Dhá Ts'edinintth'I: Oral and Written Interpretations of the Yukon's Past* (1991); Penny Petrone, *Native Literature in Canada: From Oral Tradition to the Present* (1990); and Ruth Holmes Whitehead, *The Old Man Told Us: Excerpts from Micmac History, 1500–1950* (1991).

There are many excellent regional histories of the involvement of Aboriginal people with European explorers, fur traders, and early missionaries. These studies also consider how these entanglements affected intertribal relations. For the Beothuk see *A History and Ethnography of the Beothuk* (1996). The Mi'kmaq experience is explored in Alfred Goldsworth Bailey, *The Conflict of European and Eastern Algonkian Cultures* (1969) and Leslie Francis Stokes Upton, *Micmacs and Colonists: Indian–White Relations in the Maritimes* (1979). The participation of the Iroquoian speakers is examined in Carol Blackburn, *Harvest of Souls: The Jesuit Missions and Colonialism in North America, 1632–1650* (2000); Conrad Heidenreich, *Huronia: A History and Geography of the Huron Indians, 1600–1650* (1971); Cornelius J. Jaenen *Friend and Foe* (1976); Bruce G. Trigger, *The Children of Aatientsic: A History of the Huron People to 1660* (1976); and Bruce G. Trigger, *Natives and Newcomers: Canada's "Heroic Age" Reconsidered* (1985). The changing relationship of the Anishinabe with the Iroquois is investigated in Peter S. Schmalz, *The Ojibwa of Southern Ontario* (1991).

The key studies of the central and western Subarctic and Plains people are Kerry Abel, *Drum Songs: Glimpses of Dene History* (1993); Charles A. Bishop, *The Northern Ojibwa and the Fur Trade: An Historical and Ecological Study* (1974); Kenneth Coates, *Best Left As Indians: Native-White Relations in the Yukon Territory, 1840–1950* (1984); Daniel Francis and Toby Morantz, *Partners in Furs: A History of the Fur Trade in Eastern James Bay, 1600–1879* (1983); Laura Peers, *The Ojibwa of Western Canada* (1994); Arthur J. Ray, *Indians in the Fur Trade* (1998); and Arthur J. Ray and Donald B. Freeman, *Give Us Good Measure: An Economic Analysis of Relations Between the Indians and the Hudson's Bay Company before 1763* (1978).

Extensive discussions of early contact on the Pacific slope are included in Robin Fisher, *Contact and Conflict:*

Indian–European Relations in British Columbia, 1774–1890 (1992); Robert Galois, *Kwakwaka'wakw Settlements, 1775–1920* (1994); James R. Gibson, *Otter Skins, Boston Ships, and China Goods: The Maritime Fur Trade of the Northwest Coast, 1785–1841* (1992); Erna Gunther, *Indian Life on the Northwest Coast of North America, As Seen by the Early Explorers and Fur Traders during the Last Decades of the Eighteenth Century* (1972); Richard Mackie, *Trading Beyond the Mountains: The British fur Trade on the Pacific, 1793–1843* (1997); and Dianne Newell, *Tangled Webs of History: Indians and the Law in Canada's Pacific Coast Fisheries* (1993).

Histories of social dimensions of contact and the emergence of the Métis are available in Jennifer Brown, *Strangers In Blood: Fur Trade Company Families in Indian Country* (1980); Jacqueline Peterson and Jennifer S. H. Brown (editors), *The New Peoples: Being and Becoming Métis in North America* (1984); D. Bruce Sealey and Antoine Lussier, *The Métis: Canada's Forgotten People* (1994); and Sylvia Van Kirk, *Many Tender Ties: Women in Fur Trade Society in Western Canada* (1980). For a glimpse of Prairie Métis life, see Guilhaume Charette, *Vanishing Spaces: Memoirs of a Prairie Métis* (1980).

Histories of Native involvement in European struggles for control of eastern North America are provided by Robert S. Allen, *His Majesty's Indian Allies: British Indian Policy in the Defence of Canada, 1774–1815* (1992); Cohn G. Calloway, *Crown and Calumet: British-Indian Relations, 1783–1815* (1987); and Francis Jennings, *The Ambiguous Iroquois Empire* (1984).

Colonization and Conflict:
New France and its Rivals, 1600–1760

Notable surveys of early Canadian history include those of Marcel Trudel, who in his multi-volume *Histoire de la Nouvelle-France* and other works displays a first-name knowledge of everyone who lived in seventeenth-century New France. Among English-language surveys, *The French in North America* by William Eccles (most recent edition: 1998), *La Nouvelle France* by Peter Moogk (2000), and *The People of New France* by Allan Greer (1997) are useful.

Much can be gleaned from the first five volumes of *The Dictionary of Canadian Biography*, from *The Historical Atlas of Canada*, Volume 1 (1987), and from such journals as *Canadian Historical Review, Revue d'histoire de l'Amerique française, Histoire sociale/Social History* and *William and Mary Quarterly*. A growing number of websites, including www.canadiana.org and www.civilization.ca, offer texts and references about early Canada.

Notable eyewitness accounts of early Canada include *The Jesuit Relations*, Champlain's *Works*, the *Voyages* of Jacques Cartier and of Pierre Radisson, and the letters of Marie de l'Incarnation, published as *Word from New France*, edited by Joyce Marshall (1967).

Literature on colonist–Native relations includes Bruce Trigger, *The Children of Aatientsic: A History of the Huron People to 1660* (1987); Richard White, *The Middle Ground* (1991); Daniel Richter, *The Ordeal of the Longhouse* (1992); and John Demos, *The Unredeemed Captive* (1994).

Studies of the social history of New France include *Habitants and Merchants of Montreal* by Louise Dechêne (1994); *Peasant, Lord, Merchant* by Allan Greer (1985); *La Noblesse de Nouvelle-France* by Lorraine Gadoury (1992), *Religion and Life in Louisbourg* by A. J. B. Johnson (1984), *Les communautés religieuses de Montréal* by Micheline d'Allaire (1995); *Acadia of the Maritimes*, edited by Jean Daigle (1995); *The New People: Being and Becoming Métis*, edited by Jacqueline Peterson and Jennifer Brown (1985); and the demography project of Université de Montréal (www.genealogy.umontreal.ca).

On the war of the conquest, see *Crucible of War* by Fred Anderson (2000); *Quebec 1759* by C. P. Stacey (1984); and *Dictionary of Canadian Biography*, Volume III (1974).

Canada is well provided with historic sites and museums of early history, including Vieux-Québec, Vieux Montréal, the Forges de Saint-Maurice (near Trois-Rivières), and Fortress of Louisbourg National Historic Park (websites include www.virtualmuseum.ca and www.parcscanada.ca/nhs). Readable glimpses of life in New France can be found in Christopher Moore's non-fiction *Louisbourg Portraits: Life in an Eighteenth Century Garrison Town* (2000) and in Brian Moore's novel *Blackrobe* (1985), which inspired a notable feature film of the same name.

On the Margins of Empire, 1760–1840

This chapter is distinguished by its close attention to place and space, and its consistent effort to assess the imprint of human activities upon the land of British North America. It draws from a wide range of sources. In addition to "standard" histories of British North America or parts thereof—such as Hilda Neatby, *Quebec, 1760–1791* (1966); Gerald M. Craig, *Upper Canada: The Formative Years, 1784–1841* (1963); Fernand Ouellet, *Lower Canada, 1791–1840* (1980); and W. Stewart MacNutt, *The Atlantic Provinces, 1712–1857* (1965)—it is indebted to R. Cole Harris and John Warkentin, *Canada Before Confederation: A Study in Historical Geography* (1974) and *The Historical Atlas of Canada* Volume I, *From the Beginning to 1800*, ed. R. Cole Harris, and Volume II, *The Land Transformed, 1800–1891*, ed. R. L. Gentilcore (1987 and 1993). Also helpful was R. Louis Gentilcore and C. Grant Head, eds., *Ontario's History in Maps* (1984). Other works whose information and insights have been incorporated into several parts of the chapter are: Douglas McCalla, *Planting the Province: The Economic History of Upper Canada 1784–1870* (1993); Fernand Ouellet, *Economic and Social History of Quebec, 1760–1850: Structures and Conjunctures* (1980); and Suzanne E. Zeller, *Inventing Canada: Early Victorian Science and the Idea of a Transcontinental Nation* (1987).

A small handful of books by fellow historical geographers provide inspiration, information and fine examples of the sort of work upon which this chapter is based. They are Serge Courville, *Entre Ville et Campagne. L'essor du village dans les seigneuries du Bas-Canada* (1990) and Serge Courville, *Atlas historique du Quebec: Population et territoire* (1996); Eric Ross, *Beyond the River and the Bay* (1970); Stephen J. Hornsby, *Nineteenth Century Cape Breton: A Historical Geography* (1992); Thomas F. McIlwraith, *Looking for Old Ontario: Two Centuries of Landscape Change* (1997); J. David Wood, *Making Ontario: Agricultural Colonization and Landscape Re-creation before the Railway* (2000).

The opening section of the chapter owes something to Simon Schama, "The Many Deaths of General Wolfe," pp. 3–70 of *Dead Certainties* (1992), and to the following: Olive P. Dickason, *Canada's First Nations: A History of Founding Peoples from Earliest Times* (1997); A. J. Ray, *Indians in the Fur Trade: Their Role as Hunters, Trappers and Middlemen in the Lands Southwest of Hudson Bay, 1660–1870* (1974); C. Grant Head, *Eighteenth Century Newfoundland. A Geographer's perspective* (1976); W. Gordon Handcock, *Soe longe as there comes noe women. Origins of English Settlement in Newfoundland* (1989); and Suzanne E. Zeller, "Nature's Gullivers and Crusoes: The Scientific Exploration of British North America, 1800–1870," in John L. Allen (ed.) *North American Exploration, Volume 3 A Continent Comprehended* (1997), pp. 190–243.

Discussion of the adjustments in trade and policy after 1760 rests, in part, upon the author's own research published in "A Province Too Much Dependent on New England," *Canadian Geographer*, 31 #2 (1987), pp. 98–113; "A Region of Scattered Settlement and Bounded Possibilities," *Canadian Geographer* 31 #3 (1987), pp. 319–38; and *Timber Colony: A historical geography of early nineteenth century New Brunswick* (1981). For an understanding of colonial administration in the late eighteenth and early nineteenth centuries, there is no better source than Philip A. Buckner, *The Transition to Responsible Government. British Policy in British North America, 1815–1850* (Westport, CN; Greenwood Press, 1985). For discussion of American-British influences on Upper Canada in the early decades of the nineteenth century see Jane Errington, *The Lion, the Eagle and Upper Canada. A Developing Colonial Ideology* (Kingston and Montreal: McGill-Queen's University Press, 1987). For the rebellions see Allan Greer, *The Patriots and the People. The Rebellion of 1837 in Rural Lower Canada* (Toronto: University of Toronto Press, 1993) and Mary B. Fryer, *Volunteers & redcoats, rebels & raiders: a military history of the rebellions in Upper Canada* (Toronto: Dundurn Press, 1987).

The story of immigration and settlement is an important one for this period. The classic, still unrivalled, work here is Helen Cowan, *British Emigration to British North America. The First Hundred Years*, Rev. ed. (1961), first published in 1928, but it has, thankfully, been followed by a small bookshelf full of more narrowly focused works. Chief among those used here are Donald H. Akenson, *The Irish in Ontario: A Study in Rural History* (1984); W. Cameron and M. M. Maude, *Assisting Emigration to Upper Canada: The Petworth Project 1832–1837* (2000); W. Cameron, S. Haines, and M. M. Maude, *English Emigrant Voices. Labourers Letters from Upper Canada in the 1830s* (2000); Bruce S. Elliott, *Irish Migrants in the Canadas: A New Approach* (1988); Cecil. J Houston and W. Sheamus Smyth, *Irish Emigration and Canadian Settlement: Patterns, Links, and Letters* (1990); Hugh J. M. Johnston, *British Emigration Policy 1815–30: Shovelling Out Paupers* (1972); Marianne McLean, *The People of Glengarry: Highlanders in Transition, 1745–1820* (1991); Peter Thomas, *Strangers from a Secret Land. The Voyages of the Brig 'Albion' and the Founding of the First Welsh Settlements in Canada* (1986); and Catherine A. Wilson, *A New Lease on Life: Landlords, Tenants and*

Immigrants in Ireland and Canada (1994). Other more general treatments of value include J. M. Bumsted, *The People's Clearance: Highland Emigration to British North America, 1770–1815* (1982). The cholera epidemic is dealt with by Geoffrey Bilson, *A Darkened House: Cholera in Nineteenth-Century Canada* (1980). My overall sense of the patterns of cultural loss and retention among immigrants to British North America derives from John J. Mannion, *Irish Settlements in Eastern Canada: A study of Cultural Transfer and Adaptation* (1974).

The sketches of work and life and the detailed discussions of particular settings that follow rest on a wide range of materials, including several articles to be found in *Canadian Papers in Rural History* Volumes 1–10, ed. D. H. Akenson (1978 to 1996), contemporary accounts, and such works as G. P. de T. Glazebrook, *Life in Ontario. A Social History* (1968) and Jane Errington, *Wives and Mothers, Schoolmistresses and Scullery Maids: Working Women in Upper Canada, 1790–1840* (1995). I owe a particular debt to Allan Greer's *Peasant, Lord and Merchant: Rural Society in Three Quebec Parishes, 1740–1840* (1985) for my discussion of the Allaires; to Peter M. Ennals, *Land and Society in Hamilton Township, Upper Canada,* 1791–1861, PhD dissertation, University of Toronto, 1978, for my treatment of Hamilton Township, and to the reprint of *Gubbins' New Brunswick Journals, 1811 & 1813,* edited by Howard Temperley, (1980) for my New Brunswick discussion. My debt to Margaret Atwood's *Journals of Susanna Moodie* (1970) is also clear.

The discussion of early towns can be extended from a variety of sources, including materials in the *Historical Atlas of Canada*; Yvon Desloges, *A Tenant's Town. Quebec in the Eighteenth Century* (1991); Serge Courville et Robert Garon, *Atlas historique du Quebec: Quebec, Ville et capitale* (2001); Phyllis Lambert and Alan Stewart, eds., *Opening the Gates of Eighteenth Century Montreal* (1992); Donald Kerr and Jacob Spelt, *The Changing Face of Toronto* (1969); J. M. S. Careless, *Toronto to 1918: An Illustrated History* (1984); Peter Ennals, "Cobourg and Port Hope: The Struggle for Control of 'The Back Country'," in J. David Wood, ed., *Perspectives on Landscape and Settlement in Nineteenth Century Ontario* (1975), pp. 183–96. T. W Acheson, *Saint John: The Making of a Colonial Urban Community* (1985). Finally, Eric Ross, *Full of Hope and Promise: The Canadas in 1841* (1991) offers a finely wrought portrayal of a large part of the territory considered here, and Samuel V. LaSelva's *The Moral Foundations of Canadian Federalism: Paradoxes, Achievements, and Tragedies of Nationhood* (1996) grapples intriguingly with matters barely caricatured in the concluding sentences of the chapter.

Between Three Oceans: Challenges of a Continental Destiny, 1840–1900

For the sixty years of such changes as Canada went through from 1840 to 1900, the available books are now considerable and varied. There are substantial histories in the multi-volume Centennial Series of which the most useful are: J. M. S. Careless, *The Union of the Canadas, 1841–1857* (1967); W. L. Morton, *The Critical Years, 1857–1873* (1964); P. B. Waite, *Canada, 1874–1896: Arduous Destiny* (1971); R. C. Brown and Ramsay Cook, *Canada, 1896–1921: A Nation Transformed* (1974); and Morris Zaslow, *The Opening of the Canadian North, 1870–1914* (1971). Several of these have useful bibliographies for further exploration.

The Confederation movement was a principal theme in the Morton book noted above. Others include D. G. Creighton, *The Road to Confederation* (1964) and P. B. Waite, *The Life and Times of Confederation* (1962). A useful background to Confederation is Paul G. Cornell, *The Alignment of Political Groups in Canada, 1841–1867* (1962). Ged Martin, *Britain and the Origins of Canadian Confederation, 1837–67* (1995) is a recent account.

One way of getting the feel of this period is from biography and autobiography. History's raw material is men and women's lives and there are some exceptional biographies for Canada 1840–1900. The most important is D. G. Creighton, *John A. Macdonald* (1952) and *The Old Chieftain* (1955), republished in 1999 in a one-volume paperback. It can be considered the finest biography in English in Canada. The redoubtable founder and editor of the Toronto *Globe*, George Brown, is the subject of J. M. S. Careless, *Brown of the Globe* (1959) and *Statesman of Confederation* (1963). Brian Young offers a frank and vigorous appreciation of *George-Etienne Cartier: Montreal Bourgeois* (1981). On Sir Wilfrid Laurier see O. D. Skelton, *Life and Times of Sir Wilfrid Laurier* (2 vols. 1921); Joseph Schull, *Laurier: The First Canadian* (1965); and Réal Bélanger, *Wilfrid Laurier: quand la politique devient passion* (1986). Sir John Thompson, an important guardian of Canada's national sanity as Minister of Justice, 1885–1894, is the subject of P. B. Waite, *The Man from Halifax: Sir John Thompson, Prime Minister* (1985). Another Nova Scotian, Sir Charles

Tupper, has not yet received a decent full biography; the best is Phillip Buckner's study in the *Dictionary of Canadian Biography* [*DCB*], Vol. XIV.

The *DCB* is lovely for browsing. It is organized by dates of death of the subject, so one needs to know that in order to get the right one of the 14 volumes. For biographies in short compass there is no better source. For example, Joseph Howe's life is sketched in lively detail in Volume X; Volume XIII (1910–19) contains a fine biography of Sir Hector Langevin; and Volume XIV (1911–20) is the best place to find an authoritative life of Edward Blake (1833–1912), the leader of the Liberal Party before Laurier, and of Sir William Van Horne (1843–1915), one of the builders of the Canadian Pacific Railway.

Railway history in Canada is a big subject: the railway age began in the 1850s and continued until after the First World War. For the Grand Trunk Railway, G. R. Stevens, *Canadian National Railways. vol. 1: Sixty Years of Trial and Error* (1966) is a lively recital of the line's adventures. W. K. Lamb, *A History of the Canadian Pacific Railway* (1977) is well-written and sensible and Pierre Berton's two volumes, *The National Dream: The Great Railway, 1871–1881* (1970) and *The Last Spike: The Great Railway, 1881–1885* (1971) are flamboyant and vigorous.

On the promotion of development of western Canada see Douglas Owram, *The Promise of Eden: The Canadian Expansionist Movement and the Idea of the West* (1980). The best introduction to the prairie west is Gerald Friesen, *The Canadian Prairies: A History* (1984). George F. G. Stanley, *Louis Riel* (1963) is still the surest approach to that controversial figure but it should be balanced with Thomas Flanagan, *Louis 'David' Riel: 'Prophet of the New World'* (1979), R. C. Macleod's excellent *The North-West Mounted Police and Law Enforcement, 1873–1905* (1976) and Bob Beal and Rod Macleod, *Prairie Fire: The 1885 North-West Rebellion* (1984). Maggie Siggins, *Riel: A Life of Revolution* (1994) adds new material and drama to the Métis struggle to retain their way of life. Further west, the history of British Columbia is well developed in Margaret A. Ormsby, *British Columbia: A History* (1971) and Robin Fisher, *Contact and Conflict: Indian–European Relations in British Columbia, 1774–1890* (1977) is a refreshing study on aboriginal–white relations.

For Quebec, *Quebec, a history, vol 1. 1867–1929* (1983) is a translation of the excellent *Histoire de Québec contemporain, 1867–1929* (1979) by Paul-André Linteau, René Durocher, and Jean-Claude Robert. A. I. Silver, *The French-Canadian Idea of Confederation, 1864–1900* (1982) is valuable as is Susan Mann Trofimenkoff, *The Dream of Nation: A Social and Intellectual History of Quebec* (1982). Robert Rumilly's multi-volume *Histoire de la Province de Québec* (1940–69) is a delight to read for those who read French.

The volumes in the Centennial Series noted above contain valuable accounts of Canada's relations with the Empire and the United States in this period. These should be supplemented by C. P. Stacey, *Canada in the Age of Conflict: A History of Canadian External Policies, vol. 1, 1867–1921* (1977) and Desmond Morton, *A Military History of Canada* (1985). Kenneth Bourne, *Britain and the Balance of Power In North America, 1815–1908* (1967) surveys Imperial policy and David L. M. Farr, *The Colonial Office and Canada, 1867–1887* (1955) covers the institutional aspects of Anglo-Canadian relations. A classic study of Canadian imperial ideas is Carl Berger *The Sense of Power: Studies in the Ideas of Canadian Imperialism, 1867–1914* (1967). R. C. Brown, *Canada's National Policy, 1883–1900* (1964) is a standard study of Canadian–American relations in the period while Canadian attitudes towards the United States are sketched in R. C. Brown and S. F. Wise, *Canada Views the United States: Nineteenth Century Political Attitudes* (1967).

The Triumph and Trials of Materialism, 1900–1945

General studies of these fifty years include R. C. Brown and Ramsay Cook, *Canada 1896–1921: A Nation Transformed* (1974); John Thompson and Allen Seager, *Canada 1922–1939: Decades of Discord* (1985); and J. L. Granatstein, *Canada's War: The Politics of the Mackenzie King Government, 1939–1945* (1975).

Political biographies include Joseph Schull, *Laurier: The First Canadian* (1965); Robert Craig Brown, *Robert Laird Borden* (1975 and 1980); and McGregor Dawson and H. Blair Neatby, *William Lyon Mackenzie King* (1958, 1963 and 1976). Less important but no less interesting figures include Kenneth McNaught, *A Prophet in Politics: A biography of J. S. Woodsworth* (1959); John T. Saywell, *"Just call me Mitch": The Life of Mitchell F. Hepburn* (1991); and Conrad Black, *Render unto Caesar: the life and legacy of Maurice Duplessis* (1998). Michael Bliss, *A Canadian Millionaire: The Life and Business Times of Sir Joseph Flavelle* (1978) and David Frank, *J. B. McLachlan: a biography* (1999) portray a major businessman and a radical labour leader. Mary Hallett, *Firing the Heather: The Life and Times of Nellie McClung* (1993) and Hélène Pelletier-Baillargeon *Marie Gérin-Lajoie* (1985) set out the careers of social reformers and women's rights activists. Robert Rumilly, *Henri Bourassa* (1953) and Ramsay Cook, *The Politics of John W. Dafoe and the Free Press* (1963) deal with the lives of influential journalists. Maria Tippett, *Emily Carr: A Biography* (1979) and Michael Bliss, *Banting: A Biography* (1984) present lives in the arts and medical science.

Northern Enterprise (1987) by Michael Bliss summarizes business development. Christopher Armstrong and H. V. Nelles, *Monopoly's Moment: The Organization and Regulation of Canadian Utilities, 1830–1930* (1886) and Christopher Armstrong, *Blue Skies and Boiler Rooms* (1997) examine public utilities and the stock market. Vernon C. Fowke, *The National Policy and the Wheat Economy* (1957); Ronald Rees, *New and Naked Land: Making the Prairies Home* (1988); and James Gray, *Men Against the Dessert* (1967) and *The Winter Years* (1966) tell the story of western agriculture. H. V. Nelles, *The Politics of Development: Forests, Mines and Hydro-Electric Power in Ontario, 1849–1941* (1974) and Janet Foster, *Working for Wildlife* (1978) and *L'éologisme retrouvé* (1994) describe aspects of resource policy and the early conservation movement.

Studies of working class history include Robert Babcock, *Gompers in Canada* (1974); Craig Heron, *Working in Steel* (1988); David Bercuson, *Confrontation at Winnipeg* (1974); Irving Abella, *Nationalism, Communism and Canadian Labour* (1973); Joy Parr, *The Gender of Bread Winners* (1986); Terry Copp, *The Anatomy of Poverty: The Condition of the Working Class in Montreal, 1897–1929* (1974); and Michael Piva, *The Condition of the Working Class in Toronto, 1900–1921* (1979).

Examples of immigration and ethnic history are Joy Parr, *Labouring Children: British Immigrant Apprentices to Canada, 1869–1924* (1980); Howard Palmer, *Patterns of Prejudice: A History of Nativism in Alberta* (1982); Peter Ward, *White Canada Forever: Popular Attitudes and Public Policies toward Orientals in British Columbia* (1978); John Zucchi, *Italians in Toronto* (1990); France Swripa, *Wedded to the Cause: Ukrainian Women and Ethnic Identity* (1993); George Woodcock and Ivan Avakumovic, *The Doukhobors* (1977); and Gerald Tulchinsky's two volumes on Canadian Jewish history, *Taking Root* (1992) and *Branching Out* (1998).

Catherine L. Cleverdon, *The Woman Suffrage Movement in Canada* (1950) and Veronica Strong-Boag, *The New Day Recalled* (1988) examine the suffrage and post-suffrage history of women. Ruth Pearson, *"They're Still Women After All"* (1986) discusses women in World War II. Marty Danylewycz, *Taking the Veil* (1987) and Andrée Lévesque, *Making and Breaking the Rules* (1994) consider women in Quebec.

Social reform is the subject of Ramsay Cook, *The Regenerators* (1984) and Nancy Christie and Michael Gauvreau, *A Full Orbed Christianity* (1996). James Gray, *Red Lights on the Prairies* (1971) and *Booze* (1972); W. L. Morton, *The Progressive Party in Canada* (1950); Ernest Forbes, *Maritime Rights* (1979); and David Laycock, *Populism and Democratic Thought in the Canadian Prairies, 1910–1945* (1990) describe regional protest movements.

The history of Native people is surveyed in Olive Dickason, *Canada's First Nations* (1992) and J. R. Miller, *Skyscrapers Hide the Heavens* (1989). J. Brian Titley, *A Narrow Vision* (1986); Sarah Carter, *Lost Harvests: Prairie Indian Reserve Farmers and Government Policy* (1990); Helen Buckley, *From Wooden Ploughs to Welfare* (1993); and J. R. Miller, *Shingwauk's Vision* (1996) critically examine government policy.

C. P. Stacey, *Canada in the Age of Conflict, 2 vols.* (1977 and 1984) surveys foreign policy. Carl Berger, *The Sense of Power* (1970) and H. V. Nelles, *The Art of Nation Building* (1999) explore Canada's relations with the British Empire. John H. Thompson and Stephen Randall, *Canada and the United States: Ambivalent Allies* (1994) surveys Canadian–American relations. The world wars are treated in Desmond Morton, *Marching to Armageddon: Canadians and the Great War, 1914–1919* (1989) and J. L. Granatstein, *A Nation Forged in Fire: Canadians in the Second World War, 1939–1945* (1989). *Secret Agent: The Pickersgill Letters* (1978), edited by George H. Ford, is the tragic story of one young man's war.

Denis Reid, *Concise History of Canadian Painting* (1973) surveys visual art. A. J. M. Smith, ed., *The Oxford Book of Canadian Verse* (1960) prints a selection of French and English poetry. Some of the best works of fiction are Sara Jeannette Duncan, *The Imperialist* (1904); Stephen Leacock, *The Arcadian Adventures of the Idle Rich* (1914); Ringuet, *Trente Arpents* (1938); Sinclair Ross, *As For Me and My House* (1941); Gabrielle Roy, *The Tin Flute* (1947); W. O. Mitchell, *Who Has Seen the Wind* (1947); John Marlyn, *Under the Ribs of Death* (1957); Colin McDougall, *The Execution* (1958); Roch Carrier, *La Guerre, Yes Sir!* (1968); and P. B. Heibert, *Sarah Binks* (1947).

Strains of Affluence, 1945–2000

Contemporary history gains in texture and loses in certainty. Evidence multiplies out of control; confidence that we know what happened or what matters fades. Barred from sources by security or privacy regulations or by their proliferation, historians share their strengths and limitations with journalists. Among the major sources for the period, particularly in its earlier, less pretentious years is John Saywell *et seq.* (eds.) *The Canadian Annual Review* (various) not to mention the continuing *Canada Year Book* from Statistics Canada, which also grows lovelier but more laggard and much less comprehensive. *Maclean's, le Magazine Maclean,* and its heir, *L'Actualité* are also invaluable.

Two volumes of the McClelland and Stewart Centennial Series cover part of this period: D. G. Creighton's *The Forked Road, Canada, 1939–1957* (1976) is shaped by the author's despair at American influence and Jack Granatstein's *Canada, 1957–1967: The Years of Uncertainty and Innovation* (1986) stops midway. Other survey texts go farther: Margaret Conrad and Alvin Finkel, *History of the Canadian Peoples* (1998) conscientiously avoids politics to promote social and cultural themes; J. L. Granatstein, I. M. Abella, David Bercuson, Craig Brown, and Blair Neatby, *Twentieth Century Canada* (2nd ed., 1986), preserve the political issues that united and divided Canadians. The postwar history of a province "unlike the others" is sensibly summarised in Paul-Andre Linteau, René Durocher, Jean-Claude Robert, and Francois Ricard, *Quebec Since 1930* (1991). Valuable chiefly for what most historians bypass is Norah Story's *Oxford Companion to Canadian History and Literature* (1967) and William Toye's *Supplement* (1973).

Post-war Canada is described by Desmond Morton and Jack Granatstein, *Victory 1945: Canada from War to Peace* (1995) and Barry Broadfoot's collected memories *The Veteran Years: Coming Home from the War* (1985). Veterans' policies are recalled in Peter Neary and J. L. Granatstein, *The Veterans Charter and Post-World War II Canada* (1998). A splendid recent book on life in the 1950s is Valerie Korinek's *Roughing it in Suburbia: Reading Chatelaine Magazine, 1950–1969* (1999) while and Joy Parr describes the material background of a more affluent life in *Domestic Goods: The Material, the Moral and the Economic in the Postwar Years* (1999).

Canada's post-war birthrate quietly transformed its history. The case initially made in *The Big Generation* and echoed by David Foot's best-selling *Boom, Bust and Echo: How To Profit from the Coming Demographic Shift* (1996) took historical share in Doug Owram's *Born at the Right Time: A History of the Baby Boom Generation* (1996). A major post-war outcome of Foot's "boom" and "bust" was the feminist revolution which began in 1970 with publication of the *Report* of Florence Bird's Royal Commission on the Status of Women. See Dawn Black, *Twenty Years Later* (1990) and Susan Trofimenkoff and Alison Prentice, *The Neglected Majority: Essays in Canadian Women's History* (1985). An institutional consequence began in Saskatchewan with Medicare. The best account of its evolution is Malcolm G. Taylor, *Health Insurance and Canadian Public Policy: The Seven Decisions that Created the Canadian Health Insurance System and their Outcomes* (1987). Working lives led in post-war industrial struggle are described individually by Bob White, *My Life on the Line* (1987) and collectively by Charlotte Yates, *From Plant to Politics: The Autoworkers Union in Postwar Canada* (1993). A wider history of workers and unions is Desmond Morton, *Working People: An Illustrated History of Canadian Labour* (4th ed., 2000).

A major lifestyle change came with television. See Frank Peers, *The Public Eye: Television and the Politics of Canadian Broadcasting, 1952–1968* (1979) and Paul Rutherford's *When Television was Young: Primetime Canada, 1952–1967* (1990). Its advent coincided but hardly intersected with a revival of high culture. See Paul Litt, *The Muses and the Massey Commission* (1992).

In *Louis St-Laurent: Canadian* (1967) Dale Thomson introduced his chief. In *True Patriot: The Life of Brooke Claxton, 1898–1990* (1993), David Bercuson presents one of several able ministers; even better known was the subject of Robert Bothwell and William Kilbourn, *C. D. Howe: A Biography* (1979). See also Reg Whitaker, *The Government Party* (1977) in their period of most assured power. The most engaging memoir of politics in the 1950s is Dalton Camp's *Gentlemen, Players and Politicians* (1970), a good preparation for Peter Newman's devastating biography, *Renegade in Power: The Diefenbaker Years* (1976), now replaced by Denis Smith's *Rogue Tory: The Life and Legend of John Diefenbaker* (1995).

Newman tried to repeat his feat with Lester Pearson but the Liberal leader found a more sympathetic biographer in John English. See *The Worldly Years: The Life of Lester Pearson,* vol. II, *1949–1972* (1992). The best known premier of the period found a serious biography from Stephen Clarkson and Christina McCall, *Trudeau and Our Times,* vol. I, *The Magnificent Obsession* (1990); vol. II, *The Heroic Delusion* (1994); and a mid-life biography, Richard Gwyn's *The Northern*

Magus (1980). The Mulroney and Chrétien years still offer little more than campaign biographies and memoirs, notably Ian MacDonald's *Mulroney* (1994) and Jean Chrétien's best-selling and ghosted *Straight from the Heart* (1985). Filling some of the gap is Jeffrey Simpson's *The Anxious Years: Politics in the Age of Mulroney and Chrétien* (1996).

Among memorable books on national politics are John C. Crosbie, *No Holds Barred: My Life in Politics* (1997); Thomas Flanagan, *Waiting for the Wave: The Reform Party and Preston Manning* (1995); and contrarians, Sidney Sharpe and Don Braid, *Storming Babylon: Preston Manning and the Rise of the Reform Party* (1992). On other parties, see George Perlin, *The Tory Syndrome: Leadership Politics in the Progressive Conservative Party* (1980); John Laschinger and Geoffrey Stevens, *Leaders and Lesser Mortals: Backroom Politics in Canada* (Toronto, Key Porter Books, 1992); Gad Horowitz, *Canadian Labour in Politics* (1968); and Maurice Pinard, *The Rise of a Third Party: A Study in Crisis Politics* (1964). Canada's regional politics have spawned many important memoirs and analyses, among them Richard Gwyn's *Smallwood* (1968); Seymour Martin Lipset's *Agrarian Socialism: The Co-operative Commonwealth Federation in Saskatchewan* (1968); Roger Graham, *Old Man Ontario: Leslie M. Frost* (1990); and Jonathan Manthorpe, *The Power and the Tories: Ontario Politics, 1943 to the Present* (1974).

After 1945, Canadians were conscious of their role in the world menaced by Cold War and nuclear annihilation. They could follow a deadly game in a series of annual reviews, *Canada in World Affairs*, published by the Canadian Institute for International Affairs and later (and under different titles) by Carleton University. Able diplomats wrote memoirs and tried to educate fellow citizens, among them John Holmes, *The Shaping of Peace: Canada and the Search for World Order, 1943–57* (1982); Escott Reid; *Time of Fear and Hope* (1977); and George Ignatieff, *The Making of a Peacemonger* (1985). Others commented as scholars, among them Albert Legault and Michel Fortmann, *A Diplomacy of Hope: Canada and Disarmament, 1945–1988* (1992).

Much of Desmond Morton's *Military History of Canada: From Champlain to Kosovo* (4th ed. 1999) covers post-1945 developments. David Bercuson's *Blood on the Hills: The Canadian Army in the Korean War* (1999) joins H. F. Wood's *Strange Battleground* (1966), while Richard Gimblett and Jean Morin, *Operation Friction: Canadian Forces in the Gulf War* (1996) provides an official version of the second conflict of the period. Adequate histories of Canada's peace-keeping experience are in progress. Meanwhile Carol Off's *The Lion, the Fox and the Eagle* (2000) and David Bercuson's *Significant Incident: Canada's Army, The Airborne, and the Murder in Somalia* (1996) have different views of such operations.

Canada's relationship with Washington intensified after 1945. Joseph Jockel's *No Boundaries Upstairs: Canada, the United States and the Origins of North American Air Defence, 1945–1958* (1987) describe a vital partnership as did Jon B. McLin, *Canada's Changing Defence Policy, 1957–1963* (1967). For the 1980s, see Stephen Clarkson, *Canada and the Reagan Challenge: Crisis in the Canadian-American Relationship* (1985). At the same time, Richard Gwyn's *The 49th Paradox: Canada in North America* (1985) recognized Canada's readiness for free trade. John H. Thompson and Steve Randall's *Canada and the United States: Ambivalent Allies* (1997) provides a comprehensive treatment of issues while J. L. Granatstein's *Yankee Go Home? Canadians and Anti-Americanism* (1996) contradicts some old myths.

Canada's relations with Quebec sometimes seemed a foreign affair. Many books appeared in French and English. Among the more influential in English were Conrad Black, *Duplessis* (1976); Richard Jones, *Community in Crisis* (1967); Pierre B. Trudeau, *Federalism and the French Canadians* (1968); Ramsay Cook, *Canada and the French Canadian Question* (1970); Peter Desbarats, *René: A Canadian in Search of a Country* (1976); and, in light of English Canada's widespread echoing of Trudeau's constitutional strategy, Guy Laforest's *Trudeau and the End of a Canadian Dream* (1995). In 1970, Trudeau proposed to end an old grievance by abolishing the Indian Act. A different view of history changed his mind. See Harold Cardinal, *The Unjust Society: The Tragedy of Canada's Indians* (1969). In J. R. Miller's *Skyscrapers Hide the Heavens: A History of Indian–White Relations in Canada* 2nd ed. (1991) the modern chapters are useful. So is Alan B. Cairns's *Citizens Plus: Aboriginal Peoples and the Canadian State* (1999); On the North, see Robert Page, *Northern Development: The Canadian Dilemma* (1986).

Meanwhile, two members of the Royal Commission on Bilingualism and Biculturalism helped push Canada into multiculturalism. On immigration, see Ninette Kelley and Michael Trebilcock, *The Making of the Mosaic: A History of Canadian Immigration Policy* (1998). On the consequences, scores of book appeared, among them, Franca Iacovetta, *Such Hardworking People: Italian Immigrants in Postwar Toronto* (1992); Jean Burnet and Howard Palmer, *"Coming Canadians": An Introduction to the History of Canadian Peoples* (1988) and William Kaplan (ed)., *Belonging: The Meaning and Future of Canadian Citizenship* (1993).

Acknowledgement of Picture Sources

Sources of black-and-white illustrations are as below. For reasons of space the following abbreviations have been used.

A: Provincial Archives of Alberta, Edmonton;
AO: Archives of Ontario, Toronto;
EC: Erindale College Photo Collection, Mississauga, Ontario;
GM: Glenbow Museum, Calgary;
MM: McCord Museum of Canadian History, McGill University, Montreal;
MM/N: ———, Notman Photographic Archives;
MQ: Musée du Quebec, Quebec City;
MTL: Metropolitan Toronto Library, Toronto;
MTL/C: ———, Canadian History Dept.;
MTL/JRR: ———, ———, John Ross Robertson Collection;
N: National Museums of Canada, National Museum of Civilization, Ottawa;

NGC: National Gallery of Canada, Ottawa;
NS: Nova Scotia Museum, Halifax;
PAC: Public Archives of Canada, Ottawa;
PAC/AP: ———, Documentary Art & Photography Division;
PAC/NMC: ———, National Map Collection;
ROM: Royal Ontario Museum, Toronto;
ROM/C: ———, Canadiana Dept.;
ROM/E: ———, Ethnology Dept.;
SSC: Supply & Services Canada, Photocentre, Ottawa;
YU: York University, Toronto;
YU/C: ———, Cartographic Office, Dept. of Geography

COVER
Windsor Station by Molly Bobak, reproduced by the kind permission of the artist.

FRONT MATTER
Foreword (p.v): Medal struck to commemorate Confederation, 1867; AO. *Table of Contents (p.xvii): Les Progrès de la Vie Economique de 1608 à 1875* (polychromed wood, 1875) by Jean-Baptiste Côté; MQ (S.321).

COLOPHON
Joyfully I See Ten Caribou (stonecut) by Pootagok. Dept. of Northern Affairs & Natural Resources, Ottawa.

CHAPTER ONE
Page 1: PAC/NMC, original in John Rylands University Library of Manchester, England; *3:* Environment Canada—Parks, Atlantic Region, Halifax; *4:* MQ (34.12P), photo Patrick Altman; *6:* PAC/AP (C-11201); *7:* YU/C; *11:* N (K75-1); *13:* PAC/AP (C-2264); *15:* PAC/AP (C-5528); *16:* PAC/AP (C-2167); *19:* GM (MM.58.6); *21* PAC/AP (C-3165); *25:* PAC/NMC (NMC-1908); *26:* PAC/AP (C-113066); *28:* Art Gallery of Windsor, Windsor, Ontario (*top,* 67:39; *bottom,* 67:43); *31* PAC/AP (C-403); *32:* PAC/AP (C-33615); *34:* ROM/E, Edward Morris Collection (977 x 1.3); *36:* NGC (22); *37:* MM/N (2157&2158 view); *38:* N (J-10196); *41:* PAC/AP (PA-37756); *42:* PAC/AP (C-2821); *43:* Peabody Museum, Harvard University, Cambridge, Mass. (41-72-10/499, N27995); *45:* Musée des Beaux Arts de Montréal (967.1567); *46:* ROM/E (912.1.92); *49:* British Museum, Dept. of Prints & Drawings, London, England (ECM 63&64), reproduced by courtesy of the Trustees of the British Museum; *50:* MTL/C; *52:* PAC/AP (C-94140); *56:* PAC/AP (C-1912); *54:* Musée des Beaux Arts de Montréal (974.Aa.2); *56, left:* ROM/E (HD12635/922.1.29); *top right, left to right:* N (VII-C-329); Musée de l'Homme, Paris, France (81.22.1); photo, Hilary Stewart; *bottom right:* N (K-75-493); *57:* Hudson's Bay Company Archives, Provincial Archives (HBCAP-385.N9033); *58:* Provincial Archives of Manitoba (N12578); *62:* PAC/AP (C-17338); *70:*

Hudson's Bay Company, Winnipeg (C-25); *72:* MM (M965.9); *74:* PAC/AP (C-38948); *78* PAC/NMC (NMC-3295); *79:* PAC/AP (C-41292); *83:* Provincial Archives of British Columbia, Victoria, B.C. (pdp2244); *90:* NGC (5777); *91:* Provincial Archives of Newfoundland & Labrador (A17-110), photo courtesy Ray Fennelly; *92:* YU/C; 93: AO (6287 s 8243).

CHAPTER TWO

Page 95: PAC/NMC (NMC-15661); *97:* National Library of Canada, Rare Book Division, Ottawa (NL-8760); *98:* National Library of Canada, Rare Book Division, Ottawa (NL-8759); *100:* PAC Library, Ottawa (*left,* C-133067; *right,* C-133065); *102:* National Library of Canada, Rare Book Division, Ottawa (NL-6643); *107:* PAC/AP (C-107624); *108:* Huronia Historical Parks, Ontario Ministry of Tourism & Recreation; *119:* PAC/NMC (6340); *123:* Société du Musée du Séminaire de Québec, Quebec City (PC84.1 R277); *115:* PAC/NMC (C-3686); *116:* ROM/C (957.91); *118:* Musée des Ursulines, Quebec City, photo courtesy Ministère des Communications du Québec (MCQ-87-114F1); *122:* National Film Board Collection, Ottawa; *125:* Archives Nationales du Québec, Quebec City; *126:* MQ (A 42 57 P), photo Patrick Altman; *127:* PAC/NMC (NMC-26825); *129:* PAC/AP (C-1225); *134, top:* PAC/AP (C-30926); *bottom left:* Archives Nationales, Paris, France, Fond des Colonies (C11A, vol.19, fol.43–43v); *bottom right:* PAC/AP (C-62182); *135:* PAC/AP (C-12005); *140, left:* Environment Canada—Parks, Fortress of Louisbourg, Louisbourg, Nova Scotia (74-318); *right:* PAC/AP (C-17059); *144:* YU/C; *155:* PAC/AP (C-107626); *147:* MQ, Collection des Réligieuses Hospitalières de Saint-Joseph, Montreal; *148:* Petitot et Compagnie, Paris, France; *149, top:* photo courtesy Robert Stacey; *bottom:* photo courtesy C.W. Jefferys Estate Archives, Toronto; *152:* YU/C; *161, top:* MQ (A58.187P); *bottom:* PAC/AP (C-100376); *156, top:* NGC (7792); *bottom:* ROM/C (960.106); *157:* National Film Board Collection, Ottawa; *158:* ROM/C; *163, left:* MM (M.21231); *right:* PAC/AP (C-113742); *168:* NS (P21/80.11, copy neg. N-14,638); *169:* MTL/JRR (T16045); *171:* PAC/AP (C-5907); *176:* PAC/AP (C-27665); *180:* ROM/C (940x54).

CHAPTER THREE

Page 181: ROM (949.128.34); *184:* ROM (940x26.12); *187:* PAC/AP (C-41605); *190:* Art Gallery of Nova Scotia, Halifax (82.41); *191:* NGC (6286); *193:* PAC/AP (C-3257); *198:* AO (Simcoe Sketch no.202); *199:* Law Society of Upper Canada, Toronto (87-128-2); *205, left:* Government of Ontario Art Collection, Queen's Park, Toronto (MGS606898); *right:* MQ, photo Patrick Altman (G52.58p); *206, left:* PAC/AP (C-13392); *right:* MTL, reproduced from *Upper Canada Almanack for the year 1837,* Toronto; *207:* The Right Hon. the Earl of Elgin and Kincardine, Broomhall, Dunfermline, Scotland, photo courtesy NGC (69-388A); *208, top:* ROM/C (955.217.15); *bottom:* PAC/AP (C-276); *212:* PAC/AP (C-2001); *213:* National Library of Wales, Cardiff; *217:* PAC/AP (C-41067); *220:* NGC (7157); *222, left:* National Portrait Gallery, London, England; *right:* reproduced from *A Gallery of Illustrious Literary Characters (1830–38),* London, England, 1873; *223:* PAC/AP (C-17); *227:* PAC/AP (C-105230); *228:* PAC/AP (C-10531); *232:* ROM/E (912.1.31); *233:* MTL/JRR (T31492); *235:* PAC/AP (C-19294); *238:* AO (2096); *244:* PAC/AP (C-251); *245:* PAC/AP (C-252); *250:* PAC/AP (C-11811); *252:* NS (79.146.3 N-9411); *260:* PAC/NMC (NMC-17026); *261, top:* MTL/JRR (T10248); *bottom:* ROM/C (960.58.2); *263:* PAC/AP (C-12649); *264:* PAC/AP (C-2394); *268, left:* NGC (17,920); *right:* The Winnipeg Art Gallery, Winnipeg, photo Ernest P. Mayer (G57-133); *269:* ROM/C (956.77); *270:* Queen's University Archives, William Morris Collection, Kingston, Ontario (2139, Box 3); *271:* MTL, Fine Arts Department, Picture Collection; *273, left:* York Pioneer & Historical Society, Toronto; *right:* Dundurn Castle, Dept. of Culture & Recreation, Hamilton, Ontario; *274:* PAC/AP (C-520); *275:* AO (97).

CHAPTER FOUR

Page 277: GM (NA-2222-1); *279, left:* Dr. Owen Beattie/University of Alberta, photo Canapress, Toronto; *right:* ROM/C (955.141.2); *281:* PAC/AP (*top,* C-31277; *bottom,* C-31278); *285:* NS (36.70); *286:* MTL/JRR (T12188); *289:* British Museum, London, England; *290:* Château Ramezay Museum, Montreal; *291:* MM (M11588); *294:* MM/N (88,087-II); *295:* ROM/C (951.158.14); *296:* PAC/AP (C-37218); *297:* PAC/AP (PA-45005); *298:* AO (S.4308); *300:* MM/N (7226 view); *301:* PAC/AP (*top,* C-16525; *bottom,* C-16524); *305, top:* PAC/AP (C-62715); *middle:* NGC (239); *bottom:* Government of Ontario Art Collection, Queen's Park, Toronto (MGS 622107); *308:* MM/N (76,319-I); *309:* PAC/AP (C-63484); *311:* ROM/E (SSC 952.72.1); *316:* PAC/AP (C-78979); *317:* left, *Grip Magazine* (Vol. 19, no. 12, 1882); right, *Grip Magazine* (Vol. 18, no. 15, 1882); *325:* PAC/AP (*left,* C-26415; *right,* C-7158); *327:* NGC (9990); *331:* top left, *Picturesque Canada,* bottom right, National Archives; *332:* PAC/AP (C-88917); *336:* PAC/AP (C-8449); *337:* PAC/AP (C-41603); *341:* MM/N (28901-I); *342:* MTL/JRR (T10914); *343:* PAC/AP (C-95470); *345:* MM (3362); *346:* National Archives (NAC C1011); *347:* PAC/AP (C-58640); *350:* MTL/JRR (*top,* T16532; *bottom,* T15907); *352:* GM (NA-2246-1); *353:* GM (NA-1063-1); *355:* PAC/AP (C-22249); *356:* PAC/AP (C-86515); *357:* PAC/AP (C-1875); *359:* PAC/AP (PA-31489); *360:* GM (NA-2365-34); *361, top:* CP

Rail Corporate Archives, Montreal (CP.12576); *363, top:* PAC/AP (C-3693); *bottom:* Vancouver City Archives (CAN.P78.N.52); *364:* PAC/AP (C-5142), photo E.A. Hegg; *inset:* A (A5125); *364:* PAC/AP (C-20318); *366, top:* PAC/AP (C-33881); *bottom:* Provincial Archives of Manitoba, Marguerite Simons Collection, Winnipeg (C-36/5); *367:* Wilson Studio; *368:* NS (N-585); *372:* Lawrence Lande Collection of Canadiana, Dept. of Rare Books & Special Collections, McGill University Libraries, Montreal; *376:* Canada Post Corporation, Ottawa.

CHAPTER FIVE

Page 377: PAC/NMC (NMC16411); *379:* AO (S1243); *380:* photo courtesy Michael Bliss, Toronto; *382:* MTL Board; *386:* GM (NA-1473-1); *387:* PAC/AP (C-14658); *388, top:* A/Wells Studio (WS3038), photo courtesy PAC/AP (C-38693); *bottom:* PAC/AP (C-6605); *389:* A/Ernest Brown Collection (B.219); *390:* Saskatchewan Archives Board, Regina (R-B329); *391:* PAC/AP (C-63482); *392:* GM (NA-2676-6); *394:* PAC/AP (PA-115432); *395:* EC; *398:* PAC/AP (*top,* C-6389; *bottom,* C-27791); *401: left,* Archives de l'Institut Notre-Dame du Bon-Conseil; *top right:* GM (NA-273-2); *bottom right:* private collection; *404:* Government of Ontario Art Collection, Ministry of Government Services, Queen's Park, Toronto (MGS619724), photo T.E. Moore; *405:* PAC/AP (C-27358); *410:* N/Canadian War Museum, Ottawa (8,949); *412, top:* AO (acc. 11595); *bottom:* PAC/AP (C-7492); *416:* City of Toronto Archives, James Collection (640); *420:* PAC/AP (PA-57515); *422:* PAC/AP/David Millar Collection (WS-83); *424, top:* NGC (4881); *bottom:* PAC/AP (C-88566); *425:* McMichael Canadian Collection, Kleinburg, Ontario (1969.4.54); *426, top left:* Art Gallery of Ontario, Toronto (1335); *bottom left:* AO, William Colgate Papers (S12842); *right:* NGC (82-2847); *427:* photo courtesy Thomas Fisher Rare Book Library, University of Toronto; *429:* private collection, photo T.E. Moore; *431:* NGC (6666); *433:* PAC/AP (PA-138867), photo Cobourg Skitch Studio; *438:* AO (S15001); *440:* Hudson's Bay Company, Winnipeg; *444:* Collection of Ramsay Cook, Toronto; *446:* Canapress, Toronto; *448:* A (A3742); *450:* *Toronto Star* Collection, Toronto (016120-9000); *455:* PAC/AP (C80134); *457:* PAC/AP (C-9447); *461:* PAC/AP National Film Board Collection (PA-116874, NFB 1980-121 66-346); *464:* N/Canadian War Museum, Ottawa (11,786); *466:* EC; *467, top:* PAC/AP (PA-137013); *468:* N/Canadian War Museum, Ottawa (12,722); *469:* PAC/AP (PA-119766); *470:* PAC/AP (C-11550); *471:* PAC/AP (PA-114440).

CHAPTER SIX

Page 473: National Air Photo Library, Ottawa; *475:* PAC/AP (C-22716); *477:* Saskatchewan Archives Board, Regina (R-B2895); *478:* PAC/AP (PA-128080); *479:* SSC (62-819); *483:* YU Archives, *Toronto Telegram* Collection, Downsview, Ontario; *484:* PAC/AP (PA-154607), photo Walter Curtin; *486, top:* photo Peter Croydon; *bottom:* PAC/AP (C-128763), photo L. Jacques; *488:* EC; *492:* PAC/AP (C-79009), photo MacLean; *497:* PAC/AP (C-74147); *500:* Dept. of National Defence; *501:* YU Archives, *Toronto Telegram* Collection, Downsview, Ontario; *504:* reprinted with permission—The Toronto Star Syndicate; *506:* PAC/AP (C-53641), *The Gazette,* Montreal; *509:* SSC (67-10471); *511:* EC, photo S. Jaunzems; *512:* *The Globe and Mail,* Toronto (66104-38); *513:* SSC (78-369), photo Egon Bork; *514:* photo courtesy Brian Pickell; *515:* Victoria University Library, Toronto; *516:* courtesy Mrs. Marshall McLuhan, Toronto; *517, left:* Gilbert Studios, Toronto; *right:* PAC/AP (PA-137052), photo courtesy Walter Curtin; *518:* PAC/National Film, Television & Sound Archives, Stills Collection, Ottawa (*top:* 3283; *bottom:* S-6850); *519, left:* photo Peter Esterhazy, courtesy Jocelyn Laurence, Toronto; *right:* photo Editions Boréal Express, Montreal, courtesy Dr. Carbotte, Quebec; *523, left:* University of Toronto; *right:* National Research Council, Ottawa, photo Dan Getz; *524:* PAC/Duncan Cameron Collection; *526:* PAC/AP, United Steelworkers of America Collection (C-98715); *527:* SSC (75-6674); *529:* EC; *530, top:* PAC, *Montreal Star* Collection (PA-152448); *bottom:* PAC, *Montreal Gazette* Collection (PA-117477); *534:* *News of the North,* Yellowknife, N.W.T., *539, both:* Canapress, Toronto; *542:* *Toronto Star* Collection, Toronto (S209-26); *543:* Ontario Dept. of Tourism & Information, Toronto (6-G-1464); *547:* New Westminster, B.C., *Labour News* (B 7973-4), photo Jack Lindsay/Canadian Association of Labour Media, Vancouver; *548, top:* PAC/AP (PA-145608), photo B. Korda; *bottom:* photo John Reeves, Toronto; *549:* University of British Columbia Museum of Anthropology, Walter & Marianne Koerner Collection, Vancouver; *550:* courtesy Dimo Safari; *552:* *The Globe and Mail*/Tibor Kolley; *554:* SSC (75-2242), photo George Hunter; *556:* Canapress Photo Service/Ryan Remiorz; *547:* Canapress Photo Service/Fred Chartrand; *561:* Canapress Photo Service/Fred Chartrand; *562:* Canapress Photo Service/Shaney Komulainen, *562:* Canapress Photo Service/Canadian Forces; *564:* Canapress Photo Service/John Felstead; *571:* Canapress Photo Service/John Hyrniuk; *573:* Canapress Photo Service/Ryan Remiorz; *574:* CP Picture Archive/Andre Pichette; *566:* CP Picture Archive/Robert Galbraith; *568:* CP Picture Archive/Nick Procaylo; *570:* CP Picture Archive/Marin Chamerland; *590:* AP Photo/Charles Dharapak; *591:* Reuters/Shaun Best/Canada.

Index

survey, 201–202; cholera epidemic, 218, *220*; corporate colonization ventures, 220–221; dislocated people, 271–272; in early 1760s, 189–190; ecology, impact on, 273–275; everyday life, 242; farming, 237–241, 267; fishing industry, 225–228; fragmentation in, 265–276; "Free Ports," 197; fur trade, 228–233; government system, 287–292; governors, authority of, 200–201, 202; "Indian Territory" proclamation, 184, 185; late 18th century challenges, 193–194; law and justice, *301, 302*; Loyalists, 212–215; medical advances, 303–306; mercantilism, 195–198; mortality, 303–307; Native peoples, attitudes towards, 194–195; politics in, 302, 307–308; population, 1840, 278; Quebec Act, 185, 186; rebellions in, 210; scientific knowledge, 194; self-sufficiency, 195–197; settlement, 184–185, 211–215; smaller towns, 262; society in, 267–268, 271–273, 300–302; St. Lawrence River, settlement along, 186; steamships, 308–312; timber industry, 197–198, 233–237; transatlantic migration, 215–223; transportation, 282–287; unionization plan, 205; urban society, 257–265; War of 1812, 93, 185, 207–209, *208*; work and life in, 224–225; worsening of economic circumstances, 204
British North America Act, 322–323, 333, 443, 538
Brittain, Miller, 472
Broadbent, Ed, 541, *542*, 543, 553
Brock, Isaac, 208, *208*
Brock, J.A., *359*
Brown, Anne Nelson, 317
Brown, Ernest, *388, 389*
Brown, George, 286, 303, 306, 313, 314, 317, 318, 321, 324, *325*
Brown, Richard, *461*

Brown, Rosemary, *542*
Brown, William, 39
Bruce, Charles, 266
Bruderheim (Alberta), school in, *392*
Brûlé, Etienne, 101, 102–103, 131, 144
Buchanan, James, 310
Buck, Tim, 452
Buenos Ayrean (steamship), 310
buffalo: grasslands, 10–11; horses, impact of, 80; jumps, 31–32; pemmican, 82; Plains peoples and, 30–33; robe, painted, *34*; "surround" technique, 32
A Buffalo Pound (Back), 32
A Buffalo Rift (Miller), 31
Bunker Hill, 186
bunkhouse men, 389, *394*
Burning of Parliament (Légaré), *291*
Burns, E.L.M., 495
Burrowes, Thomas, *275*
Bush, George H., 585
Bush, Jack, *486*, 487
Bush Farm Near Chatham (Bainbrigge), *250*
Bushell, John, 167
Business Council on National Issues, 556
Butler, Charles, 250
Byng, Lord, 434, *440*

C
Cabot, John, 3–4, 55, 57
Cadet, Joseph-Michel, 171
Calgary (Alberta), 395
Callaghan, Morley, 470
Calumet Dance (Heriot), *28*
Cameron, Wendy, 221
Campbell, Kim, 569
Campbell, Sir Alexander, 286
Campeau, Jean, 563, 567
Campeau, Robert, 557, 559
Canada (*see also* Canada (specific years)): federal government, power of, 325–326; flag, 507; "food desert," 9; fragmentation, 265–275; geographical diversity, 8–12; name, 62; as province (*See* Canada (Province of))

the *Canada*, 368–369
Canada (1840-1900): Boer war, 375–379; creation (*See* Confederation); depression of 1870s, 339; franchise, 334; House of Commons, 334–339; independence from Great Britain, 373; Macdonald's government (*See* Macdonald, Sir John A.); Manitoba school question, 370–371; National Policy, 340–343; Parliament, 338–339; peace with Native peoples, need for, 349–350; political life, changes in 1890s, 369–376; productivity (1840-1900), 344; two languages, 374–375; Western Canada, 348–358; work life (1840-1900), 344–347
Canada (1900-1945): the arts and culture, 423–427; Borden's government, 409–416; Canadian-American relations, 407–409; Christian reformism, 399–403; civic populism, 397–399; Diefenbaker's government (*See* Diefenbaker, John); economic growth in early 1900s, 380–384; ethnic relations, vertical character of, 393–394; foreign investment, 381; Great Depression, 448–453; immigration policy after 1896, 385–394; international community and, 442; Laurier's government, 403–409; Mackenzie King (*See* Mackenzie King, William Lyon); modernist sensibility, emergence of, 379–380; mosaic, 393–394; nationalism (*See* nationalism); Native peoples, marginalization of, 439–442; overseas trade, growth of, 381–382; politics, post-World War I, 431–436; popular culture in 1920s, 446–447; population growth, 384–385; post-war reconstruction, 421–423; religion in post-World War I, 437–439; research, 426–427; the twenties,

Duquesne, Governor, 175
Durham, "Radical Jack." *See*
    Lambton, John George (Earl of
    Durham)
Dussault, René, 580

E
the *Eaglet*, 68
Economic Council of Canada,
    510–511
economy: in 1920s, 428–431; in
    1930s, 448–453; continued
    growth in 1960s, 511; growth in
    1970s, 531; growth in early
    1900s, 380–384; inflation, 525,
    529, 531, 537–538, 547; oil-price
    shock, 532; post-war prosperity,
    474–482; recession, 543,
    544–549, 578; recovery in 1993,
    579–580; World War I, 414, 416
Edmonton (Alberta), 395, *513*
education: as assimilation vehicle,
    391–392; baby boom demand,
    484; changing attitudes and,
    517; in Quebec, 1960s, 507, 508;
    separate-school system, 314,
    370–371; student loans, 572;
    universities, 486, 572; veterans'
    benefits, 484
Edward VIII, King of England, *419*
Eisenhower, Dwight, 492, 493
elections: equal representation,
    291–292, 313–314; federal (*See*
    federal election); Montreal, 1860
    or 1861, *300*; open voting, *300,*
    302; representation by popula-
    tion, 314, 318; women, 334, 400
electricity, 365, 396, *398*, 398–399
*Elevating the Standard - the Young
    Wilfrid Laurier* (Julien), *337*
Elgin, Lord, 285, 289
Elizabeth, Queen of England, 508,
    544
Ellice, Jane, *206*
*Emigration: The Advantages of
    Emigration to Canada*
    (Catermole), 221
Employment Insurance (EI), 572
Empress of India, 360
Encampment of the Loyalists at

*Johnstown, A New Settlement, on
    the Banks of the St. Lawrence, in
    Canada* (Peachey), *212*
Encampment of Woodland Indians
    (Martin), *19*
engagés, 118, 226
England. *See* Great Britain
English Canadians (*see also* Upper
    Canada): British Empire, identi-
    fication with, 373, 406;
    nationalism in 1890s, 371–372
"English Chief," 85
the environment, 273–275,
    519–520, 576, 579
Epaves Bay, *3*
equal representation, 291–292,
    313–314
Erasmus, George, 563, 565, 580
Erebus, 278–279
Ericsson, Leif, 3
the Erie, 23, 110
Esquimaux Building a Snow-Hut
    (Lyon), *50*
Essay on the Principle of Population
    (Malthus), 215
Estai, 576
Esterhazy, Peter, *519*
eulachon, 40–41
European contact: commercial
    nature of activities, 59; disease,
    58; horses, 79–80; initial con-
    tact, 55; Maritimes, 57; Native
    Canada, map of, *7*; regular con-
    tact, establishment of, 56–57;
    trade, 57–58, 60–61; trading
    posts, 58–59
European immigrants, 387–394
Experimental Stations, 426
Expo '67, *509*

F
factories, 344
Fagundes, Joao Alvares, 4
Fairley, Barker, *426*
family allowances, 469, 475, 482
Family Compact, 203, 204, 206
farmer's movement, growing mili-
    tancy of, 432
farming. *See* agriculture
farming Native groups, 23–30

Fathers of Confederation, 312, *323,*
    324
federal election: of 1872, 334–336;
    of 1878, 341; of 1896, 371, 375;
    of 1911, 409; of 1917, 418–420;
    of 1921, 433–434; of 1925, 434;
    of 1926, 435; of 1930, 454; of
    1935, 458; of 1940, 464; of 1945,
    469, 475, 481; of 1949, 481; of 1958,
    498; of 1962, 502; of 1965, 504;
    of 1968, 522; of 1974, 532; of
    1979, 536, 541; of 1980, 537,
    541; of 1988, 558; of 1993,
    569–570; of 1997, 583; of 2000,
    585
feminism, 520
Fer, Nicolas de, *115, 127*
Fernandes, Joao, 4
Ferryland (Avalon Peninsula), 116,
    117
Fessenden, Reginald A., *446*
Fielding, W.S., 431
filles du roi, 118–119
film industry, 447
Filmon, Gary, 555
Fines, Clarence, *477*
firearms, 73–76, 88, *102*
First Play in Canada (Jefferys), *149*
Fish Creek, 356
*Fish Market, Below Front Street,
    Toronto* (after Bartlett), *261*
fishing industry: credit exchange
    ("truck") system, 228; dry cod,
    production of, *227*; and family
    life, 226; in Gulf of St. Lawrence,
    226–227; in Newfoundland,
    225–228
fitness, 514
Fitzgerald, LeMoine, 472
Five Nations. *See* League of the Five
    Nations
flag, 507
Flavelle, Joseph, *380*, 416
Fleming, Donald, 499
Fleming, Sandford, *289*, 333, *363*
Fonyo, Steve, 514
Food Prices Review Board, 531–532
Ford Macleod, *352*
forest peoples. *See* northern forest
    Native groups

Contributors

CRAIG BROWN, the Editor, is a Professor Emeritus of History at the University of Toronto. He is the author of several major works in Canadian history, including *Robert Laird Borden, A Biography*. He has been President of the Canadian Historical Association, President of the Academy of Humanities and Social Sciences of the Royal Society of Canada, and a Senior Killam Scholar. He is Editor for the Champlain Society and lives in Toronto.

The six scholars who have collaborated on *The Illustrated History of Canada* are all distinguished authorities in their field:

RAMSAY COOK won the 1985 Governor General's Award for *The Regenerators*. He is a Professor Emeritus of History at York University, A Fellow of the Royal Society of Canada, a former Senior Killam Scholar, and Past President of the Canadian Historical Association. He is the author of several books and one of Canada's best known historians. He is General Editor of the *Dictionary of Canadian Biography* and lives in Toronto.

CHRISTOPHER MOORE is a Toronto writer on historical subjects and a columnist for "The Beaver" magazine. His works include the Governor General's Award winning *Louisbourg Portraits, 1867: How the Fathers Made a Deal*, the children's history *The Story of Canada*, and the best-selling photo history *Canada: Our Century*. He lives in Toronto.

DESMOND MORTON writes political, military, and industrial relations history. A former principal of Erindale College, University of Toronto, and founding Director of McGill's Institute for the Study of Canada, he is a Fellow of the Royal Society of Canada and an officer of the Order of Canada. He is the author of many books including *A Short History of Canada* and *When Your Number's Up: Canadian Soldiers and the First World War*. He lives in Montreal.

ARTHUR RAY is Professor of History at the University of British Columbia, specializing in the historical geography of the Native peoples of Canada. He is a Killam Fellow and the author of several books including *Indians and the Fur Trade* and *I Have Lived Here Since the World Began: An Illustrated History of Canada's Native People*. He lives in Vancouver.

PETER WAITE is Professor Emeritus of History at Dalhousie University. He is an officer of the Order of Canada, a Fellow of the Royal Society of Canada and Past President of the Canadian Historical Association. He is the author of many books including *The Man From Halifax: Sir John Thompson, Prime Minister*. He lives in Halifax.

GRAEME WYNN is a Professor of Geography at the University of British Columbia. Since 1990 he has been Associate Dean of Arts and Head of the Department of Geography at British Columbia and Visiting Senior Research Fellow at St. John's College, Oxford. He is the author of *Timber Colony* and a contributor to numerous historical and geographical journals and *The Historical Atlas of Canada*. His research and writing is centred on the environmental histories of Canada and New Zealand. He lives in Vancouver.